[redacted]

Pierre Attaingnant
Royal Printer of Music

Frontispiece A French printing shop about the year 1530. Miniature from "Chant royal du drapier" (MS fr. 1537). By courtesy of the Bibliothèque Nationale, Paris.

Daniel Heartz

Pierre Attaingnant
Royal Printer of Music

A Historical Study and Bibliographical Catalogue

University of California Press

Berkeley and Los Angeles

1969

University of California Press
Berkeley and Los Angeles, California

University of California Press, Ltd.
London, England

SBN 520-01563-0

Library of Congress Catalog Card Number: 68-13959
Printed in the United States of America

To F. Lesure and G. Thibault

PREFACE

A BOOK about books is patently indebted to libraries and librarians. Having haunted so many of both, in New World and Old, while pursuing the work, I could not, short of several pages, enumerate all the persons and institutions deserving mention; perhaps failure to do so may be pardoned on account of that *brièveté raisonnable* particularly appropriate in a work concerning French music and the more pertinent in one dealing with the age of Rabelais (who had a devastating way with pedants and their lists). A few debts are too specific to be passed over. Attempts, over a period of more than ten years, to examine at first hand every copy surviving from Attaingnant's press have been generously supported by the University of California, Berkeley, which also made it possible to acquire photographic reproductions of all material described and to secure assistance with the inventorying, collating, and indexing. To these last tasks Miss Paula Morgan, at present Music Librarian of Princeton University, brought endless patience and skill. Mme Jeanne Veyrin-Forrer, Conservateur of the Réserve des Imprimés at the Bibliothèque Nationale, has been most gracious with her aid. As a result of many exchanges of information, the catalogue of Attaingnant's works offered here is in substantial agreement with the list in Volume I of the great work initiated by Philippe Renouard, *Imprimeurs et libraires parisiens du xvi*^e *siècle* (Paris, 1964—), and carried out under the direction of Mme Veyrin-Forrer. Archivists in France were equally generous, and it is to Mme Pietresson de Saint-Aubin, Conservateur of the Archives du Nord, Lille, and Mme Madeleine Jurgens, Conservateur of the Archives Nationales, Paris, that I am particularly indebted for help in deciphering some of the key documents contributing to Attaingnant's biography. Thanks to Albi Rosenthal and Jean Cortot, the early prints belonging to the Cortot succession were made available for inclusion.

The Historical Study, like the Bibliographical Catalogue, has seen many stages, and through them all a few friends have borne stoically with the writer and his writing. Charles Cushing and Leonard Johnson were among the earliest readers; H. Colin Slim has read or listened to most of the study, as has William Emboden, who also served as artistic consultant and drew the map reproduced as figure 5. Three professors at Berkeley, Bertrand H. Bronson, Vincent Duckles, and Joseph Kerman, were kind enough to recommend the work to the University of California Press.

". . . Considering for a long while to whom in particular I might dedicate this work of mine, you were the first who occurred to me, in fact you alone seemed fitting." (Dedication by Attaingnant of his folio Masses of 1532.) Inscribing the present work with the names of François Lesure and Geneviève Thibault seemed no less fitting. Much of it depends on their bibliographical studies, their many other contributions illuminating the period, and, most of all, their personal friendship and encouragement, without which the task would have been neither begun nor finished. May it please them and all others whose passions include a love for Paris, early music, and fine books.

DANIEL HEARTZ

CONTENTS

CONTENTS

LIST OF ILLUSTRATIONS

PLATES

(*following p.* 204)

FIGURES

The initial letters at the beginning of the five sections of the Historical Study are from Attaingnant's Noyon Missal **(142)**. *By courtesy of the Trustees of the British Museum.*

TRANSLATION, SYMBOLS, AND DATES

DOCUMENTS form one basis for this work. They appear in their original languages in the Appendix of the Historical Study. Those in Latin are translated there, while those in French are provided with summary captions in English. Original languages or translations are given in the Historical Study as seemed fitting to the case. Whether the original is accessible—both as to source and meaning—has served as a guide in the matter, rather than any rigid consistency of practice. Spelling in old texts has been modernized according to the procedures described in the Prefatory Note to the Bibliographical Catalogue. Translations are by the author unless otherwise specified.

Symbols and abbreviations are abhorrent by nature in a work of prose, but the convenience of a few has outweighed the author's repugnance toward them. The many references to French moneys have led to adoption of symbols for pound (*livre*) £, shilling (*sous*) *s.*, and pence (*denier*) *d.* These abbreviations stand for the standard French currency of the time, the livre tournois (l.t.) and its subdivisions unless otherwise specified, and should not be read in terms of British monetary values. (According to Cotgrave's *Dictionarie of the French and English Tongues* printed in 1611, the livre tournois amounted at the time to but two shillings sterling.) Items in the Bibliographical Catalogue are referred to by their numbers, set in bold type (e.g., **33**). Another numerical system, in the form of an equation, describes the dimensions of music type by measuring the proportion of staff-height to minim.

All dates have been transcribed according to New Style (year beginning January 1). French notarial documents as well as most Paris printing followed Gallican Style (year beginning at Easter) throughout the first half of the sixteenth century.

In the case of French terms whose English equivalents would be misleading or inexact, the original has been retained (e.g., Parlement—a royal court of law, but not a parliament).

INTRODUCTION

THE APOGEE of French printing coincides very nearly with the reign of Francis I (1515–1547). Badius, Colines, Estienne—these are names that conjure up printing's finest moment, just as Tory, Garamond, and Granjon betoken excellence in type design, and the name of the collector-diplomat Grolier stands for the ultimate refinement in bookbinding. Under Francis I, Paris succeeded in wresting supremacy in book production from Venice and Basel, the two most influential centers of publication shortly after 1500. It became not only the capital of France in a new and quite modern sense, but also the European "capital of fine book-making," to borrow a phrase from the British Museum's recent exhibition catalogue, *Printing and the Mind of Man* (1963). The consequences of the new eminence have been put succinctly by Stanley Morison in *The Typographic Book, 1450–1935*, also published in 1963: "That sixteenth-century printing everywhere is indebted more to France than to any other country is manifest." Morison sees the end of the great period coming after 1560 and remarks that by the end of the century "the typography of all Europe had, largely on account of the wars of religion, sunk to a very low level in comparison with the golden age of Simon de Colines, Robert Estienne, and Geofroy Tory." Earlier, Daniel Berkeley Updike had used the same descriptive phrase in his *Printing Types: Their History, Forms and Use* (1922): "The first sixty years of the sixteenth century may be considered the Golden Age of French typography."

Among the many achievements of that golden age was the invention of a new method for printing music. Quickly overcoming all others, it proved so apposite and functional as to dominate the field for more than two hundred years, until the innovations of Breitkopf and Fournier, around 1750. The invention and its application furnish the subject of this book, as does the repertory gathered by the first French music publisher, who, like his Parisian colleagues, left his mark on the tastes of the time. To place such an achievement in cultural context has been the chief aim of the Historical Study. The concluding Bibliographical Catalogue will, it is hoped, preserve from further destruction what knowledge is left of a once far vaster *œuvre*, and will also fill the need for a practical guide to the location and contents of the surviving originals as well as to modern editions.

Printing is a subject with an immense literature of its own, and much of interest has been written about its relationship to human progress. If it was the bellwether of intellectual change that many claim, there ought to be consequences to be drawn for the history of music. Here we run up against the notion of "Renaissance music," a terminological fable much mouthed these days. In fields of study laying stronger claims than musicology to the title of discipline, terms such as

"Renaissance" are not lightly invoked. Rather, they are reserved to works having certain demonstrable and well-understood ideals. In other words, terms are used conceptually, not as unthinking historical counters. When the accumulation of philosophical-theoretical constructions put upon the "Renaissance" is cleared away, as has been done so trenchantly by Kristeller, what remains is the humanist movement and its efforts to restore good letters in general, and Ciceronian Latin and Greek in particular. The situation in France with regard to this movement is particularly clear-cut. Under Francis I the weight of a popular monarchy and centralized political power was brought down firmly on the side of the humanist scholars. The Royal Professorships were created in accordance with their wishes, and so were the offices of Royal Printer. The distinction "Imprimeur du Roy," that "proudest typographic title" as it has been called, was something to which many aspired but few attained. Bestowing it for the printing of music raised the art to official status within the rebirth so much talked about at the time. The other royal printers were exalted figures like Tory and Estienne, men who were themselves in the thick of the linguistic revival and purification of letters. While these preoccupations offer the surest index of specifically Renaissance phenomena, there were other, more general aims espoused in the same circles. Diffusion of knowledge and culture was ardently championed by partisans of the New Learning. It can be no accident then, that the greatest strides in music printing, as in general printing, were made in Italy and France, where the humanist commitment was strongest.

There is a converse to the proposition that music printing and the humanist movement formed a natural alliance. Spain and England, two countries that lingered longer in their nostalgic dalliance with the Middle Ages, saw music printing develop only slowly and late. The ramifications of this are worthy of note. In spite of flourishing schools of composition and performance, neither country made inroads on the international musical scene during the sixteenth century. Spain set the tone in dress and fashions from about 1550 on and England enjoyed an unparalleled expansion under Elizabeth I. Yet Spanish and English music remained of only local significance until late in the century. Might this be read as a commentary on the peculiar power of the printing press during its heyday? The main axis of sixteenth-century music printing ran between Antwerp and Venice, traversing Paris en route. Few would argue that the mainstream of music history lay far afield of the same axis; what is cause and what effect in this relationship might, on the other hand, stir up some lively debate.

The adventurous approach to printing music that developed in Paris has a concomitant in the modernity of the music printed. One of the central theses of the Historical Study is that Attaingnant's production closely parallels what was sung and played in the Chapel Royal and at court. Turning this thought around and pursuing it further, we may believe that no inducement could persuade Francis I to listen to music as old as that of Ockeghem, the great master who had been the favorite of the French royal house under Charles VII, Louis XI, and Charles VIII. As for Josquin, Févin, and Mouton, the favorites during the immediately preceding reign of Louis XII, little of their music was heard—clearly, they were out of fashion. What pleased was the newer music, more elegant and simple in style, by Claudin, Janequin, and Certon. To King Francis himself, the period's "Dieu débonnaire," as Clément Marot put it, must go much credit for supporting the changes in taste, whether in music, letters, or the arts.

The ensuing Historical Study is divided into five sections, each of which is divided into parts. Conflict between the chronological and the topical, the historian's perpetual dilemma, has been resolved in a series of compromises between and within the sections, with results that are, I hope, not too desultory for the reader's convenience. The first section offers a broad picture of the Parisian scene and brief sketches of some of the personalities connected with the main figure. Sections two and three are mainly chronological and commence with a panorama of the reign at beginning and midpoint respectively. The fourth section interrupts the story with an excursus on the publishing trade, while the final section resumes and concludes, beginning with a vignette of the reign's end.

I

RENASCENT PARIS

"LUTETIA, GALLIAE urbs maxima et nobilissima, magnitudine et frequentia certat cum maximis Europae urbibus." Thus did Robert Estienne describe Paris in the dictionary of proper names he published in 1541. For generations the reputation of the city and its university had drawn scholars from many lands to the banks of the Seine in order to learn from the "Mother of Studies." At Paris, during the thirteenth century, scholasticism attained its zenith with Albertus Magnus of Cologne and with the Italian, Thomas of Aquinas, while Louis IX (later Saint Louis) reigned as King of France. The scholarly reputation persisted, but the fortunes of the university did not always prosper. Plagues, the disasters of the Hundred Years' War, and English occupation depopulated the capital, reduced the income of the colleges, and hindered communications with the rest of the Continent. With the return of stability and relative prosperity under Louis XI and Charles VIII, Paris gradually recovered its traditional place as European crossroads. Students again gathered from every corner of Christendom. A new peak of activity was reached in the first half of the sixteenth century. Robert Goulet, professor at one of the colleges, wrote in 1517 a Latin description, the title of which might be translated as "Compendium Recently Published on the Multiform Magnificence of the University of Paris, on its Dignity and Excellence, on its Founding, and on the Extraordinary Reputation of its Subjects, Officers, and Colleges." Of the last he named no fewer than eighteen. In 1546 the Venetian ambassador Cavalli estimated the number of students at between sixteen and twenty thousand. The colleges all clustered in a small area of the Left Bank. Many of them may be identified on the woodcut map of Paris about 1550 by Truschet and Hoyau, a detail of which is reproduced as Figure 1. Three main arteries flowed through the teeming Latin Quarter, so named for the preponderance there of the universal scholarly tongue. On the map these appear from top to bottom as: the street beginning at the Place Maubert and winding up the Montagne Sainte-Geneviève to the Porte Bordelle; in the center the "Grande Rue Saint-Jacques," starting at the Petit Pont and leading to the Porte Saint-Jacques, main gateway to the South; just below, leading to the Porte Saint-Michel, the "Grande Rue de la Harpe."

French music printing began in these surroundings, inconspicuously, probably with a little book of part-songs that appeared on April 4, 1528. Two months earlier Ignatius of Loyola had arrived from Spain to take up residence in the austere Collège de Montaigu ("Montecu" on the Truschet-Hoyau map, near the Porte Saint-Jacques). Young Jean Calvin of Noyon spent four years (1524–1528) in this same college, where three decades earlier Erasmus of Rotterdam had been a pensioner. From Poitou had come François Rabelais, who in 1528 was attending courses and living in the Hôtel Saint-Denis, Rue Saint-André des Arts. These and other students destined for fame were stirred by such daring figures as Lefèvre d'Étaples, a severe critic of the medieval scholastics for their faulty transmission of the Church Fathers, and Guillaume Budé, the Royal Librarian, who illuminated the ancient classics with a knowledge of Greek unsurpassed in his day. Intellectual Paris was in a ferment which had not been equaled since the time four centuries earlier when Abélard, in revolt, led his students from the cloister of Notre Dame Cathedral to the vineyards of the Montagne Sainte-Geneviève, establishing the location of the future university.

In the middle of the turmoil, figuratively and literally, were the printers and publishers of the Quarter. Schoolboy texts such as the 1534 broadside reproduced as Plate I furnished them much business. Some of their number—the scholar-printers like Josse Badius, Henry Estienne, and Estienne's son Robert—were not so much followers as leaders of that New Learning which excited the best minds of the time. The once famed Theological Faculty (synonymous with the Sorbonne) had, over the centuries, gradually declined.[1] Sophistries occupied the heirs of Scotus, Aquinas, and Ockham, and the decadent spectacle they presented to the world has been vividly described by the Swiss humanist, Henry of Glaris (Glarean). Attracted to Paris like so many others eager for knowledge and fame, he wrote to his mentor Erasmus, telling of his delight at meeting Budé and Lefèvre d' Étaples. In the same letter, dated as of Paris, Rue Saint-Jacques, August 5, 1517, he complained:

> How disappointed am I, come to Paris to practice Greek ("ut grecarer"). There is no one here, in private or in public, who lectures on an important Greek author, at least to my knowledge; crowds of sophists are clamoring all about. I recently attended a formal debate at the Sorbonne ("disputatione Sorbonicą") where I heard loud applause, as if it were in the theater at Pompeii. I could not keep from laughing or, rather, I kept myself from laughing only with great effort. But there no one laughed. An imposing dispute took place about goat's wool ("pugna magna de lana caprina"). They were very irate with Adam, our first father, for having eaten pears instead of apples, for which these supercilious disputants could hardly contain their indignation. But theological gravity won out over anger: Adam was able to retire unscathed from the fray. I left, when I had enough of such asininities. Now I remain at home, and pass my time in singing, or, alone, I delight in my Horace, or laughing with Democritus at the folly of the world.[2]

[1] On the nature and organization of the University at the time see the first chapter of Augustin Renaudet's *Préréforme et Humanisme à Paris pendant les premières guerres d'Italie* (*1494–1517*) (2d ed.; Paris, 1953).

[2] *Opus Epistolarum Des. Erasmi Rotherdami*, ed. P. S. and H. M. Allen and H.W. Garrod (Oxford, 1906–1958), Vol. III, no. 618.

1 Detail of the Left Bank about 1550. From *Plan de Paris sous le règne de Henry II* (Paris, H. Champion, 1877) (reduced).

The reputation of the University for disputatious foolery was widespread. There was a saying current in Flanders at the time that: "You may send any stupid ass to Paris; if here he is an ass, he won't be a horse there."[3]

Notwithstanding the scholastics—in fact, in their very midst—a coalition of forces had formed that was by slow degrees overcoming the old ways. From the Collège de Sorbonne itself came the call of an enlightened few who in 1470 were responsible for bringing three printers from Germany. The first book to be printed, significantly, was a collection of epistles by an Italian humanist, intended to teach students good Latin style and replace medieval usage. To this collection the printers added as a concluding flourish the following well-turned distichs:

Ut sol lumen sic doctrinam fundis in orbem,
  Musarum nutrix, regia Parisius
Hinc prope divinam, tu, quam Germania novit,
  Artem scribendi suscipe promerita.
Primos ecce libros quos haec industria finxit
  Francorum in terris aedibus atque tuis.
Michael, Udalricus Martinesque magistri
  Hos impressevunt ac facient alios.

[As the sun spreads the light, Thou pourest forth learning upon the world, O royal Paris, nursemaid of the muses. Receive, deserving city, the nearly divine art of writing that Germany has invented. Behold the first books which this industry has produced on the soil of France and in its edifices. Masters Michael, Ulrich, and Martin have printed them and will print others.]

The high praise for Paris, its arts and its learning, is less than convincing, coming from three foreigners who had known only the small towns of the Rhine Valley and who, besides, were probably eager to flatter their patrons. But the attitude toward printing, that "nearly divine" invention, rings altogether true. Later the same year, in a letter accompanying the second book, Guillaume Fichet, professor at the Sorbonne, elaborated upon this theme, mentioning a certain Gutenberg of whom the three printers told, saying that such a man ought to be honored like a god, and that humanity owed more to him than to Bacchus or Ceres, because he made it possible that "whatever one says or thinks can quickly be set down, diffused, and fixed forever in the memory of man."[4] A keener appreciation of the immense consequences of printing would be difficult to find. Printing was considered as God-given that man might be led into a better age. This attitude is clearly reflected in the law approved by Louis XII on April 9, 1513, granting

[3] Thus, in Flemish and Latin, reads the caption of a Brueghel satire called "The Ass at School" and engraved by H. Cook in 1557, reproduced in *Graphic Worlds of Peter Brueghel the Elder*, ed. H. Arthur Klein (New York, 1963). The ass is depicted attempting to read musical notation.

[4] Anatole Claudin, *Histoire de l'imprimerie en France au XVe siècle* (Paris, 1901), Vol. I, p. 26.

dispensation from taxes to those connected with the industry, "in consideration of the great good which has descended upon our realm by means of the art and science of printing, an invention which seems more divine than human, and which, God be thanked, has been found and invented in this our era."

Francis I, Maecenas

The consciousness of a new and better era became acute after 1515, with the accession of the monarch who was one of the most gifted men ever to occupy the throne of France. Just a few years before, Baldassare Castiglione had predicted great things of François d'Angoulême in his *Cortegiano*, prophesying that he would raise the dignity of letters to the level enjoyed by the profession of arms. The quotation that follows is from the English translation by Sir Thomas Hoby published in 1561:

> If Monseigneur de Angoulesme have so good luke that he may (as men hope) succede in the Crowne, the glory of armes in France doth not so florish nor is had in such estimation, as letters will be, I believe. For it is not long sins I was in France, and saw this Prince in the Court there, who seemed unto mee beside the hansomnesse of person and bewtie of visage, to have in his countenance so great a majestie, accompanicd neverthelesse with a certaine lovely courtesie, that the realme of Fraunce shoulde ever seeme unto him a small matter. I understood afterwarde by many gentlemen both French and Italian, verie much of the most noble conditions, of the greatnesse of courage, prowesse and liberalitie that was in him: and among other things, it was tolde me, that hee highly loved and esteemed letters, and had in very great reputation all learned men, and blamed the Frenchmen themselves that their mindes were so far wide from this profession, especially having at their doores so noble an universitie as Paris is, where all the world resorteth.
>
> *The Book of the Courtyer*, I

Francis took the words of Castiglione almost as a program of action, or so it would seem. Having returned from his first Italian campaign, he conceived the notion, with the prompting of Budé, of a college of ancient languages directly under royal patronage. Budé wrote to Erasmus on February 5, 1517, offering him the directorship. Erasmus temporized, making such statements as "no study can do more than that of ancient letters to illuminate all the sciences . . . I attribute this worthy program above all to the excellent King Francis," and recommending in his stead his pupil, Glarean.[5] The King, perplexed by the tactics of Erasmus,

[5] *Opus Epistolarum*, Vol. II, no. 529. Erasmus praised Glarean as a man of every talent, singling out music, cosmography, and mathematics as his strongest points.

allowed the program to be pushed into the background by more pressing matters, and further attempts in 1521–1522 were also unavailing. Francis was sincerely devoted to this project, nevertheless, and even in the darkest days of his reign, after the defeat at Pavia in 1525, his intentions on behalf of the humanists were not forgotten. With the King out of the country, the Sorbonne thought the time opportune to settle accounts with Lefèvre d'Étaples and others suspected of new ideas. From the depths of his prison in Madrid, with no Budé to urge him this time, Francis wrote to the Parlement of Paris on November 12, 1525, commanding that the charges be dropped, and adding that he was "more resolved than ever to treat honorably men of letters." Meanwhile, other centers of study had taken the initiative that lagged in Paris. Under Leo X, Rome maintained several chairs of ancient languages. Louvain had a college of three ancient languages by 1517; Greek was regularly taught at Strasbourg from 1524, at Zurich from 1526, and at Basel from 1529. Only when peace returned with the Treaty of Cambrai in 1529 did the moment seem propitious for Budé to pursue the matter further with King Francis, this time with success. Royal chairs of Greek and Hebrew were the first to be established, followed later by a chair of Latin, and the regius professors began their lectures by March of 1530. Oronce Finé became Royal Professor of Mathematics a few months later, and it is not impossible that the little musical-mathematical treatise by him, printed in 1530 **(21)**, had a direct connection with the course of instruction during his first year.[6]

From 1530 on, humanists did not spare their praises of Francis, and the notion of a revival grew apace. Commenting upon the royal chairs, Erasmus wrote on March 13, 1531, "I judge that France is infinitely more fortunate now than if all of Italy were in her power."[7] In 1532 appeared the *Pantagruel* of Rabelais, which described the new atmosphere, with characteristic hyperbole, in Gargantua's letter of paternal advice to Pantagruel, gone up to Paris for his university studies:

> In the old days of my father, times were still dark and redolent of the misfortunes and calamities of the Goths, who destroyed all good literature . . . Now all the disciplines are restored, the languages established: Greek, without which no person can call himself learned, Hebrew, Chaldean, Latin. Printed books, of such elegance and correctness are in use, an invention of my day and of divine inspiration, just like that of gunpowder, of infernal inspiration. Everywhere you find learned people, wise preceptors, and bookstores of great amplitude and in my opinion neither in the time of Plato, nor of Cicero, nor of Papinian, was there such convenience of study as seen now.
>
> *Pantagruel*, Book II, chap. viii

[6] Abel Lefranc's *Histoire du Collège de France* (Paris, 1893) is still the authority for all matters touching the regius professors.

[7] The letter, to James Tusanus, is no. 2449 of the *Opus Epistolarum*.

What seemed to have flourished all at once with a little group of royal professors (the nucleus of the future Collège de France) had long been prepared. The printed book was both harbinger and indispensable ally of the revival, as Rabelais implies.

Inventories of books owned by students provide another intimation of the alliance of New Learning and the printing press. One such inventory, taken down in 1528 by a none too literate notary, records the belongings of a certain Francis Benson, "student at Paris, native of England": *Lexicon grecum, Ambrosius Callepinus, Cicero, Theodore, Chronique de Phillipe de Commines, Demosthenes, Horace, Virgil, Terence, Salluste, De conjuratione Katerine* (*Catilenae?*), *Livre en grec intitulé . . . , Urbany grammatices institutione, Celestinum, Les faiz maistre Allain Chartier.*[8] Hardly a model of Christian piety, to judge from his library, this student owned not a single scholastic philosopher. A generation of scholar-printers would seem to have had effect, and that before the royal professors took up their posts.

The reaction of the University's scholastic theologians to the signs of change was predictable. They struck back, attempting to suppress the royal chairs, but without success. Their greatest weapon was censorship of the press, a power which repeatedly brought the humanist movement to grief. The show of strength against Lefèvre d'Étaples in 1524–1525 had to do with his publication of the New Testament. Because of censorship the great scholar was forced to see his commentaries deleted; he wrote on the occasion to a disciple: "You very rightly complain about our press. I am complaining too, and so is our brother Robert [Estienne] . . . Some time yet God will grant that we see the pure light. At the moment—at the moment there is nothing but darkness (at least, the exceptions are few) at Paris, once of noble fame."[9]

The moment of darkness passed, happily, and printers and scholars alike were largely free during the two decades that followed to pursue their work. Late in 1534 an uncomfortable time followed the profanation of the Mass by the extremists, using printed "placards" brought in from outside the realm. Someone had the audacity to post a placard in the apartments of the King, whose furious reaction must have been foreseen. But even this coarsest of provocations was weathered after a few months, and the policy of repression urged by many was abandoned.

The scholar-printers depended on the support of the Crown, as is apparent from the career of the greatest of them, Robert Estienne, regarded even in his own day as the "prince of printers." This indefatigable searcher after truth wrote a detailed account of what the New Learning and its diffusion in France owed to the Monarch:

[8] In Ernest Coyecque, "Inventaire Sommaire d'un minutier parisien," *Bulletin de la Société de l'histoire de Paris et de l'Ile-de-France* XX-XXIII (1895–1896).

[9] As translated in Elizabeth Armstrong, *Robert Estienne, Royal Printer* (Cambridge, 1954), p. 13.

> If of old it was said truly by Plato, gravest of authors, that it would at last go right nobly well with mankind when the Philosophers reigned or the Kings turned Philosophers, then we may most justly vaunt France to be greatly blessed in having, as our King, Francis the First. . . . In the first place, offering rich remuneration, he has appointed as Masters of the best arts and studies in this University (the greatest in the world, to which all resort for study from every part) great scholars. . . . Then he has at great cost furnished and is daily furnishing a noble library of every kind of book, Hebrew, Greek and Latin, so that therein he has surpassed the efforts of the kings Ptolemy and Eumenis [and,] far from grudging to anyone the records of ancient writers which he at great and truly royal cost has procured from Italy and Greece, he intends to put them at the disposal and service of all men. With this in mind he has ordered that new and accurately copied forms of letters should be cut by distinguished craftsmen, in all the languages above-mentioned so that, by this method of writing, born and invented within the last hundred years, every excellent book—multiplied in any number of copies—might come into all men's hands.[10]

What Estienne claims has been substantiated. By the end of the reign, the royal library had acquired 560 Greek manuscripts, and the King on several occasions had written personally to facilitate the quest in foreign countires; among the letter-types mentioned are the famous Royal Greeks, still in existence, cut at the King's expense by Claude Garamond. But it is the last part of the statement that is truly revealing, betraying as it does the interconnection between the various parts of the royal scheme. Francis provided "his" printers what they needed by adding it, if possible, to "his" library, with the aim of enhancing the teaching of "his" professors.

Concerning the King's own intelligence and quickness Estienne is no less precise. His words carry the conviction and authority of one who had frequent personal contact with the sovereign:

> There is in the mind of the man a kind of inborn Philosophy. Witness to that if it was needed (but indeed of witness there is plenty) the frequent conversations concerning literature and every sort of study, which he has almost daily with the most learned men whenever he has a moment of time. To the astonishment of all who stand by, while they watch the King—and a King who necessarily is always extremely busy in the most important matters—, he pronounces from memory and promptly (as each subject happens to come up for discussion) upon things which are hardly possible even to men who have had complete leisure to devote all their lives to study![11]

The picture drawn by anyone else would appear overdone, but Robert Estienne was incapable of flattery and, to his later chagrin, incapable of untruth or compromise. One of the most revealing, yet little known, portraits of King Francis

[10] *Ibid.*, pp. 125 f.

[11] *Ibid.*, p. 148.

shows him in a light similar to the scene Estienne describes (Pl. II). A miniature, it was executed to adorn the translation of the Greek historian Diodorus Siculus made by Antoine Macault, royal secretary. Conventionally, such scenes showed the writer kneeling in homage before the dedicatee, his work in hand, but here Macault, erect, reads from his work while the King listens. So does, perforce, the rest of the assemblage, including the Dauphin Francis and his younger brothers Henry and Charles, as well as many of the great of the realm. Prominent by their cardinal's hats (red in the original, light-toned in Pl. II) are the portly chancellor, Antoine Duprat, on the King's left, and on his right, with hand pointing to the King, Jean de Lorraine (see also Pl. III). The cleric behind the King's left shoulder has been identified as Guillaume Budé, which would give further significance to the occasion, an actual historical event that took place in Lent, 1534.[12] By his example, as much as by anything else, Francis encouraged intellectual striving.

When Francis I was succeeded in 1547 by his second son, the morose Henry II, the intellectual climate of Paris began to change rather noticeably. Although Henry attempted to continue the patronage of his father, it was with a different spirit. When he created a Royal Printer of Mathematics by letters dated February 13, 1553, it seems that he did so as much out of a sense of rivalry as out of dedication to learning:

> . . . Our late king and father, for several good causes and considerations known to everyone, appointed a certain number of lectors, learned men and connoisseurs of all arts, sciences, and languages, in order that they might teach students and others who love such things, which learned men—and one, indeed, who taught the art and science of mathematics [Finé]—he wished to make residents of our good city of Paris, on account of the great affluence in scholars that he saw, come from every province and all nations, and in order to carry out the design that he had to make letters flourish and revive, after they had become entirely bastardized . . . Since in the time of our late king and father and up to the present no one has been chosen or provided with the status of printer and bookseller in mathematics, it has seemed to us a very useful thing and commodious to the republic that we appoint someone our printer in the said mathematics.[13]

These words to which Henry II signed his name cannot but seem ironic. No more than a few months after his accession, Henry followed bad advice and bowed to the antihumanist forces which his father for twenty years had imperiously held in check. By December, 1547, Robert Estienne had been thrown to the theological

[12] L. Delisle, *Traductions d'auteurs grecs at latins offertes à François Ier et à Anne de Montmorency* (Paris, 1900), pp. 20–23. A woodcut after the miniature painting, and rather crude in comparison with it, was included in the printed version of the translation: *Les Troys premiers livres de l'historie de Diodore Sicilien, historiographe Grec. Translatez de Latin en françoys par maistre Anthoine Macault, notaire, secretaire et valet de chambre ordinaire du Roy, François premier* (Paris, heirs of G. Tory, 1535).

[13] Georges Lepreux, *Galliae Typographicae Documenta* (Paris, 1910), no. 22.

wolves, his Latin Bible—the first philologically grounded Vulgate—having been placed on the Index. The great printer thought himself in sufficient danger to plan his exile, which he eventually carried out by removing to Geneva in 1551. It is true that neither Francis I nor his brilliant sister, Marguerite de Navarre, could save Clément Marot from exile and Etienne Dolet from the stake. But with the hindsight of history, we know that they held back for a long time the clouds that were gradually closing in on Paris. Humanism brought the printing press to Paris; the printing press fanned religious passions into flames that could be controlled less and less. The moderate position, the toleration of reasonable diversity and of free inquiry that characterizes the reign of Francis I gave way under the stresses of the ever more acrimonious religious question. By 1550 the new age, inaugurated so auspiciously in an aura of optimism and tolerance, began to yield before another spirit, partisan and violent. The stage was being set for the wars of religion.

For a certain generation of French intellectuals, at least, "Renaissance" meant all the marvels the term implies. They spoke often of renewal and saw in Francis I a prime mover. Not merely had Paris surpassed its earlier fame: it had been specifically chosen as heir to the glories of classical antiquity. Jean Lemaire de Belges paid homage to the place of his studies, calling it "the very noble royal city, seated on the River Seine, most fortunate Paris, capital and crown of France, mother and sovereign mistress of the studies of the whole world, more than formerly any Athens or Rome had been, city where I suckled so much (whatever little) of the milk of literature that enlivens my spirit."[14] Paris in competition with Athens or Rome, or Athens and Rome outdone, as Lemaire de Belges would have it—the comparison was constantly on the lips of humanist, poet, and printer. Geofroy Tory (who was all three) insisted in his *Champfleury* (1529) that the French language, no less than French learning, was "aussi belle et bonne qu'une autre." Such a novel idea became a kind of creed among the little group of scholars gathered aroung Jean Dorat in the Collège de Coqueret, including, toward 1545, Ronsard, Antoine de Baïf, and Joachim du Bellay, the core of the future Pléiade. Du Bellay, setting forth a program for French letters in *La Deffense et illustration de la langue françoyse* (1549), proclaimed the equality of his language with Italian as a vehicle for reviving and surpassing the poetry of the ancients. He also had kind words for the nonliterary arts: "I shall not mention the many industries, arts, and sciences which flourish among us, such as music, painting, sculpture, architecture, and so forth, scarcely less than they flourished formerly with the Greeks and Romans" (Book II, chap. xii). The printer-author Etienne

[14] *Illustrations de Gaule*, Book I. chap. xvi. See Jean Frappier, "L'Humanisme de Jean Lemaire de Belges," *Bibliothèque d'Humanisme et Renaissance* XXV (1963), 289–306.

Dolet charged the cultural revival directly to the King in *Les Gestes de Françoys de Valois* (1540): "Only since thou hast had the government of the French did letters begin to flourish in France to such a degree that Greece does not surpass us." Another printer, Robert Granjon, designed a handsome cursive type with the express intention of creating something specifically national and worthy of the new eminence; he explained that "Now, by a vicissitude of things, our France is having its turn, whether in arms, in laws, in the eloquence of its language, or in all the other disciplines."[15]

The Regius Professor of Mathematics also made his contribution to the mystique of rebirth. Like Tory, Oronce Finé was a complete Renaissance man—scientist, humanist, artist, and the author of the little musical-mathematical treatise mentioned above. His diverse accomplishments merited him a laudatory chapter in André Thevet's *Les vrais Pourtraits et vies des hommes illustres* (Paris, 1584), illustrated by a handsome metal engraving showing the mathematician of intense mien, compass in hand, and described by Thevet as "the portrait done from life by master Jean Janet, painter to King Francis I, according to the true resemblance of our Dauphinois in his thirty-sixth year."[16] Finé was born in 1494 and would have been thirty-six in 1531. At the same time of being depicted by the Royal Painter he was seeing through the press a collected edition of his essays, the *Protomathesis* (Paris, 1532), for which he designed borders, illustrations, and a set of large decorative initials.[17] The work was dedicated to King Francis and began with an elaborate salute, quoted here first in the original Latin.

> Foelices eos semper existimare vel ipso jure compellimur, Francisce Rex Christianissimus, qui postpostis humanae fragilitatis illecebris, bonarum artium tum propriis, tum emendatis aliorum inventis et laboribus promovere vel quae hominum socordia inclementiave temporum, durissimam subiere jacturum *in pristinum candorum et ornatum restituere* conantur . . . (Italics added.)

> Francis, Most Christian King, justice itself compels us to regard as forever fortunate those who, putting aside human frailty's allurements, strive either to promote zeal for the liberal arts, both in their own works, and in others' impeccable works and studies; or *to restore to original clarity and beauty* what, by the negligence of man and the ravages of the ages, has endured the severest loss . . .

Restoration of the arts to their (imagined) original state was a theme long familiar

[15] Preface to Innocenzio Ringhieri, *Dialogue de la vie et de la mort* (Lyons, 1557) as quoted in H. de la Fontaine Verwey, "Caractères de civilité et propagande religieuse," *Bibliothèque d'Humanisme et Renaissance* XXVI (1964), 11–12.

[16] There is an excellent reproduction in *French 16th Century Books*, compiled by Ruth Mortimer under the supervision of Philip Hofer and William A. Jackson (Harvard College Library Department of Printing and Graphic Arts, Catalogue of Books and Manuscripts, Part I) (Cambridge, Mass., 1964), Vol. II, p. 634.

[17] *Ibid.*, Vol. I, no. 225. See also A. F. Johnson, *Decorative Initial Letters* (London, 1931), no. liv.

in Italian humanist writings, albeit new to France (note the similarity to the contemporaneous passage from Rabelais quoted earlier). Besides the content and style of Finé's discourse, its very terminology was conventional to the New Learning—Italian-inspired, but international in scope. Glarean furnishes another example with his ἀναζωπυρεῖσθαι which he renders in Latin as "pristino splendori restituere."[18]

Final word on Francis I should go to the greatest poet of the age, Clément Marot, who had the audactity in 1534 to publish the statement: "Point ne suis Lutheriste, ne Zuinglien, encores moins Papiste." More than a humanist, he was a humanitarian and wrote the most vehement attack on penal torture before Voltaire's.[19] An indomitable singer of love and personal freedom, Marot was in many respects the alter ego of his master the King. And it is true that direct royal intervention was repeatedly necessary to rescue him from imprisonment and certain punishment.

> Roy des Françoys, François premier du nom,
> Dont les vertus passent le grand rénom,
> Et qui en France en leur entier ramaines
> Tous les beaux arts et sciences romaines,
> O de quel grand bénéfice, estendu
> De Dieu sur nous, a nous il t'a rendu . . .
>
> Epigramme 133, *De la convalescence du Roy* (1537)

Scholar-Printers and Merchants

The printing press became the powerful agent of the New Learning, as later of the Reformation and Counter-Reformation. At the same time it was an industry that succeeded only insofar as it secured a livelihood to its various practitioners. The latter aspect provides a necessary complement to the world of ideas and ideals just sketched and may now be approached in the context of the Paris book-trade.

The scriptoria of Paris were among the most active of all during the Middle Ages. Their task was to provide copies of the texts upon which masters lectured and students toiled. With the gradual replacement of the manuscript by the printed book after 1470, many features of the older craft passed to the younger. For both the chief commodity was paper; parchment was used only rarely, on account of its great cost. The paper industry in France had been developing on a large and successful scale since the fourteenth century, when the University of

[18] From the dedication of Glarean's *Isagoge in Musicen* (Basel, 1516). For a facsimile see Frances Turell, "The *Isagoge in Musicen* of Henry Glarean," *Journal of Music Theory* III (1959), 110.

[19] Clément Marot, *Les Epîtres*, ed. C. A. Mayer (London, 1958), "Notice biographique," p. 24.

Paris was accorded priority to the products of the paper mills of Troyes, in Champagne, and of Essonnes, a village south of Paris. In 1415 the University took its paper-makers under direct protection. The privileges and protection accorded the *papetiers* by the University were extended also to the other artisans involved, from the *écrivains*, who copied texts, and the *enlumineurs*, who decorated the copies, to the *relieurs*, who bound the books and those merchants who finally sold them, the *libraires*. All were officers of the University and were subject to its jurisdiction, like the academic population of the colleges. Before being appointed to office, a man had to give evidence that he was qualified, and then be sworn before the Rector of the University—hence the terms *papetier juré de l'Université*, *libraire juré*, and so on. The number of official booksellers was maintained by tradition at twenty-four, from which body the *quatre grands libraires jurés* were appointed to supervise the others and to determine book prices. Other booksellers, *non-jurés*, were nonetheless subject to the University in the matter of prices; their books could be sold only at open stalls. As mentioned earlier, the original Sorbonne printers were the three Germans who were brought to Paris in 1470, and their task was directly connected with the program of instruction. These printers took two apprentices, who in 1473 set themselves up for business nearby in the Rue Saint-Jacques, at the sign of the Green Bellows (Soufflet Vert), to be followed soon by their masters, setting up a rival press a few doors away at the sign of the Golden Sun (Soleil d'Or).[20]

Within a few years printing shops lined the Rue Saint-Jacques from one extremity to the other. Paris boasted no fewer than sixty of them by 1500. In March, 1489, Charles VIII confirmed the rights and privileges of the University, and on the list of those "privileged," besides masters, scholars, and regents, were the following: twenty-four libraires, four parchemineurs, four papetiers of Paris, seven papetiers of divers other localities, two enlumineurs, two écrivains, and two relieurs. Only a few scribes and illuminators survived the so recently flourishing trade in manuscripts. The numerous papermakers were kept busy not by scribes, obviously, but by the ever more voracious printing press. Many of the "twenty-four" booksellers—the wealthiest and most powerful members of the industry—had procured one or more presses by 1500, as an adjunct to their business. Those who did not own presses were almost certain to be publishers; that is, they commissioned various "jobbing" printers in order to fill their shelves with whatever the season demanded. Clienteles other than the academic one began to appear, and the market soon expanded to include books destined for

[20] For the location of these and other printers' addresses see the "Table des adresses classées par rues" in Philippe Renouard, *Imprimeurs parisiens, libraires, fondeurs de caractères, et correcteurs d'imprimerie* (Paris, 1898).

courtiers, townspeople, the rural clergy, and others. Yet the book trade continued to depend mainly on the University and its four faculties of Theology, Law, Medicine, and Arts.

The career of one of the grands libraires may serve to show how the business of books worked together with the interests of the University. Poncet Le Preux was a bookseller of note who exercised his trade for more than six decades, commencing in 1498. His shop, well situated to do a good trade with students, was first at the sign of the Pewter Pot (Pot d'Étain) in the Rue Saint-Jacques, opposite the Chapelle Saint-Yves. By 1512 he had prospered sufficiently to move down the street a few houses into a larger establishment at the sign of the Wolf (du Loup) which was eventually acquired in its entirety through transactions in 1513, 1534, 1551, and 1554—a reflection of the continuous expansion his enterprise enjoyed. From this vantage point in the very heart of the Left Bank, Le Preux over his long lifetime must have witnessed the whole procession of printers, pedants, humanists, and artists giving life to the Parisian Renaissance. At first designated merely as libraire, he became in turn one of the libraires jurés and, in 1525, a grand libraire juré. His stock would have included hundreds of titles and thousands of copies from the numerous presses in Paris, and more than a few editions from other printing centers such as Lyons and the Rhenish cities. Some aspects of his occupation emerge from a lawsuit in 1529 involving two of his colleagues: "Henequin de Breda, German bookseller resident in Paris, gives over to Christian Wechel [another Paris libraire] his rights, by sentence of the Provost of Paris, to prosecute Poncet Le Preux in order to recover the merchandise or the value of three casks of books sent by Breda to Lyons in 1526, which books Le Preux had managed to intercept by an agent at Lyons, Catherin Jean; Wechel may deduct what Breda owes him from whatever he can recover in the affair."[21] Unlike Breda, a merchant of little account, Wechel was a prominent figure among booksellers. He operated in the Rue Saint-Jacques at the Écu de Basle, an appropriate ensign for his business since it was the Parisian outlet for the Basel publishing house of Conrad Resch. (Resch had his own shop in Paris until 1526 and is significant for his connections with the Protestant movement beyond the Rhine.) When Wechel acquired presses himself in 1526, it was for a sum payable at Frankfort on the Main. That is, in keeping with the bartering system then prevalent, Wechel's creditors in Paris were to receive payment in merchandise—meaning in all probability books from Frankfort, that great center of trade renowned for its fairs.

[21] Ernest Coyecque, *Recueil d'actes notariés relatifs à l'histoire de Paris* (Paris, 1905), Vol. I, no. 1104. Le Preux also served as the Paris outlet for the publisher Huguetan, of Lyons. See Philippe Renouard, *Bibliographie des impressions et des œuvres de Josse Badius Ascensius* (Paris, 1908), Vol. III, p. 287.

A far-flung web of communications united the book trade of Europe in the early sixteenth century, a web dependent essentially on a few very large publishing houses. This was the era of international syndicates run by families. For instance, there was the Giunta family, operating mainly out of Venice, with book depots and accounts in Frankfort, Antwerp, Lyons, Paris, and several Spanish cities. The Kobergers of Nuremberg represented an even larger network, with agents and representatives in all the important towns of the Continent. It was with "the business tycoons of the Amerbach, Froben, and Koberger class" that Le Preux belonged.[22] One document reveals him as the possessor of a valuable stock of books from abroad and as a distributor of such books to other firms: "Nicholas Boucher, bookseller, acknowledges to Poncet Le Preux, merchant, one of the four great sworn booksellers of the University, citizen of Paris, the sum of 965 l.t. he owes for books printed in Paris, Lyons, and Germany, of many kinds and many sizes, that he has had from Le Preux, for a year or thereabouts, in order to set up and stock his bookshop in the University. This sum has already been the object of a promissory note, now expired without payment, made on the day of St. Mathias."[23]

Books traveled in considerable numbers (though not with great ease) from one country to another. There is a famous example in 1519, when Johann Froben of Basel shipped 600 copies of Luther's writings to France. That the Paris publishers in their turn counted on the export market appears from the account by Josse Badius of the "foreign" distribution of Noël Béda's *Annotationes in Fabrum et Erasmum* in 1526 (an attack on Lefèvre d'Étaples and Erasmus that caused the scholarly printer some embarrassment). From an edition of 625 copies, the following were sent off by Badius:

45 to divers great personnages (complimentary copies)
32 to Melchior Koberger in Nuremberg
50 to an agent in Lyons, for distribution in Italy
50 to another agent (unspecified, but probably in the printer's native Low Countires where he retained many contacts)
62 to Conrad Resch of Basel
40 to François Viremond, distributor in England
6 to Rouen
6 to Orleans[24]

[22] The phrase is that of S. H. Steinberg in a review for the *Journal of the Printing Historical Society* I (1965), 101. Further on the commercial empires see Oskar von Hase, *Die Koburger* (2d ed.; Leipzig, 1885) and Hans Widmann, *Die deutsche Buchhandel in Urkunden und Quellen* (Hamburg, 1965).

[23] Coyecque, *op. cit.*, Vol. II, no. 4878, dated Feb. 18, 1548, Old Style.

[24] Renouard, *Bibliographie . . . de Josse Badius*, Vol. I, pp. 57–59.

An atmosphere of free trade such as has hardly existed since emerges from the business dealings of men like Badius and Le Preux.

A further idea of the scale on which a Le Preux might operate is suggested by the litigation which developed in 1538 between the University and its papetiers jurés. Guillaume Merlin, like Le Preux one of the four grands libraires jurés, testified that as publisher he ordinarily kept in operation thirteen or fourteen presses employing 250 workers and needed about 200 reams of paper a week (a ream consisted of 500 folios). From the same lawsuit it emerges that the papetiers were among the proudest merchants of the age; one obdurate member of their guild scandalized the University by his impertinence when he raised his voice as his indictment was begun in Latin, crying: "Parlez, parlez bon françois et je vous répondrai."[25]

The printer-publisher of the sixteenth century faced numerous impediments to his trade. Travel was not easy, communications often broke down, and money once invested in an edition often took a long while to return. Much of the capital that kept this risk-laden business going came from the wealthy booksellers. Le Preux's name was continually appearing on books printed either to his account or in momentary association with one or more of the other libraires jurés—with Jean Petit, Galliot du Pré, the Marnefs, the Regnaults, or others of his neighbors.[26] Plate III offers an example of the printing in a commentary on Pliny's Natural History that appeared in 1530. According to the title page this highly artistic book was to be had "apud Poncetum le Preux, sub insigni Lupi, via ad divum Jacobum." Only the colophon reveals that it was, characteristically, a collaborative venture: "In omnes C. Plinii secundi Naturalis Historiae... Commentaria: Typis ac caracteribus Petri Vidouaei impressa. Impensis honestorum virorum Ponceti le Preux et Galioto à prato [Galliot du Pré] Universitatis Parisiensis Bibliopol." One reason for the many partnerships, established often for a single publication, was the high cost of paper, which has been estimated as equal to the total of all other production costs—copy, presses, types, ink, labor, and so on.[27]

Le Preux used at least two printer's marks to identify his products. A smaller device showed a tree with an owl, its trunk surrounded by two dragons supporting

[25] César Boulay, *Historia Universitatis parisiensis* (Paris, 1665–1673), Vol. VI, pp. 314–321.

[26] Renouard's manuscript catalogue of Paris printing lists under Le Preux's name 225 publications from 1507 to 1559 (Bibliothèque Nationale, Réserve des Imprimés, MS. J4). As early as 1504, however, Le Preux joined with Gaspard Philippe to publish a Greek primer.

[27] Lucien Febvre and Henri-Jean Martin, *L'Apparition du Livre* (Paris, 1958), pp. 166–173. Similar conclusions are reached by Robert Kingdon, "The Plantin Breviaries: A Case Study in the Sixteenth-century Business Operations of a Publishing House," *Bibliothèque d'Humanisme et Renaissance* XXII (1960), 146.

2 Printer's mark of Poncet Le Preux. From a Froissart edition of 1530. By courtesy of Harvard College Library.

an escutcheon with the initials P L P.[28] A larger and later device repeated the scene with the shield now showing a wolf with a lamb on its back (Fig. 2). The reference, we may be sure, was to the sign that hung outside the Maison du Loup and served to identify it. Further elaboration was offered by the architectural frame, with its inscription "Quisquit agas, sapientur agas; respice finem," "Do wisely whatever you do; look to the end." While the wolf and the defiant monsters suggest valor ("Le Preux" means "the valiant one") the chosen motto proclaims the tempering virtue of prudence. Both qualities were essential to the business. Ordinary printers worked on commission, with funds guaranteed before the job and distribution assured afterward. The great booksellers put up the money and made the decisions. The choice of what to print coincided necessarily with what

[28] Renouard, *Les Marques typographiques parisiennes des XVe et XVIe siècles* (Paris, 1926), nos. 632–633.

3 Printer's mark of Philippe Pigouchet. From the Sarum Hours of 1502. By Courtesy of the Pierpont Morgan Library, New York.

could be sold quickly. Le Preux had to stock his shop with fast-moving items else his capital would be tied up on the shelves. Yet the situation was not unfavorable to a Badius, in whom the printer-publisher was second to the humanist. In those fruitful days of intellectual renewal men of different lights could be reconciled—Le Preux and Badius did, indeed, collaborate. It took both merchant and scholar to bring about what is now admired as the golden age of French printing.

Twice a year, on May 6 and December 27, the printers and publishers of Paris shut their shops in celebration of the feast days of their patron saint, John the Evangelist. The Confrérie de Saint-Jean would then assemble at the church of Saint-André des Arts, hearing Mass in the morning and Vespers in the afternoon,

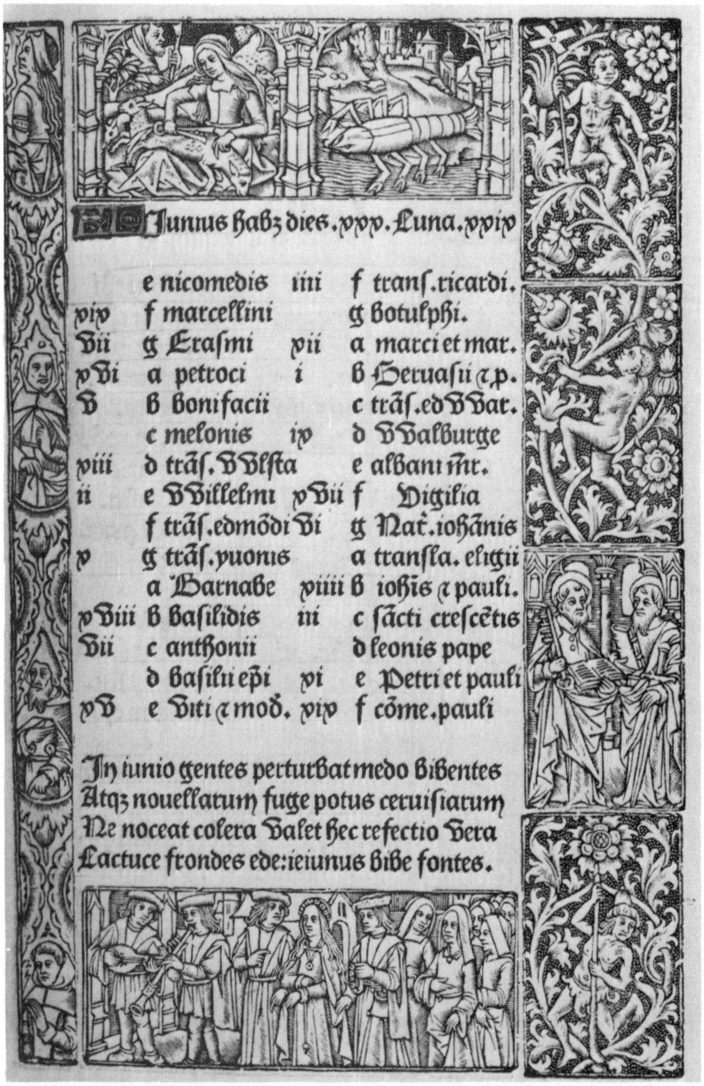
Junius habz dies.xxx. Luna.xxix

e nicomedis iiii f transl.ricardi.
xix f marcellini g botulphi.
vii g Erasmi xii a marci et mar.
xvi a petroci i b Geruasii et p.
v b bonifacii c trãs.ed vvar.
c melonis ix d vvalburge
viii d trãs.vvlsta e albani mr.
ii e vvillelmi xvii f Vigilia
f trãs.edmõdi vi g Nat.iohãnis
x g trãs.yuonis a transla.eligii
a Barnabe xiiii b iohis et pauli.
xviii b basilidis iii c sãcti crescẽtis
vii c anthonii d leonis pape
d basilii epi xi e Petri et pauli
xv e viti et mod. xix f cõme.pauli

In iunio gentes perturbat medo bibentes
Atqz nouellarum fuge potus ceruisiarum
Ne noceat colera valet hec refectio vera
Lactuce frondes ede: ieiunus bibe fontes.

4 The month of June from Pigouchet's Sarum Hours of 1502. By courtesy of the Pierpont Morgan Library.

celebrated "with chorus and organ" at the expense of the guild.[29] Professional matters were aired in what came eventually to be a kind of biannual business meeting, followed by an elaborate banquet and copious winebibbing. It is a further testimony to the stature of Poncet Le Preux that he attained the rank of governor and master of the brotherhood in or before 1523.[30]

One distinction led to another in the case of Le Preux, his nomination as a grand libraire juré of the University following close upon the governorship of the Confrérie. How did such a career get started? For the aspiring young printer or bookseller there was nothing so likely to ensure success as a strategic marriage within the industry. Widows well provided or daughters with dowries offered the readiest avenue to fortune, for they brought wealth with them—not necessarily in money, but in presses, materials, paper, and clients. Many publishers' fortunes were started or made in just this way. Henry Estienne married Guyonne Viart, the widow of John Higman, who had been one of the apprentices at the original Sorbonne press. Widowed again on the death of her second husband many years later, Guyonne, still prized, was sought in marriage by Simon de Colines, the excellent printer and type cutter whose editions are among the most elegant of the period. Robert Estienne married the daughter of Badius. It was by marrying a printer's daughter that Adrian Le Roy established his firm at the sign of Sainte-Geneviève in the Rue Saint-Jean de Beauvais. The instances are so legion as to suggest that enterprises were rarely founded otherwise. While the biography or, at least, the origin of many a printer remains obscure, the biography of business establishments is apt to be well documented and often can be traced from century to century at the same location.

Poncet Le Preux provides a typical case in that nothing is known of his origins or early life before his appearance on the Parisian scene as a libraire in 1498. His career benefited from his marriage (at a date thereafter which cannot be ascertained) to the daughter of a great Paris printer, Philippe Pigouchet. Active from about 1490 until 1514, Pigouchet is especially noted for his highly artistic Livres d'Heures, decorated throughout with ornamental borders and illustrations. According to Douglas Percy Bliss, Pigouchet is "the most delightful of all the printers of Hours."[31] Bliss comments further, referring to the printer's mark of the woodwose and his mate (Fig. 3), that "any book bearing the famous device of the Wild Man and Wild Woman, so carefully shaded and dotted, is a book to treasure. While

[29] Paul Mellotée, *L'imprimerie sous l'ancien régime, Histoire économique de l'imprimerie*, Vol. I (Paris, 1905), pp. 147–155. For the equivalent guild at Lyons, Dominique Phinot wrote a piece celebrating "la noble imprimerie." See V. L. Saulnier, "Dominique Phinot et Didier Lupi: Musiciens de Clément Marot et des Marotiques," *Revue de Musicologie* XLIII (1959), 61–80, no. 37.

[30] Coyecque, *op. cit.*, Vol. I, no. 420.

[31] *A History of Wood-Engraving* (London, 1928), p. 67.

Pigouchet continued to work, the Gothic fragrance still clung to the Horae, the designs were light, sensitive, and unassuming." The dotted or "criblé" style, with which Pigouchet is identified, may be seen to advantage in the marginal cuts of a page from his Sarum Hours of 1502 (Fig. 4), printed for the publisher Simon Vostre. In keeping with his position as an artist of the book, Pigouchet worked mostly on commission and left the commercial side in the hands of entrepreneurs like Vostre. William Ivins refers to this pair as "two of the five really great men in the early history of Paris printing, Pigouchet being one of the remarkable printers of all time."[32] He sees in Pigouchet a quintessentially French artist and remarks his "direct contact with life" and his will to "see it in much the same clear-visioned and slightly acrid way that is still the heritage of the French—the ability to find joy and poetry in a presentment of life which glosses over nothing." The remark might apply as well to many of the chansons listed in the Bibliographical Catalogue.

A coincidence of location seemed destined to link Le Preux to the Pigouchets. Le Preux faced the short Rue des Mathurins from his house at the sign of the Wolf, in the Rue Saint-Jacques, and Pigouchet faced the other end of the little street from his atelier in the Rue de la Harpe, on the corner across from the Church of St. Comos and St. Damien. Le Preux, already well established on his own at an early time, did not move into the quarters of his father-in-law upon marrying Germaine Pigouchet. Another and presumably younger daughter, Claude, brought the paternal premises with her in marriage. Her hand went to a younger man than Le Preux, with the odd name of Pierre Attaingnant.

[32] William M. Ivins, Jr., *Prints and Books: Informal Papers* (Cambridge, Mass., 1926). See the chapter on "Pigouchet's Horae of 1498," pp. 34–38.

II

BEGINNINGS OF A PUBLISHING HOUSE

PIERRE ATTAINGNANT established himself in Paris at least as early as 1514. The time was a fateful one in French history. King Louis XII, last descendant of the Valois-Orleans line, failed rather suddenly in 1514, just a few months after English alliance was secured by his marriage to young Mary Tudor. Expiring during the night of December 31, 1514, he was succeeded on New Year's Day by his son-in-law, François d'Angoulême, from a younger branch of the House of Valois. Crowned at Rheims as Francis I on January 25, 1515, the new king, aged twenty-one, made his Joyeuse Entrée into Paris on Thursday, February 15. A month later the University of Paris came before the court in the person of one of its doctors, to swear allegiance and request confirmation of the academic privileges. The worthy organized his lengthy harangue around the five reasons why France had cause to rejoice: the succession was natural and legitimate; the King was young and "beau prince"; he was prudent, valiant, and battle-tested; peace prevailed within and without the realm; great hopes existed for continued peace and tranquility on account of royal prudence. Jean Barrillon set down a vernacular version of the entire speech in his Journal and reported the second, rather unscholastic, reason in these terms: "Besides, you have achieved the right noble crown of France while being of great physical beauty, nature having left you no impairment at all, so that you are one of the handsomest and best formed persons anywhere, not only in your court but in the entire realm." In giving the Crown's reply to the oration, Chancellor Duprat dwelt upon the University's responsibilities as an organization at once national and international, turning the scarcely veiled political counsel of the last point back upon its authors. He told the scholars in effect to look to their own peace: "In order to continue the studious fervor and follow the customs of your predecessors, you must first live in amity with each other, without lawsuits and squabbles, if possible. By this means will you set your scholars good example and animate them toward fruitful learning, which is why they were given into your charge." Duprat concluded by admonishing the University to stay out of politics: "Take care not to meddle in public affairs and confine yourselves strictly to private affairs and those concerning your discipline. This way you may pursue uninterrupted study and give no cause to your scholars for being contentious and unruly; and the foreigners in your midst, whose "study" is often how to harm the realm whatever way they may, will have no occasion to do, say, or advise bad things to the French nationals and other royalists at the University, who, on account of their youth, frivolity, and limited understanding cannot tell good from bad and seek only new sensations."[1]

[1] *Journal de Jean Barrillon, Secrétaire du chancelier Duprat. 1515–1521*, ed. Pierre de Vaissière (Société de l'Histoire de France, 88) (Paris, 1897), Vol. I, pp. 39–54.

Between interests of state and the academic temperament the gulf was ever wide, it seems.

The young sovereign had other diversions besides listening to speeches. He was widely praised for dealing magnanimously with his predecessor's servants and officials. At the same time he quickly established the reputation for being a pleasure-loving spendthrift. Until the court left the capital on April 24 there was round after round of celebrations: bonfires throughout the city in the public squares, festive renditions of "Te Deum Laudamus" in the Cathedral of Notre Dame and the other great churches, proclamations by royal heralds to the sounds of trumpets and clarions, joustings and tourneys by day, banquets and masquerades by night. In the printers' quarter a platform stage in the Place Maubert offered "jeux et novalitez, c'est assavoir sottye, sermon, moralité et farce."[2] The entertainments went too far in alluding to the King's dalliances with the Parisiennes, with the result that several of the players were chastised. All Paris was agog at the doings of its dashing new sovereign and an atmosphere of great gaiety quickly prevailed over the sobriety that characterized the reign of Louis XII and Anne de Bretagne.

The international situation of 1515 was most promising. It so happened that the houses of Tudor and Hapsburg had also produced brilliant young princes—Henry VIII and Charles V. All three grew up in an atmosphere of late medieval chivalry and were impregnated with the ideal of "courtesie." Nothing seemed impossible to the three youthful knights and indeed nothing was, as long as they could maintain good relations. Prospects for stability within France became even brighter with the birth in 1517 of a Dauphin, named for his father. In a spirit of friendly regard, Francis named the second royal scion (b. 1518) after his cousin Henry, and the third (b. 1522) after cousin Charles.

Prince Charles of Hapsburg came of age on January 6, 1515. As Archduke he ruled the quasi-monarchical state formed in the region of the Low Countries by his Burgundian ancestors, Philip the Good and Charles the Bold, a hegemony contested repeatedly by the predecessors of Francis. His territories included Flanders and Artois, provinces that at the same time were held as fiefs of the French Crown. In amicable recognition of this suzerainty, Charles sent Henry of Nassau and a large embassy to Paris early in 1515 in order to do homage for the two provinces which had once formed a part of the royal domain. The dual allegiance of Flanders and Artois and the complicated and shifting relationship between Burgundian-Flemish lords and French overlords had considerable importance for musicians. For these were the provinces which, together with

[2] *Le Journal d'un Bourgeois de Paris sous le règne de François Ier (1515–1536)*, ed. V. L. Bourrilly (Paris, 1910), p. 14.

royal Picardy and archducal Brabant and Hainaut, formed the cradle of that commanding group of composer-singers, the "Franco-Flemish school."

Attaingnant's Origins

The date of birth and place of origin of the first French music publisher have long remained obscure. A biographical sketch by Georges Lepreux (who was, incidentally, a direct descendant of Poncet Le Preux) suggested that Attaingnant must have been Parisian by birth, and that he learned his trade as an apprentice to Philippe Pigouchet.[3] The conjecture is plausible, the more so because apprentices, once they had attained their brevet as journeymen, often married printers' daughters. Against the supposition of Parisian origin is the absence of any family with the name traceable in the capital. The name itself is of the rarest, meaning, literally "attaining," an importance underscored by the printer when he Latinized his name not by transliteration, but by translation, using the present participle "attingens." (Appendix, 8.) Without trace of such a family in Paris it seems as likely that Attaingnant came from the cathedral town in Picardy whose Chapter provided his presses work on several occasions **(1, 98, 138–139)**, that is from the then prosperous center of Noyon, in the valley of the Oise, about sixty miles to the north of Paris. The place-name Attigny, near the confluence of the rivers Aisne and Oise, is also suggestive. An attractive theory this, since it would place Attaingnant in the company of such prominent Picards in Paris as Lefèvre d'Étaples and Jean Calvin. The composer Claudin de Sermisy has been claimed for Picardy also—he may have been born in the village of Sermoise near Soissons and he had ties that are documented with Cambron, near Amiens, and also with the clergy of Saint-Quentin.[4] Unfortunately for this hypothesis, no Attaingnants have turned up in Noyon or its vicinity. There was, however, a family by the name of Lepreux at Noyon during the fifteenth century.[5] Moreover, Pigouchet printed books for Noyon, among many other towns; thus the connection could have come through him. Caution is in order about deducing the origin of a Paris printer from the liturgical commission he received. Paris was the leading supplier to the dioceses of England, Northern France, and the Low Countries, and had been since long before Attaingnant's day. Thus, in the years before or around 1500, Hopyl printed missals for Liège, Higman for Utrecht, Regnault for Rheims,

[3] Georges Lepreux, *Gallia Typographica* (*Revue des Bibliothèques*, Série Parisienne, Supplément 1) (Paris, 1911), *s.v.*

[4] Isabelle Cazeaux, "The Secular Music of Claudin de Sermisy" (Unpublished Ph.D. dissertation, Columbia University, 1961), Vol. I, pp. 6–9.

[5] *Collection des Inventaires-sommaires des Archives départementales antérieures à 1790: Archives de l'Oise*, Ser. G, No. 1553.

and Henry Estienne for Cambrai. The only substantial competition in the field came from the presses at Rouen, especially those of Martin Morin, who printed a beautiful Noyon Missal in 1506 and one for Arras in 1517.[6]

Did Attaingnant invent his name? Were this the case it would be quite in keeping with the playful and rhetorical mentality of the earlier sixteenth century, with its love of *devises*, riddles, emblems, and pseudonyms. But it is not the case. A family of Attaingnants, apparently quite large, flourished at the time. They were situated as far north of Noyon as Noyon was of Paris, in the old royal province of Artois, near the border of present-day Belgium.

An Antoine Attaingnant was collector of rents for the Abbey of Saint-Vaast in Arras from 1529 to 1542; Jeanne Attaingnant, a rich bourgeoise of Arras, lived until 1586; there was also a Philippe Attaingnant, curate of Sainte-Croix at Cambrai, around the middle of the century.[7] More to the point, there was a Simon Attaingnant who filled the office of canon at the collegiate church of Saint-Amé, Douai, from 1485 until the early years of the sixteenth century. He left a testament dated October 3, 1503. (Appendix, 1.) Mention is made of a debtor nephew, Jean, living at Vitry, a town midway between Arras and Douai, and of a Sire Simon Attaingnant. (The title "sire" used in this way betokened a merchant or tradesman, according to Cotgrave's *Dictionarie of the French and English Tongues.*) Canon Simon provided for his colleagues' refreshment at his funeral ("five sous each and no more"). Then, after the usual pious donations, ending with a small bequest to the godchildren, comes the main bequest: the entire rest of the estate went in halves to Jeannet de Gournenflo (possibly the son of the Gournenflo who received £40) and to a young man designated as Pierotin (a familiar diminutive for Pierre). The few words of the last clause tell much. A young Pierre Attaingnant lived at Douai in 1503 as a ward of his wealthy relation, Canon Simon. The boy's father (Jean Attaingnant?) was alive, as is evident in the provision for executors so that Pierre's inheritance "should not fall into the hands of his father."

Were Attaingnant a common name, the information might be considered as being of only possible relevance. Given the great rarity and curiosity of the name, there is every likelihood that the Pierre Attaingnant who was a minor in 1503 is the one encountered in Paris as early as 1514. At the very least, the surname

[6] Eduard Frère, *De l'Imprimerie et de la librairie à Rouen, dans les xve et xvie siècles, et de Martin Morin, célèbre imprimeur rouennais* (Rouen, 1843). See also the same author's *Manuel du Bibliographe normand* (Rouen, 1858), pp. 151–152. Rouen printers vied with those of Paris for the English market, printing missals for the use of Hereford, Salisbury, and York.

[7] *Inventaire sommaire, Pas de Calais* (Arras, 1902), Ser. H, Nos. 199, 203 (Antoine); Jean Lestocquoy and Albon de Selliers de Moranville, *Les Patriciens d'Arras sous la Renaissance* (Arras, 1950), p. 170 (Jeanne); *Archives départmentales du Nord: Répertoire numérique* (Lille, 1960), Ser. G 6, G69 (Philippe).

suggests an origin in or around the Artois. Names beginning "Att" are common to the region, not surprising in view of its Roman name—Attrebatum. A further circumstance substantiates the regional tie. One of the high points of Attaingnant's publishing career was the handsome series of motets by Claudin, Certon, and Lupi, printed in 1542 with special types upon a special paper larger than that ordinarily used for quartos. The paper, which does not occur elsewhere in Attaingnant's production, may be identified by its watermark, the Gothic initials P S on a shield surmounted by a crown. The same paper turns up in Arras and, specifically, was used for the accounts of the Abbey of Saint-Vaast in 1539 (and thus by its rent-collector, Antoine Attaingnant, presumably).[8] The normal suppliers of Paris printers were the paper mills of Troyes in Champagne. Attaingnant was no exception, his folio Masses of 1532 having been printed on a paper showing a *pot* surmounted by a cross—the "filigrane parlante" of Pothier, a miller dynasty of Troyes.[9] Use of an unusual paper, made in or for the Artois, thus helps confirm the connection between Attaingnant and the homonymous family in the north.

Supposing the Pierre Attaingnant of Douai and of Paris to be the same, we may inquire what chain of events led him from the banks of the Scarpe to the banks of the Seine. The Artois, as a border province, was ever subject to contest. Ceded to France by the Treaty of Arras in 1482, it was taken ten years later by Maximilian of Hapsburg. French suzerainty was still valid until the Treaty of Cambrai (1529), when the province was detached completely from France. A person growing up in Douai around 1500 would have owed first allegiance to the Count of Artois, Philip the Handsome (son of Maximilian and father of Prince Charles) or to his sister Marguerite of Austria, who assumed the regency of the Low Countries after the untimely death of Philip in 1506. Beyond the archducal family the inhabitants of the old royal provinces looked to Paris, to a greater or lesser degree, depending on the politics of the moment. Louis XII maintained good relations with both Philip and Marguerite and there were few impediments to concourse up to 1515. Scholars, artists, and merchants circulated freely. The peregrinations of Erasmus confirm this, as does the loan of royal craftsmen to Marguerite for the construction of her memorial church in Brou.

[8] Charles Moïse Briquet, *Les Filigranes. Dictionnaire des marques de papier* (Paris, 1907), No. 9667. A similar mark appears in the paper used for MS additions at the end of the Mazarine chansonniers. See **73.**

[9] Briquet, *op. cit.*, No. 12502. See Anne Basanoff, "L'emploi du papier à l'Université de Paris, (1430–1473)," *Bibliothèque d'Humanisme et Renaissance* XXVI (1964), p. 311, n. 5. Several other watermarks appear in papers used by Attaingnant, none as yet permitting positive identification. The mark of a compass on a shield appearing in **119, 132–133** and **141** may be connected with the Le Bé firm at Troyes. See Briquet, Vol. II, p. 271.

Douai was situated in the middle of the musical "belt" so prolific of Franco-Flemish masters. (See the map, Fig. 5.) It was not so large or famous a center as nearby Cambrai, city of Dufay, Tinctoris, and Agricola, which, in the early years of the sixteenth century, sent Louis Van Pullaer to be *Magister puerorum* at Notre Dame of Paris. (The power of Cambrai and its bishop was temporal, in that the Cambrésis formed a little state unto itself, as well as spiritual—hence financial—in that its very large diocese stretched the entire length of the River Scheldt (Escaut), from headwaters to its mouth at Antwerp, including parts of Artois and Flanders, most of Hainaut, and much of Brabant.) Nor could Douai claim as lively a commercial life as its close neighbor upstream on the Scarpe, episcopal Arras, which had sent Antoine de Févin to the French court, where he became Louis XII's favorite singer. Yet Douai maintained an artistic life of its own, particularly in the collegiate churches of Saint-Pierre and Saint-Amé. The older and wealthier was Saint-Amé, whose crypt was dedicated in 1024 and whose members included a provost, dean, treasurer, cantor, and *écolâtre* (instructor of religion), all elected by the chapter, twenty-one prebendaries and forty chaplains.[10] Musical services were elaborate, and the flourishing choir school probably afforded young Douaisiens as good training as could be had anywhere. By the second half of the sixteenth century Douai was able to boast having nurtured the musicians of the Regnart family as well as a specialist in music printing, Jean Bogard.

Several dioceses in the old royal provinces of northern France maintained scholarships for their choirboys at the University of Paris. The diocese of Arras, which included Douai, had connection with the Collège de Dainville, founded in the early fourteenth century by Michel de Dainville, Archdeacon of Arras. Dainville's executors were the cathedral chapters of Arras and Noyon.[11] The two bishoprics were contiguous, as seen in Fig. 5, a map showing diocesan boundaries from the Middle Ages until the Council of Trent (1559) in the territory between Paris and Antwerp.[12] Though small in extent, at least when compared

[10] G. Deghilage, "Les Doyens du Chapitre de St-Amé," *Bulletin de la Société d'études de la Province de Cambrai* XLIII (1950), 32–41, and De la Fons-Melicocq, "La Collégiale de St-Amé à Douai aux XIV, XV, et XVIèmes siècles," *Archives historiques et littéraires du Nord de la France et du Midi de la Belgique* (Ser. 3) (Valenciennes, 1885) V, 161–195.

[11] Michel Félibien, "Fondation et statuts du collège de Dainville," *Histoire de la Ville de Paris* (Paris, 1725), Vol. I, p. 509.

[12] The map relies primarily on Baudrillart, *Dictionnaire d'histoire et de gèographie ecclésiastique* (Paris, 1912——), Vol. VII, article "Belgique," with accompanying map opposite p. 528. For a more detailed description and analysis of the northernmost dioceses see E. de Moreau and J. Deharveng, *Circonscriptions ecclésiastiques . . . en Belgique avant 1559* (Brussels, 1948), with atlas. An equivalent study is lacking for the dioceses in the southern part of the map, which relies upon a later source, Sanson's *Atlas géographique* (Paris, 1670). These dioceses, roughly outlined on the map, were not subject to Tridentine reform. A manuscript "Description de la France" of the late sixteenth century allows the diocese of Noyon "235 fiefs et ariere fiefs, 404 paroisses et 36200 familles, feux contés," (British Museum, Sloane MS 557, *s.v.* Picardy.)

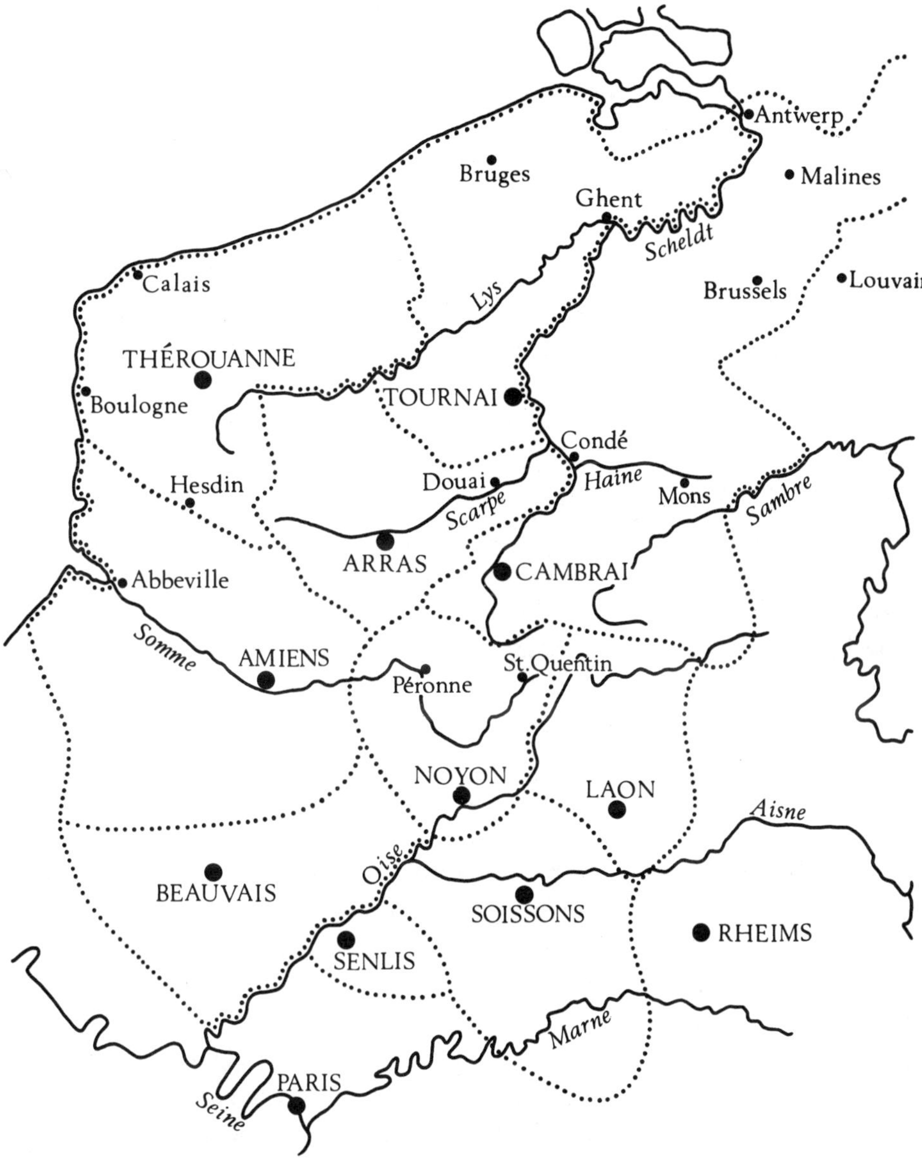

5 Dioceses between Antwerp and Paris before 1559.

with Cambrai, the episcopal sees of Arras and Noyon were wealthy in souls and industries. Noyon's territory included the two flourishing towns celebrated in a fifteenth-century chanson: "Entre Péronne et Saint-Quentin." According to the terms of Dainville's founding statutes, Noyon and Arras were to name six scholars apiece to Paris. Until dissolution of the Collège de Dainville during the French Revolution, nomination remained subject to approbation of the two chapters.

In order to enter the Collège youths had to be "tonsured, freeborn, and not servile, aged at least fourteen." Among their duties were obligatory lessons in plainchant, given in the chapel. The chapter of Arras maintained its support of the young scholars as long as they continued their studies, and if a lad chose to abandon school for a trade, it supported him throughout his apprenticeship.[13] The latter practice is especially suggestive with regard to Attaingnant. It can hardly be a coincidence that the premises he was to occupy adjoined the Collège de Dainville, from which they were rented. Attaingnant, like Pigouchet before him, was in direct, unavoidable contact with the landlord masters of the Collège de Dainville (hence with the chapters of Arras and Noyon). Not unlikely, it was this connection which first brought the boy to Paris—a scholar from the diocese of Arras. Once installed in the college, it would have been impossible for him not to be aware of the great craftsman whose printing shop crowded the walls of the college. When Attaingnant was established as proprietor of the shop, perhaps after an apprenticeship to Pigouchet, it would be natural that he print liturgical works on commission from Noyon, as Pigouchet had done before him, and as his son-in-law, Gilles Gourbin, would do after him.[14] Possibly he might have enjoyed the trade of the Arras chapter too, had not Rouen printers preëmpted the field.

The chain of circumstances is imposing: a prominent family named Attaingnant lived in Arras and Douai; mention is made in 1503 of a young Pierotin Attaingnant who lived with his well-to-do relation, Canon Simon; ties existed between the chapter of Arras and the Pigouchet-Attaingnant premises in Paris; Attaingnant, extraordinarily, used a paper connected with the Artois. All point to the same conclusion: Attaingnant, by origin, was an Artesian.

Attaingnant, man of the North—the likelihood opens various perspectives. It was to the North that the royal musical organizations turned when replacements were needed. In 1508, during a typical foray, musicians had to be sought for the Sainte-Chapelle "because the King, the Queen, and Monseigneur de Bourbon took the former singers into their services." Chaplain Henry Forin was instructed "to go to Soissons, Noyon, Saint-Quentin, Laon, Rheims, Sedan, and Arras and fetch the best and foremost singers that could be found."[15] All towns mentioned were episcopal seats with the exception of Saint-Quentin, which had a remarkable musical tradition of its own, and Sedan, which fell within the archdiocese of

[13] Georges Coolen, *Le collège de Dainville à Paris* (Bulletin historique de la Société des Antiquaires de la Morinie, No. 300) (Saint-Omer, 1938), p. 9.

[14] E. Morel, "Les livres liturgiques imprimés avant le xviie siècle à l'usage des diocèses de Beauvais, Noyon et Senlis," *Bulletin historique et philologique*, 1902, 185–196. Pigouchet's Book of Hours dated from 1498, Gourbin's Ritual from 1560 (p. 194).

[15] Michel Brenet, *Les Musiciens de la Sainte-Chapelle du Palais* (Paris, 1910), p. 49.

Rheims. All were within the then political realm of France, exception made in the single case of Arras. Whatever the circumstances that brought Attaingnant to Paris, he could hardly have failed to find there numerous countrymen—musicians with connections in the various royal establishments. Diocesan ties, a little-tapped resource for music history, surely figured in his career. Their importance may be gauged in another way from the care taken to mark the episcopal towns on Attaingnant's geographical broadsheet; these are designated by a small "e" while the archepiscopal seats are marked by a small "a" (see Pl. XIII). A further distinction was observed between less and more important towns by means of lower- and upper-case initial letters. (Note that Brussels, at the time, did not rate along with neighbors like Antwerp, Malines, and Louvain.) Perhaps "Gaule Belgique" occupied the first place on Attaingnant's sheet for more than one reason.

Early Years in Paris

The man named Pierre Attaingnant who comes to light in Paris in 1514 does so by an odd quirk. A business contract, one of the rare early ones to survive, shows him in possession of a press for hire (Appendix, 2). He is qualified as a libraire, suggesting a person of some means, presumably not less than about twenty years of age. Let us assume that he was born about 1494, a year otherwise illustrious for having produced Oronce Finé, Francis I, and Rabelais. The same birth date applied to Pierotin Attaingnant of Douai would make him about nine in 1503. (As a minor, he had to be less than fifteen at the time.) With nonage passed he would be ready for college about 1509. On this hypothetical schedule there would have been time before 1514 for an apprenticeship, which generally lasted from two to five years.

The contract is typical of the time in its complication and contains a wealth of informative detail. Jean de la Roche, a printer and typecaster, rented use of a press for five months from Attaingnant, agreeing that, should Attaingnant present him with "Dominoes, excommunications, or pardons," he would print them, his labor being deductible from the rent; should Attaingnant want the press for his own use, La Roche must give it up on fifteen days' notice. Worthy of note in passing is the crucial role of paper and its cost. La Roche, like so many printers of the time, was an itinerant jobber. Four years later he was in Orleans, hiring his services to the diocese and contracting to print three reams of Confessionals for the sum of £6.[16] Young Attaingnant obviously had some connection with an ecclesiastical jurisdiction, or hopes of obtaining one. No traces of this early activity remain. Excommunications or pardons and other publications of the

[16] Philippe Renouard, *Documents sur les imprimeurs parisiens, 1450–1600* (Paris, 1901), *s.v.*

moment, often only a single sheet, rarely outlasted their immediate purpose—there is no reason why they should. "Dominoes" offered more interest to collectors. In his *Trésor de la langue française* of 1606 Jean Nicot defined a *dominotier* as "celuy qui fait et vend des dominos, c'est à dire des images et œuvres de portraicture peintes et imprimées en papier, et gravées en bois ou cuivre." Given the context, the product may be translated freely as "religious pictures," which were produced in vast quantities for the edification of the faithful. The years between 1514 and 1525 surely saw orders for such devotional material placed with Attaingnant, although nothing of the kind now survives. The selling of prints secured a livelihood for countless libraires, and rare was the bookseller who did not also publish them if he owned a press and could get commissions.

Attaingnant's exact location in 1514 would have considerable bearing on the chronology of the early years. Unfortunately, it occurs on the missing upper right edge of the original document (Appendix, 2). His address would tell, for example, whether he was already established in Pigouchet's shop (and, by implication, whether he had already married Claude Pigouchet). The year of Pigouchet's demise has obvious bearing here.[17] For more than two decades, Pigouchet's presses were among the most active in Paris. Then all activity stopped. The last dated work is a Book of Hours for Langres that appeared in 1514. On January 30, 1515, the printer resigned his post as libraire juré, perhaps because of illness.[18] There is no good reason to believe he survived this year. In 1518 he is mentioned as deceased. (Appendix, 3.) It is not impossible that Attaingnant had already inherited all or part of the business by 1514, and that the press he rented out was in actuality located in the "Rue de la Harpe près de l'église Saint-Côme." In any case, the young libraire took Claude to wife soon after, if not before. (A parallel that would not have escaped the couple was that Francis I, on May 18, 1514, also married a Claude, the daughter of Louis XII and Anne of Brittany.) As with the marriage of Le Preux to Germaine Pigouchet, the contract has not been located. Yet another sister, Collette, (the familiar form of Nicole), was aged seventeen when she married the merchant Jean Béguin in March, 1519 (Appendix, 3). From the same document we learn that there were at least four Pigouchet children, of whom three then survived, while a son, Robert, had died. Germaine was married already to Le Preux, but any mention of Claude or her husband is mysteriously absent. Fifty years later the descendants of the three Pigouchet

[17] The year 1526 is frequently encountered in the literature. It stems from a misreading of the date on Olivier Maillard's *Quadrigesimale opus declamatum parisorum*, an error found in the Renouard MS and in the *Catalogue des Imprimés* of the Bibliothèque Nationale. The colophon in question reads "Philippi pigoucheti . . . anno xpiane. salutis M. cccc. xxvi Junii"—i.e., June 26, 1500.

[18] Philippe Renouard, *Répertoire des imprimeurs parisiens, libraires, fondeurs de caractères, et correcteurs d'imprimerie* (Paris, 1965), *s.v.*

daughters were still dividing and subdividing the estate (Appendix, 34). By this time deaths and remarriages had intervened to obscure still further a complicated series of relationships. The family tree placed at the conclusion of the Appendix is constructed with a view to untangling the various branches.

The marriage with Claude could not have taken place much later than 1520. By 1537 one of the two daughters of the couple, Germaine, was already marriageable, and perhaps even married, as Attaingnant's business partnership with his son-in-law, Hubert Jullet, would seem to indicate. In January, 1541, children were born to both Germaine and Marie Attaingnant (Appendix, 12–13). Pigouchet's widow, Jeanne Ponceau (or Du Pont), lived a number of years beyond 1520, and the rent paid for the premises in the Rue de la Harpe in 1528 shows that she lived with Attaingnant, not Le Preux (Appendix, 5). This circumstance may serve to banish the scruples expressed by the author of *Gallia Typographica* as to whether Attaingnant occupied the exact same location as Pigouchet. Both rented from the Collège de Dainville, as we have seen, and Pigouchet often included mention of this in his address: "*In locatiis Collegii vulgariter nuncupati de Dainville.*" Rent contracts between printer and college survive for the years 1506–1509 (see p. 120). In some citations Pigouchet approximated the address that his son-in-law was to adopt: "*In vico Citharae prope ecclesiam beatorum Cosmae et Damiani.*" The little church of St. Cosmos and St. Damian, situated directly on the Rue de la Harpe, and across the Rue des Cordeliers from the shop, was more easily found by prospective customers than the Collège de Dainville, situated between the small side-streets "des Cordeliers" and "Pierre Sarrazin." Saint-Côme was a landmark for several reasons. Both saints of its title were known for their miraculous cures, as was Saint Roch, to whom a chapel in the building was dedicated (later Attaingnant would print dances on a tune called "Saint-Roch"; see **16,** 13). The church had been erected in 1212 as a dependency of the abbey of Saint-Germain-des-Prés; in 1345 it passed to the jurisdiction of the University. It was the seat of a Confrérie de Saint-Côme et de Saint-Damien, an organization of barbers and surgeons (the distinction was made much later) who offered gratuitous treatment to the poor on the first Monday of every month.[19] The family church of the Pigouchets and Attaingnants was not here but at Saint-Benoît le Bétourné, in whose school the poet Villon had been raised. (See Pl. XII*b*). At this modest edifice, close by the Rue Saint-Jacques, the children of Germaine Attaingnant and Hubert Jullet were baptized (Appendix, 12, 15).

Scant traces of the sixteenth century remain in the neighborhood today. Saint-Benoît was demolished to make way for the Rue des Écoles (1852–1855) and Saint-Côme gave way to the Rue Racine (1836). The tiny Rue Pierre Sarrazin

[19] Aubin Louis Millin, *Antiquités nationales* (Paris, 1790–1799), Vol. III, Art. xxxv, p. 18.

survives yet, bearing the same name, and it still boasts the little Gothic tower on the corner of the Rue Haute Feuille, across from the old Collège des Prémontrés (see Pl. XVI). The Rue des Cordeliers, widened, now bears the name Rue de l'École de Médecine, preserving at least this link with the practitioners of old Saint-Côme. Just off it, the Cordeliers' church still stands. The Rue de la Harpe in this vicinity has disappeared altogether, having been absorbed by the Boulevard Saint-Michel. By a stroke of fate somehow appropriate, the location of the old Pigouchet-Attaingnant shop today houses the flourishing business of Joseph Gibert, one of the larger textbook stores in the University Quarter (26, Boulevard Saint-Michel). The sixteenth-century house would have occupied no more than the broad sidewalk in front of the store, now given over to open bookstalls.

The first datable publication of Attaingnant is the result of a commission from the cathedral chapter of Noyon for a Breviary. The order, which also involved Poncet Le Preux, was made on July 14, 1525. This is known from the receipt for payment, witnessed by Attaingnant and by Germaine Pigouchet acting in lieu of her husband, "momentarily absent from the city" (perhaps on one of his business trips to Lyons or abroad) (Appendix, 4). The price agreed upon was a substantial sum, £400, and the representative from Noyon, Canon Jean Poupart, declared that he had received the 320 copies for the six months of Wintertide, as agreed in the bargain. More than this number of copies must have been printed; some remained with the publishers, as shown by the inventories of later years. What survives from the breviary is not the *Pars hiemalis* mentioned in the contract, but a *Pars estivalis* **(1)**. Attaingnant's name is the only one to appear on the title page and he is styled not as an *imprimeur de livres*, as in the contract, but merely as an "honest man," leaving us in doubt as to whether his own or someone else's presses were used. The breviaries were, in any case, "on sale in his bookstore." A comparison with the prices charged for printing various liturgical books at the time reveals that the sum paid by the Noyon authorities must have been for both parts, Winter and Summer. Even so the charges were rather high. By comparison, other Paris publishers supplied:

600 Breviaries, Nevers usage, for £300, in 1523
400 Missals, Senlis usage, for £350, in 1524[20]

The publication of 1525, joined with the earlier documentary evidence, shows Attaingnant to have been a publisher-bookseller and not merely a printer.[21]

[20] Ernest Coyecque, *Recueil d'actes notariés, relatifs à l'histoire de Paris* (Paris, 1905), Vol. I, nos. 435 and 533, respectively.

[21] Yvonne Rihouët [Rokseth] suggested conclusions exactly opposite in her debut article, "Note biographique sur Attaingnant," *Revue de Musicologie* VIII (1924), 70–71. She relied on the contract of 1525 and did not take into consideration its published consequence, the Noyon Breviary **(1)**.

For the one surviving liturgical publication of the early years there must have been many companion volumes, now lost. A later inventory mentions missals, manuals, breviaries and Books of Hours (Appendix, 28). No Books of Hours for Noyon usage have come down to the present, nor have the publications for the use of Paris, listed in the same inventory. Ecclesiastical broadsides like those mentioned in the 1514 document also must have provided work during the early years. While nothing of this nature survives, there do remain, miraculously, a couple of didactic sheets, one dated 1534 and the other defective as to date **(58, 59)**. In the shadow of one college and surrounded by many others, the bookstore in the Rue de la Harpe was well placed to capitalize on the student trade. Pigouchet, a University bookseller, had done so earlier when printing items such as *Les Principes en françois*. One of the surviving sheets by Attaingnant is a vade mecum to the many divisions of knowledge (Pl. I), not excluding Magica, with its five sub-branches: Joculatoria, Mathematica, Maleficium ("quod fit per incantationes"), Sortilegium, and Prestigium. The other, possibly of more use to scholars today, gives the vernacular names and Latin equivalents of the major towns and rivers of the three parts of Gaul, as we have seen (Pl. XIII). For Paris, Attaingnant indulged in a small descriptive encomium, declaring it the "most famous city and university of Christendom." Many printers in the University Quarter offered similar material for sale, and competition must have been lively. The two outline sheets were presumably aimed at the younger and rawer students, doing their Latin grammar with the Faculty of Arts—the necessary "undergraduate" preparation for studies under one of the other faculties. Even distinguished printers like Colines turned out didactic broadsides. It has been suggested that they served not only during the lessons, but also as advertisements for them.[22]

Nothing in Attaingnant's early years predicts a career in music publishing. There is no documentary indication that he differed in any respect from scores of other booksellers living in the University. Yet it is quite possible that he had already established a music trade in addition to that in liturgical books. Someone in Paris must have handled the music books that were destined for, or closely connected with, French musical circles. A case in point is the four-volume series of *Motetti della Corona* printed by Petrucci in 1514–1519. These appeared after the printer returned to the duchy of Urbino, and the first volume (1514) mentions the reigning duke, Francesco della Rovere, who was an ally and comrade-in-arms of Francis I during the first Italian campaign of 1515. A motet of Févin in this volume sets the tone and leaves no doubt about which royal house was involved: "Gaude Francorum regia corona" (later printed by Attaingnant in **63**). The

[22] Philippe Renouard, *Bibliographie des éditions de Simon de Colines* (Paris, 1894), p. 249.

volumes of Masses by Mouton and Févin that Petrucci printed in 1515 also show a turn to a more French than "Burgundian" repertory and were perhaps motivated by the same political considerations. Urbino underwent trying times in the next few years. Pope Leo X assigned the state to his nephew Lorenzo de' Medici on August 18, 1516, and sent troops to wrest the duchy from its rightful heirs. After a year of war the attempt, with outside help, was successful, and King Francis gave it a stamp of approval when he granted the hand of a Bourbon princess, Madeleine de La Tour, to the Medici captain. The marriage, which took place at Amboise on January 28, 1518, was scorned in France because of the high birth of the lady and the low birth and base character of the newly "noble" Medici. If the match was not successful in shoring the King's position in Italy, it did call into being the magnificent musical collection known as the Medici Codex, as well as a child, Catherine, the future wife of Francis's second son, Henry.[23] Lorenzo de' Medici died on May 4, 1519. Petrucci's second, third, and fourth volumes of "Crown Motets" appeared in the same year, on June 17, September 7, and October 31, with reference to neither Medici nor Rovere. Did the volumes originate as commissions of the French Crown? Were this the case some mention probably would have been made. The more plausible explanation is that Duke Francesco encouraged the series initially as a compliment to his northern ally and a reminder of little Urbino. What more fitting way than to join the glories of the King's music with the art of an outstanding native of the duchy, Ottaviano dei Petrucci, "famoso stampatore"? A comparable instance of politics via music printing would be the collection of French pieces, now lost, printed by Francesco Marcolini in 1537 and dedicated to Count Guido Rangone, to whom the poet Niccolò Franco wrote commenting on the appropriateness of the choice of repertory "during this the hour of your valor, when appear the victorious signs of the Most Christian Crown [of France]."[24] Italian music printing depended upon export trade to make a profit, and upon France in particular, as we shall see. Petrucci's "Crown Motets" with their direct bearing on the French Royal Chapel were logical choices for export to Paris. Once arrived, no bookstore in the capital provided a more likely outlet for them than that of Attaingnant.

There is another hint of French activity in music publishing during the early years of Francis I. Marcantonio Cavazzoni's *Recerchari Motetti Canzoni* (Venice, 1523) reproduces a papal privilege that makes the following warning: "Cautum est a Christianissimo rege francie ne quis per decennium hos excudat poena

[23] Edward E. Lowinsky, "The Medici Codex: A Document of Music, Art and Politics in the Renaissance," *Annales Musicologiques* V (1957), 61–176.

[24] Scipione Casali, *Gli Annali della typografia veneziana di Francesco Marcolini da Forli* (Bologna, 1861; 2d ed., 1963), no. 23, p. 45.

amissionis librorum ac arbitraria a sua regia maiestate taxanda."[25] In other words, those subject to the Most Christian King were prohibited from printing the pieces, under threat of confiscation and censure. The Cavazzoni keyboard score of 1523 was reproduced by relief process from woodcut plates. Perhaps plans were afoot in France to print similar woodcut music, or such music may actually have appeared. Otherwise the explicit stricture of the privilege would seem pointless. One volume of woodcut music that must have come out in France before or around 1530 has been largely overlooked. The British Museum's tenor part of Antico's octavo collections of 1521 concludes with an unsigned fifth volume, containing motets and distinguished by a fleur-de-lis on the title page. The music pages resemble those of Antico in their layout. Yet the paper is different, showing no watermark, unlike the preceding volumes, and so are the text types. One text, "Signasti Domine," calls upon Saint Francis to "protect our King, Francis." Another piece, "Ave virgo sanctissima," has recently been identified by Frank D'Accone with the setting by Layolle in *Cantiones triginta* printed by Montanus and Neuber (Nuremberg, 1568). The printing device of the lily had earlier led Chapman to suggest Lyons as the place of publication.[26] There are other reasons to substantiate a Lyonese origin. The ornamental side- and tailpieces decorating the title page were used as borders at Lyons between 1526 and 1530.[27] Such skillfully cut music-plates as the motets display were not within the province of many artists. The staves and notes are, if not identical in size with those of the 1521 volumes, very close in style. The question inevitably arises whether the master engraver himself, Andrea Antico, did not sojourn for a time in France. His whereabouts in the late 'twenties are not confirmed by any signed publications.

Another of the lesser mysteries surrounding the debut of music printing in France remains unsolved. There were four two-voiced pieces in an unsigned

[25] The entire document is reproduced in Claudio Sartori, *Bibliografia della musica strumentale italiana stampata in Italia fino al 1700* (Florence, 1952), pp. 3–4.

[26] Catherine Weeks Chapman, "Andrea Antico" (Unpublished dissertation, Harvard University, 1964), pp. 167–170. Mrs. Chapman rightly discounts the implausible ascription of the volume—British Museum, K.8.b.7.(5)—to Buglhat and his associates at Ferrara, whose prints differ in format, text-types, paper, and printing technique (being reproduced by single impression from type). She suggests that the volume at London is the sole survivor of a series of six motet books devoted to Layolle and printed at Lyons around 1530; see "Printed Collections of Polyphonic Music Owned by Ferdinand Columbus," *Journal of The Americal Musicological Society* XXI (1968), 53–54, Appendix 132–137.

[27] In impressions by Antoine Blanchard for Barthélemy Trot. See Baudrier, *Bibliographie lyonnaise*, Ser. 5, pp. 100, 106. The borders also occur in Cocles, *L'Art de chyromancie* (Lyons: Jacques Moderne, n.d.) (Bib. Nat. Rés V. 2259). In all these examples the borders are without surrounding straight lines. Also, they occur in the position for which they were intended, unlike the music book, which because of its oblong shape makes the sidepieces into head- and tailpieces, and the tailpiece (with shield for coat of arms) into an awkward perpendicular sidepiece.

collection entitled *Se ensuyvent les Nouelz nouvaulx de ce présent an mil cinq cens et douze dont en y a plusieurs notez à deux parties dont l'une n'est que le plain chant. Avecq quatre histoires par personnaiges . . . Composez par maistre François Briand, maistre des escolles de Sainct Benoist en la cité du Mans.* The modern editor, Chardon, neglected to say how the music was reproduced and the original is now lost.[28] If the date of 1512 holds for the printing as well as the contents, woodcut plates would seem the most likely resort. Since Le Mans was not a printing center, publication probably took place elsewhere. In this connection it should be noted that Pigouchet printed "Heures à l'usage du Mans," in 1497, 1500, and 1510.

In addition to selling liturgical books and schoolboys' syllabuses, Attaingnant kept a stock of music paper in his shop. The "papier reglé" mentioned at a later date (Appendix, 28) was presumably paper on which staves had been printed by rule. Did he, in the early years, offer more to the musical public? Good business-man that he was, Attaingnant certainly would have wished to capitalize on the music market during the long and costly time of trial while perfecting his own printing method. The likelihood is that he did sell music, whether manuscript or printed, from his own press or that of someone else.

The transition between generations in the Rue de la Harpe raises questions, finally, about the survival of typographical materials from the distinguished older firm. Had more than a single Breviary remained from the years between 1514 and 1528 the problem might be less difficult of resolution. As yet, the Breviary has not been identified typographically with anything from Pigouchet's press. Given the very conservative nature of liturgical printing in the sixteenth century we may suspect the decorative material in the Noyon Missal **(98)** and Ritual **(139)** to be of much earlier origin. Traditionally, missals began with an illustration for the first Sunday of Advent showing the soul, in the form of a small body, literally being lifted up, in keeping with the Introit's words "Ad te levavi animam meam." The Noyon Missal complies, offering a crude woodcut representation in a style decades older than the imprint.[29] (See Pl. V.) Far from crude are the surrounding borders. The two sidepieces on the right, showing floral arabesques and grotesques on a criblé background, are in the Pigouchet style. They match the head- and tailpiece and the decorative initial so well that it is difficult to conceive of anyone less than a Pigouchet as inventor of the whole. Note in particular the

[28] Henri Chardon (ed.), *Nouelz nouvaulx de ce présent an* (Paris and Le Mans, 1904). The Bibliothèque Communale of Bourg-en-Bresse, where Chardon found the work, disavows any knowledge of it at present.

[29] The cut made the round of liturgical printing houses. It appears also in Jean Amazeur's *Missale Romanum* (Paris, 1554); see Renouard, *Imprimeurs et libraires parisiens*, Vol. I (Paris, 1964), pl. A 15. The cut of the Crucifixion in the *Manuale* for Noyon **(139)** is identical with that in Jean Adam's *Missale Parisiense* (Paris, 1516) reproduced in Renouard, *op. cit.*, pl. A 4.

use of the cone-shaped flower in both initial and borders, the playful evocation of the same in the merman's jaunty hat, mockingly enhanced by the reverse curve of his tail. Liturgical books in folio printed by Pigouchet are not now known. The sidepieces resemble those in the small Books of Hours (see Figs. 2–3), yet match none that we have seen. Pigouchet's artistry was much appreciated and he printed, on command, Hours for the use of Amiens, Angers, Arras, Besançon, Chalons, Chartres, Clermont, Coutances, Evreux, Langres, Le Mans, Lisieux, Lyons, Maçon, Nantes, Noyon, Paris, Poitiers, Rennes, Rheims, Rome, Rouen, Saint-Malo, Salisbury, and Verdun, among other places; a comparative study remains to be attempted. As for the larger criblé initials ornamenting the Noyon Missal and Ritual, they too are in an older style, based upon Gothic letter-shapes and a particular convention that might be termed "ossiferous," since the circular holes and indentations often suggest bones. The genre was very widespread, both before and after 1500. Examples published by Poncet Le Preux (Pl. IV) show a characteristically sixteenth-century lightening—an evolution away from the form's earlier heaviness. How much lighter and more graceful still is the floriated "A" in the Noyon Missal! (Five other letters from the same set were chosen to introduce the sections of this Historical Study.) Highly stylized, the alphabet expresses that interplay of tradition and innovation, of fantasy and finesse, that is so characteristic of Parisian art in the earlier sixteenth century. Quite contrary to the imported and officially proclaimed doctrines of renewal after decay and barbarism, some of the era's best artistic efforts drew upon the strength of medieval tradition. The delicate tracery of the windows in Saint-Merry, the ineffable grace of Philibert de l'Orme's choirscreen in Saint-Estienne—these are glories that may also serve to illuminate the music once heard within the same walls. Like Attaingnant's floriated initials, they are at once direct outgrowth and sublime transformation of the Gothic past.

Attaingnant possessed a smaller, related set of criblé initials which he used in the same books (Fig. 6). The example, from the Noyon Ritual, also shows his material for printing chant. Two printings were required, with staves done in red from short lateral segments and notes in black. This process betrays another tradition that reached back before 1500. It was to flourish throughout the sixteenth century and long beyond. Innovation was attempted, nevertheless, even in this most traditional area, notably in the very Paris shop in question.

A New Method of Printing

The spread of early music printing followed rather closely the geographical pattern established by the printers of liturgical chant. Centers for these were:

6 Plainchant from Attaingnant's *Manuale* for Noyon use **(139)**. By courtesy of the Bodleian Library, Oxford.

Venice, Rome, the towns in or near the Rhine Valley, Lyons, and Paris. Indeed, "Paris, with nineteen books with printed music during the incunabula period cedes first place only to Venice," according to one student of the subject.[30] Already in the late fifteenth century the Paris printer Michel Toulouze became something of a specialist in music. From his address in the Clos Bruneau at the sign of the Hart's Horn, he signed the *Art et instruction de bien dancer* (1496 or earlier), which has examples of mensural notation poorly printed from movable type upon separately printed red staves. Thus Toulouze actually preceded Petrucci although he in no sense rivaled him, for his notes were badly coordinated with the staves, while the Venetian prints achieved perfect registration. Perhaps

[30] Kathi Meyer-Baer, *Liturgical Music Incunabula* (London, 1962), p. xxxii. She believes that printing chant on staves separately reproduced from short lateral segments is one of the earliest methods: see pp. xxv–vi.

Petrucci knew of the abortive efforts in Paris—he claimed, when applying to the Signoria for a privilege in 1498, "to have discovered, with much expense and searching care, that which others, *not only in Italy but also elsewhere*, had long sought in vain: a most convenient way of printing music" (our italics). About 1500 Toulouze used his music types again, with no greater success, printing the *Utilissime musicales regulae* of his neighbor, the music teacher Guillaume Guerson de Villelongue.[31]

Subsequent attempts in Paris were inconclusive. Three months after Attaingnant rented his press to La Roche, two experienced University printers brought out another edition of Guerson's *Regulae* (Regnault and Marnef, April, 1514). They printed chant examples with red notes on four-line black staves, reproduced from type in short lateral segments, and with a modicum of success in registration. When they came to the part called "Explicit secundus liber qui est de contrapuncto," demanding mensural notation, they printed the notes but did not even attempt to supply staves (a staff, of four lines, appears only in the demonstration of mensural signs, accidentals, and rests). The minims (9.5 mm. in height) look to be printed from type, while some larger values appear woodcut. Concurrently, mensural music was being reproduced from type, in two or more impressions, not only by Petrucci, but also by Oeglin of Augsburg and Schoeffer of Mainz. Was it so staggering a task to achieve as much? The answer must be yes, when specialists were not about who could supply the typographical material. Numerous French printers mastered the printing of chant from type, but no one in France appears to have passed the barrier offered by printing mensural music from type until Attaingnant.

When music books did appear in Paris—the earliest dated examples to survive are from 1528—they showed an altogether new solution to the vexing problem of aligning notes and staff. A short vertical fragment of the staff combines with the note on the *same* piece of type. Thus the old problem was obviated while a set of new ones emerged. How manage the vertical segments so that they line up exactly on the page, giving the illusion of a continuous staff? Pierre Simon Fournier comments upon this in his *Manuel typographique*, written in the eighteenth century, but under consideration of the same method: "The difficulty is to cut the punches with the traversing lines so evenly spaced apart that when the type is cast and composed, representing notes in various positions, each character shall

[31] Hans Haase, article "Guerson" in *Die Musik in Geschichte und Gegenwart*, Vol. 5 (Kassel and Basel, 1956). In her article "A Fifteenth Century Dancing Book," *Journal of the English Folk Dance and Song Society* III (1937), 100–110, Margaret Dean-Smith offers an apt translation of the self-advertisement Guerson placed in his books: "Here he sits, a teacher of singing, with his music books. He will teach you everything with a merry countenance. Therefore young men, run hastening hither."

join up with the next, and four straight lines of even thickness shall be formed across the entire width of the page."[32]

The technical processes of typography may need some explanation at this point, for those readers little familiar with its special language. To produce type, three steps were necessary: (1) "cutting" the symbols on the head or "eye" of steel punches ("poinçons"), a very specialized task, generally carried out by master engravers, who were often goldsmiths by trade; (2) making indentations on a copper matrix with the punches, called "striking a matrix"; (3) pouring a hot liquid alloy such as lead into the matrix, which has been fixed in a mold, in order to produce a character—that is, "casting." Typefounding, a term often employed loosely to the whole process, should properly apply only to the last. When Fournier speaks of music type, he traverses, in one sentence, all the activities noted and one more beside: cutting the punches with minute exactitude, casting the type (also exacting and physically demanding as well), and composing the characters on the plate for printing. Small failures in any area could compromise the whole. Success depended upon mastery in all: punchcutting, casting, and printing.

Peculiarities of the new method are best grasped by an examination of the punches and matrices themselves. Many from the time still survive, especially at the Plantin-Moretus Museum in Antwerp and at the University Press, Oxford. Failing the opportunity for first-hand examination, the student may profit from images struck directly off early punches. Figure 7 illustrates a set of punches preserved in the Plantin-Moretus Museum. The medium-sized notes of the two top lines were cut by Robert Granjon before 1565.[33] Segments of unoccupied staff such as at the beginning of the first line were vital to the compositor for spacing; these "spaces" came in various sizes. The larger, tending toward square form, were called "cadrats." It will be noticed that some punches have as many as seven or eight surrounding staff-lines. These provided not ledger lines, but opportunities to make one punch do for several notes, depending upon what line or combination of lines was removed (possibility of any note being used upside down further extended the range from a single punch). In the words of one authority, "it was left to the caster to choose the five lines to be reproduced by fixing the matrix in one of four possible positions in the mould. By this treatment some seventy matrixes would yield all the sorts needed for mensural

[32] An annotated translation of the *Manuel* (1764–1766) was published by Harry Carter under the title *Fournier on Type-founding* (London, 1930). See p. 50. Mention is made of four lines because Fournier speaks here of printing chant; the problem is the same with mensural music.

[33] Their identifying number at the museum is ST 71. See H. D. L. Vervliet *et al.*, "Typographica Plantiniana II: Early Inventories of Punches, Matrices and Moulds in the Plantin-Moretus Archives," *De Gulden Passer* 38 (1960), p. 59.

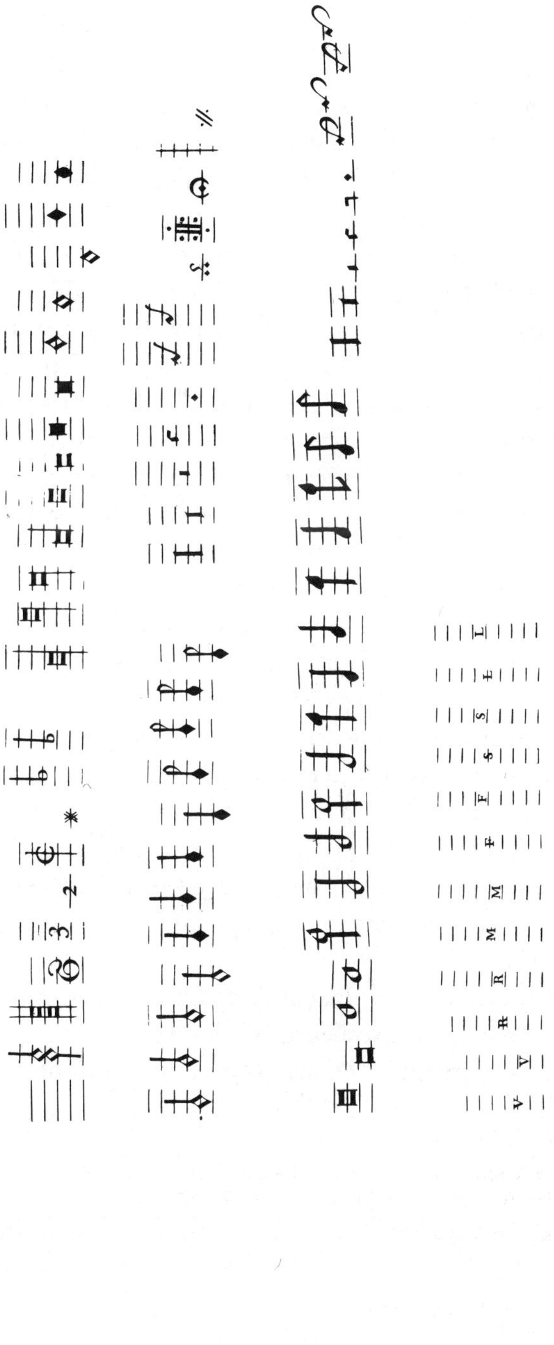

7 Specimens of music type made from Granjon's matrices. By courtesy of the Plantin-Moretus Museum.

music, nearly 200."[34] The third line in Fig. 7 shows some of the punches remaining from a cursive Civilité type, also cut by Granjon, and used by him in his music-books of 1558–1559;[35] the last line shows a few examples from a letter tablature. When the artist involved is a Granjon, it is difficult to know which to admire most, the ingenuity of the whole system or the abstract beauty of its single parts.

The *Chansons nouvelles* of April, 1528, furnish the earliest example of the new method. There are some tenuous reasons for believing these were in truth the firstlings from Attaingnant's press. If so, the choice was appropriate, for they showed the world not only a radically different method of printing but a musical genre that was prophetic in its simple, yet telling harmonic language—the "new" or "Parisian" chanson, as coined particularly by Claudin de Sermisy, who has the lion's share of the pieces. Both modernities were to have enormous consequences. The printer who stepped before the wider public with this collection was not the striving beginner that his name must have suggested, but a master. In technical perfection Attaingnant did not exceed the music printed in 1528. Such mastery presupposes years of preliminary trials. Similarly, Petrucci had spent several years in Venice at work on his method before applying for privilege in 1498; published results waited another three years and when appearing, as the *Odhecaton*, verged upon perfection. The steps leading to fruition of Attaingnant's method are less well known. No privilege was sought before publication, or, at least, no mention of privilege occurs in the earliest books. No contracts for labor or material survive to help elucidate the various phases either. It is thus not surprising that disagreement could arise concerning one of the first steps—engraving the punches.

In the earlier sixteenth century, punchcutters were rarely in business on their own account. They worked, rather, in close association with the large printer-publishers, often on the premises of the latter.[36] A few of the great Parisian printers were, like Simon de Colines and Geofroy Tory, originally, or primarily, engravers by trade. They supplied punches and matrices to other printers not specialized in the art, particularly to the smaller firm that could not afford to employ a punchcutter. It is typical of the situation of the time that uncertainty surrounds the origin of the three fonts of roman that Robert Estienne began using in 1531, establishing at once a standard of excellence that prevailed for a whole decade. Estienne's italic may have been cut by Claude Garamond, and the Royal Greeks,

[34] Harry Carter, review of Hyatt-King's *Four Hundred Years of Music Printing* (London, 1963) in *The Library*, Ser. 5, XX (1965), 154–157.

[35] ST 71a. See Harry Carter and H. D. L. Vervliet, *Civilité Types* (Oxford Bibliographical Society Publications, N.S., Vol. XIV) (Oxford, 1966), p. 22.

[36] Daniel Berkeley Updike, *Printing Types: Their History, Form and Use* (Cambridge, Mass., 1922), Vol. I, p. 191.

perhaps the most famous types of the century, were certainly cut by him, a fact known because the original contracts survive. Types were not signed. Once designed, they became the property of the printer who commissioned them and paid for them. Only toward the middle of the century did craftsmen like Garamond, Granjon, and Guillaume le Bé become sufficiently famous and sought-after to operate as free-lance punchcutters, and they were the first to do so. In the earlier years we should hardly expect to know who cut punches for Attaingnant, if he did not engrave them himself. But information on this subject does survive owing to a most peculiar circumstance.

Pierre Simon Fournier le Jeune has already been drawn upon for the description of single-impression music in his typographical manual. This engraver, referred to henceforth simply as Fournier, had attempted to improve music type, and so doing, ran afoul of the two-hundred-year-old monopoly held by the Ballards, official custodians of the "new method" and, indeed, of all French music printing from type. The old material (still relying on lozenge notes!) was hopelessly antiquated and inadequate to eighteenth-century needs, yet the Ballard family, like the Corporation of Minstrels satirized by Couperin, persisted in its moribund ways. Fournier, a man of superior wit, took the offensive verbally in support of his own contributions, writing one of those vivacious pamphlets so characteristic of the time: *Traité historique et critique sur l'origine et les progrès des caractères de fonte pour l'impression de la musique, avec des épreuves de nouveaux caractères de musique, presentés aux imprimeurs de France* (Berne and Paris, 1765). The polemical intent comes to the fore in the very first sentence:

> L'art d'imprimer les Caractères de Musique, ainsi que tous les autres en usage dans l'Imprimerie, vient des Graveurs en caractères: ce sont eux seuls qui ont inventé l'Art Typographique tel que nous l'exerçons, et qui l'ont enrichi dans tous les temps du fruit de leur travaux.

The account maintains a similar verve throughout. A tone of self-justification infiltrates the "historical" part, moreover, when Fournier explains the relationship of the typecutter Haultin (*his* spiritual ancestor) to the early printers, including Attaingnant (direct predecessor of his archenemies, the Ballard dynasty). It is as if the above premise needed exemplification. Fournier was at no loss to provide some:

> La première impression de la Musique est due à la Typographie. Pierre Hautin, Graveur, Fondeur et Imprimeur à Paris, en fit les premiers poinçons vers 1525. Hautin grava des Caractères de Musique de plusieurs grosseurs. Les notes et les filets étoient représentés sur la poinçon, par conséquent, le tout étoit imprimé en une seule fois. Il en fit usage lui-même, et en vendit à plusieurs autres imprimeurs qui les mirent en oeuvre.

He then mentions as clients the printers Attaingnant and Susato, in the same phrase, as if to suggest that he believed them contemporaries. He does not mention among the buyers Nicolas du Chemin, but says that this "graveur, fondeur, et imprimeur s'attacha principalement à l'impression de la musique: il grava lui-même plusieurs Caractères de Musique, et il en fit graver pour lui par Nicolas de Villiers et Philippe Danfrie." In some points Fournier's "history" is demonstrably awry. Du Chemin *did* acquire material from Haultin, as a contract of 1547 proves.[37] Susato, on the other hand, is unlikely to have had dealings with the French engraver (see p. 161). As for the earliest music-printing in Paris, "plusieurs grosseurs" were not used from the beginning, which Fournier's second and third sentences, read together, seem to suggest. And Haultin did not make use of the types himself, to present knowledge, until fifty years later.[38] There is no source besides Fournier claiming the invention for Haultin. In the face of so little positive evidence and so many contradictions, skeptical views of the claim have been expressed by both François Lesure and Harry Carter.[39] Doubts did not await the twentieth century to find expression. In 1766 the prominent type-founder, Nicolas Gando, with his son Pierre François, published some trenchant *Observations* on the *Traité*. Particularly irksome to Gando were the pretensions of Fournier, "historian":

> M. Fournier, pour prouver qu'il est véritablement l'inventeur des caractères dont il a donné des épreuves à la fin de son ouvrage, remonte jusqu' à l'origine des notes de musique, et descend, de génération en génération, à l'époque de l'invention qu'il s'attribue. Chemin faisant, on n'a pas épargné les traits qui peuvent contribuer à sa gloire, sans trop s'embarrasser de dégrader l'honneur des autres artistes qui courent avec succès la même carrière que lui. Il ne veut pas même qu'on les regarde comme des artistes; ce ne sont à ses yeux que des *ouvriers*: c'est l'idée qu'il prétend que le public en doit prendre, et qu'il espère même transmettre à la posterité, à laquelle il destine sans doute son morceau de l'histoire de l'Imprimerie. (pp. 5–6)

The criticism did not stop at generalities. Gando made an issue of the origins of the Ballard material, attempting to demolish his adversary's credibility at a blow. Countering Fournier's assertion that Le Bé cut a keyboard music, to be printed in

[37] The material included "poinçons et matrices d'une notte de musique" and cost 32 écus d'or. F. Lesure and G. Thibault, "Bibliographie des éditions musicales publiées par Nicolas du Chemin," *Annales Musicologiques* I (1953), 270 f.

[38] A facsimile may be seen in Louis Desgraves, *Les Haultin (1571–1623)* (L'Imprimerie à La Rochelle, Vol. II) (Geneva, 1960), p. 14.

[39] Lesure, article "Haultin," *Die Musik in Geschichte und Gegenwart*, Vol. 5; Carter, "The Types of Christopher Plantin," *The Library*, Ser. 5, XI (1956), 175.

two impressions, he wrote:

> Le Bé engraved some music characters for Adrian Le Roy and Robert Ballard to be printed with one impression and he cut only the punches of a large note, and a lute tablature to be done with two impressions . . . these two kinds being printed not on staves all of a piece but on detached segments, which we call cadrats. This manner did not diminish by very much the gaps to which printed music has always been subject. (p. 9.)

Debates in the mid-eighteenth century about the inventions of two hundred years earlier would be incomprehensible were not the typographical preëminence of the earlier period held in awe then, just as much as it is today. The Fourniers, the Gandos (with whom they were related by marriage), and other Paris firms belonged to the direct succession. They knew, in some cases possessed, material and mementos from the great period. The disputes were in a sense familial, much concerned with the honor of the French tradition, and the individual's relationship to it. From the viewpoint of the present study, the question comes down to determining exactly what sources these latter-day gladiators had at their disposal. Gando, with almost modern fussiness, hastens to inform the reader in a footnote that his facts are drawn from an inventory of November 30, 1639, after the decease of Pierre Ballard, where "all names of engravers working on music for the Ballards are cited, beside each kind of music."[40] Fournier had at hand an even earlier document, the specimen sheets collected and annotated by Guillaume Le Bé, which he referred to in a letter of 1756 as among his treasured possessions.[41] Well might they be. Le Bé's first music specimen, showing large and beautifully stylized notes for folio printing, represents a high point of the new method (see Pl. XIV). His annotations read: "J'ai fait et taillé ceste musique grosse, en l'an 1555, pour Me Adrian Le Roy et Robert Ballard, imprimeurs du Roy en musique," and at the bottom, "Il n'y avoit que cecy de taillé quand ceste espreuve fut faitte, et faut veoir des messes d'Orlande esquelles y a de telles sortes."[42] Close inspection is required to perceive that the music is composed of tiny

[40] The inventory has been an object of fruitless search by Mme Madeleine Jurgens among notarial records at the Archives Nationales. It is not preserved in any of the notaries' "études" that the Ballards were known to frequent. Thirty such "studies" of the period 1600–1650 are in course of publication by Mme Jurgens at the Imprimerie Nationale and will include much material on the Ballards and on musicians. The first volume appeared in 1968.

[41] The notebook subsequently passed to the Départment des Manuscrits of the Bibliothèque Nationale, as Nouvelle acquisition française, 4528. See the study cited below in note 45, p. 4.

[42] Presumably a reference to *Missae variis concentibus ornate ab Orlando de Lassus,* a collection in folio published by Le Roy and Ballard in 1577. The large notes for folio printing had been used by the firm since 1557. Mouton's canonic chanson "En revenant de Lyon" had been printed earlier by Attaingnant in **3.**

segments, so close is the fit, so straight the staff-lines. Only Granjon achieved an equal degree of refinement—not Haultin whose types are somewhat looser fitting, not even Hendrik van den Keere, whose fine "Moyenne Musique" for Plantin (1577–1578) is illustrated in Plate XV. As for the contest between Gando and Fournier, neither has the whole truth. Gando was correct about the large note for two impressions. The second music specimen in Le Bé's notebook, annotated "filets d'une seule pièce," shows notes that are indeed printed separately upon solid staff-lines and identical in size with those in the first specimen.[43] Fournier, for his part, correctly referred to the double-impression keyboard music, which Le Bé made in large and small sizes for Le Roy and Ballard, the second one dated 1559.[44] These must have had special interest for Fournier, because the rounded notes, with shorter values united by beams, adumbrated eighteenth-century reforms.

Fournier had other material at his disposal that came down from the Le Bé family. His older brother, Jean-Pierre, inherited a Memorandum on the history of typography, the first part of which had been written or dictated by Guillaume Le Bé junior, about 1643, shortly before his death. The account describes the work of Colines, Henry and Robert Estienne, Garamond, Haultin, Granjon, and Guillaume Le Bé, "mon père." Its remarks on Haultin deserve quotation at length, for Fournier based much of his historical tale on this precious relic, which he eventually came to possess.[45]

> Pierre Haultin, the letter-cutter and typefounder, worked in Paris in 1545 and 1550. He may have begun about 1500, and finished his apprenticeship about 1510. The first matrices on which he worked were for a Pica or Small Pica Greek, for which there were a great many punches; and since he had not previously worked

[43] Nouv. acq. fr. 4528, fol. 22vo–23, "Sois moy, Seigneur, ma garde." To make matters more confusing, there is a third specimen, "Gaudeamus omnes," of single impression like the first, on fol. 23vo–24. It is partly illustrated by Henri Omont, "Spécimens de caractères hébreux, grecs, latins et de musique gravés à Venise et á Paris par Guillaume Le Bé (1545–1592)," *Mémoires de la Société de l'histoire de Paris et de l'Isle de France* XV (1888), 273–283. Gando's reference to the large notes for double impression lends credence to the existence of the inventory of 1639 that he cites (see note 40). Whether the notes were accompanied by staves printed from rules or from small segments, as Gando mentions, was at the printer's discretion.

[44] Nouv. acq. fr. 4528, fol. 24vo–25, illustrated (reduced) in F. Lesure and G. Thibault, *Bibliographie des éditions d'Adrian Le Roy et Robert Ballard* (*1551–1598*) (Paris, 1955), plate following p. 18. The opposite side of the plate illustrates folio 26 (at the bottom, with printed page-number "3") and folio 26vo (at the top, with printed page-number "4"). These seem to be uncorrected proof-sheets for a book.

[45] *Sixteenth-Century French Typefounders: The Le Bé Memorandum*, ed. Harry Carter, with a Foreword by Stanley Morison (Documents Typographiques Français, III) (Paris, 1966). On the history of the MS see Carter's Introduction, especially pp. 4–5. I am indebted to Mr. Carter for a set of proofs of his edition, given, along with much welcome counsel, upon a visit to the University Press, Oxford, in May, 1966.

> on a face of the kind, it was long in suspense, for he began the punches in 1530. With this type was printed the New Testament in Greek, 16°, in 1549 and 1550. At the time when it was finished he dwelt in the Rue St. Jacques, opposite the graveyard of Saint Benoît, at the sign of the Fox's Tail . . . He was at work after that as late as 1561, when, upon the issue of the edict about the religious disturbances, he left Paris and went to La Rochelle. He was active there for a long time, until 1578 or 1580, when he died.

Guillaume Le Bé II was about eighty when composing these recollections and they are correspondingly vague on many points. Several dates are off by as much as a decade or more. Harry Carter warns, "the traditional memory is not to be trusted for dates," and "assertions that Haultin finished his apprenticeship about 1510 and that he gave employment to Garamond do not accord well with documentary evidence of the time, which suggests for Haultin an active career lasting from 1545 to 1587, later by a good twenty year's than Garamond's."[46] Fournier might have derived from this account that Haultin was operative in the first quarter of the century (the statement that he began his first punches in 1530 is categorical, however). What he did not and could not derive from Le Bé is any word about Haultin's punches for music. Yet Le Bé, like his father, well knew the special problems of music type, having cut it himself. He did not forbear to remark the music and tablature cut by Granjon. If he believed Haultin an innovator with regard to music type, would he have omitted so exceptional a feat? Not likely; his silence on the point shows only that the traditional memory did not burn brightly enough to illuminate the beginnings of French music printing. Another generation or two and the beginnings were even dimmer. In a continuation of the Memorandum, copied by the elder Fournier from material written by Pierre Cot about 1700, the first Jacques de Sanlecque (d. 1648) is given credit for having "cut and cast the first music types with the stave-lines that we had in France."[47] The error, its ludicrousness notwithstanding, is dutifully repeated and embroidered by Fournier in his earlier historical account on French typecutters, serving as a foreword to the *Modèles de caractères* of 1742:

> C'est lui [Sanlecque] qui a gravé et fondu les premiers Caractères de Musique portant ses règles; avant lui on les imprimoit à deux fois, les règles les premières, et ensuite la note, comme on fait encore aujourd'hui pour le pleinchant rouge et noir.

Fournier never corrected this explicitly. In his *Manuel Typographique* (1762–1764) he speaks of single-impression music, which he calls "Huguenot music," as

[46] *The Le Bé Memorandum*, p. 8.

[47] *Op. cit.*, Introduction, p. 9; transcript, p. 22 and note 57. Updike reproduces some examples of single-impression music from the Sanlecques in his *Printing Types*, Fig. 150, showing both chant and mensural notation.

"devised by our ancient letter-cutters, reformed and perfected by the two Sanlecques, father and son, and used in France since their time."[48] No hint appears yet of the revelation to come in the *Traité* of 1765. It seems that, without looking further into the matter, although relevant documents were not lacking, Fournier relied once again on his not inconsiderable power of invention. Needing a bona fide engraver to sustain the thesis about printers' eternal indebtedness to typecutters, he cited a man who appeared to have the proper qualifications. Perhaps he was influenced by his own term "Huguenot music" to settle upon Haultin. It did not matter, in the heat of the attack on the Ballards, that Haultin's work with music type, like the Huguenots, came along quite a few years later than 1525. He made his point. Taken subsequently as a scientific statement of fact and sanctified by endless repetition, that point will surely continue in life as long as there is lexicography.

An even more precious document was copied by the elder Fournier from the Le Bé records—an Inventory of punches and matrices owned by the firm after the death of the first Guillaume Le Bé in 1598, drawn up by his son in the early years of the seventeenth century.[49] Various alphabets occupy most of the Inventory. There are romans and italics, and ranges of Greek, Hebrew, and others, by most of the greats, including Granjon and Colines as well as Haultin and Garamond. There is also a section devoted to musical material. It is reproduced here, after the original in the Archives Nationales, on Pl. VI–VII. Plate VI shows a page from the first part of the Inventory, that devoted to matrices, while Pl. VII comes from the second part, devoted to punches. Each item is preceded by an identifying siglum—important sometimes as a commentary on the appearance of the original type—and followed by an arabic numeral indicating the number of punches (p) or of matrices (m) on hand, and finally by another numeral pertaining only to the disposition of the material at the Le Bé foundry. The cursive copying hand of the elder Fournier is clear enough (probably clearer than the document he inherited) although some blotting obscures the sigla. A comparison of punches and matrices shows many correspondences in the first two categories, "nottes" for chant, and "musique," but no punches on hand for the third, "Musique venues de Lion." The implication is that the first two originated in Paris, where the punches were first struck, while the out-of-town material could be had only in the form of matrices—punches ordinarily did not travel. Some of the types may be readily identified. The first item under "musique" must be that cut by Du Chemin and

[48] H. Carter, *Fournier on Typefounding* (London, 1930), p. 62.

[49] Archives Nationales, Minutier Central des Notaires, Etude LXV, liasse 229. A transcript and introductory commentary by Stanley Morison was published as *L'Inventaire de la fonderie Le Bé selon la transcription de Jean Pierre Fournier* (Documents Typographiques Français, I) (Paris, 1957).

used to print his folio Masses (between 1552 and 1568); the next, "Musique des nottes de Colin, Viliers," must refer to Pierre Colin's two volumes of motets printed by Du Chemin in 1561, while "Viliers" must be the Nicolas de Villiers whom Du Chemin had employed to cut type.[50] "Musique des chansons 4⁰," qualified as "Viliers" in the corresponding punches, was presumably another item in Du Chemin's material, which, if we may believe Fournier's *Traité*, passed altogether to the Le Bés. The next item, "Musique moienne hautin, maigre," further qualified as "vielle" in regard to the punches, could be translated as Haultin's "skinny, medium-sized notes, which are worn," and must have reference to those for which Du Chemin paid 32 golden crowns in 1547. The "danfrie" mentioned at the conclusion of the following entry is again an engraver, Philippe Danfrie, who worked in Paris as an assignee of Granjon, and who also became involved with the Le Preux family when buying a part of their house "du Loup" in the Rue Saint-Jacques in 1561.[51] The designation "Airs" and the small format point to later in the century (Le Roy and Ballard?), as do the following examples of "little music for psalms" and a "Cicero" (i.e., Pica) for psalms. The final item in the section is not the least valuable, being the "tablature for lute and guitar, Granjon," that superb material cut in Paris around 1550 and used immediately thereafter in several guitar books.[52] Of the various matrices from Lyons, the first set, by Granjon, has the most interest here, as it may correspond to the punches illustrated at the top of Fig. 7, above.

The "nottes" for the printing of plainchant have fewer typecutters' names. They rely for identification more upon the variety of service-book—antiphonary, processional, Hours with notation, or missal—together with formats, which range from 16⁰ to folio. Some of the material came from Du Chemin, it may be assumed, as in the case with mensural types; in the Le Bé Memorandum he is described as having "cut a great many punches for music and plainchant."[53] In the Inventory Le Bé supplies names in only two cases. The material designated

[50] F. Lesure and G. Thibault, "Bibliographie des éditions musicales publiées par Nicolas du Chemin,' *op. cit.* (in note 37 above), no. 75, *Petri Colin . . . Modulorum.* The volumes are of an odd size, 37.3 × 24 cm., and presumably required a special type for this reason. The same is not true of Colin's *Cinquante pseaulmes de David* printed by Du Chemin in 1550, in regular quarto.

[51] Renouard, *Répertoire des Imprimeurs parisiens* (Paris, 1965), *s.v.* "Danfrie." Fournier mentions that Danfrie cut type for Du Chemin. The Gando *Observations* ascribe to Philippe Danfrie the "musique en copie arrondie" used for the *Ballet du Roi*, Pierre Ballard, 1617. See also Carter and Vervliet, *Civilité Types*, pp. 24–28 on Danfrie.

[52] D. Heartz, "Parisian Music Publishing under Henry II: A propos of Four Recently Discovered Guitar Books," *The Musical Quarterly* XLVI (1960), 448–467. The tablature was also used by Le Roy and Ballard (*ibid.*, p. 454). It was equally serviceable for five-line lute tablature and four-line guitar tablature, the difference being made in the casting.

[53] *The Le Bé Memorandum*, transcript, p. 25; translation, p. 35.

as "Corniches, Antiphonary, 4°" with regard to its matrices has punches qualified as "Notte. mon pere," which means it was cut by the first Guillaume Le Bé, while the date 1608 to the right records that only fifteen punches remained at that date. The other case is truly exceptional, being a "Notte de gros Plainchant portant ses reglets," "large chant note carrying its staff," which is to say, devised for single impression. The corresponding punches follow the same description, and in addition, at the final position where engravers' names always appear, their inventor is mentioned: "atteignant."

Pierre Attaingnant, designer and engraver of type? There is no other way of reading Le Bé's Inventory. The oddity of what he had wrought is stressed, even, by the unusually complete description. It is borne out further in later descriptions. Most of the same "musics" were still on hand when an evaluation of the foundry was made after the death of the third Le Bé. This is the "Inventaire et estimation faitte ded. poinsons, matrices justiffiez et non justiffiez, moules et autres ustancilles servant a l'art de fonderie de lettres d'imprimerie trouvés apres le decedes et en la maison de Monsieur Guillaume Le Bé, fondeur de lettre d'imprimerie, et marchant libraire à Paris demeurant rue St Jean de Beauvais."[54] It was compiled by Philippe Cottin, another typefounder, and terminated as of Paris, September 28, 1685. Use of the same sigla and many of the same short titles facilitates comparison with the earlier inventory. Thus the first item on Pl. VI is described as:

> Une grosse notte de plainchant pour travailler rouge et noir. cotte notte antipho. p. folio marqué ♀ . . . contenant 29 matrices justiffiez prisés la somme de 12 l.t.

The other matrices for chant from the earlier inventory are likewise described, and qualified in the same way as "for working in red and black." The exception is what interests:

> Nottes portant ses Reglets. Une notte pour travailler tout noir au plainchant, Contenant 38 matrices justiffiés, marqués ♁ Et prisés la somme de 20 l.t.

This, of course, is the Attaingnant material, and it has acquired two more matrices than were present earlier, suggesting that it was put to use betweentimes. The value assigned is rather high relative to the inventory as a whole and this too implies that the matrices were still in good shape, capable of producing type. Not so much can be said of Haultin's "Musique moienne maigre," the matrices of which were still identical in number:

> Item une autre musique marquée # contenant 86 matrices justiffiées prisées la somme de 11 l.t. laquelle est de moindre valleur que celle cydesus.[55]

[54] Archives Nationales, Minutier Central, Etude LXX, liasse 182.

[55] Those "mentioned above" most immediately were the "Musique p. Messe f^{o} du Chemin," whose 78 justified matrices were valued at 20 l.t., and the "Musique des Nottes de Colin, Viliers," whose 66 justified matrices were worth 15 l.t.

It has been impossible so far to trace the material beyond 1685. Already by this time the punches were getting into serious disarray. They are not identified by sigla. Yet one item must be that cut by Attaingnant:

> Une boette cotte de la grosse notte portant son reglet dans lequel ils s'est trouvé le nombre de 20 poinsons prisés la somme de 3 l.t.

Note that only half the earlier number of punches remained. The section devoted to the musical material ends by lumping together several different punches:

> Une autre boette cotte Moienne musique et tablature de luth dans laquelle s'est trouvé Six pacquetes de poinsons plus petits que celles cy desusd. laquelle a esté prisé la somme de 9 l.t.

Only three liturgical books survive from Attaingnant's press: the breviary of 1526 (reprinted in 1546), the missal of 1541 and the ritual of 1546. More are known to have been published. Out of the hundreds of copies printed, the survivors cling to life by virtue of unique copies. The slender thread that makes the difference between existence and extinction, evident in all fields of early printing, is nowhere more keenly felt than with liturgical books. No single example from Du Chemin's press is known.[56] The high mortality is due in part to the small fascination exerted upon bibliophiles, until comparatively recent times, by the lovely old Gothic types, even when enhanced by red ink. A monochrome service book would be, if anything, less attractive to the collector than the more elaborate two-color publications. Of the two Attaingnant books with notated chant, the missal and ritual, both display the older two-color printing, illustrated above in Fig. 6. They are not large volumes, as service books go. The "grosse notte" was probably for large antiphonaires and like volumes, ponderous choirbooks of a type which does survive from the time, although just barely. Such publications have been but poorly served by modern bibliography. Hopes of finding an example of the earliest single-impression chant type are the livelier for this reason. Even if all record of such types as used by their creator were irrevocably lost, chances are good, given the continuity of French typography over many generations, that later occurrences could be found. The invention merits at least a thorough search.

Printing chant "all black" constituted as significant a departure as single-impression mensural music. It must have entailed corresponding economies in labor, time, and material. Was the new method worked out first with chant and later adapted to mensural music? The hypothesis is attractive, especially in that it

[56] According to *The Le Bé Memorandum*, p. 36, he had printed in 1574 "canonical Hours of Paris use, 16^{0}, with red and black notes, revised and augmented by M. Antoine Brunel, canon prebendary of the church of Notre Dame of Paris."

might provide an explanation of what Attaingnant was doing during the first decade in Paris. That he was an engraver is beyond reasonable doubt. It only remains to enquire why Fournier did not pick up the item referring to Attaingnant in Le Bé's Inventory. By the time of the *Traité*, Fournier had spirited this document away from the foundry of his older brother, to the latter's understandable dismay.[57] Neglect of the relevant item could be willful. Attaingnant may have seemed to Fournier too much of a printer-engraver, not enough of an engraver-printer. Or, what is more likely, Fournier simply did not study his historical materials with anything approaching a system.

The conclusion deduced here from the circuitous reconstructing of various kinds of evidence can also be read off the royal letter of June 18, 1531, as a simple statement of fact (Appendix 7). The Crown, taking cognizance of the "humble petition of our well-loved Pierre Attaingnant, printer-bookseller dwelling in the University of Paris, stating that no one in our realm before Attaingnant had endeavored to cut, found and compose ("graver, fonder et addresser") notes and characters for printing mensural music or tablature because of the great expense, investment and labor necessary thereto," proclaims that the supplicant should be rewarded for his "long thought, invention, his very great expense of time, labor and means." Hearsay or conjecture need have no place in this document, so closely contemporary with the invention itself. Put whatever interpretation upon it we may, the document was official, widely diffused by publication in the folio Masses of 1532, and witnessed by the powerful Cardinal de Tournon, Master of the Royal Chapel and a figure from whom Attaingnant hoped greater favors. In these circumstances, there was nothing to gain by compromising the truth and perhaps much to lose. The claims went unprotested, as far as is known. Subsequent events proved their justness. Attaingnant did bring to publication examples of all the genres mentioned, from organ tablatures to works for flute, from chansons to motets, hymns, and Masses, "in great volumes and small." He did own a typefoundry. An agreement of 1544 mentions not only "printing material such as large presses, chases, and friskets," but also "all the utensils of founding, such as furnaces, spoons, knives, files, hammers, anvils, [and] punches, matrices and casts, both for letters and notes" (Appendix, 18). He was, finally, an engraver, as the Le Bé Inventory testifies. Even if we did not know that he was an engraver, and did not read "graver les nottes et caractères" in the privilege, he should still be considered the inventor—whether he or someone else cut the first punches. It was he, as printer-publisher, who assumed the responsibility and the cost. Reform in design was not customarily the province of typecutters (*pace* Fournier). When

[57] *The Le Bé Memorandum*, Introduction, p. 5.

Plantin wanted a new cursive type he commissioned the calligrapher Pierre Hamon to draw it, while Haultin merely cut it; Plantin's instructions to Le Bé and the sketches he sent of Hebrew letters are similarly instructive.[58] The attitude of printer to typecutter emerges also in a letter of Plantin to a Parisian friend in July, 1567: "I pray you, also, get me from Haultin a truly complete strike of his Greek that we call *Cicero* or Median . . . And I must have it by the end of this present month or early in August or by mid-August at the latest for I bound myself at the last Frankfort fair to send this Greek of Haultin's or to take it with me, to Frankfort. But this you need not tell Haultin, lest he grow proud and enhance his price . . ."[59] To the financiers of the field like Plantin and Robert Estienne must go much of the credit for instigating typographical reforms. Attaingnant was an impresario of their kind, as well as an engraver-typefounder. On either score he deserves credit for the new method.

The later reformers of music printing took great pride in their accomplishments and wrote voluminously about their own merits. J. G. I. Breitkopf expressed himself in a letter to Fournier of September 12, 1761, with typical attention to detail:

> I have loved and practised music since my childhood, and founder and printer that I am, I knew soon enough the short-comings of our art in this field. Having therefore the advantage of a letter cutter, docile enough, in our house, I meditated how to find a way of improving and bringing to perfection music characters and the method of printing them. Comparing the range of music with the technique of casting it and printing it I saw quite well that in looking for a way that was new I should have to devise a technique of casting and printing entirely novel and never previously used. I made, therefore, a draught of a method which I had thought out and judged practicable, and at Easter in the year 1754 my letter cutter started to work according to my patterns; but I encountered two obstacles, one that the letter cutter understood nothing about music and the other that I did not wish to impart to him the whole scheme—fearing an accident and in order not to risk the fruit and glory of my invention . . .[60]

[58] Harry Carter, "Plantin's Types and Their Makers," *Gedenkboek der Plantin-Dagen 1555–1955* (Antwerp, 1955), p. 262.

[59] *Ibid.* The translation is Carter's.

[60] H. Edmund Poole, "New Music Types: Invention in the Eighteenth Century, I," *Journal of the Printing Historical Society* I (1965), 21–38. The translation, which is Poole's, is on p. 29. To avoid confusion it is perhaps best to retain the term "new method" for the sixteenth-century invention, and "improved music types" for the eighteenth-century advance, as in A. Beverly Barksdale, *The Printed Note: 500 Years of Music Printing and Engraving* (Toledo, Ohio: Toledo Museum of Art, 1957). Poole introduces as an example of early single-impression music a line from the song "Tyme to pass with goodly sport" from *The nature of the iiii elements*, attributed to the London printer Rastell. In it "the faults of the single impression type are clearly shown" (p. 26). Faults are evident, certainly, but they stem mostly from striking the matrix twice, a primitive method not characteristic of the Continent. See. p. 163, below.

Breitkopf achieved publication with his new characters in 1755. Meanwhile Fournier had been working on his own and in 1756 offered his *Essai d'un nouveau Caractère de fonte, pour l'impression de la musique, inventé et executé, dans toutes les parties typographiques par Fournier le Jeune*, explaining that "for the glory of French printing I could risk the essay which I present, and for which I have been obliged to be the inventor, the cutter, the founder, the compositor and the printer."[61]

More than two hundred years earlier, upon the last significant advance in music printing from type, there was no talk of glory—personal or national—merely of proper return upon investment. The cult of the personality was less advanced. Recognition there was at the time, nevertheless, for the man who established the first music firm in Paris and developed a new method of printing. Posterity has been more niggardly in honoring Attaingnant's "longue excogitation et travail d'esprit." Geofroy Tory, who took from 1524 to 1528 to produce his epochal work on typography and design, *Champfleury*, has, on the other hand, received magnificent tribute. Stanley Morison writes of his work:

> By 1525 the French renaissance, though originally Italian in almost every line, had come to possess a soul of its own. The designers, craftsmen and decorators imported from Italy by Francis I penetrated architecture and the handicrafts, but they did more than duplicate Florentine and Venetian details. In Parisian book-production it was a native born genius who effected in an incredibly short time the change from gothic type and decoration to the roman type which occupied almost two hundred years in England. The work of Geofroy Tory marks a new epoch in cisalpine printing . . . In many parts of the Continent reflections of Tory's style flourished for generations. It was the first international style. It was French, but not exclusively Parisian.[62]

The parallel with what Attaingnant accomplished is not only temporal. He too evolved something that was soon to become international; indeed, it was to become the first international style of music printing; his efforts, similarly protracted and arduous, were perhaps no less inspired by the achievements of Italian artists, and success required as much zeal, perserverance, and taste. With both printers the will to inform and improve—a peculiarly Renaissance will, to be sure—is manifest. The royal privilege of 1531 set down Attaingnant's aims in all clarity, describing the invention in terms of "serving the churches, their ministers, and generally all men, and for the very great good, utility and enjoyment of the republic."

[61] Poole, *op. cit.*, p. 31, note.

[62] *The Typographic Book, 1450–1935* (London, 1963), pp. 36–38.

III

THE PRODUCTIVE YEARS

FRANÇOIS PREMIER personified to a remarkable degree the mercurial temperament of the French. The salamander was his device and "nutrisco et extingo" his motto. Like the impetuous creature that survived even fire, he dared much, withstood much, and proved enormously resilient. In terms of another widespread notion of the time, he knew the extremities of Fortune's wheel—that inevitable machine bringing those who had known the heights down to the lowest depths. From stunning victory over the Swiss and Imperial armies at Marignano in 1515, it was exactly ten years until the overwhelming defeat by the forces of Charles V at Pavia. Imprisoned, he saw fit to accept the Treaty of Madrid (1526), the harsh terms of which could only raise the conflict anew. To gain his freedom he had to renounce Burgundy and suzerainty over Flanders, Artois, and the city of Tournai, a promise he had not the slightest intention of keeping. He was also obliged to place his two eldest sons, Francis and Henry, as hostages in Spanish hands.

The grim events inspired a number of moving expressions on the part of the Chapel Royal. One such was a piece by Claudin, the text of which refers to the King's captivity (or to the subsequent captivity of the Dauphin): "Quousque non reverteris pax orba Gallis, pax bonorum solamen potentibus semper odiosa. Quousque non descendes caelestis gratia, quae pacis olivam huic regno producas, sic ut concordia floreat. Revertere, in terram nostram pax sanctissima. *Et redde nobis lilium nostrum, suis radicibus avulsum spinis circumdatum.* Da nobis, Domine, pacem tuam, pacem diu desideratam, et miserere populi tui gementis. Miserere precamur, Domine Deus noster" (italics ours). In translation: "When wilt thou return, bereft peace, to the Gauls—peace the consolation of good men, ever hateful to the powerful? When wilt thou descend, O heavenly grace, that produces the olive branch of peace for this realm, so that concord may flourish? Come back, most holy peace, to our land. *Return to us our lily, torn up by its roots and surrounded by thorns.* Give us, Lord, Thy peace, so long desired, and have mercy on Thy lamenting people. Have mercy we pray Thee, Lord, our God." This version of the text opens the Newberry Library Manuscript, a collection prepared during the siege of Florence in 1528–1529, and interpreted as an entreaty by the city to King Henry VIII for aid.[1] One line (placed in italic) furnished all too vivid a reminder of royal misfortune, or so it would seem from later emendations. When, ten years after Pavia, Attaingnant assembled many political motets in the *Liber undecimus* **(63)** the passage in question was replaced with another: "Te duce vivat lilium nostrum suis radicibus aeternum spinis

[1] By H. Colin Slim, who obligingly communicated the variant text and whose study of the Newberry Library MS is in progress.

circumdatum"; "With your guidance may our lily flourish forever surrounded by its roots and thorns." Many other political pieces must have undergone similar neutralization, rendering them less precise, hence longer-lived.

The personal (and national) nadir of 1525, however odious it seemed at the time, provided the spur that resolved the King to higher purposes. His reign reached a new high point by 1530, the year of the first Regius Professors, whose appointment was of incalculable significance in the awakening of the country. At the same time France could once again look forward to an era of peace and stability. Hopes were never higher than after the "Paix des Dames" at Cambrai (1529), worked out by Louise of Savoy, acting for her son Francis, and Marguerite of Austria, acting for her nephew, Charles V. By the terms agreed upon, Charles renounced all claims to Burgundy while Francis renounced suzerainty over Flanders and Artois. Bereft of his first wife in 1524, he was to marry the Emperor's sister, Eleanor of Austria. For an enormous sum of ransom, the Dauphin and the Duke of Orleans, held hostage in Spain since 1526, were to be set free.

Throughout the early months of 1530 Paris awaited the tidings that the long negotiations were at last terminated and that the two little princes, aged nine and ten, had crossed from Spain into France. How the report arrived and the effect it had upon arrival are told in the diary of a Parisian commoner under Francis I.[2] On Tuesday, July 4, 1530, about two in the morning, a messenger of the King reached Paris, having ridden direct from Bayonne with letters for the Parlement. At daybreak the contents of the message were made public in all the city squares and at the Royal Palace by the town criers: "De par le Roy nostre sire—on vous faict assavoir que noz seigneurs les enfans de France sont, Dieu aidant, delivrez . . ." A great crowd gathered in the Cathedral of Notre Dame to hear *Te deum laudamus* sung "à chantres et orgues" followed by a solemn Mass of Our Lady. Similar services took place at the Sainte-Chapelle and the other churches, all of which let such a pealing of bells as was a marvel to hear, says the anonymous diarist, and beneath all the others sounded the great bourdon of the cathedral. Officials at the Hôtel de Ville gave a feast with "trompettes, clerons, bucinnes, tabours et autres instrumentz musicaulx"; all "honnestes gens" were welcome. The city blazed with "feux de joie" and in the streets tables were set up with food and drink. At the Royal Palace a platform stage offered entertainment, including "chantres chantans bien melodieusement." Little children cried incessantly: "Vive le Roy et ses enfants!"

The doings at Paris on this day of rejoicing having been duly described, the diarist concludes by saying: "these things were printed and sold the next day,

[2] *Le Journal d'un Bourgeois de Paris sous le règne de François Ier*, ed. V.-L. Bourrilly (Paris, 1910), pp. 340–342.

Wednesday the fifth of July." Not everyone had passed the previous twenty-four hours celebrating. Some of the city's printers must have been in furious activity. Wednesday did, in fact, see the publication of a pamphlet relating events on the previous Sunday: *La Grande triumphe et entrée des enfants de France et de madame Alienor en la ville de Bayonne.* The modern news-journal was close to being born when communications were so swift as this and presses so efficient. Throughout the joyful summer of 1530, triumphal entries of the royal party into Bordeaux, Angoulême, and other cities on the slow journey northward were diffused by the Paris press.[3] The new music-publishing house, quick to join the current, added its peculiar resources to the chorus of rejoicings. *Trente et six chansons* of 1530 opens with an ode to joy, set by Janequin, celebrating the return of the princes:

Chantons, sonnons, trompetes
Tabourins, phifres et clérons
Sy faisons la grant feste.
Plus nous ne craindrons le son de la trompete
Puisque les enfans et paix avons.
Chantés, dancés, jeunes filettes
Bourgeoyses et bourgeoys.
Faites sonner voz doulces gorgettes
Disant a haulte voix:
"Vive les enfans du noble roy Françoys."

The casual nature of the prosody suggests that the text was hastily assembled (by the composer himself?). The event celebrated helps establish a chronology within Attaingnant's publications dated 1530—the volume in question **(19)** must fall in the second half of the year. Janequin's paean would seem a natural choice to ornament one of the pageants honoring the royal progress through France. Most likely it was sung at Bordeaux, because the composer himself was then there. He had already apostrophized the King in his battle-piece celebrating Marignano, with its resounding last line, "Victoire au noble roy François!" (**4,** 2) and although his name figures on no official account, he styled himself "chantre du roi" in a document notarized on March 20, 1531.[4] Janequin left Bordeaux for Angers in 1531, and Angers for Paris years later. Attaingnant's contact with this prominent composer residing at a distance from Paris raises questions about the printer's source of supply, a topic that will be explored in larger context below.

Besides producing an abundance of news pamphlets, 1530 was a year of great publishing activity in other categories. A picture of the year's output in Paris is made possible by virtue of Renouard's special study, "L'Edition française en

[3] Jean-Pierre Seguin, *L'Information en France de Louis XII à Henri II* (Geneva, 1961), lists nine pamphlets on the subject; the one dated July 5, 1530, is his no. 93.

[4] F. Lesure and Paul Roudié, "Clément Janequin, chantre de François Ier (1531)," *Revue de Musicologie* XL (1957), 201–205.

1530." [5] Out of a total of more than 400 items, religion led all other subjects with 82 publications, and was followed closely by classical authors, with 73 (40 in Greek, 33 in Latin), and by pedagogical works, numbering 64 (only three of which were in French). Then came historical works, with 15 on ancient history and 25 on modern; law, 36 publications; liturgical books, 28; scientific works, 26; medicine, 23; philosophy, 18; imaginative tales, 16; works by Neo-Latin poets, 16; biographies, 4; plays, 3; and geographical works, 2. Music swelled the year's total with several more items. The calendar year of 1530 (until Easter, 1531) reached its culmination with the ceremonies attending the coronation and entrance of the new Queen, described in the usual way with a printed pamphlet: *L'Entrée triumphante et sumptueuse de Treshaulte, trespuissante, tresnoble et illustrissime Dame Madame Lyenor d'Austriche, seur aisnée de l'Empereur, Royne de France, en la noble ville et cité de Paris, capitalle dudict Royaume* (March, 1531).

A general feeling of resurgence gripped Paris around 1530. Expanding activities in the newly established music industry are to be seen against this background. By 1529 Attaingnant had begun to diversify his production, adding chansons à 3, motets, and lute tablature to his lists. The following year brought the first dances for instrumental ensemble as well as diversity in typography. The lute books of 1529–1530 had shown that the new method of printing with the segmented staff could be applied to other purposes besides mensural notation. A new and daring departure in 1531 proved that it could also be employed for keyboard scores. Here the problem was not only that of dealing with the characteristically ornate melodic style which the medium had evolved, but also that of setting in type several simultaneous tones on one staff—the first chords printed from type. The event of the year 1532 was the publication of the Masses in folio. With the appearance of a new format in connection with the impressive motet series of 1534–1535, the chief lines of Attaingnant's publishing activity were established.

Typography

The earliest chansonniers printed by Attaingnant were oblong part-books in octavo, measuring about 15 × 10 centimeters (or 6 × 4 inches), a format that Andrea Antico had introduced in 1520. Without altering the size of his books, Attaingnant adopted smaller music-types in 1530, beginning with *Vingt et neuf chansons* **(18)**. The change from a "première typographie" to a "seconde typographie" has made it possible to establish the chronology of several prints that Attaingnant had neglected to date.[6] In form, the earliest notes, called henceforth

[5] In *La Bibliographie de la France—Chronique* (1931), nos. 45 ff.

[6] D. Heartz, "La Chronologie des recueils imprimés par Pierre Attaingnant: La Période gothique," *Revue de Musicologie* XLIV (1959), 176–192.

Typography I, were thin and peaked, making an elongated, "Gothic" effect, further enhanced by the extreme length of the stems. The proportion of the height of the five-line staff to the minim was almost equal: 10/9.5 or 10 millimeters.[7] The subsequent material (Typography II) employed a more compact, quasi-rounded note; the proportion of staff-height to minim was 10/6.

Without an external reason for cause, such as a new format, why change to a new typography? The same question could be asked about the abandonment of the tablature types used in the *Très brève et familière Introduction* of October, 1529 **(13)**. Four months later, for *Dixhuit basses dances* **(16)** the earlier set, which used only upper-case letters, was replaced by a material using lower-case letters exclusively. If the material were worn by repeated use the change could be more easily understood. There may in fact have been more editions, and perhaps more tablatures as well, than have survived. Reference to what must be another edition of the *Introduction*, dated 1528, occurs in an old catalogue (see p. 132). It is true that types had to be replaced often in the sixteenth century. Paul Manutio, heir to the Aldine dynasty, wrote in 1570 asking that new characters be used at the beginning of any volume; otherwise the types would be worn out within four months, just when the compositor arrived at the middle of his work.[8] With Attaingnant's Typography II it was not simply a matter of pouring new types but of making new punches and matrices. This is not quite as extensive a change as it might have been, for with height of staff kept constant, the same "spaces" could be used, and other items from Typography I also remained in service: mensuration signs, breves, longs, flats, rests, congruential and hold signs. Also, for printing the texts, Attaingnant continued using the same *lettre de somme* with which he began, while his title-pages made do with the same two founts of *lettre bâtarde*.[9] The striking change was in a new slanted clef, replacing the earlier perpendicular model, and, above all, in those strangely tiny notes for all values below the breve.

Typography II answered a particular need, which may explain why it was called into existence. In the keyboard scores dating from 1531 notes were required of a size capable of being fitted together one above the other. The large note-bodies of Typography I permitted no such juxtaposition. Chords of two and three notes on the same staff were formed by combining characters having few or no surrounding staff-lines; in other words, individual characters of Typography

[7] D. Heartz, "Typography and Format in Early Music Printing, with Special Reference to Attaingnant's First Publications," *Notes* (Journal of the Music Library Association) XV (1967), 702–706.

[8] Antoine-Augustin Renouard, *Annales de l'imprimerie des Alde* (3d ed.; Paris, 1834), letter of May 10, 1570.

[9] For illustrations of the older French alphabets see Daniel Berkeley Updike, *Printing Types: Their History, Forms and Use* (Cambridge, Mass., 1922), Vol. I, fig. 135.

II were cut down. Difficulties inherent in printing the first chords from type emerge abundantly on the printed pages of the keyboard books: the chords on one staff do not always line up well vertically (alignment between the two staves, representing right and left hands, was barely attempted); gaps between staff-segments are frequent and sometimes large—the "fit" is less good than average; typographical errors abound in the series, culminating with the confusion of *Quatorze Gaillardes* **(28),** plagued by every kind of mistake a printer can make. Typography II served all the part-books printed from mid-1530 to March 1534, the last volume so composed being *Vingt et huyt chansons* **(45).** (An exceptional case, **41,** was set partly in Typography I and Typography II.) No later than April, 1534, Attaingnant returned permanently to larger notes, printing the quarto volumes that inaugurated his numbered set of motets **(46).** The little notes remained available for use, however. They reappeared in 1535 for a special purpose. A certain kind of dialogue-chanson, represented by Janequin's "Ma fille, ma mere," and "La plus belle" with occasional voice-pairing in a high range, had earlier been printed with two-note "chords" in one part, the Tenor joining the Superius for short stretches (see **40**). Again for Janequin's similar "Fyez-vous" in *Vingt et six chansons* **(62)** it was necessary to combine two voices in the Superius, with the result that the little notes served again, now surrounded by larger notes. They were still on hand in 1536 when Attaingnant reprinted "Fyez-vous" in the *Tiers livre* **(73).** (See Fig. 8.) The instance reinforces our notion that the little notes of Typography II were first created with combination in mind.

The most important event of Attaingnant's career was the publication in 1532 of an imposing collection of Masses in large choirbooks. Great effort and many months of work had to precede the appearance of the folio Masses. The title-pages alone required four sizes of lettres de forme (not to mention the specially executed woodcuts), the Dedication a new roman face, and the Privilege a lettre bâtarde. (See Pls. IX, X.) Whoever has seen the unique complete copy at Boston in the Athenaeum must account it one of America's graphic treasures. (It is "American" in an additional and odd sense, having come from the library of Henry Knox, Secretary of War to President George Washington.) An entirely new musical material had to be fabricated in order to suit the format. In form the notes show a distinct affinity with the softened contours of its contemporary, Typography II. (See Pl. XI.) Their size, 17.3/13.5, confirms the relationship, representing a ratio closer to 10/6 than to 10/9.5. Also, slanted C clefs, as in Typography II, contribute significantly to the visual effect (note also the coil-like G clef). Instead of filling out lines with "spaces" Attaingnant staggers individual staff-lines of different size, thus doing away with vertical gaps. Types were also combined here, not to form chords as in Typography II, but to render the ligatures

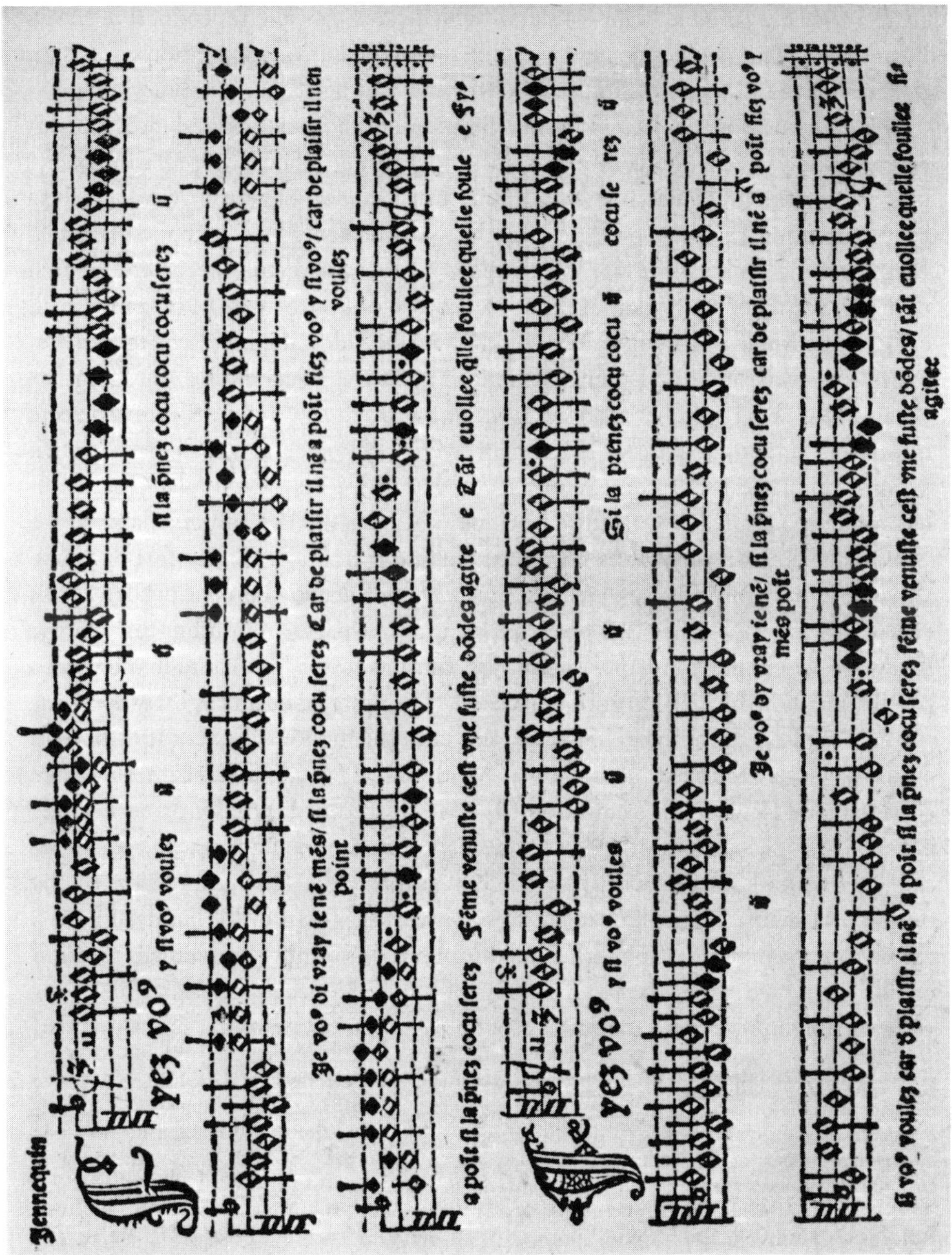

8 Janequin's "Fyez vous" in the *Tiers livre* (**73**) showing Typographies I and II. By courtesy of Bibliothèque Mazarine, Paris. (*Photo Giraudon.*)

characteristic of sacred music. Attaingnant's manner of making corrections is also exemplified on the same page; the ligature in the middle of the final line was pasted over the original print—a detail which photographic reproduction shows but faintly. The point is a small one but revealing out of proportion to its size, prompting the short digression that follows.

Typographical error, as old as printing and with equally good prospects of eternal life, was very frequent in early music printing. There were various ways of coping with it. The more unscrupulous let a deal of error stand. Others called attention to what had escaped the proofreader by inserting corrigenda. Formschneider in his *Lieder* of 1534 placed a verbal "Correctur" at the end of each part along with a note explaining that "when we looked the part over, a few small errors were found; although they could be readily identified and changed by an expert, we have indicated them all here in order to obviate long searching." [10] Attaingnant advertised his *Chansons nouvelles* of 1528 as "nunc primum correcte impresse," implying (falsely) that errors were no longer to be found after his proofreading, and perhaps implying as well that the pieces had circulated earlier in less accurate (printed?) versions. Various other early chansonniers claim to be "correctement" or even "très correctement imprimés," the latter formula, like all qualification, inspiring less rather than more confidence. Four early part-books **(10, 12, 14,** and **15)** offer lists of errors on the title-pages, reminding us that the first page was printed last of all. But the usual practice for Attaingnant was to patch, literally, what needed to be corrected. The practice occurs as early as *Trente et quatre chansons* of January, 1529 **(5),** and runs throughout his activity. In **5** an entire page was replaced, as is the case with *XII Motets* **(12),** which also have corrigenda. Elsewhere it is common to see a replaced line, phrase, or even single note.[11] The inaccuracies of *Quatorze Gaillardes*, mentioned above, and a similar carelessness marking the works of the last years give a false impression of the output as a whole. Printing cancel slips and pasting them in by hand bespeak a considerable solicitude of publisher for his public. No more convenient solution could be adopted, from the latter's point of view. Concern for utility and convenience might be instanced also by attempts to keep prices low, a subject treated

[10] "Da man den Tenor auffs new ubersehen/seind etlich gering errores funden/welche ob sie gleich von einem netlichen hetten leichtlich mügen uñ geendert werden/haben wir sie doch hie alle angezeigt/auff das wir dich des langen suchens uberheben." The corrections were entered in the music by the early owner of the Berlin copy, who was presumably the "Jacob Fücher" (Fugger) who wrote his name and the date 1534 inside the cover.

[11] Moderne also used printed cancel slips. See H. Colin Slim (ed.), *Musica Nova* (Monuments of Renaissance Music, I) (Chicago, 1964), pp. xxxi-xxxii, and *French 16th Century Books*, compiled by Ruth Mortimer under the supervision of Philip Hofer and William A. Jackson (Harvard College Library Department of Printing and Graphic Arts, Catalogue of Books and Manuscripts, Part I) (Cambridge, Mass., 1964), no. 144.

elsewhere, and by the "elucidations" on title-pages like **49,** telling a choirmaster immediately what he needed to know, or again by the hints as to what kind of instrument—flute or recorder—best suited certain chansons **(41, 42).** All these things point to a man of practical bent, interested in serving to his best the practice of music. The Masses of 1532, with their frequent patch corrections, show great care in every matter touching production. They represent an eminently practical, as well as beautiful, collection of music.

In one matter the two surviving copies of the Masses seem to be deficient. The space reserved for decorative capital initials in the music is left vacant, although appropriate woodcut initials were supplied for the Dedication and Privilege. From their absence we may deduce that the cathedrals, colleges, and churches throughout France forming the major market for such volumes were expected to have their own illuminators supply decoration. The copies at Vienna and Boston show no signs of having been used, in which they are probably the exception, explaining both their deficiency and their survival. It goes without saying that Attaingnant would have had the initials added in copies prepared for presentation to the dedicatee and other patrons.

Following the Masses of 1532 the most consequential innovation was the turn to quarto format for printing part-books. Possibly Attaingnant's first quarto publication was that devoted to Janequin's motets of 1533 **(43),** now among the many lost books. (An inverse ratio exists between the popularity of music prints and their chance of survival: surely among the most popular and influential items in the catalogue were those now lost or only partly preserved, such as **2, 3, 43, 65, 66, 67,** and **130.**) The typical oblong quarto measured about 20 × 16 centimeters (or 8 × 6 inches), resulting in an appearance quite different from the octavos. The quarto offered room for more staves per page—six, as opposed to four—and each line could be longer. In this new setting the music type looked strange at first, although "très proche de celle de 1528–1529."[12] The closeness to Typography I, upon being measured, proved extreme. *Chansons nouvelles* of 1528 showed staves and minims in the proportion 10/9.5; minims on the space (instead of on the line) often achieved an overall length of 10 millimeters. Changes in the initial musical material must have taken place as early as 1529, when a slightly shorter stem appeared more and more frequently. The notes in the lute songs of the *Très brève introduction*, for instance, vary between 9 and 9.5 for the minim on the line and between 9.5 and 10 for the minim on the space. From April, 1534, date of the first surviving quarto, the notes are in the proportion 10/9 (with the minim on the space extending to 9.5). They could have come from the same

[12] "La Chronologie des recueils imprimés par Pierre Attaingnant," *Revue de Musicologie* XLIV (1959), 180.

punches and matrices in use from the beginning, with the difference explained by trimming. The distinctness and pointed edges evident from 1528 to 1531 disappear, but this might also be explained in terms of wear and tear upon some of the older punches. Additional material was added over a period of years, which would account for the slight variations in note-forms after 1534. The later characters represent an accumulation, with notes from or like Typography I, slanted C clefs from Typography II, and some new items, such as a G clef like that in the folio Masses. This medley was destined to serve through the great series of numbered chansonniers, the *Danceries*, and on down to the last music of the widow Attaingnant. Le Febure's chanson printed in *Le Dieugard de la ville de Paris* of 1558 **(174)** still betrays notes in the proportion 10/9 (9.5 for the minim on the space). In the present state of knowledge it is more appropriate to envision a continually refurbished Typography I, rather than a separate and distinct "third Typography." If there were quartos still earlier than 1533, Typography I may have led a continuous existence from the beginning. In any case the small notes of Typography II were truly secondary, representing no more than a brief interlude. Conversely the notes with which Attaingnant began were primary in all senses. They formed the standard material for his entire career.

One altogether new musical note did emerge in the second half of Attaingnant's activity. It was occasioned by a special paper-size used for the three motet volumes of 1542 **(103–105)**, resulting in a larger oblong quarto (25.5 × 19.4). From Claudin's lead volume **(103)** the title and one page of music are splendidly reproduced in the Renouard catalogue, showing that the music, 14/12.5, was cut in proportion to the format.[13] No further use of these types is now known. They may thus be considered, like those in the folio Masses, a special creation with limited purpose. The following table sums up Attaingnant's various music-types, how and when they were used, and proposes new names for the two "special" types.

TABLE OF ATTAINGNANT'S MUSIC TYPES

Typography I	10/9–9.5	1528–1531	octavo	**2–17**[+**41**]
		1534–	quarto	**46–**
Typography II	10/6	1531–1534	octavo	**18–45**
Mass Type	17.3/13.5	1532	folio	**33–39**
Motet Type	14/12.5	1542	quarto	**103–105**

Once the quarto format had been established for sacred music in part-books, further possibilities suggested themselves in the realm of the chanson. Beginning in early 1536 Attaingnant started a series of chansonniers in quarto, which allowed

[13] *Imprimeurs et Libraires parisiens du XVIe siècle* (Paris, 1964), plates A 34–35.

for "le tout en ung livre" **(69)**. The music-type in these volumes—which is to say that observable in the sole surviving set at the Bibliothèque Mazarine—looks very worn, but this is compensated by the charming "Flemish-style" initials gracing the beginning of each piece. With four voice-parts beginning on the double page there was need to repeat the same capital three times, an opportunity seized by the printer to delight the eye, using subtle variations in the form. Letters from this "entrelacs" alphabet are illustrated in Janequin's "Fyez-vous," (Fig. 8) above, and in items **81** and **85** of the Bibliographical Catalogue. Placing all four voices on the double page meant that the verso of the final page went unused. With a view to the music lover's possible convenience, Attaingnant printed blank staves here, using staff-segments of different size.

The firm took a major departure in 1537 with the appearance on the scene of Hubert Jullet. The first book to bear both printers' names contained revised versions of Janequin's program chansons (made in all likelihood by the composer himself), a collection unique among the secular prints for using separate part-books in quarto.[14] Then began a period unusually fertile in chansonniers during which several series went on at once, some signed by the partners, others by Attaingnant alone; some with gothic types, others with italic; some "en ung volume," others "en deux volumes," and still others "en un volume et en deux." It is the last kind of distinction which was paramount and according to which the following table is arranged. Volumes of identical or similar content are placed parallel to one another.

In the face of such multiplicity the question arises whether some volumes are merely different issues of the same edition, with title pages changed. Consider first the volumes in categories A and B. Of prints "in one volume" there are none from 1537 to 1543. Did the works in category B, advertised as "in one volume and in two" take their place? Possibly, but every surviving copy using this formula is in two books. Could the title be intended as a coverall for the two dispensations? If so it would seem an odd economy inasmuch as the same plates could not be used to print both two and four voice-parts per volume. Separate editions were mandatory. When the enigmatic formula stops appearing on title pages **(113)**, prints "in one volume" are again found (with the 15th Book, **118**). Within category B there are two distinct series, one using gothic for titles and texts, the other using italic. There is no question as to the priority of the former—the dates show the italic series to be later editions, not to speak of the contents, which are revised, sometimes extensively (see, for example, **97**). By 1542 gothic was abandoned; the italic volumes concluding category B represent the direct line, not reprints.

[14] See A. Tillman Merritt, "Janequin: Reworkings of Some Early Chansons," in *Aspects of Medieval and Renaissance Music*, ed. Jan LaRue (New York, 1966), pp. 603–613.

TABLE OF SURVIVING CHANSONNIERS 1536–1546

A *En un livre* (Attaingnant)	B *En un volume et en deux* (Attaingnant + Jullet)	C *En deux volumes* (Attaingnant)
69 1er livre, 1536		
70 1er livre . . . chansons esleues, 1536		
71 2nd livre . . . chansons esleues, 1536	**78** 2nd livre . . . chansons vielles, 1538	**76** *2nd livre . . . chansons vielles*, 1537
72 2nd livre, 1536		
73 Tiers livre, 1536	**79** Tiers livre . . . chansons vielles, 1538	
	80 1er livre . . . chansons nouvelles, 1538	**140** *Ier livre . . . chansons nouvelles*, 1546 (M)
81–84 2nd–5^{e} livres, 1538	**94–97** *2nd–5^{e} livres*, 1540 (revision) (M)	
86 6^{e} livre, 1539		**87** *6^{e} livre*, 1539 (M)
88 7^{e} livre, 1539	**89** *7^{e} livre*, 1540 (revision) (M)	
90 8^{e} livre, 1540		**91** *8^{e} livre*, 1539 (M)
92 9^{e} livre, 1540	**106** *9^{e} livre*, 1542 (revision) (M)	
99 10^{e} livre, 1541		**100** *10^{e} livre*, 1541 (M)
101 11^{e} livre, 1541	**107** *11^{e} livre*, 1542 (M)	**108** *11^{e} livre*, 1542
	109 *12^{e} livre*, 1543	**110** *12^{e} livre*, 1543 (M)
	112 *13^{e} livre*, 1543	**111** *13^{e} livre*, 1543 (M)
	113 *14^{e} livre*, 1543	**113bis** *14^{e} livre*, 1543 (with Jullet)
		114 *14^{e} livre*, 1543 (M)
118 *15^{e} livre*, 1544 (with Jullet)		**116** *15^{e} livre*, 1544 (with Jullet)
		117 *15^{e} livre*, 1544 (M)
125 *16^{e} livre*, 1545		**123** *16^{e} livre*, 1545 (with Jullet)
		124 *16^{e} livre*, 1545 (M)
127 *17^{e} livre*, 1545		**126** *17^{e} livre*, 1545
129 *18^{e} livre*, 1545		**128** *18^{e} livre*, 1545
136 *19^{e} livre*, 1546		**135** *19^{e} livre*, 1546
		137 *20^{e} livre*, 1546

(M = items from the set in Munich)

Between the volumes in categories B and C priority is not so easily established. Attaingnant kept a series "in two volumes" running under his own name, and profits therefrom were presumably not shared with his junior partner. (Another, less plausible explanation, is that Attaingnant reprinted the volumes after Jullet's death, retaining their original dates on the title pages.) The distinction breaks down in 1543 when Jullet also began to sign works "in two volumes" (13th–16th Books). Nevertheless Attaingnant continued to use his name exclusively on matching chansonniers. With two exceptions, the books signed by the partners run concurrently, bearing the same dates as those signed by Attaingnant alone. Up to 1542 the distinction between them is sharp, for one series is gothic throughout, using lettres bâtardes for texts and the handsome "Flemish" initials encountered earlier, while the other employs italic and plain black capitals well chosen to enhance the text type. All music was reset. The gothic series is better printed than the italic, particularly with regard to eliminating vertical gaps between staff-segments. Yet the italic series, with its severely simple initials and "modern" text types, was the more influential.[15] At the beginning of the concurrence is a 1537 reprinting of the second volume of "old songs" **(76).** Choice of so unprepossessing a collection to inaugurate the italic series (and to announce the appointment of Attaingnant as Royal Printer) makes no sense and must be charged to the vagaries of source preservation. Immediately at issue here is not what has been lost but the relation in time between the two editions, **76** and **78.** The gothic **78** bears the date "February, 1537" (Old Style) and thus could conceivably have been anterior to its italic twin, dated simply "1537," although were this the case Attaingnant might be expected to follow an earlier habit of his and qualify the latter "avant Pâques." In order for **78** to take precedence we must assign **76** to the one remaining month during (Old Style) 1537 that followed the date of **78.** The beginnings of both series are too imperfectly known for so arbitrary an action. With the 11th Book of new chansons the circumstances are different. Here the gothic **101**—the last surviving chansonnier to use the older text types—bears the date 1541, while the italic **108** is dated 1542. The parallel italic work "in two volumes" signed by both partners **(107)** must be a matter merely of different title page, surely. But no, here too the plates are different. The same is true of the various versions, all italic, of the 12th to 16th Books. There is not a single case of a divergent issue made from the same plates. Every book in the table represents a separate edition. From this it may be concluded that the public for printed chansonniers was very numerous around 1540.

The table of surviving chansonniers from 1536–1546 also allows some notion of what has not survived. Losses at the beginning of both gothic and italic series must be heavy; otherwise it is difficult to explain the strange isolation of **76** and **78.** Why reprint in two volumes the second (and not the first or third) book of the one-volume 1536 series? Why reprint a book of "old chansons" and not those of "new chansons"? Lack of any italic volumes whatsoever dated 1538 is surely an accident. The heavily revised editions after 1540 raise the possibility that all, not

[15] Du Chemin's chansonniers are in direct imitation. Late in the century Haultin still retained a design of remarkable similarity, including plain black initials. See Louis Desgraves, *Les Haultin (1571–1623)* (Geneva, 1960), p. 14.

just some, of the early volumes were brought up to date. We must rely here mostly upon a single set—that at Munich. Munich's thirty-five Books survive in two very thick volumes, still protected by the original sixteenth-century binding, showing gold arabesques on green and brown leather, and represent Attaingnant's stock as it was at mid-century (the copy of the 35th Book is dated 1550). A composite from different series, it begins with a late reprint of Book 1 **(140),** continues with revised editions of Books 2–5, 7, and 9, unrevised editions of Books 6 and 8, and a secondary edition of Book 11 **(108).** The last is of special interest because it bears the printer's signature "XI." In two other provable cases of later edition, **76** and **140,** roman numerals corresponding to the volume number are used as signatures. This suggests a convention for signing reprints (as distinct from revised editions, which were not so signed). In consequence, all Munich copies, from the 14th to the 35th Books, would belong to later than first editions. Whether the series "in one volume" (column A) went beyond the 19th Book is a moot question. The disposition of all the voices in one book remained in favor, as evident from the *Danceries* (1547–1557), whose sole surviving set is also made up partly of reprints (the 2d to 5th Books are signed with roman numerals and, of these, the 3d Book **(172)** is patently a reprint because of its date). The lesson to be drawn from all this is clear: at least as many editions are lost as have survived.

Gothic types gradually disappeared from chansonniers between 1537 and 1542. Volumes devoted to sacred music reflected the same trend. In 1539 the 14th Book of Motets, containing pieces by Pierre de Manchicourt, still relied on the old text types as we have seen. For the motet series of 1542, Attaingnant employed roman face throughout. Three years later, when Manchicourt's motets were brought out again **(119),** the texts were set in italic, just as in the contemporaneous books of chansons. Subsequently the older type-faces were used only in liturgical books.

The gradual demise of gothic types around 1540 has a wider significance. In the second quarter of the century, Paris printing in general went through the process of replacing the lettres bâtardes and lettres de forme with italics and romans. Humanist works published by the scholar-printers had led the way, but soon many other areas of printing joined the swing. Liturgical books, one of the greatest Paris specialties, resisted change the longest. Types are thus a function of subject matter, and, far from being of merely antiquarian interest, furnish an invaluable index of changing styles and attitudes. It was no accident that the learned Dedication in Latin heading the folio masses of 1532 was set in roman, with initial in an appropriately Renaissance style, while the vernacular and prosaic legal jargon of the Privilege was set in gothic, and enhanced by a "grotesque" initial. No coincidence either, surely, was the turn to italic at the same time a brilliant new chapter in Attaingnant's career began.

Privilege and Patronage

All the sworn booksellers of the University were privileged, in the general sense that they enjoyed tax exemption, like the rest of the academic community. Unlike Le Preux, Attaingnant was not a libraire juré and his career was begun without this kind of financial support. Privilege in the specific sense was a particular kind of protection, defined by Robert Estienne in his *Dictionarium latino-gallicum* of 1542 as "a special law for or against someone." The first music books make no mention of privilege. Most printers up until around 1530 relied on the Provost of Paris or the Parlement of Paris when they wanted a legal statement protecting their publications. Infringements would then come under the jurisdiction of one or the other of these two bodies of justice. That Attaingnant did not secure a privilege for the Noyon breviaries is understandable, the market being small and presumably saturated by the printing he did in 1525–1526 in conjunction with Le Preux. The first music books of 1528 also found an open market with no competition in sight. But in mid-1529, after a year of printing music and a dozen or more collections, Attaingnant must have applied for protection. Did he see the threat of competition? It is not unlikely, and were the names of the journeymen printers in his shop known, we might find that among them were some who soon afterward would be printing music elsewhere. In any case, Attaingnant besought the authorities to prohibit other printers from copying his publications. He went not to the Parlement or the Provost of Paris, but directly to the Crown. In so doing he was following the example of the scholar-printers, notably Robert Estienne. Letters patent to Attaingnant are not extant—no documents of the kind survive in the original from any period of his life. Thus we must rely on extracts printed here and there whenever he deemed it necessary. Upon first mention, in October, 1529, on the title-page of the *Très brève Introduction*, the Privilege is quoted as prohibiting the printing of music or lute tablature for the next three years. This blanket protection is not borne out in the more extended and, no doubt, more accurate quotation from the same Privilege (Appendix, 6) in **22.** Here it says that "no one may print the music, lute or keyboard tablatures *that Attaingnant has printed* for the time of three years." The difference is between "none may print music" and "none may print them"—that is, the books first brought out by Attaingnant. A trifling matter of one omitted pronoun, *les*, but on its account another printer might be put off from attempting to print music. To thwart such misquotations, frequent enough, to be sure, a law was passed in 1561 requiring privileges to be reproduced in entirety, word for word.

Calculating three years after the date of every print, protection of the earliest volumes, printed early in 1528, would have run out by the spring of 1531. The *Chansons nouvelles* (April, 1528) would be without protection from April, 1531, and so on. The meager sources of information about privileges complement the surviving printed collections in this case. Attaingnant applied for a new privilege in the spring of 1531, and as a result he received the letter of June 17, 1531, dated from Saint-Germain-en-Laye, where the King and court had arrived a few days earlier (Appendix, 7). The timing of the new privilege offers a reason for believing that no collection antedates the *Chansons nouvelles* (and consequently that the fragment of canonic pieces **(3)** came later in the year 1528). The second royal Privilege extends the period of coverage to six years for "what has been printed and is to be printed," mentioning "books and booklets (*cahiers*) of Masses, motets, hymns, chansons, whether for lute, flutes, or organ, in great or in small volumes." Thus the Masses in folio were already planned and possibly the motets of 1534–1535 as well. Intentions with regard to the flute came to fruition in the two chansonniers that were "convenable à la fleuste." **(41, 42,** also **67.)**

The Privilege of 1531 evidently satisfied all needs, for Attaingnant was content to renew it periodically, when the six-year periods were due to expire (Appendix, 9,16,22). So far as is known, he never prosecuted a rival printer for infringement. Such prosecutions were not rare, and Attaingnant probably would have had good cause to seek legal redress against some of his contemporaries, notably Jacques Moderne of Lyons and Nicolas du Chemin, whose activities will be discussed later.

The granting of privileges was a form of patronage that cost nothing to the dispensing authority. What it cost the supplicant is another question. To win a privilege from the King required at the least some well-placed friends at court. Merely obtaining an audience to present the plea would imply good connections. Of these matters the magnificent title page of the folio Masses is telling. The woodcut depicting the court at Mass (Pl. VIII) reveals much about the structure of French musical life and Attaingnant's relation to it.

In the center, singing from an open choirbook, is the Chapel Royal. Presumably their number would have included the musical director, Claudin de Sermisy. The cut is very attentive to detail, as for instance in the attempt to convey the contents of the double-page opened before the singers. The words "O Salutaris Hostia" begin the last verse of the hymn "Verbum supernum prodiens" by Thomas Aquinas and they are appropriate to the moment of the service depicted —the Elevation of the Host. Not content with just words, the artist went out of his way to include the appropriate melody in the very small space at his disposal.[16]

[16] The chant is similar to one still in use today and found in the *Vesperale romanum*, edition of 1945, p. 111.

Center foreground is occupied by the Swiss Guards, always attendant upon the sovereign; one of their halberds bears the letter F. Numerous clerics and laymen fill the same area. Here the artist had difficulty trying to reconcile multitude (suggested by the many small bumps representing heads) and perspective. The King's whippets, in the far foreground, guard between them the letters F I, which could stand for Francis I—articles pertaining or belonging to him were often sprinkled with this monogram.[17] They might also be the signature of an artist or engraver.

The artist places other hints on the title-page, and in a most significant place. A right sidepiece shows Saint Peter, identified as was customary by his key (Fig. 9). The choice of Peter might be interpreted as a compliment to the publisher, by reference to his patron saint. Saint Paul, with his sword, was a mandatory choice for the balancing left side-piece—the two saints were traditionally paired, to the extent that their feasts were celebrated together, on June 29 (see Fig. 4 for Pigouchet's rendering of the saints). Also not immaterial to the choice, perhaps, was the dating of the Privilege on June 18 and the Dedication on the ides of July. Next to Peter's feet is another F like those in the main cut. In this case there is no particular reason to explain the letter as a reference to Francis. Rather more likely is a reference, unobtrusive and almost private, as it were, involving Saint Peter—by extension, his namesake, Pierre—and an artist named F—. Under the pedestal supporting the saint the artist planted another clue. Two dolphins with personified heads occupy what space is available on either side. The dolphin, used as a decorative element, points to the Royal Professor of Mathematics, Oronce Finé. The allusion was to his native province of Dauphiné (the root is the same in French for both fish and locality) but may have had another reference as well; *the* Dauphin was of course the heir to the throne, the eldest son of France (depicted at the King's right in Pl. VIII, and in Pl. II).

9 Saint Peter, from the title page of *Viginti missarum musicalium* **(33).** By courtesy of the Boston Athenaeum.

Finé, who had his *Epithoma musice instrumentalis* printed by Attaingnant in

[17] See Charles Samaran and Robert Marichal, *Catalogue des manuscrits en écriture latine* (Paris, 1949–) Vol. I, p. 59.

1530, designed numerous architectural borders, illustrations, diagrams, and initials, for his own works as well as those of others, and was called upon by various Paris publishers from 1515 on.[18] A. F. Johnson describes his style as follows:

> As a decorator of books, Finé belongs entirely to the Renaissance and has nothing of the medieval manner of the previous generation at Paris. He took his dolphins, salamanders and grotesques and his architectural details from the art of the Italian renaissance, and yet the result is very different from that obtained by his contemporary Tory, who was inspired by the same source. Much of Finé's work has the appearance of being an imitation of metal work, and it is this fact which makes his decorative style so easily recognizable.[19]

Similarities of detail, and of general style too, leave no doubt that the hand responsible for the sidepieces also executed the main cut, as well as the Annunciation at the bottom of the title page, which is repeated at the top of the Privilege[20] (see Pl. X). Compare the winged cherubs' heads in Fig. 9 with those in the middle of the framing columns, Pl. VIII; or the coats of arms at the top of Pls. VIII and X; or the quality of line at the base of the flowerpot in Pl. X with the treatment of the pedestal in Fig. 9. Most telling of all are the stylized dolphin snouts at the base of the columns in Pl. VIII. An identical detail occurs on the title-page of Guillaume Budé's *Altera aedito annotationum in pandectas* (Paris, J. Badius, 1532), with borders attributed to Finé, and in a cut from Finé's own *Protomathesis* (Paris, G. Morrhé, 1532) showing the mathematician in company with Urania, under a celestial sphere.[21] Finé must have been a busy man from 1530 to 1532, when these various works were in preparation. Besides his decorative work for several presses, his teaching, and his voluminous writings, he served the King as cosmographer, in which role he drew an important map of the world, dated 1531 in an address to the reader, and printed by Antoine Augereau for Jean Petit and Galliot du Pré in 1532.[22] A personal favorite of King Francis, Finé had his portrait done by Jean Janet, royal painter, in 1531. Perhaps the mathematician-artist welcomed a commission to portray, in his own turn, both King and royal family for Attaingnant's title page. All things considered, the monogram F I in Pl. VIII may allude to more than the obvious: it could be read also as "Fineus Inventor" and perhaps this very ambiguity explains why it was used.

[18] *French 16th Century Books*, nos. 224–232. For the 1515 work see no. 432.

[19] "Oronce Finé as an Illustrator of Books," *Gutenberg Jahrbuch*, 1928, 107–109.

[20] The traditional association of the lily with Annunciation scenes may explain the choice of subject. An Annunciation figured in the last pageant at the entry of Mary Tudor into Paris in 1514, which, like the 1532 cut, represented both King and Queen; the printed pamphlet called attention to "ung beau lis." See Charles Read Baskervill, *Pierre Gringore's Pageants for the Entry of Mary Tudor into Paris* (Chicago, 1934), p. 26.

[21] *French 16th Century Books*, nos. 120 (Budé) and 225 (Finé; see illustration, p. 276).

[22] *Ibid.*, no. 387.

The royal family is accorded the same attention to detail seen in connection with the Chapel Royal. On the ladies' side the main figure is Queen Eleanor, identified by her coat of arms above, showing her Hapsburg lineage. Just below the Queen are some smaller persons, probably intended to represent the royal princesses, daughters of her predecessor, Queen Claude, who died in 1524. Of the four daughters, Louise (1515–1517), Charlotte (1516–1524), Madeleine (1520–1537) and Marguerite (1523–1574), the two surviving at the time of the woodcut would have been eleven and eight in age. The mature woman in the foreground may be intended to represent the King's sister, Marguerite de Navarre. The King himself faces the Queen from the opposite side of the chancel and is accompanied by his coat of arms—the triple fleur-de-lis to which he alone was entitled. Three beardless faces to his right must represent the Dauphin François, Henri Duc d'Orléans, and Charles Duc d'Angoulême, aged fourteen, thirteen, and nine, respectively (compare their costumes in the miniature painting of the court, Pl. II). It is tempting to see the bearded layman in left foreground as a depiction of the publisher. Comparison suggests, however, that this person is identical with the courtier placed directly above the head of the reader in the 1534 miniature, a man who has been identified as the powerful Anne de Montmorency, Grand-Maître de France.[23] Two additional figures are called to the viewer's attention by use of heraldry.

The armorial bearings of the figure nearest the King are those of the House of Lorraine. Surmounted by the broad hat of a Prince of the Church, they identify John, Cardinal of Lorraine (1498–1550). Second in line to his older brother, Duke Anthony, the reigning head of the house from 1508 to 1544, John came to benefit from the extensive power wielded by his family, which claimed descent from the Kings of Jerusalem. Elected Bishop of Metz in 1505 at the age of seven, owing to the pressures exerted by his father, René II, John was created a cardinal in 1518 by Leo X, just before attaining his twentieth year.[24] As papal legate he made frequent trips to Rome and earned a reputation for his fine knowledge of Italian.[25] Among the many writers he patronized was Luigi Alamanni, who celebrates his liberality in the first *Selva* of the *Opere toscane*, printed at Lyons in 1533. Lazare de Baïf's treatise, *De re vestiaria*, dedicated to him, touted another aspect of the man—cynosure of fashion. Poets and scholars often addressed him when seeking some royal protection or preferment.[26] Marot wrote to him with

[23] Chantilly, Musée Condé, MS 721. The identifications are the collective work of several scholars and are to be seen at Chantilly in the form of a labeled transparent drawing accompanying the MS. It was the prerogative of the Grand-Maître to make all appointments in the royal household.

[24] Augustin Calmet, *Histoire ecclésiastique et civile de Lorraine* (Nancy, 1728), Vol. II, pp. 1228–33.

[25] Emile Picot, *Les Français italianisants au XVIe siècle* (Paris, 1906–1907), Vol. I, pp. 54 f., 58.

[26] Lorraine as patron is the subject of Albert Collignon's monograph, "Le Mécénat du cardinal Jean de Lorraine," *Annales de l'Est* XXIV, No. 2 (1910).

the greatest deference, asking him to intercede with Montmorency:

> Mais d'où provient que ma Plume se mesle
> D'escrire à vous? Ignore ou présume elle?
> Non pour certain: motif en est Mercure
> Qui, long temps a, de me dire print cure
> Que vous estiez des bien aymez amans,
> Des dicts dorez et des rymez rommans,
> Et de science, et divine et humaine.
>
> *Epistre au Reverendissime Cardinal de Lorraine* (1528)

Lorraine had no lack of means with which to encourage the legend of "loving and being well loved" by the Muses. He accumulated title and revenue of eight bishoprics, four archbishoprics, as well as several of the realm's wealthier abbeys (including Cluny). As one wag of the time put it, he needed, in order to attend a Church council, merely to commune with himself. A member of the Council of State from 1530 on, he spared his numerous flocks the embarrassment of his choosing among them by residing almost exclusively at court.

An anonymous painting of the man in his mature years is preserved in the Musée Lorraine at Nancy (Pl. III). It shows, under a cardinal's biretta, a mien—sensitive and aristocratic, though hardly ascetic—that is recognizably similar to the figure of the prelate pointing to the King in the 1534 miniature (Pl. II). His features are also captured, insofar as the medium allows, in the 1532 woodcut, where he is again placed on the King's right hand. This was a bit of astuteness on Attaingnant's or Finé's part. An ordinance of June 11, 1528, had established the order of precedence to be observed at ceremonies at which the royal person was present: "le Roy, le Roy de Navarre, et monseigneur le Cardinal de Lorraine. . . ."[27] Throughout the reign, as the royal party moved from château to château, Lorraine was the King's close companion. He was at the meeting with Henry VIII at the Field of the Cloth of Gold in 1520. When the two sovereigns met again in 1532, it was Lorraine who accompanied the Tudor monarch to the festive Mass celebrated at Notre-Dame de Boulogne.[28] As abbot of Cluny, this princely figure occupied the Hôtel (now Musée) de Cluny, which had been completed in 1498. He decorated it in such high fashion that the King did not hesitate to lodge James V of Scotland there upon his visit in 1536, come to wed Princess Madeleine. The royal wedding took place in the same edifice.

Boon companion, "social secretary," confidant—Lorraine was all these things to Francis I. Brantôme celebrates his ability to please the King whether at the

[27] *Ordonnances des Rois de France: Règne de François Ier*, Vol. V (Paris, 1936), no. 486.

[28] P. A. Hamy, *Entrevue de François premier avec Henry VIII à Boulogne-sur-mer en 1532* (Paris, 1898), p. 68.

chase, the dance, the masquerade, or in amatory embassies, of which the Cardinal himself was evidently the not infrequent beneficiary, and concludes: "... he had many great virtues and perfections, which obfuscate one little imperfection, if making love can be called an imperfection."[29] Like Marot and Rabelais, he was untrammeled by any puritan meanness.

By saluting Jean de Lorraine, Attaingnant was making a gesture toward France's most prodigal patron of art. At the same time he was honoring the prince who was his near neighbor; the Hôtel de Cluny, located in the middle of the Rue des Mathurins, was within earshot of the music house in the Rue de la Harpe. Besides, the Cardinal was avidly fond of music; witness the sums paid singers and players in the household accounts of Lorraine.[30] He retained a troupe of violinists—Italians, apparently, from their names—who were favored by a royal gift in 1543.[31] Florent Copin, one of the Cardinal's shawm players, dedicated a collection of poems to His Eminence, apologizing for his inadequacy to the task of sufficiently gratifying his master:

> Car pour assez, o des princes le prime
> Joyeulx te rendre oyant beaulx vers en rithme
> Un sainct-Gelais, poete tant supreme
> Omere grec, Marot ny maro mesme [i.e., Virgilius Maro]
> Ne suffiroient a te donner plaisir.
>
> (Chantilly, Musée Condé, MS 530)

Clément Janequin speaks of having enjoyed the Cardinal's "singulières affections et bonne volonté" in the dedication of his *Inventions musicales* (Du Chemin, 1555) to François de Lorraine, Duke of Guise.[32] Marot, in a curious *chant pastoral*, consoles the Cardinal on the absence of his favorite flute-player, Michel Huët (the effect was perhaps ambiguous, considering the Prelate's reputation for denying his favors to none of God's creatures). Attentions paid to musicians by the Cardinal went so far as the abduction of youths from choir-schools.[33] Nothing was denied His Grace, it would seem, and no adulation was spared him.

The ultimate in flattery was undoubtedly reached by that "scourge of princes" and literary scoundrel without equal, Pietro Aretino, who was a client of Lorraine over a long period and addressed him repeatedly. Typical of the genre and dating

[29] *Les Dames galantes*, ed. Maurice Rat (Paris, 1955), p. 300.

[30] Albert Jacquot, *La Musique en Lorraine* (3d ed.; Paris, 1886), pp. 43 f., 53 f.

[31] "Don à Vincent Maudin, Cyprien Renelio, Michel Sauzel et Marc-Antoine Gayardel, violons du cardinal de Lorraine, des biens de Thomas Roquadelle, échus au roi par droit d'aubaine." *Catalogue des actes de François Ier*, Vol. VII (Paris, 1896), no. 27265.

[32] F. Lesure, "Clément Janequin: Recherches sur sa vie et son oeuvre," *Musica Disciplina* V (1951), 164.

[33] Janequin, *Chansons polyphoniques*, ed. A. T. Merritt and F. Lesure, Vol. I (Monaco, 1965), pp. iii f.

within two years of the folio Masses, the following letter will round off our portrait:

To the Illustrious Cardinal of Lorraine:

I do not grieve, Sire, to be born in these times, because I have witnessed a prelate who is the issue of kings, not of priests (who may be cardinal in habit but never in spirit). One must be born to it. One must bear the greatness of royal blood like yours from swaddling robes. What generosity could one of these puppets have, arrived at such dignity by way of money or by chance? What manners, what delicacies, what qualities, what princely airs could tradesmen and common people possess? To you, My Lord, all the episcopal sees, monasteries, and orders are becoming because you know how to dispense so well that, from being the richest prelate in God's church (saving the Pope) you find yourself still the poorest, considering as credit the debts to which you are and will always be held on account of the generosity with which you have stupefied this mighty city, giving to everyone with a gracious humility that bespeaks receiver, not giver. Then, too, there is evident in you a sweetness so marked, I myself believe that twenty-five saints have been canonized for less. You do not live in order to be loved by others so much as to incarnate love and benevolence. And I say this in order to speak the truth, not to pay you with praises for the hundred crowns sent me from France and the hundred given me here, along with the great fringed gown of purple velvet, covered with silver mail and gold inlays, the gleaming of which is like the light of glory that illuminates your name for what you have done, which is pleasing to God and to me.

Venice, November 21, 1534

John of Lorraine had the reputation for being one of the more liberal churchmen of the day in matters of theology. Not so the other cardinal, placed in the foreground of the 1532 woodcut. His arms identify him as Francis of Tournon (1489–1562). Although his revenues were less extensive than those of his colleague of Lorraine, he was a more important statesman. In fact, no political figure under Francis I was more powerful than Tournon, who chose for himself the device "Non Quæ super Terram."[34] It was Tournon who negotiated the Treaty of Madrid and who managed the successful campaign against the Imperial incursions into Provence. Named a cardinal by Clement VII in 1529, he was a frequent minister plenipotentiary for French affairs in Italy. Like Lorraine, he enjoyed a perfect command of Italian and was at home in the world of letters. He tried his hand at poetry as did nearly every other courtier, with the difference that his verses

[34] For a general study see Michel François, *Le Cardinal de Tournon, homme d'état, diplomate, mécène et humaniste (1489–1562)* (Bibliothèque des Ecoles françaises d'Athènes et de Rome, CLXXII) (Paris, 1951). Picot's *Les Français italianisants* has additional information *s.v.* There is no satisfactory study of either Tournon or Lorraine as patrons. French scholars have been unaware of the 1532 dedication.

were considered worthy of being set to music by composers like Claudin, Cadéac, and Pierre Colin. Examples are "Or sus, Amor, puisque tu m'as attaint," "L'oeil dict assez s'il est entendu," and "L'oeil trop hardy." His love-poetry notwithstanding, he was a relatively sober and orthodox prelate. As abbot of Saint-Germain-des-Prés, he occupied the palatial residence of this monastery outside the walls of Paris (from 1534 on), and one can imagine the atmosphere there being considerably less *joyeuse* than at the Hôtel de Cluny, although not necessarily less artistic. Marot, addressing Tournon in his capacity as governor of Lyons (through which the poet intended to pass in 1536 after his brief exile in Italy), brought forth the same conceit he had earlier tried on Lorraine: "... amy tu es, et bien aymé, de l'assemblée aux Muses tressacrées." (*Epistre à Monseigneur Le Cardinal de Tournon.*) Attention to the Muses is evident as well from the dedication of two Lyonese prints to the Cardinal—Pierre Joly's Psalms, printed by the Beringen brothers in 1552, and the lute tablature of Valentin Bacfarc, printed by Moderne in 1553.[35] More specifically to the point here, Tournon's relations with the musical world had an official basis. As titular head of the Chapel Royal he was a figure whose good will was essential for great undertakings in music. Attaingnant's homage to him did not stop with the representation of his person and his arms on the title-page. An elaborate Latin address overleaf is directed exclusively to Tournon and signed "Petrus Attingens, typographus musicus" (Pl. IX). Fully "Renaissance" in effect, the page is graced with a white, roman-style initial P on a white ground with arabesques—similar to Geofroy Tory's "lettres fleuries" (and an example, perhaps, of Finé imitating Tory). The careful layout and integration of all graphic elements show that Attaingnant, when occasion demanded, could rival the innovations of the great designers and printers who had put Paris in the vanguard of the printing art. Noteworthy, and in keeping with the use of roman face, is the dedicatory epistle's style, its classical allusions, its bow to the ancients, "both Greek and Latin." (See the transcription and translation in Appendix, 8.) The disquisition—part eulogy, part genealogy—seems to have as its main (but unstated) aim the securing of the King's favor through the good graces of Tournon. Mention is made of the Cardinal's "authority and influence" with the King, who has "never denied you aught." Tournon is a "most successful student of the art of music," a "prince of the Muses," but most important of all, "Master of the Royal Chapel."

Not content with his own effusive praises, Attaingnant must have sought out a versifier who would further decorate the occasion. He found one in the person of Nicolas Bourbon (1503-ca. 1550), native of Vandoeuvre in Champagne and a

[35] See F. Lesure in *Revue de Musicologie* XLVII (1961), 198–199.

Neo-Latin poet who served as a preceptor in the Tournon family.[36] Bourbon was educated at the Collège de Montaigu, among other places, and was perhaps in Paris when Attaingnant procured from him the laudatory Sapphic ode which follows the Dedication. In the poet's words, the Mass volume "breathed forth melodies similar to those of Thracian Orpheus." Whatever its merits, the verse may be the earliest printed from Bourbon's pen, as his first collection of *Nugae* was published only in 1533 (by one of the great Paris printers, Michel Vascosan). The *Nugae* (or *Bagatelles*) were more than slightly redolent of anti-Sorbonne, Reformation ideas, and the Parlement of Paris reacted to them by committing the poet to prison. Freeing him required the combined efforts of Marguerite de Navarre, the King himself, and the Cardinal of Lorraine.

Between Lorraine and Tournon Attaingnant could hardly have made a wrong choice. The two were the most likely patrons in the realm for furthering his ends. He may have pondered which to choose and speaks, in fact, of "considering for a long time" to whom the Masses might be dedicated. Putting both in the cut on the title page, Lorraine next to the King and Tournon to the forefront, must have seemed a very diplomatic solution, the efficacy of which is borne out in the subsequent fortunes of the printer. A complimentary copy of the Masses went to Tournon, of course. Other copies, we may suppose, went to Lorraine and to the separate households of the King, the Queen, and the Dauphin. Remuneration was the normal outcome of presenting anything so lavish as these Masses. Yet Attaingnant relied only this one time on the usual dedicatory path to wealth and success. Much more important to him than a purse of money was the esteem and favor of the Crown, which came to pass in an unprecedented appointment a few years later. Meanwhile, the King should have been favorably reminded of his "well-beloved Pierre Attaingnant" by the inclusion of several ceremonial motets having to do with the royal family, printed in the *Liber undecimus* **(63)** or by the ditty praising him by name in an anonymous chanson:

France, par consolation
Rejouys-toy du cueur courtoys,
Honneur, louenge, par renom
Au tres noble Roy François.
Banny sommes a ceste foys
Hors de soucy
Puisque France a flory

[36] V. L. Saulnier, *Les Bagatelles de Nicolas Bourbon* (Paris, 1945). See the concluding "Note Bio-bibliographique," pp. 129 f. Holbein drew Bourbon's portrait in 1535 and a woodcut copy attributed to Georges Reverdy was made the following year. See *French 16th Century Books*, no. 117. The cut, in addition to another portrait dated 1538, is also reproduced in *Catalogue des livres composant la bibliothèque de Feu M. Le Baron James de Rothschild*, ed. E. Picot, (Paris, 1912), Vol. IV, no. 2788.

Par quoy chantons a hault:
"Vive le Roy des fleurs de lys."

Vingt et huit chansons, 1532 **(31)**

King's Printer

The greatest honor to which a French printer could aspire was nomination as an "imprimeur et libraire du roy," a distinction which fell to Attaingnant no later than 1537, when the phrase first appears in the title of a collection **(76).** The office was specifically qualified with the words "en musique." Letters patent do not survive, but they must have been directed to Attaingnant alone, not to the new partnership of Attaingnant with his son-in-law, Hubert Jullet, also begun in 1537. The joint publications do not begin to bear the phrase until more than two years later (Appendix, 11). Two offices were covered by the double title "imprimeur et libraire." (In succeeding to the title, Le Roy and Ballard inherited only the first.) There had been royal booksellers since at least the last years of Louis XII as is known from the use of this title by the Parisians Guillaume Eustace, (1514), Jean de Sansay (1522), and Claude Chappuis (around 1540).[37] As purveyor of books to the King—it goes without saying that no one "sold" books to the Crown—Attaingnant could expect not only to remit a copy of every important new musical publication to the royal library at Blois, but also to receive at any moment the visit of his sovereign in the Rue de la Harpe. The penchant of Francis for roaming the streets of his capital was legendary, and La Caille has gathered a pleasant tale about a visit to another of the royal printers, Robert Estienne.[38] Arriving one day at the shop of the scholar-printer in the Rue Saint-Jean de Beauvais, Francis found the head of the enterprise absorbed in correcting proof and, rather than disturb him, insisted that the task be finished while majesty waited.

The office of King's Printer was the more important. Printing at its inception in France awakened little interest at the court, perhaps because of its too narrowly didactic purposes. Only once in the fifteenth century is the title of royal printer encountered: Pierre Le Rouge, famous for his beautiful illustrations, so styles himself in 1488; but, according to Auguste Bernard, this is merely a solitary instance and a slip for what should have read "libraire du roy."[39] In 1531 Francis I bestowed the title of imprimeur du roy on Geofroy Tory, whose typographical accomplishments paralleled Attaingnant's, as has been mentioned. Tory was

[37] Auguste Bernard, *Geofroy Tory, peintre et graveur, premier Imprimeur Royal* (2d ed.; Paris, 1865), pp. 393–396.

[38] Jean de La Caille, *Histoire de l'imprimerie et de la librarie* (Paris, 1689), p. 87.

[39] Bernard, *op. cit.*, p. v, note.

simultaneously named libraire juré, the University deferring to the wishes of the Crown to the extent of creating a special post, because none was vacant among the traditional twenty-four. Clearly, the motive behind this was to gain for Tory the indirect benefit of tax exemption enjoyed by all members of the University. The next to be named King's Printer was Attaingnant, whose appointment preceded that of Conrad Neubar, King's Printer in Greek (by letters of January 17, 1539) and that of Estienne, King's Printer of Hebrew and Latin (by letters of June 24, 1539, now lost) and, upon Neubar's death in 1541, of Greek as well. Two main policies guided the choice of a royal printer in these appointments: recognition for past distinction, especially true of Tory and Estienne, and support for printers involved in producing something specialized and costly, as was Neubar. Attaingnant could lay claim to the title on either score. Was it Tournon who reminded the King what distinction the music printer of Paris had achieved in a decade's production? Or Lorraine?

As in the case of Estienne, letters patent do not survive for Attaingnant or for the Attaingnant-Jullet partnership. But the content of the letters was probably similar to that of the letter to Neubar, wherein the salient points were that Francis intended to promote learning, and specifically to do so by subsidizing Greek printing because of the high degree of specialization and expense involved. Three clauses treated the printer's duties, which were: (1) to submit all copy to the University for prior approval—a provision meant for theological works, (2) to deposit a copy of each original work in the royal library, and (3) to sign every work with his title of King's Printer. As his reward he was to receive one hundred crowns annually and enjoy tax exemption and the other privileges granted to the University of Paris, "in order that he draw greater advantage from his enterprise and acquire more easily all that is necessary for a typographical establishment." Finally, all others were prohibited for five years from printing or selling any books printed abroad that Neubar should wish to print, with the usual warning of punishment, confiscation, and so on against infringers.[40] Thus Neubar, too, was promoted to status equivalent to that of the tax-exempt libraires jurés even though he was not formally received by the University, as Tory was. The nomination of Attaingnant surely meant no less.

Further details about the post and specifically on the charge as "imprimeur du roy en musique" come from the letters patent given to Le Roy and Ballard on February 16, 1553.

> . . . Acknowledging that we, having regard for the good and pleasing services already done by our well beloved Adrian Le Roy and Robert Ballard, music printers

[40] The Latin original is quoted in G. Lepreux, *Galliae Typographicae Documentae* (Paris, 1910), no. 6; a French translation is given in Bernard, *Geofroy Tory*, Appendix VI.

> dwelling at Paris, and in consideration of this and their sense, sufficiency, probity, and good experience, have retained them and do retain them by these present letters in the status and office of our printers in order to print every kind of music, vocal as well as instrumental, and in the said occupation to serve us from now on, with the accustomed honors, authority, prerogatives, freedoms, liberty, privileges, profits, revenues, and emoluments, *such as and like unto those that the persons were accustomed to enjoy who had previously been named by us to the said charge*, and moreover we have permitted them and do permit them for ever and always to print every kind of music, vocal or instrumental, by any composers whosoever, notwithstanding all letters to the contrary that have been obtained and will be obtained which by our express will and by these present letters we have abrogated and do abrogate in regard to things that have not been printed, and on which the time has expired . . . [Italics added.][41]

Those who held the charge previously were, of course, Attaingnant and Jullet. To form an idea of the "accustomed honors, authority, prerogatives," and so on, we may have recourse to the gloss of these terms made by Lepreux in *Gallia Typographica.*

Honneurs derived from the fact of being attached to the person of the King, being his officer, and having access to his table and to the court.

Autorité was the power, not enjoyed by other printers, to call oneself in all things, everywhere and always, by the title of King's Printer.

Prérogative meant precedence, the evident superiority which decided the King's choice, and, as a consequence, the superiority over other printers in the fact of being King's Printer.

Franchise meant exemption, in general, from certain taxes which the printer enjoyed as a domestic officer of His Majesty, and, in particular cases, from certain other taxes.

Privilège and *Droit* referred to the function of printing edicts, ordinances, and other official acts of the sovereign power, to the exclusion of all other printers, for a certain time-span.

Profit was the benefice resulting from the exercise of the privilege and of the rights (i.e., by the sale of the publications).

Revenus and *Émoluments* betokened the special wages attached to the charge and belonging to it; in some cases these were specifically mentioned in the letters of the award.

The holder's access to the sovereign, and his special function of printing royal edicts are known from the activities of Attaingnant's successors. Adrian Le Roy was frequently at the court of Charles IX, and among the official publications was

[41] Quoted in Michel Brenet, "La Librairie musicale en France de 1653 à 1750," *Sammelbände der Internationale Musikgesellschaft* VIII (1906), 404.

the annual announcement of the Puy d'Evreux.[42] Also, under Charles IX, Le Roy and Ballard were put on the royal payroll as domestic officers and paid (irregularly) from the accounts of the Chapel Royal. Under Henry III these wages were continued and augmented by highly interesting letters patent of May 6, 1576, which bestowed the annual sum of 120 livres tournois upon each partner (previously each had received 50 l.t. per annum), to be paid now from the general tax receipts of Paris.[43] Payment was made with the intention of "favorably treating the said Le Roy and Ballard, both in consideration of their services and for the great care, diligence, and large expense that they employ in order to make their publications correct, and in order to give them means to continue on with even better . . . " Whether Attaingnant in his day received an outright subsidy from the Crown is questionable. More vital than "revenus" and "émoluments" was the access enjoyed by the royal printers to the household of the King and thus to the other institutions directly dependent thereupon. With Attaingnant as with Le Roy and Ballard this meant close contact with the Chapel Royal and the Sainte-Chapelle du Palais. What such an intimacy implied in regard to the sources of printer's copy may now be explored in the context of the nearly two hundred musicians' names appearing in Attaingnant's books.

Composers

The principal responsibilities of a press, said Robert Estienne in his will, were the correction of proof and provision of copy.[44] In the complex world of the printing business one easily loses sight of the man responsible for there being something to print—the author or composer. Attaingnant, upon inaugurating an entirely new industry so far as his country was concerned, had to establish a *modus vivendi* with his composers in an area where no precedent existed. The matter of providing copy raises the question of just what sort of relationships he did work out with composers. Was he a composer himself, and in this sense on equal terms with the musicians whose works he printed? It would seem not, for there is no single piece signed with his name over the span of a quarter century's activity. Andrea Antico, Antoine Gardane, and Tielman Susato were not hesitant about bringing occasional pieces of their own into the light of publication, whatever the compositional merit. Had Attaingnant been without any musical competence, on

[42] F. Lesure and G. Thibault, *Bibliographie des éditions d'Adrian Le Roy et Robert Ballard* (Paris, 1955), pp. 14, 17.

[43] Lepreux, *op. cit.*, nos. 46, 48. The 1576 letters are reproduced as no. 60.

[44] Antoine-Augustin Renouard, *Annales de l'imprimerie des Estienne* (2d ed.; Paris, 1843), pp. 578–582.

the other hand, some record of his dependence on hired assistants ought to have survived in the form of contracts. Such is the case with Nicolas du Chemin, who had his editor, Nicolas Regnes, give him lessons in how to sing and to "hold his part."[45] For negative reasons we may assume that Attaingnant was musician enough to serve as his own corrector. Only during the last days of the firm, in 1550, does an editor and corrector emerge, in the person of Claude Gervaise—so far as title pages allow us to tell **(164, 165, 172)**. Gervaise also arranged music; witness his three-part chansons adapted from well-known chansons *à 4* **(166)** and his settings of dance tunes **(170)**. For such arrangements the press must be held responsible. In fact, we have here some of the earliest music written expressly for publication. A few years later one of Du Chemin's editors filled a similar need for arrangements: "Loys Bisson has reduced from four parts *en duo*, without changing the Superius, except for a few rests, the music of several excellent chansons."[46] In 1541 the Venetian printer Scotto commissioned Jehan Gero to write his two-voiced madrigals and *canzoni francesi*.[47] The sixteenth-century "Duo" seems to be one genre which the publisher had called into life. The more regrettable from this point of view is the loss of Attaingnant's duos, which were among the earliest and most copied **(65, 66, 67)**. The duo offers an exceptional case in the relations between composer and publisher. Normally the copy procured for printing was not written on command, but was derived from what was currently sung at court and in the great chapels.

In Attaingnant's case this meant the royal music, as is clear from a mere counting of the names occurring in his collections. In order of frequency they are: Claudin de Sermisy, music director of the Chapel Royal; Pierre Certon, master of the children at the Sainte-Chapelle du Palais; and Clément Janequin, a royal musician of sorts too, as appears from the title "chantre du roi" (1531), and a dependant at some time of the Cardinal of Lorraine, as we have seen. Nomination as King's Printer merely made official a situation that existed from the beginning. Enjoying good relations with the main musicians of the Chapel Royal and Sainte-Chapelle, Attaingnant naturally profited from the repertory of these organizations, which furnished his mainstay. In the early years, access to the manuscripts used by the royal musicians was perhaps by way of the mysterious P.B. of *Dixhuit basses dances* **(16)**, who has been identified with the Pierre Blondeau serving the function of scribe to the Chapel Royal in 1532.

More than any other musician, Claudin seems to have been influential in

[45] F. Lesure and G. Thibault, "Bibliographie des éditions musicales publiées par Nicolas du Chemin (1549–1576)," *Annales Musicologiques* I (1953), 273 f.

[46] *Ibid.*, no. 87, p. 337.

[47] Alfred Einstein, *The Italian Madrigal* (Princeton, N.J., 1949), Vol. I, p. 264.

Attaingnant's success. A veritable dean of French musical life during the second quarter of the century, he was a key figure on the international scene too, as instanced by his correspondence with the Duke of Ferrara about exporting singers to Italy.[48] Michel Guilliaud, a preceptor at the Parisian Collège de Navarre, upon dedicating his *Rudiments de Musique* to Claudin in 1552, declared the composer an Apollo, remarking: "King Francis, father of the Muses and protector of all who love them, for this reason elevated you in honor, and since then the music planted by you in France has taken such a growth that many good spirits have striven to cultivate it more and more."[49] (The figure might be extended by remarking the importance of the music press in the ever more flourishing garden.) Another testimony, written while Francis still reigned, confirms that the King, hearing Mass every day, took particular pleasure in the art of his music director:

> Le Roy ne fault ung seul jour d'ouyr messe,
> Et conferment la créance et promesse
> Faicte au baptesme et depuys tant jurée,
> Et par plusieurs sacremens asseurée.
> Chantres y sont qui ont voix argentines,
> Psalmodiant les louanges divines,
> Et de David recitant des chansons,
> Avec motets de diverses façons,
> Soit de Claudin, pere aux musiciens
> Ou de Sandrin, esgual aux anciens.
>
> Claude Chappuys, *Discours de la court*, 1543

The dedication which Pierre Certon addressed to Claudin in 1542 speaks even more eloquently of the widespread love and respect for the "père aux musiciens" and implies, moreover, that Claudin was responsible for publication of Certon's motets by Attaingnant (Appendix, 14). Claudin's music helped inaugurate the publishing firm with the *Chansons nouvelles* of 1528, and his pieces were chosen almost invariably when lute or keyboard arrangements were undertaken. Weighty as was his contribution to the new-style chanson, his Masses and motets came to have a preponderant part in the publisher's operations. The question arises, inevitably, of a possible liaison between the King's music director and his music printer. Certainly Claudin was close enough to Attaingnant to insure superior readings of his own works. In the motet "Quare fremuerent gentes," for example, one of the master's longest and most impressive compositions, the printed version

[48] The original document in the archives at Modena is transcribed in Henry Prunières, *L'Opéra italien en France avant Lulli* (Paris, 1913), p. xv. English translation in D. Heartz, "Les Goûts Réunis, or the Worlds of the Madrigal and the Chanson Confronted," in James Haar (ed.), *Chanson and Madrigal 1480–1530* (Cambridge, Mass., 1964), p. 109.

[49] F. Lesure and G. Thibault, "Bibliographie . . . Du Chemin," p. 281.

of 1542 offers a more polished musical text than does the earlier Newberry Library Motet MS, as H. Colin Slim will show in his forthcoming study of the latter. There is little else to go on, yet some significance may attach to the following circumstance. Nearly two-thirds of Claudin's secular composition falls in his earliest period, before 1536, after which there is a great slackening in the number of chansons; his production by decades has been summed up as follows:[50]

	Secular works	*Sacred works*
1526–1536	122	39
1537–1547	42	33
1548–1559	2	26

In 1533 Claudin was nominated to the eleventh canonry of the Sainte-Chapelle, with which office went a domicile in Paris as well as a goodly stipend. Was it increasing material prosperity that turned him away from secular composition? If so, this might suggest that he received financial remuneration for the many chansons of the early years. The hypothesis, however, receives little support from what is known generally about relations between publishers and authors at the time.

Rarely was an author paid for his manuscript, at least in France. Authorship, in Boileau's phrase, was thought to be a "divine art," not to be degraded into a "mercenary craft."[51] Only men so renowned as Erasmus or so feared as Aretino could demand payment from printers—and they did not always obtain it. The typical payment throughout the sixteenth century, if payment there was, consisted of a certain number (usually small) of printed copies. Even in the early seventeenth century Descartes received only two hundred copies in payment for his *Discours de la méthode.* With some astutely calculated personal dedications a composer or author might hope to profit from his allotted copies. But the main profit, as well as the risk, devolved upon the publisher. He made the decisions. An example is offered in the person of the poet-composer Eustorg de Beaulieu (ca. 1500–1552), who attempted repeatedly to have his polyphonic pieces published. He promised in his *Divers Rapportz* (1537) that twelve of his chansons would be published "en note musicallement à 3 et 4 parties," but only three seem to have been printed—in Moderne's first and second *Parangon des chansons* (1538).[52]

[50] Isabelle Cazeaux, "The Secular Music of Claudin de Sermisy" (Unpublished Ph.D. dissertation, Columbia University, 1961), Vol. I, p. 28.

[51] David T. Pottinger, *The French Book Trade in the Ancien Régime, 1500–1791* (Cambridge, Mass., 1958), p. 95.

[52] Nanie Bridgman, "Eustorg de Beaulieu the Musician," *The Musical Quarterly* XXXVII (1951), 61–70.

In 1540 he tried to persuade the printer Mathias Apiarius of Berne (earlier associated with Peter Schoeffer the Younger at Strasbourg) to bring out some Psalm-settings; this failed too, it seems.[53] Finally, in his *Chrestienne Resjouyssance* (1546), Beaulieu says that he has set thirty-nine of the poems to music and would like to print them, if only he could find an "imprimeur commode," To be sure, Beaulieu was no Claudin, so far as can be judged from the three pieces that Moderne printed. By way of another example, it may be noted that the appearance of Glarean's *Dodecachordon* was delayed eight years (from 1539 to 1547) because a publisher could not be found.[54]

Composer-publisher relationships during the sixteenth century are described in minute detail in the remarkably extensive archives surviving from the Plantin firm at Antwerp. Faced with the necessity of disposing of a vast quantity of expensive paper in "royal" format, Plantin began printing mensural music in 1578, publishing the Masses of George De la Hèle, a young musician much in favor with Philip II of Spain. The composer was obliged to put his signature to the following terms before his manuscript was published:

> I, the undersigned, recognize and confess having made an agreement with Christopher Plantin, printer to the King [of Spain] to wit: I promise that, once the work is printed, I will buy forty copies at the price charged booksellers, with whatever additional rebate Plantin may be gracious enough to give me. The copies will be delivered by the half-dozen and paid for immediately, before dispatch of the other obligatory copies, all copies to be received and paid for within the term of a year. Made without fraud or deceit at Antwerp, on August 21, 1578.[55]

The trade price of these folio volumes was 16 florins; at retail they sold for 18 florins. De la Hèle was not able to carry out the compact fully, with the results that complaints were made by Plantin. In a letter of 1582 the composer sought to excuse himself: ". . . were it not for these injurious times and the dangers of travel, all the copies would have been sold; they are so much in demand that a hundred copies or more could have been sold had I only been in Italy—a letter from Rome written by one of the first musicians of Italy informs me that the writer alone would like 150 copies." De la Hèle then goes on to chide his publisher by saying that the volume especially prepared for presentation to Philip was so poorly bound that two of the Masses could not be sung.[56] Plantin demanded

[53] Pierre Pidoux, *Le Psaultier Hugenot* (Basel, 1962), Vol. II, p. 5.

[54] Clement Miller, "The *Dodecachordon*: its Origins and Influence on Renaissance Musical Thought," *Musica Disciplina* XV (1961), 161.

[55] The contract is printed in J. A. Stellfeld, *Bibliographie des éditions musicales Plantiniennes* (Académie Royale de Belgique, Classe des Beaux-Arts, *Mémoires*, Vol. III, No. 3) (Brussels, 1949), pp. 28 f.

[56] *Ibid.*, pp. 30 f.

similar agreements from other composers. Thus Jacobus de Brouck promised to take 162 copies of his *Cantiones* (1579), Severin Cornet a hundred copies of his pieces (1581), while even the internationally famous Jacobus de Kerle had to buy twelve copies of his Masses in folio (1582) and the venerable Philippe de Monte was expected to advance money before the printing of his music began in 1586.[57]

If the initiative in a printing venture came from the composer he was obliged both to pay the cost of paper, types, and proofreading and to guarantee a certain sum to the printer—in other words, to take over the function of publisher. This is precisely what happened in the case of Elzéar Genet (alias Carpentras), a wealthy composer whose involvements with the press are described below under "The Avignon Contracts." When a printer offered money for manuscript music, as did Du Chemin to Regnes in 1548, there was some special reason.[58] With Du Chemin it was a case of attempting to break into a business for which he lacked background and connections, having never printed music and not being musician himself. This instance notwithstanding, it is abundantly clear that the French composer ordinarily could expect little if any profit from having his work printed and was without protection comparable to a copyright. The ten-year privileges granted to Lassus and Claude le Jeune by Henry III in 1581–1582 provide early examples of "composers' rights" in France. (A recent work on musical copyright suggests that a modern system of protection was already widespread in the sixteenth century, but does not make it clear that the study, purportedly comprehensive, is based almost entirely on German sources.[59] This explains why a Frenchman, writing on the same subject, could arrive at the contradictory position that authors' rights in regard to music had to await the eighteenth century before being fully established.[60] In France they did.)

If a Claudin or a lesser figure consigned his music to Attaingnant, his motive was probably not financial; he had merely the hope of honor and fame. This is the attitude which emerges from the prefaces of Manchicourt and Certon (Appendix, 10,14). Having few tangible rewards to gain from publication, not every sixteenth-century composer or author sought the celebrity of print. As the court poet Mellin de Saint-Gelais well knew, what the press had once diffused could never again lay claim to being novel or exclusive. He and probably many others held back from publication for this reason.

Poets may have been reluctant about publication, but they were eager to see musical setting—an important part of the Renaissance mystique was the union of

[57] *Ibid.*, pp. 48, 65, 77, 96.

[58] Lesure and Thibault, "Bibliographie . . . Du Chemin," pp. 273 f.

[59] Hansjörg Pohlmann, *Die Frühgeschichte des musikalischen Urheberrechts (ca. 1400–1800)* (Basel, 1962), p. 20.

[60] Raoul Castelain, *Histoire de l'édition musicale* (Paris, 1957), p. 57.

verse and music, for which Plato's authority was frequently invoked. Some went so far as to dedicate their verses to the hoped-for source of musical "illustration." Thus François Habert, author of the political chanson printed by the widow Attaingnant in 1558 **(174),** addressed an earlier effort, apparently futile, to one Jacques Copain, organist, explaining in some liminary couplets:

Or reçoys donc (amy) ce petit livre
Ou maint rondeau et dixain, je te livre
Car en musique il seront par toy mis
Sans qu'il en soit ung seullement omis,
Dont tes accords plains de perfection
Donneront lustre a mon invention
Te suppliant de si bon gré le prendre
Comme ay voulu entre tes mains le rendre.

Les Ballades . . . et chansons du Banny de lyesse (Paris, Lotrian, n.d.)

One hundred and seventy-five composers are named in the surviving publications of Attaingnant. Any attempt to group them according to time, place, or affiliation must be subject to cautionary warning. The tables below are no more reliable than the current state of biographical information, which is to say, very inadequate. The numeral next a composer's name betokens the number of *different* pieces ascribed to him in what is left of Attaingnant's output. Names are standardized in spelling according to the form adopted in the Composer Index. Christian names are added only when deemed helpful for clarification.

Older Generation of Franco-Flemish Composers:

Agricola	1	Pierre de La Rue	5
Brumel	2	Jean Mouton	21
Divitis	3	Pipelaire	1
Antoine de Févin	5	Jean Prioris	2
Josquin des Prés	33	Total	73

Most surprising about this list of "great names" from around 1500 is the paucity of their pieces. Even Mouton, "chantre du roy" until his death in 1522, is scantily represented and almost entirely by sacred works, the last of which was printed in 1535. The total from the group would be nearly halved were it not for the late and faulty edition of Josquin's chansons **(162),** which could have come in part from an earlier Susato edition. Relations between the "Prince of Musicians" and France constitute one of the greater enigmas of music history. At various times, and perhaps in various capacities, Josquin had ties with Louis XII;

thus he too was a royal musician.[61] Other links might have existed with Paris. As liturgical printer to the diocese of Noyon Attaingnant also served Saint-Quentin, one of its chief cities and a reputed music center—the Collegiate church there could boast a tradition that included canons Philippe de Vitry and Guillaume Machaut in the fourteenth century, Josquin, as choirboy, in the mid-fifteenth, and canon Loyset Compère, buried within its walls in 1518, as was canon Jean Mouton four years later. A Picard from the Vermandois region around Saint-Quentin, if not from Saint-Quentin itself,[62] Josquin late in life returned north, accepting the post of provost at Condé on the Escaut river, a few miles from Douai. He died there, probably in 1521. We might expect the music press begun in Paris shortly thereafter to be close to the master in every sense. The truth of the case is otherwise. After a single chanson in 1529 (in **5**, and probably by Benedictus) no other music attributed to Josquin appeared for four years—no motets and not a single Mass in the seven-volume series. "Mille regretz," printed in 1533 (**41**, the earliest surviving source for the piece) carries the name not of Josquin, as elsewhere, but of "J. Lemaire." Is this a reference to Jean Lemaire de Belges, the prominent poet of the first quarter of the century? If so, did poet's and composer's names become exchanged? The case reinforces the impression that Attaingnant was out of touch with the great generation preceding his own.

With the Northern masters who were his contemporaries it was a different matter. Included in this group are Gombert and Clemens, but not Willaert, Arcadelt, and others whose careers took them to Italy, for which special tabulation is made.

Franco-Flemish Composers after 1525:

Benedictus Appenzeller	3	Jean du Moulin	1
Jachet Berchem	3	Gombert	27
François Bourguignon	5	Lupi	42
Canis	2	Manchicourt	36
Clemens non Papa	11	Rogier Patie	5
Courtois	13	Loyset Piéton	1
Crecquillon	2	Richafort	17
Delattre	1	Total	169

[61] For an interpretation combining biographical and musical evidence see Howard M. Brown "The Genesis of a Style: The Parisian Chanson, 1500–1530," in Haar (ed.), *Chanson and Madrigal 1480–1530*, pp. 11 f.

[62] The latest suggestions as to the composer's birthplace are the Vermandois village of Prez (Henry Leland Clarke, "Musicians of the Northern Renaissance," in *Aspects of Medieval and Renaissance Music*, pp. 76 f.) and the village of Beaurevoir, five leagues from Saint-Quentin (Félix Raugel, "Notes pour servir à l'histoire musicale de la Collégiale de Saint-Quentin depuis les origines jusqu'en 1679," in *Festschrift Heinrich Besseler zum sechzigsten Geburtstag*, [Leipzig, 1961], p. 53).

The composers who were active in Italy have been grouped in the following list, according to the place with which they are most firmly identified.

Composers Resident in Italy:

FLORENCE		ROME, PAPAL SERVICE	
Verdelot	14	Arcadelt	19
MANTUA		Conseil	17
Jacquet of Mantua	2	Festa	1
MILAN		Hilaire Penet	2
Werrecore	2	Ninot le Petit	1
VENICE		Andreas de Silva	3
Gardane	20	ROME, SAN LUIGI DE' FRANCESI	
Willaert	22	L'Héritier	12
		Total	115

Of the composers resident in the French realm it will be convenient to divide those in Paris or in royal service from those who inhabited other centers.

Composers Who Were Singers in the Chapel Royal:

Guillaume Belin	12	Rousée	8
Jean Bouchefort	2	Sandrin	50
Guillaume Nicolas	5	Sermisy	230
Jacotin [Le Bel]	32	ALSO IN ROYAL SERVICE:	
Didier La Chenet	3	Pierre d'Auxerre	1
Le Brun	2	Gascongne (?)	17
Antoine de Longueval	1	Jean Le Gendre	5
Pierre Moulu (?)	6	Gosse (?)	13
Romain	5	Janequin (?)	178
		Total	570

Composers Whose Main Connection was with the Sainte-Chapelle:

Hector Boucher L'Enfant	1	Du Hamel	3
Barra (?)	5	Mornable	82
Blancher	2	Tetart	1
Certon	188	Vermont	13
Cibot	5	Ysoré	7
Dorle	1		
Duboys	1	Total	309

Other Composers Resident at Some Time in the Capital:

Alaire	9	Regnes	12
Boyvin (?)	11	Wauquel (?)	5
Du Tertre	25	NOTRE DAME DE PARIS:	
Gervaise	33	Jean Herissant	1
Goudimel	2	Pagnier	4
Jodon	1	Sohier	22
Mittou	2	Total	127

Composers Resident at Length in Other French Cities:

AMIENS		LYONS	
Vulfran Samin	14	Layolle	1
ANGERS		Fresneau (?)	4
Janequin		Villiers (?)	13
AUCH		NANCY	
Pierre Cadéac	7	Lasson	7
AUTUN		NEVERS	
Pierre Colin	7	Morel	14
AVIGNON		NOYON	
Gabriel Coste	1	Nicholas de Marle	8
L'Héritier		Sohier	
BEAUVAIS		POITIERS	
Jean Doublet	2	Senterre	4
Godard	12	ROUEN	
Hesdin	18	François Dulot	5
BORDEAUX		Magdelain	5
Janequin		G. le Roy	2
BOURGES		ST-FLORENT EN ROYE	
Bastard	1	Wauquel	
Le Bouteiller	6	TOURS	
CHARTRES		Le Heurteur	45
Nicole Groussy	1		
Jean Guyon	11	Total	202

Finally, there is an intriguing number of names that cannot yet be attached to any town or institution. The list has been restricted to those composers represented by four or more pieces. Most would seem to have been French by their names.

Bon Voisin	5	Mittantier	22
Decapella	5	Morpain	7
Delafont	15	Passereau	24
Ebran	15	Pelletier	4
Garnier	4	Pellison	4
Gentian	19	Puy	5
Goudeaul	4	Roquelay	5
La Fage	4	Symon	23
L'Huyllier	11	Vassal	6
Maille	20	Total	251
Meigret	29		

Although such lists can give a very approximate picture at best, they do throw into relief three cardinal bases upon which Attaingnant built his publishing career: his reliance on the royal organizations, his modernity, and his position as a truly national printer. Regarding the last, it is noteworthy that English, German, and Italian composers are entirely absent from his offerings (except for one piece by Festa, who may have been trained in France). The only "foreign" element is that represented by the contemporary Franco-Flemish musicians. This is to be expected because of the eminence of composers like Clemens, Gombert, Lupi, and Manchicourt. It may be construed as evidence that the music of "Burgundian" composers continued to find favor in Paris, and that the old ties between music at the French court and in the northern provinces remained vital. In all likelihood, composers remote from Paris or outside the realm did not actually send their pieces to Attaingnant. It probably sufficed that their works were in the repertory of the Chapel Royal or the Saint-Chapelle to make them available to the printer. One Franco-Flemish master who may have had direct dealings with Attaingnant was Pierre de Manchicourt, phonascus of Tournai and Canon of Arras.[63] He kept his motets to himself before publication, if we may believe the dedication he wrote in 1539 to Remigius Ruffus (Remy Roussel), Canon of Tours (Appendix, 10). Printing arrangements may have been carried out by way of Claudin, whose nephew Gilles (Egidius) contributed the verses comparing Manchicourt to Orpheus. It is perhaps significant that Tournai was an old French possession

[63] The term "phonascus" is probably meant as a synonym for musician. Glarean used it in a more specific sense, however, as he explained in a letter of 1538 to Johannes Aal: "I call a *phonascus* the inventor of a single melody in some mode, a *symphoneta* the one who adds the remaining voices." Clement Miller, "The *Dodecachordon* . . . ," *Musica Disciplina* XV (1961), 160.

(until 1523)—a pocket within Hapsburg lands that was an issue of contention between Francis I and Charles V. At the same time it should not be overlooked that Manchicourt's office at the neighboring cathedral town of Arras provides a link with the seat of the Attaingnant family.

The term "foreign" is misleading when applied to relations between royal France and the territories to the north under Hapsburg control, especially in regard to cultural matters. Francis I and Charles V, although in frequent political conflict, were linked by language, religion, and education. Both were French princes, and Charles had been reared in much the same way as his Valois cousin. The rivalry between them, always keen, extended to artistic matters. Even their musicians competed with each other, according to a letter describing the Emperor's visit to Paris in 1540 (see p. 140). Relevant here is the expression of the letter-writer characterizing the musicians of both princes as comprising "all those of our France." The boundaries of Attaingnant's musical realm may be understood with similar latitude. They embraced all those parts of Gaul which the printer himself described in a broadside **(59)** as being "bounded by the Rhine, the Alps, the Pyrenees, the Atlantic, and divided into Belgian, Celtic, and Aquitanian portions." (See Pl. XIII.)

It was to Valois France, nevertheless, to the royal territories, that Attaingnant owed the vast majority of his pieces. Paris formed the center of his musical universe, and to this center the northern provinces without the realm were as tributary as the southern provinces within. Another way of looking at the geographical situation is provided by the frequent topical allusions in chanson-texts. The northern provinces offer many. There are, for example, "Les bons frères de Thérouenne" (in Flanders), rivaling "Les filletes de Tournay" (in Hainaut). The chief city of Artois furnished the locale for Willaert's "Dessus le marché d'Arras." Immediately south lies the province celebrated in the drinking song "Ceux de Picardie," set by the Picard, Claudin. The cathedral town whose Chapter Attaingnant supplied is represented by "En venant de Noyon." Paris itself figures numerous times, and such texts are set by Janequin, among others, as in "Gros Jean menoit hors de Paris en croupe ung jour d'esté sa maistresse jouer." The immediate environs of the capital also come into play, as in the chanson "En m'en venant de Nanterre" (a village near Saint-Germain-en-Laye). In the valley of the Loire, the capital of Touraine, with its patron saint, are the subject of "En Tours la feste Sainct Martin." Neighboring Nivernois contains the town referred to in the query "Estes-vous de Clamessy, dame?" France's second city figures in the text of a canon by Mouton, "En venant de Lyon." Toulouse in Languedoc is represented by a piece that shifts, with obvious delight, into local dialect:

Chacune d'un Toulouzan pas compra ha! ha!
Laise sabbaton de cordoven los casignolet
Haribouriquet bouriquet bouriquet . . . (**31**, 28)

Still farther afield, at the Spanish border, was the setting for "En m'en venant de la Fontarabie." The texts, in sum, offer a colorful variety of local allusions and dialects, the richness of which has been barely suggested. They help define, after their own fashion, the extent of Attaingnant's musical domain.

Texts tell another tale when considered together with their authors. Music books, careless enough about composers' names, almost never mention authors. Some have been identified (see the Indexes of First Lines). Many more could be through intensive study of contemporary verse collections—mainly manuscripts in the Bibliothèque Nationale. The task is fundamental to a history of the chanson and, along with prosodic analysis and textual criticism, must provide the framework for studies of the music. From the identifications that have been made, as recorded in the Index of First Lines, it is apparent again how close the Attaingnant repertory was to the court. The poets Clément Marot and Mellin de Saint-Gelais lead all others in frequency. Both held appointments in the royal household and played a vital part in its daily social life. Equally significant are the numerous verses that can be ascribed to persons of higher station. In MS fr. 1700 "Si vostre amour ne gist qu'en apparence" (set by Sandrin) is attributed to "Monseigneur le dauphin," meaning probably the future Henry II. Mention has been made of Cardinal Tournon's poetic efforts, set, among others, by Claudin. Claudin also set "Si ung oeuvre parfait doibt chacun contenter," ascribed to "La R. de Navarre" in MS fr. 1667 and to "Le Roy" in MS fr. 2335. Marguerite de Navarre receives the attribution as well of "Pour vous rendre parfait contentement" (in MS fr. 1667), and we may suspect that other of the more polished lyrics flowed from the pen of the lady who was the court's literary jewel. Her brother the King was a prolific versifier and the most represented poet after Marot and St.-Gelais. Claudin and Janequin made rival settings of his "Je n'ose etre content de mon contentement," together with its response, "Las que crains tu, amy, de quoy as déffiance." The two masters rivaled each other on several other verses, for example "O cruaulté logée en grand beaulté," and "Martin menoit son pourceau," (both by Marot), "Ayez pitié du grand mal" (attributed to Heroët and Chappuys) and "Dites sans peur ou l'ouy ou nenny" (Francis I or St.-Gelais). A number of texts were set in common by Certon and Claudin too; still more were shared by Certon and Janequin, including "Frere Thibault" and "Plus ne suys," both by Marot and "Un jour que madame dormait" by St.-Gelais. Not uncommonly did three or more composers take up the same lyrics; one text, "Las qu'on cogneust mon vouloir," offers the spectacle of a competition among the four leading masters of the Parisian chanson: Claudin, Janequin, Certon, and Sandrin.[64] Parallel settings like these provide an attractive approach to the artistic personalities involved. The poems of Francis I and their musical settings also deserve no less than a full-scale critical study. Some go back to the King's captivity—for example, "Si la fortune et la diversité," described as "La chanson que le roy fist luy estant a madride en espaigne" in *La fleur des chansons*[65] and printed, with considerable textual variation, in an anonymous musical setting **(9,** 3**)**. Some probably stemmed from courtly entertainments, such as the (masker's?) song "Vous qui voulez sçavoir mon nom," set by Claudin. Not surprising in the least, it was Claudin who set more of the King's verses than did anyone else; the same is true of Marot's verses. What more logical chain than from royal pen to royal chapel director, to royal music-printer? Francis I may have other claim to being included in a section on composers. When Attaingnant printed "Puisque donc ma maitresse n'a pas pitié" (**15,** 12), he ascribed it simply to "Françoys." Given the King's wide talents and celebrated melomania, the piece may be his, *verbo et cantu*. Could he do less, after all, than compete with another royal scribbler of music, "cousin" Henry VIII?

Between a poem's origin, its musical setting, and the latter's publication, the time was often short. It is characteristic that many of Marot's early chansons saw print in musical versions by Claudin before they came out in the poet's *Adolescence Clementine*, first printed by Geofroy Tory on August 12, 1532. Claudin's setting of Marot's "Amour me voyant sans tristesse" appeared in **42** within the year of its first edition in *La Suite de l'Adolescence Clementine*, dated late 1533. Janequin's quick response to the return of the royal princes in 1530 has been discussed above. Marot's delightful epigram "Du Beau Tétin," written in late 1535, while the poet was in exile at Ferrara, appeared in Janequin's setting in April 1536 **(72)**. These and many similar cases suggest that the leading poets and composers were in as close touch as was Attaingnant with his composers.

Few glimpses of personal contacts between the royal printer and his composers survive in documents. The extraordinary significance of Claudin to Attaingnant has been touched upon. With Certon—the second musician of the realm, in a sense—a special relationship is no less likely. Certon was the protégé of Claudin, as emerges very clearly from the Dedication of the motet volume of 1542 (Appendix, 14). Still more revealing and eloquent is the *Déploration* of the older master which Certon set to music:

[64] Claudin's setting does not survive in Attaingnant's extant publications, unlike the others, but may be found in Moderne's *Parangon . . . Tiers Livre* (Lyons, 1538).

[65] See Jean Rollin, *Les Chansons de Clément Marot* (Publications de la Société Française de Musicologie, Ser. 3, Vol. I) (Paris, 1951), p. 254, no. 58.

Musiciens, chantres melodieux,
En piteux chants jettez larmes des yeulx
Pour ce grand maistre, expert et magnifique
Compositeur, le thrésor de Musique:
Hélas, hélas, c'est l'excellent Claudin,
Que mort a pris, ayant mis de sa main
Plusieurs Mottets, et Messes par escrit,
En si doulx chants: prions à Jesus-Christ
Qu'un *Libera* luy soit bien tost donné
Et requiem aeternum Domine.

Les Meslanges de maistre Pierre Certon, 1570

On September 16, 1542, Certon joined the Attaingnant family in their parish church of Saint-Benoît in order to hold the child of Hubert Jullet and Germaine Attaingnant over the baptismal font (Appendix, 15). On the same occasion one godmother was the wife of Mathurin Le Beau, *procureur en Parlement*. The circumstance that this highly placed lawyer was a close friend of Janequin provides another reason for believing the composer to have been in close contact with Paris, even while holding posts at Bordeaux and Angers.[66] Mathurin Le Beau became sole executor of Janequin's last will and testament.

The Attaingnant shop must have provided a common meeting-ground not only for the stellar trio of Claudin, Certon, and Janequin, but also for countless other musicians and music lovers from all parts. For this reason, if for no other, Francis I's music printer may be said to have established a new institution in the cultural life of the nation. The role of the music press as a clearinghouse for ideas and as an arbiter of taste was something to be reckoned with henceforth in French music.

[66] F. Lesure, "Clément Janequin: Recherches sur sa vie et son oeuvre," *Musica Disciplina* V (1951), 171.

IV

MUSIC AND THE BOOK TRADE

EARLY MUSIC PUBLISHING affords an unusual view of the interworkings between art and commerce. Scholarly attention has centered heretofore mainly on the very act of printing. The publisher, then as now, had several additional concerns. Editorial copy, financing, distribution, publicity, and the customer all required attention. Publication, properly speaking, comprised the manifold stages intervening between producer and consumer—between composer and collector.

Compared with other specialty trades in the publishing business, music was a late-comer. The volumes brought out by Petrucci at Venice between 1501 and 1512 represent the incunabula in the field and have, on account of their clarity and beauty as well as their age, been accorded an esteem beyond all others. When Anton Schmid wrote his monograph on early music printing more than a century ago he entitled it, in keeping with the Great Man approach to history of the time, with the single name of the printer seen at once as creator and acme. Opinion today would wish to give much more credit to the fifteenth-century printers of chant for preparing the way; and it detracts nothing from Petrucci to notice that others, using his methods, produced equally beautiful books, or that Antico, using woodcut, achieved comparable excellence, as did Granjon and Le Bé in engraving punches for single impression. Yet what Petrucci offered must have struck the public by its novelty. It also struck in a rather vulnerable spot, namely the purse. Ferdinand Columbus (1488–1539), son of the explorer, left records of his book-buying over three decades, precious documents to which we shall recur later. When in Rome in 1512–1513 Columbus bought several of Petrucci's volumes, and for the price of any one of them he might have acquired several literary works of equivalent size. The extreme luxury of the Petrucci prints went against the trend toward utility in contemporary general printing. In the same year of the first music print another Venetian printer, Aldus Manutius, launched his series of classic authors in octavo, employing a new cursive type which later came to be called italic. The innovation proved epochal in regard to both the reduced format, permitting a price reduction, and the abandonment of the international gothic for the more modern type. The aims and methods of Manutius were soon followed in music printing; a similar reduction in format and price was achieved by Andrea Antico, who stated in a request for a privilege in 1513 that he wished to print for those "learned in the liberal arts and especially students of music." Petrucci's *Magnificat* was purchased by Columbus for 81 quattrini in 1521, while the small Antico part-books which had just come out cost only 31 quattrini.[1] The equivalent of the smaller sum in French money of the

[1] Catherine Weeks Chapman, "Andrea Antico" (Unpublished Ph.D. dissertation, Harvard University, 1964), p. 46. I am indebted to Mrs. Chapman for much information on the early Italian printers and for generously communicating the results of her research when it was still in progress.

time was 10 sous tournois, or half a livre tournois. There is evidence, to be presented below, that Attaingnant, like Antico, was able to keep the price of a set of part-books down to half a livre or even less.

The success of the new and cheaper format perhaps had something to do with Petrucci's withdrawal from the field. Having removed to his native Fossombrone in 1513, he printed music only sporadically and then gave up all together after 1520, although he lived until 1539. Petrucci had difficulties keeping in business. Some of the reasons for this emerge from the renewal of his original privilege granted by the Venetian authorities in 1514.[2] The printer, styled as "primo Inventor de stampar libri de canto figurato," claimed that he would fall upon hard times if his privilege were not extended. Reason therefor was that "in printing such [musical] works there was need for much capital, and not having much, Petrucci, being a poor man, took as partners Signor Amadeo Scotto, bookseller, and Signor Nicolò de Raphael, who together brought out many music books . . ." Because of wars and turbulences, the partners were not able to export their books; thus they had "tied up their capital, to their great loss and sacrifice." The emphasis upon the export market is noteworthy, as is the overriding importance of quick sales and return upon investment. The luxurious Petrucci volumes did, indeed, linger on booksellers' shelves for a number of years, as we know from the record Columbus left of his acquisitions. Besides being dependent upon others for capital, Petrucci was not entirely self-sufficient in editorial matters. The *Odhecaton* was compiled and edited for him by Petrus Castellanus. In another instance one of his correctors, Hieronymus Posthumous, placed a note at the end of a nonmusical volume of 1513, disclaiming responsibility for a number of misprints on the grounds that the printer was a man of little learning; he complained, furthermore, that one Johannes Baptista, a beardless Ethiop youth and beginner in the art of printing, had been engaged in the work.[3] The reliance upon unskilled pressmen says much about the precariousness of Petrucci's ventures, as does the reliance upon outside capital. Petrucci's strong point was design; he was a master engraver in metal and the first specialist in music printing. He was not a music publisher in the sense that Attaingnant was later to become.

Andrea Antico was neither publisher nor printer. He worked as a craftsman in wood, on commission from others, and had the added advantage over Petrucci

[2] Anton Schmid, *Ottaviano dei Petrucci da Fossombrone, der erste Erfinder des Musiknotendruckes mit beweglichen Metalltypen und sein Nachfolger im sechzehnten Jahrhunderts* (Vienna, 1845), p. 19. The privilege is reprinted in Claudio Sartori, *Bibliografia delle Opere Musicali stampate da Ottaviano Petrucci* (Florence, 1948), p. 19.

[3] F. J. Norton, *Italian Printers 1501–1520: An Annotated List, with an Introduction* (Cambridge Bibliographical Society, Monograph No. 3) (London, 1958). See p. xxii.

of being an experienced musician, even a composer. Documents survive concerning the publication of the *Liber quindecim missarum* (1516), the plates of which he executed.[4] When the 1,008 copies of this magnificent folio volume were finished, they were put in the hands of Ottaviano Scotto, the publisher; the printer, Antonio Giunta, received payment by the piece for his work. Three papal singers were present as witnesses to the agreement: Gilles Carpentier, Gilles de Hamedin, and Jean van der Tyende (from the dioceses of Amiens, Cambrai, and Tournai, respectively). The position held by these three hints that the Masses were derived from, as well as destined for, the repertory of the Papal Chapel. But copies had to be sold far and wide to meet the expenses of publication—the terms mention specifically France and other "ultramontane parts." Wherever sold, the volumes were to be priced at 20 giulii retail, and 15 giulii wholesale. Converted into French money of the time, the cost of a single volume would be about £7 6*s*.—almost fifteen times the 10*s*. that Columbus paid for the octavo *Chansons à troys* (1520).[5] But then, the pages of the Mass volume "in royal folio" are almost eight times as large and its 162 leaves make it twice as long as the combined total of the three little part-books. The two formats were worlds apart, yet there was perhaps some similarity of intention in the guiding mentality behind them. Both were well designed to serve practical music-making, a consideration by which Petrucci seemingly put little store. His many quarto publications with all the parts in a single volume were not ideally suited either for intimate secular groups or for use by large church choirs. In some other features having to do with performance, such as the matter of texts, Petrucci showed himself less solicitous for the musician than the latter might wish. Was he out of touch with practical aspects of music? The question is, in any case, academic. Only a few, very wealthy collectors could have afforded his de luxe editions. It is symptomatic that these survive in a greater number of copies than do Antico's music prints, showing that Petrucci always had a place of honor—on the library shelf.

In the two decades between 1510 and 1530 several other printers followed in the paths of the two pioneers. As early as 1507, Oeglin of Augsburg had succeeded in printing mensural music with movable type, using two or more impressions, and the same was accomplished by Peter Schoeffer the Younger of Mainz in 1513.

4 Chapman, *op. cit.*, pp. 55–57.

5 One giulio was equivalent to 24 quattrini, according to the calculations of Chapman (*op. cit*, p. 58). The quatrino was valued at 420 to the gold ducat in 1530, as Ferdinand Columbus noted on the Petrucci volumes he bought that year in Perugia. The same collector noted on the French translation of Virgil (Paris, 1532) that the gold ducat was worth 47*s*. 6*d*. See Jean Babelon, *La Bibliothèque française de Fernand Colomb* (*Revue des Bibliothèques*, Supplement X) (Paris, 1913), no. 269.

Imitators were not lacking in Italy, either. Pasoti of Rome carried on the Petrucci method, while Sambonetto of Sienna and Caneto of Naples imitated Antico's small woodcut books. Woodcuts were also used by Arnt of Aachen for the books of lieder printed at Cologne about 1519. One of the most beautiful imitations of a Petrucci print was done by the anonymous craftsmen responsible for *XX. Songes* (London, 1530). Another stunning volume of the early followers was a folio choirbook edited by the composer Senfl and published at the expense of Grimm and Wyrsung as the *Liber selectarum cantionum* (Augsburg, 1520). The model of Antico is visible here with regard to layout as it is in the *Contrapunctus seu figurata musica super plano cantu missarum solennium totius anni* (Lyons, Gueynard, 1528).

The prestige of such resplendent folio volumes matched their price. One French musician, Carpentras, decided to produce a series of such volumes "in royal folio" devoted entirely to his own *œuvre*. Up to this time no other composer's works had been so published. Negotiations concerning the feat took place over a number of years. They provide some of the most remarkable documents of the kind to survive and will be considered in detail.

The Avignon Contracts

Elzéar Genet, known as Carpentras (after his native town in Provence), had been a singer in Avignon in 1505 and had subsequently gone north to serve at the court of Louis XII. Sent by the King to Leo X in 1513, Carpentras had the good fortune to satisfy this Medici pope, a lover of music as well as every other pleasure, and as a result became a very rich man. The victim of a mysterious and unnamed illness, he returned to Avignon in 1526 to pass his remaining days, having amassed several prebends, three canonries, nine priories, and two vicarships. A few years later, while serving in his capacity as dean of Saint-Agricole, he began negotiations toward the monumental edition of his compositions. Although no local printer had attempted mensural music, the composer must have been persuaded that his aims could be accomplished by Jean de Channey, a craftsman of some distinction active at Avignon between 1511 and 1540. The original agreement between the two, dated January 2, 1531,[6] is here summarized:

(1) Channey agrees to print within the term of six months the four volumes of music, using 120 reams of paper in royal format furnished by Carpentras (referred to always as "my lord Dean"), who will also furnish a man to correct proof, for the price of £4 per ream.

(2) The music must be well printed, correct, and of good form, "according to

[6] The document in the original French is printed in Pierre Pansier, *Histoire du Livre et de l'Imprimerie à Avignon du xivme au xvime siècle* (3 vols; Avignon, 1922), Vol. III, no. 108.

the art and use of fine printers," and it is especially important that the notes be exactly placed in height and width so that musicians who sing from it will not need to guess the pitch because of the ambivalence of the notes' location.

(3) After the design and accuracy of the first leaves are approved by the corrector or by the composer as being well arranged and well printed, with the notes properly situated, the whole will be drawn to the number of 500 copies. And if the results are found otherwise, Channey will be responsible for reprinting in proper fashion, and for whatever paper is spoiled.

(4) Channey must fashion the characters and notes so that they are distinct and well located in relation to the lines and spaces, as in the sample given him where the words are *In animabus nostris* and in another sample to be given him.

(5) Channey must hire a journeyman printer-musician ("companion imprimeur chantre") who has had experience in the field for the placement of the characters and notes, in order that measure [the tactus] not be violated at the end of the line and that no errors appear in the edition.

(6) Channey promises to print on parchment four copies [dedication copies] of each collection, according to the composer's wishes, each volume containing in addition thirty leaves of paper in royal format, and to print these gratis.

(7) If all the articles of this agreement are not met satisfactorily, Carpentras need not accept the work, and Channey must return all funds paid him within the month.

(8) Once the work is finished and acceptable, Channey must give Carpentras the notes and characters necessary thereto, without holding back any with which to print other music, and the value of said notes and characters will be estimated by men who are expert in such things, chosen by Carpentras, which sum will then be paid Channey.

(9) Channey must give up all the copies of what he prints to Carpentras reserving only four of each to himself, under pain of £300 penalty.

(10) Channey may not print other music for himself or anyone else for three years after the termination of the present work, without the license of Carpentras, under pain of £500 penalty.

(11) As often as Carpentras wishes to print other music, he may, upon a month's notification, and by bringing the music types, oblige Channey to print for him at the price of £2 10*s*. per ream, anticipating 500 copies of 30 folios each.

(12) Before printing anything else whatsoever, Channey must give Carpentras a month's notice; if Carpentras wishes to employ him, his needs must be served first.

(13) If by chance Channey wishes, with the consent of Carpentras, to print other music, he may rent the music types and pay in silver, by the ream, whatever shall be agreed between them; the volumes must be in royal format.

(14) It is agreed that Carpentras advances Channey £150 so that preparations necessary to the work may be begun.

(15) Once Channey has begun to print, Carpentras must see that there is no lack of paper, copy, or corrector.

(16) Channey may not make new music types similar to those here used for the duration of four years, under pain of £500 penalty.

The contract was, from the point of view of Carpentras, airtight. Even if the venture failed, responsibility was put on the printer (art. 7), who would, of course, in such a case be utterly ruined. Channey had little choice in the matter since he was already indebted to his Lordship for a loan of money the previous year. On January 13, a few days after the signing of the contract, Carpentras advanced Channey £100. Identical sums were handed over on March 13 and August 7.[7] By then the six months had passed. The first samples (art. 3) must have been ready in the course of the same year. They were a disaster. Far from satisfying the requirements of accuracy and legibility (arts. 2–5), Channey could not get notes and staves to fit at all. We learn this from a document dated December 14, 1531, mentioning that Carpentras had lent great sums to Channey for "lead, metal, paper, and all the other things necessary to printing," and that the printer "had been unable to make the note types fit or proceed correctly, on account of which the work lies unfinished, to the great loss of my lord Dean."[8] This document was the new contract adding a third partner, one Stephan Bellon, a Dominican preacher, who agreed to show Channey how to ensure that the "notes and spaces should proceed correctly and equally, as written in the original manuscript." For this Bellon was to receive a quarter of the edition, subject to the following provisos:

(1) Bellon was to provide a quarter of the cost, to be paid in halves, one half immediately and the other at or toward the middle of the operation.

(2) The sale price was to be determined together, not separately.

(3) Bellon could, on his option, receive his quarter in books or wait for his money until all the books were sold.

(4) One partner could not transfer his part of the merchandise without the consent of the others.

(5) If Carpentras wished further editions of the same music, or other music, he must so indicate to Bellon, who could on his option participate at the same rate established above (arts. 1–4); if Bellon did not wish to participate, this must also be established by formal agreement before any further printing was undertaken.

[7] *Ibid.*, Vol. II, p. 186.

[8] The document, in Latin, is in Pansier, Vol. III, no. 109 bis.

(6) Bellon must supply a quarter of *all* expenditures, those made and those to be made, for the cutting of the characters and for metal, type, and other necessities.

(7) From the funds supplied by Bellon, books were to be printed as far as these funds and the money remaining from previous investments should allow.

The intervention of Bellon proved efficacious as well as timely, and the first volume finally appeared on May 15, 1532. Its five Masses were printed by movable type in two impressions. The handsome types had been created by Stephen Briard, according to a liminary poem in the volume. A second volume, containing Lamentations, appeared a few months later, bearing the publication date of August 14, 1532. The title pages of both volumes bear the legend "Cum Gratia et Privilegio," no specification being made as to the source of such grace and privilege. Since the volume was dedicated to the reigning pontiff, Clement VII, it is likely that privilege had been requested of him, but there are no letters to this effect surviving. Avignon was far from Rome, and though it belonged to the Papal See (as it continued to do until the Revolution) it was surrounded by the royal territories of Languedoc, Dauphiné, and Provence. Some more practical protection must have seemed desirable to Carpentras. The following year, on June 4, 1533, he paid Constant Fradin, a libraire of Lyons, a certain sum in order to secure the *privilegium regium*.[9] Fradin promised that within the month he would secure it from Francis I. The court was then at Lyons, having witnessed the entry of Queen Eleanor on May 27, and of the Dauphin Francis the following day. The King was on his way to the Interview of Marseilles with Clement VII, which would make the Pope's niece, Catherine de' Medici, a bride of the second son of France, Henry—an engagement despised by the French nobility almost as much as that of 1517 which had sent a Bourbon princess, Catherine's mother, to wed a "mercantile" Medici. Politics, however, required it, the immense power of the Hapsburgs causing Francis to seek allies where he could find them (not excluding the German Protestants and the Grand Turk!). Although it was but a few days' journey from Marseilles to Avignon, the dedicatee of the Carpentras Masses did not choose to visit his subjects there. But the royal party did pass through the city on the way to and from Marseilles. What came of the attempts to get a royal privilege we know not. Yet it speaks for the efficacy of such a privilege that Carpentras was willing to pay an intermediary twenty crowns just to seek it. To obtain it, he probably would have had to pay even more into the King's coffers. Did sales of the first two volumes encounter hindrances in France? If so, Jacques Moderne or Attaingnant might have been directly involved. Nothing in Attaingnant's privilege of 1531 expressly forbade Carpentras from publishing

[9] *Ibid.*, Vol. II, pp. 187 f.

his own music and selling it in France. Had he used the single-impression method, the case might be different, for the document could be interpreted as forbidding the method to others. Attaingnant had never printed any music by Carpentras and was, as far as is known, never to do so, which means merely that the composer was more successful than most in keeping his compositions out of circulation.

Operations in Avignon went smoothly enough in 1533, and Channey received £122 10*s.* on October 11 of this year.[10] The undated third volume, containing the hymns of Carpentras, must have come out either in this year or the next, since it was dedicated to Cardinal Ippolito de' Medici, who died in August, 1534. The undated fourth and last volume, containing Magnificat sections, appeared later, perhaps in 1536. Volumes III and IV both bear the unspecific "Cum Gratia et Privilegio," suggesting that Fradin's attempt to get a royal privilege had been bootless. Difficulties arose between Carpentras and his printer during 1534, but both parties agreed to submit the matter to arbitration.[11] Another complication arose when Bellon wished to withdraw from the partnership and settle for costs. The settlement he proposed in 1536 was finally accepted by Carpentras three years later.[12] Total costs had risen to £1,260 1*s.* 11*d.* Bellon, who had contributed £200, claimed that by his calculation he was due to receive 81 copies of each volume. His contribution was thus a little less than one-sixth of the total, not the quarter share agreed upon. It appears that 500 copies were printed as planned, for the 81 copies claimed by Bellon would be very close to one-sixth of that total. Since Bellon had received only 51 copies of Volume 1, 30 more of these were due him, as well as 81 each of Volume II and Volume III, or altogether 192 copies (he did not participate in Vol. IV, according to Pansier). He was willing to accept 100 golden "sun" crowns (£225) in lieu of his 192 copies, that is, about 24*s.* per copy.[13] The sale price per copy, however, was probably at least twice that amount. A contract for the publication of the French translation of Thucydides, printed by Badius in 1527, provides an instructive comparison.[14] The Thucydides volume was in royal folio and consisted of 298 leaves. Total printing costs for 1,225 copies were reckoned at £612 10*s.* (£208 7*s.* for paper alone); the sale

[10] *Ibid.*, p. 74.

[11] *Ibid.*, Vol. III, nos. 110, 111.

[12] *Ibid.*, no. 111 bis.

[13] The value of the "écu soleil" had been fixed at 45*s.* by a royal edict of March 5, 1533. *Ordonnances des Rois de France: Règne de François Ier*. Vol. V (Paris, 1936), no. 616. At the same time the "écu couronne" was fixed at 43*s.* 6*d.*

[14] Philippe Renouard, *Bibliographie des impressions et des œuvres de Josse Badius Ascensius, imprimeur et humaniste, 1462–1535* (3 vols.; Paris, 1908), Vol. I, pp. 58 f. When inventoried in a private library a generation later, the value of the Thucydides had fallen to £12 6*s.* See Françoise Lehoux, *Gaston Olivier, aumonier du roi Henri II (1552)*, (Paris, 1957), no. 749.

price per copy was set at 20*s*., which was twice the cost of production. This suggests that the prospective customer for one of the Avignon volumes could have expected to pay a sum near £2 10*s*., or twice the amount for which Bellon settled. In comparison with Antico's *Liber quindecem missarum*, having 162 folios and retailing at about £7 6*s*., Carpentras offered five Masses (94 folios of music) in Volume I—cheaper by the page but equally dear by the Mass.

Carpentras' venture into publishing shows that music was not something with which the general printer could easily cope. It did not suffice to be a good craftsman, as Channey was, in order to solve the technical problems of getting notes, staves, and texts together in proper fashion. The printer had to be a specialist, as Carpentras found out to his chagrin, after pouring "very large sums" into his edition. The somewhat disingenuous Dean also failed to take into consideration the hard realities of bookselling, or so it would seem from his efforts to obtain a royal privilege a year after the first two volumes were printed. His money was again spent to little avail.

Another factor to emerge from the protracted negotiations is the crucial role of paper—that prime material of the printing industry. This was the first subject to be regulated in the original contract, the composer agreeing to furnish 120 reams in royal format, which at £4 a ream represented an investment of £480. The situation had not changed a few decades later when Plantin began his music editions. After receiving a commission from Philip II to print a plainsong antiphonary he bought a large stock of fine-quality paper in royal format. Difficulties with cutting types led to more expense than the King's treasury could bear and the project was abandoned, leaving Plantin with a fortune invested in paper.[15] It was in order to use this paper that Plantin became a music printer, having secured types from his fellow citizen Tielman Susato. No more telling evidence exists to show that paper remained a touchstone in the printing business.

Labor was a factor of less cost than paper in the working of the press. The Avignon contracts supply few details in this matter, but they may be complemented by records of general printing. The typecutter Stephan Briard, who came from Bar-le-Duc, presumably was an independent agent and not otherwise connected with the printer Channey. He accomplished his task by making a careful copy of the rounded notes just then beginning to be used in manuscripts, probably taking as his model the very pieces that Carpentras submitted as specimens (see Fig. 10), and in so doing anticipated the Civilité music types of Granjon and Danfrie.[16] His notes are beautifully proportioned to the folio page, with

[15] J. A. Stellfeld, *Bibliographie des éditions musicales plantiniennes* (Académie Royale de Belgique, Classes des Beaux-Arts, *Mémoires*, Vol. V, no. 3) (Brussels, 1949), pp. 12–16.

[16] See Harry Carter and H. D. L. Vervliet, *Civilité Types* (Oxford Bibliographical Society Publications, New Series, XIV) (Oxford, 1966), p. 22.

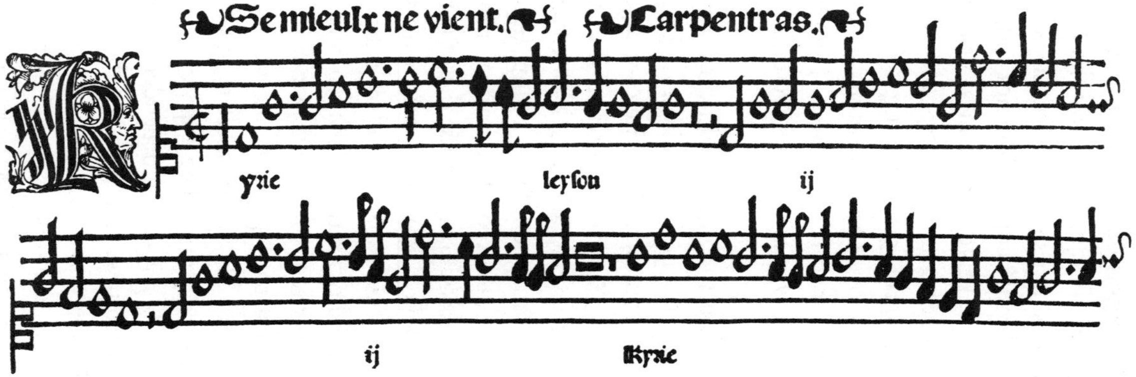

10 Excerpt (reduced) from the Masses of Carpentras, printed by Channey in 1532. By courtesy of Geneviève Thibault, Comtesse de Chambure.

staff-height and minim in the relation of 18/16 mm. Although not recorded, Briard's wages must have been covered by the sums given Channey for "metal, type, and other necessities." Was the "journeyman printer-musician" called for by article 5 of the original contract actually engaged by Channey? A man with experience in a music-printing shop probably could not be located short of searching other centers, of which Lyons would have been the nearest. The failure of the first attempts suggest that this part of the agreement was not, or could not be met. We may recall that Petrucci had to use a raw "Ethiop youth" in his presswork after returning to Fossombrone, which like Avignon was no great center of printing.

Managing a Press

Keeping a press in operation required several skilled hands. The man who performed the physically demanding task of "pulling" the press worked in conjunction with an inker, as we witness in the miniature painting of a press in operation dating from about 1530 (see Frontispiece). A compositor was also essential in order to place the type on the plates from which printed pages were drawn. In the sixteenth century the font of type was small, no more than enough to compose a few dozen pages. Thus printers were forced to disperse their characters frequently and reëmploy them often. The compositor never lacked for work while a book was in the press; in the miniature of about 1530 we see him, rule in hand, sitting before his type font beside two persons reading proof, another essential task that would have to be done quickly. One of the proofreaders depicted would have been the foreman or owner of the press; the other was perhaps an author or an employed *correcteur*. The master printer took upon himself the task of reading proof in most good houses. This was true of the finest Paris printers—of Badius, Colines, and Robert Estienne.[17] There is no reason to believe that it would have been any different with Attaingnant.

The several people necessary to the operation of a press took their midday meal in the home of the master printer, which was generally over the shop, in the same house. Henry Estienne, the son of Robert, speaks in one passage of a staff of ten sitting down with the family at table.[18] Young apprentices were housed as well as fed on the premises. Student boarders were also very frequent, especially in Paris, where they often served as correctors and consultants in exchange for their board. Young Claude Goudimel, while a student at the University of Paris between 1551 and 1555, had some such arrangement with Nicolas du Chemin.

[17] Lucien Febvre and Henri-Jean Martin, *L'Apparition du Livre* (Paris, 1958), p. 197.

[18] Elizabeth Armstrong, *Robert Estienne, Royal Printer* (Cambridge, 1954), pp. 15 f.

After an apprenticeship of two to five years, during which marriage was forbidden, a young man might expect to receive his brevet as a journeyman (*compagnon*), upon which occasion he would usually establish his own household. The journeyman was paid for his work, unlike the apprentice. At Lyons in 1539 a compositor received 6*s*. 6*d*. per day, or a little more than £7 for a month of twenty-four working days.[19]

The personnel at the Attaingnant shop may have included, besides those directly concerned with printing, someone to tend the bookstore. When Fezandat and Granjon formed their brief partnership in 1551 they hired a certain Gervais Fleurant to care for their establishment and to sell their books, which were priced at £1. His wages were a commission of fifteen per cent, or 3*s*. per volume.[20]

The investment represented by a press was surprisingly small. At Paris a small press and equipment was valued in 1512 at about 60 livres parisiis (l.p.); an establishment in 1520 with three presses, eight fonts, and matrices for four alphabets was worth 351 l.p.; three years later the value of Hopyl's large firm, including many fonts, matrices, and punches, was set at 700 l.p.[21] As we saw, a single Badius volume cost £612 10*s*. to print in 1527, and costs of the Carpentras publications had mounted to £1,260 by 1536. If a printer did not own a press he could rent one for a modest sum. La Roche paid Attaingnant only 2 l.p. for a half year in 1515 (Appendix, 2).[22] About 1540 the rent had risen to between £6 and £8 per year; to buy a press in good condition required from £23 to £30 during the decade 1540–1550. By way of contrast, purchase of a font of type could amount to as much as £225 if artists like Granjon or Garamond were involved.[23] Haultin sold Du Chemin a set of music punches and matrices in 1547 for 32 crowns, that is, upward of £70. The average printer-publisher employed more than one press—there is evidence that Robert Estienne had three presses in 1531. The maximum for the time was probably six; the University of Paris printer, Claude Chevallon, had this many in 1538, as is known from a proofreader's note at the end of Pachymera's *Paraphrasis* mentioning that the printing had been done "sex praelis dietim sudantibus."[24] In 1565 Plantin's firm, the largest in northern Europe, employed twenty-one printers, eighteen compositors, three

[19] Febvre and Martin, *op. cit.*, p. 200.

[20] Ernest Coyecque, *Recueil d'actes notariés* (Paris, 1905), no. 5846. On the Granjon-Fezandat partnership see D. Heartz, "Parisian Music Publishing under Henry II," *Musical Quarterly* XLVI (1960), 448–467.

[21] Febvre and Martin, *op. cit.*, pp. 163 f. The livre parisiis was equal to 25 sous tournois, or £1 5*s*.

[22] *Ibid.*, pp. 164 f. The authors err by reporting the duration of the 1515 contract as a year and the sum in sous tournois instead of sous parisiens.

[23] Armstrong, *op. cit.*, pp. 47 f.

[24] *Ibid.*, p. 46 and p. 47, n. 3.

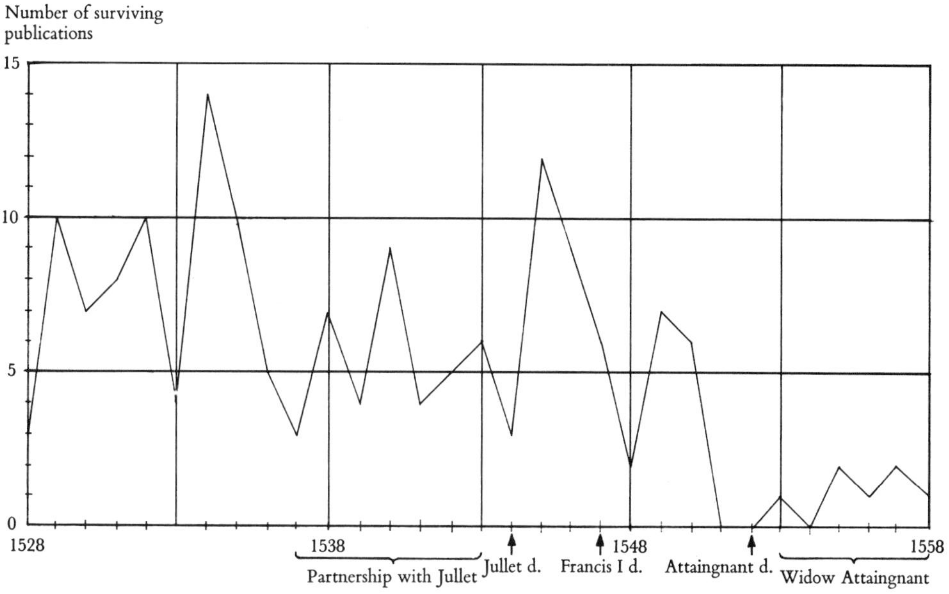

11 Attaingnant's surviving music books, by year.

apprentices, two typefounders, and a shopboy, together with five press-correctors.[25] This large force allowed him to bring out, on an average, about forty-five publications annually. Armstrong has shown that Colines at his height produced about thirty publications a year and that the output of Robert Estienne over his quarter century in Paris would average eighteen a year.[26] Attaingnant, who combined printing with publishing like his two contemporaries just named, achieved as many as fourteen music publications a year (not counting liturgical and other nonmusical works). (See Fig. 11.) If the peak years are taken as an indication of capacity, it would seem that Attaingnant had more than one press. The inventory of 1544 confirms this by mentioning *des grosses presses* (Appendix, 18). The folio Masses of 1532 were separated from works in octavo by a few months, if at all, suggesting that two presses were already in operation at this date. In the case of Plantin we know that a folio choirbook of 95 leaves occupied a single press for four months.[27] When Hubert Jullet joined the Attaingnant firm

[25] Max Rooses, *Le Musée Plantin-Moretus* (Antwerp, 1914), p. 162.

[26] *Op. cit.*, p. 27.

[27] Gaucquier's *Quatuor Missae* were begun February 11, 1581, and finished June 3. Stellfeld, *op. cit.*, pp. 55 f.

in 1537 he had a share in only part of the business, as shown by the continued appearance of Attaingnant's name alone on several works. Jullet's interest may have been tied to the production of one or some, but not all, of the presses. Were he a mature and established printer at the time he joined the partnership, his advent might have meant an additional (and third?) press in the Rue de la Harpe's music shop.

When Attaingnant agreed to settle the inheritance of Jullet at £2,000 in 1547, he gave evidence of a remarkable prosperity (Appendix, 23). Presses, founding materials, and fonts could not have accounted for even half of this fortune; a good part of it must have been in merchandise, the valuable music-books figuring importantly, along with debts owed him for them. It is very difficult to translate the value of such sums into modern terms, but a few prices may give a relative idea. For the several livres tournois that it took to buy a folio music-book, a considerable collection of musical instruments could be had. Thus in various inventories of the time a consort of four wooden flutes was valued at 45*s.* (1544), three *violons* with bows at 40*s.* (1551), a spinet three feet long at 40*s.* (1556), and a lute with its case at 20*s.* (1557); a livre also fetched a sheep, while two livres bought a barrel of good red wine containing 200 liters.[28] The rent paid for the premises in the Rue de la Harpe gives a further idea of monetary value and of rising prices during the century:

Per Annum Rent for the Pigouchet-Attaingnant Premises

1506–1509	£25	(Archives Nationales, M. 120)
1510	30	(Archives Nationales, M. 120)
1528	30	(Appendix, 5)
1548	44	(Appendix, 24)
1573	60	(Appendix, 34)

The Attaingnant fortune did not cease to multiply after its founder left the scene. In 1571, when a special tax was levied on the inhabitants of Paris to pay for the Joyeuse Entrée of Charles IX, the widow of Attaingnant had to pay £6 (Appendix, 32). Du Chemin was taxed only £3, while Adrian Le Roy paid £5.

Edition and Distribution

In the earliest days of European printing, books were published only in small editions of from 100 to 500 copies. Toward the end of the fifteenth century, when

[28] F. Lesure, "La Facture instrumentale à Paris au seizième siècle," *Galpin Society Journal* VII (1954), 11–52; the references are from pp. 21, 22, 24, 26. The prices of staples are after V.-L. Saulnier, *La Littérature française de la Renaissance* (Paris, 1942), pp. 13 f.

syndicates had organized an international market, much larger editions were forthcoming. Koberger regularly commissioned editions of 1,500 copies. During the sixteenth century the number of copies in a normal edition remained between 1,000 and 1,500. These figures held good for all countries. The usual number of copies did not increase in the seventeenth century, and actually fell off owing to the general decline of the book trade and of European population.[29] There seems to have been no technical reason for not printing larger editions. Rather, the limitation had to do with financing. A publisher would be wary of risking money on more copies than he might expect to sell in a reasonably short time. He could not afford to see his capital, represented by the expensive commodity of paper, tied up on the shelves. Speculation was inevitably involved in the decision of what to publish, and the danger of pirated editions was always present. With copyright laws in a very rudimentary and ineffectual state, the publisher of the time lived in constant fear of seeing his latest enterprise duplicated by a rival publisher. The market might then be saturated, to the detriment of both, or the pirate publisher might have calculated correctly in thinking it could absorb another edition. Often the only revenge possible was to retaliate in kind when the opportunity arose. Pirating was very widespread in Paris until about 1530, when the authority of royal privileges became more effective. Poncet Le Preux was not above a commercial venture of the kind, although it was one of his duties as grand libraire to prevent this very thing. That the book trade maintained even a modicum of order required a good many gentlemen's agreements. Subterfuge and guile were essential to success in this business. An anonymous set of "rules for publishers" from a manuscript of the time includes these two cardinal points:

(1) Keep all projects under cover, so that others learn of them solely by their execution.

(2) Authors, correspondents, and workmen must be maintained in a dependent state as much as possible; rely on them as little as possible.[30]

The uncertainties of the business perhaps had something to do with the modest size of editions (and had at the same time the effect, paradoxically, of encouraging imitations). Another reason for the stabilization at what by modern standards would be a rather small edition had to do with the printer. His interests were best served by keeping the working force constant and not allowing the presses to remain idle. In England the Stationers' Company in the second half of the century set limits of 1,250 or 1,500 copies so that compositors would not lack for work.[31]

[29] This information and much more that is pertinent to the subject is found in Febvre and Martin, *op. cit.*, chap. vii, "Le commerce du livre"; see also pp. 233 ff.

[30] Bibliothèque Nationale, the Guillaume Le Bé MS (Nouv. acq. fr. 4528, f. 28).

[31] Marjorie Plant, *The English Book Trade* (London, 1939), p. 87.

An edition of about 1,200 copies was the average quantity for books of general interest. Smaller editions were made of more specialized books. Badius printed 1,225 copies of the French translation of Thucydides in 1527, as we have seen; he printed only 625 copies of Noel Beda's theological *Annotationes* against Lefèvre d'Étaples and Erasmus in 1526. Since music was a kind of specialty printing, it might be expected to approach the lower rather than the higher figure. Such, however, was not the case. The small edition of 500 copies of the Carpentras volumes was an exception. In 1516 the *Quindecim missarum* was published in an edition of 1,008 copies. Other evidence shows this figure to have been close to the norm for French music printing. On February 12, 1552, Guillaume Morlaye, lutenist, obtained from Henry II the privilege of publishing the works of his teacher, Albert de Rippe.[32] Two months later he signed a contract with the printer Michel Fezandat, who promised to print, once the proofs were corrected by Morlaye, 1,200 copies, and no more, of whatever tablature Morlaye should supply. The edition was then to be divided, 600 to the printer and 600 to Morlaye. Fezandat promised also not to make any further editions without Morlaye's consent. A few decades later the *Obras* of Cabezòn (1578) were printed in an edition of exactly the same number; 1,023 copies of Dowland's *Second Book of Ayres* were printed in 1600.[33] These few documented cases suggest that the normal edition for music in the sixteenth century was around or slightly more than a thousand copies. In one other documented case, which seems to be exceptional, the edition was larger. Robert Granjon, after returning to Lyons from Paris, contracted in 1557 with Jean Hiesse and the composer Guillaume Gueroult to print music in 1,500 copies, which were to be divided equally between the three associates. Within a year Granjon was suing his partners for not providing enough music to print, and was being sued in turn by them for secretly printing outside the contract.[34]

Who made up the public for several million music-books? Multiplying the items in our Bibliographical Catalogue by the conservative figure of 1,000 yields a total of 174,000 prints that Attaingnant alone was responsible for putting on the market. Sixteenth-century Paris, the most populous European city by far at the

[32] Jacques Prod'homme, "Guillaume Morlaye, éditeur d'Albert de Rippe," *Revue de Musicologie* VI (1925), 157–160.

[33] Gustave Reese, *Music in the Renaissance* (New York, 1954), pp. 627, 840. For more on music editions the size of which is known see F. Lesure, "Histoire d'une édition posthume: Les 'Airs' de Sébastien le Camus (1678)," *Revue Belge de Musicologie* VIII (1954), 126–128.

[34] Claude Dalbanne, "Robert Granjon, imprimeur de musique," *Gutenberg Jahrbuch* XIV (1939), 226–232. Plantin, in contrast, regularly restricted his music editions to 500 or less; see Stellfeld, *op. cit.*, p. 46.

time, counted no more than 300,000 souls.[35] Only a small minority of these were literate, and still fewer would have been able to read notes. To publish in such volume Attaingnant had of necessity to build or hire a commercial network to sell his books in other cities and countries. If he were not himself directly engaged in business with one of the international syndicates, he probably operated through the business of his more commercially active brother-in-law. Le Preux, with whom he collaborated on publishing ventures as early as 1525–1526, is known to have had a stock of the music books (Appendix, 17). The most likely places for arranging exports were the trade fairs held every spring and fall. The most important during the first half of the sixteenth century were those at Lyons, where Le Preux had business connections. (Was this the reason for his "absence from the city" in April, 1526? Appendix, 4.) The rival Frankfort fairs, especially favored by Italians, are known to have drawn booksellers from Paris and Lyons as well. In 1557 at Frankfort there were, for example, four libraires from Paris and two from Lyons, and also two from Geneva and five from Antwerp. One Parisian visitor, Henry Estienne II, left his impressions of the Frankfort fair in the form of a delightful book.[36]

Dealers' catalogues were another means by which publishers sought to sell their stock. Such lists go back to the beginnings of printing. Some early catalogues advertised the simultaneous availability of items in different places: for example, the volume published by Albrecht de Memmingen as *Libri venales Venetiis, Nurembergae et Basilae* (1500), offering 2,000 titles. Even more modest firms such as those of Colines and Robert Estienne printed catalogues of their books.[37] The first trade bibliographies (involving many publishers) began appearing at the Frankfort fairs in 1564; similar catalogues of the Leipzig fairs, destined to supplant those of Frankfort in importance, commenced in 1600.[38]

Trade lists are among the rarest of all sixteenth-century books today—so practical yet ephemeral a tool was obviously destined for quick destruction. Did any of the music publishers of Attaingnant's day resort to such means in order to advertise their works? No music lists survive before those of two Venetian

[35] Eugene Rice, "Recent Studies on the Population of Europe, 1348–1620," *Renaissance News* XVIII (1965), 180–187. Other populous centers were Venice (170,000 by 1540), Antwerp (100,000 by 1560) and Rome (100,000 by 1600).

[36] *Francofordiense Emporium* (Paris, 1574), translated and edited by James Westfall Thompson as *The Frankfort Book Fair* (Chicago, 1911).

[37] An example from the Estienne press is reproduced in Albert Flocon, *L'Univers des Livres* (Paris, 1961), Figs. 124, 125.

[38] For an example from the Frankfort fair see *Die Musik in Geschichte und Gegenwart* (Kassel, 1949—), I, 1833–34. See also Albert Göhler, *Verzeichnis der in Frankfurter und Leipziger Messkatalogen der Jahre 1564 bis 1759 angezeigten Musikalien* (Leipzig, 1902).

firms in the late sixteenth century.[39] But there must have been earlier ones for the larger publishers in the field. If something of the kind had been preserved representing the books offered for sale by Le Preux, we should undoubtedly see listed many of the titles in our Bibliographical Catalogue as well as many others, now lost, that belong there.

When books traveled, as they had often to do, they followed the established trade routes. The main export markets of the Paris printers were northern France, England, Germany, and, to a lesser degree, northern Italy (by way of Lyons). The markets for Lyons, on the other hand, were primarily southern France, Italy, Germany (by way of Switzerland) and the Iberian peninsula. A near monopoly of the Spanish trade was long the province of Lyonese printing. (The trade route in this case was not the Rhone Valley, as one might expect, but overland to the Loire, down the valley to the port of Nantes, and by ship to Spain.) Between 1557 and 1564 André Ruiz, a merchant banker, had 1,057 trunks of books shipped from France to Spain, of which 919 came from Lyons and only 103 from Paris.[40] Thus there is nothing exceptional in the fact that Jacques Moderne published several Spanish composers while Attaingnant, as far as is now known, printed no music by Spaniards.

England, being without a first-class scholarly press and also without a specialist in music printing, provided a logical market for scholarly and musical works from Paris, as it did also for liturgical books—particularly Books of Hours, a Parisian "specialty." In spite of heavy protective tariffs, books traveled in considerable numbers from Paris to England, and quickly. Polydore Virgil's *De Inventoribus rerum* (1529) reached an Oxford college in the year of its publication.[41] Commerce with Germany was also very lively. In 1545 Robert Estienne sent his son Francis to Strasbourg so that he might "study the market and become familiar with the German language"; Estienne's trade connections were already so well ordered that on August 28, 1535, Melanchthon could write about seeing in Wittenberg Budé's *De transitu hellenismi ad christianismum*, first published in Paris on March 5 of the same year.[42] Trade with Italy was much more difficult, but this did not prevent Italians from acquiring Parisian chansons. In one instance a printer in Venice, Francesco d'Asola, had to protest that a package of books which he caused to be sent from France (with the intention of reprinting them) was confiscated at Turin; one of the prints seized was described as "uno libretto di canto canzon'

[39] G. Thibault, "Deux catalogues de libraires musicaux: Vincenti et Gardane (Venise, 1591)," *Revue de Musicologie* X (1929), 177–183 and XI (1930), 7–18.

[40] Febvre and Martin, *op. cit.*, p. 338.

[41] Armstrong, *op. cit.*, p. 29.

[42] *Ibid.*, p. 32.

venti nove di Paris."[43] The book can be none other than the *Vingt et neuf chansons* of 1530 **(18)**.

The territories to the north under control of the Spanish Hapsburgs were in constant and lively trade with Paris. An attempt to break off commercial relations in 1528 for political reasons was soon obviated by French merchants, who stood to lose much from any such rupture. Two purchases of the Collegiate Church of Saint-Amé in Douai throw light on the acquisition of music at the time.[44] In 1529 François Castelain was paid £24 8*s*. for a manuscript songbook on Lombard paper "en chose faicte ou sont escript xxxiii magnificat"; the sum is so high as to suggest that Castelain was paid to copy (or illuminate?) the music. Toward 1560 the same church paid £10 for "XII messes en musique imprimées à Paris pour servir de chanter en choeur," which would seem to be Du Chemin's *Missae Duodecim*, a collection in folio printed in 1554. The price was high—compared with about £2 for five Masses of Carpentras, or about £7 for Antico's *Quindecim missarum*—but not inconsistent with generally rising prices in the mid-century, and was, even so, considerably less than would have been paid earlier for a manuscript. Attaingnant probably sold few motets and Masses in the Franco-Flemish North, to judge from surviving records or surviving copies. If so, the reason was perhaps not commercial but artistic. The clientele for such volumes as the folio Masses—the choir-schools of cathedrals and other large churches—was supplied by the still flourishing local school and by its music copyists who turned out manuscripts in series. Herbert Kellman has been able to establish a family of fifty manuscripts of the early sixteenth century connected with the Hapsburgs and the "Burgundian Chapel."[45] These manuscripts traveled in all directions from the center of production at Malines and, like the ubiquitous Hapsburgs, were encountered far and wide—at Vienna, Prague, and Budapest, as well as at Valladolid and Lisbon. The industry of the Northern copyists represented a kind of "publication" which was in fact a potent rival to the early music press.

[43] G. Thibault, "De la vogue de quelque documents français à Venise," *Bibliothèque d'Humanisme et Renaissance* II (1935), 61–65. On the general topic of trade and musical relations between France and Italy see D. Heartz, "Les goûts réunis," in James Haar (ed.), *Chanson and Madrigal, 1480–1530*, (Cambridge, Mass., 1964), especially p. 98.

[44] De La Fons-Mélicocq, "La collégiale de St-Amé à Douai aux XIV, XV et XVIèmes siècles," *Archives historiques et littéraires du Nord de la France et du Midi de la Belgique*, Ser. 3, V (1855), 161–195. The two items are on pp. 169 and 181.

[45] "Illuminated Choirbooks and the Manuscript Tradition in Flanders in the Early 16th Century," paper read at the annual meeting of the American Musicological Society, Columbus, Ohio, 1962, and "The Role of the Empire in the Radiation of the Northern Repertory, 1500–1530," paper read at the annual meeting of the American Musicological Society, Ann Arbor, Mich., 1965.

Collectors

Early collectors of music can be identified in a number of ways: a few left records of their purchases; many wrote their names in books that have come down to the present; still others copied out pieces from printed books, which copies sometimes survive while the models used do not. Inventories after decease offer another resource. One such inventory describes what may well have been a typical Paris collection besides giving information on the value of music books at the time.

Jean de Badonvilliers was a member of the Royal Chancellery and an adviser to Francis I. He belonged to one of the wealthier bourgeois families of Paris. Upon his death in 1544 the appraisal of his large collection of books of all sorts was entrusted to the experienced printer Galliot Du Pré, libraire juré of the University and a frequent joint publisher with Le Preux. We list the musical volumes in the collection and the value ascribed by Du Pré:[46]

Quinze messes, reliées en 4 parties, en moyen vol.	25*s.*	[? *Liber quindecim missarum*, Nuremberg, Petrejus, 1539]
Trente quatre chansons musicales, reliées en 4 petits volumes	20*s.*	[**5**, or **29**]
Vingt huit chansons nouvelles en musique reliées en 4 petits volumes	20*s.*	[**31**]
Ung Enchiridion musices	2*s.*	[? Nicolas Wollick, Paris, J. Petit, 1512]
De arte cantande	2*s.*	[? Seybald Heyden, *De arte canendi*, Nuremberg, 1540]
Editio motetorum Claudii de Sermisy en quatre parties, blanc, non reliés	12*s.*	[**103**]
Motetti Johannes Lupi, aussi en blanc en quatre parties, non reliés	8*s.*	[**105**]
Plusiers livres de motets et chansons, blancs, non reliés	5*s.*	

Here the 1542 motets of Claudin and Lupi give the closest approximation of what it would have cost to buy music in Attaingnant's shop. They were relatively new compositions and were unbound. It is puzzling that Claudin's motets should be valued a third again as much as those of Lupi, the volumes being of identical size. The popularity of Claudin in Paris, as against the "foreign" status of

[46] Jérome Pichon and Georges Vicaire, *Documents pour servir à l'historie des libraires de Paris* (Paris, 1895), pp. 24–32. For a list and general description of inventories see Roger Doucet, *Les Bibliothèques parisiennes au xvi*^{e} *siècle* (Paris, 1956).

Lupi, may help explain why. Part of the value of the two chansonniers undoubtedly lay in their bindings. Bound or not, music books were worth considerably more than other types of books, even when the others were imported volumes. Some selected items from the same collection are listed for comparison:

Quatre paires d'heures à l'usage de Paris, grosses lettres de forme, blanches, non reliées.	8*s.*
... Dictionnaire latin, françois et allemand relié en parchemin	6*d.*
Deux livres de Champfleury, en blanc, non reliez	8*s.*
La science de pourtraicture	3*s.*
Ung breviaire à l'usage de Paris relié en grand vol.	15*s.*
Libro de Cortegiano, impression de Venise relié et doré en ung grant volume	15*s.*

The price range evident here is confirmed in sale catalogues issued by Paris printers about 1540. Paul Mellottée summarizes this data as follows: "The little grammar books brought from 2*d.* to 8*d.*, according to size; ordinary octavo volumes ranged between 1*s.* and 6*s.*, the costliest being Cicero commentaries, which went as high as 7*s.* or 8*s.* . . . Quarto volumes averaged from 10*s.* to 12*s.*, while volumes in folio reached 15*s.* to 25*s.*"[47]

The library of Badonvilliers, which passed to his immediate descendants, has not survived intact, and the music books are presumably lost. A few other copies of Attaingnant publications, however, have led a continuous existence in or near Paris. Manuscript additions in the books at Versailles show early or original French ownership (see **11**). The Mazarine chansonniers (**69–74**) also have a lengthy manuscript addition and are inscribed with the name "Lois Gonory" (see **73**). The set of motet books now in the Bibliothèque Sainte-Geneviève has a Parisian history and was kept at one time in the little church of Saint-Germain le Vieux on the Ile de la Cité, a few steps from the Petit Pont (see **141**). An old French hand provided the set of early chansonniers now in the Bibliothèque Nationale with an index of first lines. When Sébastien de Brossard visited the Ballard firm in 1701–1702 he saw several Attaingnant books, including **120–121** and **133–134**; he himself also owned a number (see **169**).

Elsewhere in France the volumes must have once decorated many a collection. They no longer do. Tours possesses no copy of the Manchicourt motets dedicated to one of her canons. Bordeaux and the lively musical circle around Janequin celebrated by Eustorg de Beaulieu fail to be commemorated today in holdings of printed music.[48] The copy of the set of *Danceries* now in Paris (see **148**) once

[47] *L'imprimerie sous l'ancien régime* (*Histoire économique de l'imprimerie*, Vol. I) (Paris, 1905), pp. 440 f.

[48] In a poem of about 1530 addressed to Bernard de Lahet, Crown lawyer at the Parlement of Bordeaux, Beaulieu mentions part-music in a fashion that might refer to a printed chansonnier: "Si tu trouvois de Musique aulcung Livre, Toy, Blaise et moy chantions jusque à my nuict." *Les Divers Rapportz*, ed. M. A. Pegg (Geneva, 1964), p. 45.

belonged to an inhabitant of Langres, the city of Canon Jehan Tabourot, alias Thonoit Arbeau, who recommends the same publications in his *Orchésographie* (1589). It is possible that the copy once belonged to Arbeau himself (see **170**). Jacques Moderne must have had his hands on several publications by his colleague in Paris. Antoine du Verdier and La Croix du Maine, who published rival bibliographies at Lyons in 1584–1585, mention several Attaingnant volumes, including a lost introductory treatise on music **(130).**

Italy provided an eager but difficult market, as we saw above in the case of the Venetian printer whose imported chansonnier got only as far as Turin. Several chansonniers must have reached Venice successfully, however, judging from the use made of Parisian chansons by printers there. Also, manuscript copies of chansons are very numerous in Italian libraries.

Of the several Attaingnant books presently in Italy, most can be traced back to the sixteenth century. The Accademia Filarmonica at Verona purchased its nine chansonniers already bound in 1548, paying £3 12*s*., that is, 8*s*. per individual collection (see **86**). Copies of the 1534–1535 motets now in the Milan Conservatory once formed part of the extensive music collection at Santa Barbara in Mantua. An Italian amateur, Geronimo Fieravanti, possessed the books preserved in the Florence Conservatory (see **76**). The motet books of 1542 in the Vatican Library belonged to Cardinal Augustani (Otto von Waldburg), patron of Lassus and a sponsor of the Tridentine musical reforms.

Two of the three motet volumes of 1542 found their way to the Spanish royal chapel under Philip II. The inventory of 1606 describes the extensive music holdings and mentions:

"Otros quatro libros ympressos em Paris, de motetes enquadernados en pargamino, de Claudeyn y Lupi."[49]

In Portugal, the royal library at Lisbon constituted one of the richest collections of printed music until destroyed by earthquake in 1755. A catalogue was made in the first half of the seventeenth century under the music-loving monarch, John IV. It revealed substantial holdings from all countries and periods, including some of the earliest Paris prints:[50]

Item 269	MOTTETES.	
	Quinque, et viginti musicales. Claudin, & outros. a 4. lib. 1	**(46)**
	Quatuor, et viginti musicales. A. Willart, & outros. a 4. lib. 2	**(47)**
	Viginti musicales. Pienton [sic], & outros. a 5. 6. &. 8. lib. 3	**(49)**

[49] Edmond Van der Straeten, *La Musique aux Pays Bas avant le XIXe siècle*, Vol. VIII (Brussels, 1888) p. 380.

[50] *Primeira Parte do Index da Livraria de Musica do Rey Dom João IV*, ed. J. Vasconcellos (Lisbon, 1873).

MAGNIFICAS.

Liber quintus 12. trium priorum tonum Magnificat continent. Cibot, & outros. a 4. **(52)**

Liber sextus 13. quinque ultimorum tonorum Magnificat continent. Ioão Mouton, & outros. a 4. & 5. **(53)**

Item 930 XXIV. CANÇOENS MUSICAES.

Compostas por Clement Jenequin, a 4. **(40)**

XXVII. CANÇOENS MUSICAES.

Impressas em Paris por Pierre Attaingnant, a 4. **(42)**

MOTETTES.

Novamente compostos, a 4. & 6. Impressos em Paris, por o mesmo. **(11)**

XII. MOTETTES MUSICAES.

Claudin, & outros, a 4. & 5. **(12)**

England should by all rights be a rich repository for Attaingnant prints, as it is for the other products of the Paris press. Yet the only large holding is the set of the 1538 chansonniers at Oxford, Christ Church, and this bears hints of original French ownership (see **90**). The Parisian chanson certainly made its way in England even earlier. Although the chansonniers of 1528–1530 are no longer there to prove it, copies from them were made in such English manuscripts as Royal Appendix 56 and 58.[51] The numerous English chapels and cathedrals should have provided an excellent market for volumes of Masses and motets. If they did, all traces of the copies are lost. A possible reason for this is the extreme religious reform under Edward VI (1547–1553) which would have rendered Latin church-music useless, and foreign, "papist" publications particularly suspect.

To judge from the surviving records, the largest export trade was carried on with German-speaking lands. Conrad Gesner, the celebrated scholar and bibliographer of Zurich, cited a score of Attaingnant volumes in his *Pandectarum* of 1548. (See Fig. 12.) He included the Masses in folio, described as *Missae praestantissimorum Musicorum uno volumine excusae, Lutetiae*, and gave a detailed description of the thirteen motet books of 1534–1535, expressing his approbation of the whole in the following terms: "Hoc opus plurimum a Musicis commendari

[51] John Ward, "The Lute Music of MS Royal Appendix 58," *Journal of the American Musicological Society* XIII (1960), 117–125; Kenton Parton, "On Two Early Tudor Manuscripts of Keyboard Music," *Journal of the American Musicological Society* XVII (1964), 81–83. Parisian chansons were copied in a vast number of English and Continental MSS. For a partial list see D. Heartz, *Preludes, Chansons, and Dances for Lute* (Neuilly-sur-Seine, 1964), p. lxiii.

The 1609 catalogue of the Lumley library has the following entry under item 2583: "16. Chansons nouvelles à 4 parties, composees par Clement Jenniquin a Lyon, anno domini 1540, 4 volum." Nothing meeting these specifications survives from Moderne's press, nor from Attaingnant, whom the modern editors suggest; see Sears Jayne and Francis R. Johnson, *The Lumley Library* (London, 1956), p. 285.

¶ *Cantiones Gallicæ.*

Les chansons cõposees par maistre Clement Iennequin. De la Guerre, La chasse, Le chant des oyseaux, La louette, Le rossignol. Secundo excusæ Parisijs per Petrum Attaignant, & Hubertum Iullet.

Motetti tribus uocibus Ioannis Mouton, & aliorum.

Composita quædam per Gombertũ & alios excellentissimos Musicos duabus uocibus, Lugduni.

Chansons. Iacques Moderne dict grãd Iacques, pres nostre Dame de Confort à Lyon, 4. uocibus.

Psalmi ecclesiastici Gallice excusi Lugduni, 4. uocibus.

Quarante & quatre chansons à deux, ou duo, chose delectable aux fleustes. Petrus Attaignans excudebat Parisijs.

La courone & fleur des chansons à troys, liber excusus Venetijs.

Trente & une chansons Musicales à trois parties en ung liure imprimees per Pierre Attaignant à Paris.

Viginti cantiunculæ Gallicæ quatuor uocũ & 5. Petrus Schœffer & Matthias Apiarius excudebant Argentorati.

12 Excerpt from the section devoted to music in Conrad Gesner's *Pandectarum* of 1548.

audio: Et alia plura ab eodem typographo in arte Musica publicata esse." It is possible that Gesner owed the musical entries to his friend Glarean, then established at Freiburg im Breisgau. Or, as a student in Paris at the time of their publication he may have seen them there. In either case the volumes were known in this part of the world. Another humanist in the same circle was Boniface Amerbach of Basel, who played the keyboard and lute and possessed tablatures for these instruments wherein several Parisian chansons figured prominently.[52]

Two German bibliophiles of the sixteenth century had particularly rich music holdings. Raimund Fugger the Younger of Augsburg (1528–1569) amassed more than 250 music books, some inherited from his father (1489–1535) and the majority acquired before 1566, when an inventory was made.[53] In the inventory are two entries pertinent here:

Item 214. Mutettorum Libri 1.2.3.4.5.7.8.10.12.
cum 4 voc. *Impressis* Paris.

Item 215. Chansons Eleues libri 1.2.3.4.5.6.7.8.9.
10.11.12.13.14.15.16.17.18.19.20.
21.23. tout à 4 parties.

The motet books must be those of Attaingnant from 1534–1535, as no other Paris printer before 1566 edited so long a numbered series. Possibly this is the same as the copy in the Austrian State Library showing the Fugger arms on the binding and the initials G.F. for Georg Fugger (1518–1569), older brother of Raimund (see **46**). The numbered chansonniers, also ascribable to Attaingnant, survive in the same library, but are now incomplete, consisting of only the eleventh through the seventeenth volumes.

Another patrician family of Augsburg, the Herwarts, formed an equally impressive music library, now the nucleus of the collection of early music prints in the Bavarian State Library at Munich. A manuscript catalogue of their holdings was made about 1586.[54] It commences with this item: "Chansons nouvelles à quatre parties, en deux volumes imprimées par Pierre Attaingnant, libraire à Paris." An early hand, using the same ink, has crossed out this item. Its place was taken by the subsequent entry: "Trente cinquiesme livre des chansons nouvelles, à quatre parties, en deux volumes, imprimées par Pierre Attaingnant./à Paris. 1546/in 4." The title corresponds with **160,** while the date was evidently

52 MSS in the University Library, Basel: F.IX.22, Nos. 47–50; F.IX.58, No. 7A; F.IX.56 (lute).

53 Richard Schaal, "Die Musikbibliothek von Raimund Fugger d.J.," *Acta Musicologica* XXIX (1957), 126–137.

54 Bavarian State Library, Munich, Cod. Bav. cat. 115. This catalogue will be the subject of a forthcoming article by H. Colin Slim, to whom I am indebted for communicating the information included here.

calculated upon the first volume of the set, the 1546 reprint of the *Premier livre* **(140).** It is to the Herwarts then, that we owe the great numbered series of chansonniers, surviving as a thirty-five volume set only at Munich. Many other, earlier books derived from the same source. The catalogue describes a collection of "63 French songs in four volumes commencing with Six Gaillardes . . ." This must correspond with the first four items in the former Musica Pratica 31 at Munich (stolen in 1963), which would indeed account for the necessary total:

	Chansons	
(17)	Six gaillardes . . . treize chansons	13
(20)	Neuf basses dances	0
(40)	Vingt et quatre chansons	24
(62)	Vingt et six chansons	26
	Total	63

The catalogue also lists, in sequence, the titles of **12, 31, 45,** and **44,** and these still exist in the same order, forming Musica Pratica 40/5–8. Herwart-owned copies of the Manchicourt motets **(85)** and the 1537 Janequin volume **(75)** also survive at Munich.

The choir-school of Saint Anne in Augsburg once possessed a fine collection of music prints, incorporating some earlier holdings of the Fuggers. Knowledge of it survives today only through a detailed catalogue made by the composer Adam Gumpelzhaimer, cantor of the school from 1581 to 1625.[55] On folio 36 verso he listed the *Premier-septiesme livres de chansons* printed by Attaingnant and Jullet in 1538–39 **(80, 81, 82, 83, 84, 86, 88)**; on the next leaf appear all thirteen books of motets from 1534–1535 and the *Liber Decimus quartus* (by Manchicourt) of 1539. Under didactic books (folio 29,) we encounter: "Frantzösische Music-büechl Mense Julio 1528. Tres Familiare." No less than the first French lute tablature can be meant. The entry shows that there was another and earlier edition (dare one say first?) dating from more than a year before the one preserved **(13).** The copy was bound with the *Brevis musicae isagoge* of Johann Frisius (without specification of date or place—the earliest known edition is that of Zurich, 1554, but Frisius was a student at Paris in the thirties and the possibility of still earlier editions should not be dismissed). Saint Anne's library also contained the numbered chansonniers printed by Du Chemin between 1549 and 1554 (fol. 25 verso). Outstanding among the other early French material is the "Gsangbuech lang median quart . . . Dreyzehen Büecher französische alte guete Stücklein von dem besten Autorn mit vier Stimmen. 1539.40.41.43.44.45." (fol. 12).

[55] Richard Schaal, *Das Inventar der Kantorei St. Anna in Augsburg* (Kassel, 1965).

"Lang median quart" would seem to refer to the unusual format of Jacques Moderne's *Parangon des chansons*, which once included many more volumes than the ten now surviving.

What amounts to a nearly complete set of the chansonniers from 1528–1533 traveled to Germany at an early time. This is apparent from the Contratenors now in the library of Eichstätt (which also possessed the seven keyboard tablatures of 1531 before these were preempted by Munich in 1870). An early owner started to index the volume of Janequin's program chansons, translating titles into German: "1. Vogelgesang, 2. Die Schlacht," and so on. The Eichstätt set preserves the chronological order of original publication, except for placing the motet volumes **11** and **12** at the end. A set of Superius parts, formerly at Castell and now belonging to the Cortot succession, includes many of the same works. The order is also chronological, with the same exception of placing **12** at the end. In both sets the two early chansonniers **5** and **9** are present in their secondary editions as **29** and **32**.[56]

Contents and order are strikingly similar in both. And Eichstätt (near Nuremberg) is not very far from Castell (near Würzburg). Yvonne Rokseth suggests

[56] A table will facilitate comparisons:

		Eichstätt Contratenor	*Cortot Superius*
3		No. 1	
4		2	
5	(in the reprinted edition, **29**)	3	No. 1
6		4	2
7		5	3
8		6	4
9	(in the reprinted edition, **32**)	7	5
11	(Motetz)	15	. . .
12	(XII Motetz)	16	22
14		8	. . .
15		9	6
17		10	7
18		11	8
19		12	9
20		13	10
30		14	11
31			12
40			13
41			14
42			15
44			16
45			17
54			18
55			19
62			20
65			21

that when the Attaingnant organ tablatures reached the Eichstätt library (between 1803 and 1870) they came from some monastery in the vicinity;[57] possibly they were accompanied by the closely contemporary Contratenor parts. Could the Contratenor and Superius have once been companions in the same set of part-books? Lack of two initial volumes in the Superius and several volumes at the end of the Contratenor might be explained by the frequent attrition working its way towards the middle of old sets. Recall that the Bass and Tenor are altogether lost or destroyed. Difficult of explanation yet would be the missing **11** and **14** in the Superius. The hypothesis breaks down altogether with the reading of the inscription in the Superius and the consecutive numbering throughout in the same early hand, showing that the twenty-two volumes formed an entity from the beginning of their existence and have never been disturbed. This is further confirmed by the manuscript additions at the end, again in the same hand (see **12**). The information jotted down by the first owner on the inside cover tells much in few words (see **29**): "bought at Paris with the other three parts for 2 crowns, $10\frac{1}{2}$ sous in the year 1539. T.W. H[einrich] G[raf] u[nd] H[err] zu Castell." Henry of Castell (1525–1595) was one of the century's most avid bibliophiles. According to the sketch of his life by his direct descendant, Prosper Graf zu Castell-Castell, he owned many Aldines—not surprising since as a young man (1533–1548) he studied at Bologna and Padua as well as at Ingolstadt and Dôle.[58] The possibility that he also studied in Paris is discounted by Count Prosper in favor of occasional visits there during his numerous travels. As for the chansonniers bought at Paris, they have led a relatively placid existence. Ludwig Friedrich of Castell (1707–1772) exchanged them, and a substantial part of his inherited library, for contemporary theological books with his father-in-law, the Count of Stolberg-Wernigerode. The family of the latter kept the chansonniers at Wernigerode until about 1930, when financial difficulties forced their sale and they passed into the hands of another great collector, Alfred Cortot. Count Henry purchased not only the set of early octavos when at Paris in 1539, but also five quarto chansonniers which had just been printed—the *Premier-Sixieme livres* of 1538–1539 (omitting for some inexplicable reason the *Cinquieme livre*). He neglected to record the price in these, but did use the same abbreviation for his name in the surviving Contratenor-Bassus part, which has never left Castell (see **80**). For the twenty-two early octavos he paid 97*s*. 6*d*., figuring the crown at 43*s*. 6*d*. (see note 13, above). This sum, nearly five livres, makes the individual collection worth 4*s*. 5*d*. apiece. They were undoubtedly unbound, like the part-books in

[57] *La Musique d'Orgue au XVe siècle et au début du XVIe* (Paris, 1930), p. 212.

[58] Article "Castell" in *Neue deutsche Biographie*, Vol. III (Berlin, 1957). The subsequent information was kindly supplied by communication from Count Prosper.

large quarto valued at from 8*s.* to 12*s.* five years later, upon the inventory of the Badonvilliers library. In price the octavos were relatively low, a bargain perhaps on account of their age. That Attaingnant still had in stock chansonniers dating back a decade is precious knowledge in itself. That he sold these in the order he did adds reinforcement to the testimony of the Eichstätt set. The evidence of both sets shows that the prints were sold in an order closely approximating their chronology.

Other, more modest German collectors also procured French secular works. Johannes Semler of Nuremberg once owned the *15ᵉ livre* (see **118**) Another citizen of that flourishing *Reichstadt* possessed the copy of Moderne's *Parangon des chansons* now in the British Museum, as is evident from the inscription on the flyleaf: "Anno 1541 idi 3 Augusti In Lyon in Frannckreych hab ich Sebastian Grolandi Diss Buch gekauuft umb XIII golt krane. Sebastian Grolandi Von Nurnberg Nº 8." (Moderne's music books came very dear if the thirteen crowns paid by Groland for nine volumes is a fair indication.) The copy of the *36ᵉ livre* now at Uppsala, containing Josquin's chansons, was earlier held in Mainz (see **162**).

The largest and most international private collection in the early sixteenth century was that of Ferdinand Columbus (Fernand Colón). His remarkable library, put together in the course of numerous tours around Europe, is known through the elaborate manuscript catalogues that he prepared, or had prepared, many of which still survive at the Biblioteca Colombina in Seville. Columbus owned no fewer than 37 different Attaingnant publications, which is to say over half those printed up to 1535. There is evidence to show that he acquired a copy of *Trente et six chansons* at Louvain in September 1531, within two months of its earliest possible publication (see **19**); the rest he bought at Lyons in October, 1535.[59] Of all these volumes there now remains in Seville one Contratenor part of one chansonnier **(20).**

The destruction and dispersion still continue. Well into modern times one of the richest collections of books signed with the name Attaingnant must have been that in the little wooden *librairie* adjoining the north apse of Notre Dame de Noyon. This charming building, constructed in 1506 to house the books of the chapter, is one of the rarest of its kind.[60] (See Pl. XIIa.) Noyon as a town suffered grievous damage in the First World War, from which it has still not recovered. Its shell-pocked Gothic cathedral is no longer the seat of a bishop, and the library,

[59] Catherine Weeks Chapman, "Printed Collections of Polyphonic Music Owned by Ferdinand Columbus," *Journal of The American Musicological Society* XXI (1968), 52–53.

[60] André Masson, "La 'Librairie' du Chapitre de Noyon et l'architecture des bibliothèques françaises à la fin du Moyen Age," *Bulletin des Bibliothèques de France* II (1957), 95–110.

stripped of many of its treasures, stands a forlorn monument to a more flourishing past.

Even less survives of the collection that once must have been the most well provided of all—that of Francis I and his successors. Not a single copy of an Attaingnant volume seems to be of royal provenance. The course of subsequent French history and taste helps to explain this. People in the Grand Siècle conceived a haughty disdain for the "bizarre" artifacts of the previous century. Particularly with the tonal art it was a case of an older style, intricate and subtle, becoming not only outmoded but also quite unintelligible. Few in France took an interest in preserving useless musical relics before Brossard, and by his day it was probably too late. Even the luxurious court manuscripts and dedication copies that must have existed in great number had all but disappeared. The music of the French Renaissance would be close to a lost art were it not for the bibliomania of a few private collectors.

V

FINAL YEARS: FOLLOWERS

GREAT REIGNS END with disenchantment sometimes, their principal figures having tarried over long—Louis XIV provides a case in point. Not so Francis I, who quit the stage with the timing of an actor as the first half of the century was drawing to a close. To the Parisians who witnessed the public spectacle on May 22, 1547, it must have seemed as if an entire era was passing. On this day a life-like effigy of the King, bearing the crown and scepter, entered in state. The pageantry belied the plain hearse that went before, drawn by twenty black-caparisoned horses. According to long-standing traditions, the dead King was received in triumph—he was making another Joyeuse Entrée. No effort was spared to impress the subjects of the Crown with the eternal majesty of royalty, as if to demonstrate the truth of two proverbial French sayings: "Le Roi ne meurt jamais," and its even more paradoxical equivalent, "Le Roi est mort, vive le Roi." Francis had seen to it that his funeral would excel those of his predecessors in pomp and splendor, just as, living, he had been more splendid and munificent. Newly crowned kings entered the city from the north, having come from coronation at Rheims; sovereigns on their way to burial at Saint-Denis entered Paris from the south. The ceremonial route on this occasion followed the Rue Saint-Jacques to the Petit Pont and then to the Cathedral of Notre Dame. Every house along this way—truly the printers' row of Paris—had been draped with royal blue and funereal black. Burning torches decorated with the arms of the city illuminated the strange raiment of the narrow thoroughfare. At each of the numerous crossroads the twenty-four town criers near the front of the procession stopped to intone the following exhortation: "Priez Dieu pour l'âme de très-haut, très-puissant, et très-magnanime François, par la grace de Dieu Roy de France très-chrestien, premier de ce nom: Prince clément, Père des arts et des sciences." The cortege was more than a mile long. It included effigies as well as the mortal remains of the two sons who had predeceased the King, Francis (d. 1536) and Charles (d. 1545). The surviving son, Henry, watched in secret from a house in the Rue Saint-Jacques; he did not display himself publicly until after the burial, for there could never be two kings of France on view at the same time. The reactions of the multitude of onlookers can well be imagined. Le Preux and Attaingnant had a choice vantage point from the "maison du Loup." In summing up the day the Marquis de Vieilleville wrote: "Never was such funereal pomp witnessed before in all the histories of our kings, nor in all Europe."[1]

It was not only the *Père des arts* who was passing from the scene. One by one

[1] Ralph E. Giesey, *The Royal Funeral Ceremony in Renaissance France* (Travaux d'humanisme et Renaissance, XXXVII) (Geneva, 1960), chap. i, "The Funeral of Francis I." The quotation from Vieilleville appears on p. 10.

the great figures who had commanded the center of attention for a long generation were disappearing. Clément Marot had died in 1544, and Luther in 1546. Henry VIII breathed his last in January 1547, and this event is reported to have severely shaken Francis I, who expired at Rambouillet three months later, on March 31. His beloved sister, Marguerite, did not survive 1549, the same year in which the third great dynastic prince, Charles V, began plans to abdicate. France's most prodigal patron of art, John, Cardinal of Lorraine, rounded out his life of pleasure in 1550.

The last years of this generation were characterized by a musical fashion quite different from anything that seems likely to have caught on during the early years. A veritable mania developed for singing the Psalms in the vernacular. The mellifluous translations of Clément Marot had initiated the practice, and the musical world was eager to second his efforts. Marguerite of Navarre was also involved; the first Marot translation to be printed was Psalm 6 ("Je te supplie, ô Sire") which was appended to the *Mirroir de la tres chrestienne princesse Marguerite*, printed by Antoine Augereau (Paris, 1533) and subsequently identified with her.[2] Cultivation of the Psalms in the vernacular showed a more than slightly Protestant bias, and the Sorbonne reacted as might be expected—Augereau was burned in the Place Maubert, after the affair of the placards in 1534. The situation changed according to the politics of the moment. A few years later Marot was given royal permission to have printed his translations of the first thirty psalms, which were then published by Roffet (Paris, 1541), prefaced by a long and eloquent dedication to Francis I. The special connection of Psalm 6 with Marguerite could not have been lost upon Attaingnant when he placed it as the very first piece in the collection of *Trente et un psaumes*, the earliest printed part-books devoted to the Psalms in French **(142)**. Moreover, every one of Marot's *Trente Psaumes* was included, as set to music by Certon or Mornable, in this and the subsequent volume (*Livre second*, **143**). The vogue of polyphonic psalm-settings seems to have begun around 1540, when Charles V made a trip through France, meeting a final time with Francis. According to the account of an eyewitness—a letter written some years later to Catherine de' Medici by Villemadon, one of Marguerite de Navarre's retainers—the King had asked Marot to present his guest of honor with the still unpublished psalm-translations.[3] The Emperor was so pleased with them that he gave Marot two hundred doubloons, encouraged him to continue his labors and in particular to send a translation of "Confitemini Domino" as

[2] Philippe Renouard, *Imprimeurs et libraires parisiens au xvie siècle*, Vol. I (Paris, 1964), nos. 562 f. A separate publication of the same translation was bought for 4*d* by Columbus at Lyons in 1535; see Jean Babelon, *La Bibliothèque française de Fernand Colomb* (*Revue des Bibliothèques*, Supplement X) (Paris, 1913), no. 128.

[3] Pierre Pidoux, *Le Psautier Hugenot* (Basel, 1962), Vol. II, *Documents et Bibliographie*, pp. viii f.

soon as he could. "Upon seeing and hearing this, the musicians of the two Princes, which is to say all those of our France, began to see who could best set the Psalms to music, and everyone sang them." From this intriguing statement Villemadon went on to say how fond the Dauphin Henry was of the Psalms, his favorite being "Bienheureux est quiconques" (Psalm 128 as translated by Marot). To this he composed his own tune, we are told. It is possible that Mornable, in setting the Dauphin's favorite psalm, (**143,** 11) had recourse as well to the royal melody. In any event, polyphonic settings were being made very early.[4] Villemadon's letter mentions an episode in 1543 at which several polyphonic psalms were sung. Marguerite had sent her retainer to visit Prince Henry in order to inquire about his illness. The Dauphin, restored to health, was reported as singing psalms "with lutes, viols, spinets, and flutes, mixed with the voices of his singers." From this concert Henry then sent back to his aunt Marguerite by the same messenger "le chant *et les parties*." Finally, it emerges from the letter that the Dauphine Catherine had her favorite, too, which was "Vers l'Eternel des oppressez" (Psalm 142), causing Marguerite to remark the curiosity of her choice, "since it was not one of Marot's translations."

Royal musicians, as well as the royal family, were inextricably associated with the first song settings of the Psalms in French. That the practice was courtly in origin is beyond all reasonable doubt. Without adequate records of musicians attached to the household of the Dauphin, or, for that matter, of the King, it is difficult to place a more precise interpretation on the relation of Certon and Mornable to the court. In the case of Mornable, the act of setting Henry's favorite psalm and printing it with the Royal Printer hints at some kind of official relationship. Attaingnant first printed motets by Mornable in 1534, when the composer must have been quite young—he left the Sainte Chapelle in 1530 at the mutation of his voice. Nothing is known of his subsequent positions until the 1546 title-page, placing him in the service of Guy, Count of Laval.

A few more details about psalm singing at court are furnished by Florimond de Rémond, writing much later, on the basis of information supplied him by Pierre Cayer.[5] Several other prominent persons had their identifying Psalms, he says. Diane de Poitiers, Henry's *maîtresse en titre*, claimed for her own Psalm 130, "Du fond de ma Pensée," a setting of which figured in the first book (**142,** 7); the husband of Marguerite de Navarre, Antoine, chose Psalm 43, "Révenge-moy,

[4] An isolated instance occurs in Moderne's *Parangon* VI (Lyons, 1540), which opens with a setting of Marot's translation of "Super flumina" (Psalm 137) attributed to "Abel" (a pseudonym?). The piece, which is not mentioned by Pidoux, *op. cit.*, is the more interesting since its tenor uses the tune first printed in *Aulcuns pseaulmes et cantiques mis en chant* (Strasbourg, 1539; facsimile reprint, Geneva, 1919) and subsequently adopted by the Calvinists for settings of "Estans assis aux rives aquatiques."

[5] *Histoire des progrès et décadence de l'Hérésie* (Paris, 1610). See Pidoux, *op. cit.*, Vol. II, p. ix.

prends la querelle" (**142,** 21). In sum, the Marot verses served as another and unique kind of "devise" with the great personages around Francis I. By publishing two volumes containing several of the favorites Attaingnant demonstrated anew his entrée at court.

In the midst of all this activity was the fascinating and complex personality of the King. Had he failed to encourage his "valet de chambre" and poet in the enterprise of translation there probably would have been no fashion of psalm settings. Inevitable from Marot's pen in the Dedication of *Trente Psaulmes* were metaphors in which one king, David, was embodied by another, Francis; furthermore, Marguerite linked the two kings in a New Year's poem she sent her brother in 1543.[6] Artists often made the same transfer when depicting David, by lending him the royal ensigne of the fleur-de-lis. The illustration in Attaingnant's Noyon breviary seems to have gone even further (Fig. 13).[7] King David here bears an uncanny resemblance to Francis I—compare, for example, the long-nosed Valois and the beard he wears in the woodcut of 1532 (Pl. VIII).

The significance of the portrait may have eluded those for whom the breviary was intended in 1525. When Attaingnant reprinted the same two decades later **(138),** could any Frenchman have failed to see the point? The year was 1546, date of the part-song settings of Marot's Psalms, and Francis was in the last year of his life. The long reign that had begun with such *joie de vivre* ended in a more introspective aura, singing psalms in preference to "sottes chansons." Repeated misfortune overcame the three gallant princes of Valois, Tudor, and Hapsburg. Their division—the ensuing division of Christendom—had wrought much damage and destroyed most of the fair hopes of 1515.

Misfortunes also began to strike the music firm of Paris after 1540. Claude Pigouchet, as she was still called late in life, as if to honor the great artist who was her father, must have died in the late spring of 1543. An inventory was necessary to settle the division of goods (Appendix, 17). Another Pigouchet heir, Germaine,

[6] "Epistre II envoyée par la Royne de Navarre avec un David au Roy Françoys, son frere pour ses estreines." The significance of the poem is discussed in Michel Jeanneret, "Marot traducteur des Psaumes: entre le Neo-platonisme et la Réforme," *Bibliothèque d'Humanisme et Renaissance* XXVII (1965), 630 f.

[7] The cut was used as early as 1516, in Missals printed by Kerbriant and Jean Adam for Jean Petit; see Renouard, *Imprimeurs et libraries parisiens* Vol. I (Paris, 1964), nos. 2, 271. A closely related cut was used by Thielman Kerver in his octavo *Horae* of 1517; see *French 16th Century Books*, compiled by Ruth Mortimer under the supervision of Philip Hofer and William A. Jackson (Harvard College Library Department of Printing and Graphic Arts, Catalogue of Books and Manuscripts, Part I) (Cambridge, Mass., 1964), no. 300. I am indebted to Miss Mortimer of the Houghton Library for pointing out the resemblance. There is no adequate iconography of Francis I. A partial one may be found in *Les Quatres siècles du Collège de France*, Exposition, Bibliothèque Nationale (Paris, 1931), pp. 25–30.

13 King David (Francis I?), from Attaingnant's Breviary for Noyon use (**1**). By courtesy of the Bibliothèque Nationale.

wife of Poncet Le Preux, had preceded her in death, and this meant that Attaingnant was obliged to give his brother-in-law that portion of the inheritance that had come to Claude from Germaine. The debt was acquitted partly in cash, partly in goods (Appendix, 18). After the death of Claude the two Attaingnant daughters, Marie and Germaine, were entitled to a fraction of the inheritance. Marie and her husband, Pierre Aleaume, took their part in cash, while Germaine and her husband, Hubert Jullet (still in partnership with Attaingnant), seem to have taken theirs in books. Jullet and Aleaume discharged their father-in-law from all obligation in the matter, with one reservation—a certain Arthus Sandrin of Noyon had a quantity of missals and a large unpaid debt from them (Appendix,

18). The printing of new books slackened considerably in 1543, a year which saw only the twelfth, thirteenth, and fourteenth chansonniers in the numbered series added to the roster of publications. The situation was not ameliorated in the following year, during which a plague began to ravage Paris. It was still raging in July, 1545, when Parlement enjoined the University to assign members of its Faculty of Medicine to devote themselves exclusively to the afflicted. Hubert Jullet, who may have been one of the victims, succumbed sometime between March, 1544, and the following spring, perhaps early in 1545, since one volume signed with his name has this year-date **(123).** In this bleak situation with first his wife and then his son-in-law and chosen successor taken from him, Attaingnant allowed his production to come to a near halt. Only one new publication, the *Quinziesme livre*, bears the date 1544.

Production climbed in 1545, however, and soon resumed a nearly normal rate. In April of this year we first encounter the mention of Marie Lescalloppier as wife of Pierre Attaingnant (Appendix, 20). She was a person of property, holding title to a house and garden in Saint-Germain-des-Prés. When Attaingnant settled the inheritance of Jullet upon the remarriage of Germaine in 1547 he agreed to pay the princely sum of £2,000 as her share of the property. The figure is so much larger than the amounts mentioned in the inventory of 1543 as to suggest that union with Marie Lescalloppier was financially very advantageous. Prosperity continued in succeeding years, which saw the printer involved in various commercial transactions. But the artistic side of his operations was not maintaining the level he himself had established. Also, competition by rival printers became more and more telling after 1547. It had begun much earlier.

A Rival at Lyons

Jacques Moderne was born in the little town of Pinguente on the Istrian peninsula, not far from Andrea Antico's native Montona. Like many a printer of the time, he was attracted to the great trading center at the confluence of the Rhone and the Saône, an international crossroads second to none and the seat of a large Italian colony. His first dated book was an edition of Vallo's *Du Faict de la Guerre et Art Militaire* (1529), a particularly appropriate subject in the city that had served as the staging point for the French campaigns in Italy.[8] Throughout his career Moderne continued to print books of many kinds, with an emphasis upon medical, devotional, and popular literature, the last being something of a specialty with the printers at Lyons. Another local specialty was the reprinting of works from other places, especially Paris—both Robert Estiennes had complaints to

[8] Jean Vial, "Un Imprimeur lyonnais méconnu, Jacques Moderne," *Gutenberg Jahrbuch*, 1962, 256 f.

make on this score.[9] A generous number of Moderne's publications were reprints, whether general books, books about music (e.g., Guerson's *Regulae musicales*), or music itself.[10] The edition of Morales was an exact copy of one published by the Doricos in Rome. *Musicque de Joye* was copied in part from the Venetian *Musica Nova* (1540) while another part duplicated pieces in Attaingnant's *Second livre* **(148).**

The earliest music from Moderne's press was probably the folio *Liber decem missarum.* In the extant copies the dedication bears the date 1532. Yet Columbus entered it in his catalogue as follows: "Misse 10. prima p. moulu de s. stephano. 10ª F. de layole de salutaris hostia cum tribus motetis. 13451. L[yons] 1531." The volume is, by any standard, a remarkably ugly book. Its pages are crowded with ornament, placed with no view to the effect of the whole. Initials in the newly popular "Basel" style, associated with Holbein, vie with late-Gothic grotesques, and still more strange, with a few examples of the ultra-refined Parisian initials of Tory. Assuming that Columbus was exact in his annotation, some copies of the Masses, perhaps an entire edition, appeared in 1531, and thus antedated the collection of motets in parts called *Motetti del fiore*, begun in 1532. The "flower" of the title may be explained by the printer's adopted mark of the fleur-de-lis. As a symbolic device the lily did double service, pertaining both to the French realm and to Florence (which city received it as a "gift" from France). The choice of Italian for the title seems to reinforce the Florentine allusion and was perhaps dictated by the composer Francesco de L'Aiollo, who left his native city for France about 1520. Among other duties in Lyons he assumed responsibility as Moderne's music corrector, as is known from a note printed in the folio Masses. Previously he may have had some connection with Estienne Gueynard, an important printer of liturgical books working at Lyons since the end of the fifteenth century and the publisher, with Guillaume Gobert, of *Contrapunctus seu figurata musica*, the privilege for which is dated August, 1528.[11] A choirbook in folio, the *Contrapunctus* contained plainchant and figural music of the Mass Propers for thirteen major feasts. The only signed pieces are by Layolle—the concluding three settings of "Salve Virgo," "Media vita," and "Ave Maria." Besides a dedication, "Bernardus Guarnerus Typographus, Bernardo Altovitae Patricio Florentino," the volume contained addresses headed "Guillelmi Goberti item Chalcographi, Dialogus" and "Idem chalcotypi ad lectorem," reflecting the significance of the work and the occasion. Decorated with uniform "Flemish-style" initials and the same headpieces throughout, *Contrapunctus* is masterly in

[9] Elizabeth Armstrong, *Robert Estienne, Royal Printer* (Cambridge, 1954), p. 44.

[10] H. Colin Slim (ed.), *Musica Nova* (*Monuments of Renaissance Music*, Vol. I) (Chicago, 1964), p. xxxii.

[11] H. L. and J. Baudrier, *Bibliographie lyonnaise*, Ser. 11 (Lyons, 1914), *s.v.* "Guaynard."

both design and printing; its staves were reproduced from rules, while the notes, whether plainchant or mensural, were printed separately from type (15/15). For all its excellence the work was to have no successors, the types created for it having never found further employment, to present knowledge. Gueynard's death in late 1529 or early 1530 may provide the explanation for this and also for the decision of Moderne (at Layolle's instigation?) to start a music "line" in addition to his other specialties. Layolle was the musical luminary of Lyons to his death about 1540 and a natural choice to be Moderne's "artistic director," as Lesure calls him. It was perhaps natural too that Moderne, one of whose mainstays consisted of cheaply manufactured "popular" books, should reject the costlier multiple impression method in favor of the technique recently originated at Paris.

By printing mensural music in a single impression from type, Moderne produced the first datable examples following Attaingnant. To the Masses in folio of 1531–1532 he soon added his "flower" motets, partbooks in quarto (21.5 × 16.5 cm.), and later a collection of chansons—*Le Parangon*—using a larger oblong quarto (23.7 × 17.5 cm.). Regardless of format or genre Moderne used a single musical note for all these volumes (13/13). Its body was extremely narrow (ca. 2.5 cm.) relative to the height (ca. 5.5 cm.), producing an exaggerated, typically Gothic, elongation. Rather odd in appearance, the single typography was too large for the quartos and too small for the folios. Moderne remedied the lack of folio-size type later by adding a larger note (16.5/16.5); it appears in his *Harmonides Ariston* of 1548. Between the staff-segments in the Masses of 1531–1532 there are large gaps, showing that the new technique was not mastered easily or at once. The motets represent an improvement in this regard (as well as in design), but Moderne never achieved the close "fit" of Attaingnant's best work. In some aspects Moderne showed himself quite independent. His *Parangon*, in keeping with its distinctive title, offered an unusual, yet practical disposition of the voices, all on the double-page (which explains the slightly oversize format).

Tenor	Altus
Superius	Bassus

From the beginning of Moderne's activity as a music printer there were a certain number of pieces shared with Attaingnant. The latter's motet series of 1534–1535 has in common as many as fifteen compositions with the three volumes of motets that Moderne printed in 1532, as Samuel Pogue has shown.[12] Fifteen

12 Samuel F. Pogue, "Jacques Moderne as Music Publisher" (Unpublished Ph.D. dissertation, Princeton University, 1968), pp. 46 ff. Exchanges of information concerning Attaingnant and Moderne have taken place over a number of years, with the result that both studies are in substantial agreement.

represents a small fraction in a collection of more than 250 pieces, and the concordances are not concentrated in any one or two of the Paris volumes. Were the composers involved those who are particularly identified with Moderne, such as Layolle, Villiers, or Colin, there might be reason to suspect some direct borrowing. The motets in common, on the contrary, are by international figures such as Verdelot, Willaert, and Gombert—masters whom Attaingnant had printed from the time of his earliest volumes. His sources in 1528–1529, as later during the fourteen-volume series of motets, surely derived from the Chapel Royal. When Moderne resumed his series of motets in 1539 he printed a few pieces found in the Attaingnant books of 1534–1535. No direct borrowing need be assumed here, either.

It is a different matter with the chansonniers that Moderne began to print in 1538. For the next few years there was a lively competition between Paris and Lyons, many chansons being printed in one place within the same year as in the other, raising some vexing questions as to priority. Moderne introduced the chansons of a group of people unknown previously in Attaingnant's collections; besides Layolle, Villiers, and Clérеau, there were many less well-known names such as La Moeulle, Coste, Benoist, Cavillon, Fresneau, the poet-composer Eustorg de Beaulieu, and "F. de Lys"—the last name perhaps a whimsical fiction of the editor. Along with these Moderne printed the pieces of many Paris masters and Franco-Flemish musicians resident in the Low Countries, Spain, or Italy. In his first *Parangon*, for example, there are six chansons by Sandrin, every one of them duplicated in Attaingnant's *Second* or *Tiers livre*, also dated 1538. A survey of the concordances in the first three volumes of the *Parangon*, below, reveals some conflicting attributions, adding another imponderable to the question. (Attaingnant's attribution, if conflicting, is given in parentheses under the relevant item.)

PARANGON I (1538)

1. Sandrin	**81**,9	10. Mornable	**81**,18	19. Mornable	
2. La Moeulle		11. Villiers		20. Cadéac	
3. E. de. Beaulieu		12. Mornable	**81**,6	21. Cadéac	
4. Villiers		13. Layolle		22. Mornable	
5. Cavillon		14. Cadéac		23. Mornable	
6. Villiers	**82**,7	15. Sandrin	**81**,3	24. Sandrin	**81**,11
7. E. de Beaulieu		16. Sandrin	**82**,16	25. Villiers	
8. Sandrin	**81**,4	17. Sandrin	**81**,7	26. Cadéac	
9. Villiers	**96**,14	18. Gombert		27. Villiers	

Parangon II (1538)

1. Claudin		12. Passereau	**29**,15	23. Villiers	**95**,6
2. Claudin		13. Villiers		24. Cavillon	
3. Layolle	**96**,28	14. Mouton		25. Layolle	
4. Cadéac		15. Cassa sol la		26. Sandrin	**80**,7
5. Gombert		16. E. de Beaulieu		27. Villiers	
6. Lupus		17. Hesdin	**80**,12	28. Gombert	**69**,15
7. Villiers	**95**,29	18. La Moeulle		29. G. Coste	
8. Arcadelt		19. Cassa sol la		30. Janequin (Clemens)	**81**,26
9. Certon	**81**,8	20. Villiers	**95**,10		
10. Manchicourt		21. G. Coste		31. Layolle	
11. Villiers		22. Richafort			

Parangon III (1538)

1. Fresneau		9. Benoist		18. Villiers	**96**,13
2. Arcadelt	**79**,19	10. Cadéac	**82**,12	19. J. Buus	
3. Claudin (Sandrin)	**81**,13	11. R. Patie	**84**,26	20. Passereau	
		12. Benoist		21. G. Coste	
4. Certon	**83**,1	13. Janequin (Bon Voisin)	**83**,13	22. Fresneau	**82**,23
5. G. Coste				23. Villiers	**94**,14
6. Claudin	**83**,9	14. J. Buus		24. Certon	**84**,7
7. Villiers	**84**,22	15. Layolle		25. Arcadelt	
8. Claudin (Sandrin)	**83**,9	16. Fresneau		26. Layolle	
		17. Maillard	**96**,15		

Can so many duplications be explained as coincidence? The twenty-four concordances with Attaingnant chansonniers of 1538 **(78–84)** involve composers who were associated with Paris or had previously been printed there (except for Fresneau). Yet Moderne makes different ascriptions in several cases besides offering versions sometimes different in musical detail, which might be interpreted to mean that he used separate and distinct sources. The two Claudin pieces placed prominently at the beginning of the second *Parangon* reinforce this theory. These were the latest chansons of the Parisian master, it seems, or at least they had not been printed previously, to the extent of present knowledge. The first chanson had the added distinction of being a setting of Marot's "Pourtant si je suis brunette," which had just seen print for the first time in the *Oeuvres* edited by Dolet (Lyons, 1538). Those concordant pieces printed later by Attaingnant (in **94–96,** dated 1540) are mostly by Villiers and they present a different aspect of the problem, which will come under discussion after we have outlined the contents of the remaining volumes of the *Parangon.*

PARANGON IV (1538) 1–16 à 2, 17–32 à 3

1. Layolle		12. Gardane		23. Gosse	**65**,6
2. Gardane		13. Pelletier		24. Willaert	
3. Layolle		14. Certon		25. Claudin	**65**,14
4. Gardane		15. Gardane		26. Anon.	
5. Claudin	**65**	16. Layolle		27. Anon.	**65**,2
6. Heurteur		17. Pignard		28. Claudin	**65**,11
7. Gardane		18. Layolle		29. Willaert	
8. Claudin	**65**?	19. Layolle		30. Claudin (Anon.)	**65**,22
9. Gardane		20. Willaert			
10. Heurteur		21. Claudin	**65**,8	31. Cosson	
11. Pelletier		22. Mouton		32. Claudin	**65**,20

PARANGON V (1539)

1. Layolle		10. F. de Lys		20. Bourgeois	
2. V. Sohier		11. G. Coste		21. Clέreau	
3. Villiers	**96**,24	12. Villiers	**96**,10	22. Heurteur	**84**,16
4. Fresneau		13. Clέreau		23. Maillard	**84**,13
5. Clέreau (Certon)	**86**,2	14. Janequin	**84**,5	24. G. Coste	
		15. G. Coste		25. Belin	**84**,28
6. G. Campis		16. Sandrin	**84**,1	26. Certon	
7. G. Campis		17. Bourgeois		27. F. de Lys	
8. Fresneau		18. Sandrin	**84**,2	28. Layolle	
9. Bourgeois		19. Maillard	**84**,6		

PARANGON VI (1540)

1. Abel		9. Lupi		18. Cordeilles	
2. Villiers	**94**,12	10. La Moeulle		19. G. Coste	
3. A. Francon		11. J. Buus		20. F. de Lys	
4. Cordeilles		12. Villiers	**96**,8	21. Bourguignon	**86**,12
5. Fresneau		13. G. Coste		22. Certon	**84**,4
6. F. de Lys (Quentin)	**94**,10	14. De Porta	**84**,10	23. Certon	**86**,27
		15. Lupi	**42**,17	24. Maillard	**86**,7
7. G. Coste		16. Berchem		25. Janequin (Clemens)	**86**,11
8. Cordeilles		17. F. de Lys			

Moderne continued the series with chansons à 2 and à 3, a combination that must have been very popular and which Attaingnant had cultivated in 1535. At least one of the duos had been printed in the missing section of **65** (and perhaps the other duo by Claudin too?), while several of the trios duplicate pieces in **65,** albeit in transposed versions.[13] Volumes V and VI show a suspiciously large number of concordances with **84** and **86,** which appeared in 1538 and 1539 respectively, although there are still conflicting attributions, including one in

[13] D. Heartz, "Attaingnant's Two- and Three-part Chanson Arrangements of 1535," paper read at the annual meeting of the American Musicological Society, New Haven, Conn., December, 1968.

which Moderne's enigmatic "F[leur?] de Lys" is identified by the name "Quentin." By the time of Volume VII the supply of fresh chansons in Lyons must have been running low. Except for a few token pieces, mostly at the beginning and end, the volume comprises pieces previously printed in Paris. The main sources appear to have been the *Tiers livre* of 1536 **(73)** and the *Septiesme livre* of 1539 **(88)**; six of the concordances had also been printed much earlier by Attaingnant. The succeeding *Parangon* VIII is equally derivative. Earlier, in Volume III, Moderne had called the chapel master of the Brussels court "R. Patie"; in Book VII he becomes "Rogier," exactly as in Attaingnant.

PARANGON VII (1540)

1. La Moeulle		10. Janequin	**73**,3	20. Maillard	**88**,11
2. Berchem		11. Janequin	**73**,4	21. Cordeilles	
3. Cadéac (Heurteur)	**62**,24	12. Sandrin	**88**,10	22. Morpain	**88**,14
		13. Passereau	**73**,21	23. Le Hugier	**88**,20
4. Certon	**86**,10	14. Mittantier	**86**,20	24. Berchem	**89**,21
5. Artins	**86**,16	15. Claudin	**82**,10	25. Patinge	**88**,22
6. Janequin	**73**,1	16. Fresneau		26. Tetart	**88**,29
7. Rogier	**86**,15	17. Maille	**88**,13	27. Barte	
8. Janequin	**73**,10	18. Sandrin	**88**,17		
9. Janequin	**73**,6	19. Coste			

PARANGON VIII (1541)

1. Villiers		12. De Lattre	**92**,5	22. Maillard	**92**,20
2. Maillard	**92**,3	13. Mittantier	**92**,21	23. Lupi	
3. Villiers		14. Certon	**92**,9	24. Sohier	**92**,22
4. La Moeulle		15. Maille	**92**,24	25. Maille	**92**,19
5. G. Coste	**89**,3	16. Villiers (also Certon)	**89**,7	26. Mornable	**92**,16
6. Forestier				27. Godart	**83**,26
7. G. Coste		17. Le Hugier	**92**,27	28. Certon	**92**,1
8. Forestier		18. Berchem	**89**,24	29. P. Messins	
9. Sandrin	**84**,23	19. Villiers	**89**,23	30. P. Messins	
10. Mornable	**92**,10	20. Lupi	**92**,13		
11. Berchem	**89**,9	21. Mornable	**92**,15		

The ninth and tenth volumes marked a return to a more independent repertory. With the tenth volume many of the chanson *texts* are found in earlier Paris collections; printed music books were a frequent literary source for composers of the time, and one publication without music, *La fleur de poésie françoyse . . . mis en nottes musicalles par plusieurs autheurs* (Paris, Lotrian, 1542), was admittedly derived from music books.

Parangon IX (1541)

1. Villiers		12. Sandrin	**80**,15	23. Carpentras	
2. G. Coste		13. Certon	**82**,18	24. Lupi	
3. Sandrin	**84**,3	14. Janequin	**90**,4	25. L'Héritier	
4. Gombert		15. Sandrin	**99**,16	26. Mostiers	
5. F. de Lys		16. J. Buus		27. Villiers	**137**,10
6. Maillard		17. Villiers	**106**,12	(Puy)	
7. Certon	**92**,18	18. J. Buus		28. Gombert	
8. G. Coste		19. Maillard	**88**,25	29. Villiers	
9. J. Buus		20. Maille		30. Villiers	
10. Maillard	**88**,26	21. Carpentras		31. Maillard	**95**,25
11. Claudin	**88**,4	22. Maillard			

Parangon X (1543)

1. De la Farge		12. Crequillon		22. James	**101**,28
2. Gardane		13. Crequillon		(Lupus)	
3. Claudin	**101**,25	14. Lupi		23. F. de Lys	
4. Crequillon		15. Lortin	**83**,8	24. Caulz	
5. L'Héritier		(Godart)		25. Gardane	
6. La Moeulle		16. Crequillon		26. F. de Lys	
7. Payen		17. Maillard		27. Crequillon	
8. Doussera		18. Renes		28. G. Coste	
9. L'Archier		19. Villiers		29. Gardane	
10. J. Buus		20. Crequillon		30. La Saigne	
11. Villiers		21. Gardane			

Eighteen volumes of the *Parangon* once existed, according to Du Verdier's *Bibliothèque* (1585). An eleventh volume survived in the Bibliothèque Royale, Brussels, until the Second World War, at which time it was stolen.

There can be little doubt that Moderne made direct use of some Paris chansonniers, particularly in his seventh and eighth volumes. On his part, Attaingnant must have seen some of the *Parangon*. His new *Second Livre* of 1540 **(94)** added two chansons, both found in *Parangon* VI (nos. 2,6). The new *Tiers Livre* **(95)** added five pieces; the three by Villiers could have been conveniently found in one place, *Parangon* II. Attaingnant's penchant for Villiers emerges again in the revision of the *Quart livre* **(96)**. Twelve of the old chansons were dropped, to be replaced by thirteen new ones. Seven of the substitutes are in the *Parangon*, Volumes I–IV, including five pieces by Villiers. An irony may have been intended by concluding the renovated *Quart livre* with Layolle's "Ce me semblent choses perdues." It was one of the very few times his music was printed in Paris.

Moderne, upon reediting his *Parangon* II in 1540 (after Layolle's death?), removed the composer from his usual place of honor at the conclusion of the book and substituted in his stead an old Claudin chanson, "Martin menoit son pourceau" (**62**,14).

Moderne brought out another secular collection under the title *Le Difficile des chansons*, printed in four part-books. The first volume, bearing no date, has been assigned by Samuel Pogue to 1540 or 1541 on typographical grounds. It is devoted entirely to Janequin, the first sixteen pieces duplicating those in Attaingnant's *Huitiesme livre* **(90),** which is dated 1540 and must have appeared early in that year because the printers' signatures follow directly upon those in the *Septiesme livre*, dated 1539 **(88).** After this group of pieces Moderne places the five "program chansons" printed by Attaingnant in 1537 **(74),** four of which had been printed, in slightly differing form, in the early Janequin book of 1528 **(4).** For the second *Difficile des chansons* (1544) Moderne seems to have found a more independent repertory—only one piece, Dambert's "Secouez moy," stands out as figuring earlier in what has survived of Attaingnant's output. The correspondences between *Musicque de Joye* and Attaingnant's *Second livre* of dances dating from 1547 have been mentioned. Although Moderne's collection is dated about 1544 by Pogue, it still cannot be proven to represent a prior publication of the concordant pieces. Use of Roman numerals as printer's signatures in the 1547 *Second livre* hints that it had been printed in an earlier edition by Attaingnant (see p. 76).

After 1547 Moderne printed a number of lute tablatures, employing the Italian system of ciphers rather than the letter system known as French tablature—another testimony of physical and artistic proximity to Italy. One of the tablatures is devoted to pieces by Valentin Bacfarc (1553) and was dedicated to Attaingnant's old patron, the Cardinal de Tournon. Moderne used dedications only rarely in his musical works. He also did without privileges throughout most of his career. The Bacfarc tablature is exceptional in this regard, a privilege having been secured from the civic authorities to protect the volume for three years.

Moderne's repertory differed from Attaingnant's in some important respects aside from the obvious one of featuring Lyonese music. Moderne printed many pieces on Italian texts, which is not surprising since Lyons led the country in Italian-language publications. Also, he offered a greater proportion of Franco-Flemish masters, especially those in Hapsburg service. Characteristically, it was Moderne who printed the epitaph of Erasmus, "Plangite pierides" (in *Motetti del fiore* III, 1538), set to music by the Netherlander Benedictus (Appenzeller). Lupi's chanson in *Parangon* VI on the "Plus ultra" device of Charles V is another piece conspicuous by its absence in Paris collections. Moderne took a certain amount from Attaingnant in the way of repertory. More significant was his success in duplicating the manner of printing. He showed by example that the new method could be copied with equanimity, even in France. The lesson was not long lost on others.

Concurrents Abroad

The Royal Privilege of 1531 states that Attaingnant had "opened to other printers and booksellers the way and industry of printing music" (Appendix, **7**). Specific reference was intended to the new method. But in general, whether considering method, layout, format, or repertory, no music printer was more imitated during the two decades after 1530 than Attaingnant.

German printers, ever among the most active in the music field, became increasingly numerous in the second quarter of the century. Two years after the first chansonnier of 1528, Peter Schoeffer the Younger (*ca.* 1480–1547) brought out a collection of "twenty French songs" at Strasbourg. Conrad Gesner refers to this lost collection in his *Pandectarum* of 1548 as follows: "Viginti cantiunculae gallicae 4 vocum, excusae Argentorati apud Petrum Schoefferum 1530. in 12. per transversum, maiori forma folii, chartris 16." The contents probably consisted of the new "Parisian" chanson, although it is not impossible that Schoeffer went back to the older repertory diffused by Antico in his two collections of 1520 containing chansons. Schoeffer had reprinted from Italian models as early as 1513 at Mainz, when he republished the entire *Canti. B. numero Cinquanta* of Petrucci (1501).[14] Printers in Germany, of course, had nothing to fear from the strictures of the Venetian Senate's privilege. Yet 1513 was the very year that Petrucci acquired from Leo X a wider privilege, supposedly protecting his work from imitation by all Christians, under pain of excommunication. Such papal pretensions were taken lightly outside of Italy, evidently. In 1532 Badius claimed specifically that privileges granted Italian printers by the Pope were not binding in France.[15] And in 1528 Attaingnant had reprinted Antico's canonic chansons and motets of 1520 while these were still under papal protection. When reproducing *Canti B* Schoeffer adopted a different format, employing separate part-books in octavo, but he clung to multiple impression and, as in his model, he supplied only incipits. Full texts were probably omitted for technical reasons, as they would

[14] Walter Senn, "Das Sammelwerk 'Quinquagena Carminun' aus der Offizin Peter Schöffers d.J.," *Acta Musicologica* XXXVI (1964), 183–185.

[15] Philippe Renouard, *Bibliographie des impressions et des oeuvres de Josse Badius Ascensius* (Paris, 1908), Vol. III, pp. 354 f.

have required still further impressions and greater cost.[16] As late as 1539 Schoeffer was still using double impression, his *Cantiones quinque vocum* of that year offering a selection of motets, mostly by Franco-Flemish masters. He was one of the last to employ the older method, along with Castelliono of Milan[17] and a pair of Antwerp printers, as we shall see below.

In other German centers, meanwhile, printers were turning increasingly to music. At Leipzig, Nicolas Faber published a collection of Virgil settings, the *Melodiae prudentianae* (1533), reproduced from woodcut plates. The distinguished printer Christian Egenolff (1502–1555) established a firm in Frankfort on the Main and became prominent in the publication of Lutheran Bibles. He inaugurated his music offerings in 1532 by returning to the Horatian Odes set by Tritonius—the pieces with which Oeglin had begun the printing of mensural music in Germany more than twenty years earlier. The work was accomplished with movable types in a single impression, probably the earliest employment of the method outside France.[18] By comparisons with music prints signed by Egenolff such as the *Reutterliedlein* and *Gassenhawerlin* (1535), Nanie Bridgman has been able to ascribe three unsigned part-books containing secular songs to the same press and to the years 1532–1535.[19] Indeed, the three part-books and the Odes betray the identical music-type (8.5/7.5). The part-books are distinctive for being printed in 16° and are therefore unusually small (no larger than 7.3 × 9.7 cm.). Although they are decorated with finely made cuts and initials, the music itself is very primitive in its reproduction, a criticism made by Eitner and Riemann that is discussed and somewhat tempered by Bridgman. Egenolff was a typecutter and presumably made his own notes. He was unable to achieve good registration with them. The extremely disjunct staff-segments and faulty inking fall beneath the general standard of this fine printer, suggesting that he had a particular clientele (perhaps University students?) in mind for his music series. The repertory is older than Attaingnant's or that of the contemporary Italians, comprising chansons and lieder from the turn of the century. Such musical backwardness is the more curious for emerging in the liveliest trading city of central Europe. Slightly more successful as music prints are those in a set of four unsigned volumes of lieder

[16] Absence of full texts cannot be construed as evidence that the music was intended for instrumental performance, as is often claimed, and most recently by Senn, *op. cit.*, p. 184; all part-music was so intended in the sense that it was considered "apt" for instruments as well as voices.

[17] *Mutetarum divinitatis liber primus quae absolutae vocibus ex multis praestantissimorum musicorum academiis collectae sunt* (Milan, 1543). The publisher was Bernardus Calaschus.

[18] A facsimile may be seen in Caroline Valentin, *Geschichte der Musik in Frankfurt am Main* (Frankfort, 1906), p. 62.

[19] "Christian Egenolff, Imprimeur de Musique," *Annales Musicologiques* III (1955), 88–177. Articles on Egenolff and most of the other printers discussed here are to be found in *Die Musik in Geschichte und Gegenwart.*

which have also been ascribed to Egenolff.[20] These are in octavo, which might raise doubts as to the attribution. Yet the music-types leave no place for doubts, being identical with those in the Odes of 1532 and the three part-books in 16⁰.

The German city destined to become the greatest center of early music printing was Nuremberg.[21] Here, by 1534, Heinrich Formschneider (Grapheus) had succeeded in bringing out a collection of lieder as well as Senfl's *Carmina*, making skillful use of the new method, which was employed again for the lieder of Heinrich Finck (1536). All are in octavo. The notes have a rather stubby appearance, explained partly by their proportions (10.5/8.5). Formschneider followed Attaingnant, knowingly or not, when he turned to quarto for his series of motets, beginning with those printed in 1537. Like his Parisian counterpart he made do with the original octavo types, merely increasing the number of lines per page (from three to five). Formschneider prepared the way for other Nurembergers, such as Johannes Petrejus who began printing mensural music as early as 1537, when he brought out Seybald Heydn's *Musicae, id est Artis canendae*, using for the examples rather small and very neat type (9.5/7.5). With his motets in quarto (from 1538) Petrejus introduced larger type (11/10.5). Another Nuremberg firm was inaugurated in 1542 by Berg (Montanus) and Neuber, a partnership which was to have a long and fruitful course. Berg, a native of Antwerp, had studied in Paris for three years before going to Germany in 1541.

There was no lack of communication with France during the years when Nuremberg was becoming a center of music publishing. One of the leading Nuremberg figures was Seybald Heydn (1499–1561), whose didactic treatise, just mentioned, probably reached Paris soon after being printed. Heydn was rector of St. Sebald's from 1525 and an influential Protestant writer as well as a teacher of music. At the French court the Reformation party that centered around the King's sister paid Heydn the compliment of having one of his essays published (at Alençon in 1531). The essay, moreover, was translated into French and placed alongside Marguerite's *Mirroir* and Marot's Psalm 6 in the 1533 editions, mentioned above. Protestant sentiment made many inroads in the printing and musical worlds of the French capital, as is well known. By printing the musical settings of Marot's Psalms in 1546 Attaingnant may have taken more of a position than we

[20] Munich, Bavarian State Library, Musica Pratica 46. In the *Répertoire international des sources musicales.* Vol. I, *Recueils imprimés XVIe–XVIIe siècles*, ed. F. Lesure (Munich, 1960), the four works are described under items [1536]8, [c. 1535]13, [c. 1535]15, [c. 1535]12. Schoeffer and Apiarius also edited the first of these, employing an odd format (12.5 cm. square) and the same types for double impression that Schoeffer had used earlier (10/11.5). A Vagans in the British Museum assigned in the *Répertoire international* . . . to what is called the "Egenolff ré-édition" belongs to the Schoeffer-Apiarius edition.

[21] See Paul Cohen, *Die Nürnberger Musikdrücker im sechzehnten Jahrhundert* (Erlangen, 1927).

realize today. His family circle was, in any case, not without converts: during the repressions of the 1560's both sons of Poncet Le Preux were banished as heretics and so was the family of Hubert Jullet's sister Claude.[22] The channels of communication between Paris and the Protestant cities of Germany were never more lively than during the reign of Francis I, a ruler for whom religious considerations weighed less than political ones.

Mention should be made of a few other German printers who turned to music during the first half of the century. Georg Rhaw of Wittenberg, after printing some early self-tutors with woodcut music, began to use the new method, commencing with a collection of Passion music printed in 1538. His types are identical with those used by Formschneider from 1534, the matrices probably having been procured directly from the Nuremberg firm. Melchior Kriesstein "native of Basel, citizen of Augsburg," as he described himself, arrived upon the music-printing scene with considerable flourish, his *Selectissimae necnon familiarissimae cantiones* (1540) laying down a barrage of preliminary poems and addresses. In one of the latter the printer begged favor of his public on grounds of the particular diligence and exertion required by music printing: "Cum cantuum Impressiones, Candidi Lectores, maiorem diligentiam et laborem desiderent, quam aliae librorum impressiones, valde vos oro et obsecro, ut Primam hanc meam Impressionem boni consulatis . . ." His invention did not extend to all domains of music publication, it seems, for the types correspond with the smaller set used by Petrejus (9.5/7.5), while much of the music, including some Parisian chansons, was indeed most familiar in the sense of having seen print before.

The list of German concurrents may be brought to an appropriate close with the printing of Glarean's *Dodecachordon*, one of the publishing events of the century. Although the treatise was finished by 1539, a satisfactory typographer could not be found, particularly for the numerous musical examples; by 1545 the cost of printing was estimated at the enormous sum of 900 gold florins.[23] The great scholar, having retired some years earlier to the small university town of Freiburg im Breisgau, was not in so good a position as he was earlier to negotiate with the world of commerce. The burden of publication was assumed, finally, by Heinrich Petri of Basel, and the elaborate work appeared as a folio volume of nearly 500 pages in 1547. The musical examples, both chant and mensural, were printed (with many errors) from single-impression types. Like Kriesstein, another Basler, Petri employed the small types for mensural music (9.5/7.5) that had seen use in Nuremberg ten years earlier by Petrejus, from whom matrices may have

[22] Philippe Renouard, *Répertoire des imprimeurs parisiens, libraires, fondeurs de caractères, et correcteurs d'imprimerie* (Paris, 1965), p. 269 and article "Hercule François."

[23] Clement A. Miller, "The *Dodecachordon* . . . ," *Musica Disciplina* XV (1961), 161.

been procured.[24] Graced with plain black initials and a roman face for the texts, the musical examples emerged looking quite similar to Attaingnant's 1542 motet series.

The uniform appearance of much German music printing after 1550 probably reflects the continued importance of a few firms in Nuremberg and Frankfort as supply houses. With further study along the lines attempted here it may prove possible to establish wider correspondences involving both German and French typography. Were this the case, it would be quite in line with what is known of general printing. The specimen books published by Egenolff's successors offered buyers a large selection from the "classic" matrices of such French masters as Garamond and Granjon.[25]

In Italy the new method made a delayed but quick conquest. It was introduced by northerners, either German or French. The earliest datable example displaying the method is a collection of three part-books in octavo entitled *Canzone, Villanesche alla Napolitana*, the colophon of which offers the following information: "Stampata in Napoli per Joanne de Colonia alli xxiiii de Octobris. M.D.XXXVII." The identity of this "John of Cologne" is unknown. His types are small (8/7) and bear resemblance to those of Egenolff. The notes with tails often lean in one direction or the other, which crudity points to the use of two punches—one for the note and one for the staff-segment—in striking the matrix. A few months later a group in Ferrara brought out a collection in quarto, *Liber (vocum) quatuor triginta novem motettos habet* with types well designed and employed (10/10.5). Dated March, 1538, the work was dedicated to Duke Hercules II of Ferrara, from whom a privilege had been obtained. It offered a largely French repertory, including Janequin, Claudin, and other masters identified with Paris—hardly surprising since the Duchess of Ferrara, Renée de France, had gathered a circle of her countrymen (and was, besides, very receptive to Reformation tendencies emanating from the French court). The printing and publishing were accomplished "In aedibus Francisci Rubei, de Valentina, Expensis e Labore Joanne de Buglhat, Henrici de Campis, et Athonii Hucher, Sociorum." Buglhat on account of his name would seem to have been of German origin, while Campis and Hucher could have been French.[26] A second volume of motets was printed by the associates in 1539.

[24] The original examples are reproduced in facsimile in *Heinrich Glarean: Dodecachordon*, translation, transcription and commentary by Clement A. Miller (Musicological Studies and Documents, 6) (American Institute of Musicology, 1965). They are not to scale.

[25] A *Specimen Characterum* of 1592 survives. See Daniel Berkeley Updike, *Printing Types: Their History, Forms, and Use* (Cambridge, Mass., 1922), Vol. I, pp. 286 f.

[26] Campis probably functioned as music editor, as his name does not appear in non-musical works printed by Buglhat and Hucher. He is cited as *cantor* in the accounts of the ducal chapel between 1534 and 1550 according to George Nugent, to whom I am indebted for communicating the information.

The chief Italian center of printing had long been the great and wealthy port of Venice. While Venetian printing was in a general decline between 1510 and 1540, the city's presses even so were more active during these decades than those of any other Italian city. A lost volume of *Musica in canto figurato formata da Francesi Autori* printed by Francesco Marcolini in 1537 may have introduced the new method to the Serene Republic, if the manner of printing was as French as the contents.[27] Marcolini had used double impression in his tabulature of 1536, however, and claimed that he was able to achieve this and penetrate the "secret" of Petrucci only by dint of Herculean efforts. Most likely it was not Marcolini but the French musician Antoine Gardane (1509–1569), who first produced new-style music prints at Venice. According to the *Biographie universelle* of Fétis, Gardane began his activities in 1537 by reprinting Attaingnant's *Liber septimus* of 1534, but of such a publication there is no trace. He did use mostly Paris pieces in *Venticinque Canzoni francesi* of April, 1538, dedicated to Leone Orsini, Bishop of Fréjus, whence the lion and bear of his printer's device (an ingenious reading pointed out to the writer by Geneviève Thibault). The following year he reprinted Moderne, as he freely admits in the playful title of *Fior de mottetti tratti dalli Mottetti del fiore*. His *Canzoni francese a due voci* (1539) are also derivative, at least in part. In *Venticinque canzoni* Gardane employed italic type for the text while preserving Flemish-style initials, lending the visual aspect a peculiar blend of Northern and Southern; the rather large notes (10/10.5) seem ill fitted to the octavo format. Subsequently Gardane printed in quarto, using the same music type, which he handled so well as to nearly eliminate white spaces between the staff-segments. Gardane had ties with southern France, as is evident from his name, his patron, and because Moderne printed his music already in *Liber decem missarum* of 1531–1532. Yet it was Attaingnant's Typography I that he copied, not the more Gothic style of Moderne's notes.

There are various factors other than commercial that might have led a Frenchman to Venice. The republic was noted for its considerable tolerance in religious matters—it was the choice of Clément Marot from June to November, 1536, after his unorthodoxy had made him suspect in Ferrara. Getting established in business was no easy task for a new arrival like Gardane. His first venture outside music, a volume of *Pistole vulgari de M. Nicolo Franco* (1539), caused financial difficulties, if we may believe Aretino, who wrote that "il Gardane francese" had been ruined by Nicolo Franco, "sodomito," to whom the printer had lent money (presumably in the form of credit toward the publication expenses).[28] The same

[27] Simone Casali, *Gli Annali della typografia veneziana di Francesco Marcolini da Forli* (Bologna, 1861; 2d ed., 1953), no. 23.

[28] *Tutte le opere di Pietro Aretino: Lettere*, ed. Francesco Flora (Milan, 1960), p. 595 (letter of Oct. 7, 1539).

year Gardane, far from being finished, lashed out at the wickedness of printers, with particular reference to a pirated Milanese edition (now lost) of Arcadelt's first book of madrigals.[29] He noted with scorn that even the errors of his own edition had been slavishly copied, excusing himself at the same time for having made the errors originally by blaming his typesetters ("i miei compositori"). The true challenge for Gardane was Venetian, however, and came from the well-entrenched publishing family of the Scottos. Before 1500, Ottaviano I Scotto had published many liturgical volumes, with the chant being printed from movable type in so skillful a manner as to merit acclaim equal to that accorded Petrucci's invention. Amadeo Scotto, a nephew, had been one of Petrucci's associates in 1512–1514. During the years between 1533 and 1539 Ottaviano II Scotto, from a younger branch of the family, published a distinguished series of woodcut collections, devoted mostly to Verdelot's madrigals and French chansons and executed by Andrea Antico. A brother, Gerolamo Scotto, is usually credited with beginning his new-method music prints in 1539. Yet he may have printed the 1538 volume of *Madrigali di M. Constantio Festa Libro Primo*, and therefore have adopted the new method as soon as, or not long after, Gardane.[30] Although he began by printing relatively fresh material, he soon resorted to what looks to be extensive borrowing. According to Sartori, he repeatedly pirated Gardane's newest music-books and the two engaged in a price war that led to a decline in the quality of Venetian music printing, if not the quantity.[31] The evidence of the music type used by both puts a slightly different light on their competition. An opportunity in May, 1966, to place side-by-side the British Museum's copies of Gardane's 1538 Motets and Scotto's 1540 Masses revealed other similarities. The initial musical typography of both men is identical (10/10.5). Not only this, the two collections utilized the same italic types for the texts. If Scotto were not markedly less successful in achieving horizontal continuity with his staff segments we might hypothesize that the presswork of the two firms was done in common. At the least, their sharing of types raises the possibility that the relationship was one of collusion more than competition. The common source at its origin was almost certainly Gardane, whose very skillful printing, together with his French origins, offer the most plausible explanation for the new method's arrival in Italy. Gardane may have had some preparation in the art of printing as well as in the

[29] For a facsimile of the original see *Die Musik in Geschichte und Gegenwart* VIII, 1427.

[30] A copy is in the Harding Library, Chicago. The ascription to Scotto is after Catherine Weeks Chapman, "Andrea Antico" (Unpublished Ph.D. dissertation, Harvard University, 1964), p. 165.

[31] Article "Scotto" in *Die Musik in Geschichte und Gegenwart* and "La Famiglia degli Scotto," *Acta Musicologica* XXXVI (1964), 19–30. Thomas Bridges questions Sartori's conclusions in his dissertation on Arcadelt (in progress at Harvard University) which should eventually clear up the issue of priority between Scotto and Gardane.

musical art; or, he may have brought craftsmen with him to Venice. The music-types of Buglhat and his associates in Ferrara may also have come from Gardane, for they are remarkably close to, if not identical with, those used by Gardane and Scotto from 1538 to 1540. The successors of Gardane and of Scotto were still competing late in the century, by which time many firms had come and gone. With the exception of a few copperplate engravings, especially favored for keyboard music, the new method sufficed Italian music during its great flowering around and after 1600.

After Venice, Paris, and Nuremberg, the city that was to prove the most congenial home of early music printing was Antwerp. The development seemed inevitable, given the musical, artistic, and commercial importance of the Low Countries, in which region Holland was then a largely agricultural tributary, while Flanders was the thriving center, and Antwerp the most populous and flourishing of Flemish cities. Here the *Lofzangen* in honor of Prince Charles of Hapsburg and his grandfather Maximilian had been printed in 1515. Woodcut plates were used in this work, printed handsomely by Jan de Gheet, although the notes show none of Antico's ability to counterfeit printing types. Another printer at Antwerp, Willem Vosterman, used woodcut musical illustrations in the French translation of Wirdung's *Musica Getutscht*, brought out in 1529; Columbus acquired the volume for his library and his copy is now unique.[32] During the earlier years of the century, the dioceses of the Low Countries depended mostly on Paris for their printed missals. A trend toward local printing may be observed in the third decade, however, chiefly in the person of Christophorus Ruremundensis of Antwerp, who printed plainchant with the customary two impressions; an example from a *Processionale ad usam Sarum* of 1528 is reproduced by H. D. L. Vervliet in his *History of Typography in the Low Countries*.[33] The smaller type with square heads in the *Processionale*, for which a Parisian origin is suggested by Vervliet, was used subsequently in Symon Cock's *Ghestelijche Liedekens ende Leysenen* (Antwerp, 1539). Cock also used diamond-shaped notes, reproduced by double impression, in his *Souter-liedekens* (Antwerp, 1540).

The years around 1540 were filled with activity at Antwerp, as several persons explored the possibilities of reproducing mensural music from type. On August 22, 1541, Charles V granted a privilege to Henry Loys and Jehan de Buys for the time of three years allowing them to print "toutes les oeuvres de musicque faictes par les maistres, nommées en cestuy ottroy, tant messes, mottés que chansons

[32] Howard Mayer Brown, *Instrumental Music Printed Before 1600. A Bibliography* (Cambridge, Mass., 1965), no. 1529.[2] Catherine Weeks Chapman, "Printed Collections of Polyphonic Music Owned by Ferdinand Columbus," *Journal of The American Musicological Society* XXI (1968), no. 170.

[33] I am indebted for being allowed to study this work in proof. Further mentions of Mr. Vervliet refer to the same work, which is in process of publication.

licites et honestes . . ." In the same month the two printers brought out *Chansons a quatre parties composez par M. Benedictus: M. de la Chapelle de Madame la Regente*, a fine example, in quarto, of double impression printing (15/13.5). The partners, from the terms of their privilege (known only from the extract in the printed *Chansons*), must have envisaged other "masters" in imperial service and other genres; further volumes, if printed, have not survived. In any case, there would have been little future for such lavish volumes with their large types and corresponding restriction to four lines of music per page. At the same time a practical musician who was about to become a printer was planning a music series along more modern lines. Thielman Susato, who settled in Antwerp in 1529, was a music copyist and instrumentalist, as well as a composer. In 1542 he entered partnership with Hendrik Verbruggen and Willem van Vissenaeken for the purpose of creating type with which to print music by single impression. It soon came into dispute. According to Vervliet's reading of the exceedingly complicated litigation, the types fell to Susato, who commenced printing on his own by 1543, date of his *Premier livre des chansons a quatre parties*, a volume in quarto with large, clear notes (13/9.5). In another volume, undated, but ascribed to the same year, *Vingt et six chansons musicales*, Susato claimed in a little rhyme that the means of printing music had been discovered to him only after arduous studies and the expenditure of much time and effort.[34] As with Marcolini in Venice, it was necessary to invent anew techniques that were nevertheless being employed widely in several centers. Who cut the punches for Susato is not known. They were probably done at Antwerp, since the availability of the punches is mentioned in the lawsuit. An allusion in the famous passage of Fournier's *Traité* suggests that the craftsman was Haultin, a claim that was questioned even by Goovaerts and is rejected by Vervliet. Susato's former partner, Vissenaeken, succeeded in bringing out a collection of motets with his own types in 1542, a volume in quarto, although the staves (14.7/11.5) would have been large enough for a folio. He seems to have preceded Susato in introducing the new method to the region, but nothing more is known from his press.

Until Philip II founded a university at Douai in 1560, there was but one institution of higher learning in the Spanish-dominated southern Low Countries (comprising Flanders, Hainaut, Brabant and Artois—see Fig. 5, above). This was at Louvain. Knowing the ties between printing and universities elsewhere, we are not unprepared to find a firm plying the music trade there. In 1545, Pieter Phalesius, sworn bookseller of the University of Louvain, commissioned a series

[34] Reproduced in part by Alphonse Goovaerts, *Histoire et Bibliographie de la Typographie musicale dans les Pays Bas* (Antwerp, 1880), p. 29, and in entirety by Edmund Van der Straeten, *La Musique au Pays Bas*, Vol. V (Brussels, 1880), pp. 259 f.

of lute tablatures of the printers Bathen and Velpen, employing the letter system associated with Paris and lifting, moreover, a number of pieces from Attaingnant's tablatures of 1529–1530.[35] Louvain was no center of music to compare with Antwerp or Paris, and Phalesius, throughout his career, compensated for this by liberally helping himself to whatever previously printed material he pleased. Even so, the magnetism of Antwerp must have made itself felt. Toward the end of his life Phalesius formed a partnership with Jan Bellerus, an important printer whose Antwerp address appears on the music volumes from 1570 on. Pieter Phalesius the Younger, who took over upon his father's death in 1573, moved to Antwerp in 1581, and was to continue printing there for many decades.

Among other music-printing enterprises in Antwerp were those carried on by the composer Waelrant, in partnership with the printer Van Laet (from 1559 to 1567), and by the city's greatest pride, Christopher Plantin. A native of Touraine, Plantin had been at Lyons as a youth and was proprietor of a house in the Rue Saint-Jean-de-Latran in Paris from 1546 until 1549, when he settled in Antwerp, probably quitting Paris, like Robert Estienne, in consequence of the less tolerant regime of Henry II. He turned to music printing in 1578 after having brought out many distinguished liturgical books. With the "architypographicus," to give him the title bestowed by Philip II, we reach a high point in the history of new-method music printing, before its decline at the hands of lesser men.

England and Spain had no specialists in music printing until later, but both saw some fine early instances. Vihuela tablatures were printed by the new method, beginning with Luis Milán's *El Maestro* in 1536, and mensural notation was printed with one impression at least as early as the *Delphin de musica* of Narváez (1538). It may be recalled that England produced a remarkable imitation of Petrucci, the *XX Songes* of 1530. The type was so large (15.5/14.5) that only three lines of music per page could be accommodated, for the most part, to the octavo format. This luxury item, which had no successors, must have been the work of craftsmen with small musical experience: the clefs are too small in proportion to the staves; note-stems frequently go in the wrong direction; accidentals are often omitted at the beginning of the line, then supplied later, in the middle of the line, as if in afterthought. Another early English example that has attracted much attention occurs in the play by John Rastell, *The Nature of the iiii elements*, a three-voiced closing song printed in score, by single impression (16/13). Rastell wrote the play in 1516–1517 when in Ireland preparing an expedition to the New

[35] For concordances see the modern edition cited under **13** and **16.** The musical typography used by Phalesius from 1563 for folio volumes is identical with Attaingnant's Mass Type according to Vervliet, *History of Typography in the Low Countries* (in press).

World. It may have been performed on his private stage at London (one of the earliest) in 1527. The date of printing has yet to be ascertained.[36] Rastell is known to have employed French printers, and the possibility that his music types came from this source may not be excluded. His types are not, strictly speaking, produced by the new method. Fragments of the staff sometimes peep through the white notes, and the tails lean to the right or left without the staff-segment's showing a corresponding incline. These imperfections occur because the workmen struck the matrix twice, once with the staff-segment, and once with the note (or other symbol). The method is crude in comparison with that used to create the first French matrices, which were evidently made from a single strike. It may be the result achieved by a workman who, lacking apprenticeship in the process, took his departure from a printed book. Harry Carter restores a proper perspective to the question of "priority," writing as follows: "If a date about 1527 for John Rastell's use of a single-impression type in London is correct, there can be little doubt that the technique had an earlier origin in Continental Europe."[37] Contacts between the printing worlds of London and Paris at the time offer a fascinating topic for exploration, indeed. One should like, for example, to know more about Richard Grafton, a King's Printer and one of the first in London to engage regularly in music printing. He was sent to Paris in 1537 by Thomas Cromwell to supervise the production of an English Bible (a testimony to the continuing eminence of Paris printers in one of their specialties).[38] Grafton was later to print Merbecke's *Booke of Common Praier noted* (1550), using black notes printed from movable type upon red staves. Wherever part-music was printed after 1550 the new method was invariably adopted. Its sway was not broken until the reforms of Breitkopf in Leipzig and Fournier in France, working independently during the years 1740–1750. In more remote locations the older practices survived much longer. American songbooks of the nineteenth century commonly display the method which Attaingnant first popularized.

By the second half of the sixteenth century it was no longer necessary for each printer to "discover" how notes and staves could be joined and printed. Music types (or, more accurately, their matrices) became available commercially and were advertised in specimen books. Among his other lines of endeavor, Plantin sold material to smaller firms. A *Specimen Characterum* dating from about 1578

[36] Attempts have been made by Robert Steele, *The Earliest Music Printing* (London, 1903), p. 3 and W. W. Gregg, "Notes on Some Early Plays," *The Library*, Ser. 4, XI (1930), 49–50. A. Hyatt King adopts the position of the latter in *Five Hundred Years of Music Printing* (London, 1964), p. 16. Further clarification of the subject is expected from Mr. King, to whom I am indebted for the information about Rastell.

[37] Review of King's *Five Hundred Years of Music Printing* in *The Library*, Ser. 5, XX (1965), 154–157.

[38] William Gamble, *Music Printing and Engraving* (London, 1923), pp. 30–32.

displays, with many types for Greek, Latin, and Hebrew and other texts, the special characters he was prepared to supply for music (Pl. XV). Plantin's distinctions between *Grande*, *Moyenne* and *Petite musicque* are also encountered in inventories of type such as that of the Le Bé firm. Music types, together with their employment, had become quite standardized by this time. The largest notes were for choirbooks in folio, like Plantin's own Masses. *Moyenne musicque* approximated the size and shape of Attaingnant's Typography I and was widely used for volumes in quarto. The smallest notes (even smaller than Attaingnant's Typography II) were especially popular for psalms and served in many "pocket book" editions. With such serviceable and beautiful types as these available, the decisions facing later printers and publishers differed markedly from those of the pioneers—no longer *how* to print, but mostly *what* to print.

Paris Successors

The change of regime from Francis I to Henry II occurred in mid-1547. During the following year Attaingnant's production fell off distinctly, editions of the 26th and 27th chanson books being the only survivors to bear the date 1548. It was customary for a new sovereign to renew the rights and privileges granted by his predecessor, although such was not always the case. Upon his accession in 1461, Louis XI dismissed many of his father's pensioners, including Nicolas Jenson, who had been sent to Mainz to acquire the "secret" of printing—Jenson in consequence betook himself and his skills to Venice instead of Paris. There must have been some doubt in Attaingnant's mind about his standing with the new generation come to power. He took care to seek renewal of his six-year privilege, which was not due to expire until 1549 (Appendix, 22). Possibly he planned no new works until the renewal was granted, which would explain the slackening of production in 1548.

As long as King Francis reigned, privileges for music were granted only to Attaingnant. The sole exception is Gueynard's *Contrapunctus* of 1528, which bears the legend: "Cum privilegio Regio per quinquenium." Under the new monarch the situation quickly changed. Francis had been buried scarcely two months before a privilege was given on August 4, 1547, to the Beringen brothers at Lyons to print psalms, chansons, and motets.[39] Nicolas du Chemin received a privilege on November 7, 1548, to print "all new music that has not been printed

[39] For a facsimile see *Die Musik in Geschichte und Gegenwart*, II, 161. Pidoux, *Le Psautier Huguenot*, Vol. II, p. 37, gives the date of the privilege incorrectly as April 4, 1547, and contradicts this with the correct date on p. 73. As to typography, the Beringens used a small note (9.5/7.7) very similar to, if not identical with, one used by Petrejus, Kriesstein, and Petri, and discussed above.

before," which he quickly proceeded to do, beginning with the Janequin Psalms of 1549. In anticipation he had bought music punches and matrices from Pierre Haultin in February, 1547. They produced characters (10/9) nearly indistinguishable from Attaingnant's Typography I, as may be seen in the chansonniers that began appearing in 1549.

Du Chemin was an engraver by trade. His qualifications for the new task he set himself were purely typographical; that he was not able to read music is clear from the contract with his first music editor, Nicolas Regnes.[40] Why, then, was Du Chemin determined, as he says in the same contract, to "print books after the fashion and format of those printed by Attaingnant"? There was at least one person close to him with experience in a bookstore where music was sold and who might have convinced him of the profitability of such a business. In November of 1545 he had married Catherine Delahaye, whose one distinction mentioned in the marriage contract was that she served as "une pupille de Poncet le Preux."[41] This connection with the inner Attaingnant circle may have been put to good use. Janequin's Psalm-settings were new, but much else that Du Chemin brought out did not fall into the category of "music previously unpublished." His *Livres du Recueil* (1549–1551) not only contained "chansons antiques," as he called them, but also duplicated almost piece for piece the retrospective collections of *Chansons esleues* (1549–1550) advertised by Attaingnant as "beaucop [sic] plus correcte."

Privileges were meanwhile being sought by others. Early in 1550 Robert Granjon received permission to print "all kinds of music, including tablatures for lute, guitar, and other instruments." On August 14, 1551, the partnership of Adrian Le Roy and Robert Ballard received a privilege for "all books of music, instrumental as well as vocal." The distinguished printer Michel Fezandat turned to music after receiving a privilege on January 18, 1552, to print "Chansons, Masses, motets, tablatures for lute, guitar and other instruments." Within a month the lutenist Guillaume Morlaye had succeeded in obtaining permission to print or have printed the works of his master, Albert de Rippe, as well as "works for guitar, *espinette*, or other instruments." Morlaye engaged Fezandat in the execution of his projects and the two agreed on April 19, 1552, upon an edition of 1,200 copies, to be divided evenly. During the reign of Henry II France could pride itself not only on the achievements of the great music houses of Paris, but also upon numerous activities at Lyons, where music was printed by Granjon,

[40] F. Lesure and G. Thibault, "Bibliographie des éditions musicales publiées par Nicolas du Chemin (1549–1576)," *Annales Musicologiques* I (1953), 273 f.

[41] Ernest Coyecque, *Recueil d'actes notariés relatifs à l'histoire de Paris* (Paris, 1905), Vol. II, no. 3882.

the Beringens, Giovan' Pullon da Trino, Michel du Bois, and Simon Gorlier, as well as by Jacques Moderne.

The near monopoly in music printing, maintained for almost a quarter of a century, had been broken. No new music books from Attaingnant appeared in 1551. Yet in this year appeared a volume of commentaries on Pliny **(167)** by Léger du Chesne de Quercu, rector of the Parisian college of Sainte-Barbe. Heavy competition in the music field may explain this attempt to capture part of the market for academic textbooks. The humanist Léger du Chesne was perhaps a relation of the Guillaume du Chesne de Quercu who was corrector for Pigouchet.[42] Another possible factor in the liaison was the Regius Professorship. Like Oronce Finé Léger du Chesne belonged to the small band of scholars directly appointed by the Crown. And Attaingnant was still Royal Printer—so he signed himself on the 1551 title page. It was his last volume. He must have died not long afterwards. A contract was witnessed as late as October 3, 1551 (Appendix, 26). Early in 1553 the title of King's Music Printer was bestowed elsewhere.

Funeral services presumably would have been held in the parish church of the Attaingnant family, Saint-Benoît-le Bétourné. (See Pl. XIIb.) Burial was not unlikely in or near the same twelfth-century edifice. Millin states that a list of printers buried at Saint-Benoît would provide "presque une histoire abregée de l'imprimerie et de la librairie," but mentions no music printers by name in his partial inventory of tombs.[43] The grave of another typographical great, Claude Garamond, is described with a touching attention to detail in Le Bé's Memorandum: "Garamond died in November 1561 and was buried in the Cemetery of St. Benoît, where the fountain is now . . . The place of his grave was under the spouting gutter of the Collège de Cambrai, and at the second spout."[44] Like so many of the oldest buildings in Paris, Saint-Benoît gave way to ninteenth-century progress—it was demolished upon the piercing of the Rue des Ecoles. Some conception of the old neighborhood is still possible, thanks to the many fine panoramic maps of Paris made during the *ancien régime*. A detail from the so-called Plan de Turgot, executed by Bretez and printed in 1739, may serve to close the subject, allowing the reader to travel in imagination the way "from Saint-Côme to Saint-Benoît," trod so often by Attaingnant in life and probably traversed a final time in the winter of 1551–1552. (See Pl. XVI.)

The Crown showed no inclination to bestow the royal title on widows. Thus when Conrad Neubar, King's Printer of Greek, died in 1540, his widow had to

[42] See Renouard, *Répertoire des imprimeurs parisiens*, *s.v.* Du Chesne, Guillaume.

[43] Aubin-Louis Millin, *Antiquités nationales* Vol. III (Paris, 1791), chapt. XXIX.

[44] Harry Carter (ed.), *Sixteenth-Century French Typefounders* (Documents Typographiques Français, III) (Paris, 1966), p. 31.

yield the title to Robert Estienne. Similarly, Marie Lescalloppier was not able to retain her husband's title. The male heirs were not yet of age. Jullet's son Pierre might conceivably have rebuilt the business later, having been raised by the libraire Guillaume Guiolin. But he became instead an apothecary (Appendix, 29, 30). The son of Attaingnant and Marie Lescalloppier, also named Pierre, aimed no higher, becoming a bailiff of the Parlement of Paris. And so the industry built up over a generation—the reputation to which a lifetime of effort had been devoted—scarcely outlived the man.

Little new music issued from the presses of the widow Attaingnant after they were started again in 1553 with the editorial help of Claude Gervaise. The *Danceries* of the last years were probably reprints of works first published when Attaingnant was still alive; the *Troisiesme livre* **(172)** certainly was. The firm might have attempted to profit from the vast repertory pouring forth from other publishers in Paris. But Le Roy and Ballard, who began to dominate the field increasingly, sought and obtained tighter regulations in their privilege of 1555, which states that "no printers of the realm, whoever they are, may extract any part of their books, or counterfeit their music characters." The commentaries of Léger du Chesne, continuing for a number of years, provided the mainstay of the much reduced firm. The last book with music **(174)** included one chanson and was evidently designed to court favor with the mighty, being a celebration by François Habert of the capture of Calais, addressed to the all-powerful Duke of Guise. The last work of any kind—again by Du Chesne—bears the date 1567.[45]

The Paris successors, in the strictest sense, were Adrian Le Roy and Robert Ballard, to whom the royal title was given by letters patent of February 16, 1553. It had been many years since Attaingnant merited the distinction "Imprimeur du Roi." New initiatives were few after 1546—almost lacking if the second half of the numbered set of chansonniers now at Munich were merely reprints, as we have suggested. The volumes of 1548–1551 are not only small in number, but poorly printed, their worn type and careless design being substandard for the house. Volume 36 of 1551, devoted to Josquin, is noteworthy mostly for its misattributions. Whether for reasons of ill health or whatever, Attaingnant showed none of the vigor of the new generation arriving on the scene—of Du Chemin, Fezandat, Granjon, and Le Roy and Ballard, extraordinarily fine printers all, whose books rivaled each other for a few years in both beauty and musical interest. Competition was particularly keen in instrumental tablatures, perhaps because Attaingnant had neglected them so long. The decline and end of the first French

[45] Some copies from the widow Attaingnant displayed the address of Benoît Rigaut of Lyons. See Renouard, *Imprimeurs et libraires du xvie siècle,* I (1964), no. 457 bis. Did Rigaud, who edited a music collection in 1568, obtain typographical material from Paris?

music publisher thus signaled the advent of a new flourishing, destined in its turn for quick demise.

The first sixty years of the sixteenth century have justly been called the golden age of French typography. In terms that are the most pertinent, the period embraced three reigns: Louis XII (1498–1514); Francis I (1515–1547); Henry II (1547–1559). During the first, which corresponded to the generation of Pigouchet, the development of graphic arts reached a very high point, providing the fund of skills necessary to such specialized lines of printing as music. Attaingnant was in every way a creature of the second, having risen with the fortunes of the Crown, prospered under royal smiles, and declined when the King died. The last was a brief but glorious epilogue before the ineluctable catastrophe of the civil wars. The followers of Attaingnant, in the wider sense of all those who took after him, exceeded what he had done in some respects. Like worthy children, they may be considered no small part of his attainment.

APPENDIX:

DOCUMENTS, DEDICATIONS, AND PRIVILEGES

1. October 3, 1503

Resumé of the testament by Simon Attaingnant, canon of Saint Amé, Douai

Il demande à être enterré en l'église Saint Amé devant la chapelle Sainte Anne.

4 livres pour son service à Saint Amé.

Célébrations de 40 messes à Saint Amé le jour de son service au chapelain du doyen de Saint Amé 8 sols, au clerc paroissial 4 sols, à la fabrique 40 livres à prendre moitié sur les biens de son exécution testamentaire, moitié sur Jean Attaingnant, son neveu, demeurant à Vitry, qui devra payer sur ce qu'il doit au testateur.

Aux chanoines de Saint Pierre de Douai pour venir à son service 40 sols, aux frères prècheurs 20 sols, aux frères mineurs 20 sols, aux frères de la Trinité 10 sols; à chaque porteur de son corps 2 sols; à ses confrères pour faire récréation ensemble au diner après le service 5 sols et non plus, aux chapelains pour semblable cause 4 livres.

À l'hôpital des Chartreux 40 sols, à l'hôpital Saint Thomas 40 sols; à l'église de Sortel [?] 60 sols.

À sire Simon Attaingnant 10 livres.

À sa servante 1 livre, une bonne paire de draps et 16 aunes de toile.

Il quitte à André Le Vairrier 6 livres sur les 12 qu'il lui avait prêtées.

Il donne 12 livres aux pauvres.

À sire Antoine Charlet 8 livres.

À l'église de Sortel pour une chasuble pour son service en ladite église 8 livres.

À Gournenflo 40 livres.

À la paroisse de l'église d'Orchies 60 sols.

18 livres pour 4 trentains de messes.

À ses filleules et filleuls nés à Douai, à chacun 1 écu 48 sols.

Tout le surplus de ses biens à Pierotin Attaingnant qui a demeuré avec lui et à Jeannet de Gournenflo par moitié, la part dudit Pierotin demeurant aux mains des exécuteurs testamentaires afin qu'elle ne vienne pas aux mains de son père.

[Archives du Nord, 1 G 155 fol. 206^{v}–208]

2. January 13, 1514

Jean de La Roche rents the use of a press from Pierre Attaingnant, for whom he agrees to print "dominoes," excommunications, and pardons, if required

Jehan de La Roche, imprimeur et fondeur de lectres à imprimer, demour[ant à Paris], rue des Poirées, prent à loage de Pierre Ataignant, libraire, demourant à Paris, rue [. . . . .], une presse garnye de platine de fer, trois frisquettes, une casse, deux ays [. . . . .] tremper le papier, ung ays à bouter encre dessus et ung aultre à bouter le rouge av[ec . . . . .] chassis de boys telz qu'il les vouldra choisir entre ceulx là qu'a ledict Ataignant [le tout] bon, loyal et marchant, lesquelles choses ledict de La Roche prent à louage dudict Ataignant du jour d'huy jusques au jour Sainct-Jehan-Baptiste prochainement venant moyennant que ledict de La Roche sera tenu de payer audict Ataignant, pour les dessus dictes choses, vingt solz parisis à Pasques et aultres vingt solz parisis à la Sainct-Jehan-Baptiste, le tout prochainement venant, avec aussi que ledict de La Roche sera tenu rendre audict Ataignant le tout en aussi bonne valeur comme icelluy Ataignant les luy a baillés et livrés. Et, oultre plus, si ledict Ataignant vouloit faire des dominos ou excomunimens ou pardons ou aultre chose semblable, icelluy de La Roche sera tenu les luy faire, c'est asscavoir composer et imprimer pour le pris de six solz tournoiz par chacune rame de papier commun, et, s'il les faict de papier bastard, il doi[t . . . . .] demy franc de la rame et doit changer à chacune rame de piece nouvelle ainsi qu'il semblera audict Ataignant et aussi ledict Ataignant sera tenu de faire faire audict de La Roche journée entiere sur lesdicts dominos ou aultre chose au dessusdict pris. Et oultre est tenu ledict de La Roche rabatre [. . . . .] dessusdict, c'est asscavoir pour l'impression de chacune rame dessusdicte audict Ataignant, sur et entant moins de certain obligé en quoy ledict de La Roche est obligé envers [ledict] Ataignant à besongner d'impression, sauf les dix francs qu'il est tenu bailler [audict] Ataignant en argent comptant dedens le jour de caresme prenant. Et si ledict Ataignant avoir à faire de sadicte presse et utensilles pour besongner pour luy, pourveu qu'il ne la veulle louer à aultres que audict de La Roche, en [. . . . .] le faisant ascavoir audict de La Roche quinze jours devant, ledict de La Roche sera tenu rendre et livrer le tout audict Ataignant en aussi bo[nne] valeur comme il les a receues et si ledict de La Roche faict faire aulcune choze a [ladicte] presse, comme coffre, tympans ou aultres chozes, le tout demeurera audict Ataignant.

Faict à la presence de Patrix et Jehan le Charpentier et autres. Promectant etc. [obligeant etc], renonceant etc. Faict le vendredi XIIIe janvier V^{C} XIII.

[Archives Nationales, Minutier central, XXXIII, 1]

NOTE: The right side of the document is torn and partly missing; in some of the bracketed passages the sense of the matter permitted a partial reconstruction.

3. March 12, 1519

Contract of marriage between Collette Pigouchet and Jean Bégin

Contrat de mariage de Jean Begin, marchand et bourgeois de Paris, et de Collette Pigouchet, agée de dix-sept ans, fille de feu Philippe Pigouchet, libraire et bourgeois de Paris, et de Jeanne du Ponceau, et soeur de feu Robert Pigouchet et de Germaine Pigouchet, mariée à Poncet Le Preux, libraire et bourgeois de Paris.

[Ernest Coyecque, *Recueil d'actes notariés relatifs* à *l'histoire de Paris et de ses environs au xvi*ᵉ *siècle* (Paris, 1905), Vol. I, no. 79.]

4. April 18, 1526

Receipt by Germaine Pigouchet and Attaingnant of final installment from the Cathedral chapter of Noyon, for 320 breviaries

Reçu par Germaine Pigouchet, femme de Poncet Le Preux, libraire, bourgeois de Paris, momentanément absent de la ville, et par Pierre Attaingnant, imprimeur de livres, à Paris, au chapitre de Noyon, représenté par Jean Poupart, prêtre, chanoine de Noyon, de 100 l.t. somme restant due sur les 400 l.t. constituant le prix des bréviaires commandés le 14 juillet 1525, "desquelz brevyaires led. Poupart a confessé avoir esté receu par lesd. de chappitre seize vings demy temps d'iver, ainsi que contenu est oud. marché."

[Coyecque, *Recueil d'actes notariés*, Vol. I, no. 620.]

5. March 28, 1528

Rent-contract for the house in the Rue de la Harpe for twelve years

Bail pour douze ans, par le collège de Dainville à Ponce Le Preux, libraire juré en l'Université, bourgeois de Paris, agissant pour sa belle-mère, Jeanne Ponceau, veuve de Philippe Pigouchet, et à Pierre Ataignant, libraire, à Paris, gendre de ladite Jeanne Ponceau, d'une maison, rue de la Harpe, "en laquelle led. Atignant est à present demourant et ainsi que luy et lad. vefve l'ont tenue par cy devant." Prix: 30 l.t. l'an.

[Coyecque, *Recueil d'actes notariés*, Vol. I, no. 768.]

6. 1529, before October

First Royal Privilege—three years (extract)

Le Roy a donné permission et privilege audit Attaingnant des livres qu'il a par cy devant imprimez et espere imprimer cy apres tant en musique, jeux de Lutz, Orgues, et semblables instruments que nul ne les pourra imprimer, contrefaire ne aulcune partie d'iceulx vendre, ne distribuer jusques a troys ans apres l'impression de chacun d'iceulx. Et tout sur la peine de confiscation et d'amende arbitraire.

[Quoted from **22;** shorter extracts from the privilege, with slightly different phrasing, in **12, 13,** and **18.**]

7. June 18, 1531

Second Royal Privilege—six years

Françoys, par la grace de dieu Roy de France, au prevost de Paris, Baillifz et Seneschaulx et a tous noz aultres justiciers et officiers ou a leurs lieutenans, salut et dilection. Receu avons l'humble supplication de nostre bien amé Pierre Attaingnant, imprimeur libraire, demourant a l'Université de Paris, contenant que, comme par cy devant nul en cestuy nostre royaulme ne se seroit entremis de graver, fondre et addresser les nottes et carracteres de l'impression de musicque figurée en choses faictes, ensemble des tabulatures des jeuz de lutz, flustes et orgues, tant pour la difficile imagination et longue consumption de temps que pour les grans fraiz, mises et labeurs qu'il y convenoit faire et appliquer, ledit suppliant par longue excogitation et travail d'esperit et a tres grans fraiz, labeurs, mises et despens ait inventé et mis en lumiere la maniere et industrie de graver, fondre et imprimer lesdictes nottes et carracteres, tant de musicque et choses faictes comme desdictes tabulatures des jeuz de Lutz, Flustes et Orgues, desquelles il a imprimé et faict imprimer et espere faire cy apres plusieurs livres et cayers, tant de messes, motetz, hymnes, chansons que desditz jeuz de Lutz, Flustes et Orgues, en grans et petitz volumes, pour servir aux eglises, ministres d'icelles et generalement a toutes personnes, et pour le tres grant bien, utilité et soulaigement de la chose publique. Toutesfoys il doubte que, apres avoir mis en lumiere sadicte invention et ouvert aux aultres imprimeurs et libraires la voye et industrie d'imprimer ladicte musicque et jeuz, iceulx imprimeurs et libraires se voulsissent semblablement entremetre d'imprimer ladicte musique en choses faictes et jeuz de Lutz, Flustes et Orgues. Et par ce moyen ledit suppliant perdist totalement le merite de ses labeurs et recouvrement des fraiz et mises qu'ilz a faitz et exposez a l'invention et composition des caracteres desusdictz si par nous ne luy estoit sur ce pourveu et survenu, de nostre grace humblement requerant icelle. Pour ce est il que nous, ces choses considerées, non voulans ledit suppliant demourer inutilles ses labeurs, application de temps, fraiz et mises par luy supportées audit affaire, ains a en emporter et sentir commodité. Pour ces causes et aultres a ce nous mouvans, avons voulu et ordonné, voulons et ordonnons que, durant le temps et terme de six ans prochainement venans a compter du jour et datte de ces presentes, Aultre que ledit suppliant ou ceulx qui auront charge de luy ne puissent imprimer ne exposer en vente lesditz livres et cayers de musicque en choses faictes et tabulature des jeuz de Lutz, Flustes et Orgues dessus declarez. Si vous mandons et commettons par ces presentes et a chacun de vous sur ce requis que de nostre presente grace, ordonnance et ottroy vous faictes ledit suppliant jouyr et user plainement et paisiblement. En faisant inhibitions et deffenses de par nous a tous libraires et aultres personnes generalement quelzconques de non imprimer ne exposer en vente lesditz livres et cayers de musicque et tabulature des jeuz dessusditz, ledit temps de six ans durant, sans expres povoir et consentement dudit suppliant, et ce sur grans peines a nous a appliquer et deperdition et confiscation desditz livres et cayers. Et a ce faire et souffrir contraignez ou faictes contraindre tous ceulx qu'il appartiendra et qui pour ce seront a contraindre par toutes voyes et manieres deues et raisonnables, car ainsi nous plaist il estre faict. Nonobstant quelzconques ordonnances, restrictions, mandemens ou deffenses a ce contraires. Donné a Sainct Germain en Laye, le dixhuitiesme jour de Juing, l'an de grace mil cinq centz trente ung, et de nostre regne le xvii. Par le Roy. Le Cardinal de Tournon, maistre de la Chapelle dudit seigneur present. Signé J. Hamelin.

[Quoted from **33,** fol. 1; facsimile of the original and translation in D. Heartz, "A New Attaingnant Book and the Beginnings of French Music Printing", *Journal of the American Musicological Society* XIV (1961), 9–23, Pl. V and Appendix.]

8. July 15, 1532

Attaingnant addresses the Cardinal de Tournon, dedicating to him the Masses in-folio: poem of Nicolas Bourbon in praise of Tournon

Reverendissimo in Christo Patri ac Domino Domino Francisco a Turnone Cardinali meritissimo Petrus Attingens, typographus musicus, s[alutem] p[lurimam] d[icit.]

Plurimum vereor, Reverendissime pater, ne temeritatis et arrogantiae arguar, qui te tantum heroa tantisque rebus occupatum interpellare ausus sim. Sed ego spero te non aegre laturum, adeo humanus es et benignus, nec dubito quin in bonam partem accepturus sis hunc librum quem sub tuo illustrissimo nomine in lucem edo. Nam cum mecum diu cogitarem cui potissimum hunc laborem meum dedicarem, tu primus occurristi, imo vero solus mihi dignus visus es, cui musae universa opera sua consecrarent. A musis musica dicta est, de cuius artis laudibus tacere satius est quam pauca dicere. Hoc unum tamen non praeteribo, quod prisci illi, tam graeci quam latini, cum hominem significare vellent in omni disciplinarum genere excellentem, eum musicum appellabant. Sed haec ut alia quaeque optima nemo te melius novit. Cum igitur videam te nostri saeculi decus esse, artisque musicae foeliciter studiosissimum, opusculum hoc missarum musicis accentiunculis notatarum tuae celsitudini nuncupandum duxi, quod ut aequi bonique consulas oro, interim dum meliora parabuntur. Potero enim et meliora et majora praestare, si tuae benignitatis favor accesserit. Scio quantum valeas authoritate et gratia apud hunc principem, ut a qui repulsam nunquam passus sis. Nemi est qui non admiretur egregias tum animi tum corporis dotes, quibus Deus te prae caeteris mortalibus decoravit. Quare mirum non est, si principes te amant, si universa Gallia te in primis venerat. Turnonia domus et antiquissima est et nobilissima, nempe a Trojanis originem ducens. Tu eam ex noblissima reddis nobiliorem et fulgentiorem, qui primus tam insigni familiae sacram purpuram attulisti. O utinam nunc viverent Justus et Gaspar, germani tui, quorum ille pro patria pugnando fortiter occubuit, hic vero pastor vigilantissimus ecclesiae Valentinae (cui praeerat) moriendo incredibile sui desiderium reliquit. Sed supersunt adhuc Dominus Claudius Turnonius Vivariensis episcopus, et nepotes tui Dominus Carolus Vivarensis designatus, Dominus Jacobus Castrensis episcopus. Justus justi filius, (qui a sancto Justo generis vestri consorte nominatur), Turnonii dominus, Henricus item, natu minimus, Arlenci dominus. Ii omnes stellae sunt ac tanquam lucidissima sidera in domo Turnonia ut caetera taceam innumerabilia gentis tuae lumina. Tu autem, velut sol inter stellas, omnium oculos in te convertis. Sed vereor ne sim justo prolixior; quare finem facio laudandi tui, ne id laudare velle videar quod satis nunquam laudari potest. Tibi igitur tanquam principi musarum et regii sacelli moderatori modulos meos offero, parvum quidem munus et indignum tanto vertice, sed abunde magnum si animum dantis inspicias. Vale foeliciter, Francisce, antistes ornatissime, musarumque ac virtutum omnium parens. Ex officina nostra, Parisiis. Idibus Juliis M.D.XXXII.

Nicolai Borbonii Vandoperani Ad R[everendum] P[atrem] D[omino]
Franciscum Cardinalem Tornonium

Carmen Sapphicum

Thracius tigres, fluvios, et ornos
Traxit, et rupes, fidibus canoris
Fretus: et mores hominum ferinos
Leniit orpheus.

Hic liber tales modulos, et omnes
Gratias, omnes veneres canendi
Spirat: haec doctae tibi dant sorores
Munera praesul.

Te sibi solum statuere regem.
Purpuratorum columen refulgens,
Atque Turnonae domui dederunt
Nomina musae.

[From **33**, verso of title-page.]

8a.

To the most reverend Father and Lord in Christ Francis, most worthy Cardinal of Tournon, greetings from Pierre Attaingnant, musical typographer.

I am very much afraid, most reverend father, that I may be accused of temerity and arrogance, for having dared to interrupt you who are so great a personage and occupied with such undertakings, but I hope you will not take it amiss—you who are so civilized and kind, and I do not doubt that you will receive in good part this book which I am publishing under your most illustrious name. Whereas I was considering for a long time to whom in particular I might dedicate this work of mine, you were the first who occurred to me, in fact you alone seemed fitting, a person to whom the Muses might consecrate all their works. Music is named from the Muses; about the praises of this art it is better to be silent than to say too little. This one thing, however, I will not pass over, namely, that when the ancients, both Greek and Latin, wanted to show that a man was outstanding in every branch of study, they called him a *musicus*. But these things, as all the other best things, no one knows better than you. Since therefore I see that you are the ornament of our century and a most successful student of the art of music, I have considered this collection of Masses notated with type should be dedicated to Your Eminence. I beg that you take it in good part in the meantime until better things are produced. I shall be able to supply bigger and better works if I meet with the favor of your kindness. I know how great your authority and influence are with this Prince, since he has never yet denied you aught. There is no one but admires the outstanding qualities of mind and body with which God has endowed you beyond other mortals. So it is no wonder that Princes love you, that all France honors you in particular. The house of Tournon is very ancient and noble, drawing its origin from the Trojans. Most noble as it is, it is rendered even more noble and more splendid by you, first to bring the sacred purple to so eminent a family. If only your brothers Juste and Gaspar were alive, of which the former died bravely, fighting for his country, the latter, as the most watchful pastor of the church of Valence (of which he had charge) left upon his death an unbelievable sense of loss. But there still survive Claude de Tournon, Bishop of Viviers, and your nephews Charles, named to Viviers also, and Jacques, Bishop of Castres, Juste II, son of Juste (who are named from the St. Juste connected with your family), baron of Tournon, and likewise Henri, master of Arles. These are stars, and, as it were, the brightest heavenly bodies in the house of Tournon, to say nothing about the countless other lights of your family. But you, as the sun among planets, turn all eyes to yourself. But I am afraid that I am more prolix than proper. Therefore I make an end of praising you so that I may not seem to wish to praise that which can never be praised sufficiently. To you therefore, as the prince of the Muses, Master of the Royal Chapel, I offer my works, a small gift to be sure, and unworthy of so great a leader, yet sufficiently great if you consider the spirit of the giver. Farewell, Francis, most distinguished prelate, father of all the Muses and the virtues. From our office, Paris, 15 July 1532.

NICOLAS BOURBON OF VANDOEUVRE TO THE REVEREND FATHER IN GOD, FRANCIS, CARDINAL OF TOURNON

A Sapphic Poem

Thracian Orpheus relying on his melodious lyre
Moved tigers, rivers and mountain ashes
And rocks, and softened the beast-like hearts of men.
This book breathes forth similar melodies
And all the Graces and Charms of singing;
These gifts the learned sisters give you, O prelate.
The muses have established you as their sole sovereign—
You, gleaming bulwark of the wearers of the purple—
And have given fame to the house of Tournon.

9. 1537, presumably June or thereafter.

First Renewal of 1531 privilege for six years. Attaingnant named royal printer

Prorogation du privilege du Roy, de nouvel obtenu par ledit Attaingnant pour les livres ja par luy imprimez et qu'il imprimera cy apres jusques a six ans.

[From the title-page of **76.**]

NOTE: on the same title-page appears the first mention of the title "imprimeur et libraire du Roy en musique." (Letters patent do not survive.)

10. 1539.

Pierre de Manchicourt dedicates his motets to his patron, Remy Roussel, canon of Tours. Poem of Gilles de Sermisy in praise of Manchicourt

Integerrimo ac doctissimo Viro Remigio Ruffo Candido insignis Ecclesiae Turonae canonico meritissimo P[etrus] Manchicourtius s[alutem] d[icit.]

Non erraverunt, mea quidem sententia, Stoici Remigi eruditissime, qui, quae in terris gignuntur, ad usum hominum omnia creari existimarunt, homines autem hominum caussa esse generatos, ut ipsi inter se, alii aliis mutatione officiorum prodesse possent Quod perpendens Terentianus ille Chremes, objurganti Menedemo seni, scite ad modum respondit, homo, inquit sum humani a me nihil alienum puto Et sane quia hominem nudum fragilemque Deus formaverat, ut eum sapientia bene institutum melius insigniret: praeter caetera hunc amorem illi pietatis insevit, ut homo hominem tueatur, diligat, foveat, contraque omnia pericula et accipiat, et praestet auxilium: Summum igitur inter se hominum vinculum est humanitas Quae profecto praeter raras animi tui ingeniique dotes, multorum animos cum perstrinxisset, magna familiaritate sibi conjunxit. Et ut interim taceam, quae, erga omnes doctos, et indignitate fortunae male acceptos, tuae humanitatis officia extant: ego vel solus amplissimum argumentum esse possum, qualis quantusque semper fuerit tuus ille singularis morum candor, et melioris vitae non omittenda constitutio. Tu enim vix bene cognitum, et diversis fortunae flatibus objectum adeo benigne, et re, et consilio fovisti: ut tibi jure acceptum ferre debeam, quod etiam nunc res nostrae incolumes stent maxime: quas in extremum fere discrimen, invidia ipsa cum adduxisset, tuum Petrum laborantem, velut facto gradu, sustentasti servasti, asservisti. Nec licet quoque silentio nunc praeterire, qua animi honestate, tua nos opera uti volveris: quosque labores ultro in rem nostram impenderis. Profecto si ut conatum praestitisti, ita coeptis fortuna respondisset, meliore vento navigaremus: quem in hac maris tranquillitate confido brevi non defuturum. His igitur tot tuae humanitatis beneficiis affectus, magnopere sollicitor quo pacto tuis in me meritis gratiam referre possim. Et quamvis in solidum atque aliqua ex parte haud fieri posse satis id intelligam, nihilominus tamen adjuncto aino impense laborandum est, ut sic saltem tibi homini longe omnium gratissimo interiores bonae mentis affectus ostendantur. Quamobrem aliquot nostras musicae artis cantiones tibi ut patrono dicamus, Remigi humanissime, nostrae erga te benevolentiae testimonium fidelissimum: quas cum amici pene quotidianis a me convitiis postularent, neque eas, citra magnum laborem, quis facile (omnibus obsequendo) exscribere posset, neque etiam id consilii foret, eorum expectationem diutius protrahere, operae precium me facturum putavi, eas sub tui nominis tutela praelo committere: quo facilius omnium voluntati satisfacerem, et hoc officio simul omnes amantissimos mei demereri possem. Neque id tibi mirum videri debet, si quae tibi, itidem et illis privatim dicata sunt, omnibus communiter exposuerim, quin omnino par est, ut quem pari amore complectimini, ita ejusdem vigiliis gaudere et oblectari possitis. Quae si vobis gratae fortassis videbuntur, aequi bonique velim consulatis. Si minus tamen jucundae: dedisse me operam, conatumque omnem praestitisse, quaeso, sufficiat qui sicut plerisque in rebus vel solus laudi datur. Ita eum ad veniam mihi libenter speraverim profuturum. Vale.

EGIDII DE SERMISY AD P[ETRUM] MANCHICOURTIUM

Delphin per siculos evexit Ariona fluctus
  Tangentem Aoniae plectra sonora lyrae
Muri olim Thebes Amphionis arte manebant:
  Junctaque saxa suis quaeque reposta locis.
Ad styga festinans Orpheus dulcedine movit
  Tergeminum, Eurydices victus amore, canem.

Petre tamen, Phoebo vel certent judice, vincis,
Et tua nescio quid cantio majus habet
Cui dulcedo omnis, cedant et pocula divum,
Si quid et Ambrosia dulcius esse potest
Haec sunt fida tui studii monumenta, nec ullum
Invida posteritas est habitura parem.

[From **85**; also in **119.**]

10a.

Pierre de Manchicourt greets the very upright and learned Remy Roussel the Honest, most worthy canon of the distinguished church of Tours.

Those men did not err, at least in my opinion, most erudite Stoic Remy, who were of the opinion that all things which are brought forth on earth were created for the use of men, but that men were created for the sake of men, so that, just among themselves, some could be useful to others by an exchange of courtesies. Considering this, Chremes (that well-known character in the plays of Terence) cleverly replied to the reprimanding old man Menedemus in this way: "I am a man; nothing pertaining to man do I consider foreign to me." And that is the truth, because God had formed man naked and frail, so that He might place a more distinguished mark on man as being well provided with wisdom; in particular, He implanted this sense of duty so that men might always look after, love, and cherish each other, and so that against all dangers they might receive and offer aid to each other. The supreme bond, then, between men is their common humanity. Since this very humanity (not to mention your spiritual and intellectual endowments) had reached the hearts of many men, it was joined with great intimacy. Let me for the time being keep silent about the kindnesses which your humanity has bestowed on all learned men as well as on those who have been badly treated by the outrages of fortune; for even I alone can stand as more than ample proof of both the quality and the extent of your constant and unique sincerity of character—and let me not forget how you provide a better life. For example: I, a man not very well known to you and one buffeted by the countless blasts of fortune, was so kindly supported by you, both with money and advice, that I rightly owe you an accounting for the extreme soundness of my present circumstances. Although malice itself almost brought those circumstances into extreme danger, you supported, preserved, and attended to your striving Pierre just as if he were in an established position. Nor is it right to bypass in silence your nobility of spirit in wanting to employ us in your service; of your own accord you paid advantageously for these labors. If fortune had given your undertakings an answer comparable to the efforts you have expended, we would surely be sailing with the breeze of prosperity; and I am confident that it will be some time before that breeze fails on this calm sea. And so, touched by the numerous kind acts of your humanity, I am quite upset as to how I can possibly repay your services to me. And although I realize that for this to be done with fitting thoroughness is in some sense impossible, yet I must at least make a whole-hearted effort to show you, who are by far my dearest friend, my profound feelings of good will toward you. Let me therefore dedicate to you, as my patron, several of my compositions, my very generous Remy; they are a most faithful proof of my feeling of good will for you. Although my friends kept up virtually a daily clamor asking me for these pieces, there was none who could easily copy them, except with great labor, and still please everyone. Since I thought it unadvisable to keep people waiting any longer, I felt it would be worthwhile to entrust them to the press under the protection of your name; thus it would be easy to satisfy the expectations of all and, by this service, to be able to oblige all my best friends at once. And you should not think it odd but, rather, quite appropriate if I have placed before the general public pieces which were privately dedicated to both you and my friends; I explained jointly to all that it is entirely suitable: just as you embrace a person in mutual love, so you could rejoice and take delight in his waking hours. And if these pieces are by chance to your liking, please be fair and honest in your consideration of them. If, however, they are not too pleasing, let it, I beg you, be enough that I have taken pains and summoned forth my utmost efforts. Just as he, even alone, is praised in most undertakings, so I might gladly expect that he would be favorable to the indulgence I seek. Farewell.

Gilles de Sermisy to Pierre de Manchicourt

A dolphin carried Arion through the Sicilian billows
  As he was plucking the tuneful strings of the Muses' lyre.
Once the art of Amphion made Thebes' walls stand firm;
  The stones were joined, each placed in its proper spot.
Overcome by love of Eurydice, Orpheus, hurrying toward the Styx,
  Moved Cerberus by his charm.

But, my Pierre, let them have a contest, even with Apollo as judge,
  And you will emerge victorious.
Your music has something great in it, second to no charm, not even to the goblets of the gods,
  If there can be anything more sweet than ambrosia.
These are faithful memorials of your pains,
  And envious ages to come are not likely to have any equal.

11. 1540

Attaingnant and Jullet named "Libraires et imprimeurs de musique du Roy"

(Letters patent do not survive; first inclusion of the title for both men is found in an edition of the *Sixiesme livre* with revised title, **86,** bearing the date "1539," like the first edition, but probably issued in 1540 because some publications dated 1540 do not bear the new title.)

12. January 1, 1541

Baptism of a daughter, Claude, born to Germaine Attaingnant and Hubert Jullet

Du 1er Janvier 1540, Claude, fille de Mr Hubert Juillet, maitre imprimeur, et Germaine Atteignant. Parrain: Pierre Alleaume, bonnetier. Marraines: Denise Begin, femme de Monsieur Vincent Mustel, docteur en médecine; et Antoinette Adam, femme de Nicholas Barbette, tavernier.

[Parish-registers of Saint-Benoît, No. 1; extracted in the Fichier Laborde, Bib. Nat. MS. nouv.acq.fr. 12127, no. 36.626]

13. January 31, 1541

Baptism of a daughter, Jeanne, born to Marie Attaingnant and Pierre Aleaume

Lundi. 31 Janvier 1540, Jehanne, fille de Pierre Aleaume, bonnetier, demourant sur le pont Notre Dame. Parrain: maistre Regnault Aleaume, chirurgien; Marraines: Jehanne Magdelain, femme de Pierre Petit, marchand de vin, Claude Pigouchet, femme de Pierre Atignant, imprimeur de musique.

[Parish-registers of St.-Jacques-de-la-boucherie, no. 3; extracted in the Fichier Laborde, Bib. Nat. MS. nouv.acq.fr. 12046, no. 1030.]

14. 1542.

Pierre Certon addresses and thanks Claudin de Sermisy

Petrus Certonius, Phonascus, Sancti Sacelli Parisiensis Claudio de Sermisy submagistro regii Sacelli foelicitatem perpetuam exoptat.

Habunde magnam animo laetitiam antea conceperam (Claudi musicorum doctissime et doctissimorum amicissime) qui ita comiter mecum egisses ut amicitiam nostram non aspernarere. Nam si rei nullius thesaurus putetur jucundior quam amicorum (quoniam ubi amici ibi opes) videbar mihi vel Croeso locupletior, cui amicus contigisses sine fuco. Nuper vero cumulus laetitiae major accrevit, cum rescivissem modulos meos musicos fuisse non mediocriter laudatos abs te viro nunquam satis laudato. Cujus judicium cum in caeteris, tum in re musica pluris fecerim, quam vel Amphionis vel Orphei. Neque verbis apud te exprimere possim quam impense mihi arriserim qui tam candide de meis naeniis censueris ut pene pro Certonio factus sim Suffenus. Itaque vel si uni tibi placerent nostrae quisquiliae facile tamen patere caeteris displicere. Neque diutius delitescent in capsulis, cum visum sit tibi ut in hominum aures veniant. Venient autem ea lage ut tuo patrocinio tutiores bonis auspiciis in publico versentur. Quae fiducia si me non fallat, et si huic meo partui tuus dexter genius profuerit, dum foetura gregem suppleverit aureus esto. Vive et Vale.

[From **104.**]

14a.

Pierre Certon, Musician of the Sainte-Chapelle of Paris, wishes eternal prosperity to Claudin de Sermisy, submagistrate of the Royal Chapel.

My heart had previously been extremely happy (Claudin, great scholar among musicians and great friend of scholars) that you had treated me so kindly in not spurning our friendship. For if the treasure that is one's friends should be considered more pleasing than all else (for friends are a bulwark of wealth), then I would consider myself wealthier than Croesus himself, since it was in friendship that you so openly had reached out to me. Recently, however, the extent of my happiness became even greater, when I had learned that my musical pieces had received no small amount of praise from you, who have yourself never received the praise due you. Your judgment in music—not to mention other matters—I have valued more than I would that of an Amphion or Orpheus. My words could not express for you how greatly pleased I was at your very candid judgment of my pieces: it has made me a veritable Suffenus. In short, even though you were the only one who liked our humble trifles, I should still find it an easy matter to put up with the cavil of others. No longer will these pieces lie hidden in my closet, since you have decided that they deserve a general hearing. But they will be heard only on one condition: that, guaranteed by your patronage, they be circulated before the public under good auspices. Unless my faith in this method of publication deceive me, and if, while my travail has been adding to the flock, the kindness of your guiding spirit will have proved of advantage to these my musical offspring, then you shall surely be golden.

May you live long and be well.

15. September 16, 1542

Baptism of a daughter, Marie, born to Germaine Attaingnant and Hubert Jullet. God-parents are Pierre Certon and the wife of Mathurin le Beau

Du 16^{e} Septembre, 1542, Marie, fille de M. Hubert Jullet, libraire, et de Germaine Attaingnant. Parrain: Maitre Pierre Certon, Maitre des enfants de la Ste Chapelle. Marraines: Marie de la Rue, femme de Mathurin le Beau, procureur; Jaqueline La Caille.

[Parish-registers of Saint-Benoît, No. 1; extracted in the Fichier Laborde, Bib. Nat. MS. nouv.acq. fr. 12127, no. 36.682]

16. 1543

Second renewal of 1531 privilege for six years

Avec prorogation du privilege du Roy, de nouvel obtenu par ledit Attaingnant pour les livres ja par luy imprimez et qu'il imprimera cy apres jusques a six ans.

[From the title-page of **114.**]

17. September 13, 1543

Attaingnant cedes to Aleaume and Jullet the rights that his late wife, Claude Pigouchet inherited from her sister, the late Germaine Pigouchet, wife of Poncet Le Preux, in consequence of books received by Le Preux from Attaingnant. Aleaume and Jullet assume funeral expenses of Germaine Pigouchet, and promise to settle with Jean Beguin who has claim to half of the estate of Germaine Pigouchet, in the name of his wife, Collette Pigouchet

Honnorable homme Pierre Atignan, marchant libraire, bourgeois de Paris, demourant rue de la Herpe, confesse avoir ceddé, quicté, transporté et délaissé en tout a tousjours a honnorables personnes Pierre Aleaulme, marchant bonnetier, Marye Attignan, sa femme, et a maître Hubert Jullet et Germaine Atignan, sa femme, filles dud. Pierre Atignan et de feue Claude Pigouchet, jadis sa femme, lesd. femmes absentes et lesd. Aleaulme et Jullet ad ce présens et acceptans tant pour eulx que pour leursd. femmes, leurs hoirs, tous telz droictz qui aud. ceddant a cause de lad. deffuncte Claude Pigouchet, sa femme, qui a esté héritiere pour moictié de feue Germaine Pigouchet, jadis femme de Poncet le Preux, pevent . . . compecter et apartenir tous et chacuns les biens meubles, debtes, créances et autres biens généralement quelzconques demourez apres le déces et trespas de lad. deffunte Germaine Pigouchet, seur de lad. deffuncte Claude Pigouchet, de laquelle Germaine icelle deffunte Claude Pigouchet a esté héritiere pour moictié comme dict est, quelque part et en quelque lieu que lesd. biens seront trouvez et assis, ensemblement ceddé et transporté la somme de XXXI l. XIIs. t., restant de la somme de XLVIII l. VIIIs. t. a luy deue par led. le Preux, a cause de marchandise de livres par led. Attignan baillez et délivrez aud. Poncet le Preux; pareillement leur a ceddé et transporté toutes les actions demandées et poursuittes qu'il avoit et povoit avoir a cause de ce qui est, tant a elle que dud. le Preux que tous autres . . . Cestz cession et transport faictz a la charge que lesd. Aleaulme et Jullet ont promis et seront tenuz acquiter led. ceddant de toutes et chacunes les debtes, obsecques et funérailles, en quoy led. Attignan eust peu et pourroit, est tenu a cause de ce . . . Fait et passé triple comme dessus.

Honnorable homme Jehan Began, marchant, bourgeois de Paris, lesd. Aleaulme et Jullet confessent avoir respectivement promis et promectent l'un d'eulx a l'autre de fournir . . . aux fraiz et mises qu'il conviendra, chacun en leur regard, fournir et frayer en certain proces intenté allencontre de Poncet le Preux, pour raison de la succession de feue Germaine Pigouchet, jadis femme dud. Poncet le Preux, de laquelle led. Began a cause de Collette Pigouchet, sa femme, est héritiere pour moictié et lesd. Alleaulme et Jullet, tant en leurs noms a cause de leurs femmes que comme ayans droict par transport de Pierre Atignan, leur pere, pour l'autre moictié . . . Faict et passé triple comme dessus.

[Arch. Nat., Minutier central, LXXIII, 3; F. Lesure, "Pierre Attaingnant: notes et documents," *Musica Disciplina* III (1949), 34–40, no. 3.]

18. March 31, 1544

Agreement between Attaingnant, Aleaume, and Jullet to recognize the inventory of goods made at the house in the Rue de la Harpe, June 11–25, 1543, after the decease of Claude Pigouchet. Aleaume and Jullet each inherit household goods, printing and founding materials, music-books and other books; not included in the division of goods are a certain quantity of Missals of the Noyon usage, in the possession of Arthus Sandrin at Noyon. Aleaume receives his part in cash

Du XXXI et dernier jour de mars mil V^{c} XLIII avant Pasques. Furent présens en leurs personnes honnorables hommes Pierre Attignant, marchant libraire et imprimeur de musique, bourgeois de Paris, d'une part, Pierre Aleaulme, marchant bonnetier, a cause de Marye Attignant, sa femme, et Hubert Jullet, aussi imprimeur de musicque, a cause de Germaine Attignant, sa femme, lesd. Marye et Germaine, héritieres de feue Claude Pigouchet, leur mere, jadis femme dud. Pierre Attignant, leur pere, d'autre part, lesquelz . . . confesserent . . . qu'ilz respectivement auroient et ont bien agréable ung inventaire faict faire a leur requeste le lundy XI jour de juing l'an mil V^c^ quarente troys par Nicolas Dupuys et Denis Dryet, freppiers et priseurs de biens jurez a Paris, et autres dénommez en la titulation dud. inventaire des biens demourez apres le déces et trespas de lad. deffuncte et qui estoient entre led. Attignant et lad. deffuncte au jour de son trespas, lequel inventaire a la requeste des dessusd. Pierre Attignant, Aleaulme et Jullet, apres que led. Attignant a affermé ne scavoir autres biens apartenant a la succession de lad. deffuncte Claude Pigouchet, jadis sa femme, que ceulx inventoriez aud. inventaire, a esté signé des notaires au Chastellet de Paris soubzsignez, voullans et consentans par lesd. parties que led. inventaire vaille et sortisse son plain et entier effect, force et vertu, et comme s'il avoit esté par deux notaires du Chastellet de Paris . . . se sont tenuz et tiennent pour bien contens, comme d'inventaire bien, deuement, justement et solempnellement faict . . . Lesd. Aleaulme et Jullet confesse avoir eu et receu dud. Attignant, leurd. beau-pere, chacun leur juste part et portion de tous et chacuns les biens meubles, ustancilles d'hostel, d'imprimerye, fonderye, livres de musicque et autres livres, biens meubles, debtes, lettres et créances . . . Iceulx Aleaulme et Jullet pour leursd. portions se sont tenuz et tiennent pour bien contens et en ont quicté et quictent led. Attignant . . . , a la réservation touteffois de certaine quantité de *Messelz* usage de Noyon estans en la possession de maitre Arthus Sandrin, aud. Noyon, et d'une ceddulle monitoire a la somme de cent LXIIII l. XIXs. t. . . . Fet et passé triple comme dessus.

Led. Aleaulme confesse avoir eu et receu dud. Attignant la somme la quarente sept livres huict solz neuf deniers t., assavoir la somme de XXXV l. XVIs. t., pour telle part et portion des ustancilles cy apres déclarez qui luy apartenoit a cause de lad. Marye, sa femme, par la succession de lad. deffunte Claude Pigouchet. C'est assavoir les ustancilles d'imprimerye, comme des grosses presses, chassis, frisquettes, autres nottes, casses, matieres a fondre, lesd. livres et nottes, et de tous les ustancilles de fonderye ayant fourneaux, cuillieres, estocz, lymes, marteaulx et enclumeaulx servans au mestier d'imprimerye et fonderye qui furent prisez et inventoriez par l'inventaire qui en fut faict le lundi XXV jour de juing mil V^c^ XLIII, d'une part, et unze livres douze solz neuf deniers tournois, aussi pour telle part et portion que a cause que dessus luy povoit apartenir en autres ustancilles d'imprimerye et fonderye, comme poinçons, matrices, moslles a fondre lettres et nottes, et autres ustancilles d'imprimerye et fonderye qui, lors dud. inventaire, furent oublyez a inventorier . . . Fet et passé double comme dessus.

[Arch. Nat., Minutier central, LXXIII, 4; Lesure, "Notes et documents," no. 4.]

19. April 18, 1545

Germaine, widow of Jullet, and Attaingnant, acting as guardians for Jullet's children, secure promise that some money paid for wheat not delivered will be repaid

Furent presens et comparurent en leurs personnes honnorable homme Pierre Atygnant, libraire, bourgeois de Paris, demourant rue de la Harpe, et Germaine Atignant, veufve de feu Hubert Jullet, en son vivant imprimeur et libraire a Paris, demourant en lad. rue de la Harpe, en leurs noms, led. Atignant et veufve comme tuteurs et curateurs des enffans myneurs d'ans dud. deffunt Hubert Jullet et de lad. vefve, d'une part, et Françoys Charbonnyeres, laboureur demourant a Saint-Germain-des-Prez-lez-Paris, a présent prisonnyer es prison du Chastelet de Paris, d'autre part, disant lesd. Pierre Atignant et Germaine Atignant esd. noms que pour le paiement de quatre muys de bled, froment venduz ausd. Atignant et Jullet par led. Charbonnyeres et une nommé Julle Bersan . . . venduz moyennant la comme de cent livres . . . led. Charbonnyeres, personne retenue es prison, et sa femme de luy auctorisée en ceste partie, qui s'est dit aagée de XXV ans dans le moys de may mil V^{c} quarente quatre dernier passé, et vénérable et discrette personne maitre Vallentin Charbonnyeres, prebtre, demourant a Moyssy l'évesque, ad ce présent ont confessé et confessent debvoir bien et loyaulment ausd. Atignant et vefve . . . la somme de six vingtz livres t. pour les causes cy-apres déclairées, laquelle somme ilz ont promis et seront tenuz, promectent et payent chacun pour le tout . . .

[Arch. Nat., Min. centr., CXXII, 1312; Lesure, "Notes et Documents", no. 5.]

20. April 21, 1545

Marie Lescalloppier, wife of Attaingnant, renews her title to a house in the Rue de Casset, Saint-Germain des Prés

Honnorable femme Marye Lescailloppier, a présent femme de honnorable homme Pierre Attaignant, marchant libraire, bourgeois de Paris, et avec lequel elle dict n'estre commune en biens, confesse que au lieu de Nicollas Junel, mercier demourant a Paris, elle est a présent détempteresse et propriéteresse d'une maison et petit jardin servant de court, le lieu ainsi qu'il se comporte assis a Sainct-Germain-des-Prez-les-Paris, rue de Casset . . . sur laquelle maison dessud. déclarée Raoulline Cheradame, vefve de feu Estienne Rolliers, a ce présent a droict de prendre et percepvoire par chacun an a tousjours aux quatres termes a Paris accostumez quatre livres tournois de rente . . . Faict l'an mil V^{c} XLV, le mercredi XXI jour d'avril.

[Arch. Nat., Min. centr. XLIX, 30; Lesure, "Notes et Documents," no. 6.]

21. March 22, 1546

Marie Lescalloppier renews her title to the house in Saint-Germain des Prés

Du mardi XXII jour de mars V^{e} XLV. Honnorable femme Marye Lescallopier, femme de honnorable homme Pierre Attaignant, marchant imprimeur, bourgeois de Paris, confesse quicte aux ayans droict de maitre Anthoine Dumesnil, est de présent détenteresse et propriéterresse d'une maison, court et jardin, le tout cloz de muraille, tant alentour le lieu comme il se comporte assis a St-Germain-des-Prez-lez-Paris au lieu du *Casset,* tenant d'une part aux héritiers et ayans cause feu Honnoré Chevalier, d'autre a Guillaume Mareschal, maitre scelier lormier, bourgeois de Paris, a cause de l'acquisition par lui fete de Ysrael Roze, aboutissant d'un bout aud. Mareschal et d'autre bout aux héritiers feu maitre Jehan Cherondance, led. Mareschal comme ayant droit dud. Roze a droict de prandre et percepvoir par chacun an . . . quarante cinq s. t. de rente.

[Arch. Nat., Min. centr., LXXIII, 7; Lesure, "Notes et Documents," no. 7.]

22. 1547

Third renewal of the 1531 privilege for six years

Avec prorogation du privilege du Roy, de nouvel obtenu par ledit Attaingnant pour les livres ja par luy imprimez et qu'il imprimera cy apres jusques a six ans.

[From **148;** see also **149–151.**]

NOTE: Accession of Henry II in April, 1547 may explain why Attaingnant sought renewal of his privilege two years before it would have expired, in 1549.

23. December 7, 1547

Contract of marriage between Germaine Attaingnant, Jullet's widow, and Jean Matheau. Attaingnant promises to pay 2,000 livres tournois to the couple in settling the inheritance of Jullet

Furent présens en leurs personnes Jehan Matheau, marchant boucher, demourant a St-Germain-des-Prez-lez-Paris, pour luy et en son nom, d'une part, et Germaine Attaignant, vefve de feu maitre Hubert Jullet et fille de honnorable homme Pierre Attaignant, marchant bourgeois de Paris, aussi pour elle et en son nom, d'autre; lesquelles parties . . . en la présence et du consentement dud.

Attaignant, pere de lad. Germaine, honnorables personnes Jehan Begin, marchant bourgeois de Paris, et Nicole Pigouchet, sa femme, tante de lad. Germaine, et de Pierre Aleaulme, beau-frere d'icelle Germaine et aussi en la présence de honnorable homme Pierre Tubeuf, marchant boucher, bourgeois de Paris, demourant aud. St.-Germain-des-Prez, beau-frere dud. Matheau, recongneurent et confesserent avoir promis et promectent prandre l'un d'eulx l'autre par loy et nom de mariage . . . en faveur et contemplation duquel mariage led. Pierre Attaignant a promis . . . payer ausd. futurs maryez . . . la somme de deux mil livres tournois . . . et ce pour tous et chacuns les biens meubles, debtes et créances, de quelque qualité qu'ilz soient, héritages, rentes et arrérages d'icelles qui pouroient et peuvent comporter et apartenir a lad. Germaine a cause de la communaulté d'entre elle et led. deffunt maitre Hubert Jullet, jadis son mary, assis tant au pays de Bourgoigne que ailleurs, avec les arrérages, deniers et despens a lad. vefve deubz par Poncet le Preux, a cause de la maison en laquelle il est demourant, la part et portion a lad. Germaine apartenant en lad. maison, touteffois demourant en proportion a lad. Germaine; desquelz biens meubles, héritages, rentes, arrérages et deniers a lad. vefve apartenant a cause de lad. communaulté comme dit est, lesd. futurs maryez feirent et par ces présentes font cession et transport aud. Pierre Attaignant au nom et comme tuteur et curateur des enffans myneurs d'ans dud. deffunct Jullet et de lad. Germaine, . . . Et oultre, moyennant lad. somme, ont iceulx futurs maryez ceddé et transporté aud. Attaignant oud. nom de tuteur la somme de cent solz t. de rente a lad. vefve apartenant de son propre et icelle deue par Guillaume Tron et Nicolas Attaignant, demourant a Saigy, pres Ponthoise, pour en joyr par led. Attaignant pour et au nom d'iceulx myneurs . . . Et partant a led. Matheau doué et doue lad. Germaine, sa future espouse de la somme de six cens soixante et six livres t. en douaire préfix et pour une fois payer . . . Et ne sera led. Attaignant tenu rendre aucun compte ausd. myneurs dud. deffunct Jullet et de lad. vefve des arréages des rentes a eulx apartenant . . . Faict et passé multiple l'an mil cinq cens quarentes sept, le mercredi septiesme jour de décembre.

[Arch. Nat., Min. centr., LXXIII, 11; Lesure, "Notes et Documents," no. 8.]

24. January 2, 1548

Rent-contract for the house in the Rue de la Harpe for nine years

Bail passé à Pierre Attaingnant, imprimeur, devant Cruce, notaire à Paris, pour neuf ans du jour de Pasques 1548, moyennant quarante quatre livres de loyer.

[18th-century copy of the original contract, Archives Nationales MM 391 Liasse XXII, no. 3.]

25. July 7, 1548

Sale by Pierre Chalemeaulx, Esme Chevillart, and Nicole Ezelin of the rights to 25l.t. worth of rent annually to Attaingnant

Pierre Chalemeaulx, advocat a Herny-le-Chastel, y demourant, Esme Chevillart, advocat en la Court de Parlement a Paris, et Nicole Ezelin, procureur au Chastelet de Paris, confessent avoir vendu et constitué . . . a honorable homme sire Pierre Attaignant, marchant libraire, imprimeur de musicque, bourgeois de Paris, a ce présent achepteur et acquesteur pour luy, ses hoirs, vingt cinq livres t. monnaies courantes et présentes de rente annuelle . . . , et speciallement y a led. Ezelin obligé et ypothecqué, oblige et ypothecque une maison a luy apartenant . . . rue de la Harpe, ou pend pour enseigne *Le Pillier vert* . . .

[Arch. Nat., Min. Centr., LXXIII, 12; Lesure, "Notes et Documents," no. 9.]

26. October 3, 1551

Attaingnant renews the title to the house in the Rue Casset, Saint-Germain des Prés, acting in the name of Clément de Cot. Loys Bocart has the right to take 65 s.t. in annual rent on the same house

Honnorable homme Pierre Attaignant, marchant bourgeois de Paris, au nom et comme procureur de maitre Clément de Cot, praticien suyvant le Grand Conseil, confesse oud. nom estre detempteur et propriétaire d'une maison, court et jardin . . . a St-Germain-des-Prez-lez-Paris, au lieu dict *Casset,* qui fut et appartint a Marye Lescaloppier, femme dud. Attaignant . . . , et que sur lad. maison et lieu honnorable homme Loys Bocart, sergent a verge, . . . a droict de prendre et prenoyt par chacun an au jour St-Remy soixante et cinq solz t. de rente annuelle . . . .

[Arch. Nat., Min. centr., LXXIII, 45; Lesure, "Notes et Documents," no. 10.]

27. December 26, 1553

Marriage contract between Marie Attaingnant and Gilles Gourbin

Contrat de mariage de Gilles Gourbin, libraire, rue Saint-Jean-de-Latran, avec Marie Attaignant, veuve de Pierre Alleaume, bonnetier. Témoins: Michel de Vascosan et Oudin Petit, libraires-jurés, naguères maîtres de Gourbin, et Guillaume Cavellat, libraire.

[Arch. Nat., Y 106, fol. 390^v^; Philippe Renouard, *Documents sur les imprimeurs, libraires* (Paris, 1901), p. 111.]

28. June 25, 1554

Sale by Jean Matheau to Marie Lescalloppier of various goods, including missals, manuals, breviaries and Books of Hours, all of the Noyon usage, and Books of Hours of the Paris usage, as well as large motets, large Masses, and ruled paper, for 210 l.t.

Honnorable homme Jehan Matheau, marchant boucher, demourant a St-Germain-des-Prez-lez-Paris, confesse avoir vendu et promect garentir a honnorable femme Marye Lescalloppier, bourgeoise de Paris, vefve de feu Pierre Attaignant, en son vivant marchant libraire, imprimeur de musicque, aussi bourgeois de Paris, plusieurs sortes de marchandises comme Messelz, manuelz, Brevieres et Heures, le tout usage de Noyon, et Heures de Paris, grans Motetz, grans livres de messe et papier reglé que lad. vefve a confessé avoir eu et receu dud. Matheau et icellui avoir en sa possession pour en joyr. Ceste vente faicte moyennant la somme de deux cens dix livres t. que pour ce lad. vefve en promect . . . payer aud. Matheau en argent content . . . .

[Arch. Nat., Min. centr., LXXIII, 20; Lesure, "Notes et Documents," no. 11.]

29. June 17, 1558

Pierre Jullet, grandson of Attaingnant, is under the guardianship of Guillaume Guiolin, bookseller

Guillaume Guiolin, libraire rue St-Jean-de-Latran, est tuteur et curateur de Pierre Jullet, fils mineur de feu Hubert Jullet et de Germaine Attaingnant, jadis son épouse.

[Arch. Nat., Min. centr., LXXIII, 52; Lesure, "Notes et Documents," no. 12.]

30. August 17, 1567

Marie and Pierre Jullet, children of Germaine Attaingnant, sell their share in the house of Le Preux at the sign of the Wolf

Jean Robeline, bonnetier, et Marie Juillet, sa femme, vendent à Gilbert Chapelle, banquier, propriétaire de la maison voisine, un huitième de la maison du Loup, rue Saint-Jacques; les autres propriétaires de la maison sont les ayant-cause de feu Poncet Le Preux, Vincent Mustel, docteur en médecine, et Gilles Gourbin, libraire, à cause de sa femme. Pierre Juillet, compagnon-apothicaire, avait vendu sa part, le 17 juillet précédent, à Jean Robeline.

[Arch. Nat., S 904, fols. 191^{v}–192; Renouard, *Documents sur les imprimeurs*, p. 169.]

31. August 24, 1569

Marriage contract between Catherine Attaingnant and Jean Charron the younger

Contrat de mariage de Catherine Attagnant, fille de feu Pierre Attagnant, marchand, bourgeois de Paris, et de Marie Lescalloppier, bourgeoise de Paris, et de Jean Charron le jeune, maître imprimeur demeurant rue des Carmes à l'image Saint-Jean.

[Arch. Nat., Min. centr., LXXIII, 36; Philippe Renouard, *Imprimeurs et libraires parisiens du xvie siècle* (Paris, 1964), Vol. I, pp. 117–118.]

32. 1571

Marie Lescalloppier is taxed six pounds on the sum of 300,000 pounds

La veuve Pierre Attignant, rue de la Harpe, est taxée à 6 livres au don de 300,000 livres.

[Bib. Nat., ms. fr. 11692, fols. 286 & 391^v^; Renouard, *Documents sur les imprimeurs,* p. 3.]

33. November 15, 1572

Agreement to a rent division between Gilles Gourbin and Marie Lescalloppier, acting for Pierre II Attaingnant, aged twenty-two years

Gilles Gourbin, libraire de Paris, et Marie Attaignant sa femme, héritiere pour moitié de Catherine Attaignant sa soeur, femme de Jehan Charon le Jeune, imprimeur, et Marie Lescallopier, bourgeoise de Paris, veuve de Pierre Attaignant, tutrice de Pierre Attaignant son fils agé de 22 ans, héritier pour l'autre moitié de ladite defunte le partagent 15 l. de rente.

[Arch. Nat., Min. centr., LXXIII, 39.]

34. May 18, 1573

Public sale of Le Preux's house "du Loup" and division of the sum between the descendants, including Marie Attaingnant, the children of Le Preux and of Béguin

Répartition du prix de la maison du Loup, vendue aux enchères publiques et achetée par Etienne Chapelle: Vincent Mustel, docteur-régent à la Faculté de médecine, pour lui, Claude, Vincent et Nicolas, enfants qu'il a eus de Denyse

Béguin, sa femme, reçoit 1,250 l.t. pour un quart; Jacques Chappelain, notaire, et Marguerite Le Preux, sa femme, à cause d'elle, et au nom de Jean Le Preux qui était aussi adjudicataire de la part de François Le Preux, leur frère, reçoivent pour la moitié 2,500 l.t., Gilles Gourbin, libraire et Marie Attignant, sa femme, à cause d'elle reçoivent pour un huitième 625 l.t., et Gilbert Chapelle, banquier, aussi pour un huitième, la même somme.

[Arch. Nat., S 904, fol. 197; Renouard, *Documents sur les imprimeurs*, p. 169.]

35. August 6, 1573

Rent contract for the house in the Rue de la Harpe for nine years

Bail passé à Marie L'Escalopier veuve dudit Pierre Attaingnant, devant Philippe L'Amyral, Notaire à Paris, pour neuf ans du premier Octobre 1573, moyennant 60 livres de loyer.

[18th-century copy from the original document, Arch. Nat. MM 391 Liasse XXII, no. 4.]

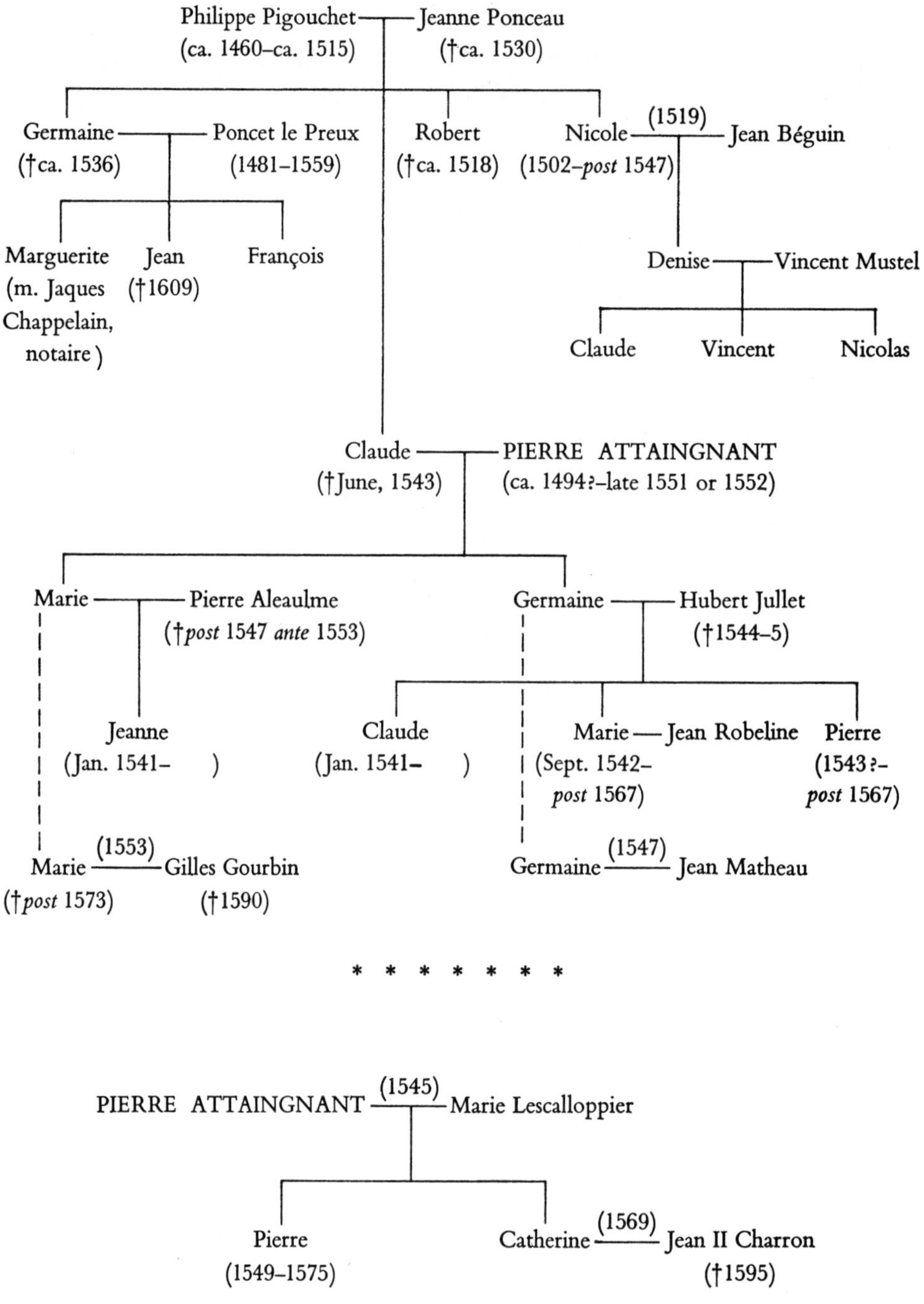

14 Genealogical chart

INDEX TO THE HISTORICAL STUDY

INDEX TO THE HISTORICAL STUDY

INDEX TO THE HISTORICAL STUDY

INDEX TO THE HISTORICAL STUDY

INDEX TO THE HISTORICAL STUDY

INDEX TO THE HISTORICAL STUDY

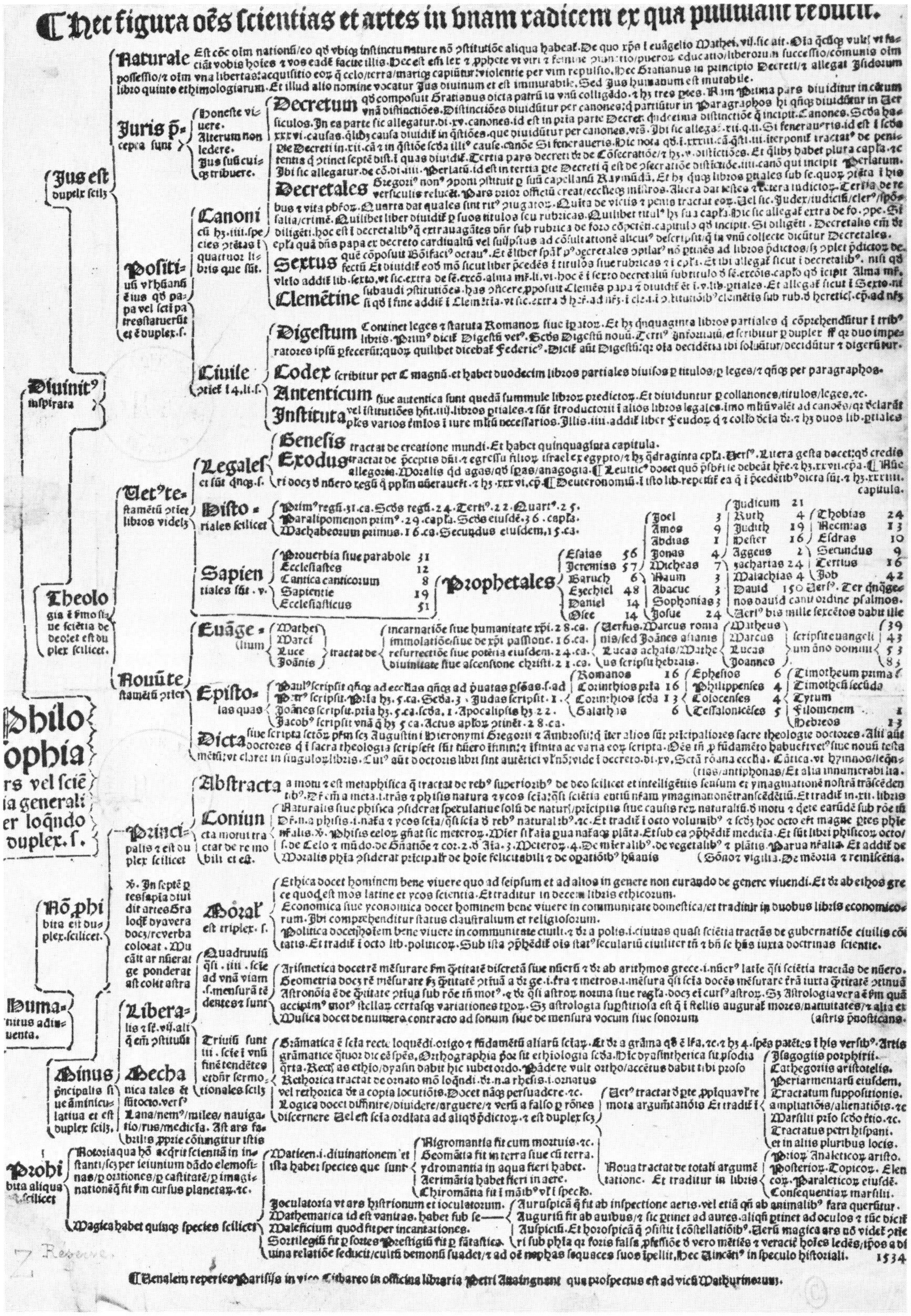

I *Philosophia*, didactic broadside printed in 1534 **(58)**. By courtesy of the Bibliothèque Nationale, Paris.

II Francis I with his sons and counselors. By courtesy of the Musée Condé, Chantilly. (*Photo Giraudon.*)

III John Cardinal of Lorraine (1503–1550). Anonymous oil portrait, by courtesy of the Musée Lorraine, Nancy.

CAPVT .XXI.

AETITES LAPIS, &c. Eſt lapis velúti prægnans cum quatitur alio in vtero ſonante. Grauidis continet partus, cum ſunt lubricæ vuluæ, & parum tenaces ſi ſiniſtro brachio alligetur furem deprehendit, authore Dioſcorid. libro quinto. MVSEA, &c. Muſeum opus, quod in ædificijs ex pumicibus dependens quod fit arte ad reddēdam imaginem. Pumices enim eroſos Pumicea vocant. Eſt etiam Muſeum muſis dicatum domicilium. Aetites

CAPVT .XXIIII.

CALCIS ET MEDICINA, &c. Fit potiſſimum è glebis lapidum crematis, nec non è vili marmore vis omni calci in commune ignea, mordens, adurens & cruſtas inducens abſu= mit, diſſipat, vlcera ad cicatricem perducit, authore Dioſcori. libro quinto. Gypſum autem habet vim adſtringendi, ſangui nis eruptiones cohibet at'que ſudores, ſed potum ſtrangulat. Calx.

CAPVT .XXV.

PAVIMENTA ORIGINEM, &c. Victruuius de his ſic agit. Aſaroton oecon ad Theatri vſum habentur, quo ſe populus recipiebat cum imber repētinus ludos interpellabat. Pauimenta certè, aut ſub tecto, aut ſub dio. Subdialia veteres poſt coaxationem filicem potius quàm paleam inducebant, deinde ſtatumen ex ruderatione, qui de his plura volet, adeat Victruuium. Pauimē ta.

CAPVT .XXVII.

IGNIS ACCIPIT, &c. Hoc parum habet nubili, putarim tamen male legi, vbi legitur. Vt licet viderint gla= diatores cum deluſerint, &c. Legerim deluxati ſint. Nam paulò ſuperius dixit. Inde enim cinis luxatis potus medetur. Ignis.

Commentariorum in Triceſimumſextum Plinij Secundi,
Naturalis hiſtoriæ, ſcriptoris argutiſſimi,
FINIS.

nn iiij

IV (above) Page from a Pliny Commentary published by Poncet Le Preux in 1530. By courtesy of the Plantin-Moretus Museum, Antwerp.

V A page from the Noyon Missal (**142**). By courtesy of the Trustees of the British Museum, London.

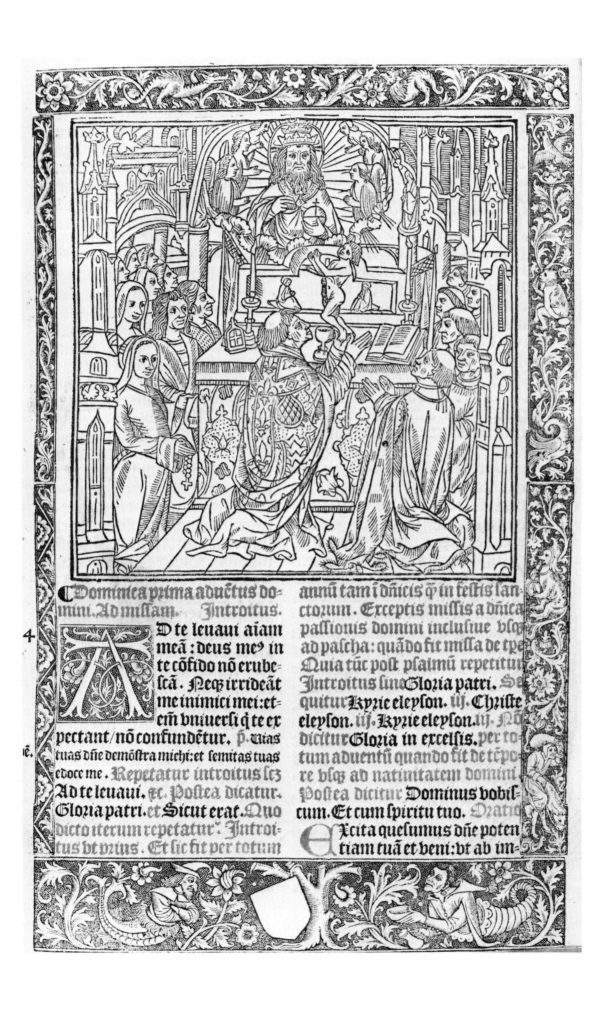

Dominica prima aductus domini. Ad missam. Introitus.

4 Ad te leuaui aiam meã: deus me⁹ in te cõfido nõ erubescã. Neq irrideãt me inimici mei: etenĩ vniuersi q̃ te expectant / nõ confundẽtur. ℣. Uias tuas dñe demõstra michi: et semitas tuas edoce me. Repetatur introitus scz Ad te leuaui. ꝛc. Postea dicatur. Gloria patri. et Sicut erat. Quo dicto iterum repetatur. Introitus vt prius. Et sic fit per totum annũ tam ĩ dñicis q̃ in festis sanctorum. Exceptis missis a dñica passionis domini inclusiue vsq ad pascha: quãdo fit missa de tpe. Quia tũc post psalmũ repetitur Introitus sine Gloria patri. Sequitur Kyrie eleyson. iij. Christe eleyson. iij. Kyrie eleyson. iij. Nõ dicitur Gloria in excelsis. per totum aduentũ quando fit de tẽpore vsq ad natiuitatem domini. Postea dicitur Dominus vobiscum. Et cum spiritu tuo. Oratio

Excita quesumus dñe potentiam tuã et veni: vt ab im-

ϕ	Notte de Plainchant Antiph. folio	27	m	36
o⫲	Notte de Plainchant Process. 8°.	73	m	36
♀	Notte de Plainchant heme notteé 16°.	62	m	36
o⫲⫲	Notte de Plainchant Missel 8°.	60	m	37
δ	Notte de Plainchant encor de meme			37
♁	Notte de Plainchant Cornicher Antiph. 4°.	15	m	37
♁	Notte de gros Plainchant portant ses Reglets	34	m	37

♂	Musique p. Messe f°. du Chemin	92	m	38
≡	Musique des Nottes de Colin, Viliers	67	m	38
≡	Musique moienne des chansons 4°.	94	m	38
#	Musique moienne hautin, maigre	86	m	39
≡	Musique des airs 16°. danfrie	47	m	39
≡	Musique petite pour psaumes 3e	28	m	39
≡	Musique petite aussi pour psaume	20	m	39
◇	Musique en blanc de Cicero	18	m	40
◆	Tablature de lut et Guitare, Granjon	55	m	40

Musique venues de Lion

≡	Musique in 4° Granjon	50	m	40
≡	Musique encor de meme	64	m	40
≡	Musique des airs 16°. plaine	55	m	41
≡	Musique petite pour airs	70	m	41
≡	Musique de Coppie moyenne	34	m	41
#	Musique petite po.r psaume	23	m	41
✕	Musique telle quelle	28	m	41

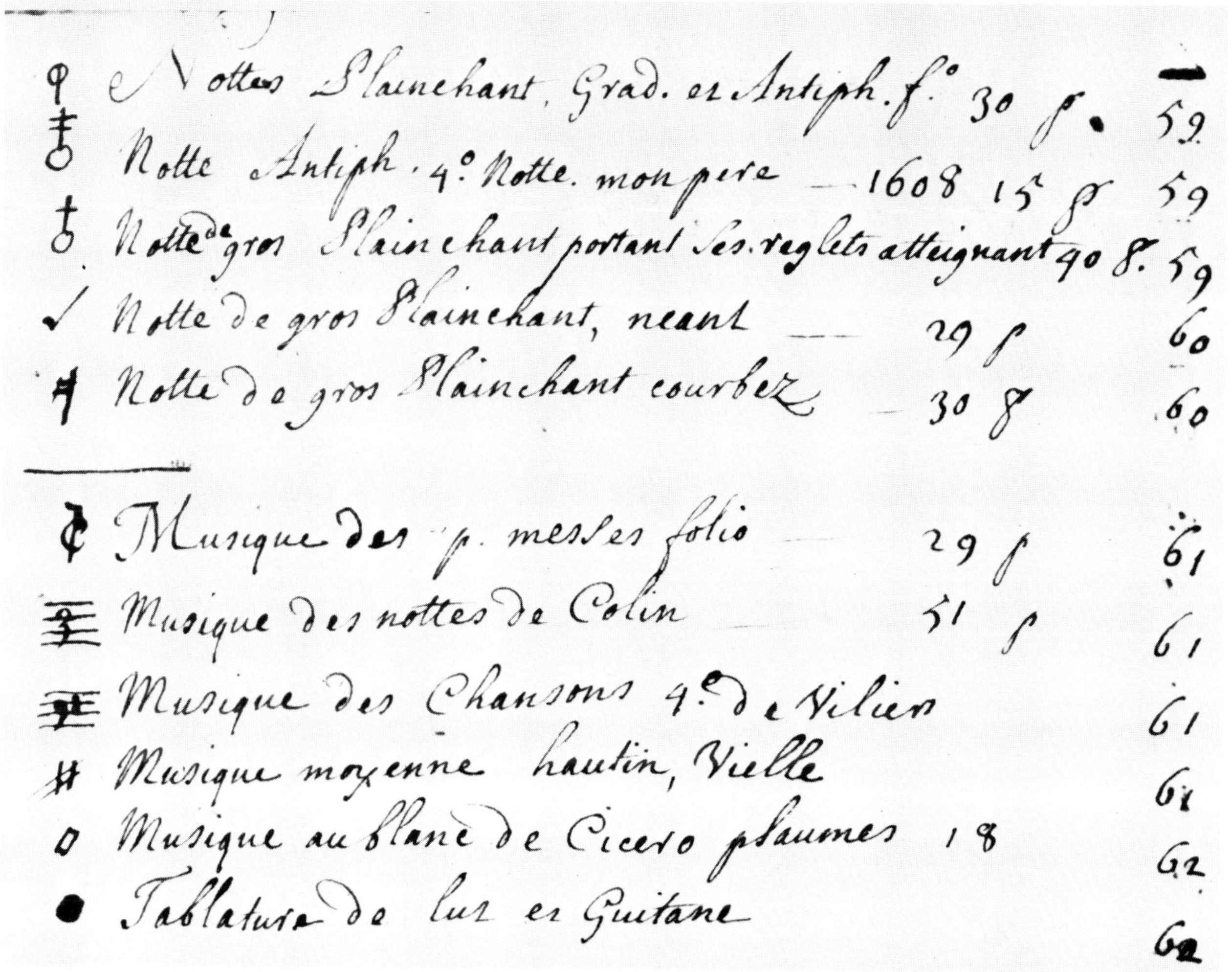
Nottes Plainchant, Grad. et Antiph. f° 30 p. 59
Notte Antiph. 4° Notte. mon pere — 1608 15e p 59
Notte de gros Plainchant portant ses reglets atteignant 40 p. 59
Notte de gros Plainchant, neant — 29 p 60
Notte de gros Plainchant courbez — 30 p 60
Musique des p. messes folio — 29 p 61
Musique des nottes de Colin — 51 p 61
Musique des Chansons 4° de Viliers 61
Musique moyenne hautin, Vielle 61
Musique au blanc de Cicero plaumes 18 62
Tablature de lut et Guitane 62

VI–VII (left and above) Inventory of matrices (m) and punches (p) for music from the Le Bé succession. By courtesy of the Archives Nationales, Paris.

VIII–XI (following pages) *Viginti missarum musicalium* **(33)**. By courtesy of the Boston Athenaeum.

VIII Title woodcut of the court at Mass.

IX Dedication to the Cardinal of Tournon.

X Royal Privilege of 1531.

XI Excerpt from Mouton's "Messe d'Allemaigne."

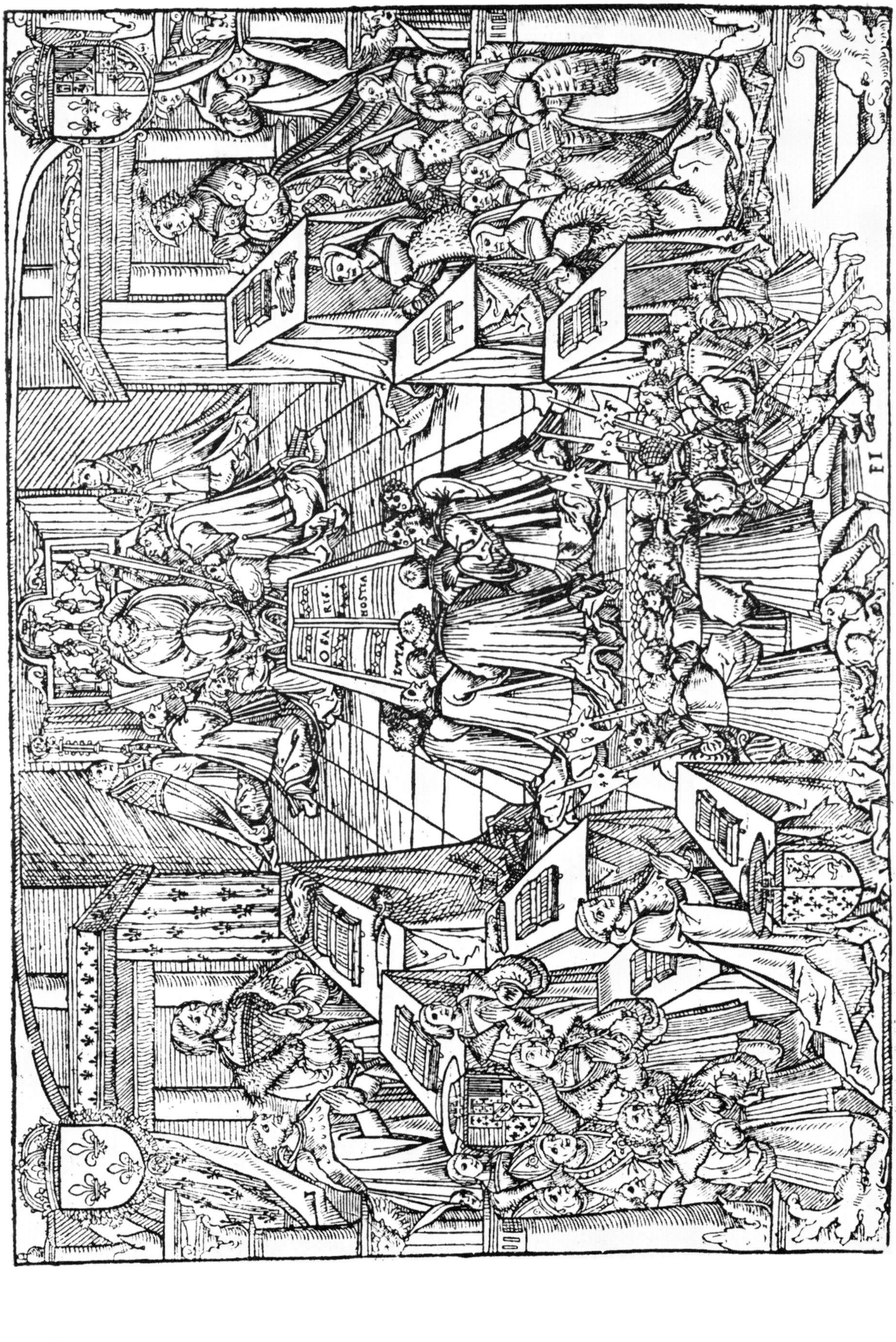

REVERENDISSIMO IN CHRISTO PATRI AC DOMINO
D. Francisco a Turnone Cardinali meritissimo
petrus Attingens typographus
musicus S. p. D.

PLurimum vereor Reuerendissime pater, ne temeritatis et arrogantię arguar, qui te tantum heroa tantisq; rebus occupatum interpellare ausus sim. Sed ego spero te nō ęgre laturum, adeo humanus es & benignus. nec dubito quin in bonam partem accepturus sis hunc librum quem sub tuo illustrissimo nomine in lucem edo. Nam cū mecum diu cogitarem cui potissimum hunc laborem meum dedicarem, tu primus occurristi, imo vero solus mihi dignus visus es, cui musę vniuersa opera sua consecrarent. A musis musica dicta est, de cuius artis laudib⁹ tacere satius est, q̄ pauca dicere. hoc vnum tamen non prętereibo, quod prisci illi tam gręci q̄ latini, cum hominē significare vellent in omni disciplinarum genere excellentem, eum musicum appellabant. Sed hęc vt alia queq; optima nemo te melius nouit. Cum igitur videam te nostri seculi decus esse, artisq; musicę fœliciter studiosissimum, opusculum hoc missarum musicis accētiunculis notatarum tuę celsitudini nuncupandum duxi. quod vt ęqui boniq; consulas oro, interim dum meliora parabuntur. potero enim & meliora & maiora pręstare, si tuę benignitatis fauor accesserit. Scio quantum valeas authoritate & gratia apud hunc principem, vt a quo repulsam nunq̄ passus sis. Nemo est qui non admiretur egregias tum animi tum corporis dotes, quibus deus te prę cęteris mortalibus decorauit, Quare mirum non est, si principes te amant, si vniuersa gallia te in primis venerat̄ Turnonia domus & antiquissima est & nobilissima, nempe a Troianis originem ducens. Tu eam ex nobilissima reddis nobiliorē & fulgentiorem, Qui primus tam insigni familię sacram purpuram attulisti, O vtinam nunc viuerent Iustus & Gaspar germani tui, quorum ille pro patria pugnando fortiter occubuit, Hic vero pastor vigilantissimus ecclesię Valentinę (cui prę erat) moriendo incredibile sui desyderium reliquit, Sed supersunt adhuc, D. Claudius Turnonius Viuarieñ episcopus, & nopotes tui D. Carolus Viuarieñ. designatus, D. Iacobus Castreñ. episcopus, Iustus iusti filius, (qui à sancto Iusto generis vestri consorte nominatur) Turnonij dominus, Henricus Item natu minimus Arlenci domin⁹: Ij omnes stellę sunt ac tanquā lucidissima sydera in domo Turnonia. vt cętera taceam innumerabilia gentis tuę lumina, Tu autem velut sol inter stellas omniū oculos in te cōuertis. Sed vereor ne sim iusto prolixior. Quare finem facio laudandi tui, ne id laudare velle videar quod satis nunq̄ laudari potest. Tibi igitur tanq̄ principi musarum & regij sacelli moderatori modulos meos offero, paruum quidem munus & indignum tāto vertice. sed abunde magnum si animum dantis inspicias. Vale fœliciter Francisce antistes ornatissime, musarumq; ac virtutum omnium parens. Ex officina nostra parisijs. Idibus Iulijs M. D. xxxij

Nicolai Borbonij Vandoperani Ad R. p. D.
Franciscum Cardinalem Turnonium
Carmen Sapphicum

Francoys par la grace de dieu Roy de France

Au preuost de Paris Baillifz et Seneschaulx et a tous noz aultres iusticiers & officiers/ou a leurs lieutenās salut et dilection. Receu auons lhumble supplication de nostre bien ame Pierre Attaingnant imprimeur libraire demourant a luniuersite de Paris contenant que comme par cy deuant nul en cestuy nostre royaulme ne se feroit entremis de grauer fondre et addresser les nottes et caracteres de limpression de musicque figuree en choses faictes. ensemble des tabulatures des ieuz de lutz flustes et orgues tant pour la difficile imagination et longue consumption de temps que pour les grans fraiz mises et labeurs quil y conuenoit faire & appliqr/ ledit suppliant par longue excogitation et trauail desperit et a tresgrās fraiz labeurs mises et despēs ait inuente et mis en lumiere la maniere et industrie de grauer fondre et imprimer lesdictes nottes et caracteres tant de musicque et choses faictes comme desdictes tabulatures des ieuz de Lutz Flustes et Orgues desquelles il a imprime & faict imprimer & espere faire cy apres plusieurs liures et cayers tant de messes/motetz/hymnes/chansons que desditz ieuz de Lutz Flustes et Orgues en grās et petitz volumes pour seruir aux eglises ministres dicelles/et generalemēt a toutes personnes. et pour le tresgrant bien vtilite & soulaigement de la chose publique. Toutesfoys il doubte que apres auoir mis en lumiere sadicte inuention et ouuert aux aultres imprimeurs et libraires la voye et industrie dimprimer ladicte musicque & ieuz iceulx imprimeurs & libraires se voulsissent semblablement entremetre dimprimer ladicte musique en choses faictes & ieuz de Lutz Flustes et Orgues. Et par ce moyen ledit suppliant perdist totalement le merite de ses labeurs et recouurement des fraiz et mises quilz a faitz et exposez a linuention et composition des caracteres desusdictz si par nous ne luy estoit sur ce pourueu & suruenu de nostre grace humblement requerant icelle. Pource est il. Que no⁹ ces choses considerees non voulās ledit suppliant demourer inutilles ses labeurs: application de temps: fraiz et mises par luy supportees audit affaire. Ains a en emporter et sentir commodite. Pour ces causes et aultres a ce nous mouuās auōs voulu et ordonne: voulons et ordonnons que durant le temps et terme de six ans prochainement venans a compter du iour et datte de ces presentes Aultre que ledit suppliant ou ceulx qui auront charge de luy/ne puissent imprimer ne exposer en vente lesditz liures & cayers de musicque en choses faictes: et tabulature des ieuz de Lutz Flustes et Orgues dessus declarez. Si vous mandōs et commettons par ces presentes: et a chacun de vous sur ce requis que de nostre presente grace ordonnance et ottroy vous faictes ledit suppliant iouyr et vser plainement et paisiblement. En faisant inhibitions et deffenses de par nous a tous libraires & aultres personnes generalement quelzconques de non imprimer ne exposer en vēte lesditz liures et cayers de musicque/et tabulature des ieuz dessusditz ledit temps de six ans durant. Sans expres pouoir et consentement dudit suppliant. Et ce sur grans peines a no⁹ a appliquer et de perdition et confiscation desditz liures et cayers. Et a ce faire et souffrir contraignez ou faictes contraindre tous ceulx quil appartiendra et qui pour ce seront a contraindre par toutes voyes et manieres deues et raisonnables: car ainsi nous plaist il estre faict. Non obstant quelzconques ordonnances/restrictions mandemens ou deffenses a ce contraires.

Dōne a sainct Germain en laye le dixhuitiesme iour de Juing. Lan de grace mil cinq centz trente vng. Et de nostre regne le. xvii

Par le Roy   Le Cardinal de Tournon maistre de la Chapelle dudit seigneur present.   Signe   J. Hamelin

Messe Dallemaigne
Osanna
osanna
in excelsis
in excelsis
Benedict9 tacet
Osanna
osanna
in excelsis
in excelsis

XIIa (above) The "Libraire" adjoining Notre Dame de Noyon, built in 1506 to house the Chapter Library.

XIIb (below) Saint-Benoît, Paris, the parish church of the Attaingnant family. From Millin, *Antiquités nationales*, Vol. III (Paris, 1791).

[G]aule est clo[se]
[e]nuirōnee du fleu[ue]
[d]u rhin/des alpes/
[de]s mōs pyrenees/et
[l]a mer occeane/& est
[d]iuisee en troys pties
[a]ssauoir Gaule

Belgique cōmēce aux riuieres de marne & seine & finist au Rhin du coste de septētrion & partie du coste doriēt/et du coste doccidēt est close de la mer occeane: en la quelle partie sont les cites villes princi-palles et fleuues de renom qui sensuyuēt. Cestassauoir

Cologne colonia a
Traict Tratectū e
Magunce Magūcia a
Treue Treueris a
Confluence confluentia
Basle Basilea
Constance Constantia
Suisse Sueuia
Juliers iuliacum
Cleues Cliuia
Embrique embrica
Rees res
Vuesalie Vuesalia
lesperon calcar
Gueldres Gueldria
Noymage nouimagū
arne arna
ruremūde ruremunda
vvalaf
zelande zelandia
meldebourg meldeburgū
ziericze
bryelle brielis
penisle peninsula
Holande Holandia
leyde leydis
harle harla
austerdame austerdamᵍ
derdraque derdracum
lyege leodium e
hastale hastalum
hoye hoyum
dynam dynantum
bouine bouina
bruxelles bruxelle
nyuelle nyuella
Anuers Antuerpia
bergues berga
Malinnes Machlinia
Louuain Louanium
bosduc boscusducis
Mōs en haynaut Mons in hanonia
Valētiēnes valentine
Quesnoy le conte quēnayum comitis

auenne auenna
Gand Gandauum
aldenarde aldenardum
Bruges Bruge
lescluse sclusa
courtray curtracum
tēdremōde teneramūda
ypre ypre
Tournay Tornacum e
Lisle insula
orchie orchie
douay duacum
saint omer s. Audomarus
graueligñes grauelingua
ostende ostenda
neufport nouusportus
Therouēne morinum e
aere aeria
perne perna
Hesdin hisdinum
Bethune bethunia
S. Paul S. Paulus
dorlen dorlenum
huissant icius portus
Bologne Bolonia
mōstercul mōsteriolum
Arras attrebatū e
bapaulme bapalma
Cambray cameracū e
S. quentin S. quintinus
peronne perona
corbie corbeia
Amiens ambianus e
Abbeuille abbatisuilla
S. riquier S. richarius
crotoy Croteium
Clermont clarusmons
crail creolium
Beauuais Bellouacū e
Senlis siluanectū e
compiegne compendiū
mondidier mōdiderium
roye roya
Pontoise pontisara
S. Denis S. dionysius
Rouen rothomagᵍ a

dieppe dieppa
fescamp. fiscānᵍ
harefleur. harfleu
Noyon Nouiomᵍ e
Soyssons suessio e
Meaulx meldis e
chasteautierri castrumthericum
Reims remis a
aspreñay aspreneiacum
Chalons cathalannū e
sandiger sandigerium
Langres lingonis e
bar barrum
ligny ligniacum
La marche marchia
chaumont caluusmons
Metz mete e
nammurch nāmurchum
luxēbourg luxēburgus
Nancy nancium
montrolant mōtrolandᵍ
Marcheneuf nou̅ mercatᵍ
verdun virdunum e
Tou tullum e
mōtbelliard monsbelliardus
Beaulne belna
besanson bisentium e
dole dola
saline salina
losane losana e
Geneue gebana e
Chamberi chāberiacum
Fleuues portās Bateaux
Seine sequana
Somme somma
Aise isara
Lyse lysa
Scalde scaldis
Enne enna
Meuse mosa
Moselle mosella
Dube dubis
Sagonne sagona
Le rhin rhenus

Paris cite & vniuersite la plus fameuse de chrestiētez chef du royaulme de france Parisius e
Sens senonis a
nemours nemoracum
Moret moretum
troys trece e
Auxerre altissiodorᵍ e
Autun heduum e
Digeon diuio
beaulne belna
germonne germona
arge argilis
Mascon matisco e
Chalons cabilo e
anse ansa
Lyon Lugdunū a
Ambrun ebredunū a
S. saphorin Sanctus simphorianus
Vienne vienna a
daulphine delphinatus
grasse grassa e
Grenoble grationopolis
Valence valentia e
montlimart mōslimardus
Diees diena e
viueres viuarium e
aurange aurasicum
S. esprit sctūs spiritus
Auignon Auinio
villeneufue villa noua
Carpētras carpētracū e
tarascon tarasco
arle aralata a
Marseille marsilia e
eaux aquesexte e
apres aptea
Regene regena e
Vapinte vapina e
sistarique sistarica
fourville forūiullium e
Tollon tollona e
nice nicia e
Cauali cauallcū e
Vason vasio e
Tricaste tricastinum e
biterre biterris
lunal lunellum
Mōtpellier mōspessulanᵍ
pesena pesignianum

Celtiq̄ cōmēce a la riuiere de Seine & sestēd iusq̄s a Loyre/mais elle court depuis la riuiere de marne iusq̄s au rosne/& si cōprēt vne ptie de la puīce de Narbōne/& fine es ptie a la mer ligustiq̄ & ptie aux mōtaignes de sauoye en laq̄lle sōt les villes & fleuues q̄ sensuyuēt

Aquitanique cōmēce a la riuiere de Loyre et sestend iusques aux mons pyrenees qui sont la separation des espaignes. Les villes & fleuues plus renommees sont

Bourges bituris a
meuge magdunum
dun le roy dunū regis
Clermōs clarusmōs e
vsson vsson
monete moneta
brioude briouda
Le puy podium e
S. flour S. florus e
Limoges lemouice e
tulle tutella e
cahors cathurcū e
rochemadour/rocamadorᵍ
Rouargue ruthenū e
vabre vabra e
Alby albia e
nimay nimatum
montauban mōtalbanū e
casteau cordō/castrum cordue
galace galiacum
Carcassonne carcasona e
Toulouze tolosa a
appamer appamara e
riuene riuena e
S. paul sctūs paulᵍ e
lombecs lombaria e
monlion monlionus
mirepoys mirapice e
fois fuxus
vaurene vaurena e
conues conuene
mirande miranda
lestore lectorium
Condon condoniū e
Aux auscus a
baguiere baiguera
conserant conserana e
Tarbe tarba e

Oleron olera e
Vasas vasata e
Lascure lascura e
mōtmarsant mōsmarsanᵍ
morlois morlanum
hortois hortesion
batone batona
alebret lebretum
rigene rigena
Adure adura e
agede agatha e
Vics vtica e
Electe electa e
limoy limosum
S. pons sctūs pōtᵍ e
chasteau barri castellum barri
elne elna
Lodesue Lodeua e
Tours turonus a
chinon chino
vendosme vindocinum
bloys blesa
Chastelerault castrūlerum
lomelle lomella
Poictiers pictauis e
partenay partenayum
maillesaiz malesaca e
La rochelle rupella
le lude ludum
touars touarsus
Luxon luxiona e
Xaintes xantona e
angolesme angolisma e
cognac cognacum
Perigort petragoricū e
Pierrebuffiere petrabuffiera
bergerat bergeratum

Sarlat sarlata e
Agen agena e
Condon condona e
lisignem lisigniacum
lebourg burgus
blaye bloya
ville roy villa regalis
liborne liburna
Bordeaux burdigala a
S. Jehā dangeli. S. Johannes angeliacus
Tailleborg tailburgus
la guierche laguiersa
Nantes nonetum e
Renes redonis e
fougeres fougera
S. Paul sctūs Paulus
lamballe lamballa
S. malo S. maclouᵍ e
Dolle dola e
dinam dinantum
S. brieuc S. briocus e
cornouaille cornubie e
Vennes venete e
Lcon leona e
Triguet Trecorum e

Les fleuues & riuieres de renom sont
Loire ligeris
Le loir lalerius
Le cher carus
La chalante chalantum
Dordonne dordonna
Gironde garunna

Neuers niuernum e
Molins molinum
clugni cluniacum
S. gengon s. gēgulphus
Motargis mōsargis
chastillon castillio
Orleans aurelie e
Janville ianuilla
Estampes stampe
chartres carnotum e
bonneual bonauallis
Eureux ebroice e
Sees sagium e
Lysieur lexouium e
argenten argentonū
Fallaise fallisia
hōnefleu hōneflorus
caen cadomum
Bayeux baiote e
pontorson pontorsonus
Auranches abrince e
Constāces constantia e
et aulcunes villes de bretaigne armorique
Le mans cenomania e
Alencen alencentum
Mortaigne mauritania
Mante medonta
Vernon verno
Meulan meulānum

Les fleuues portās bateaux. Le ne qui separe les belges et les celtes.
Loire ligeris
Vianne viana
Yonne iona
Dobe oba
le rosne rodanus
Sorde sorda
Durante durantia

En ceste figure ne sont compris grant multitude de petites villes/bourgs/chasteaulx/fo[rteresses] de Gaule/ne aussi plusieurs petis fleuues et riuieres desquelz ledit pays est arrouse ... vins/fruictz/bestiail/bestes saulvaiges/pastouraiges ... choses ... places pour la tuition & deffense dudit pays ... en bons fourmens
Il est a noter que quant vous trouueres a/deho[rs] ...
On les vend a Paris en la rue de la Harpe deuant ...

XIII Geographical primer in French and Latin **(59)**. By courtesy of the Bibliothèque Universitaire, Paris.

1554. C 53
Mouton.
EN venant de Lyon, & bō bō bō, trouuay en vn buiſon Robin & Marion, qui lui leuoit ſon peliſſon, et bō dnn

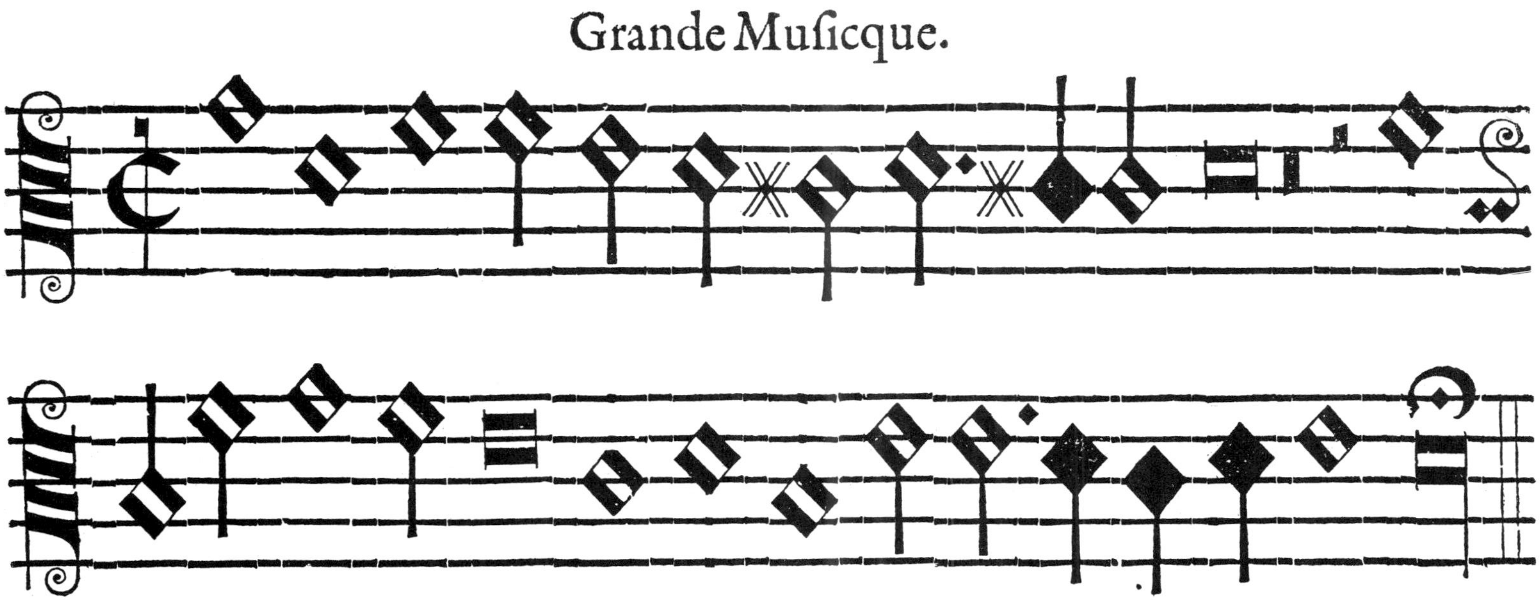

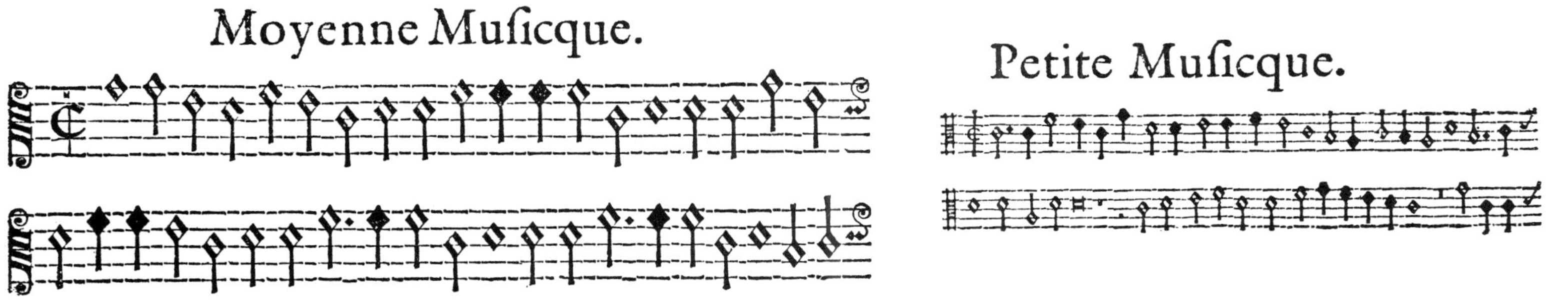

XIV (above) Specimen of folio music cut by Guillaume Le Bé. By courtesy of the Bibliothèque Nationale.

XV (below) Specimens of music type from the Plantin firm. By courtesy of the Plantin-Moretus Museum.

XVI (overleaf) The Latin Quarter, from Saint-Côme to Saint-Benoît. Detail from the "Plan Turgot." (*Photo Giraudon.*)

SORBONE
CORDE
Rue des
S.T COME
Col. des Prémontrés
Rue Pierre Sarazin
Rue de Sorbonne
S.T BENOIT
Cloître S.t Benoit
Rue des Mathurins
H.Cluni
Rue de la Harpe
R. des deux Portes
MATHURIN
Rue du Foin
Col. de Me Gervais
Rue de la Parcheminerie
S.T YVES
Rue Poupée

BIBLIOGRAPHICAL CATALOGUE

PREFATORY NOTE

ALL PUBLICATIONS of Attaingnant are described, including some that have survived only as titles. Of Attaingnant's widow's production only the music books have been included.

The title-pages are quoted verbatim, after the Superius part, or the Superius-Tenor, where this applies. Important variants in other parts such as the addition of a date, or mention of a privilege, occur immediately under the Superius title. There follows the description of a perfect copy (or the copy that is closest to being perfect), with signatures given in the order S, A, T, B. Variants in individual copies are included below, immediately following the place of conservation and call number. In long series such as the 1534–1535 motets the call numbers are not repeated for every volume subsequent to the first. The terms quarto, octavo, and folio are used in their precise technical sense.

In giving text incipits an attempt has been made to include the first line in entirety. The numbering to the left of the incipits is editorial. Attributions to composers that come en masse from a later reprint have been included without brackets and with a statement as to their source. For attributions in brackets that are not otherwise explained under the entry in which they occur, see the Index of First Lines.

Contractions and abbreviations in the text incipits (unlike those in the title-page) have been replaced by the words for which they stand. Differentiation has been made between *i* and *j*, and between *u* and *v*. Otherwise spelling is unchanged. In French texts the standard editorial modifications have been made: commas, to set off expletives or appositions, apostrophes, the cedilla, and the acute accent; hyphens and the diaeresis are applied selectively in order to help clarify textual meaning. Proper names and place names have been capitalized in both French and Latin. Spellings are given after the Superius except for typographical errors, in which case correction is made from one of the other parts. Composers' names are spelled variously, as they occur in the original.

For modern editions that are cited by short titles, consult the list of sigla, which follows.

SIGLA FOR MODERN EDITIONS

Anthologie	*Anthologie de la Chanson Parisienne au XVIe Siècle*, ed. François Lesure. Monaco, Editions de l'Oiseau-Lyre, 1953.
Arcadelt	*The Chansons of Jacques Arcadelt*, ed. Everett Helm. Smith College Music Archives, No. 5. Northampton, Mass., Smith College, 1942.
Chanson and Madrigal	*Chanson and Madrigal 1480–1530*, ed. James Haar. Cambridge, Mass., Harvard University Press, 1964.
Chansons polyphoniques	*Chansons polyphoniques du XVIe siècle*, ed. Marc Honegger. Paris, Les Editions Ouvrières, 1963–1965.
Chansons und Tänze	*Chansons und Tänze*, ed. E. Bernoulli. Munich, C. Kuhn, 1914.
CMM 3	*Adriano Willaert: Opera Omnia*, ed. Hermann Zenck and Walter Gerstenberg. *Corpus Mensurabilis Musicae, 3.* American Institute of Musicology, 1950——.
CMM 4	*Jacobus Clemens non Papa: Opera Omnia*, ed. K. Ph. Bernet Kempers. *Corpus Mensurabilis Musicae, 4.* American Institute of Musicology, 1951——.
CMM 6	*Nicolas Gombert: Opera Omnia*, ed. J. Schmidt-Görg. *Corpus Mensurabilis Musicae*, 6. American Institute of Musicology, 1951——.
CMM 20	*Pierre Attaingnant Transcriptions of Chansons for Keyboard*, ed. Albert Seay. *Corpus Mensurabilis Musicae, 20.* American Institute of Musicology, 1961.
Chorwerk, Vol. 15	*Johannes Lupi: Zehn Weltliche Lieder*, ed. Hans Albrecht. Das Chorwerk, Vol. 15. Wolfenbüttel, Möseler Verlag, n.d.
Chorwerk, Vol. 61	*Zwolf Französische Lieder aus Jacques Moderne: Le Parangon des Chansons* (*1538*), ed. Hans Albrecht. Das Chorwerk, Vol. 61. Wolfenbüttel, Möseler Verlag, 1957.
Chorwerk, Vol. 73	*Clement Janequin: Zehn Chansons*, ed. Albert Seay. Das Chorwerk, Vol. 73. Wolfenbüttel, Möseler Verlag, 1959.
Chorwerk, Vol. 82	*Pierre Certon: Zehn Chansons*, ed. Albert Seay. Das Chorwerk, Vol. 82. Wolfenbüttel, Möseler Verlag, 1962.
Deux livres d'Orgue	*Deux livres d'Orgue parus chez Pierre Attaingnant en 1531*, ed. Yvonne Rokseth. Paris, Publications de la Société Française de Musicologie, Première Série, Tome I, 1925.
French Chansons	*French Chansons*, ed. Albert Seay. Evanston, Ill., Summy-Birchard Publishing Co., 1957.
GMB	*Geschichte der Musik in Beispielen*, ed. Arnold Schering. Leipzig, Breitkopf und Härtel, 1931.
HAM	*Historical Anthology of Music*, ed. A. T. Davison and Willi Apel. Vol. I. Cambridge, Mass., Harvard University Press, 1946.
Josquin	*Werken van Josquin Des Prés*, ed. A. Smijers. Amsterdam, G. Alsbach & Co., 1925——.
Masterworks	*Masterworks of Yesterday*, ed. Albert Seay. Colorado Springs, Colorado College Music Press, 1955——.

MMRF	*Les Maîtres Musiciens de la Renaissance Française*, ed. Henri Expert. Paris, Alphonse Leduc, 1895–1908.
Pariser Tanzbuch	*Pariser Tanzbuch aus dem Jahre 1530*, ed. F. J. Giesbert. Mainz, B. Schotts Söhne, n.d.
Preludes, Chansons	*Preludes, Chansons and Dances for Lute. Published by Pierre Attaingnant, Paris (1529–1530)*, ed. Daniel Heartz. Neuilly-sur-Seine, Société de Musique d'Autrefois, 1964.
Quinze Chansons	*Quinze Chansons Françaises du XVIe Siècle*, ed. Maurice Cauchie. Paris, Rouart, Lerolle, 1926.
Theatrical Chansons	*Theatrical Chansons of the Fifteenth and Early Sixteenth Centuries*, ed. Howard M. Brown. Cambridge, Mass., Harvard University Press, 1963.
Thirty Chansons (1960)	*Thirty Chansons for Three and Four Voices from Attaingnant's Collections*, ed. Albert Seay. New Haven, Department of Music, Yale University, 1960.
Treize Livres de Motets	*Treize Livres de Motets parus chez Pierre Attaingnant en 1534 et 1535*, ed. A. Smijers and A. Tillman Merritt. Paris, Monaco, Editions de l'Oiseau Lyre, 1934–1963.
Treize Motets	*Treize Motets et un Prélude pour Orgue parus chez Pierre Attaingnant en 1531*, ed. Yvonne Rokseth. Paris, Publications de la Société Française de Musicologie, Première Série, Tome V, 1930.
Trente Chansons (1928)	*Trente Chansons à Trois et Quatre Voix de Clément Janequin*, ed. Maurice Cauchie. Paris, Rouart, Lerolle, 1928.

1

¶ Breuiarium scd'm vsum in=/signis eccl'ie Nouiomẽsis auctoritate / Reuerẽdissimi dñi epi/necnõ venera/biliũ dñoꝝ. Decani & capti/eiusdẽ / ecclesie/nup. correctũ/emenda=/tu/ac multis in locis abbre=/uiatũ. Impressum &o im=/pensis honesti viri Pe=/tri Attaingnant. An=/no domini Mille/simo quingẽtesi/mo 'vicesimo / quinto ∴ / ✠ / ¶ Venale reperies Parisiis in vico Cytha/reo/in officina libraria dicti Attaingnant / vico Mathurinorum directe opposita. / ¶ Pars Estiualis. /

1 vol. in-16°, 9 × 14.5 cm.; 52 f. unnumbered, 94 f. numbered i–xciiii, 136 f. unnumbered.
Sign.: $✠^{8}$; a^{8}–d^{8}; e^{10}; $¶^{2}$; A^{8}–L^{8}; M^{6}; A^{8}–R^{8}

Paris: Bibliothèque Nationale, Rés., Vélins 1.614 (MS. inscription on the title page: Bellement)
Illustration on verso of f. ¶2: King David kneeling (see fig. 13 above).
Title page and a page of text reproduced in Renouard, *Imprimeurs et libraires parisiens du XVIe siècle*, Paris, 1964, Vol. I, plate 32.

1528, APRIL 4

2

Chansons nouuelles en musique / A quatre parties: naguere iprimees a Paris p. Pierre attaingnant=/libraire demourant en la rue de la Harpe deuant le bout de la rue des / Mathurins pres leglise de sainct Cosme. / ¶ Cantiones musicales cũ quatuor vocibus a doctis=simis in Musica / magistris nuper edite. Et a Petro attingente librario Parisiis ĩ vico / Cithareo in domo vie Mathurinorum directe opposita commorãte / nunc primũ correcte impresse. Anno virginei partus 1527 / Altus. Tenor. /

[2] vol. in-8° obl., 15 × 10 cm.; 32 f. numbered [1]–32 (Altus, i.e., Superius-Tenor [1], [2], 3,–[4], 5, 8, 7, 6, 9, 10)
Sign.: a^{4}–h^{4}; [A^{4}–H^{4}?]
RISM–I, 1528^{3}

The Hague: Koninklijke Bibliothe,, I D 16(Altus-Tenor; incomplete.)
Versailles: Bibliothèque Municipale, Fonds Goujet, 8° G. 32 (1) (Altus-Tenor)

*1.	Secourez moy, ma dame, par amours	Claudin	1^{v}
*2.	Tant que vivray en aage florissant	[Claudin]	2^{v}
*3.	Dont vient cela, belle, je vous supply	Claudin	3^{v}
*4.	Vivray-je tousjours en souci pour vous	Claudin	4^{v}
*5.	Joyssance vous donneray, mon amy	Claudin	5^{v}
*†6.	Si j'ay pour vous mon avoir despendu	Claudin	6^{v}
*7.	Il est jour dit l'alouette, allons jouer	Claudin	7^{v}
*8.	Le content est riche en ce monde	Claudin	8^{v}
9.	De resjoyr mon povre coeur veu sa douleur		9^{v}
10.	Quant tu chanteras pour ton ennuy passer		10^{v}
11.	Le triste cueur puis qu'avec vous demeure		11^{v}
12.	Ma bouche rit et mon coeur pleure		12^{v}
*13.	Las, voulez-vous que une personne chante	[Vermont]	13^{v}
*14.	Mon cueur est souvent bien marry	Claudin	14^{v}
*15.	Le départir de cil que tant j'aymoy		15^{v}
*16.	Veu le gref mal ou sans fin je labeure		16^{v}
17.	Puis que j'ay mis tout mon entendement		16^{v}
‡18.	Serpe et serpette, les serpiers et le serpillon T: Vive la serpe	Claudin	18^{v}
*19.	Changeons propos, c'est trop chanté d'amours	Claudin	19^{v}
*†20.	J'atens secours de ma seule pensée	Claudin	20^{v}
*21.	Languir me fais sans t'avoir offensé	Claudin	21^{v}
22.	A mon resveil ung oyseau j'ay oy		22^{v}
*23.	C'est a grant tort que moy povrette endure	Claudin	23^{v}
*24.	Aupres de vous secretement demeure	[Claudin or Jacotin]	24^{v}
*25.	Ung jour Robin alloit aux champs jouant gallant	Claudin	25^{v}
*26.	Longtemps y a que je viz en espoir		26^{v}
*27.	N'auray-je jamais réconfort de vous	Jacotin	27^{v}
§28.	Réconfortez le petit cueur de moy	Janequin	28^{v}
*29.	Le cueur est bon et le vouloir aussi		29^{v}
*30.	J'ay contenté ma voulenté suffisamente	Claudin	30^{v}
*‖31.	Las, je my plains, mauldicte soit fortune	Claudin	31^{v}

Folio 32^{v}: ¶La table des chansons servant pour les deux livres / [Table] / 4 aprilis. 1527. aū Pascha /

MS inscription on the title page of the Versailles copy: "Biblioteque La Montrouge—La Luttrye 1690". The Hague copy has the Ex libris of Scheuerleer inside the front cover. It is mentioned in *Catalogus der Musiekbibliotheek van D. F. Scheurerleer* Vol. I (S' Gravenhage, 1893) p. 287, with no indication that the copy is a facsimile, and incomplete, consisting of title page, f. 1^{v}–4, 5^{v}–6, 20^{v}–22, 19^{v}–20, 26^{v}–27, 30^{v}–31. A brittle modern paper is used except for f. 1^{v}, 30^{v} and 31, which are on a soft paper printed on one side only (unlike the original, as exhibited in the Versailles copy.) Although a facsimile, the copy possesses the interest of an original, having been made from an exemplar now unknown (not that at Versailles, as may be surmised from the lacking library stamp and other details.)

* Modern edition in *CMM 20*
† Modern edition in *Chanson and Madrigal.*
‡ Modern edition in *Quinze Chansons.*
§ Modern edition in *Trente Chansons* (*1928*).
‖ Modern edition in *Anthologie.*

Attributions from **32**.
The collection is reprinted, with corrections, in **9** except for nos. 23 and 24, which appear in **5**, and no. 26, which appears in **6**.
Title page of the Versailles copy reproduced in *MGG* II, col. 1055–1056 (reduced) and in *La musique française. Moyèn Age à la Revolution.* Paris, 1934, p. 72.

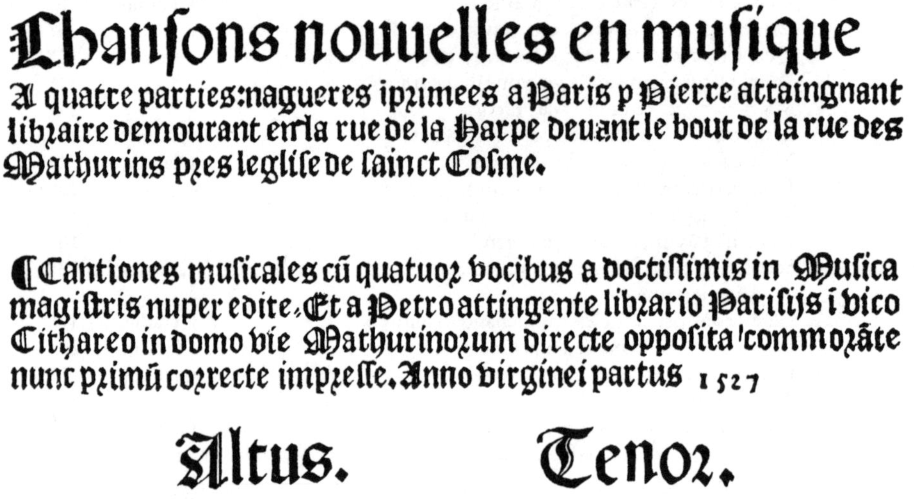
Chanſons nouuelles en muſique
A quatre parties: nagueres ip̄rimees a Paris p Pierre attaingnant libraire demourant en la rue de la Harpe deuant le bout de la rue des Mathurins pres legliſe de ſainct Coſme.

¶ Cantiones muſicales cū quatuor vocibus a doctiſſimis in Muſica magiſtris nuper edite. Et a Petro attingente librario Pariſijs i vico Cithareo in domo vie Mathurinorum directe oppoſita commorāte nunc primū correcte impreſſe. Anno virginei partus 1527

Altus. Tenor.

15 Title page of *Chansons nouvelles* **(2)**. By courtesy of the Koninklijke Bibliotheek, The Hague.

[1528]

3

[Chansons et motets en canon a quatre parties sur deux]

1 vol. in-8° obl., 15 × 10 cm.; 4 f. numbered 41–44 (folios 1–40 lacking) Sign.: ✠ 11[4]
Eichstätt: Staatliche Bibliothek, Lit. O No. 38, no. 1

1.	Ave Maria, gratia plena—In diapenthe	[Prioris]	41
2.	En disant une chansonnette—Duo		41v
[1]3.	Christi virgo dilectissima—I	[Willaert]	42v
	Quoniam peccatorum molle premimur—II		43v
4.	En venant de Lyon	[Mouton]	44v

¶ Finis

The Eichstätt set of 16 books (see Section IV above, note 56) is bound in a single volume, with old leather-covered boards, stamped in gold: CONTRATENOR. The volume

[1] 42v: Canon In subdiapason; 43: Ad tertiam; 43v: Secunda pars; 44: Canon In diapason.

was sent in 1960 to the "Reparierungsatelier" at Munich, where the restorers described it as "Französische Bindeart." Still discernible is an older shelf mark: H / I / 16

Attributions are from *Motetti novi et chanzoni franciose a quatro sopra doi*, Venice, Antico, 1520.

The title is cited after an entry in one of the Colombine catalogues. See Catherine Weeks Chapman, "Printed Collections of Polyphonic Music Owned by Ferdinand Columbus," *Journal of the American Musicological Society* XXI (1968), 73, no. 92. The entry gives the additional information that there were 41 pieces, beginning and ending in an alphabetical sense with "Adieu mes amours" and "Tout d'un accord." Both pieces are among the 32 double canons in Antico's *Motetti novi*, which occupied 38 folios. Assuming that Attaingnant reprinted the Venetian collection in its entirety, his additional 9 pieces, probably simple duets like no. 4, would have to be confined to about 6 folios. There are discrepancies between the Colombine descriptions and the surviving editions to be noted. Thus **6** (Chapman no. 93) is said to begin with "Le trop long temps," and **10** (Chapman no. 96) with "Tout a loisir."

Facsimile of the fragment in D. Heartz, "A New Attaingnant Book and the Beginnings of French Music Printing," *Journal of the American Musicological Society* XIV (1961). 9–23 (Plates I–III). *Ibid.*, transcription of pieces 2 and 4.

[1528]

4

Chansons de maistre Clement Ja/nequin Nouuellemet et correctemēt imprimeez a Paris par Pierre / attaingnant demourāt a la rue de la harpe deuāt le bout de la rue des / mathurins pres leglise saint Cosme. / Superius. /

4 vol. in-8° obl., 15 × 10 cm.; 16 f. numbered [1]–16 (B: 4 unfoliated; T & B: 13 16, 15, 14)

Sign.: a^4–d^4; aa^4–dd^4; AA^4–DD^4; A^4–D^4 (Ct: cc i, c ii; T: A ii, B, B ii, CC; B: AA ii, BB, BB ii)

Eichstätt: Staatliche Bibliothek, No. 2 (Ct: folios i^v & 2, 3^v & 4 labeled T)
Paris: Bibliothèque Nationale, Rés. Vm^7 181
Versailles: Bibliothèque Municipale, Fonds Goujet, 8° G. 32 (2) (S)

Folio 16: ¶ La table de ceste presente partie. / [Table] /
For reprint see **75.**
Modern edition in *MMRF*, Vol. VIII. Includes facsimiles of title page, 5^v, and 6 of Ct.
A complete edition of Janequin's chansons is in course of publication by A. Tillman Merritt and François Lesure for Editions de l'Oiseau-Lyre. The first volume, including the above pieces, appeared in 1965.

5

Trete et quatre chãsos musicales / **a quatre parties imprimees a Paris le. xxiii. iour de ianuier mil. v. c.** / **xxviii. par Pierre Attaingnãt demourãt en la rue de la Harpe pres le/glise sainct Cosme. desquelles la table sensuyt.** / [Table] / **Superius.** /

4 vol. in-8° obl., 15 × 10 cm.; 16 f. numbered [1]–16 (S: 1 2 3 2; Ct: 9 10 11 10; B: a printed page pasted over original, f. 11)
Sign.: e^4–h^4; ee^4–hh^4; EE^4–HH^4; E^4–H^4
RISM-I, 1529[3]

Paris: Bibliothèque Nationale, Rés. Vm[7] 175.

			5, 29
1.	Venés ça ho dictes ung petit		1^v
2.	Qui veult raison en raison se contente		2
*3.	Aupres de vous secretement demeure	[1]Claudin or Jacotin	2^v
†4.	De mon triste et desplaisir a vous belle	Richafort	3
‡5.	Le Dieu d'aymer m'a mis au bas		3^v
6.	Qu'esse d'amour bien le vouldroie sçavoir		3^v
7.	Esse raison que pour une asseurance		4
*8.	Le coeur de vous ma présence désire	Claudin	4^v
*9.	Aller my fault sur la verdure	Jennequin	5
[2]*10.	A mes ennuyz que si longtemps je porte		5^v
11.	A demy mort chacun me peult juger		6
12.	Amy, héllas, ostés-moy de la presse		6^v
§13.	Amour et mort me font oultrage		7
*14.	Celle qui m'a tant pourmené	Claudin	7^v
15.	Ce fut amour dont je fus abusée	[3][Passereau]	8
16.	C'est grant plaisir d'estre amoureux		8^v
17.	C'est grant pitié quant argent fault a ceulx qui boivent voluntiers		9

* Modern edition in *CMM 20.*
† Modern edition in *Theatrical Chansons.*
‡ Modern edition in *Chansons polyphoniques.*
§ Modern edition in *Thirty Chansons (1960).*

[1] Attributions from **29**. On the conflicting attribution see François Lesure, "Les Anonymes des Recueils imprimés français du xvi[e]s.," *Fontes Artis Musicae* I (1954), 80.
[2] "En mes ennuyz" in **29**.
[3] Attribution after *Le Parangon des Chansons*, II, Lyons, Moderne, 1538, fol. 13.

‖18.	Assouvy suis mais sans cesser désire	[Janequin]	9^{v}
*19.	Contre raison vous m'estes fort estrange	Claudin	10
#20.	Coeurs désolez par toutes nations	[4]Josquin des prés	10^{v}
21.	De nuyt et jour il fault estre amoureux	Consilium	11
22.	De bien aymer j'en ay faict l'entreprise		11^{v}
23.	D'estre amoureux jamais ne seray las		11^{v}
*24.	De retourneur, mon amy, je te pri		12
25.	Du temps me deulx et non de vous amye		12^{v}
*26.	De toy me plaintz non sans cause et raison		13
27.	En devisant au gratieux pourpris		13
28.	Esse bien fait, dictes-moy, belle amye		13^{v}
29.	En vous aymant je languis a poursuyvre		14
30.	Fait ou failli ou du tout riens qui vaille	Claudin	14^{v}
*31.	C'est a grant tort que moy povrette endure	Claudin	15
32.	Si plusieurs jours comme le bon veneur		15^{v}
§33.	C'est grant erreur de cuider présumer		16
*34.	Il me souffit de tous mes maulx	Claudin	16^{v}

Finis

Contents same as **29**.

Facsimile of Superius fol. 1^{v} in *Enciclopedia della Musica Ricordi*, IV, pl. cxxxv.

‖ Modern edition in *Trente Chansons (1928)*.
Modern edition in *Josquin*, Bundel III.

[4] The piece is printed in the *Chansons a quatre parties par M. Benedictus*, Antwerp, 1541, an authoritative edition of Benedictus Appenzeller deserving more weight than Attaingnant's attribution.

[1529]

6

Trente et cinq chãsons musicales / a quatre parties nouuellement et correctement imprimees a Paris / par Pierre Attaingnãt demourant en la rue de la Harpe pres leglise / sainct Cosme. desquelles la table sensuyt. [Table] / [Corrigenda] / **Superius.** /

4 vol. in-8° obl., 15 × 10 cm.; 16 f. numbered [1]–16 (S: [1] 2 4 4; T: 9 12 11 12; B: 9 12 11 12)
Sign.: i^4–m^4; ii^4–mm^4; II^4–MM^4; I^4–M^4
RISM–I, [c. 1528][7]

Eichstätt: Staatliche Bibliothek, No. 4 (Ct)
Lausanne: Succession A. Cortot, (olimWernigerode, fürstlich Stolberg Bibliothek) (S.) "Le seconde Livre"
Munich: Bayerische Staatsbibliothek, Mus. Pr. 31/13
Paris: Bibliothèque Nationale, Rés. Vm^{7} 176

1.	Le coeur de moy ne fut jamais repris	1^{v}
2.	Tout a loysir j'ay malheure combatu	1^{v}

*3.	Vignon vignette, qui te planta		2
4.	Petit coeur franc et gratieux		2v
5.	Miculx quc congnue est ma félicité		3
6.	Fortune, héllas, as-tu mis en oubly		3v
*7.	Ung grant plaisir Cupido me donna		4
8.	Estre loyal je le tiens a follie		4v
*9.	A bien grant tort vous faictes ce partaige		5
10.	Est-il déduit ou autant y aist d'aise		5
11.	Je suis tout seul, madame la dict		5v
12.	Qui veult entrer en grace des dames		6
13.	Vous avez tort du mal qu'ainsi j'endure		6v
14.	Las, fortune, de toy je fais mes plainctes		7
15.	Le chant plaisant fortifie l'affection		7v
16.	Le temps me vengera de ta grande finesse		8
17.	L'eureux travail qu'en sa fin et plaisante		8v
*18.	Longtemps y a que je vis en espoir		8v
*19.	L'heur de mon bien et vray contentement		9
20.	Las, il fauldra que ung estranger la maine		9v
21.	Le coeur est mien ou tout malheur abonde		10
22.	Je fus cité d'aversité en court d'Amours		10v
*23.	Maulgré moy viz et en vivant je meurs	[Claudin]	11
*24.	Le jaulne et bleu sont les couleurs		11v
25.	Impossible est que je puisse vivre en joye		12
*26.	Mon coeur gist tousjours en langueur	[Claudin]	12v
27.	Madame ne m'a pas vendu		13
28.	Quant j'ay beu du vin cleret tout tourne		13v
29.	Tous nobles coeurs venez voir Magdalene		14
30.	Ha hay, ha hay, estes-vous rencherie		14v
†31.	Ouy de beaulx faictes luy chere		14v
32.	Et bien, bien, il m'en souviendra		15
*‡33.	Puis qu'en deux coeurs y a vraye union		15v
34.	Si le voulés je le veuil bien		16
35.	Tant que vivray je seray vostre amy		16v
	¶ Finis		

* Modern edition in *CMM 20*.
† Modern edition in *Thirty Chansons* (*1960*)
‡ Modern edition in *French Chansons*.

[1529]

7

Trente et deux chāsōs musicales / **a quatre parties nouuellemēt et trescorrectemēt imprimees a Paris** / **par Pierre Attaingnāt demourant en la rue de la Harpe pres leglise** / **saint Cosme. desquelles la table sensuyt.** [Table] / **Superius.** /

4 vol. in-8° obl., 15 × 10 cm.; 16 f. numbered 1–16 (S: 9 10 11 10; T: 11 10 9 12)
Sign.: n^4–q^4; nn^4–qq^4; NN^4–QQ^4; N^4–Q^4
RISM–I, [c. 1528][5]

Brussels: Bibliothèque Royale, Fétis 2306 (T)
Eichstätt: Staatliche Bibliothek, No. 5 (Ct)

Lausanne: Succession A. Cortot (olim Wernigerode) (S). "Le tiers Livre"
Munich: Bayerische Staatsbibliothek, Mus. Pr. 31/10
Paris: Bibliothèque Nationale, Rés. Vm^7 174

1.	Vien tost despiteux desconfort	[1][Claudin]	1^{v}
*2.	Réveillés-vous, réveillés jeunes dames qui dormés		2
3.	Trésoriere de plaisir amoureux		2^{v}
†4.	Tous mes amys, venez ma plaincte ouyr	[Claudin]	3
‡5.	Et la mon amy, la tandis que vous y estes		3^{v}
6.	Si content suis en la foy de m'amie		4^{v}
7.	Grace, vertu, bonté, beaulté, noblesse	[Roquelay]	5
8.	Si quelque foys je me lasse d'aymer		5^{v}
†9.	Le corps s'en va et le coeur vous demeure [à 3]	[2][Consilium]	5^{v}
§10.	Renfort de gens pour aller vendenger		6^{v}
*11.	Aporte a boyre et du salé		7
12.	Croyés devray sur toutes estes celle		7^{v}
13.	Avant qu'il soit jamais dix ans		8
14.	De vous aymer il fault que m'en retire		8^{v}
15.	A quoy tient-il d'ou vient cela		9
16.	Venés regretz venés tous en mon coeur		9^{v}
17.	J'ay par trop longuement aymé		9^{v}
18.	Las, pourquoy m'estes vous si rude		10
19.	M'a-t-il laissé le traistre desloyal		10^{v}
20.	De trop aymer ne vous repentés tant		11
21.	Plaisir n'ay plus mais vis en desconfort		11^{v}
22.	Regretz, soucy et peine m'ont fait ung villain tour		12
23.	Heureux je suis par sur tous seurement		12^{v}
24.	A elle suis aussi elle est a moy		13
‖25.	Mon coeur en vous a s'amour commencée		13^{v}
26.	Tant fus au coeur de son amour espris		14
27.	Mauldit soit-il qui en vous se fira		14^{v}
28.	Le bon espoir que mon coeur a sur le temps advenir		14^{v}
‖29.	Je le disois qu'on m'a bien estrangé		15
30.	Si vostre coeur prent le tenné		15^{v}
31.	Oubli, oubli non pas de l'oublieur		16
32.	De mon amy ne me puis contenter		16^{v}

* Modern edition in *Thirty Chansons (1960).*
† Modern edition in *Preludes, Chansons.*
‡ Modern edition as *Masterworks*, Vol. 1.
§ Modern edition as *Masterworks*, Vol. 10.
‖ Modern edition in *CMM 20.*

[1] Attribution after Cambrai, Bibl. de la Ville, MS 125–128, fol. 44^{v}
[2] Attribution after *Second livre de chansons a 3 . . .*, Paris, Le Roy et Ballard, 1578, fol. 7^{v}.

[1529]

8

Trēte chāsons musicales a quatre / parties nouuellement et tres= correctement imprimees a Paris par / Pierre Attaingnāt demourāt en la rue de la Harpe pres leglise saint / Cosme. desquelles la table sensuyt. / [Table] / Superius. /

4 vol. in-8° obl., 15 × 10 cm.; 16 f. numbered 1–16 (S: 12 15 14 13 16; T: 13 14 15 19; B: 13 14 15 19)
Sign.: r⁴–v⁴; rr⁴–vv⁴; RR⁴–VV⁴; R⁴–V⁴
RISM–I, [c. 1528]⁴

Brussels: Bibliothèque Royale, Fétis 2305 (T)
Eichstätt: Staatliche Bibliothek, No. 6 (Ct)
Lausanne: Succession A. Cortot (olim Wernigerode) (S). "Le quart Livre"
Munich: Bayerische Staatsbibliothek, Mus. Pr. 31/8
Paris: Bibliothèque Nationale, Rés. Vm⁷ 172

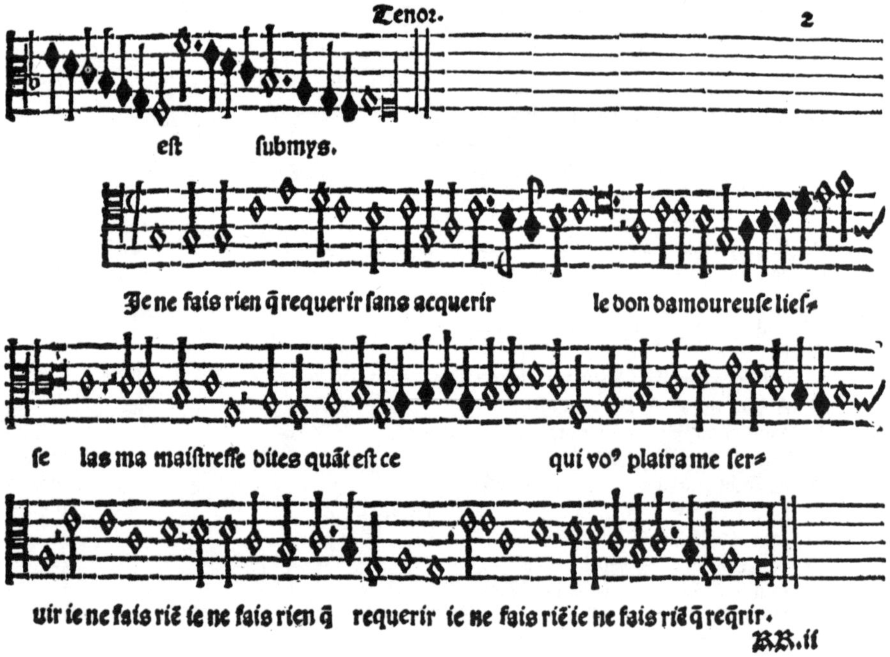

16 Music page from *Trente chansons* (**8**). By courtesy of the Bibliothèque Royale, Brussels.

1.	Du grant soulas ou espoir m'avoit mis		1ᵛ
*2.	Je ne fais rien que réquérir	[Claudin]	2
3.	Vray Dieu d'amours mauldit soit la journée		2ᵛ
4.	Doeul, double doeul a mon coeur assommé		3
*5.	D'un nouveau dard je suis frapé		3ᵛ
6.	C'est grant malheur a créature née		4
7.	Point ne flatés ne semblés la marmaille		4ᵛ
8.	Secours, héllas, par amour je vous prie		5
9.	En attendant d'amours la jouissance		5ᵛ
10.	Fortune, fortune, bien je te doibs mauldire		5ᵛ
†11.	Et d'en bon jour et dont venez vous		6ᵛ
†12.	Et d'en bon soir j'avois tousjours en espérance		7

* Modern edition in *CMM 20*.
† Modern edition as *Masterworks*, Vol. 6.

13.	Il n'est plaisir qui soit meilleur a suyvir		7^{v}
14.	Amour, tu es par trop cruelle		8
15.	Apres ta mort je ne cherche plus vivre		8^{v}
16.	Et moulinet vire tourne, moulinet tourne vire [à 5]		9
17.	En attendant que yray dancer au may		9^{v}
18.	Et je les ay, les frisques amouretes		10
19.	Amy, souffrez que je vous ayme		10^{v}
20.	Plaindre me puis d'une sans la nommer		11
[1]21.	Par fin despit je m'en yray seullete		11^{v}
22.	Le doulx acueil, le maintien gratieux		12
23.	Fleur de beaulté, dame sans per, ma maistresse		12^{v}
24.	Coeur envieux, plus dur que pierre dure		13
25.	J'ay trop aymé, vrayment je le confesse		13^{v}
26.	Trop mal me vient d'estre tenu		14
‡27.	Povre coeur, tant il m'ennuye		14^{v}
28.	Gentilz gallans adventuriers qu'en amour plaisir prenez	[2][Ninot le Petit]	15^{v}
29.	Mon desconfort me fait vivre en tristesse		16
30.	Mi larrés-vous tousjours languir		16^{v}

¶ Finis

‡ Modern edition in *Thirty Chansons* (*1960*).

[1] See **54**, No. 8.
[2] Attribution after Florence, Bibl. del Conservatorio, MS Basevi 2442, fol. 15.

[1529]

9

Trēte et sept chāsons musicales a /quatre parties nouuellement et correctemēt imprimees a Paris par / Pierre Attaingnāt demourant a la rue de la Harpe pres leglise saint / Cosme. desquelles la table sensuypt. / [Table] / [Corrigenda] / **Superius. /**

4 vol. in-8° obl., 15 × 10 cm.; 16 f. numbered 1–16 (S: 1 2 3 13; T: 1 15 3 13; Ct: 1 14 3 16; B: 1 1† 3 16; 13 1† 15 16; Table follows correct pagination)
Sign.: x^{4}–&^{4}; xx^{4}–&&^{4}; XX^{4}–*AA*^{4}; X^{4}–*A*^{4}
RISM–I, [c. 1528][8]

Paris: Bibliothèque Nationale, Rés. Vm^{7} 178

			9	**32**
1.	Secourez-moy, ma dame, par amours	Claudin	1^{v}	i^{v}
*2.	A desjuner, la belle andouille		2	xii^{v}
3.	Si la nature en la diversité		2	xiiii
4.	En attendant qui tres mal me contente		2^{v}	xv
5.	En languissant je meurs sans esperance		2^{v}	iii
6.	En souspirant les griefz souspirs d'amours		3	xii^{v}
7.	O cruaulté logée en grant beaulté	Claudin	3^{v}	ix^{v}
8.	Le grant ennuy que incessamment porte	Claudin	3^{v}	ix^{v}
9.	Si le vouloir adoulcit la douleur	Claudin	4	x
10.	Dont vient cela, belle, je vous supply	Claudin	4^{v}	iiii^{v}
11.	Vivray-je tousjours en soucy	Claudin	5	vii

* Modern edition in *CMM 20*. For other modern editions see **2**.

12.	Joyssance vous donneray, mon amy	Claudin	5	vi
13.	Si j'ay pour vous mon avoir despendu	Claudin	5^{v}	xi^{v}
14.	Il est jour dit l'alouette	Claudin	6	vii^{v}
15.	Le content est riche en ce monde	Claudin	6^{v}	v
16.	De resjoyr mon povre coeur		7	xi^{v}
17.	Quant chanteras pour ton ennuy		7^{v}	vi^{v}
18.	Le triste coeur puis qu'avec vous demeure		8	xiiii^{v}
19.	Ma bouche rit et mon coeur pleure		8^{v}	xiiii^{v}
20.	Las, voulez vous qu'une personne	[Vermont]	8^{v}	v^{v}
21.	Mon coeur est souvent bien marry	Claudin	9^{v}	ii^{v}
22.	Le départyr de cil que tant j'aymoye		9^{v}	xv^{v}
23.	Veu le gref mal ou sans fin je labeure		10	xi
24.	Je my pleins fort non pas de ma maistresse		10^{v}	viii^{v}
25.	Puis que j'ay mis tout mon entendement		11	x^{v}
26.	Serpe et la serpette, les serpiers et le serpillon	Claudin	11^{v}	viii
	T & B: Vive la serpe, les serpiers et le serpillon			
27.	Changeons propos, c'est trop chanté d'amours	Claudin	12	ii
28.	J'atens secours de ma seulle pensée	Claudin	12^{v}	xii
29.	Languir me fais sans t'avoir offensé	Claudin	13	iii^{v}
30.	A mon resveil ung oyseau j'ay oy		13^{v}	ix
31.	Ung jour Robin alloit aux champs	Claudin	14	iiii
32.	N'auray-je jamais réconfort de vous	[Jacotin]	14	xiii
33.	Réconfortez le petit coeur de moy	Jennequin	14^{v}	xvi
34.	Le coeur est bon et le vouloir aussi		15	xiii^{v}
35.	J'ay contenté ma volunté suffisamment	Claudin	15^{v}	ii^{v}
36.	Las, je my plains, mauldicte soit fortune	Claudin	16	xiii^{v}
37.	Tant que vivray en aage florissant	[Claudin]	16^{v}	xvi^{v}

¶ Finis

A revised edition of **2**, lacking nos. 23, 24, and 26; nos. 2, 3, 4, 5, 6, 7, 8, 9, and 24 are new.
Contents same as **32**; attributions from **32**.
Facsimile of no 29, Superius, in D. Heartz, "La Chronologie des recueils imprimés par Pierre Attaingnant," *La Revue de Musicologie* XLIV (1959), 181.

1529, APRIL 22

10

Quarãte et deux chãsõs musicales / a troys parties nouuellement et correctemẽt imprimees a Paris le / xxii. iour dapuril mil cinq centz vingt et neuf par Pierre Attaingnãt / demourãt en la rue de la Harpe deuant le bout de la rue des Mathu=/rins pres leglise saint Cosme. desquelles la table sensuyt. / [Table] / [Corrigenda] **Superius.** /

3 vol. in-8° obl., 15 × 10 cm.; 20 f. numbered 1–20
Sign.: ✠a^{4}–✠e^{4}; ✠AA^{4}–✠EE^{4}; ✠A^{4}–✠E^{4} (B: ✠A ii, ✠A ii)
RISM-I, 1529^{4}

Paris: Bibliothèque Nationale, Rés. Vm^{7} 180.

1.	Le trop long temps qu'ay esté sans te veoir		1v
2.	En regardant son gratieux maintien		2
*3.	D'amours je suys déshéritée		2v
4.	Mon cueur avez par subtille maniere		2v
5.	J'auroys grant tort de mespriser amours		3v
†6.	Je demeure seulle esgarée avec cent mille douleurs		4
†7.	Le cueur est mien qui oncques ne fut pris		4v
†8.	Ces facheux sotz qui mesdisent d'aymer		5
†‡9.	Je ne sçay pas coment a mon entendement		5v
†10.	C'est boucané de se tenir a une		5v
†11.	J'ay mis mon cueur en ung lieu seulement		6
†12.	Amy, souffrez que je vous ayme	[1][Moulu]	6v
†13.	Fortune, lesse-moy la vie		6v
†14.	J'ay trop aymé, vrayment je le confesse		7
15.	S'esbahist on se j'ay perdu le taint		7v
†16.	Dolent départ du lieu tant fort aymé		8
17.	Si par souffrir on peult vaincre fortune		8
†18.	Amour vault trop qui bien s'en sçait déffaire		8v
19.	Hélas, que c'est ung grant remort		9
20.	On n'en fait plus si on ne les commande		9v
21.	Mais que ce fust le plaisir de elle		10
22.	Héllas, se je vivoys mil ans		10v
23.	Incessamment je my tourmente		11
24.	Que t'aige fait desplaisante fortune		11
§25.	Belle sur toutes ma doulce amye B: Total pulchra es	[2][Agricola]	11v
* #26.	On a mal dit de mon amy	[3][Févin]	12v
*27.	C'est grant erreur de cuider présumer		13
28.	J'ay espéré ce qui point ne me appaise		13v
29.	J'ay trop loué Amour et sa noblesse		13v
*30.	Vive la marguerite c'est une noble fleur		14v
31.	Abus sert a conduire en court		15
32.	Hé, Dieu, qui mi confortera		15v
33.	Héllas, or ay-je bien perdu		16
34.	Certes, ce n'est pas gloire chevaleureuse		16v
‖35.	Au joly boys je rencontray m'amye	[4][Clemens]	17
36.	Je brusle et ars et est mon cueur espris		17v
37.	Trop se fier au promesses d'aultruy		18
38.	Héllas, héllas, je suys bany		18v
39.	Si j'ay erré et fait piteuse qu'este mon erreur		19
40.	Ainsy meurs vif et mon cueur se tourmente		19v
41.	Adieu amours, de vous suys las		20
†42.	C'est grant plaisir d'estre amoureux		20v

¶ Finis

* Modern edition in *Thirty Chansons* (*1960*).
† Modern edition in *CMM 20*.
‡ Modern edition in *Theatrical Chansons*.
§ Modern edition in *GMB*.
‖ Modern edition in *CMM 4*.
\# Modern edition in A. Tillman Merritt, "A Chanson Sequence by Févin," *Essays on Music in, Honor of Archibald Thompson Davison*. Cambridge, Mass., 1957.

[1] Attribution from *Premier livre de chansons a trois parties* . . . , Paris, Le Roy and Ballard, 1578, fol. 18.
[2] Attribution after *Canti C*, Venice, Petrucci, 1504, fol. 162.
[3] Attribution to Févin in Cambridge MS Pepys 1760, fol. 47v.
[4] Attribution after *Recueil des fleurs* . . . *a trois parties* . . . , Louvain, Phalesius, 1560, p. 4

Title page reproduced in Renouard, *Imprimeurs et Libraires parisiens du xvie siècle*, Paris, 1964, Plate 32.

[1529]

11

Motetz **nouuellemēt composez Imprimez a paris par Pierre** / **attaignāt demourāt a la rue de la harpe pres s. cosme** / **Superius.** / [Music] /

4 vol. in-8° obl., 15 × 10 cm.; 16 f. numbered 1–16 (T: 13 13 15 16; Ct: 13 13 15 15)
Sign.: *a⁴–*d⁴; *aa⁴–*dd⁴; *AA⁴–*DD⁴; *A⁴–*D⁴
RISM–I, [1528][2]

Eichstätt: Staatliche Bibliothek, No. 15 (Ct, defective, f. 14–16)
Paris: Bibliothèque Nationale, Rés. Vm⁷ 182 (B: 10 9 12 11, incorrectly bound)
[1] Versailles: Bibliothèque Municipale, Fonds Goujet, 8° G. 32 (3) (S)

1.	Girum cæli circuivi sola—I Ego in altissimis habito—II	[Claudin]	1
2.	Aspice, Domine, quia facta est desolata civitas—I Plorans ploravit in nocte et lachrymæ eius—II		2
3.	Philomena prævia temporis ameni—I Veni dulcis amica Dei noctis solatia præstans—II	[Richafort]	3
4.	Impetum inimicorum ne timueritis		4v
5.	Deus venerunt gentes in hereditatem tuam—I Effunde iram tuam in gentes—II (à 3) Adjuva nos, Domine Deus salutaris noster—III		5v
6.	Regina cæli lætare, alleluya—I Resurrexit sicut dixit, alleluya—II	[Brumel]	7v
7.	Regnum mundi et omnem ornatum sæculi		8v
8.	Deus in nomine tuo salvum me fac—I Averte mala inimicis meis in veritate tua—II		9v
9.	Emendemus in melius quæ ignoranter peccavimus—I Peccavimus cum patribus nostris—II	[Richafort]	11
10.	Deus ultionum Dominus libere egit—I Intelligite sapientes in populo—II	[Gombert]	12v
[2]11.	Da pacem, Domine, in diebus nostris—Canon in subdyatessaron (T on fol. 14)	[Brumel]	13v
12.	Ave Maria virgo virginum sanctæ Trinitatis sacrarium—[6 ss bb]		14v

La table de ceste presente partie / [Table] /

[1] Three MS folios of music plus one blank folio at end:
Folio 65–66 Superius to a chanson "Quant j'estoys a maints"
Folio 66v–67 Untexted Superius part for "Je suis desheritée (**44**–16)
A 16th-century hand has scrawled on the final page: "Je moy Pierre Garnier conoy et confesse devoir a messire Andry de Vaulx la somme de 40 livres tournois pour[———]de bons heritages ce [———]." (Date eradicated.)

[2] In Superius book only.

"Ista est specio en canon" appears only in table of Superius book.
First page of the Contratenor reproduced in Robert Brun, *La Typographie en France au seizième, siècle*, Paris, 1938, Plate XXX.

For attributions see François Lesure, "Les anonymes des Recueils imprimés français du XVIe s.", *Fontes Artis Musicae* I (1954), 79.

1529, OCTOBER 1

12

xii Motetz a quatre et cinq voix / **cōposez par les autheurs cy dessoubz escriptz Nagueres imprimees a** / **Paris par Pierre Attaingnāt demourant a la rue de la Harpe pres** / **leglise saint Cosme** / **desquelz la table sensuyt.** / [Table] / [Corrigenda] / **Superius kal. Octo. 1529** /

Tenor: **xii Motetz musicaulx a quatre et** / **cinq voix . . . Auec priuilege du Roy nostre sire pour troys ans tant pour les** / **liures ia imprimees que a imprimer.**

4 vol. in-8° obl., 15 × 10 cm.; 16 f. numbered [i]–xvi
Sign.: *e i, ✠e$^{2-4}$–✠h^{4}; *ee i, ✠ee$^{2-4}$–✠hh^{4}; *EE i, ✠EE$^{2-4}$–✠HH^{4}; *E i, ✠E$^{2-4}$–✠H^{4}
RISM–I, 1529[1]

Eichstätt: Staatliche Bibliothek, No. 16 (Ct, f. xvi lacking)
Lausanne: Succession A. Cortot (olim Wernigerode) (S). "Le XXII. Livre"
Munich: Bayerische Staatsbibliothek, Mus. Pr. 40/5
Paris: Bibliothèque Nationale, Rés. Vm[7] 183

[1]1.	Nativitas >gloriosæ virginis Mariæ Conceptio	Claudin	i[v]
2.	Sancta Maria, succurre miseris	Phi. Deslouges	ii
3.	Salve Barbara dignissima quæ in cælo	Deslogues	iii
4.	Michael archangele, veni in adjutorium	Claudin	iiii
5.	Ecce tu pulchra es, amica mea—I Venit dilectus meus in hortum meum—II	Du croc	v
6.	In illo tempore Maria Magdalene—I Sepulchrum christi viventis—II	Mouton	vi[v]
7.	Angelus Domini ad pastores—I Et invenietis infantem pannis involutum—II	Gombert	viii
8.	Quæramus cum pastoribus verbum incarnatum—I Ubi pascas, ubi cubes dic si ploras—II	Mouton	ix[v]

[1] Table: Nativitas est hodie.

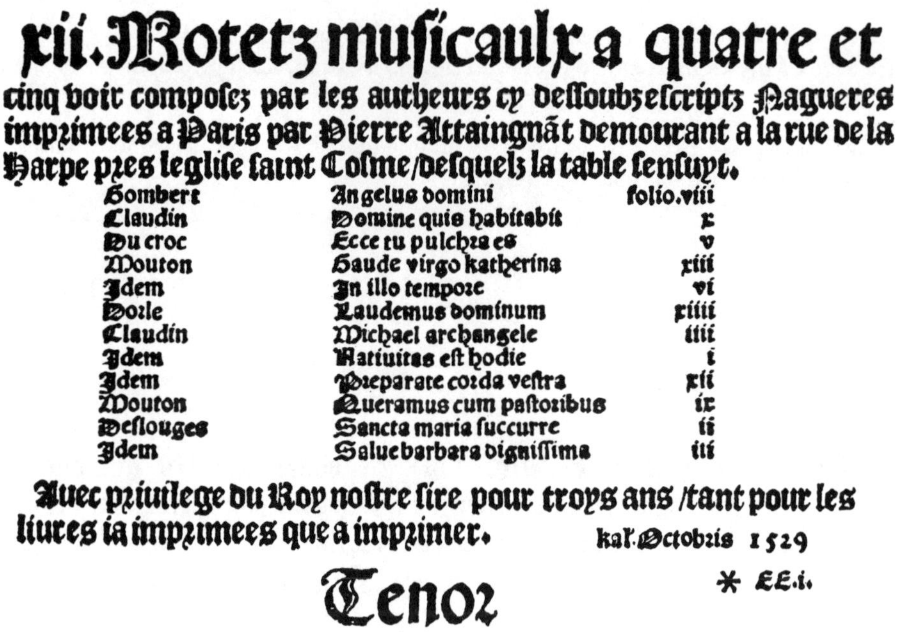

xii. Motetz musicaulx a quatre et
cinq voix composez par les autheurs cy dessoubz escriptz Naguerès
imprimees a Paris par Pierre Attaingnãt demourant a la rue de la
Harpe pres leglise saint Cosme/desquelz la table sensuyt.
Gombert Angelus domini folio.viii
Claudin Domine quis habitabit x
Du croc Ecce tu pulchra es v
Mouton Gaude virgo katherina xiii
Idem In illo tempore vi
Dorle Laudemus dominum xiiii
Claudin Michael archangele iiii
Idem Natiuitas est hodie i
Idem Preparate corda vestra xii
Mouton Queramus cum pastoribus ix
Deslouges Sancta maria succurre ii
Idem Salue barbara dignissima iii
Auec priuilege du Roy nostre sire pour troys ans /tant pour les
liures ia imprimees que a imprimer. kal. Octobris 1529
Tenor
* EE.i.

17 Title page (Tenor) of *XII Motetz* **(12)** with excerpt from the first royal privilege. By courtesy of the Bayerische Staatsbibliothek, Munich.

9.	Domine, quis habitabit in tabernaculo tuo—I Ad nichilum deductus est in conspectu eius—II	Claudin	x^{v}
10.	Preparate corda vestra Domino	Claudin	xii
11.	Gaude, virgo Katherina, quam refulsit—I Gaude, quia meruisti—II	Mouton	xiii
12.	Laudemus Dominum quem laudant angeli—I Christe redemptor omnium conserva tuos famulos—II S 1: Conserva tuos famulos beate semper virginis S 2: Omnes sancti et sanctæ Dei orate pro nobis	[2]Dorle	xiiii^{v}

In the tenor part a printed page is pasted over the original page on folio viii^{v}. Folio vi of the Tenor reproduced in Renouard, *Imprimeurs et Libraires parisiens du xvie siècle*, Paris, 1964, Pl. A33, top.

A MS addition follows the Superius part belonging to the Cortot Succession. It is written on old paper—the same make as that on which the music is printed—which has been lined with staves by hand. The contents are the Superius parts of the following:

		MS addition folio
Pavenne Gaillarde	(identical with "Bel fiore" and perhaps the lost ensemble model for the lute pavan, **16**–42)	1
Gaillarde Autre gaillarde		1^{v}
Trium. Vray dieu d'aimer		2

[2] "Drole" in Superius, f. xiv^{v}.

13

Tres breue et familiere introdu/ction pour entendre & apprēdre par soy mesmes a iouer toutes chansons reduictes en la tabu-/lature du Lutz / avec la maniere daccorder le dict Lutz. Ensemble. xxxix. chansons dont la plus / part dicelles sōt en deux sortes / cest assauoir a deux parties & la musique. Et a troys sans musiq̄. / Le tout acheue dimprimer le. vi. iour doctobre. 1529. Par Pierre Attaingnāt demourant a / Paris en la rue de la Harpe pres leglise saint Cosme. Desquelles la table sensuyt / [Table] / Avec priuilege du Roy nr̄e sire pour troys ans / que nul ne pourra / imprimer ou faire imprimer en ce royaulme la mu/sique & ieu du lutz fors le dict Attaingnant. soubz les / peines contenues es lettres dudict priuilege. /

1 vol. in-8° obl., 15 × 10 cm.; 60 f. numbered iii–lx
Sign.: A⁴–P⁴

Berlin: Stiftung Preussischer Kulturbesitz (Staatsbibliothek, West Berlin), Mus. ant. theor. F. 100

*1.	Prelude	[ii^v]
*2.	Prelude	iii^v
*3.	Prelude	iiii^v
*4.	Prelude	v^v
*5.	Alsowerdemont. A toy me rendz	vi^v
*6.	Dulcis amica	vii^v
*7.	C'est boucané [arrangement of **10**–10]	viii^v
*8.	Prelude	ix
*9.	Fortune laisse [**10**–13]	ix^v
†10.	Fortune, laisse moy la vye [idem]	x
*11.	Amy souffrés [**10**-12—Moulu]	xi^v
†12.	[A]my, souffrés que je vous ayme [idem]	xii^v
*13.	J'ay trop aymé [**10**-14]	xiii^v
†14.	[J]'ay trop aymé, vrayment je le confesse [idem]	xiiii^v
*15.	Si vostre cueur [**7**-30]	xv^v
†16.	Si vostre cueur prent le tanné [idem]	xvi^v
*17.	De retourner [**5**-24]	xvii^v
†18.	[D]e retourner mon amy je te pry [idem]	xviii^v
*19.	Languir me fais [**2**-21; **9**-29; **32**-6—Claudin]	xix^v
†20.	[L]anguir me fais sans t'avoir offensée [idem]	xx^v
*21.	Vivray-je tousjours en soucy [**2**-4; **9**-11; **32**-13—Claudin]	xxi^v
†22.	[V]ivray-je tousjours en soucy [idem]	xxii^v
*23.	J'atens secours [**2**-20; **9**-28; **32**-25—Claudin]	xxiii^v
†24.	[J]'atens secours de ma seulle pensée [idem]	xxiiii^v

* The 40 pieces so marked are for lute solo. They are edited, with the tablature, in *Preludes, Chansons.*

† The 24 pieces so marked are for lute and voice. They are edited, with the tablature, in *Chansons au Luth et Airs de Cour Français du xvie Siècle*, by Adrienne Mairy, Geneviève Thibault, and Lionel de La Laurencie. Paris, Publications de la Société Française de Musicologie, Ser. 1, Vols. IV-V, 1934.

*25.	Ces fascheux sotz [**10**-8]	xxv^{v}
†26.	[C]es fascheux sotz qui mesdisent d'aymer [idem]	xxvi^{v}
*27.	Dolent départ [**10**-16]	xxvii^{v}
†28.	[D]olent départ du lieu tant fort aymé [idem]	xxviii^{v}
*29.	Je me repens	xxix^{v}
†30.	[J]e me repens de vous avoir aymé	xxx^{v}
*31.	Je demeure seule esgarée [**10**-6]	xxxi^{v}
†32.	[J]e demeure seule esgarée avecques cent mil douleurs [idem]	xxxii^{v}
*33.	Amour vault trop [**10**-18]	xxxiii^{v}
†34.	[A]mour vault trop qui bien s'en sçait [idem]	xxxiiii^{v}
*35.	Secourés moy [**2**-1; **9**-1; **32**-1—Claudin]	xxxv^{v}
†36.	[S]ecourés moy, ma dame, par amour [idem]	xxxvi^{v}
*37.	D'ou vient cela [**2**-3; **9**-10; **32**:8—Claudin]	xxxvii^{v}
†38.	[D]'ou vient cela, belle, je vous supply [idem]	xxxviii^{v}
*39.	Il me suffit [**5**-34; **29**-34—Claudin]	xxxix^{v}
†40.	[I]l me suffit de tous mes maulx [idem]	xl^{v}
*41.	Las, las, pourquoy [**7**-18]	xli
†42.	Las, las, pourquoy m'estes vous si dure [idem]	xli^{v}
*43.	Fortune a bien couru sur moy	xlii^{v}
†44.	Fortune a bien couru sur moy	xliii
*45.	Le dur regret	xliii^{v}
*46.	Une bergerote [à 2] [**15**-30—Claudin]	xliiii^{v}
*47.	Une bergerote [à 3] [idem]	xlv
*48.	Las, il fauldra [**6**-20]	xlv^{v}
†49.	[L]as, il fauldra qu'un estranger [idem]	xlvi^{v}
*50.	Le jaulne et blanc [**6**-24]	xlvii^{v}
†51.	Le jaulne et blanc sont les couleurs [idem]	xlviii^{v}
*52.	Jouissance [**2**-5; **9**-12; **32**-11—Claudin]	xlix^{v}
†53.	[J]ouissance vous donneray, mon amy [idem]	l^{v}
*54.	D'estre amoureux	li^{v}
†55.	[D]'estre amoureux jamais ne seray las	lii^{v}
*56.	Tant que vivray [**2**-2; **9**-37; **32**-37; **74**-6—Claudin]	liii^{v}
†57.	[T]ant que vivray en aage florissant [idem]	liiii^{v}
*58.	Si j'ay pour vous [**2**-6; **9**-13; **32**-23—Claudin]	lv^{v}
†59.	[S]i j'ay pour vous mon avoir despendu [idem]	lvi^{v}
*60.	D'amour je suys [**10**-3]	lvii^{v}
*61.	De toy me plains [**5**-26]	lviii
*62.	Elle s'en va [**14**-9—Claudin]	lviii^{v}
*63.	La guerre	lix
*64.	Trésoriere [**7**-3]	lx

On fol. i^{v}–ii: "Troys breues rigles pour estre tost & facilemēt introduict en la tabulature du lutz." These folios are published in facsimile in Johannes Wolf, *Handbuch der Notationskunde*, Vol. II, pp. 72–73. Facsimiles of the title page are to be found in both modern editions mentioned.

1529, NOVEMBER 1

14

Trente et vne chanson musicales / **a quatre parties nouuellemēt imprimees a Paris p. Pierre Attain=/ gnant demourant en la rue de la Harpe pres leglise saint Cosme.** / **desquelles la table sensuyt.** / [Table] / [Corrigenda] / **1529** / **Superius** /

Tenor: **1529 kal. Nouēb. Tenor** / **Cum priuilegio.** /

4 vol. in-8° obl., 15 × 10 cm.; 16 f. numbered i–xvi (S: ix vi xi viii; T: ix vi xi viii)
Sign.: †a⁴–†d⁴; †aa⁴–†dd⁴; †AA⁴–†DD⁴; †A⁴–†D⁴
RISM–I, 1529²

Eichstätt: Staatliche Bibliothek, No. 8 (Ct)
Paris: Bibliothèque Nationale, Rés. Vm⁷ 173

1.	Mon povre cueur, héllas, que nuyt et jour souspire	Gascongne	iᵛ
2.	L'aultre jour jouer m'aloie dens ung boys	Consilium	ii
3.	My levay par ung matin plus matin que aprins que n'avoie	Janequin	iiᵛ
*4.	L'espoir que j'ay d'acquérir vostre grace		iii
*5.	Hau, hau le boys prions a Dieu le roy	Claudin	iiiᵛ
6.	Puis que fortune a sur moy entrepris	Claudin	iiii
7.	Au joly boys en l'ombre d'ung soucy	Claudin	iiiiᵛ
8.	Belle, sans sy combien que grande offense	Lombart	v
*9.	Elle s'en va de moy tant regretée	Claudin	vᵛ
10.	En espérant le printemps advenir	Dulot	vᵛ
11.	En entrant en ung jardin j'ay trouvé Guillot	Claudin	viᵛ
12.	Pour tout le moins ayez en souvenir		vii
13.	A bien parler que c'est d'amours	Consilium	viiᵛ
14.	Je ny sçauroys chanter ne rire	Gascongne	viiᵛ
*15.	Mauldite soit la mondaine richesse	Claudin	viiiᵛ
*16.	Amours partés, je vous donne la chasse	Claudin	ix
17.	J'ay cause de moy contenter	Sohier	ixᵛ
*18.	C'est une dure départie de celuy	Claudin	x
*19.	Du bien que l'oeil absent ne peult choisir	Claudin	xᵛ
*20.	J'ay le désir content et l'effect résolu	Claudin	xᵛ
21.	Ce moys de may ma verte cotte	Jennequin	xiᵛ
22.	Au verd boys je m'en iray seule	Jennequin	xii
23.	Au joly jeu du pousse avant fait bon jouer	Jennequin	xiiᵛ
24.	Seule demeure et despourveue	Deslouges	xiii
25.	Je ne fus jamais sy aise	Janequin	xiiiᵛ
*26.	Puis qu'en amours a si grant passetemps	Claudin	xiiii
27.	S'il est a ma poste il aura mon cueur	Hesdin	xiiiiᵛ
28.	Ce n'est pas trop que d'avoir ung amy	Vermonti'	xv
29.	Trop dure m'est la longue demourée	Jacotin	xvᵛ
30.	Vire, vire, Jan Jennette	Courtoys	xvᵛ
31.	A déclarer mon affection my souffit l'escripture		xviᵛ

¶ Finis

Complete modern edition in *MMRF*, Vol. VII. Includes facsimiles of title page, xvᵛ, and xvi of T.

* Modern edition in *CMM 20*.

1530, JANUARY 1

15

Trente et huyt chãsons musicales / **a quatre parties nouuellemẽt imprimees a Paris p. Pierre Attain-**/**gnant demourant en la rue de la Harpe pres leglise saint Cosme.** / **Desquelles la table sensuyt.** / [Table] / [Corrigenda] / **kal. ianua. 1529** / **Superius** / **Cum priuilegio.** /

4 vol. in-8° obl., 15 × 10 cm.; 16 f. numbered i–xvi (B: i ii ii iiii)
Sign.: †e⁴–†h⁴; †ee⁴–†hh⁴; †EE⁴–†HH⁴; †E⁴–†H⁴
RISM-I, 1530⁵

Brussels: Bibliothèque Royale, Fétis 2308 (T)
Eichstätt: Staatliche Bibliothek, No. 9 (Ct)
Lausanne: Succession A. Cortot (olim Wernigerode) (S). "Le VI. Livre"
Munich: Bayerische Staatsbibliothek, Mus. Pr. 31/16
Paris: Bibliothèque Nationale, Rés. Vm⁷ 179

1.	Nature avoit fait ung oeuvre de passé		iᵛ
2.	Trop de regretz pour vous seule je porte	[Hesdin]	iᵛ
3.	Considerant les devis tant joyeulx		ii
4.	Par toy livré suys a la mort		iiᵛ
5.	De triste dueil vivre me faict la mort		iii
6.	Héllas madame, a quoy tient-il	Hesdin	iiiᵛ
7.	Si je regrette et my complains		iiii
8.	Je l'ay requise de mes belles amours		iiiiᵛ
9.	Trop longuement avez tenu en l'air mon cueur		v
*10.	Gris et tanné me fault porter	Gombert	vᵛ
11.	Si de nouveau j'ay nouvelles couleurs	Consilium	vi
12.	Puis que donc ma maistresse n'a point pitié	Françoys	viᵛ
13.	Aymer ne puis celle que dons demande	Cybot	viᵛ
†14.	A Paris a troys fillettes te remu tu	Jacotin	vii
15.	C'est a ce coup que j'auray jouissance		viiᵛ
16.	La grant douleur que j'ay au vif		viii
17.	Sans vous changer j'attens pour tout	Ysoré	viiiᵛ
18.	Espoir je sers pensant avoir secours		ix
19.	Si mon espoir a lieu pour bien servir		ix
20.	Voicy le may le joly moys de may	Moulu	ixᵛ
21.	Veu le crédit que de moy vous avez		xᵛ
22.	Si mon amy venoit en nuyt pas je ne nye		xᵛ
23.	Une pastourelle gentille et ung berger		xi
24.	Quant vous vouldrés faire une amye		xiᵛ
25.	Or suys-je pris en merveilleux arroy		xiᵛ
26.	J'ay grant désir d'avoir plaisir d'amour mondaine		xii
27.	Possible n'est d'avoir plus de soulas		xiiᵛ
28.	Amye tu as sur moy trop d'avantaige	Cibot	xiiᵛ
29.	Bany d'amours par une oultre cuidance		xiii
‡30.	Une bergerotte prise en ung buisson	Claudin	xiiiᵛ
31.	Pis ne me peult venir que j'ay jusques icy		xiiiᵛ
32.	Quant je pense en vous, ma bien aymée		xiiii
33.	Arriere l'amoureux affaire je ne sçaurois		xiiiiᵛ
34.	D'amours me plains a bon droit et raison		xiiiiᵛ
35.	Ung vray amant doibt estre souffreteux		xv
36.	La seureté ne sera plus tant que seray envie		xvᵛ
37.	Vostre bon bruit et beaulté naturel		xvi
*38.	Boute ly ty mesme de l'enclen que main		xviᵛ
	¶ Finis		

* Modern edition in *Thirty Chansons (1960)*.
† Modern edition in *French Chansons*.
‡ Modern edition in *Preludes, Chansons*.

16

1529 Kal. Februarii / Dixhuit basses dāces garnies de / Recoupes et Tordions avec dixneuf Br̄les quatre q̄ Sauterelles q̄ / Haulberroys quinze Gaillardes et neuf Pauēnes de la pl' grāt part / desquelles le subiect est en musique. Le tout reduyt en la tabulature / du Lutz nouuellement īprime a Paris p. Pierre Attaingnāt demourāt / en la rue de la Harpe pres leglise saīt Cosme desq̄lles la table sensuyt. / [Table] / **Avec plusieurs aultres chāsons nouuelles tāt en tabulature du Lutz que en musique / Cum priuilegio regis ad triennium**

1 vol. in-8° obl., 15 × 10 cm.; 40 f. numbered i–xl
Sign.: L A4–L K4
RISM–I, 1530[7]

Berlin: Stiftung Preussischer Kulturbesitz (Staatsbibliothek, West Berlin), Mus. ant. pract. A 680

1. La magdalena. Basse dance. P.B.	i^v
2. Puis qu'en deux cueurs. Basse dance. P.B.	ii^v
3. Basse dance. P.B.	iii
4. La brosse. Basse dance. P.B.	iii^v
5. Le cueur est bon	iiii^v
6. L'espoir. B[ran]l[e]	v
7. Foués Basse dance.	v^v
8. La roque. P.B.	vi
9. Basse dance. Le corps s'en va. P.B.	vi^v
10. Tous mes amys. Basse dance. P.B.	vii
Subjectum	vii^v
11. Sansserre. Basse dance.	viii
12. Cueur angoisseux. Basse dance. P.B.	viii^v
13. Basse dance s[aint] roch	ix
Recoupe	ix^v
Tordion	x
14. Basse dance de lespine	x^v
Recoupe	xi
Tordion	xi^v
15. Basse dance	xi^v
Recoupe	xii^v
Tordion	xiii
16. Basse dance	xiii^v
Recoupe	xiiii
Tordion	xiiii^v
17. Branle gay	xv
18. Branle gay	xv^v
19. Branle	xvi
20. Branle gay. C'est mon amy	xvi^v
21. Branle	xvii
22. Branle gay	xvii^v
23. Branle gay	xviii
24. Haulberroys	xviii^v
25. Haulberroys	xix
26. B[ranle de] Poictou	xix
27. Branle [de] Poictou	xix^v
28. B[ranle de] Poictou	xix^v
29. B[ranle de] Poictou	xx
30. Branle	xx^v
31. Branle Nicolas mon beau frere	xxi
32. Basse dance Patience	xxi^v
Recoupe	xxi^v
Tordion	xxii
33. Branle gay	xxii^v
34. Branle Allez dire a c[eux] d'Amboyse	xxii^v
35. Branle gay	xxii^v
36. Basse dance Beure frais	xxiii^v
Recoupe	xxiii^v
Tordion	xxiiii
37. Branle S'il est a ma poste	xxiiii^v
38. Pavane	xxv
39. Gaillarde	xxv^v
40. Branle [de] Poictou	xxvi
41. Gaillarde	xxvi
42. Pavane	xxvi^v
Sauterelle	xxvii^v
43. Gaillarde	xxviii
44. Pavane	xxviii^v
Sauterelle	xxix

45. Gaillarde	xxix^{v}	56. Gaillarde. P.B.	xxxv^{v}
46. Pavane	xxx	Subjectum	xxxvi
47. Gaillarde	xxx^{v}	57. Pavane P.B.	xxxvi^{v}
48. Gaillarde	xxx^{v}	58. Pavane Blondeau	xxxvij
49. Gaillarde	xxxi	59. Gaillarde. P.B.	
50. Basse dance Verdurant	xxxi^{v}	Subjectum	xxxvii^{v}
Recoupe	xxxi^{v}	60. Gaillarde. Subjectum	xxxviii
Tordion	xxxii	61. Pavane P.B. [=No. 55]	xxxviii^{v}
51. Gaillarde	xxxii^{v}	62. Gaillarde [=No. 56]	xxxix
52. Pavane	xxxiii	63. Gaillarde P.B.	xxxix^{v}
53. Gaillarde. P.B.	xxxiii^{v}	Subjectum	xl
Subjectum	xxxiiii	64. La Rote de Rode	xl^{v}
54. Balle	xxxiiii^{v}	Subjectum	
55. Pavane P.B.	xxxv		

¶ Finis

Printed library mark pasted inside back cover: "Ex bibliotheca Poelchaviana"
All pieces are edited in *Preludes, Chansons.*
Pieces 31–35 follow the corrected order suggested in the critical edition. In the original a printing error was responsible for the attachment of the inner form of gathering G to the outer form of gathering F, and the outer form of G to the inner form of F.
Dances which were written on the Superius parts of chansons from Attaingnant publications are as follows:

No. 2. Puis qu'en deux cueurs	**6**-33	No. 9. Le corps s'en va	**7**-9 (Consilium)
5. Le cueur est bon	**2**-29, or **9**-34	10. Tous mes amyz	**7**-4; **74**-9 (Claudin)
6. L'espoir	**14**-4	37. S'il est a ma poste	**14**-27 (Hesdin)

Other dances find parallel settings in the pieces printed in the ensemble dance books, **17** and **20**:

1. La magdalena Basse dance P. B.	**20**-6	56. Gaillarde P. B. Subjectum	**17**-2
4. La brosse Basse dance P. B.	**20**-8	57. Pavane P. B.	**20**-49
44. Pavane-Sauterelle	**20**-47	59. Gaillarde P. B. Subjectum	**17**-1
52. Pavane	**20**-29	60. Gaillarde. Subjectum	**17**-6
53. Gaillarde P. B. Subjectum	**17**-4 and **20**-44	63. Gaillarde P. B. Subjectum	**20**-5
54. Balle	**20**-47	64. La Rote de rode Subjectum	**20**-50
55. Pavane P. B.	**20**-49		

1530 (before Easter, APRIL 17)

17

Six Gaillardes et six Pauanes / **auec Treze chãsons musicales a quatre parties le tout nouuellemẽt** / **imprime par Pierre Attaingnãt imprimeur et libraire demourant a** / **Paris en la rue de la Harpe deuant le bout de la rue des Mathurins** / **pres leglise saint Cosme. desquelles la table sensuyt.** / [Table] / **Superius** /

Tenor: 1529 / **Cum priuilegio.** /

4 vol. in-8° obl. 15 × 10 cm.; 16 f. numbered i-xvi (B: i [ii] iii iiii)
Sign.: †i^4–†m^4; †ii^4–†mm^4; †II^4–†MM^4; †I^4–†M^4
RISM–I, [c. 1528][9]

Eichstätt: Staatliche Bibliothek, No. 10 (Ct)
Lausanne: Succession A. Cortot (olim Wernigerode) (S). "Le VII. Lĩvre"
Munich: Bayerische Staatsbibliothek, Mus. Pr. 31/1

1.	Gaillarde 1		i^v
2.	Gaillarde 2		i^v
3.	3 Gaillarde		ii
4.	Gaillarde 4		ii^v
5.	Gaillarde 5		ii^v
6.	Gaillarde 6		iii
*7.	Pavane 1		iii^v
8.	Pavane 2		iii^v
9.	Pavane 3		iiii
10.	Pavane 4		iiii
11.	Pavane 5		iiii^v
12.	Pavane 6		iiii^v
†13.	A l'aventure, l'entrepris cuidant gaigner en fin le pris	Willart	v
14.	Mon cueur, mon corps, mon ame	Willart	v^v
†15.	En l'ombre d'ung buyssonnet tout au long	M. Lasson	vi^v
16.	Héllas madame, trop my donnez de peine	Moulu	vii
17.	Alleluya my fault chanter iiii. foys	Gombert	vii^v
18.	Voulez ouyr les cris de Paris	Jannequin	viii^v
19.	Jan, petit Jan, quant tu as belle femme	L'hiretier	xi^v
‡20.	Dessus le marché d'Arras, myrely, myrela, bon bas	Willart	xii^v
21.	Si vous estes m'amye je vous donneray bon temps		xiii
22.	C'est tout abus, c'est grant folye d'amours		xiiii
23.	Du feu d'amours je suis si tres espris	Jacotin	xv
†24.	Vion, viette, sommes-nous en goguette	Claudin	xv^v
25.	En regardant son gratieux maintien		xvi^v

¶ Finis

Nos. 1–12 in modern edition in *Pariser Tanzbuch.*

* Modern edition in *Chanson and Madrigal.*
† Modern edition in *Thirty Chansons (1960).*
‡ Modern edition in *CMM 20.*

1530 (after APRIL 17)

18

Vingt et neuf chāsons musicales / **a quatre parties imprimees a Paris par Pierre Attaingnāt libraire** / **demourāt en la rue de la Harpe pres leglise saint Cosme Desquelles** / **la table sensuyt. 1530** / [Table] / **Superius** / **Cum priuilegio** /

Ct, T: [Table] / ¶ **Le Roy a dōne priuilege de troys ans aud' Attaīgnāt apres līpressiō** / **de chacū liure q'l īpriera. Et deffēt a to' libraires** / **īprimeurs & aultres** / **q'lʒ nayēt a īprimer & ʒtrefaire lesd' liures p. lesd' Attaīgnāt īprimeʒ ne** / **aulcune partie diceulx sur peine de cōfiscatiō & damēde arbitraire.** /

4 vol. in-8° obl., 15 × 10 cm.; 16 f. numbered i–xvi (S: i ii ii iiii; T: i ii ii iiii)
Sign.: ‡n4–‡q4; ‡nn4–‡qq4; ‡NN4–‡QQ4; ‡N4–‡Q4
RISM–I, 1530[3]

Eichstätt: Staatliche Bibliothek, No. 11 (Ct)
Lausanne: Succession A. Cortot (olimWernigerode) (S). "Le VIII Livre"
Munich: Bayerische Statsbibliothek, Mus. Pr. 31/7
Paris: Bibliothèque Nationale, Rés. Vm[7] 171

*1.	Ma povre bourse a mal au cueur	Beaumont	iv
2.	J'ay sçeu choisir a mon plaisir complexion	Claudin	ii
3.	Tu disoys que j'en mourroys, menteuse que tu es	Claudin	iiv
4.	Tous les plaisirs que en langueur	Consilium	iiiv
5.	Autant ailleurs cela m'est déffendu	Claudin	iiii
†6.	La, la, la, l'oysillon du boys, madame	[Mouton]	iiiiv
7.	Héllas, héllas, m'avez vous oubliée		v
8.	Gris et tenné me fault porter	Claudin	vv
9.	A tout jamais me convient endurer	Claudin	vv
10.	J'ayme bien mon amy pour tant qu'il est joly	Claudin	xi
11.	Or my rendez mon karolus tant belle	G. Le heurteur	viv
12.	Vous sçavez bien, ma dame souveraine	Lupi	viiv
13.	Bien heureuse est la saison et l'année	Claudin	viii
14.	Je me vantoys, dame, n'avoir puissance	Claudin	viiiv
15.	Laissez cela, ne m'en parlez	Jennequin	ix
16.	De tant aymer mon cueur se abuseroit	Jacotin	ixv
‡17.	Faictes-le-moy, je vous prie assavoir	Jennequin	ixv
§18.	Allez souspirs enflammez au froit cueur	Claudin	xv
19.	Comme transy et presque hors du sens	Claudin	xv
20.	J'ay fait pour vous cent mille pas	Claudin	xi
21.	Moy qui ne feiz jamaiz que luy complaire	Jacotin	xiv
22.	Dictes-moy, je vous supplie, la ou je pouroys aller		xii
23.	J'ay pris pour moy le noir, non par regret	Claudin	xiiv
24.	L'ardant désir que j'ay de vous m'amye	N. Renes	xiii
25.	L'autre jour je vis par ung matin		xiiiv
26.	Dieu vous gard, ma belle amye		xiiii
27.	Sur le joly, joly jonc ma doulce amye	Passereau	xiiiiv
28.	Hé, hermite, saint hermite, oseray-je faire		xv
29.	Nous estions troys compaignons qui alions		xvv
‖30.	Amours ont changé de façon sy d'argent	[Mahiet]	xvi
31.	Ce fut en montant les degrez	N. Renes	xviv

¶ Finis

Folio xiii of the Bassus reproduced in Renouard, *Imprimeurs et Libraires parisiens du XVIe siècle*, Paris, 1964, Pl. A33, bottom.

* Modern edition in *Chorwerk, Vol. 15.* Attribution to Lupi in this edition is made after *Le Parangon des Chansons*, VIII, Lyons, Moderne, 1541.
† Modern edition in *Theatrical Chansons.*
‡ Modern edition in *Chorwerk, Vol. 73.*
§ Modern edition in *Chanson and Madrigal.*
‖ Modern edition in *French Chansons.*

19

Trente et six chansons musicales / a quatre parties imprimees a Paris par Pierre Attaingnāt libraire / demourāt en la rue de la Harpe pres leglise saint Cosme Desquelles / la table sensuyt. 1530 / [Table] / Superius. / Cum priuilegio /

4 vol. in-8° obl., 15 × 10 cm.; 16 f. numbered i–xvi (T: xiii xiiii xv vi)
Sign.: †r^4–†v^4; †rr^4–†vv^4; †RR^4–†VV^4; †R^4–†V^4
RISM–I, 1530^4

Eichstätt: Staatliche Bibliothek, No. 12 (Ct, defective)
Lausanne: Succession A. Cortot (olimWernigerode) (S). "Le IX. Livre"
Munich: Bayerische Staatsbibliothek, Mus. Pr. 31/14
Paris: Bibliothèque Nationale, Rés. Vm^7 177 (Ct fol. v–xvi bound separately after Vm^7 179)

*1.	Chantons, sonnons, trompetes, tabourins, phifres	Jennequin	i^v
2.	J'ay mes amours longuement attendu	Jacotin	ii
3.	J'ay souhaicté depuis troys moys	J. de Bechefort	ii^v
4.	Je changeray quelque chose qu'on pense	Jacotin	iii
5.	Ta grant beaulté a tant navré mon cueur	J. de Bouchefort	iii^v
6.	Par ton regart tu me fais espérer	Claudin	iii^v
†7.	J'ayme le cueur de m'amye, sa bonté	Claudin	iiii
8.	D'ung coup mortel en lieu de jouissance	Jacotin	iiii^v
9.	Doeul, double doeul, renfort de desplaisir	[Hesdin]	v
10.	Plaisir n'ay plus mais vis en desconfort		v^v
11.	La rosée du moys de may si m'a mouillée	[Rousée]	vi
12.	Le dur regret que j'ay de ma maistresse	Gobert Cochet	vi^v
13.	Je m'en voys au verd boys		vi^v
14.	Vous aurez tout ce qui est mien		vii^v
15.	Vray Dieu, las, que ferai-je		vii^v
16.	Plus vous que moy servi j'ay loyaulment	Gobert Cochet	viii^v
17.	Je n'en puys plus et n'ay qui me sequeure		ix
†18.	Tous compaignons qui beuvés voluntiers		ix^v
19.	La teste my fait si grant mal		ix^v
20.	Quant me souvient du temps passé		x
21.	N'auray-je jamais mieulx que j'ay	Claudin	x^v
22.	Sonnez my donc quant vous yrez		x^v
23.	J'ay bon vouloir de vous servir		xi^v
24.	Le mal que j'ay c'est d'avoir offensé		xi^v
25.	Par son grant art nostre mere nature	Claudin	xii
26.	Si vous voulez je le veulx bien		xii^v
27.	Hola hé, par la vertu goy, Dieu vous gart		xiii
28.	Long temps y a que je vis en espoir	[Dulot or Claudin]	xiii^v
29.	Joyeusement il fait bon vivre		xiiii
30.	N'ayés ennuy pour ceste départie		xiiii^v

* Modern edition in *Trente Chansons* (*1928*).
† Modern edition in *Thirty Chansons* (*1960*).

[1] The first piece celebrates the return of the royal princes, who had been held as hostages in Spain (1526–1530). News of the event did not reach Paris until early July.

‡31.	Quoando dormyve come la mya seignore		xiiii^v
32.	Pour le grant grief que mon esperit endure		xv
†33.	Jamais je n'aymeray grant homme		xv^v
34.	Puys qu'il est fait, de riens ne sert la plaincte		xv^v
35.	Au fons d'enfer, voire, en plus grief tourment	[2][Benedictus]	xvi
36.	Hau le boys, vignerons gentilz		xvi^v

¶ Finis

On title page of T and Ct: privilege as in **18**.
Folio iiii of the Superius is reproduced in facsimile in the article "Attaingnant" by V. Fédorov in MGG, Vol. I, col. 767–768.

‡ Modern edition in *Chanson and Madrigal.*
[2] Attribution after Cambrai, Bibl. de la Ville, MSS 125–128, fol. 122^v

1530

20

Neuf basses dances deux branles / vingt et cinq Pauennes auec quinze Gaillardes en musique a quatre / parties le tout nouuellemēt imprime a Paris par Pierre Attaīgnāt / libraire demourant en la rue de la Harpe au bout de la rue des Matu=/rins pres leglise saint Cosme. 1530 /Superius. / Cum priuilegio /

4 vol. in-8° obl., 15 × 10 cm.; 16 f. numbered i–xvi
Sign.: †x⁴–† &⁴; †xx⁴–† & &⁴; †XX⁴–† AA⁴; †X⁴–† A⁴

Eichstätt: Staatliche Bibliothek, no. 13 (Ct; xii, xvi, xiiii, xiiii, xvi)
Lausanne: Succession A. Cortot (olim Wernigerode) (S). "Le X. Livre"
Munich: Bayerische Staatsbibliothek, Mus. Pr. 31/2
Seville: Biblioteca Capitular y Colombina (Ct)

1.	1 Basse dance	i^v
2.	2 Basse dance	i^v
3.	3 Basse dance	ii
4.	4 La gatta en italien Basse dance	ii
5.	5 La scarpa my faict mal Basse dance	ii^v
6.	6 La magdalena Basse dance	ii^v
	Tourdion	iii
7.	8 Basse dance	iii^v
8.	9 La brosse Basse dance	iii^v
9.	1 Branle	iiii^v
10.	2 Branle	iiii^v
11.	1 Pavenne	v
12.	2 Pavenne	v
13.	3 Pavane	v^v
14.	4 Pavane	v^v
15.	5 Pavane	vi
16.	6 Pavenne	vi^v
17.	7 Pavenne	vii
18.	8 Pavane	vii^v
19.	9 Pavane	vii^v
20.	10 Pavane	viii
21.	11 Pavane	viii
22.	12 Pavenne	viii^v
23.	13 Pavenne	viii^v
24.	14 Pavenne	ix
25.	15 Pavenne	ix
26.	16 Pavane	ix^v
27.	17 Pavane	ix^v
28.	18 Pavane	x
	Scd's superius	x
29.	19 Pavenne	x^v
30.	1 Gaillarde	xi
31.	2 Gaillarde	xi^v
32.	3 Gaillarde	xi^v
33.	4 Gaillarde	xii
34.	5 Gaillarde	xii^v
35.	6 Gaillarde	xii^v
36.	7 Gaillarde	xiii

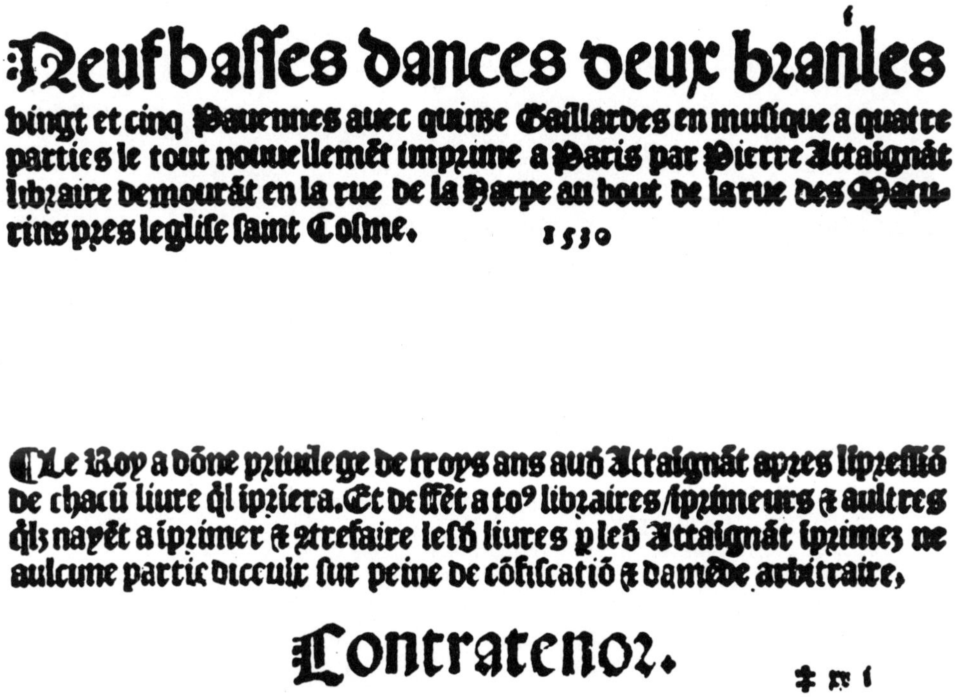
Neuf basses dances deux branles vingt et cinq Pavennes avec quinze Gaillardes en musique a quatre parties le tout nouvellemēt imprime a Paris par Pierre Attaignāt libraire demourāt en la rue de la Harpe au bout de la rue des Mathurins pres leglise saint Cosme. 1530

Le Roy a dōne privilege de troys ans audit Attaignāt apres limpressiō de chacū livre ql imprimera. Et deffēt a to⁹ libraires/imprimeurs & aultres qlz nayēt a imprimer & ctrefaire lesd livres p led Attaignāt imprimez ne aulcune partie diceulx sur peine de cōfiscatiō & amēde arbitraire.

Contratenor.

18 Title page (Contratenor) of *Neuf basses dances* **(20)** with excerpt from the first royal privilege. By courtesy of the Biblioteca Capitular y Colombina, Seville.

37. 8 Gaillarde	xiii	45. 20 Pavenne	xv^{v}
38. 9 Gaillarde	xiii^{v}	46. 21 Pavenne	xvi
39. 10 Gaillarde	xiii^{v}	47. 22 Pavenne	xvi
40. 11 Gaillarde	xiiii	48. 23 Pavenne	xvi
41. 12 Gaillarde	xiiii^{v}	49. 24 Pavenne	xvi^{v}
42. 13 Gaillarde	xiiii^{v}	50. 25 Pavenne La rote de rode	xvi^{v}
43. 14 Gaillarde	xv		
44. 15 Gaillarde	xv^{v}		

On title page of T and Ct: privilege as in **18**.
Complete modern edition in *Pariser Tanzbuch*.

R. Eitner, in *Biographisch-Bibliographisch Quellenlexikon*, Leipzig, 1900–1904, cites a copy in the Nationalsbibliothek, Vienna, dated 1538. (Vol. I, p. 230). Anton Schmid, in *Ottaviano dei Petrucci*, Vienna, 1845, p. 228, dates the Munich copy 1538. Both may be misreadings of 1530. No copy now exists at Vienna.

1530

21

Epithoma musice instrumentalis/ ad omnimodam Hemispherii seu Luthine & theoricam et practicam / Per Orontium fineum Delphinatem studiose collectum. 1530 / ¶ Venit Par̄. in officina libraria Petri Attaingnāt / in vico cythare.

1 vol. in-8° obl., 15 × 10 cm.; 7 f. unnumbered
Sign.: A^{4}–B^{3}

Berlin: Stiftung Preussischer Kulturbesitz (Staatsbibliothek, West Berlin), Mus. ant. theor. F.100 (Bound with **13**)
Vienna: Österreichische Nationalbibliothek, SA 71 F 79

Complete facsimile in *Preludes, Chansons.*

1531, JANUARY 13

22

Dixneuf chāsons musicales redui/ctes en la tabulature des Orgues Espinettes Manicordions / et telz / semblables instrumentz musicaulx Imprimees a Paris par Pierre / Attaingnāt demourāt en la rue de la Harpe pres leglise saint Cosme / Desquelles la table sensuyt. Idibus Januarii 1530 / [Table] **/ ¶ Le Roy a dōne p.missiō et priuilege aud' Attaingnant des liures q'l / a par cy deuant imprimez & espere imprimer cy apres tāt en musique / ieux de Lutz / Orgues / et semblables instrumentz q̄ nul ne les pourra / imprimer contrefaire ne aulcune partie diceulx vendre ne distribuer / iusques a troys ans apres limpressiō de chacū diceulx. Et le tout sur / peine de confiscation et damēde arbitraire. /**

1 vol. in-8° obl., 15 × 10 cm.; 40 f. numbered [i]–viii (no foliation after viii)
Sign.: ✠a4–✠k4
RISM–I, 1531[6]

Munich: Bayerische Staatsbibliothek, Mus. Pr. 235

1. Ung grant plaisir [**71**-13—Claudin]	[i^v]
2. Hau, hau le boys [**14**-5—Claudin]	iiii^v
3. Mon cueur est souvent bien marri [**2**-14, **9**-21—Claudin]	vii
4. Amour partés [**14**-16—Claudin]	viii
5. A bien grant tort [**6**-9]	[ix]
6. Celle qui m'a tant pourmené [**5**-14—Claudin]	[xi]
7. Je ne sçay point comment [**10**-9]	[xiii^v]
8. Elle s'en va de moy tant reg. [**14**-9—Claudin]	[xv^v]
9. Il me suffit [**5**-34—Claudin]	[xvii^v]
[1]10. Fors seulement—[Pipelare]	[xviii^v]
11. Le cueur est bon [**2**-29, **9**-34]	[xxi^v]
12. J'ay trop aymé [**10**-14]	[xxiii^v]
13. Au desjuner [**9**-2]	[xxv^v]
14. Mauldicte soit la mondaine richesse [**14**-15—Claudin]	[xxvi]
15. Dolent départ [**10**-16]	[xxviii]
16. Aupres de vous [**2**-24, **5**-3, **70**-18—Claudin or Jacotin]	[xxx]
17. C'est grant plaisir [**10**-42]	[xxxiii]
18. D'ung nouveau dart [**8**-5]	[xxxv^v]
19. Je le disoies [**7**-29]	[xxxviii]

¶ Finis

Facsimile edition, with **23**, **24**, and **28**, in *Chansons und Tänze*.
Modern edition, with **23** and **24**, in *CMM 20*.

[1] Attribution from various MSS. See commentary in *CMM* 20.

1531, FEBRUARY 1

23

Vingt et cinq chāsons musicales / reduictes en la tabulature des Orgues Espinettes Manicordions A / telz sēblables instrumētz musicaulx Imprimees a Paris par Pierre / Attaingnāt demourāt en la rue de la Harpe pres leglise saint Cosme / Desquelles la table sensuyt. kal. februarii 1530 / [Table] / **Auec priuilege du Roy nostre / sire pour trois ans.** /

1 vol. in-8° obl., 15 × 10 cm.; 40 f. numbered xli–lxxx (lxxv lxxiiii lxxiii lxxvi)
Sign.: ✠l4–✠v4
RISM–I, 1531[7]

Munich: Bayerische Staatsbibliothek, Mus.Pr. 236

1. Aller m'y fault sur la verdure [**5**-9, **29**-9—Janequin]	xli
2. J'ay contenté ma volunté [**2**-30, **9**-35, **32**-4—Claudin]	xliiii

3. C'est une dure départie [**14**-18—Claudin] xlv^v
4. Le cueur de vous [**5**-8, **29**-8—Claudin] xlvii
5. Contre raison [**5**-19, **29**-19—Claudin] xlix
6. L'heur de mon bien [**6**-19] li
7. Du bien que l'oeil [**14**-19—Claudin] lii
8. Mon cueur en vous [**7**-25] liii^v
9. Dessus le marché d'Arras [**17**-20—Willaert] lv
10. Tant que vivray [**2**-2, **9**-37, **32**-37, **74**-6—Claudin] lvii
11. J'atens secours [**2**-20, **9**-28, **32**-25—Claudin] lviii^v
12. Languir me fais [**2**-21, **9**-29, **32**-6—Claudin] lix^v
[1]13. Au joly bois lxi
14. Vignon, vignette [**6**-3] lxi^v
15. Le jaulne et bleu [**6**-24] lxiii
16. Le cueur est mien [**10**-7] lxiiii
17. Ung jour Robin [**2**-25, **9**-31, **32**-7—Claudin] lxv
18. C'est a grant tort [**2**-23, **5**-31, **29**-31—Claudin] lxvii
19. Changeons propos [**2**-19, **9**-27, **32**-2—Claudin] lxviii^v
20. Maulgré moy viz [**6**-23, **70**-24—Claudin] lxxi
21. Longtemps y a [**2**-26, **6**-18] lxxiii [lxxv]
22. Secourez moy [**2**-1, **9**-1, **32**-1—Claudin] lxxv [lxxiii]
23. Fortune [**10**-13] lxxvi^v
24. De toy me plains [**5**-26, **29**-26] lxxviii
25. Ces facheux sotz [**10**-8] lxxix^v

¶ Finis

For facsimile and modern edition see **22.**

[1] The tenor tune of this arrangement is related to that in **10**-35 and to the Superius in the four-voiced pavane, **17**-9.

1531, FEBRUARY 5

24

Vingt et six chansons musicales / reduictes en la tabulature des Orgues Espinettes Manicordions & / telz sẽblables instrumẽtz musicaulx Imprimees a Paris par Pierre / Attaingnãt demourãt en la rue de la Harpe pres leglise saint Cosme / Desquelles la table sensuyt. Nonã. februarii 1530 / [Table] / Auec priuilege du Roy nostre / sire pour trois ans. /

1 vol. in-8° obl., 15 × 10 cm.; 40 f. numbered lxxxi–cxx (xciil xciii xcv xcvi; final folio misnumbered cxix)
Sign.: ✠aa^4–✠kk^4
RISM-I, 1531^8

Munich: Bayerische Staatsbibliothek, Mus. Pr. 237

1. Mon cueur gist tousjours [**6**-26, **79**-3—Claudin] lxxxi^v
2. C'est boucané [**10**-10] lxxxiii
3. Las, voulez vous [**2**-13, **9**-20, **32**-10, **70**-19—Vermont] lxxxiiii
4. Je demeure seule esgarée [**10**-6] lxxxvi^v
5. Amour vault trop [**10**-18] lxxxvii^v

6. Las, je my plains [**2**-31, **9**-36, **32**-29—Claudin] lxxxix
7. Amy, souffrez [**10**-12—Moulu] xc
8. Je ne fais rien que réquérir [**8**-2, **70**-27—Claudin] xci^{v}
9. Le content est riche [**2**-8, **9**-15, **32**-9—Claudin] xcii^{v}
10. De retourner [**5**-24, **29**-24] xciiii^{v}
11. Ung grant plaisir [**6**-7] xcv^{v}
12. Si j'ay pour vous [**2**-6, **9**-13, **32**-23—Claudin] xcvii
13. Puis qu'en deux cueurs [**6**-33] xcviii^{v}
14. Puis qu'en amours [**14**-26—Claudin] c
15. Il est jour dit l'alouette [**2**-7, **9**-14, **32**-14—Claudin] cii
16. J'ay mis mon cueur [**10**-11] ciii^{v}
17. Vivray-je tousjours [**2**-4, **9**-11, **32**-13—Claudin] ciiii^{v}
18. J'ay le désir content [**14**-20—Claudin] cv^{v}
19. Veu le grief mal [**2**-16, **9**-23, **32**-22] cvii^{v}
20. L'espoir que j'ay [**14**-4] cix
21. Ma bouche rit [**71**-19—Duboys] cx^{v}
22. Dont vient cela [**2**-3, **9**-10, **32**-8—Claudin] cxii
23. A mes ennuis [**5**-10, **29**-10] cxiiii
24. Jouyssance vous donneray [**2**-5, **9**-12, **32**-11—Claudin] cxvi
25. N'auray-je jamais réconfort [**2**-27, **9**-32, **32**-28, **70**-20—Jacotin] cxvii
26. Le départyr [**2**-15, **9**-22, **32**-35] cxix

For facsimile and modern edition see **22**.

1531 (before MARCH 1)

25

Tabulature pour le ieu Dorgues / Esginetes et Manicordions sur le plain chant de Cunctipotens et / Kyrie fons. Auec leurs Et in terra. Patrem. Sanctus et Agnus dei / le tout nouuellement imprime a Paris par Pierre Attaingnant de-/mourant en la rue de la Harpe pres leglise sainct Cosme. / Auec priuilege du Roy nostre / sire pour trois ans. /

1 vol. in-8° obl., 15 × 10 cm.; 40 f. unnumbered
Sign.: †A^{4}–†K^{4}

Munich: Bayersiche Staatsbibliothek, Mus. Pr. 232

[Missa "Kyrie Fons"]	
[Kyrie]	[1^{v}]
[Gloria]	[9^{v}]
[Credo]	[18^{v}]
[Sanctus]	[21^{v}]
[Agnus]	[23^{v}]
[Missa "Cunctipotens"]	
[Kyrie]	[26]
[Gloria]	[30^{v}]
[Sanctus]	[35]
[Angus dei]	[38]

Complete modern edition, with **26,** in *Deux livres d'Orgue*. Includes facsimiles of title pages.

26

Magnificat sur les huit tons auec / Te deū laudamus. et deux Preludes / le tout mys en la tabulature des / Orgues Espinettes A Manicordions imprimez a Paris par Pierre / Attaingnant libraire demourant en la rue de la Harpe pres leglise / saint Cosme. kal. Martii 1530 / [Table] / Auec priuilege du Roy nostre sire pour trois ans. /

1 vol. in-8° obl., 15 × 10 cm.; 40 f. numbered xli–lxxx
Sign.: ✝L⁴–✝V⁴
RISM–I, 1530[8]

Munich: Bayerische Staatsbibliothek, Mus. Pr. 233

1.	Preludium	xli^v		
2.	Prelude sur chacun ton	xliiii^v		
3.	Magnificat primi toni	xlix		
	Secundus versus	l		
4.	Magnificat secundi toni	li		
	Secundus versus	lii^v		
5.	Magnificat tertius toni	liii^v		
	Secundus versus	liiii^v		
6.	Magnificat quarti toni	lv^v		
	Secundus versus	lvi^v		
	Tertius versus	lvii^v		
	Quartus versus	lviii^v		
	Quintus versus	lviiii		
7.	Magnificat quinti toni	lx^v		
	Secundus versus	lxi^v		
8.	Magnificat sexti toni	lxii		
	Secundus versus	lxiii		
9.	Magnificat septimi toni	lxiiii		
	Secundus versus	lxv^v		
10.	Magnificat octavi toni	lxvi^v		
	Secundus versus	lxvii^v		
	Tertius versus	lxix		
	Quartus versus	lxx		
11.	Te Deum laudamus	lxxi^v		
	¶ Finis			

Complete modern edition by Y. Rokseth. (See **25**.)

27

Treze Motetz musicaulx auec vng / Prelude / le tout reduict en la tabulature des Orgues Espinettes et / Manicordions et telz semblables instrumentz imprimez a Paris par / Pierre Attaingnant libraire demourant en la rue de la Harpe pres / leglise saint Cosme Desquelz la table sensuyt. kal'. April'. 1531 / [Table] / Auec priuilege du Roy nostre sire / pour trois ans. /

[1] Since Easter fell on April 9, 1531, the date on the title page should read "kal'. April'. 1530." Furthermore, April 1, 1531, is an impossible date under the Julian calendar because Easter fell in March in 1532.

1 vol. in-8° obl., 15 × 10 cm.; 40 f. numbered lxxxi–cxx
Sign.: †Aa^4–†Kk^4
RISM–I, 1531^5

Munich: Bayerische Staatsbibliothek, Mus. Pr. 234 (missing since 1963)

1.	Manus tuæ, Domine, fecerunt me	lxxxi^v
2.	Fortuna desperata	lxxxiii^v
3.	Bone Jesu dulcissime! [**63**-26—Mathieu Gascongne]	lxxxvi^v
4.	Sicut malus [Moulu]	lxxxix
5.	Sancta Trinitas [Févin]	xcii
6.	Benedictus Févin	xcvii
7.	Si bona suscepimus [**63**-10—Claudin]	c
8.	Sicut lilium [Brumel]	cv
9.	Dulcis amica Dei [**93**-1]	cvi^v
10.	O vos omnes qui transitis per viam [Compère] Secunda pars	cviii
11.	Aspice Domine [**63**-16—La Fage; **101**-16—Claudin]	cxi^v
12.	Consummo	cxv
13.	Parce Domine [Obrecht]	cxvii
14.	Prelude	cix^v

¶ Finis

Complete modern edition in *Treize Motets.* Includes facsimile of title page and folio lxxxi^v. The order of pieces has been changed as follows:

Original	*Rokseth edition*	*Original*	*Rokseth edition*
1.	V	8.	X
2.	XIII	9.	IV
3.	III	10.	VI
4.	XI	11.	I
5.	VIII	12.	XII
6.	II	13.	VII
7.	IX	14.	Initial piece, without number

Attributions of the models are made by Rokseth.

[1531 (before JUNE 18)]

28

Quatorze Gaillardes neuf Pauen / nes / sept Branles et deux Basses Dances le tout reduict de musique / en la tabulature du ieu Dorgues Espinettes Manicordions A telz / semblables instrumentz musicaulx Imprimees a Paris par Pierre / Attaingnāt demourāt en la rue de la Harpe pres leglise saint Cosme / Auec priuilege du Roy nostre / sire pour trois ans. /

1 vol. in-8° obl., 15 × 10 cm.; 40 f. unnumbered
Sign.: ✠^{4}; ✠AA^4–✠BB^4; *CC^4–*HH^4; †II^4

Munich: Bayerische Staatsbibliothek, Mus. Pr. 238

1. Pavane	[1]p. 2	16. Gaillarde	42
Gaillarde sur la Pavane	7	17. Branle	43
2. Gaillarde	10	18. Gaillarde	45
3. Gaillarde	11	19. Pavane	46
4. Branle commun	14	20. Gaillarde	47
5. Branle gay	15	21. Gaillarde	49
6. Gaillarde	17	22. Pavanne	51
7. Basse dance	21	La Gaillarde	55
8. Basse dance	23	23. Gaillarde	58
9. Branle	25	24. Pavane	60
10. Gaillarde	27	25. Gaillarde	62
11. Pavenne	31	26. Gaillarde	64
12. Gaillarde	34	27. Gaillarde	66
13. Branle [simple]	37	28. Pavane	69
14. Branle	39	29. Pavane	73
15. Branle [simple]	40	30. Gaillarde	77

¶ Finis

Complete modern edition by D. Heartz in *Keyboard Dances from the Earlier Sixteenth Century* (Corpus of Early Keyboard Music, Vol. VIII), American Institute of Musicology, 1965.

[1] Page numbers are those of the fascimile edition, *Chansons und Tänze.*

[1531 ?][1]

29

Trēte et quatre chāsōs musicales / a quatre parties imprimees a Paris par Pierre Attaingnant librai-/re demourant en la rue de la Harpe pres leglise sainct Cosme / Desquelles la table sensuyt. / [Table] / **Superius / Auec priuilege pour troys ans./**

4 vol. in-8° obl., 15 × 10 cm.; 16 f. numbered i–xvi (B: f. xvi blank)
Sign.: 34 e^4–34 h^4; 34 ee^4–34 hh^4; 34 EE^4–34 HH^4; 34 E^4–34 H^4
RISM–I, [c. 1528]^6

Brussels: Bibliothèque Royale, Fétis 2307 (T)
Eichstätt: Staatliche Bibliothek, No. 3 (Ct)
Lausanne: Succession A. Cortot (olim Wernigerode) (S). "Le premier Livre" (folio iv is in facsimile)
Munich: Bayerische Staatsbibliothek, Mus. Pr. 31/12

Contents same as **5.**

[1] After April 1530 because of typography; prior to second privilege for six years, granted June 18, 1531.

30

Trente et troys chansons nouuel/les en musique a quatre parties imprimees a Paris par Pierre At-/taingnant libraire demourant en la rue de la harpe pres leglise saint / Cosme Desquelles la table sensuypt. / [Table] / Superius. / Cum priuilegio /

Bassus: kal. Februarii 1531
4 vol. in-8° obl., 15 × 10 cm.; 16 f. numbered i–xvi
Sign.: ø a⁴–ø d⁴; ø aa⁴–ø dd⁴; ø AA⁴–ø DD⁴; ø A⁴–ø D⁴
RISM–I, 1532[12]

Eichstätt: Staatliche Bibliothek, no. 14 (Ct)
Lausanne: Succession A. Cortot (olim Wernigerode) (S). "Le XI. Livre"
Munich: Bayerische Staatsbibliothek, Mus. Pr. 31/11

1.	Ayez pitié du grant mal que j'endure	Claudin	i^v
2.	Si je viz en peine et langueur	Claudin	ii
3.	Nulle oraison ne te devroit tant plaire		ii^v
4.	J'attens l'aumosne de doulceur		iii
*5.	Dictes sans peur ou l'ouy ou nenny	Claudin	iii^v
6.	Dessoubz le marbe de dure récompense	Claudin	iiii
7.	Si ainsi est que me veuillez aymer		iiii^v
8.	De jour en jour tu me fais consumer		v
9.	La plus des plus en beaulté excellente	Le bouteiller	v^v
10.	Maintenant voy que fortune m'a prins		vi
11.	Mon povre cueur ne pourroit plus porter		vi^v
12.	Douloir me puys et non me secourir		vii
13.	Sans plus attendre, allégéz moy ma dame		vii^v
14.	Quant tu vouldras ton humble serf changer	Claudin	viii
15.	Plus ne me fault estre amoureux		viii^v
16.	Et quant je suis couchée, ô mon villain mary		ix
17.	Si vous m'aymez donnez m'en asseurance	Claudin	ix^v
18.	Mary, je songay l'autre jour	Jacotin	ix^v
19.	Si j'ay eu du mal ou du bien par oubly	Claudin	x
20.	Si mon malheur my continue	Le peletier	x^v
21.	Vostre bonheur me conduit en tristesse		x^v
22.	Je n'ose estre content de mon contentement	Claudin	xi^v
23.	Las, que crains tu, amy, de quoy as déffiance	Claudin	xii
24.	De trop penser en amour et richesse	Jacotin	xii^v
25.	Fleur de beaulté, chef d'oeuvre de nature	Consilium	xiii
26.	My larrez-vous tousjours languir	[Roquelay]	xiii^v
27.	Faulte d'argent, Dieu te mauldie		xiiii
28.	Vous aurés tout ce qui est mien [à 5]		xiiii^v
	Ct: Canon Ce que l'une faict l'autre déffaict		
29.	Le seul plaisir du désiré revoir	Claudin	xv
30.	Vueillent ou non les envieux		xv^v
31.	Tant qu'en amours tu seras ma maistresse	Jacotin	xv^v
32.	D'ung desplaisir Amour si fort my lasse	Jacotin	xvi
33.	Qui la vouldra souhaitte que je meure	Claudin	xvi^v

Finis

* Modern edition in *Anthologie*.

31

Vingt et huit chansons nouuel/les en musique a quatre parties imprimees a Paris par Pierre / Attaingnāt libraire demourāt en la rue de la Harpe pres leglise saint / Cosme Desquelles la table sensuyt. feb. 15301 / [Table] / Superius / Auec priuilege pour six ans /

4 vol. in-8° obl., 15 × 10 cm.; 16 f. numbered i–xvi
Sign.: ø e^4–ø h^4; ø ee^4–ø hh^4; ø EE^4–ø HH^4; ø E^4–ø H^4 (B: ø e i, ø E ii)
RISM–I, 1531[1]

Eichstätt: Staatliche Bibliothek, No. 15 (Ct)
Lausanne: Succession A. Cortot (olim Wernigerode) (S). "Le XII. Livre"
Munich: Bayerische Staatsbibliothek, Mus. Pr. 40/6

1.	Nous estions troys compaignons tous d'une livrée		i^v
2.	Le cueur de vous ma dame par amours	F. Dulot	ii
3.	Ung peu plus hault, ung peu plus bas mon amy	Passereau	ii^v
4.	Rire a l'entrée, plourer au départir		iii^v
5.	A bien grant deul me puis-je bien retraire		iiii
6.	A quoy tient-il dont vient cela	Gombert	iiii^v
7.	France, par consolation resjouys toy		v
8.	De bien aymer les dames je ne blasme	[Renes]	v^v
9.	Si le plaisir d'honneste jouyssance		vi
10.	Or plaise a Dieu, las, devant que je meure		vi^v
11.	Pourtant si suys ung peu jeunette d'aage		vi^v
12.	A si grant tort vous m'avés prins en haine		vii^v
13.	Mon cueur me suyt, me suyvant, me pourchasse		viii
14.	Qui mieulx ne peult, il est bien a son aise		viii^v
15.	Au port d'amours me fault user ma vie		ix
16.	Trop de tourment pour vous, dame, j'endure	Consilium	ix^v
17.	Je ne puis estre en vostre grace		x
18.	Bon jour m'amye, bon jour et bon an		x^v
19.	Aupres de vous secretement demeure [*Fricassée*]		xi^v
20.	Je suys joyeulx et languis en tristesse	[Claudin]	xii^v
21.	Celuy est sot qui de femme s'asotte		xiii
22.	De ton gent corps l'exellente facture		xiii^v
23.	Mon povre cueur plain de douleurs	Lupi	xiiii
24.	Joye et douleur, mon amy, sur mon ame	[Isoré]	xiiii^v
25.	Dieu gart de mon cueur la régente	Claudin	xv
26.	Je meurs de soif au pres de la fontaine		xv^v
27.	Prisonnier suys en prison bien profonde	Barbette	xvi
28.	Les dames se sont tailladés	Claudin	xvi^v
	T & B: Chacune d'un Toulouzan pas compra		

Finis

32

Trente et sept chãsons musicales / a quatre parties nouuellement et correctemẽt reimprimees a Paris / par Pierre Attaingnãt libraire demourant en la rue de la Harpe pres / leglise saint Cosme Desquelles la table sensuyt. Martii 1531./ [Table] / **Superius** / **Auec priuilege pour six ans** /

4 vol. in-8° obl., 15 × 10 cm.; 16 f. numbered i–xvi
Sign.: x^4–&^{4}; xx^4–& &^{4}; XX^4–AA^4; X^4–A^4
RISM–I, 1531[2]

Eichstätt: Staatliche Bibliothek, No. 7 (Ct)
Lausanne: Succession A. Cortot (olim Wernigerode) (S). "Le V. Livre"
Munich: Bayerische Staatsbibliothek, Mus. Pr. 31/15

Contents same as **9**.

Facsimile of no. 6, Superius, in D. Heartz, "La Chronologie des recueils imprimés par Pierre Attaingnant," *La Revue de Musicologie* XLIV (1959), 181.

1532, JULY 15

33

¶ **Primus liber viginti missarum / musicalium tres missas continens / Quarum nomina sequuntur,** / [Table] / **Parisiis in vico Cithare apud Petrũ Attaingnant / non procul a templo sanctor. Cosme et Damiani.** / **Cum gratia et priuilegio cuius tenorem / inuersa pagella demonstrabit.** / **M.v.xxxii** /[Description of composition of the volume]

1 vol. in-fol., 41 × 28.5 cm.; 39 f. numbered [i]–xxxviii (plus unfoliated title page)
Sign.: A^7; B^6–E^6; F^8 (Beginning with title page: A i, A ii, A ii, A iii, etc.)
RISM–I, 1532[1]

[1]Boston: Atheneum, ^{s}TUM/9 at 8
Vienna: Österreichische Nationalbibliothek SA 68 A1 (lacking title page)

[1] A small handwritten "K" in the top right corner of the title page identifies the provenance of the volume as the library of Henry Knox. The identification of the Knox volumes is made in a pamphlet by James E. Belliveau, *K equals X and Then Some*, Boston, Boston Atheneum, 1965.

1.	[Missa] Deus in adjutorium	P. de Manchicourt	iv
[2] 2.	[Missa] Philomena prævia	Claudin	xiiiiv
3.	[Missa] Nigra sum	Mattheus Gascongne	xxvv

Verso of title page: dedication to Francis, Cardinal of Tournon, dated July 15, 1532.
Folio i: privilege
For full text and translation of dedication and privilege, see Appendix, Documents 7 and 8. Facsimile of title page and folio i in D. Heartz, "A New Attaingnant Book and the Beginnings of French Music Printing," *Journal of the American Musicological Society* XIV (1961), 9–23. The article includes a translation of the privilege in appendix. See plates VIII–XI above for additional facsimiles.

Cited by Conrad Gesner, *Pandectarum*, Zurich, 1548, f. 84: "Missae praestantissimorum Musicorum uno volumini excusae, Lutetiae."

[2] Based on Richafort's "Philomena prævia," **11**-3. Other sources credit the motet to Verdelot. (Reese, *Music in the Renaissance*, p. 337.)

1532

34

¶ Secundus liber tres / missas continet / [Table] / **Cum gratia et priuilegio christianissimi / Francorum Regis ad sexenniū vt patet primo libro. / M.v.xxxij** / [Description of composition of volume]/

1 vol. in-fol., 41 × 28.5 cm.; 38 f. numbered xxxix–lxxvi
Sign.: G^6–L^6; M^8
RISM–I, 1532[2]

Boston: Atheneum
Vienna: Österreichische Nationalbibliothek

[1] 1.	[Missa] Tua est potentia	Mouton	xxxixv
2.	Missa. ix. lectionum	Claudin	lijv
3.	[Missa] Surge et illuminare	P. de Manchicourt	lxiijv

Facsimile of title page in *MGG* IX, Plate 13, following col. 224, with false identification of Queen Eleanor as Queen Claude.

Facsimile of a part of folio xxxixv in *The Printed Note: 500 Years of Music Printing and Engraving*, The Toledo Museum of Art, 1957, p. 74.

[1] Based on Mouton's "Tua es potentia," *Motetti libro primo*, Venice, Antico, 1521. (Minor, "The Masses of Jean Mouton," unpublished dissertation, University of Michigan, 1950, p. 145.)

35

¶ **Tertius liber tres / missas continet,** / [Table] / **Cum gratia et priuilegio christianissimi / Francorum Regis ad sexenniū ut patet / primo libro. / M.v.xxxij** / [Description of composition of volume] /

1 vol. in-fol., 41 × 28.5 cm.; 40 f. numbered lxxvii–cxvi
Sign.: N6–S6; T4
RISM–I, 1532[3]

Boston: Atheneum
Vienna: Österreichische Nationalbibliothek

[1]1. Missa plurium motetorum	Claudin	lxxvij[v]
[2]2. Messe D'Allemaigne	Mouton	lxxxix[v]
[3]3. [Missa] Jam non dicam vos servos	Lupus	cij[v]

[1] Among the models are:
Gascogne, "Deus regnorum," **63**-15
Consilium, "Adjuva me," **63**-7
Févin, "Benedictus Dominus," *Motetti de la corona*, Venice, Petrucci, 1514
Anonymous, "Impetum," **11**-4
Anonymous, "Deus in nomine," **11**-8
(G. Allaire, "The Masses of Claudin de Sermisy," unpublished dissertation, Boston University, 1960, p. 152.)

[2] Printed as "Missa Regina mearum" in *Missarum Joannis Mouton, Liber primus*, Petrucci, 1515.

[3] Based on Richafort's "Jam non dicam vos servos," *Secundus liber cum quinque vocibus*, Lyons Moderne, 1532. Transcribed in Kabis, "The Works of Jean Richafort," unpublished dissertation, New York University, 1957, Vol. II, p. 114.

1532

36

¶ **Quartus liber tres / missas continet,** / [Table] / **Cum gratia et priuilegio christianissimi / Francorum Regis ad sexenniū ut patet / primo libro. / M.v.xxxij** / [Description of composition of volume] /

1 vol. in-fol., 41 × 28.5 cm.; 36 f. numbered cxvii–clii (cxvii cxviii cxx cxx cxxi cxxii)
Sign.: AA6–FF6
RISM–I, 1532[4]

Boston: Atheneum
Vienna: Österreichische Nationalbibliothek

[1]1.	[Missa] O genitrix	Richefort	cxvij^v
*2.	Requiem	Claudin	cxxix^v
3.	[Missa] Osculetur me	Le heurteur	cxl^v

* Modern edition as *Musica Liturgica* No. 1:2, ed. Robert J. Snow. Cincinnati, Ohio, 1958.

[1] Based on Richafort's "O genitrix," Copenhagen Ny Kgl. Samling 1848-2°. (Kabis, "The Works of Jean Richafort," unpublished dissertation, New York University, 1957, Vol. I, p. 40; transcription in Vol. II, p. 208.)

1532

37

¶ Quintus liber tres / missas continet, / [Table] / **Cum gratia et priuilegio christianissimi / Francorum Regis ad sexenniū vt patet / primo libro. / M.v.xxij** / [Description of composition of volume]/

1 vol. in-fol., 41 × 28.5 cm.; 38 f. numbered cliii–cxc (cliii cliiii clv clii clvii clviii)
Sign.: GG⁶–LL⁶; MM⁸
RISM–I, 1532⁵

Boston: Atheneum
Vienna: Österreichische Nationalbibliothek

[1,*]1.	[Missa] Quem dicunt homines	Divitis	cliij^v
2.	Requiem	Prioris	clxv^v
[2]3.	[Missa] Panis quem ego dabo	Lupus	clxxvj^v

* Modern edition in *Das Chorwerk*, vol. 83, ed. Lewis Lockwood, Wolfenbüttel, [1961].

[1] Based on Richafort's "Quem dicunt homines," *Motetti del Fiore*, Primus liber, Lyons, Moderne, 1532. (*Das Chorwerk*, Vol. 83, ed. Lewis Lockwood.)

[2] Based on Lupus Hellinck's "Panis quem ego dabo," Cambrai, Bibl. de la Ville, MS 125–128. See Albrecht, "Hellinck," *MGG* VI, col. 108.

1532

38

¶ Sextus liber duas / missas habet, / [Table] / **Cum gratia et priuilegio christianissimi / Francorum Regis ad sexenniū vt patet / primo libro. / M.v.xxxij** / [Description of composition of volume]/

1 vol. in-fol., 41 × 28.5 cm.; 38 f. numbered cxci–ccxxviii
Sign.: NN⁶–RR⁶; SS⁸
RISM–I, 1532⁶

Boston: Atheneum
Vienna: Österreichische Nationalbibliothek

1.	Requiem	Richafort	cxcj^{v}
[1]2.	[Missa] Quam pulchra es et quam decora [à 6]	N. Gombert	cciij^{v}

[1] Based on Baulduin's "Quam pulchra es et quam decora," *Selectissimae Symphoniae*, Nuremberg Montanus & Neuber, 1546. Modern edition in *CMM 6*: III.

1532

39

¶ Septimus liber tres / missas habet, / [Table] **/ Cum gratia et priuilegio christianissimi / Francorum Regis ad sexenniū vt patet / primo libro. / M.v.xxxij** / [Description of composition of volume] /

cclxiiij^{v}: **Tabula / ¶ Index viginti missarum musicalium / hoc in volumine contentarum.** / [Table] / **Parisiis in vico Cythare apud Petrum Attaingnant ad / sanctorum Cosme et Damiani templum. / Cum gratia et priuilegio christianissimi / Francorum Regis ad sexenniū** /

1 vol. in-fol., 41 × 28.5 cm.; 36 f. numbered ccxxix–cclxiiii (ccxxix ccxxx ccxxxi ccxxxii ccxxxiii cclx)
Sign.: TT^{6}–*AA*^{6};
RISM–I, 1532[7]

Boston: Atheneum
Vienna: Österreichische Nationalbibliothek

[1]1.	[Missa] Domini est terra	Claudin	ccxxix^{v}
[2]2.	[Missa] Impetum	Le heurteur	ccxxxvij^{v}
*3.	[Missa] Da pacem	N. Gombert	ccl^{v}

* Modern edition in *Nicolas Gombert: Opera Omnia*, ed. Joseph Schmidt-Görg. Vol. I, *The Masses*. Corpus Mensurabilis Musicae, Vol. VI. Rome, American Institute of Musicology, 1951.

[1] Based on Claudin's "Domini est terra," **60**-13.
[2] Based on the anonymous motet "Impetum," **11**-4.

1533, APRIL (after the 13th)

40

¶ Vingt et quatre chansons musicales a / quatre parties composees par maistre Clement Jēnequin / et imprimees a Paris en la rue de la Harpe prez sainct / Cosme par Pierre Attaingnant. / Mense April'. m.d.xxxiii. / [Table] / **Superius. / Cum priuilegio ad sexenniū.** /

4 vol. in-8° obl., 15 × 10 cm.; 16 f. numbered i–xvi
Sign.: ø h⁴–ø l⁴; ø hh⁴–ø ll⁴; ø HH⁴–ø LL⁴; ø H⁴–ø L⁴ (S, Ct, B: ø h i, h ii; ø i, i ii; ø k, k ii, etc. T: HH i, HH ii; ø II, II ii; ø KK, KK ii etc.)

Lausanne: Succession A. Cortot (olim Wernigerode) (S). "Le XIII. Livre"
Munich: Bayerische Staatsbibliothek, Mus. Pr. 31/3

1.	Il me suffit du temps passé	iᵛ
2.	De labourer je suys cassé B: Il me suffit	ii
3.	Ma fille, ma mere, ma fille, venez a moy	iii
4.	En attendant son heureuse présence [I] De son amour me donne jouissance [II; à 3]	iiiᵛ
5.	Madame a soy non aux aultres ressemble	iiiiᵛ
*6.	La plus belle de la ville c'est moy	v
7.	Dites sans peur ou l'ouy ou nenny	vᵛ
8.	Si en aymant je pourchasse et procure	vi
*9.	Qu'esse d'amour, comment le peult on paindre	viᵛ
10.	Ayés pitié du grant mal que j'endure	viiᵛ
11.	C'est a bon droit que mon cueur se lamente	viii
12.	Au despartir triste deul appresse	viiiᵛ
*13.	De tes doux yeulx fut distillé la goute	ix
†14.	Si d'un petit de vostre bien	ixᵛ
15.	Suyvés tousjours l'amoureuse entreprise	xᵛ
16.	Elle craint cela sur tout rien qu'on la chatoulle	xiᵛ
17.	L'ermophrodite est estrange en figure	xiiᵛ
†18.	Ung vieillart amoureux est souvent mal content	xiii
19.	De vostre amour je suys déshérité [I] Las, las si je n'ay si hault bien mérité [II]	xiiiᵛ
20.	Je n'ose estre content de mon contentement	xiiiiᵛ
*21.	Las, que crains tu, amy, de quoy as déffiance	xv
22.	Mais ma mignonne aux tétins descouvers	xvᵛ
23.	Frapper en la roye, c'est ung grant plaisir	xviᵛ

¶ Finis

Facsimile of Superius, fol. iii, in Harman and Mellers, *Man and his Music*, New York, 1962, Plate XIV, following p. 176; and also in Kinsky, *A History of Music in Pictures*, New York, 1937, p. 95.

* Modern edition in *Trente Chansons* (1928).
† Modern edition in *Chorwerk, Vol.* 73.

1533, APRIL

41

Chansons musicales a quatre parties / desquelles les plus conuenables a la fleuste dallemāt sont / signees en la table cy dessoubz escripte par a. et a la fleuste / a neuf trous par b. et pour les deux fleustes sont signees / par a b. Imprimees a Paris en la rue de la Harpe debāt / le bout de la rue des Mathurins prez leglise sainct Cosme / par Pierre Attaingnant. / Mense april. MD.xxxiii. / [Table] / **Superius.** / **Cum priuilegio ad sexenniū** /

4 vol. in-8° obl., 15 × 10 cm.; 16 fol. numbered i–xvi
Sign.: ø n^4–ø q^4

Lausanne: Succession A. Cortot (olim Wernigerode) (S). "Le XIIII. Livre"

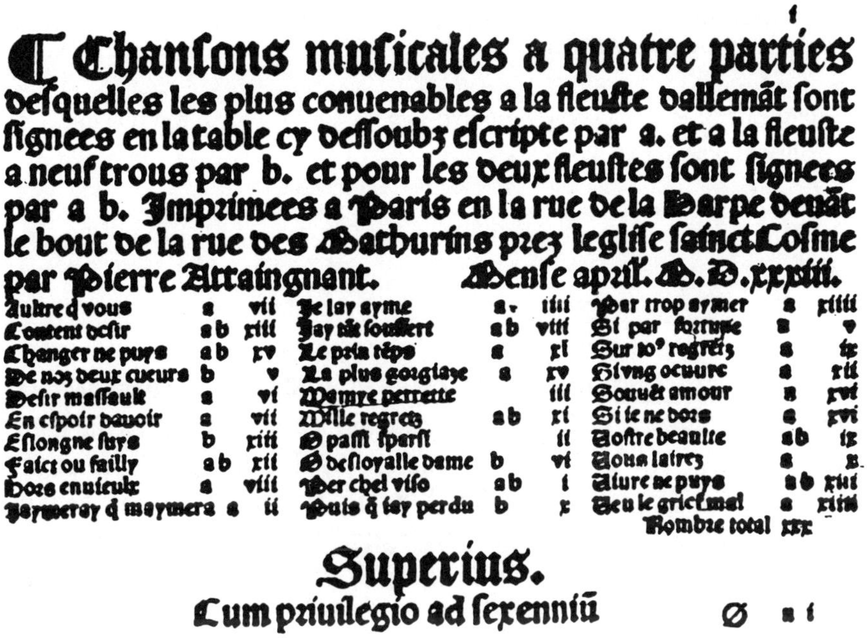
i

¶ Chansons musicales a quatre parties desquelles les plus conuenables a la fleuste dallemãt sont signees en la table cy dessoubz escripte par a. et a la fleuste a neuf trous par b. et pour les deux fleustes sont signees par a b. Imprimees a Paris en la rue de la Harpe deuãt le bout de la rue des Mathurins prez leglise sainct Cosme par Pierre Attaingnant. Mense april. M. D. xxxviii.

Aultre q vous	a	vii	Je lay ayme	a	iiii	Par trop aymer	a	xiiii
Content desir	ab	xiii	Jay tãt souffert	ab	viii	Si par fortune	a	v
Changer ne puys	ab	xv	Le prĩs tẽps	a	xi	Sur to' regretz	a	ix
De noz deux cueurs	b	v	La plus gorgiaze	a	xv	Si vng oeuure	a	xii
Desir massault	a	vi	Mamye perrette		iii	Souuẽt amour	a	xvi
En espoir dauoir	a	vii	Mille regretz	ab	xi	Si ie ne dors	a	xvi
Eslongne suys	b	xiii	O passi sparsi		ii	Vostre beaulte	ab	ix
Faict ou failly	ab	xii	O desloyalle dame	b	vi	Vous laires	a	x
Hors enuieulx	a	viii	Per chel viso	ab	i	Viure ne puys	ab	xiii
Jaymeray q maymera	a	ii	Puis q iay perdu	b	x	Veu le grief mal	a	xiiii
						Nombre total	xxx	

Superius.

Cum priuilegio ad sexenniũ ø a i

19 Title page (Superius) of *Chansons musicales*, **(41)**. By courtesy of the Cortot Succession

1. Per ch'el viso d'amor portava insegna	ab		i^v
2. J'aymeray qui m'aymera sans mélencolie	a	Gombert	ii
3. O passi sparsi, o pensier vaghi e pronti		[Festa]	ii^v
[1]4. Or vien ça, vien, m'amie Perrette		Jannequin	iii^v
5. Je l'ay aymé et l'aymeray le mien amy	a	[Certon]	iiii^v
6. De noz deux cueurs soit seulle voulenté	b	[Guyon]	v
7. Si par fortune avez mon cueur acquis	a	Certon	v^v
8. Désir m'assault et m'adresse la mort	a	Manchicourt	vi
9. O desloialle dame, la sourse de rigueur	b	Bourguignon	vi^v
10. En espoir d'avoir mieulx il faut avoir souffrance	a	Gombert	vii
11. Aultre que vous de moy ne jouyra	a		vii^v
12. J'ay tant souffert que pour plaisir avoir	ab	[Jacotin]	viii
13. Hors envieux, retirez-vous d'ici	a	Gombert	viii^v
14. Sur tous regretz les miens plus piteulz pleurent	a	Richafort	ix
15. Vostre beaulté plaisant et lyé	a	Lupus	ix^v
16. Puis que j'ay perdu mes amours	b	Lupi	x
17. Vous l'arés s'il vous plaist madame	b	Adorne	x^v
18. Mille regretz de vous abandonner	ab	J. lemaire	xi^v
19. Le printemps faict florir les arbres par nature	a	Benedictus	xi^v
20. Si ung œuvre parfaict doibt chacun contenter	a	Claudin	xii
21. Faict ou failly, ou du tout rien qui vaille	ab	Bridam	xii^v
22. Eslongné suys de mes amours	b		xiii
23. Content désir qui cause ma douleur	ab	Claudin	xiii^v

[1] Listed in the table as "M'amye Perrette."

24.	Vivre ne puys content sans sa présence	ab	Claudin	xiii^{v}
25.	Veu le grief mal ou sans repos labeure	a	Heurteur	xiiii
26.	Par trop aymer j'ay cuidé demourer	a	Benedictus	xiiii^{v}
27.	La plus gorgiase du monde, le bruit, l'honneur	a		xv
28.	Changer ne puys et aultre ne désire	ab	Lupi	xv^{v}
29.	Souvent Amour me livre grant tourment	a	Heurteur	xvi^{v}
30.	Si je ne dors je ne puis vivre	a	Le Gendre	xvi^{v}

¶ Finis

The second gathering (fol. v–viii) employs Typography I, unlike the remainder of the work, which employs Typography II.

1533, APRIL

42

¶ Vingt & sept chansons musicales a qua=/tre parties desquelles les plus cōuenables a la fleuste dal=/lemant sont signees en la table cy dessoubz escripte par a. / et a la fleuste a neuf trous par b. et pour les deux par a b. / Imprimees a Paris en la rue de la Harpe deuant le bout / de la rue des Mathurins prez leglise sainct Cosme par / Pierre Attaingnant. Mense April'. m.D.xxxiii. / [Table] / **Superius.** / **Cum priuilegio ad sexenniū** /

4 vol. in-8° obl., 15 × 10 cm.; 16 f. numbered i–xvi
Sign.: ø r^4–ø v^4; ø rr^4–ø vv^4, ø RR^4–ø VV^4; ø R^4–ø V^4
RISM-I, 1533[1]

Lausanne: Succession A. Cortot (olim Wernigerode) (S). "Le XV. Livre"
Munich: Bayerische Staatsbibliothek, Mus. Pr. 31/5

1.	De vous servir m'est prins envie	ab	Claudin	i^{v}
2.	Mirelaridon don don don daine		Heurteur	i^{v}
3.	Parle qui veult, tien seray j'en suys la	a	Claudin	ii^{v}
4.	Va mirelidrogue va quant m'en venoys		Passereau	iii
5.	A Paris prez des billettes, gentil maréschal			iii^{v}
6.	Les yeulx bendez de triste congnoissance	ab	Vermont	iiii
7.	Amours vous me faictes grant tort	a	Gombert	iiii^{v}
8.	Amour me poingt et si je me veulx plaindre	ab	Claudin	v
9.	Allons ung peu plus avant, demourrons	ab	Heurteur	v^{v}
10.	Je ne puis pas mon grant deul appaiser	ab	Heurteur	vi^{v}
11.	Tous amoureux qui hantés le commun	ab	Passereau	vii
12.	Par ung matin fuz levé devant le jour	ab	Heurteur	vii^{v}
13.	Pren de bon cueur le petit don que ton povre amy	a	P. de Manchicourt	viii
14.	Héllas, Amour qui sçais certainement	ab	Heurteur	viii^{v}
15.	Amour me voyant sans tristesse	ab	Claudin	ix
16.	Jectés moy sur l'herbette mon amy gratieulx	a	Lupi	ix^{v}

17.	Jamais ung cueur qui est d'amour embrasé	ab	Lupi	x
*18.	Troys jeunes bourgeoises aux cordeliers s'en vont	b	Heurteur	x^v
†19.	Allez souspirs enflammez au froid cueur	b	Claudin	xi
20.	Elle veult donc par estrange rigueur	a	Claudin	xi^v
21.	On dit qu'Amour luy mesmes l'aymera	ab	Vermont	xii
‡22.	Voyant souffrir celle qui me tourmente	ab	Jacotin	xii^v
23.	Hayne et amour dedans mon cueur se tiennent	a	Vermont	xiii
‡24.	Pour quoy donc ne fringuerons nous	a	Passereau	xiii^v
25.	Je n'en diray mot, bergere m'amye		Passereau	xiiii^v
26.	Je n'avoye point a bien choisir failli	a	Claudin	xv
27.	Ung petit coup m'amye, ung petit coup, héllas		[1]Passereau	xv^v
28.	Si bon amour mérite récompense	a	Jacotin	xvi^v

¶ Finis

* Modern edition in *Theatrical Chansons.*
† Modern edition in *Chanson and Madrigal.*
‡ Modern edition in *Anthologie.*

[1] Attributed to Janequin in *Venticinque Canzoni Francesi*, Venice, Gardane, 1538. See Lesure in *Fontes* I (1954), 83.

1533

43

[Jannequin Cl. Sacrae Cantiones seu motectae quatuor vocum. Parisiis, in vico Cythare prope Sanctorum Cosme et Damiani templum apud Petrum Attaingnant musice Calcographum, 1533, in quart.]

From C. F. Becker, *Die Tonwerke des xvi. und xvii. Jahrhunderts*, Leipzig, 1855, p. 23.

Fétis cites the same title.
One motet by Janequin, "Congregati sunt", possibly from this collection, is printed in *Liber cantus triginta novem motetos*, Ferrara, Buglhat *et al.*, 1538.

The Columbine catalogues contain an entry that, according to Chapman, may refer to the same lost print: "Clementis Genichin Sperantis modulatio in dimidio folio." See "Printed Collections of Polyphonic Music Owned by Ferdinand Columbus," *Journal of the American Musicological Society* XXI (1968), 53 and no. 145.

1534, FEBRUARY

44

¶ Trente chansons musicales imprimees / lan mil cinq centz trēte et troys au moys de Feburier par / Pierre Attaingnant demourant a Paris en la rue de la / Harpe pres leglise sainct Cosme Desq̄lles ensuyt la table. / [Table] / **Superius.** /

4 vol. in-8° obl., 15 × 10 cm.; 16 f. numbered i–xvi
Sign.: ø x^{4}–ø &^{4}; ø xx^{4}–ø & &^{4}; ø XX^{4}–ø AA^{4}; ø X^{4}–ø A^{4}
RISM–I, 1534^{13}

Lausanne: Succession A. Cortot (olim Wernigerode) (S). "Le XVI. Livre"
Munich: Bayerische Staatsbibliothek, Mus. Pr. 40/8

1.	Just et amer de vous la spécieuse [I]		i^{v}
	Si suys a vous et que crainte honteuse [II]		i^{v}
	Mais s'elle vient a retraicte odieuse [III]		ii
2.	Sy dire je l'osoye qu'il my fault tant souffrir		ii^{v}
3.	Qui vous vouldroit souhaiter pour s'amye	M. Sohier	iii
4.	Content je suys de madame fortune		iii^{v}
5.	Faictes sans dire et vous taisés		iii^{v}
6.	Je languiray si de vous n'ay secours	G. Ysoré	iiii^{v}
7.	Le seul plaisir de honneste présence	P. Certon	v
8.	Je suy mon bien du quel me tiens content	Certon	v^{v}
9.	Venés-y toutes et l'on vous fera mouldre	Sohier	v^{v}
10.	Entendés-vous qu'ung aultre je seconde	Certon	vi^{v}
11.	Je ny voys riens si souvent que ses yeulx	Certon	vii
12.	Prestez m'en l'ung de ses yeulx bien apris	Certon	vii^{v}
13.	En ce joly moys de septembre que l'iver commence	Sohier	vii^{v}
14.	Amour a tort de me tenir rigueur	P. Certon	viii^{v}
15.	Cruelle mort qui de rien n'est contente	Alaire	ix
*16.	Je suys déshéritée puisque j'ay perdu mon amy	Lupus [or Cadéac]	ix^{v}
17.	Mon pere my marye, c'est en despit de moy	M. Sohier	x
18.	N'aurai-je point de mon mal allégeance	[Alaire]	x^{v}
19.	Quant j'estois petite garce		x^{v}
20.	Mon petit cueur c'est voulu a donner		xi^{v}
21.	Amour voyant l'ennuy qui tant m'opresse	Claudin	xii
22.	Bien mauldit est l'estat des amoureux. *Canon*	Alaire	xii^{v}
23.	A gouverner femmes a fort affaire		xiii
24.	Puis que mon cueur fermement continue	[Morel]	xiii^{v}
25.	Triquedon daine laridaine triquedon daine laridon		xiii^{v}
26.	Sy je l'ayme c'est bien raison		xiiii^{v}
27.	Las, fauldra il soubz l'umbre d'ung mary		xv
28.	Entre vous qui aymés bon vin et bon poisson		xv^{v}
29.	Vostre amytié bien congnoistre vouldroye		xvi
30.	Triste pensif par le pourchas de rigueur	Alaire	xvi^{v}

¶ Finis

* Modern edition in *Chorwerk, Vol. 15* and *GMB.*

1534, MARCH

45

¶ Vingt et huyt chansons musicales im=/primees lan mil cinq cētz trēte et troys au moys de Mars / par Pierre Attaingnāt demourāt a Paris en la rue de la / Harpe pres leglise sainct Cosme Desq̄lles ensuyt la table. / [Table] / **Superius.** /

4 vol. in-8° obl., 15 × 10 cm.; 16 f. numbered i–xvi
Sign.: C a⁴–C d⁴; C aa⁴–C dd⁴; C AA⁴–C DD⁴; C A⁴–C D⁴
RISM–I, 1534[11]

Lausanne: Succession A. Cortot (olim Wernigerode) (S). "Le XVII. Livre"
Munich: Bayerische Staatsbibliothek, Mus. Pr. 40/7

1.	Or oüez les introites de taverne B: Or oüez les introites de la messe T: Exurge quare obdormis, Domine	Guiard	iv
2.	Dite di non, amor, quanto vi piace		iii
3.	Sans toy présent je ne vaulx moins que morte		iiiv
4.	Pleust a Jésus que je feusse a la porte		iiii
5.	Joyeulx adieu d'ung visage	Claudin	iiiiv
6.	Rions, chantons, passons temps en liesse	C. Jennequin	v
7.	Endurer fault, le temps le veult ainsy	G. Ysoré	vv
8.	Maintenant resjouissons nous	Jennequin	vi
9.	Fy, fy, metés-les hors du compte	C. Jennequin	viv
10.	Vous qui voulez sçavoir mon nom	Claudin	vii
11.	En revenant de jouer trouvay m'amye	G. Ysoré	viiv
12.	Qui du blason d'amours a congnoissance	Claudin	viii
13.	Allons, fuyons, bevons au départir	C. Jennequin	viiiv
14.	Il n'est plaisir ne passe temps au monde	C. Jennequin	ix
15.	Le framboisier que j'ay cueilli	De lestanc	ixv
16.	D'estre subject me faict ung grant oultrage	C. Jennequin	x
17.	Puis qu'il me plaist a qui doibt il desplaire		xv
18.	Si pour aymer on ne quiert que beaulté	Jacotin	xi
*19.	My levay par ung matin plus matin que l'alouette	Guyard	xiv
20.	Le deul d'amours ay par long temps porté		xii
21.	Ung compaignon gallin gallant et une fillette jolye	Passereau	xiiv
22.	A vous, command, je suys prest de servir		xiii
23.	La, mon amy, faictes tout bellement	Jennequin	xiiiv
24.	Ce qui me tient en merveilleux esmoy	G. Ysoré	xiiiiv
25.	C'est en amour une peine trop dure	Claudin	xv
26.	Il m'aviendra ce que vouldra fortune	Certon	xvv
27.	Encore la luy merray-je demain	Fescam	xvv
28.	J'ay prins a aymer a ma devise	Claudin	xviv

¶ Finis

* Modern edition in *Theatrical Chansons.*

1534, APRIL (after the 4th)

46

¶ Liber primus quinq3 et viginti musicales quatuor vo=/cum Motetos complectitur / quorum nomina tabella se=/quens in=dicat. / [Table] / **Parisiis in vico Cithare ad templum sanctorꝰ. / Cosme et Damiani apud / Petrum Attaingnant musice typographum / mense Aprili 1534 / Superius. / ¶ Cum priuilegio ad sexenniū.** /

4 vol. in-4° obl., 20.5 × 16 cm.; 16 f. numbered i–xvi
Sign.: a⁴–d⁴; aa⁴–dd⁴; AA⁴–DD⁴; A⁴–D⁴
RISM–I, 1534[3]

Jena: Universitätsbibliothek
Milan: Biblioteca Ambrosiana, SCLI 21–22 (S & B; S. lacks f. i–ii) (Old shelf-mark: P. L. 114)
[1]Milan: Biblioteca del Conservatorio, Fondo Santa Barbara No. 57
Noyon: Ancienne Bibliothèque du Chapitre
[2]Paris: Bibliothèque Sainte-Geneviève, Vm. 83 Rés (S, lacking f. i)
[3]Vienna: Österreichische Nationalbibliothek SA 76 d2

1.	Clare sanctorum senatus Apostolorum I— De Apostolis Agneli vellere qui maculas nesciens aliquas II Ct, B: Æthiopes horidos Mathæe agneli vellere	Claudin	i^{v}
2.	Viri Galilæi, quid admiramini aspicientes in cælum? I—In die Ascensionis Domini Videntibus illis elevatus est II	Couillart	ii
3.	Reges terræ congregati sunt I—In die Epiphaniæ Et venientes invenerunt puerum II	Jo. Mouton	ii^{v}
4.	Gloria, laus et honor tibi sit—In ramis Palmarum	Richafort	iii^{v}
5.	Hac clara die turma festiva dat præconia I— In assumptione beatæ Mariæ In me quomodo tua jam fient nuncia II	Richafort	iiii
6.	Alma Redemptoris mater I Tu quæ genuisti, natura mirante II	Jo. L'héritier	v
7.	Angelus Domini descendit de cælo, alleluya I Et introeuntes in monumentum II	Jo. L'héritier	v^{v}
8.	Beata es, virgo Maria, quæ Dominum portasti	L'héritier	vi^{v}
*9.	Beatus Stephanus, preciosus Dei prothomartyr I Et videntes vultum eius tanquam vultum angeli II	A. Willart	vii
10.	Maria virgo, semper lætare I Te laudant angeli atque archangeli II	Gascongne	vii^{v}
11.	Dignare me laudare te, virgo sacrata I Cum jocunditate solemnitatem beatæ Mariæ II	Gascongne	viii^{v}
12.	Gabriel archangelus apparuit Zachariæ	Verdelot	ix
13.	Caro mea vere est cibus et sanguis meus I Hic est panis qui de cælo descendit II	Gascongne	ix^{v}
14.	Salve mater Salvatoris, mater salutifera I Virga rubi appellaris, flos, fenestra, janua II		x^{v}
15.	Lamentabatur Jacob de duobus filiis suis		xi
*16.	Intercessio, quæsumus Domine, beatæ Barbaræ	A. Willart	xi^{v}
17.	Ave virgo gratiosa, stella sole clarior	Bouteillier	xii
18.	Salve Barbara dignissima quæ in cælo	Verdelot	xii^{v}
19.	Ave sanctissima Maria, mater Dei, regina cæli	Jo. Mouton	xiii
20.	Benedicat nos Deus noster Deus misereatur nostri et benedicat nos Deus—versus	Vermont primus	xiii^{v}

* Modern edition in *CMM 3*:II

[1] Bound in old paper-covered boards with the Gothic letter "A" written on all four parts. The Superius is labelled "Cantus" on the cover and the Contratenor "Altus."

[2] Concerning this set see **141**.

[3] Bound in leather stamped with a coat of arms showing two fleur-de-lis (right side, gold on a brown field; left side, brown on a gold field) surmounted by the initials "G. F." The arms are those of the Fugger family and must refer to Georg (1518–1569), son of Raimund Fugger (1489–1535).

†21.	O gloriosa Dei genitrix, virgo semper Maria I Quæ est ista quæ ascendit II	Gombert	xiiii
22.	Miseremini mei, saltem vos amici mei I Cutis mea aruit et contracta est II	[4][Jo. Mouton]	xv
23.	Postquam consummati sunt dies octo	Lupus	xv^{v}
‡24.	Salve crux sancta, arbor digna I Causa etiam vitæ foret cunctis II	A. Willart	xvi
25.	Homo quidam fecit cenam magnam	Jo. Mouton	xvi^{v}

¶ Finis

Complete modern edition in *Treize Livres de Motets*, Premier Livre. Includes facsimile of title page.

† Modern edition in *CMM 6*:V
‡ Modern edition in *CMM 3*:I

[4] Attribution from Glarean, *Dodecachordon*, Basel, 1547, Liber III, p. 323.

1534, MAY

47

¶ Liber secundus: quatuor et viginti musicales quatuor / vocum Motetos habet / quorum nomina tabella sequens / indicat. / [Table] / **Parisiis in vico Cithare ad templum sanctor. Cosme et Damiani apud / Petrum Attaingnant musice typographum / mense Maii 1534 / Superius / ¶ Cum priuilegio ad sexenniū. /**

4 vol. in-4° obl., 20.5 × 16 cm.; 16 f. numbered i–xvi
Sign.: e^{4}–h^{4}; ee^{4}–hh^{4}; EE^{4}–HH^{4}; E^{4}–H^{4}
RISM–I, 1534[4]

Jena: Universitätsbibliothek
Milan: Biblioteca Ambrosiana (S & B)
Milan: Biblioteca del Conservatorio
Noyon: Ancienne Bibliothèque du Chapitre
Paris: Bibliothèque Sainte-Geneviève, Vm. 84 Rés (S)
Vienna: Österreichische Nationalbibliothek

*1.	Pater noster, qui es in cælis—Oratio Dominicalis	Willart	i^{v}
2.	Maria Magdalene et Maria Jacobi I—[1]In die Paschæ Certe multis argumentis vidi signa resurgentis II T & B: Dic nobis, Maria, quid vidisti in via?	F. Du lot	ii
3.	Victimæ paschali laudes immolant christiani I— De Resurrectione Domini Sepulchrum Christi viventis II	Verdelot	ii^{v}

* Modern edition in *CMM 3*:II

[1] Bassus: In Resurrectione Domini.

4.	Gaudeamus omnes in Domino—In Resurrectione Domini	Verdelot	iii^{v}
†5.	Congratulamini michi omnes qui diligitis Dominum I—De Resurrectione Domini	Willart	iiii
	Recedentibus discipulis non recedebam II		
6.	Sancta Maria, succurre miseris—Salutatio communis beatæ Mariæ	Verdelot	v
7.	Christe, totius dominator orbis I	Richafort	v^{v}
	Christe, qui victa nece suscitasti II		
8.	Christus vincit, Christus regnat I—Pro rege nostro	Gascongne	vi
	Rex regum et gloria nostra II		
9.	Ave Maria, gratia plena—Salutatio angelica	Jo. L'héritier	vii
10.	Egredere ab Occidente, Gallia fidelis I—In die Epiphaniæ	Consilium	vii
	Dic matri, dic piæ, virgo clemens II		
11.	Noe, noe, magnificatus est rex pacificus—In Nativitate Domini	Claudin	viii
12.	Noe, noe, psallite noe. Hierusalem—In Nativitate Domini	Jo. Mouton	viii^{v}
†13.	Omnipotens sempiterne Deus qui huius diei—De uno apostolo	Willart	ix
14.	Benedicta es, cælorum regina I—De beata Maria	Bouteillier	ix^{v}
	Per illud ave prolatum et tuum responsum gratum II		
15.	O quam dulcis et beate N. I—Plurimorum martyrum	Richafort	x
	Ecce quam bonum et quam jocundum II		
16.	O præsul egregie, N. lux ecclesiæ I—De uno episcopo	Richafort	xi
	O plebs N. non tamquam gens II		
17.	O crux, viride lignum, quia super te I—In festo sanctæ Crucis	Mathias	xi^{v}
	Salus omnium populorum per crucem II		
†18.	Ave regina cælorum, ave domina I—Salutatio communis beatæ Mariæ	Willart	xii^{v}
	Gaude gloriosa, super omnes speciosa II		
19.	Pater, peccavi in cælum et coram te I—Pro peccatis	Consilium	xiii
	Quanti mercennarii in domo patris mei II		
‡20.	Aspice, Domine, quia facta est desolata civitas I	N. Gombert	xiii^{v}
	Muro tuo inexpugnabili circuncinge eam, Domine II		
21.	Spiritus ubi vult spirat I—In die Penthecostes	Gascongne	xiiii^{v}
	Charitas Dei diffusa est in cordibus nostris II		
	T & B: Per Spiritum sanctum qui datus est nobis		
22.	Virgo Christi egregia, pro nobis peccatoribus—De communi unius virginis	L'héritier	xv^{v}
†23.	Patefactæ sunt januæ cæli I—De sancto Stephano	Willart	xvi
	Mortem enim quam Salvator noster dignatus est II		
24.	Ave sanctissima Maria, mater Dei—De beata Maria	Verdelot	xvi^{v}

¶ Finis

Complete modern edition in *Treize Livres de Motets*, Deuxième Livre. Includes facsimile of title page.

† Modern edition in *CMM 6*:I
‡ Modern edition in *CMM 3*:V

48

Missarum musicalium quatuor vocum / Liber primus / [Table] / **Parhisiis in vico Cithare apud Petrum Attaingnant / iuxta templum sanctorum Cosme et Damiani. / Mense Mayo 1534 / Superius / Cum priuilegio ad sexennium.** /

4 vol. in-4° obl., 20.5 × 16 cm.; 16 f. numbered i–xvi (S, T: xvi^v blank)
Sign.: *a^4–*d^4; *aa^4–*dd^4; *AA^4–*DD^4; *A^4–*D^4
RISM–I, 1534^1

Jena: Universitätsbibliothek
Noyon: Ancienne Bibliothèque du Chapitre

[1]	1. Missa Le cueur est mien	M. Sohier	i^v
[2]	2. Missa Ung jour Robin	G. Le heurteur	v
	3. Missa Fors seulement	G. Le heurteur	viii^v
[3]	4. Missa Content désir	M. Joh. de Billon	xii^v

Finis

Cited by Conrad Gesner, *Pandectarum*, Zurich, 1548, f. 84: "Missarum Musicalium quatuor vocum liber primus impressis Pariis apud Petrum Attaignant."

[1] Based on the anonymous chanson "Le cueur est mien," **10**-7.
[2] Based on Claudin's "Ung jour Robin," **9**-31.
[3] Based on Claudin's "Content désir," **41**-23.

49

¶ Liber tertius: viginti musicales quinqȝ / sex / vel octo / vocum motetos habet vt sequenti tabella demonstratur. / [Table] / **Nota pro huius tabule elucidatione: q. ciffre priores partiū aut vocū numerū denotant / vine aut litere sequētes: vt. ss. duas / supremas partes: tt. 2. tenores / cc. 2. contratenores / bb duos bassos significant. Et vbi passim reperies Canon. 4. super. 2. aut / 4. sup. 1. id duas partes super vnam / aut. 4. super vnam fore canendas indicat. / Parisiis in vico Cithare apud Petrum Attaingnant musice / typographum Mense Junio 1534 / Superius / ¶ Cum priuilegio ad sexennium.** /

4 vol. in-4° obl., 20.5 × 16 cm.; 16 f. numbered i–xvi (S: xiii xvi xv xiiii)
Sign.: i^4–m^4; ii^4–mm^4; II^4–MM^4; I^4–M^4
RISM–I, 1534^5

Jena: Universitätsbibliothek
Milan: Biblioteca Ambrosiana (S & B)
Milan: Biblioteca del Conservatorio
Noyon: Ancienne Bibliothèque du Chapitre
Paris: Bibliothèque Sainte-Geneviève, Vm. 85 Rés (S)
Vienna: Österreichische Nationalbibliothek

1.	O beata infantia, per quem nostri generis I O felices panni, quibus peccatorum II 5 ss cc; In Nativitate Domini	Pieton	i^v
2.	Parasti in dulcedine tua pauperi, dulcissime Jesu I Cæleste est hoc manna, quod huius mundi II 5 ss; in festo Sacramenti	Hesdin	ii^v
3.	Ave virgo gloriosa, stella sole clarior T 2: O pia, o clemens 6 tt bb; De beata Maria	Vermont primus	iii^v
4.	Dignare me laudare te, virgo sacrata 4 super 2; Quatuor in partes opus hoc distinguere debes	Verdelot	iiii^v
5.	Ave Maria, gratio Dei plena [1]Ct 1 & 2, B	Claudin	iiii^v
6.	Nesciens mater virgo virum, peperit sine dolore 8 super 4; De beata Maria	Mouton	v
7.	Hi sancti quorum hodie celebrantur solennia I Excuset apud Dominum nostrorum lapsus criminum II 5 tt; De omnibus Sanctis	[2][Courtois]	v^v
8.	Adest nanque beati Dionysii sacratissima dies I Quem Dominus post apostolos sic honoravit II T 2, I & II: Gaude, prole Græcia 5 tt; De sancto Dionysio	Vermont primus	vi
9.	Super flumina Babylonis illic sedimus I Si oblitus fuero tui, Hierusalem II 5 tt	De la fage	vii
10.	Virgo prudentissima, quo progrederis, quasi aurora 5 tt; De Assumptione beatæ Mariæ	Hilaire Penet	viii^v
11.	Peccantem me quotidie et non me penitentem 5 ss; Canon; Pro defunctis	Mouton	ix
12.	Congratulamini michi omnes, qui diligitis Dominum I Tulerunt Dominum meum et nescio ubi posuerunt II 5 ss; In festo Paschæ	G. Le heurteur	ix
13.	Alma Redemptoris mater, quæ per via cæli I Tu quæ genuisti, natura mirante II 5 bb; De beata Maria	De Silva	xi^v
14.	Pater noster, qui es in cælis I Panem nostrum quotidianum da nobis II 5 cc; Canon; Oratio Dominicalis	[3][Richafort]	xii
15.	Omnia quæ fecisti nobis, Domine I Largire, quæsumus, Domine, fidelibus tuis II 5 cc; Pro peccatis	M. J. de Ferare	xii^v

[1] Table of Bassus book: 3 ss.
[2] Attribution after *Secundus Liber cum Quinque Vocibus . . .*, Lyons, Moderne, 1532. See Lesure in *Fontes* I (1954), 82.
[3] Attribution after London, BM Add. 19583, f. 42^v. (See Kabis, "The Works of Jean Richafort," unpublished dissertation, New York University, 1957, Vol. I, p. 41.)

16. Deus misereatur nostri et benedicat nobis I Lætentur et exultent gentes, quoniam judicas populos II 5 bb	Claudin	xiii
17. Argentum et aurum non est michi 5 ss; De sancto Petro apostolo	Hesdin	xiiii
18. Angeli et archangeli, throni et dominationes I T, B: Principatus et potestates Te gloriosus apostolorum chorus II 5 ss; In festo Omnium Sanctorum	Hesdin	xiiii[v]
19. Salve mater pietatis ac totius Trinitatis 4 super 2; Canon in epydiapason		xv[v]
20. Ave sanctissima Maria, mater Dei 6 super 3; Canon in dyathessaron	[4]Verdelot	xv[v]
21. Ave Maria, gemma virginum 8 super 4; De beata Maria	Mouton	xvi[v]

¶ Finis tertii libri

Complete modern edition in *Treize Livres de Motets,* Troisième Livre. Includes facsimile of title page.

[4] Attributed to Claudin in Contratenor.

1534, JUNE

50

¶ Liber quartus. xxix. musicales quatuor vel quinꝫ / pariū vocū modulos habet. vt sequēti indice demōstratur. / [Table] / **Parhisiis in vico Cithare in officina libraria Petri Attaingnant / musice typographi prope sanctorum Cosme & Damiani templum. / Mense Junio 1534 / Superius. / Cū grā ⁊ priuilegio xp̄ianissimi frācor. / regis ad sexēniū. /**

4 vol. in-4° obl., 20.5 × 16 cm.; 16 f. numbered i–xvi
Sign.: n^4–q^4; nn^4–qq^4; NN^4–QQ^4; N^4–Q^4
RISM–I, 1534[6]

Jena: Universitätsbibliothek
Milan: Biblioteca Ambrosiana (S & B)
Milan: Biblioteca del Conservatorio
Noyon: Ancienne Bibliothèque du Chapitre
Paris: Bibliothèque Sainte-Geneviève, Vm. 86 Rés (S)
Vienna: Österreichische Nationalbibliothek

*1. Precatus est Moyses in conspectu [Domini] Dei sui I Memento Abraham, Ysaac et Jacob II à 5; T: canon in dyapenthe	A. Willart	i[v]

* Modern edition in *CMM 3*:III.

2.	Clare sanctorum senatus Apostolorum I Thoma, Bartholomæe, Johannes, Philippe, Simon II De apostolis		ii
3.	Veniat dilectus meus in hortum meum T, Ct: Ut comedat fructum pomorum suorum De beata Maria		iii
4.	Ave, Domina mea, sancta Maria, mater Dei De beata Maria	De la fage	iii^{v}
5.	Virgo carens criminibus, te precor De beata Maria	A. de Silva	iiii
6.	Exaltare super cælos, Deus, et super omnem terram	G. Le Heurteur	iiii^{v}
7.	Adorna thalamum tuum, Syon I Suscipiens Jesum in ulnas suas II De Purificatione beatæ Mariæ	Vermont Primus	v
8.	O crux ave sanctissima, salus mundi verissima I O crux plena dulcedinis et summæ pulchritudinis II De Cruce	Courtoys	v^{v}
9.	Nesciens mater virgo virum, peperit sine dolore De beata Maria		vi^{v}
10.	Sancti Spiritus adsit nobis gratia De sancto Spiritu		vi^{v}
11.	Recordare, Domine, testamenti tui sancti Quinta pars. In dyapason. Parce, Domine, populo tuo à 5; Contra pestem	Verdelot	vii
12.	Adjuva nos, Deus salutaris noster Quinta pars. In dyapenthe. Parce, Domine, populo tuo à 5	Verdelot	vii^{v}
13.	Christum regem regum adoremus Dominum De sancto Andrea	[1][Mouton]	vii^{v}
14.	Contremuerunt omnia membra mea De Annunciatione beatæ Mariæ		viii
15.	Virgo sancta Katherina, Græciæ gemma De sancta Katherina	Gombert	viii^{v}
16.	Ave mater matris Dei, per quem salvi fiunt rei De sancta Anna		ix
17.	Infirmitatem nostram, quæsumus, Domine à 5; Primus tenor / Fors seulement	Verdelot	ix^{v}
18.	Veni in hortum meum, soror mea sponsa I In lectulo meo per noctes quæsivi II De beata Maria	Hesdin	ix^{v}
19.	Tanto tempore vobiscum sum De sancto Philippo	Verdelot	x^{v}
20.	Tempus est ut revertar ad eum I Rex gloriæ, Dominus virtutum II De Ascensione Domini	Consilium	x^{v}
21.	Cognoscimus, Domine, quia peccavimus I Vita nostra in dolore suspirat II	Richafort	xi
[2]22.	Sufficiebat nobis paupertas nostra	Richafort	xii
†23.	Virgo salutiferi genetrix intacta tonantis I Tu potis es primæ scelus expurgare II Nunc, cæli regina, tuis progentibus ora III	Josquin des pres	xii^{v}

†Modern edition in *Josquin*, Bundel VII.

[1] Attribution after *Motetti de la corona. Libro primo*, Venice, Petrucci, 1514, fol. 10.

[2] Text of Superius part is preceded by the words, "Mon souvenir."

	S & T 2, I, II, & III: Ave Maria gratia plena à 5; De beata Maria		
24.	Nigra sum sed formosa, filiæ Hierusalem De beata Maria	Consilium	xiii^{v}
25.	Ave Maria, gratia plena, Dominus tecum, toties enim oscularis I Gaude, virgo gratiosa, gaude, tellus fructuosa II T, Ct: Verbo Verbum concepisti; B: Gaude, virgo gloriosa De beata Maria	Hesdin	xiiii
26.	Surge, propera, amica mea, columba mea I Vox turturis audita est in terra nostra II De beata Maria	Mathias	xiiii^{v}
27.	Inviolata, integra et casta es, Maria De beata Maria	[3][Courtois]	xv
28.	Sancta et immaculata virginitas I Benedicta tu in mulieribus II De beata Maria	Hesdin	xvi
29.	Sancta Maria, mater Dei, succurre miseris De beata Maria	Consilium	xvi^{v}

Finis quarti libri

Complete modern edition in *Treize Livres de Motets*, Quatrième Livre. Includes facsimile of title page.

[3] Attribution after *Motteti del Fiore, Primus Liber*, Lyons, Moderne, 1532, fol. 27.

1534, JULY

51

Missarū musicaliū ad quatuor voces pares. / Liber secundus / [Table] / **Parhisiis in vico Cithare apud Petrum Attaingnant musice / typographum prope sanctorum Cosme & Damiani templum. / Mense Julio 1534 / Superius / Cū grā & priuilegio xpianissimi frācor. regis ad sexēniū. /**

4 vol. in-4° obl., 20.5 × 16 cm.; 16 f. numbered i–xvi (T, Ct: xvi^{v} blank)
Sign.: *e^{4}–*h^{4}; *ee^{4}–*hh^{4}; *EE^{4}–*HH^{4}; *E^{4}–*H^{4}
RISM–I, 1534^{2}

Jena: Universitätsbibliothek
Noyon: Ancienne Bibliothèque du Chapitre

[1,*]1.	Missa Tota pulchra	Claudin	i^{v}
[2]2.	Missa sur Fantasie Si vous avez voix de dessus / Chantes une double au dessus	Claudin	v

* Modern edition, without Credo, published by Annie Bank, Amsterdam, 1950.

[1] Based on Claudin's "Tota pulchra es," **63**-20.
[2] Table: Missa ad placitum.

[3]3.	Missa Sancta et immaculata	Allaire	vii^v
[4]4.	Missa Jam non dicam vos servos	Du moulin	xi^v

[3] Based on Hesdin's "Sancta et immaculata," **50**-28.

[4] Based on Richafort's "Jam non dicam vos servos," *Secundus liber cum quinque vocibus*, Lyons, Moderne, 1532. Transcribed in Kabis, "The Works of Jean Richafort," unpublished dissertation, New York University, 1957, Vol. II, p. 114.

1534, AUGUST

52

Liber quintus. xii. trium priorum tonorum / magnificat con=tinet / [Table] / **Parhisiis apud Petrum Attaingnant musice calco=graphum / ad templum sanctorum Cosme & Damiani. / Mense Augusto 1534 / Superius / Cum priuilegio ad sexēnium. /**

4 vol. in-4° obl., 20.5 × 16 cm.; 16 f. numbered i–xvi
Sign.: r^4–v^4; rr^4–vv^4; RR^4–VV^4; R^4–V^4
RISM–I, 1534^7

Jena: Universitätsbibliothek
Milan: Biblioteca Ambrosiana (S & B)
Noyon: Ancienne Bibliothèque du Chapitre
Vienna: Österreichische Nationalbibliothek

1.	[Magnificat] Primi toni	Cybot	i^v
2.	[Magnificat] Primi toni	Heurteur	ii^v
3.	[Magnificat] Primi toni	F. Dulot	iiii
4.	[Magnificat] Primi toni	Jo. Le brun	v
5.	[Magnificat] Primi toni	A. Mornable	vi
6.	[Magnificat] Primi toni	A. Févin	vii
7.	[Magnificat] Secundi toni	Ho. Barra	viii
8.	[Magnificat] Secundi toni	Ho. Barra	ix
9.	[Magnificat] Secundi toni	P. Manchicourt	x
10.	[Magnificat] Secundi toni	Hesdin	xi^v
11.	[Magnificat] Tertii toni	Hylaire Penet	xii^v
12.	[Magnificat] Tertii toni	Jacotin	xiiii
	Finis huius libri		
13.	Fecit potentiam—Trio I	Claudin	xv
	Esurientes implevit bonis—Trio II	Claudin	xv^v
	Sicut locutus est—Trio III	Claudin	xvi^v
	Finis		

Complete modern edition in *Treize Livres de Motets*, Cinquième Livre. Includes facsimile of title page.

53

Liber sextus. xiii. quinqȝ vltimorū tonorum / magnificat continet / [Table] / Parhisiis apud Petrum Attaingnant musice calco= graphum / ad templum sanctorum Cosme & Damiani. / Mense Septēb. 1534 / Superius / Cum priuilegio ad sexēnium. /

4 vol. in-4° obl., 20.5 × 16 cm.; 16 f. numbered i–xvi
Sign.: x⁴–&⁴; xx⁴–&&⁴; XX⁴–AA⁴; X⁴–A⁴
RISM–I, 1534⁸

Jena: Universitätsbibliothek
Milan: Biblioteca Ambrosiana (S & B)
Milan: Biblioteca del Conservatorio
Noyon: Ancienne Bibliothèque de Chapitre
Vicenza: Biblioteca Bertoliana, FF. 2.7.23(1) (S)
Vienna: Österreichische Nationalbibliothek

1.	[Magnificat] Quarti toni	Jo. Mouton	iv
2.	[Magnificat] Quarti toni	Jacotin	iiv
3.	[Magnificat] Quarti toni	Jo. L'héritier	iiiv
4.	[Magnificat] Quarti toni	Heurteur	v
5.	[Magnificat] Quinti toni	Divitis	vi
6.	Magnificat quinti toni	Du hamel	vii
7.	[Magnificat] Sexti toni	Jo. Mouton	viiiv
8.	[Magnificat] Septimi toni	M. Gascongne	xv
9.	[Magnificat] Octavi toni	Richafort	xiv
10.	[Magnificat] Octavi toni	Claudin	xiii
11.	Magnificat octavi toni	Jacotin	xiiiv
12.	Magnificat octavi toni	Du hamel	xiiiiv
[1]13.	[Magnificat] Primi toni	Jo. de Billon	xvi

Finis

Complete modern edition in *Treize Livres de Motets*, Sixième Livre. Includes facsimile of title page.

[1] Table: ad tres voces pares.

54

Trente et vne chansons musicales a quatre/ parties imprimees par Pierre Attaingnāt imprimeur de / musique demourant a Paris en la rue de la Harpe pres / leglise sainct Cosme Desquelles la table sensuyt. / Mense Septemb. 1534 / [Table] / Superius / Auec priuilege du Roy iusques a six ans /

4 vol. in-8° obl., 15 × 10 cm.; 16 f. numbered i–xvi (S: i & x xi xii; B: & x xi xii)
Sign.: C e^4–C h^4; C ee^4–C hh^4; C EE^4–C HH^4; C E^4–C H^4
RISM–I, 1534^{14}

Lausanne: Succession A. Cortot (olim Wernigerode) (S). "Le XVIII Livre"
Munich: Bayerische Staatsbibliothek, Mus. Pr. 31/9

1.	O doulce amour, ô contente pensée	Claudin	i^v
2.	Il est en vous le bien que je désire	Claudin	ii
3.	Tant ay gravé au cueur vostre figure	Jennequin	ii^v
4.	Si par souffrir l'on peult vaincre fortune	Courtois	iii
5.	La grant doulceur de ma loyalle seur	M. Lasson	iii^v
6.	L'oeil a plaisir et l'esprit se contente	M. Lasson	iii^v
7.	Amour, passion incréable	Claudin	iiii
[1]8.	Par fin despit je m'en yray seullette	Claudin	iiii^v
9.	Ung coup d'essay avant que bailler gaige	Jennequin	v
10.	J'ay congé prins sans l'avoir mérité	Gombert	v^v
11.	Souffrés ung peu que vous baise et acolle	Jennequin	vi
12.	De vray amour ne me vient que tristesse	Jennequin	vi^v
13.	Du cueur le don a le loyal amant	Certon	vii
14.	Jectés-les hors de joyeuse queste	Certon	vii^v
15.	Amour au cueur me poing	Heurteur	vii^v
16.	L'espousé la premiere nuict		viii^v
17.	Le doulx baisier que j'ai au départir	Roger Patie	ix
18.	J'ay trop d'amours et peu de récompense	Lupi	ix^v
19.	Pour ma maistresse et moy honneur garde		x
20.	Pour satisfaire a l'esperit tourmenté	M. Lasson	x^v
21.	Martin menoit son pourceau au marché	Alaire	x^v
22.	Je l'ayme bien et l'aymeray a ce propos	Hesdin	xi^v
23.	Si nostre amour ne monstre sa valeur	Certon	xii
24.	Les mesdisans qui sur moy ont envie	Certon	xii^v
25.	Cesse mon oeil de plus la regarder	Roger Patie	xiii
[2]26.	J'ay veu soubz l'umbre d'ung buisson	Rousée	xiii^v
27.	Mon confesseur m'a dict que je m'exente	Jennequin	xiiii^v
28.	L'ardant vouloir est au désir	Claudin	xv
29.	Voulant Amour, soubz baiser gracieux	Mahiet	xv^v
30.	Madame ung jour doulx baiser me donna	Heurteur	xvi
31.	Le trop dissimuler en amour et opresse		xvi^v

Finis

[1] Superius only is the same as **8**-21.
[2] Listed in table as "Remues la paille."

1534, OCTOBER

55

Vingt et huyt chãsons musicalles a quatre/ parties imprimees par Pierre Attaingnãt imprimeur de / musique demourant a Paris en la rue de la Harpe pres / leglise sainct Cosme Desquelles la table sensuyt. / Mense Octobri 1534 / [Table] / Superius / Avec priuilege du Roy iusques a six ans. /

4 vol. in-8° obl., 15 × 10 cm.; 16 f. numbered i–xvi
Sign.: C i⁴–C m⁴; C ii⁴–C mm⁴; C II⁴–C MM⁴; C I⁴–C M⁴
RISM–I, 1534[12]

Lausanne: Succession A. Cortot (olim Wernigerode) (S). "Le XIX Livre"
Munich: Bayerische Staatsbibliothek, Mus. Pr. 31/6

1.	Il est bel et bon, commere, mon mari	Passereau	iv
2.	Chose commune a tous n'est agréable	Claudin	ii
3.	Aultre que vous il n'a voulu choisir	Claudin	iiv
4.	Altro non e'l mio amor ch'el proprio inferno	Claudin	iiv
5.	Jamais je n'euz tant de soulas	Gombert	iiiv
6.	Onques amour ne fut sans espérance	Heurteur	iiii
7.	Qui peult ne veult avoir pitié de moy	Georges	iiiiv
8.	Allons jouer sur le jonc, le joly jonc		v
9.	Pour ton amour contrainct suys d'endurer	Du Hamel	vv
*10.	Et gentil ma maréschal, ferreras-tu pas mon cheval		vi
11.	Pourquoy voulés-vous cousturier aultre que moy	[1]Jennequin	viv
12.	On dit que vous la voulés prendre	Jennequin	vii
13.	En aultre avoir trop plus que toy fiance	Gombert	viii
14.	Lors demourra l'espérance asseurée		viiiv
15.	C'est a jamais a qui je me submetz	Courtoys	ix
16.	Amour peult tout, soit plaisir ou tristesse		ixv
17.	Amour ne peult en virile courage		x
18.	Les bons freres de Thérouenne	Du Croc	xv
19.	Troys fillettes estoient toutes en ung coing	Courtoys	xi
20.	Si pour sçavoir le malheur advenir		xii
21.	Plus ne me fault estre amoureux		xiiv
22.	J'ay trouvé part, adieu te dis fortune		xiii
23.	Revenés souvent m'amye, je le trouve bon	Jennequin	xiiiv
24.	Pour ung nouveau qui par doulceur te flate		xiiiiv
25.	On dit bien vray la maulvaise fortune		xv
26.	Desliez-moy, ma maistresse, m'amye		xvv
†27.	Ce sont gallans qui s'en vont resjouyr	Jennequin	xvi
28.	Du plasmateur de terre et cieulx		xviv

Finis

* Modern edition in *Quinze Chansons.*
† Modern edition in *Trente Chansons* (*1928*).

[1] Attributed to Passereau in *Venticinque Canzoni Francesi*, Venice, Gardane, 1538. See Lesure in *Fontes* I (1954), 83.

1534, NOVEMBER

56

¶ Liber septimus. xxiiij. trium / quatuor / quinqꝫ / sex de / vocum modulos dominici aduentus / natiuitatisqꝫ ei' / ac / sanctorum eo tempore occurrentiū habet. vt presens index / tibi commonstrat / [Table] / Et quia O sapientia cetereqꝫ huiusmodi anti- phone propriis carēt Magnificat / tibi opus erit recursu / ad quintū librū motetor. in quo quatuor secūdi toni Magnificat q̄ pro libito tibi canēda erūt reperies / Superius / Parisiis in vico cithare apud Petrū Attaingnant musice calcographū: / Cū priuilegio regio ad sexenniū. /

Ct.: Mense Novēb. 1534 / [Table]/

4 vol. in-4° obl., 20.5 × 16 cm.; 16 f. numbered i–xvi
Sign.: ✝a⁴–✝d⁴; ✝aa⁴–✝dd⁴; ✝AA⁴–✝DD⁴; ✝A⁴–✝D⁴
RISM–I, 1534⁹

Jena: Universitätsbibliothek
Milan: Biblioteca Ambrosiana (S & B)
Milan: Biblioteca del Conservatorio
Noyon: Ancienne Bibliothèque du Chapitre
Paris: Bibliothèque Sainte-Geneviève, Vm. 87 Rés (S)
Vienna: Österreichische Nationalbibliothek

1.	Virgo flagellatur crucianda fame religatur I O quam felices per te, sanctissima plures II T 2, I & II: Virgo sancta Katherina, Græciæ gemma 5 tt; De sancta Katherina	Vermont primus	iᵛ
2.	Conceptio tua, Dei genitrix, virgo 5 cc; De Conceptione	Gombert	iiᵛ
3.	Ecce Dominus veniet et omnes sancti eius 5 tt; Canon; De Adventu Domini	A.Willart	iii
4.	Vidi sub altare Dei animas interfectorum I Divinum acceperunt responsum II 4; In festo Innocentium	G. Le Heurteur	iiiᵛ
5.	In illa die suscipiam te servum meum I In tribulatione invocasti me II 4; De sancto Johanne Evangelista	Consilium	iiii
6.	Congratulamini michi omnes qui diligitis Dominum I Et beata viscera Mariæ Virginis II 4; In die Nativitatis Domini	Rousée	v
7.	Lapidaverunt Stephanum et ipse invocabat I Stephanus vidit cælos apertos II 4; De sancto Stephano	Jo. Rousée	vi
8.	Laudem dicite Deo nostro, omnes sancti eius I Genus electum, gens sancta II 4; De omnibus Sanctis	Rousée	vii
9.	Sospitati dedit ægros olei perfusio I Vas in mari mersum patri II 4; De sancto Nicolao	Rousée	viii
10.	O sapientia quæ ex ore Altissimi prodisti 5 bb; O Sapientia		ix
11.	Et dux domus Israel qui Moysi 5 tt; O Adonay	Certon	ixᵛ
12.	Qui stas in signum populorum 4; O radix Jesse	Hotinet	x
13.	Et sceptrum domus Israel qui aperis 6 bbtt; O clavis David	A. Mornable	xᵛ
14.	Splendor lucis æternæ et sol justiciæ 5 bb; O oriens	G. Le Roy	xi
15.	Per Christum quem meruisti tangere [1]5 cc; O Thoma Didime	Manchicourt	xiᵛ
16.	Rex et legifer noster, expectatio gentium 4; O Emanuel	Manchicourt	xii
17.	Et desideratus earum lapisque 4; O rex gentium	Hotinet	xiiᵛ

[1] Table: 5 bb.

18.	Quomodo fiet istud, quia nec primam similem 6 ttcc; Secundus contratenor / Canon in sub diapenthe; O virgo virginum	Manchicourt	xiii
19.	Gaude, virgo Katherina, quam refulsit I Gaude, quia meruisti II 4; De sancta Katherina	[2]Mouton	xiiii
20.	Andreas, Christi famulus, dignus Deo apostolus I Qui persequebatur justum, demersisti eum, Domine II 4; De sancto Andrea	Hesdin	xv
21.	Da pacem, Domine, in diebus nostris quia non est alius—3	Claudin	xv^{v}
22.	Pater noster, qui es in cælis I Panem nostrum quotidianum da nobis hodie II 3; Oratio dominicalis	A. Mornable	xv^{v}
23.	Dignare me laudare te, virgo sacrata 3; De beata Maria	Maistre Gosse	xvi^{v}
24.	Sancta Maria, mater Dei, ora pro peccatis nostris 3; De beata Maria	Maistre Gosse	xvi^{v}

Finis

Complete modern edition in *Treize Livres de Motets*, Septième Livre. Includes facsimile of title page.

[2] Attributed to Gombert in Bassus.

1534, DECEMBER

57

¶ Liber octauus. xx. musicales motetos quatuor / quinqz / vel sex vocum modulos habet. / Mense decemb. M.d.xxxiiij / [Table] / Superius / Parisiis in vico cithare prope sanctorum Cosme et Damiani templũ / apud Petrum Attaingnant musice calcographum. / Cũ priuilegio regio ad sexenniũ. /

4 vol. in-4° obl., 20.5 × 16 cm.; 16 f. numbered i–xvi
Sign.: †e^{4}–†h^{4}; †ee^{4}–†hh^{4}; †EE^{4}–†HH^{4}; †E^{4}–†H^{4}
RISM–I, 1534^{10}

Jena: Universitätsbibliothek
Milan: Biblioteca Ambrosiana (S & B)
Milan: Biblioteca del Conservatorio
Noyon: Ancienne Bibliothèque du Chapitre
Paris: Bibliothèque Sainte-Geneviève, Vm. 88 Rés (S)
Vienna: Österreichische Nationalbibliothek

1.	Nigra sum sed formosa I 6 ttcc; Sexta pars Nigra sum—Canon in diapenthe—Circumdederunt me gemitus mortis; De beata Maria	L'héritier	i^{v}

2.	Ave Maria, gratia plena	Richafort	ii
	5 tt; Salutatio angelica		
3.	Hac clara die turma festiva dat præconia I	Willart	ii^{v}
	Ct, B: Mariam concrepando symphonia nectarea		
	Cui contra Maria hæc reddit famina II		
	4; In Annunciatione aut Assumptione beatæ Mariæ		
4.	Veni, electa mea, et ponam te I	Richafort	iii^{v}
	Quia concupivit rex speciem tuam II		
	6 ttcc; De Assumptione beatæ Mariæ		
5.	Cum rides michi basium negasti I } 4	L'héritier	iiii^{v}
	Data es de lachrymis michi voluptas II }		
6.	Homo erat in Hierusalem cui nomen Symeon I	N. Gombert	v
	Et cum inducerent puerum in templum II		
	4; De Purificatione beatæ Mariæ		
7.	Saule, quid me persequeris? I	Le brun	v^{v}
	Sancte Paule apostole, prædicator veritatis II		
	T, I & II: Sancte Paule ora pro nobis.		
	5 tt; Canon. Luna te docet; De sancto Paulo		
*8.	Verbum bonum et suave I	A.Wyllart	vi^{v}
	Ave, solem genuisti, ave, prolem protulisti II		
	6 ttcc; De beata Maria		
9.	Epiphaniam Domino canamus gloriosam I	Hesdin	vii^{v}
	Aurum simulthus et myrram II		
	Ct, B: Huic magi munera deferunt præclara		
	Magi stella sibi micante prævia III		
	5 canon; T: canon in dyapason; De Epiphania		
10.	Gloriosi principes terræ quomodo in vita sua	Jo. Mouton	viii^{v}
	B, T 1: Petrus apostolus et Paulus doctor gentium		
	5 tt; De Apostolis		
11.	Cum inducerent puerum Jesum parentes eius	Consilium	ix
	4; De Purificatione beatæ Mariæ		
12.	Exurge, quare obdormis, Domine I	Rousée	ix^{v}
	Sciant gentes quoniam nomen tibi Deus II		
	6 sstt		
13.	Hierusalem, luge et exue te vestibus I	Lupus	xi^{v}
	Deduc quasi torrentem lachrymas II		
	5 tt; In die Parasceves		
*14.	Beata viscera Mariæ virginis	Willart	xii
	6 cctt; Canon in dyapenthe / Secundus Contratenor / et secundus Tenor; De beata Maria		
15.	Benedictus es, Domine Deus patrum nostrorum		xii^{v}
	5 tt; De sanctissima Trinitate		
16.	Cede fragor strepitusque omnis; terrenæ sileant I		xiii
	Ecce velut fumi consurgens virgula odori II		
	T, I & II: Sicut lilium inter spinas; B 1, II: Scandit ad æthereum		
	[1]6 cc bb; De beata Maria		
17.	Descendi in hortum meum ut viderem poma		xiii^{v}
	6 tt cc; Quinta et sexta pars: Canon; De beata Maria		
18.	Sancta Maria, regina cælorum I	Willart	xiiii
	O pia domina, per illud gaudium II		
	Quinta pars, I & II: Pulchra es et decora		
	5 ss; De beata Maria		

* Modern edition in *CMM 3*:IV.

[1]Table: 6 tt bb.

19. Ecce nos reliquimus omnia I Et omnis qui reliquerit domum vel fratres II 4; De Apostolis	M. Jo. de Ferrare	xv^v
20. Anthoni, pater inclyte, qui Paduanus diceris I O Anthoni pater, veni, clara proles II 4; De sancto Anthonio	M. Lasson	xvi

Finis

Complete modern edition in *Treize Livres de Motets*, Huitième Livre. Includes facsimile of title page.

1534

58

¶ Hec figura oẽs scientias et artes in vnam radicam ex qua pullulant reducit / [Chart] / 1534 / **¶ Venalem reperies Parisiis in vico Cithareo in officina libraria Petri Attaingnant qua prospectus est ad vicū Mathurinorum** /

Broadside, 23 × 32.4 cm.

Paris: Bibliothèque Nationale, Rés. Z. 544
Paris: Bibliothèque Universitaire, 276 a Rés. (Bound inside Chasseneus, *Catalogus gloriae mundi*, Lyons, 1529)

For facsimile, see Plate I.

[1534?]

59

[Latin and French names of the rivers and towns of the three parts of Gaul.]

Bottom: ¶ On les vend a Paris en la rue de la Harpe devant [le bout de la rue des Mathurins pres leglise de Sainct Cosme.]

Broadside, 21.9 × 30.8 cm.

Paris: Bibliothèque Universitaire, 276 a Rés. (bound inside Chasseneus, *Catalogus gloriae mundi*, Lyons, 1529)

For facsimile, see Plate XIII.

60

¶Lib. nonus. xviij. dauiticos musicales psalmos habet. / Mense Januarii. M.d.xxxiiij / [Table] / **Superius** / **Parisiis in vico cithare prope sanctorum Cosme et Damiani templu** / **apud Petrum Attaingnant musice calcographum.** / **Cū priuilegio regio ad sexenniū.** /

4 vol. in-4° obl., 20.5 × 16 cm.; 16 f. numbered i–xvi
Sign.: †i^4–†m^4; †ii^4–†mm^4; †II^4–†MM^4; †I^4–†M^4
RISM–I, 1535^1

Jena: Universitätsbibliothek
Milan: Biblioteca Ambrosiana (S & B)
Milan: Biblioteca del Conservatorio
Noyon: Ancienne Bibliothèque du Chapitre
Paris: Bibliothèque Sainte-Geneviève, Vm. 89 Rés (S)
Vienna: Österreichische Nationalbibliothek

1. Dilexi quoniam exaudiet Dominus I	Denis Briant	i^v
O Domine, libera animam meam II		
2. Fundamenta eius in montibus sanctis I	Guyon	ii^v
Nunquid Syon dicet:homo II		
3. Lætatus sum in his quæ dicta sunt michi I	Math. Gascongne	iii^v
Rogate quæ ad pacem sunt Hierusalem II		
4. Laudate Dominum, omnes gentes	M. Gosse	iiii^v
5. In convertendo Dominus captivitatem Syon I	Lupus	v
Qui seminant in lachrymis II		
6. Confitemini Domino quoniam bonus I	Jo. Mouton	v^v
Bonum est confidere in Domino II		
7. In te, Domine, speravi I 5 ss	Lupus	vi^v
Quoniam fortitudo mea II		
8. Proba me, Domine, et tenta me	Jacotin	viii
9. Credidi, propter quod locutus sum I	Jacotin	viii^v
T, B: Ego dixi in excessu meo: omnis homo mendax		
O Domine, quia ego servus tuus II		
10. In Domino confido; quomodo dicitis animæ meæ I	Vermont primus	ix
Oculi eius in pauperem respiciunt II		
11. Usquequo, Domine, oblivisceris me in finem? I	Lupus	x
Illumina oculos meos II		
12. Beatus vir qui non abiit in consilio impiorum I	Claudin	xi
T, B: Et in via peccatorum non stetit		
Non sic impii, non sic; sed tanquam pulvis II		
13. Domini est terra et plenitudo eius I	Claudin	xi^v
Hæc est generatio quærentium Dominum II		

14.	Benedic, anima mea, Domino I Qui redemit de interitu vitam tuam II	Claudin	xii^v^
15.	Deus in adjutorium meum intende	Claudin	xiii
16.	Qui confidunt in Domino sicut mons Sion I Benefac, Domine, bonis et rectis corde II	L'héritier	xiii^v^
17.	Inclina, Domine, aurem tuam et exaudi me I Deduc me, Domine, in via II [à 3] Domine Deus, miserator III	Jacotin	xiiii^v^
18.	Nisi Dominus ædificaverit domum I Cum dederit dilectis suis somnum II	G. Le Heurteur	xv^v^

Finis

Complete modern edition in *Treize Livres de Motets*, Neuvième Livre. Includes facsimile of title page.

1535, FEBRUARY

61

¶Lib. decimus: Passiones dominice in ramis palmarū / veneris sancte: necnon lectiones feriarū quinte / sexte / ac sabbati hebdomade / sancte: multaq; alia quadragesime congruentia c tinet. vt palam videre licet. / Mense Februario 1534 / [Table] / Superius / Parisiis in vico cithare prope sanctorum Cosme et Damiani templum / apud Petrum Attaingnant musice calcographum. / Cū priuilegio regio ad sexenniū. /

4 vol. in-4° obl., 20.5 × 16 cm.; 16 f. numbered i–xvi
Sign.: †n[4]–†q[4]; †nn[4]–†qq[4]; †NN[4]–†QQ[4]; †N[4]–†Q[4]
RISM–I, 1535[2]

Jena: Universitätsbibliothek
Milan: Biblioteca Ambrosiana (S & B)
Milan: Biblioteca del Conservatorio
Noyon: Ancienne Bibliothèque du Chapitre
Paris: Bibliothèque Sainte-Geneviève, Vm. 90 Rés (S)
Vienna: Österreichische Nationalbibliothek

1.	Feria quinta in Cena Domini Aleph. Quomodo sedet Gimel. Migravit Judas Zay. Recordata est	Févin	i^v^
2.	Feria sexta in Parasceves Men. Cui comparabo Samech. Plauserunt Phe. Fecit Dominus		iii
3.	Sabbato in vigilia Paschæ Thau. Reddes eis vicem Gimel. Sed ex lamyæ Zay. Candidiores	Claudin	iiii^v^

4.	Kyrie eleyson	4		vi
	Parce famulis. Christus Dominus factus est			
5.	Passio Domini secundum Mathæum	4	Claudin	vi^{v}
6.	Passio Domini secundum Johannem	4		ix
7.	In pace in idipsum dormiam et requiescam	4	L'enfant	x^{v}
8.	In pace. Si dedero somnum oculis meis	6	Moulu	xi^{v}
	T: canon—[3 in 1]			
9.	Ne projicias nos in tempore senectutis	5	Verdelot	xii
	T: canon			
10.	Ne projicias nos in tempore senectutis	6	Moulu	xii^{v}
	Ct 2: canon			
11.	O Rex gloriose inter sanctos tuos I	4	G. Louvet	xii^{v}
	Ne derelinquas nos, Deus noster II			
12.	Gloria, laus et honor tibi sit [I]	4	Divitis	xiii^{v}
	Israel es tu Rex [II]	[3]		
	Cetus in excelsis te laudat cælitus [III]	[2]		
	Plebs Hebræa tibi cum palmis [IV]	[6]		
13.	Domine, non secundum peccata nostra I	6	Jacquet	xiiii^{v}
	Domine, ne memineris iniquitatum II	[4]		
	Adjuva nos, Deus salutaris noster III	[6]		
[1]14.	Et adhuc tecum sum, alleluya	4	Claudin	xvi^{v}

Finis

Complete modern edition in *Treize Livres de Motets*, Dixième Livre. Includes facsimile of title page.

[1] Table: Resurrexi.

1535, FEBRUARY

62

¶ Vingt & six chãsons musicales a quatre / parties imprimees par Pierre Attaingnant imprimeur de / musique demourant a Paris en la rue de la Harpe pres / leglise sainct Cosme desquelles la table sensuyt. / Mense Februario. m.d.xxxiiij / [Table] / **Superius / Cũ priuilegio regio ad sexenniũ. /**

4 vol. in-8° obl., 15 × 10 cm.; 16 f. numbered i–xvi
Sign.: C n^{4}–C q^{4}; C nn^{4}–C qq^{4}; C NN^{4}–C QQ^{4}; C N^{4}–C Q^{4}
RISM–I, 1535^{6}

Lausanne: Succession A. Cortot (olim Wernigerode) (S). "Le XX. Livre"
Munich: Bayerische Staatsbibliothek, Mus. Pr. 31/4

*1.	Fyez vous y si vous voulés	Jennequin	i^{v}
2.	Pour n'avoir onc faulse chose promise	Claudin	ii
3.	Puys que sa foy l'ennemy par noblesse	Claudin	ii^{v}
4.	Las, cruel départ, veulx tu faire mourir		iii^{v}
5.	Qui par servir n'aquiert grace		iiii

* Modern edition in *Chorwerk, Vol. 73.*

6.	Faictes-vous bien sans cause dechasser		iiii^{v}
7.	Fy, fy, cela est trop maigre	Jennequin	v
8.	Es-tu bien malade, dy, mon compaignon		v^{v}
9.	De trop aymer tout homme n'est pas sage		vi
†10.	Je ne seray jamais bergere	Passereau	vi^{v}
11.	Tu pers ton temps de plus muser	Gombert	vii
[1],‡12.	Saincte Barbe, mon con, mon compere Ct & B: Nostre dince, mon con, mon compere	Passereau	vii^{v}
13.	Contre raison trop m'as voulu meffaire		viii
14.	Martin menoit son pourceau au marché	Claudin	viii^{v}
15.	C'est trop parlé de Bachus et sa tasse	Certon	ix
16.	Je suys en doubte et ne le puys sçavoir		x
17.	Quant j'estoys jeune fillete	Lupi	x^{v}
18.	Aultre que vous ne voy qui tant me plaise	Gombert	xi^{v}
19.	Pour vous donner parfaict contentement	Allaire	xii
20.	De moy avez le cueur et le corps en gaige		xii^{v}
21.	Martin menoit son pourceau au marché	Jennequin	xiii
22.	Jouer irons sur la verdure ce moys de may	Cirot	xiii^{v}
23.	Qui me vouldra a gré servir		xiiii^{v}
24.	C'est trop aymé sans avoir recompense	Heurteur	xv
25.	Sans lever le pied j'abatray la rousée	Cirot	xv^{v}
26.	Mais que ce fust secretement	Jennequin	xvi
27.	Mes bons amys ont pourchassé ma mort—*Canon*		xvi^{v}
	Finis		

† Modern edition in *Chansons polyphoniques.*
‡ Modern edition in *Thirty Chansons* (*1960*).

[1] Listed in table as *Nostre dince.*

1535, MARCH (before the 28th)

63

¶ Lib. undecim'. xxvj. musicales habet modulos quatuor / et quinqȝ vocibus editos: quorum index subsequitur. / Mense Martio. m.d.xxxiiij. / [Table] / **Superius** / **Parrhisiis in vico Cithareo p.pe sctōꝝ. Cosme & Damiani tēplum** / **in edibus Petri Attaingnant musice calcographi** / **Cū grā et priuilegio xp̄ianissimi frācor. regis ad sexēniū** /

4 vol. in-4° obl., 20.5 × 16 cm.; 16 f. numbered i–xvi (T: xiii x xv xii)
Sign.: †r^{4}–†v^{4}; † rr^{4}–† vv^{4}; † RR^{4}–† VV^{4}; † R^{4}–† V^{4}
RISM-I, 1535^{3}

Jena: Universitätsbibliothek
Milan: Biblioteca Ambrosiana (S & B)
Milan: Biblioteca del Conservatorio
Noyon: Ancienne Bibliothèque du Chapitre
Paris: Bibliothèque Sainte-Geneviève, Vm. 91 Rés (S)
Vienna: Österreichische Nationalbibliothek

1.	Quare tristis es, anima mea? I	Gascongne	i^{v}
	Quare oblitus es mie? et quare tristis incedo II		
	Dum dicunt michi per singulos dies III		
2.	Benedicite Deum cæli I	Longueval	ii
	Ipsum intelligite et cantate illi II		
3.	Vide, Domine, afflictionem nostram	De la fage	ii^{v}
4.	Exurge, quare obdormis Domine? I	Claudin	iii^{v}
	Quare oblivisceris inopiæ II		
5.	Non nobis, Domine, sed nomini tuo da gloriam I	Gascongne	iiii
	Conserva regem Franciscum II		
	T, B: Jesu, bone rex virtutum		
6.	Domine, Rex omnipotens, in ditione tua I	Claudin	v
	Exaudi orationem meam et converte II		
	Ct, B: Exaudi orationem nostram		
7.	Adjuva me, Domine, et salvus ero I	Consilium	v^{v}
	Servus tuus ego sum: de michi intellectum II		
8.	Recordare, Domine, testamenti tui I	Vermont primus	vi
	Quiescat jam, Domine, ira tua II		
9.	Da pacem, Domine, in diebus nostris. I	Claudin	vi^{v}
	Rogate quæ ad pacem sunt Hierusalem II		
10.	Si bona suscepimus de manu Domini	Claudin	vii^{v}
11.	Homo natus de muliere brevi vivens tempore I	Claudin	vii^{v}
	Homo cum in honore esset non intellexit II		
12.	Quousque non reverteris pax orba Gallis	Claudin	viii^{v}
13.	Sustinuimus pacem et non venit	Claudin	ix
14.	Unde veniet auxilium michi? I	Passereau	ix^{v}
	Auxilium meum a Domino II		
15.	Deus regnorum et christianissimi maxime protector I	Gascongne	x^{v}
	Deus a quo sancta desideria II		
	T, B: Recta consilia et justa sunt opera		
16.	Aspice, Domine, de sede sancta tua	[1]De la fage	xi
17.	Ne reminiscaris, Domine, delicta nostra I	Gascongne	xi^{v}
	Neque vindictam sumas de peccatis nostris II		
18.	Gaude Francorum regia corona	Févin	xii
19.	Antequam comedam suspiro I } 5 tt	Jo. Mouton	xii^{v}
	Ecce non est auxilium michi II } 5 tt		
	T 2, I & II: Je ris et si ay la lerme a l'oeil		
	Secondus tenor crescit in duplo / Canon		
	Dissimulare loco summa prudentia est		
20.	Tota pulchra es, amica mea	Claudin	xiii
*21.	Videns Dominus flentes sorores Lazari	Willart	xiii^{v}
22.	O dulcissime Domine Jesu Christe 5 tt	Verdelot	xiii^{v}
23.	Esto michi, Domine, turris fortitudinis I } 5 tt	Claudin	xiiii^{v}
	Non confundantur omnes qui sperant in te II } 5 tt		
24.	Rex autem David cooperto capite incedens	Gascongne	xv^{v}
25.	In manibus tuis sortes meae, Domine I	M. Lasson	xv^{v}
	Esto, Domine, propitius sorti meae II		
26.	Bone Jesu dulcissime! O Jesu clementissime!	Gascongne	xvi^{v}
	Finis		

Complete modern edition in *Treize Livres de Motets*, Onzième Livre. Includes facsimile of title page.

* Modern edition in *CMM 3*:I.

[1] Claudin in **103**.

64

¶ Lib. duodecim'. xvij. musicales ad virginē christiparā / salutationes habet. vt subscripto indice videre licet. / Mense Martio. m.d.xxxv. post pascha / [Table] / Superius / Parrhisiis in vico Cithareo p.pe sctōꝝ. Cosme & Damiani tēplum / in edibus Petri Attaingnant musice calcographi / Cū grā et priuilegio xpianissimi frācor. regis ad sexēniū /

4 vol. in-4° obl., 20.5 × 16 cm.; 16 f. numbered i–xvi
Sign.: † x^4–† $\&^4$; † xx^4–† $\&\&^4$; † XX^4–† AA^4; † X^4–† A^4
RISM-I, 1535^4

Jena: Universitätsbibliothek
Milan: Biblioteca Ambrosiana: (S & B; S. lacks f. xii, xiii, xvi)
Milan: Biblioteca del Conservatorio
Noyon: Ancienne Bibliothèque du Chapitre (S bound incorrectly, ix xii xi x)
Paris: Bibliothèque Sainte-Geneviève, Vm. 92 Rés (S)
Vienna: Österreichische Nationalbibliothek

1.	Ave regina cælorum	4	M. Sohier	i^v
2.	Ave regina cælorum	4	Maurici' Georget	ii
3.	Salve regina	4	M. Sohier	ii^v
*4.	Regina cæli	5	M. Sohier	iii^v
5.	Regina cæli—S: Canon	4	Moulu	iiii^v
†6.	Regina cæli T: Canon in subdiapenthe—I; Canon in epidiapenthe—II	5	Wyllart	iiii^v
7.	Regina cæli	8	Rousée	v^v
8.	Regina cæli	12	Gombert	vi^v
9.	Regina cæli	6	Vermont primus	viii^v
10.	Regina cæli	4	Bourguignon	ix
11.	Regina caeli—S, T: Canon in subdiapason	6	Desilva	ix^v
‡12.	Salve regina	5	Josquin	x
13.	Salve regina	6	Claudin	x^v
14.	Salve regina	5	Consilium	xi^v
15.	Salve regina—T: Canon	6	L'héritier	xii^v
16.	Salve regina	4	Hotinet Barra	xv^v
17.	Salve regina	5	Richafort	xvi

Finis

Complete modern edition in *Treize Livres de Motets*, Douzième Livre. Includes facsimile of title page.

* Transcription of the motet and negative of title page in J. Delaporte, "Le Regina Coeli de Mathieu Sohier", *Revue Liturgique et Musicale* XX (1936–37), 64–65.
† Modern edition in *CMM 3*:III.
‡ Modern edition in *Josquin*, Bundel XI.

65

¶ Trēte et une chāsons musicales a troys / parties auec quinze Duo imprimees p. Pierre Attaingnāt / imprimeur de musique a Paris en la rue de la / Harpe pres leglise saincte Cosme. Mense aprili. 1535 / [Table] / **Superius / Cū priuilegio ad sexenniu.**

4 (?) vols.[1] in-8° obl., 15 × 10 cm.; 16 f. numbered i–xvi
Sign.: ✠ f⁴–✠ i⁴
Lausanne: Succession A. Cortot (olim Wernigerode) (S) "Le XXI. Livre"

1.	Le berger et la bergere sont a l'ombre d'ung buysson	[N. Revez][2]	i^v
2.	Le cueur de vous ma présence désire		ii
3.	Amour tu es par trop cruelle		ii^v
4.	Si j'ay eu du mal ou du bien par oubly	Gosse[3]	iii
5.	Amour me poing et si je me veulx plaindre	Gosse[4]	iii^v
6.	Amour me voyant sans tristesse	Gosse	iiii
7.	J'ayme le cueur de m'amye, sa bonté et sa doulceur	[Claudin][5]	iiii^v
8.	J'ay le désir content et l'effect résolu	Claudin	v
9.	Si mon malheur my continue je ne sçay pas	Claudin	v^v
10.	Celle qui m'a tant pourmené	Claudin	v^v
11.	Aupres de vous secretement demeure	Claudin	vi^v
12.	J'ay par trop longuement aymé	[Claudin][5]	vii
13.	Je ne fais rien que réquérir	Claudin	vii^v
14.	Changeons propos, c'est trop chanté d'amours	Claudin	vii^v
15.	J'ay contenté ma volunté suffisament	Claudin	viii^v
16.	Regretz, soucy et peine m'ont fait de villains tours	Heurteur	ix
17.	C'este une dure départie de celuy ou j'ay mis mon cueur	Claudin	ix^v
18.	On en dira ce qu'on vouldra	[Claudin][5]	x
19.	Quant j'ay beu du vin clairet tout tourne	Heurteur	x^v
20.	Par fin despit je m'en iray seullette au joly boys	Claudin	xi
21.	Je suys trop jeunette pour faire ung amy	Gascongne	xi^v
22.	Il est en vous le bien que je désire	[Claudin][6]	xii
23.	Trop dure m'est la longue demourée	G. Ysoré	xii^v
24.	Vignon, vignette, qui te planta il fut preud'hom	Claudin	xiii

[1] The "Quinze Duo" [sic] presumably occupied a fourth part-book (what would normally be the Bassus) while the chansons à 3, involving the three higher voices, would have taken up the Contratenor and Tenor books besides the Superius. The latter carries throughout the running head: "Primus Superius." The duets are listed separately in the Colombine catalogues, whence it can be learned that they included "Ayés pitié," "Ung gran plaisir Cupido me donna," and "Vivre ne puis." See Catherine Weeks Chapman, "Printed Collections of Polyphonic Music Owned by Ferdinand Columbus," *Journal of the American Musicological Society* XXI (1968), 78, no. 128.

[2] Attribution after *La Couronne et fleur des chansons à troys*, Venice, Antico, 1536.

[3] Attributed to Ysoré in *Primo libro di madrigali d'Archadelt a tre voci . . . con la gionta di dodese canzoni francese*, Venice, Gardane, 1542.

[4] Attributed to Jacotin, *idem.*

[5] Attribution after the Gardane print indicated in note 3.

[6] Attribution found in the same Gardane print and in Moderne's *Parangon des chansons,* IV, Lyons, 1538.

25.	Contre raison vous m'este fort dure	Claudin	xiii[v]
26.	Par ton regart tu me fais espérer	Gosse	xiiii
27.	Content désir qui cause ma douleur	Gosse	xiiii[v]
28.	Vivre ne puis content sans sa présence	Gosse	xiiii[v]
29.	Elle veut donc par estrange rigueur		xv
30.	Qui la vouldra souhaitte que je meure	Gosse	xvi
31.	De retourner, mon amy, je te prie	Heurteur	xvi[v]

Finis.

The collection, along with **66** and **67**, furnished the subject of a paper, "Attaingnant's two- and three-part chanson arrangements of 1535," read at the Annual Meeting of the American Musicological Society, New Haven, 1968.

[1535?]

66

[Trente et une chansons Musicales à trois parties en ung livre imprimees per Pierre Attaignant a Paris.]

From Conrad Gesner, *Pandectarum*, Zurich, 1548, f. 85.

[1535?]

67

[Quarante et quatre chansons à deux, ou duo, chose delectable aux fleustes. Petrus Attaignans excudebat. Parisiis.]

From Conrad Gesner, *Pandectarum*, Zurich, 1548, f. 85.

1535, MAY

68

¶Lib. decimustertius. xviij. musicales habet modulos / quatuor quinqз vel sex vocibus editos. opus sane totius / armonie flos nuncupandum: vt indice sequeti palam est. / Mense Mayo. m.c.xxxv / [Table] / **Superius** / **Parrhisiis in vico Cithareo prope sanctorum Cosme et Damiani** / **templum: in edibus Petri Attaingnant musice calcographi.** / **Cum priuilegio regio ad sexen=nium** /

4 vol. in-4° obl., 20.5 × 16 cm.; 16 f. numbered i–xvi
Sign.: * a4–* d4; * aa4–* dd4; * AA4–* DD4; * A4–* D4
RISM-I, 1535[5]

Jena: Universitätsbibliothek
Milan: Biblioteca Ambrosiana (S & B)
Milan: Biblioteca del Conservatorio
Noyon: Ancienne Bibliothèque de Chapitre

1. O altitudo divitiarum sapientiæ et scientiæ Dei 4; De Trinitate	Roger	iv
2. Tempus meum ut revertar ad eum I Viri Galilei aspicientes in cælum II 4; De Ascensione	Cornesle Joris	ii
3. Virgo salutiferi genitrix intacta tonantis I Tu potis primæ scelus expurgare parentis II T, B: En potis es primæ scelus expurgare parentis 4; De beata Maria	Jodon	iiv
4. Factus est repente de cælo sonus I Et apparuerunt illis dispertitæ linguæ II 4; In die Penthecostes	Cornesle Joris	iiiv
5. Virtute magna reddebant Apostoli I Repleti quidem Spiritu sancto II 4; De Apostolis	M. Lasson	iiii
[1]6. Benedicat te Dominus in virtute tua 4	L'héritier	iiiiv
[2]7. Quæ corda nostra faciat habitacula I T, B: Sancti spiritus assit nobis gratia Prophetas tu inspirasti II [à 3] Tu animabus vivificandis aquas fecundas III 4; In festo Penthecostes	Claudin	v
8. Ave Verbum incarnatum I Ave corpus Jesu Christi II 6 ttbb; De Sacramento altaris	Lupus	vi
9. Beata Dei genitrix Maria I Ora pro populo interveni pro clero II 6 ttbb; De beata Maria	Colin Margot	viv
10. Gaude tu Baptista Christi I Gaude quæ reprehendisti Herodem II 5 tt; De sancto Johannis Baptista	Lupus	vii
11. Non conturbetur cor vestrum I Ite in orbem universum II 5 cc; De Ascensione	M. F. Villain	viiv
12. Caro mea vere est cibus I Hic est panis qui de cælo descendit II 5 tt; In festo Sacramenti	P. Manchicourt	viii
13. Surge Petre et indue te vestimentis tuis I Si diligis me Simon Petre pasce oves meas II 6 ttbb; De sancto Petro Apostolo	Jacquet	ix
14. Salvator mundi salva nos omnes I T, B: Sancta Dei genitrix Eya ergo advocemus gloriosam virginem II T, B: Cælorum reginam Mariam 6 ttcc; De omnibus Sanctis	N. Gombert	x

[1] Table: Benedicat te Deus.
[2] Table: Sancti spiritus.

15.	Respexit Helyas ad caput suum I Si quis manducaverit ex hoc pane II 6 sstt; In festo Sacramenti	Jarsins	xi^v
16.	Fundata est domus Domini I Benedic Domine domum istam II 6 sstt; In dedicatione ecclesie	Cadéac	xiii^v
17.	Salus populi ego sum dixit Dominus 5 tt; Pro quacunque tribulatione	Cadéac	xv^v
18.	Sancta Maria, mater Dei, ora pro nobis Canon [4 supra 1]; De beata Maria Finis		xvi^v

Complete modern edition in *Treize Livres de Motets*, Treizième Livre. Includes facsimile of title page.

1536, JANUARY

69

¶ Liure premier contenant xxix. chansous a quatre par/ties le tout en vng liure ĩprimees p. Pierre Attaingnant / imprimeur et libraire de musique demourãt a Paris en / la rue de la Harpe pres leglise S. Cosme. / Mẽse Januario M.D.xxxv. / [Table] / **¶ Cum grã et amplissimo xpianissimi frã=/corum Regis priuilegio Ad sexennium.** /

1 vol. in-4° obl., 20 × 15.5 cm.; 32 f. numbered [i]–xxxii
Sign.: A^4–H^4 (f. i unsigned)
RISM–I, 1536^4

Paris: Bibliothèque Mazarine, Rés 30345 A (2)

*1.	Amour est bien de perverse nature	Certon	i^v
†2.	La, la, maistre Pierre, la, la, beuvons don	Claudin	ii^v
3.	Je vouldroye bien mais que fusse contente	Doublet	iii^v
4.	Mon mari est allé au guet	Passereau	iiii^v
5.	En languissant avoir secours j'attens	Certon	v^v
‡6.	J'ay veu le temps qu'on me soulloyt aymer	Jennequin	vi^v
7.	Mon cueur sera tousjours soubz ta puissance	Certon	vii^v
§8.	Ung jour Colin la Colecte accula	Jennequin	viii^v
9.	Dictes, vous que ne sçay faire	Des Fruz	ix^v
10.	Vostre oeil a déceu ma pensée	Claudin	x^v
11.	Contentez-vous, amy, de la pensée	Claudin	xi^v
12.	En espérant en ceste longue attente	Claudin	xii^v
13.	Le vray amy ne s'estonne de rien	Claudin	xiii^v
14.	Ne te plains tant, amy, de ta douleur	De Villiers	xiiii^v
15.	Mort et fortune, pourquoy m'avez laissé	Gombert	xv^v

* Modern edition in *Chorwerk, Vol. 82.*
† Modern edition in *Anthologie.*
‡ Modern edition in *Chorwerk, Vol. 73.*
§ Modern edition in *Thirty Chansons (1960).*

§16.	Apres avoir, las, tout mon temps passé	Certon	xvi^{v}
17.	Espoir m'a tenu languissant	Roquelay	xvii^{v}
†18.	Sur la rousée fault aller la matinée	Passereau	xviii^{v}
19.	Le bien promis apres la longue attente	Claudin	xix^{v}
20.	Prenez le galland, couppez-luy les choses	Sohier	xx^{v}
21.	Ramonnez moy ma cheminée	Hesdin	xxii^{v}
22.	Faict-elle pas bien d'aymer que luy donne	[Senterre]	xxiii^{v}
23.	Si j'ay esté vostre amy a l'espreuve	Jennequin	xxv^{v}
‡24.	Tresves d'amours c'est une paix fourrée	Jennequin	xxvi^{v}
25.	Le voulez-vous, j'en suis tres bien contente	Jacotin	xxvii^{v}
26.	Aù joly son du sansonnet je m'en dormy	Passereau	xxviii^{v}
‖27.	Dame de beaulté, je vous prie	Morel	xxix^{v}
28.	Ne sçay pourquoy vostre grace ay perdu		xxx^{v}
§29.	Nature a faict, ainsi Dieu l'a permis	Roquelay	xxxi^{v}

‖ Modern edition in *French Chansons.*

1536, FEBRUARY

70

¶ Premier liure cōtenāt xxxi. chāsōs musicales esleues de/ plusieurs liures p. cy deuant īprimez: et nagueres reimpri/mees en vng volūe p. Pierre Attaingnant imprimeur et li/braire de musique demourāt a Paris en la rue d' la Harpe / pres leglise S. Cosme. Mēse Februario. M.D.xxxv / [Table] / **¶ Cum grā et amplissimo xp̄ianissimi frā=/corum Regis priuilegio Ad sexennium.** /

1 vol. in-4° obl., 20 × 15.5 cm.; 32 f. numbered [i]–xxxii (xv unfoliated; xxi xxii xxii xxiiii; lacks f. xxx–xxxii)

Sign.: a^{4}–h^{4}
RISM–I,1536^{2}

Paris: Bibliothèque Mazarine, Rés 30345 A (4)

*1.	La, la, la, l'oysillon du boys, madame	Mouton	i^{v}
2.	Mari, je songeois l'aultre jour	Jacotin	ii^{v}
3.	Vray Dieu d'amours mauldict soyt la journée	Jacotin	iii^{v}
4.	Le content est riche en ce monde	Claudin	iiii^{v}
5.	Le cueur de vous ma présence désire	Claudin	v^{v}
†‡6.	Si j'ay pour vous mon avoir despendu	Claudin	vi^{v}
7.	Jouyssance vous donneray	Claudin	vii^{v}
§8.	Dictes sans peur ou l'ouy ou nenny	Claudin	viii^{v}
9.	Qui la vouldra souhaitte que je meure	Claudin	ix^{v}
10.	Si j'ay eu du mal ou du bien	Claudin	x^{v}

* Modern edition in *Theatrical Chansons.*
† Modern edition in *Chanson and Madrigal.*
‡ Modern edition in *CMM 20.*
§ Modern edition in *Anthologie.*

11.	De bien aymer les dames je ne blasme	Renes	xi^v
12.	D'ung desplaisir Amour si fort me lasse	Jacotin	xii^v
13.	Veu le grief mal ou sans repos labeure	Heurteur	xiii^v
14.	Vous sçavez bien, ma dame souveraine	Lupi	xiiii^v
15.	Ayez pitié du grant mal que j'endure	Claudin	xv^v
16.	Contre raison vous m'estes fort estrange	Claudin	xvi^v
17.	My larrez-vous toujours languir	Roquelay	xvii^v
18.	Aupres de vous secretement demeure	[1]Jacotin	xviii^v
‡19.	Las, voulez-vous qu'une personne chante	Vermont	xix^v
‡20.	N'auray-je jamais réconfort de vous	Jacotin	xx^v
21.	Je n'ose estre content de mon contentement	Claudin	xxi^v
22.	Las, que crains tu, amy, de quoy as déffiance	Claudin	xxii^v
‖23.	Serpe et la Serpette T, B: Vive la serpe	Claudin	xxiii^v
‡24.	Maulgré moy vis et en vivant je meurs	Claudin	xxiiii^v
25.	Ung jour Robin alloit aux champs	Claudin	xxv^v
26.	Héllas madame, a quoy tient-il	Hesdin	xxvi^v
‡27.	Je ne faiz rien que réquérir	Claudin	xxvii^v
28.	Trop de regretz pour vous seulle je porte	Hesdin	xxviii^v
29.	De trop penser en amour et richesse (S & Ct only)	Jacotin	xxix^v
[30.	Tant qu'en amours	Jacotin	xxx^v]
[31.	Le cueur est bon	Claudin	xxxi^v]

‖ Modern edition in *Quinze Chansons.*
[1] Claudin in **29**.

1536, FEBRUARY

71

¶ Second liure cōtenāt xxxi. chāsōs musicales esleues de / plusieurs liures p. cy deuāt īprimes: et nagueres reimpri/mees en vng volue p. Pierre Attaingnant imprimeur et li/braire de musique demourāt a Paris en la rue d' la Harpe / pres leglise S. Cosme. Mēse Februario. M.D.xxxv / [Table] / **¶ Cum grā et amplissimo xp̄ianissimi frā=/corum Regis priuilegio Ad sexennium.** /

1 vol. in-4° obl., 20×15.5 cm.; 32 f. numbered [i]–xxxii (xxi xxii xxiii xxiii)
Sign.: i^4–q^4
RISM–I, 1536^3

Paris: Bibliothèque Mazarine, Rés 30345 A (5)

1.	D'ung coup mortel en lieu de jouyssance	Jacotin	i^v
2.	Hors envieux, retirez-vous d'ici	Gombert	ii^v
*3.	Longtemps y a que je vis en espoir	Dulot	iii^v
4.	Si par fortune avez mon cueur	Certon	iiii^v
5.	Par ton regart tu me fais espérer	Claudin	v^v

* Modern edition in *CMM 20.*

6.	Je l'ay aymé et l'aymeray le mien amy a qui tousjours seray	Certon	vi^v
7.	Changer ne puis et aultre ne désire	Lupi	vii^v
†8.	Content désir qui cause ma douleur	Claudin	viii^v
9.	Vivre ne puis content sans sa présence	Claudin	ix^v
10.	De noz deux cueurs soit seulle volonté	Guyon	x^v
11.	Doeul, double doeul, renfort de desplaisir	Hesdin	xi^v
12.	Grace, vertu, bonté, beaulté, noblesse	Roquelay	xii^v
*13.	Ung grant plaisir Cupido me donna	Claudin	xiii^v
14.	Je suis joyeulx et languis en tristesse	Claudin	xiiii^v
‡15.	Assouvy suys mais sans cesser désire	Jennequin	xv^v
16.	Souvent Amour me livre grant tourment	Heurteur	xvi^v
17.	J'ay tant souffert que pour plaisir avoir	Jacotin	xvii^v
§18.	Voyant souffrir celle qui me tourmente	Jacotin	xviii^v
*‖19.	Ma bouche rit et mon cueur pleure	Duboys	xix^v
20.	J'ayme le cueur de m'amye	Claudin	xx^v
21.	Mauldicte soit la mondaine richesse	Claudin	xxi^v
22.	Amours partez, je vous donne la chasse	Claudin	xxii^v
23.	Si mon malheur my continue	Le Peletier	xxiii^v
24.	Puisque j'ay perdu mes amours	Lupi	xxiiii^v
25.	Mon povre cueur plain de douleurs	Lupi	xxv^v
26.	C'est une dure départie	Claudin	xxvi^v
‖27.	Gris et tenné me fault porter	Claudin	xxvii^v
28.	J'ay le désir content et l'effect résolu	Claudin	xxviii^v
29.	C'est a grant tort que moy povrete endure	Claudin	xxix^v
30.	Celle qui m'a tant pourmené	Claudin	xxx^v
‖31.	Joye et douleur, mon amy, sur mon ame	Isoré	xxxi^v

For reprint see **76**.

† Modern edition in *Theatrical Chansons*.
‡ Modern edition in *Trente Chansons* (*1928*).
§ Modern edition in *Anthologie*.
‖ Modern edition in *Thirty Chansons* (*1960*).

1536, APRIL (after the 16th)

72

¶Second liure cōtenāt xxv. Chāsons nouuelles a quatre / parties le tout en vng liure īprimeez p. Pierre Attaingnāt / imprimeur & libraire de musique demourāt a Paris en la / Rue de la Harpe pres leglise S. Cosme. / Mēse Aprili. M.D.xxxvi. / [Table] / Cum gratia et priuilegio xp̄ianissimi / frācorū regis ad sexēniun /

1 vol. in-4° obl., 20 × 15.5 cm.; 32 f. numbered [i]–xxxii ([i] ii ii iiii; f. xxxii bound after **73**.)
Sign.: I^4–Q^4
RISM–I, 1536^5

Paris: Bibliothèque Mazarine, Rés 30345 A (3)

*1.	Ho le vilain, prenez-le	Certon	i^{v}
2.	N'espoir ne peur n'auray jour de ma vie	Claudin	iii^{v}
3.	Quant je vouldrois de vous me puys venger	Godard	iiii^{v}
4.	Du grand plaisir que le cueur a receu	Sohier	v^{v}
5.	Ung vray musicien beuvoit d'aultant	Hesdin	vi^{v}
6.	Puis qu'elle a mis a deux son amytié B: Si ne pleut dit elle, il desgoutte [à 5]; Canon Supra Tenore In subdyapente	Claudin	vii^{v}
7.	Ton feu s'estaint de ce que le myen art [à 4]; Canon Supra Bassum In epydyapason	Claudin	viii^{v}
†8.	A l'envers sur lict ou couchette	Renes	ix^{v}
9.	Rossingnollet congnoys-tu poinct m'amye		x^{v}
10.	Gracieuse en dictz et faictz plaisante	Du pont	xii^{v}
11.	Seul joyres du bien que je vous garde	Certon	xiii^{v}
12.	J'ay tant chassé que la proye m'a pris	Mitantier	xiiii^{v}
13.	Je suys a moy et a moy me tiendray	La Rue	xv^{v}
‡14.	Pour ung plaisir que si peu dure	Claudin	xvi^{v}
15.	Amy, tu te complains et moy je me lamente	Sohier	xvii^{v}
16.	Combien que j'ay doleur véhémente	Doublet	xviii^{v}
17.	Ma mere héllas, mariez-moy	La Rue	xix^{v}
‡18.	C'est grand pitié quant argent fault a bon compaignon sur les champs	Certon	xx^{v}
19.	Tétin refaict plus blanc qu'ung oeuf	Jennequin	xxi^{v}
20.	[Fricassée] S: A l'aventure Tous mes amys T: Je m'en [vois] au vert boys Ct: Amoureux suys d'une plaisante brunette B: A quoy tient il dont vient cela		xxv^{v}
§21.	Ung jour passé bien escoutoye	[Clemens]	xxvi^{v}
‡22.	Ta bonne grace et maintien gracieulx	Roquelay	xxviii^{v}
§23.	Le départir est sans département	[Clemens]	xxix^{v}
24.	Est-il possible que l'on puisse trouver	Morel	xxx^{v}
25.	Héllas madame, faictes-luy quelque bien (S and Ct only; T and B bound after **73**.)	Passereau	xxxi^{v}

Facsimile of f. xxxi^{v} in Kinsky, *A History of Music in Pictures*, New York, 1937, p. 95.

* Modern edition in *Chorwerk, Vol. 82.*
† Modern edition in *Thirty Chansons* (*1960*).
‡ Modern edition in *French Chansons.*
§ Modern edition in *CMM 4*:X

1536, MAY

73

¶ Tiers liure cōtenāt xxi. Chāsons musicales a quatre / parties composeez par Jennequin & Passereau esleues / de plusieurs liures par cy deuant imprimez: & nagueres / rimprimees par Pierre Attaingāt imprimeur & libraire / de musique demourāt a Paris en la Rue de la Harpe / pres leglise S. Cosme. / Mēse mayo M.D.xxxvi. / [Table] / **Cum gratia et priuilegio xp̄ianissimi / frācorū regis ad sexēnium** /

1 vol. in-4° obl., 20 × 15.5 cm.; 30 f. numbered [i]-xxx[1]
Sign.: r⁴– &⁴ (r i, [r ii], [r iii], r ii; z i, z ii instead of y i, y ii)
RISM–I, 1536[6]

Paris: Bibliothèque Mazarine, Rés 30345 A (6)

1.	Or vien ça, vien, m'amye Perrette	Jennequin	i^v
2.	La, mon amy, faictes tout bellement	Jennequin	iii^v
*3.	Ung coup d'essay premier que bailler gaige	Jennequin	iiii^v
4.	Mais ma mignonne aux tétins descouvers	Jennequin	v^v
†5.	Pour quoy donc ne fringuerons nous	Passereau	vii^v
‡6.	Martin menoit son porceau au marché	Jennequin	ix^v
7.	Il est bel et bon, commere, mon mary	Passereau	xi^v
‡8.	Nostre dince, mon con, mon compere	[Passereau]	xii^v
9.	Elle craint cela sur tout rien qu'on la chatoulle	Jennequin	xiiii^v
*10.	Ung vieillart amoureux est souvent mal content	Jennequin	xvi^v
11.	Ung compaignon gallin gallant et une fillette jolye	Passereau	xvii^v
12.	Laissez-cela, ne m'en parlez jamais	Jennequin	xviii^v
‡13.	Il n'est plaisir ne passe temps au monde	Jennequin	xix^v
*14.	Fyez-vous-y si vous voulez	Jennequin	xx^v
*15.	Si d'ung petit de vostre bien ma dame	[Jennequin]	xxi^v
16.	Ce sont gallans qui s'en vont resjouyr	[Jennequin]	xxiii^v
17.	Pourquoy voulés-vous cousturier aultre que moy	[Jennequin]	xxiiii^v
18.	Je ne seray jamais bergere	Passereau	xxvi^v

For facsimile of f. xx^v see fig. 8 above.

* Modern edition in *Chorwerk, Vol. 73.*
† Modern edition in *Anthologie.*
‡ Modern edition in *Thirty Chansons (1960).*

[1] Followed by a single folio, xxxii, from **72**, then eleven folios in MS, containing chansons and dances and beginning on the verso of the misplaced folio from **72**, "Héllas ma dame faictes luy quelque bien"; the staves are printed, mostly from a single rule.

Verso of f. from **72**	Pilons l'orge, pilons la	**81**-21, **94**-21 (Claudin)
MS 2^v	Puys qu'il est tel	**81**-15, **94**-15, **163**-19 (Claudin)
MS 3^v	Ung laboureur au premier chant—Certon	**81**-1, **94**-1 (Certon)
MS 5^v	L'autrier je vois dans un bosquet—Denis Brument	
MS 6^v	Je suys déshérité	**44**-16, **79**-27 (Lupus); **96**-11, **163**-13 (Cadéac)
MS 7^v	Sur le pont d'Avignon—Claudin	
MS 8^v	Domine Deus omnipotens (conclusion of Ct & B lacking)	**103**-8 (Claudin)
MS 10 lacking		
MS 11	Fini le bien (Ct & B only)	**81**-8, **94**-8, **161**-4 (Certon)
MS 11^v	Vous perdez temps (B lacking; beneath Ct, 1 line of music without text, belonging to another piece)	**82**-10, **95**-14, **161**-22 (Claudin)
MS 12^v	Two parts of an instrumental piece, titled "Paduane descant" and "Paduane" respectively and signed "Lois Gonory."	

19.	Ung petit coup m'amye, ung petit coup, héllas	[Passereau]	xxvii^v
§20.	Et gentil, ma maréschal, ferreras-tu pas mon cheval		xxix^v
‡21.	Ung peu plus hault, ung peu plus bas mon amy	Passereau	xxx^v

§ Modern edition in *Quinze Chansons.*

[1536]

74

¶ [Chansons musicales, esleues de plusieurs livres par ci=devant imprimés, le tous dans un seul livre . . . réimprimées par P. Attaignant, imprimeur et libraire de musique, Paris. 1536.]

1 vol. in-4° obl., 20×15.5 cm.; 8 f. numbered ix–xvi (f. i–viii lacking)
Sign.: cc^4–dd^4
RISM–I, 1535^7

Paris: Bibliothèque Mazarine, Rés 30345 A (1)

1.	De retourner, mon amy, je te prye (S and Ct lacking)		ix
*2.	Las, je my plains, mauldicte soit fortune	Claudin	ix^v
‡3.	Languir me fais sans t'avoir offencée	Claudin	x^v
†‡4.	J'atens secours de ma seulle pensée	[Claudin]	x^v
5.	J'ay faiz pour vous cent mille pas	Claudin	xi^v
‡6.	Tant que vivray en aage florissant	Claudin	xii^v
7.	Elle s'en va de moy tant regretée	Claudin	xiii^v
8.	Amours ont changé de façon	Mahiet	xiiii^v
§9.	Tous mes amys, venez ma plaincte ouyr	Claudin	xv^v
10.	Si vous m'aymés, donnez-moy asseurance [à 3]	Claudin	xvi^v

* Modern edition in *Anthologie.*
† Modern edition in *Chanson and Madrigal.*
‡ Modern edition in *CMM 20.*
§ Modern edition in *Preludes, Chansons.*

1537, MAY

75

Les chansōs de | **La guerre / La chasse / Le chāt des oyseaux / Lalouette / Le rossignol** | **Cōposees par maistre clemēt Jennequin**

Reimprimees par Pierre Attaingnant et Hubert Jullet / imprimeurs et libraires de musique demourās a Paris / en la Rue de la Harpe pres leglise S. Cosme. / Mense Mayo M.D.xxxvii. / Superius. / Cum gratia et priuilegio xpianis= simi / frācorum regis ad sexēniū. /

4 vol. in-4° obl., 21 × 16 cm.; 10 f. numbered [i]–x (8 folios in Bassus book)
Sign.:)(a⁴–)(b⁶;)(aa⁴–)(bb⁶;)(AA⁴–)(BB⁶;)(A⁴–)(B⁴

Munich: Bayersiche Staatsbibliothek, Mus. Pr. 52/10
Wolfenbüttel: Herzog-August-Bibliothek, 2.30 Mus.
Vicenza: Biblioteca Bertoliana, FF. 2.7.23 (3) (S)

1.	Escoutez tous, gentilz galloys, du noble roy Françoys I Fan frere le le lan fan II	i^{v}
2.	Gentilz veneurs, allez en queste au buysson I Sur tous soulas, plaisir et lyesse II [à 7]	iii^{v}
3.	Resveillez-vous, cueurs endormis	vii^{v}
4.	Or sus, vous dormez trop, ma dame jolyette	viii^{v}
5.	En escoutant le chant melodieulx	ix^{v}

Revised edition of **4**, with substitution for the fifth piece. For modern editions see **4**. No. 2 ("La chasse") is expanded by the addition of three supplementary voices in the second part. No. 3 ("Le chant des oyseaux") is condensed in this version into one part.

Title page and folio v of Bassus reproduced in *MGG*, Vol. II, col. 1057–1060.

1537

76

Secōd liure de chãsōs esleues, cotenãt xxx. / REIMPRIMEES EN DEVX VOLVMES PAR PIERRE / *Attaingnant imprimeur & libraire du Roy en musique, demourant a / Paris en la Rue de la Harpe pres leglise S. Cosme.* / 1537. / [Table] / **Superius & Tenor** / *Auec prorogation du priuilege du Roy, De nouuel obtenu par ledit attaingnant / Pour les liures Ia parluy imprimez & quil Imprimera cy apres iusques a six ans.* /

2 vol. in-4° obl., 21.4 × 16.1 cm.; 16 f. numbered [i]–xvi
Sign.: II e⁴–II h⁴; II E⁴–II H⁴
RISM–I, 1537³

Florence: Biblioteca del Conservatorio, Basevi 2496 (6)

			76	**78**
1.	D'ung coup mortel en lieu de joyssance	Jacotin	i^{v}	i^{v}
2.	Hors envyeux, retirez vous d'ici	Gombert	i^{v}	i^{v}
*3.	Longtemps y a que je viz en espoir	[1]Claudin	ii^{v}	ii^{v}
4.	Je l'ay aymé et l'aymeray Le myen amy a qui tousjours seray	Certon	ii^{v}	iii^{v}
5.	Par ton regart tu me faiz espérer	Claudin	iii^{v}	ii^{v}

* Modern edition in *CMM 20*.

[1] Dulot in **71**.

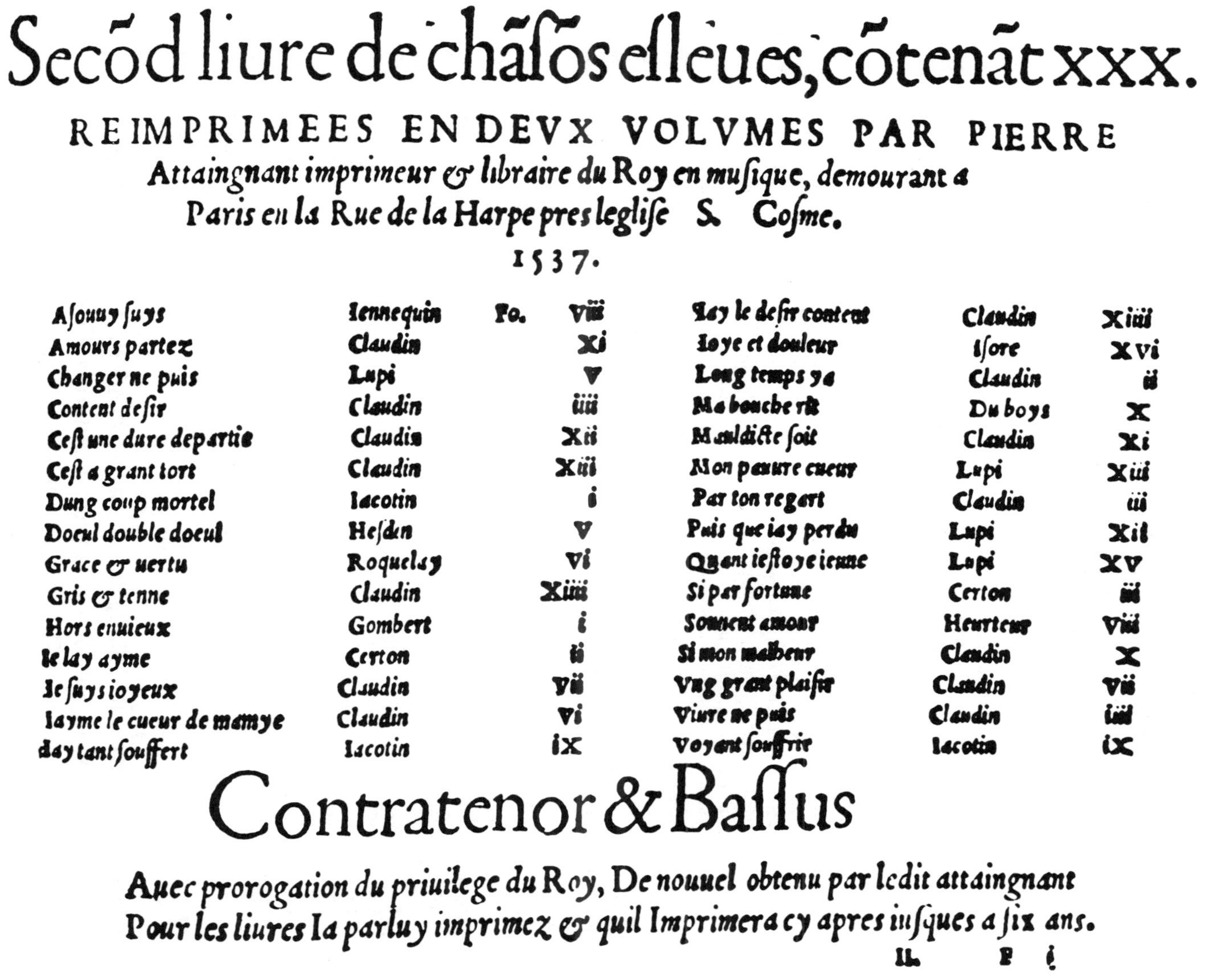

Secōd liure de chāsōs esleues, cōtenāt xxx.

REIMPRIMEES EN DEVX VOLVMES PAR PIERRE
Attaingnant imprimeur & libraire du Roy en musique, demourant a
Paris en la Rue de la Harpe pres leglise S. Cosme.
1537.

Asouuy suys	Iennequin	Fo.	Viii	Iay le desir content	Claudin	Xiiii
Amours partez	Claudin		Xi	Ioye et douleur	Isore	Xvi
Changer ne puis	Lupi		V	Long temps ya	Claudin	ii
Content desir	Claudin		iiii	Ma bouche rit	Du boys	X
Cest une dure departie	Claudin		Xii	Mauldicte soit	Claudin	Xi
Cest a grant tort	Claudin		Xiii	Mon pauure cueur	Lupi	Xiii
Dung coup mortel	Iacotin		i	Par ton regart	Claudin	iii
Doeul double doeul	Hesdin		V	Puis que iay perdu	Lupi	Xii
Grace & uertu	Roquelay		Vi	Quant iestoye ieune	Lupi	XV
Gris & tenne	Claudin		Xiiii	Si par fortune	Certon	iii
Hors enuieux	Gombert		i	Souuent amour	Heurteur	Viii
Ie lay ayme	Certon		ii	Si mon malheur	Claudin	X
Ie suys ioyeux	Claudin		Vii	Vng grant plaisir	Claudin	Vii
Iayme le cueur de mamye	Claudin		Vi	Viure ne puis	Claudin	iiii
Iay tant souffert	Iacotin		ix	Voyant souffrir	Iacotin	ix

Contratenor & Bassus

Auec prorogation du priuilege du Roy, De nouuel obtenu par ledit attaingnant
Pour les liures Ia par luy imprimez & quil Imprimera cy apres iusques a six ans.
Il. F i

20 Title page of the second book of "old chansons" **(76)**. By courtesy of the Biblioteca del Conservatorio, Florence.

6.	Si par fortune avez mon cueur acquis	Certon	iii^{v}	iii^{v}
†7.	Content désir qui cause ma douleur	Claudin	iiii^{v}	vii^{v}
8.	Vivre ne puis content sans sa présence	Claudin	iiii^{v}	vii^{v}
9.	Doeul, double doeul, renfort de desplaisir	Hesdin	v^{v}	v^{v}
10.	Changer ne puis et aultre ne désire	Lupi	v^{v}	v^{v}
11.	J'ayme le cueur de m'amye, sa bonté et sa doulceur	Claudin	vi^{v}	xi^{v}
12.	Grace, vertu, bonté, beaulté, noblesse	[2]Roquelay	vi^{v}	iiii^{v}
*13.	Ung grant plaisir Cupido me donna	Claudin	vii^{v}	iiii^{v}
14.	Je suys joyeulx et languis en tristesse	Claudin	vii^{v}	vi^{v}
‡15.	Assouvy suys mais sans cesser désire	Jennequin	viii^{v}	vi^{v}
16.	Souvent Amour me livre grant torment	Heurteur	viii^{v}	viii^{v}
17.	J'ay tant souffert que pour plaisir avoir	Jacotin	ix^{v}	x^{v}
§18.	Voyant souffrir celle qui me tormente	Jacotin	ix^{v}	x^{v}
19.	Si mon malheur my continue	[3]Claudin	x^{v}	xi^{v}
*‖20.	Ma bouche rit et mon cueur pleure	Du boys	x^{v}	viii^{v}
21.	Amours partés, je vous donne la chasse	Claudin	xi^{v}	ix^{v}
22.	Mauldicte soit la mondainne richesse	Claudin	xi^{v}	ix^{v}
23.	C'est une dure départie de celluy ou j'ay mis mon cueur	Claudin	xii^{v}	xii^{v}
24.	Puisque j'ay perdu mes amours	Lupi	xii^{v}	xiii^{v}
25.	Mon pauvre cueur plain de douleurs	Lupi	xiii^{v}	xiii^{v}
26.	C'est a grant tort que moy povrette endure	Claudin	xiii^{v}	xiiii^{v}
‖27.	Gris et tenné me fault porter	Claudin	xiiii^{v}	xii^{v}
28.	J'ay le désir content et l'effect résolu	Claudin	xiiii^{v}	xiiii^{v}
29.	Quant j'estoy jeune fillette	Lupi	xv^{v}	xv^{v}
‖30.	Joye et douleur, mon amy, sur mon ame	Isoré	xvi^{v}	xv^{v}

Finis

Revised reprint of **71** lacking nos. 10 and 30. No. 29 is new.

Bound after the five other Attaingnant prints at Florence (**122**, **119**, **161**, **159**, **163**) and three madrigal collections in four separate part-books. The binding, of the mid-sixteenth century, is leather stamped with gold tracery and with the name "Jheronimus Fioraventius." Each flyleaf bears the inscription "Geronimo Fieravanti e sue amici," apparently in the hand of the first owner.

† Modern edition in *Theatrical Chansons*.
‡ Modern edition in *Trente Chansons* (*1928*).
§ Modern edition in *Anthologie*.
‖ Modern edition in *Thirty Chansons* (*1960*).

[2] Roquelay in **78**.
[3] Le Peletier in **71**.

1537

77

[Jean-Louis Hérault. Antiphonae sacrae B.M.V. trium et quatuor vocum; Parisiis, in vico Citharae prope sanctorum Cosmae et Damiani templum apud Petrum Attaingnant musicae Chalcographum]
In 4°, gothique, 1537

From Fétis, *Biographie universelle des musiciens*, 2d. edition, Paris, 1870–75, Vol. IV, p. 298.

78

¶ Second liure contenant xxx. Chāsons vieilles esleues / de plusieurs liures: nagueres Reimprimees en vng volu/me et en deux par Pierre Attaingnāt et Hubert Jullet li-/braires et Imprimeurs de musique demourans a Paris / en la Rue de la Harpe pres leglise S. Cosme. / Mense februario, M.D.xxxvij. / [Table] / Superius et Tenor. /

2 vol. in-4° obl., 21 × 15.8 mm.; 16 f. numbered [i]–xvi
Sign.: aa^4–dd^4; AA^4–DD^4
RISM–I, 1537^3

Oxford: Christ Church, Mus. 515–516 (3)

Contents same as **76**.

1538, MARCH

79

¶ Tiers liure contenant xxx. Chāsons vieilles esleues de / plusieurs liures: nagueres Reimprimees en vng volume / et en deux par Pierre Attaingnāt et Hubert Jullet librai-/res et Imprimeurs de musique demourās a Paris en la / Rue de la Harpe pres leglise S. Cosme. / Mense Martij. M.D.xxxvij. / [Table] / Superius et Tenor. /

2 vol. in-4° obl., 21 × 15.8 cm.; 16 f. numbered [i]–xvi
Sign.: ee^4–hh^4; EE^4–HH^4
RISM–I, 1537^4

Oxford: Christ Church, Mus. 515–516 (4)

1.	Amour, voyant l'ennuy qui tant m'oppresse	Claudin	i^v
2.	Je l'ay aymé et l'aymeray a ce propos suys et seray	Hesdin	i^v
3.	Mon cueur gist tousjours en langueur	Claudin	ii^v
4.	C'est en amour une peine trop dure	Claudin	ii^v
5.	L'espous a la premiere nuyt	Bon voisin	iii^v
6.	Je suy mon bien du quel me tiens content	Certon	iii^v
7.	Amour au cueur me poingt	Heurteur	iiii^v
8.	J'ay trop d'amours et peu de récompence	Lupi	iiii^v
9.	Entendez-vous qu'ung aultre je seconde	Certon	v^v

10.	Du cueur le don a le loyal amant	Certon	v^v
11.	O doulce amour, ô contente pensée	Claudin	vi^v
12.	Il est en vous le bien que je désire	Claudin	vi^v
13.	N'aurai-je point de mon mal allégeance	Alaire	vii^v
14.	Amour me poingt et si je me veulx plaindre	Claudin	vii^v
15.	Il m'aviendra ce que vouldra fortune	Certon	viii^v
16.	Hélas, Amour qui sçays certainement	Heurteur	viii^v
17.	Voulant Amour, soubz parler gracieulx	Harchadel	ix^v
18.	Regret, soucy et peine me font de villains tours	Jacotin	ix^v
19.	Si pour aymer on ne quiert que beaulté	Jacotin	x^v
[1]20.	Par fin despit je m'en iray seullette	Claudin	x^v
21.	Ribon, ribaine tout en despit de moy	Jarsins	xi^v
*22.	Jaquin, Jaquet, Jouyn jouoit	Clemens	xii^v
23.	Mon cueur est souvent bien marry	Claudin	xii^v
24.	La rousée du moys de may si m'a moullée	Rousee	xiii^v
25.	Ce moys de may ma verte cotte	Jennequin	xiii^v
26.	Jamais je n'eu tant de soulas	Gombert	xiiii^v
†27.	Je suys déshéritée puisque j'ay perdu mon amy	Lupus [or Cadéac]	xiiii^v
28.	Madame ung jour doulx baiser me donna	Heurteur	xv^v
29.	Joyeulx adieu d'ung visage content	Claudin	xv^v
30.	Amour me voyant sans tristesse	Claudin	xvi^v

Finis

* Modern edition in *CMM 4*: X
† Modern edition in *Chorwerk, Vol. 15* and *GMB*.

[1] See **54**-8.

1538 (after APRIL 21)

80

¶ Premier liure cōtenāt xxv. Chāsons nouuelles a qua=/tre parties en vng volume et en deux īprimees par Pierre / Attaingnāt et Hubert Jullet libraires et Imprimeurs de / musique demourans a Paris en la Rue de la Harpe pres / leglise S. Cosme. M.D.xxxviij. / [Table] / Superius et Tenor. /

2 vol. in-4° obl., 21 × 15.8 cm.; 16 f. numbered [i]–xvi
Sign.: a^4–d^4; A^4–D^4
RISM-I, 1538^{10}

[1] Castell: Fürstlich Castell'sche Schlossbibliothek (Ct-B)
[2] Oxford: Christ Church, Mus. 515–516 (1) (folio v lacking)
Wolfenbüttel: Herzog-August-Bibliothek, 2.8.8 Mus.

			80	**140**
*1.	Amour est bien de perverse nature	Certon	i^v	i^v
†2.	La, la, maistre Pierre, la, la beuvons donc	Claudin	i^v	i^v

* Modern edition in *Chorwerk, Vol.* **82**.
† Modern edition in *Anthologie*.

[1] Mark of ownership: "1539 H. G. V. H. Zu Castell" (i.e., "Heinrich Graf und Herr zu Castell").
[2] All pages are ruled by hand in this and the subsequent volumes of the Oxford series.

3. Dictes, vous que ne sçay faire d'amourettes jolyettes	Des fruz	ii^{v}	ii^{v}
4. Comme inconstante et de cueur faulse et lasche	Renes	iii^{v}	iii^{v}
‡5. D'ung desplaisir que fortune m'a faict	De la Rue	iii^{v}	iii^{v}
6. Vray Dieu tant j'ay le cueur gay	Vassal	iiii^{v}	iiii^{v}
7. Vous usurpez, dames, injustement	Sandrin	v^{v}	vi^{v}
8. Le vray amy ne s'estonne de rien	Claudin	v^{v}	v^{v}
9. Contentez-vous, amy, de la pensée	Claudin	vi^{v}	vii^{v}
10. En espérant en ceste longue attente	Claudin	vi^{v}	vii^{v}
11. Mort et fortune, pourquoy m'avez laissé	Gombert	vii^{v}	vi^{v}
†12. Plaindre l'ennuy de la peine estimée	Hesdin	vii^{v}	v^{v}
Ct: Canon A quarte chantez / A cinq si voulez			
13. Ramonnez moy ma cheminée	Hesdin	viii^{v}	ix^{v}
14. Faict-elle pas bien d'aymer qui luy donne	Senterre	viii^{v}	ix^{v}
15. Voyez le tort d'amours et de fortune	Sandrin	ix^{v}	x^{v}
†16. Sur la rousée fault aller la matinée	Passereau	x^{v}	xi^{v}
17. Prenez le galland, couppez luy les choses	Sohier	xi^{v}	viii^{v}
18. Sans liberté que ung bon esprit regrette	Magdelain	xii^{v}	xii^{v}
19. Passions et douleurs qui suyvez tous malheurs	Pagnier	xii^{v}	xii^{v}
20. Le voulés-vous, j'en suis tres bien contente	Jacotin	xiii^{v}	xv^{v}
21. Si le service est reçeu pour offense	De Villiers	xiii^{v}	xvi^{v}
22. Au joly son du sansonnet je m'en dormy	Passereau	xiiii^{v}	xiiii^{v}
23. Dame de beaulté, je vous prie	Morel	xiiii^{v}	xiiii^{v}
24. Amours si m'ont cousté cent livres	Mittantier	xv^{v}	xiii^{v}
25. D'une dame je suys saisy	De Villers	xvi^{v}	xv^{v}

Finis

Contents same as **140**.

‡ Modern edition in *Quinze Chansons*.

1538

81

¶Second liure cõtenãt xxvij. Chãsons nouuelles a qua=/tre parties en vng volume et en deux ĩprimees par Pierre / Attaingnãt et Hubert Jullet libraires et Imprimeurs de / musique demourans a Paris en la Rue de la Harpe pres / leglise S. Cosme. M.D.xxxviij. / [Table] / **Superius et Tenor.** /

2 vol. in-4° obl., 21 × 15.8 cm.; 16 f. numbered [i]–xvi
Sign.: e^{4}–h^{4}; E^{4}–H^{4}
RISM–I, 1538^{11}

Castell: Fürstlich Castell'sche Schlossbibliothek (Ct–B)
Oxford: Christ Church, Mus. 515–516 (2)
Wolfenbüttel: Herzog-August-Bibliothek, 2.8.8 Mus.

1. Ung laboureur au premier chant du coq	Certon	i^{v}
2. Vostre oeil a déceu ma pensée	Claudin	i^{v}
3. Vaincre n'a peü le temps par sa rigueur	Sandrin	ii^{v}

*4.	Qui vouldra sçavoir qui je suys	Sandrin	ii^v
5.	N'espoir ne peur n'auray jour de ma vie	Claudin	iii^v
6.	Elle a mon cueur je croy qu'elle est contente	Mornable	iii^v
‖7.	Doulce mémoire en plaisir consommée	Sandrin	iiii^v
†8.	Fini le bien, le mal soudain commence	Certon	iiii^v
9.	Ce qu'il souloit en deux se despartir	Sandrin	v^v
10.	Fine affinée, remplye de finesse	Vassal	v^v
11.	Je ne le croy et le sçay seurement	Sandrin	vi^v
12.	L'heur et malheur de vostre congnoissance	Villiers	vi^v
13.	Sy mon travail vous peult donner plaisir	Sandrin	vii^v
14.	Le doeul yssu de la joye incertainne	Maillart	vii^v
15.	Puys qu'il est tel qu'il garde bien s'amye	Claudin	viii^v
16.	Qui se pourroit plus désoler et plaindre	Claudin	viii^v
17.	Ung seul désir ma volenté contente	Mornable	ix^v
*18.	L'heur d'amytié gist premier en la veue	Mornable	ix^v
[1], ‡19.	C'est trop dormy, resveillez vous	Jennequin	x^v
20.	Resveillez-moy mon bel amy	Garnier	xi^v
21.	Pilons l'orge, pilons la, mon pere my maria	Claudin	xii^v
22.	Contentement, combien que soit grande chose	Jacotin	xiii^v
23.	Ta bonne grace et maintien gracieulx	Roquellay	xiii^v
24.	Est-il possible que l'on puisse trouver	Morel	xiiii^v
§25.	Le départir est sans département	Clemens	xiiii^v
§26.	Une fillette bien gorriere embrassa ung vert vestu T & B: Tout au prez d'une riviere	Clemens	xv^v
§27.	Ung jour passé bien escoutoye	Clemens	xv^v

Finis

For reprint see **94**.

* Modern edition in *Chorwerk, Vol. 61.*
† Modern edition in *Chorwerk, Vol. 82.*
‡ Modern edition in *Trente Chansons* (*1928*).
§ Modern edition in *CMM 4*:X
‖ Modern edition in Diego Ortiz, *Tratado de glosas* (1553) ed. Max Schneider, 1913, and in Ernst T. Ferand, *Die Improvisation in der Musik*, 1938.

[1] Table: Resveillez vous.

1538

82

¶ Tiers liure cotenant xxviij. Chasons nouuelles a qua=/tre parties en vng volume et en deux īprimees par Pierre / Attaingnāt et Hubert Jullet libraires et Imprimeurs de / musique demourans a Paris en la Rue de la Harpe pres / leglise S. Cosme. M.D.xxxviij. / [Table] / **Superius et Tenor.** /

2 vol. in-4° obl., 21 × 15.8 cm.; 16 f. numbered [i]–xvi
Sign.: i^4–m^4; I^4–M^4
RISM–I, 1538^{12}

Castell: Fürstlich Castell'sche Schlossbibliothek (Ct-B)
Wolfenbüttel: Herzog-August-Bibliothek, 2.8.8. Mus.

1.	Au vert bocquet trouvay seullette ung dandrillon	Buchelli	i^{v}
2.	Au départyr m'amye a mauldit l'heure	Claudin	ii^{v}
3.	Or et argent, vous me faictes grant tort	Claudin	ii^{v}
4.	La, la, la, je ne l'ose dire	Certon	iii^{v}
5.	Or n'ay-je plus crainte d'estre surpris	Bourguignon	iii^{v}
6.	Par ton parler n'auras sur moy puissance	Mittantier	iiii^{v}
7.	En grant douleur faict son triste demeure	Villiers	iiii^{v}
8.	Le mal que j'ay rigueur le me procure	Le Moisne	v^{v}
9.	Mariez-moy mon pere, il est temps ou jamais	Godart	v^{v}
*10.	Vous perdez temps de me dire mal d'elle	Claudin	vi^{v}
11.	Tel en mesdit qui pour soy la désire	Mittantier	vi^{v}
12.	En languissant je consomme mes jours	Cadéac	vii^{v}
13.	O doulx reveoir que mon esprit contente	[1]Godard	vii^{v}
14.	Ha, quel tourment, quel peine et quel angoisse	Godard	viii^{v}
15.	Las, s'il convient si tost faire despart	Certon	viii^{v}
†16.	Puis que de vous je n'ay aultre visaige	Sandrin	ix^{v}
‡17.	Ung moins aymant aura peult estre myeulx	Certon	ix^{v}
18.	Las, qu'on congneust mon vouloir sans le dire	Certon	x^{v}
19.	Amour tu faiz a ton office injure	Colin	x^{v}
20.	Si l'amytié porte la suffisance	Mittantier	xi^{v}
21.	Si j'ay du mal maulgré moy je le porte	Claudin	xi^{v}
22.	Faisons ung coup je vous en prie	Courtoys	xii^{v}
23.	A bien compter ma joye abandonnée	Fresneau	xiii^{v}
24.	Du feu d'amour qui jamais ne termine	Le Roy	xiii^{v}
25.	L'esté passé Martine au dur téton	De porta	xiiii^{v}
26.	Amour me feist longuement souffreteur	Certon	xv^{v}
27.	Le dur travail que je porte sans cesse	Certon	xv^{v}
28.	Ce n'est a vous a qui je m'en prendray	Certon	xvi^{v}
	Finis		

For reprint see **95**.

* Modern edition published by Akademische Druck- und Verlagsanstalt, Graz, 195–.
† Modern edition in *Quinze Chansons*.
‡ Modern edition in *Chansons polyphoniques*.

[1] Certon in **161**.

1538

83

¶ Quart liure cõtenant xxviij. Chãsons nouuelles a qua=/tre parties en vng volume et en deux ĩprimees par Pierre / Attaingnãt et Hubert Jullet libraires et Imprimeurs de / musique demourans a Paris en la Rue de la Harpe pres / leglise S. Cosme. M.D.xxxviij. / [Table] / **Superius et Tenor.** /

2 vol. in-4° obl., 21 × 15.8 cm.; 16 f. numbered [i]–xvi
Sign.: n^{4}–q^{4}; N^{4}–Q^{4}
RISM–I, 1538^{13}

Castell: Fürstlich Castell'sche Schlossbibliothek (Ct-B)
Wolfenbüttel: Herzog-August-Bibliothek, 2.8.8. Mus.

1.	Frere Thibault, séjourné, gros et gras	Certon	i^v
2.	O seul espoir du cueur désespéré	Claudin	i^v
3.	Je ne menge point de porc	Claudin	ii^v
4.	Amour le veult et mon espoir attend	Garnier	ii^v
5.	Ce joly moys de may me donne grant esmoy	Passereau	iii^v
6.	Je n'en puis plus durer Marquet	Passereau	iiii^v
7.	A cent diables la vérolle	[1]Bon voisin	v^v
8.	Ce moys de may sur la rousée	Godart	v^v
9.	Mon cueur voulut dedans soy recepvoir	Claudin	vi^v
10.	En te voyant j'ay si ardant désir	Le Gendre	vi^v
11.	Elle veult donc que d'elle mécontente	Courtoys	vii^v
12.	En espérant espoir me désespére	Mittantier	vii^v
13.	Larras-tu cela, Michault	Bon voisin	viii^v
14.	Oncques amour ne fut sans grant langueur	Garnier	viii^v
15.	Ung jour au bois soubz la ramée	Courtoys	ix^v
16.	Par ung matin tout par souhait	Courtoys	x^v
17.	Tant est l'amour de vous en moy empraincté	Mittantier	xi^v
18.	Si tu voulois accorder la demande	Mittantier	xi^v
19.	Je veulx tousjours obéir et complaire	Claudin	xii^v
20.	Est-il advis qu'on doibve estimer d'elle	Harchadel	xii^v
21.	Gens qui parlez mal de m'amye	Romain	xiii^v
22.	Puis que malheur me tient rigueur	Certon	xiii^v
23.	L'oeil trop hardy si hault lieu regarda	Cadéac	xiiii^v
24.	Satisfaict suys au long de mon mérite	Certon	xiiii^v
25.	Ma passion je prens patiemment	Courtoys	xv^v
26.	Hélas Amour, je pensoye bien avoir	Godart	xv^v
27.	L'aultre jour en ung jardin soubz une treille	Forestier	xvi^v
	Finis		

For reprint see **96**.

[1] Heurteur in **96**.

1538

84

¶ Cinquiesme liure cōtenant xxviij. Chāsons nouuelles / a quatre parties en vng volume et en deux imprimees par / Pierre Attaingnant et Hubert Jullet libraires et Impri=/meurs de musique demourans a Paris en la Rue de la / Harpe pres leglise S. Cosme. M.D.xxxviij. / [Table] / **Superius et Tenor. /**

2 vol. in-4° obl., 21 × 15.8 cm.; 16 f. numbered [i]–xvi (final gathering of S–T book is Ct–B)
Sign.: r^4–v^4; R^4–V^4
RISM-I, 1538^{14}

Wolfenbüttel: Herzog-August-Bibliothek, 2.8.8 Mus.

1.	L'amour premiere en jeunesse innocente	Sandrin	i^v
2.	Quant je congneu en ma pensée	Sandrin	i^v
3.	Héllas amy, je congnoy bien que ne puis nyer mon offence	Sandrin	ii^v
4.	Vivre ne puis content sans ma maistresse	Certon	ii^v
5.	Frere Thibault, séjourné, gros et gras	Jennequin	iii^v
6.	Si comme espoir je n'ay de guarison	Maillard	iiii^v
7.	Puis que prier n'est de vous entendu	Certon	iiii^v
8.	Celle qui veit son mari tout armé	Jennequin	v^v
9.	Alix avoit aux dens la malerage	Peletier	vi^v
10.	Si j'ay aymé légierement	De porta	vii^v
11.	Je feis le feu dont l'aultre se chauffa	Maillard	vii^v
12.	Si vostre amour ne gist qu'en apparence	Sandrin	viii^v
13.	Si mon vouloir ne change de désir	Maillard	viii^v
14.	Amour cruel de sa nature	Jennequin	ix^v
15.	O cruaulté logée en grant beaulté	Jennequin	ix^v
16.	Nostre vicaire ung jour de feste	Heurteur	x^v
17.	Par ton départ regret me vient saisyr	Courtoys	x^v
18.	Ung cueur vivant en langoureux désir	Mornable	xi^v
19.	Quant je vous ayme ardentement	Alaire	xi^v
20.	Continuer je veulx ma fermeté	Bourguignon	xii^v
21.	Jamais amour ne peult si fermement	Mittantier	xii^v
22.	Veu le grief mal que longuement j'endure	Villiers	xiii^v
23.	Deux cueurs voulans par fermeté louable	Sandrin	xiii^v
*24.	L'aultrier passant par ung vert boys	Clemens	xiiii^v
25.	Puis que une mort resuscite ma vie	Soyer	xiiii^v
26.	En vous voyant j'ay liberté perdue	Rogier	xv^v
27.	Amour voyant que j'avoys abusé	Certon	xv^v
28.	Une dame par ung matin	[1]Belin	xvi^v

Finis

For reprint see **97**.

* Modern edition in *CMM 4*:X.

[1] Gentien in **97**.

1539

85

¶ Liber decimus quartus. xix. musicas cãtiones cõtinet / P. de Mãchicourt insignis Ecclesie Turonẽsis prefecto / authore. M.d.xxxix. / [Table] / **Superius** / **Parisiis in vico cythare prope sanctorum Cosme et Damiani / templum apud Petrum Attaingnãt et Hubertum Jullet.** /

4 vol. in-4° obl., 20 × 16 cm.; 16 f. numbered [i]–xvi
Sign.: *e^4–*h^4; *ee^4–*hh^4; *EE^4–*HH^4; *E^4–*H^4

Munich: Bayerische Staatsbibliothek. 4° Mus. Pr. 12/7
Noyon: Ancienne Bibliothèque du Chapitre
Vienna: Österreichische Nationalbibliothek

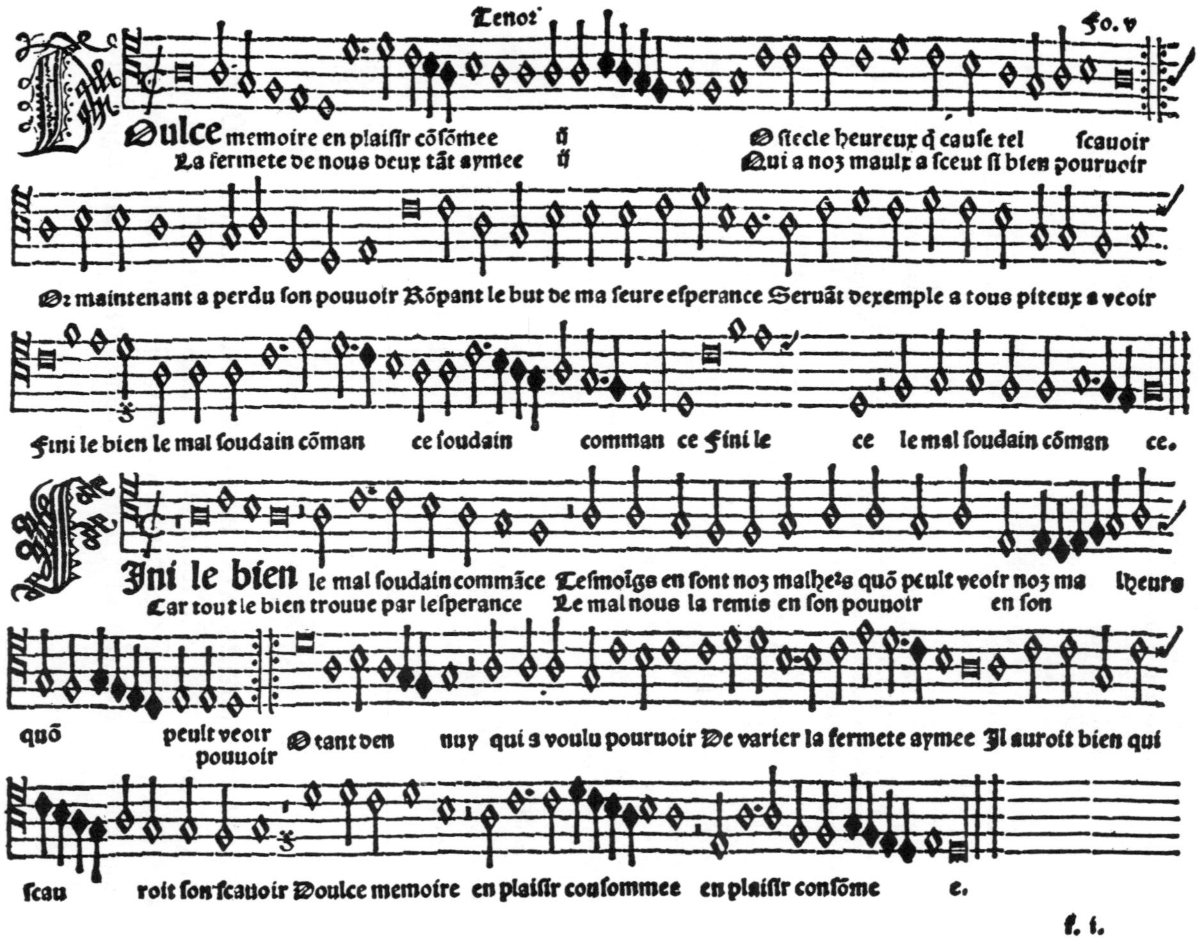

21 Music page (tenor) from the second book of old chansons **(81)**. By courtesy of the Herzog August Bibliothek, Wolfenbüttel.

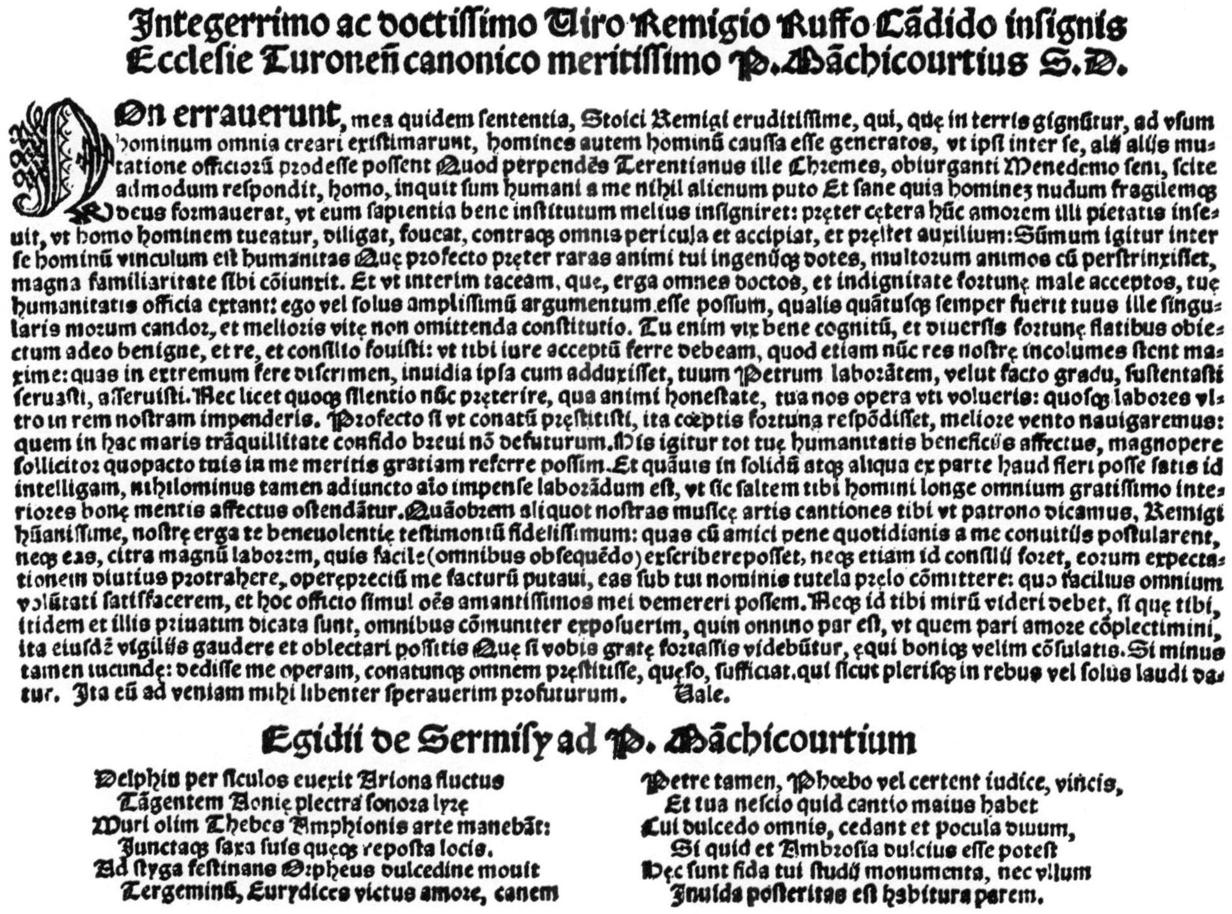
Integerrimo ac doctissimo Viro Remigio Ruffo Cādido insignis Ecclesie Turoneñ canonico meritissimo P. Māchicourtius S.D.

NOn errauerunt, mea quidem sententia, Stoici Remigi eruditissime, qui, quę in terris gignūtur, ad vsum hominum omnia creari existimarunt, homines autem hominū caussa esse generatos, vt ipsi inter se, alii aliis mutatione officiorū prodesse possent Quod perpendēs Terentianus ille Chremes, obiurganti Menedemo seni, scite admodum respondit, homo, inquit sum humani a me nihil alienum puto Et sane quis hominez nudum fragilemq Deus formauerat, vt eum sapientia bene institutum melius insigniret: prẹter cẹtera hūc amorem illi pietatis inseuit, vt homo hominem tueatur, diligat, foueat, contraq omnis pericula et accipiat, et prẹstet auxilium: Sūmum igitur inter se hominū vinculum est humanitas Quę profecto prẹter raras animi tui ingeniiq dotes, multorum animos cū perstrinxisset, magna familiaritate sibi cōiunxit. Et vt interim taceam, quę, erga omnes doctos, et indignitate fortunę male acceptos, tuę humanitatis officia extant: ego vel solus amplissimū argumentum esse possum, qualis quātusq semper fuerit tuus ille singularis morum candor, et melioris vitę non omittenda constitutio. Tu enim vix bene cognitū, et diuersis fortunę flatibus obiectum adeo benigne, et re, et consilio fouisti: vt tibi iure acceptū ferre debeam, quod etiam nūc res nostrę incolumes sint maxime: quas in extremum fere discrimen, inuidia ipsa cum adduxisset, tuum Petrum laborātem, velut facto gradu, sustentasti seruasti, asseruisti. Nec licet quoq silentio nūc prẹterire, qua animi honestate, tua nos opera vti volueris: quosq labores vltro in rem nostram impenderis. Profecto si vt conatū prẹstitisti, ita cœptis fortuna respōdisset, meliore vento nauigaremus: quem in hac maris trāquillitate confido breui nō defuturum. His igitur tot tuę humanitatis beneficiis affectus, magnopere sollicitor quopacto tuis in me meritis gratiam referre possim. Et quāuis in solidū atq aliqua ex parte haud fieri posse satis id intelligam, nihilominus tamen adiuncto aīo impense laborādum est, vt sic saltem tibi homini longe omnium gratissimo interiores bonę mentis affectus ostendātur. Quāobrem aliquot nostras musicę artis cantiones tibi vt patrono dicamus, Remigi hūanissime, nostrę erga te beneuolentię testimoniū fidelissimum: quas cū amici pene quotidianis a me conuitiis postularent, neq eas, citra magnū laborem, quis facile (omnibus obsequēdo) exscribere posset, neq etiam id consilii forei, eorum expectationem diutius protrahere, operęprecīū me facturū putaui, eas sub tui nominis tutela prelo cōmittere: quo facilius omnium volūtati satisfacerem, et hoc officio simul oēs amantissimos mei demereri possem. Neq id tibi mirū videri debet, si quę tibi, itidem et illis priuatim dicata sunt, omnibus cōmuniter exposuerim, quin omnino par est, vt quem pari amore cōplectimini, ita eiusdē vigiliis gaudere et oblectari possitis Quę si vobis gratę fortassis videbūtur, ęqui boniq velim cōsulatis. Si minus tamen iucundę: dedisse me operam, conatumq omnem prẹstitisse, quęso, sufficiat. qui sicut plerisq in rebus vel solus laudi datur. Ita cū ad veniam mihi libenter sperauerim profuturum. Vale.

Egidii de Sermisy ad P. Māchicourtium

Delphin per siculos euexit Ariona fluctus
Tāgentem Ionię plectra sonora lyrę
Muri olim Thebes Amphionis arte manebāt:
Junctaq saxa suis quęq reposta locis.
Ad styga festinans Orpheus dulcedine mouit
Tergeminū, Eurydices victus amore, canem

Petre tamen, Phœbo vel certent iudice, vincis,
Et tua nescio quid cantio maius habet
Cui dulcedo omnis, cedant et pocula diuum,
Si quid et Ambrosia dulcius esse potest
Hęc sunt fida tui studii monumenta, nec vllum
Inuida posteritas est habitura parem.

22 Dedication from the first edition of Manchicourt's motets (**85**). By courtesy of the Österreichische Nationalbibliothek, Vienna.

1.	Laudate Dominum, omnes gentes I	6 ttcc	ii
	Plaudite ergo, omnes gentes II		
2.	Regina cæli lætare, alleluya I		iii
	S: Canon. Sans souspirer ne chantez poinctz	[1]6 bbss	
	Resurrexit, sicut dixit, alleluya II		
3.	Congratulamini michi omnes I	5 tt; In Resurrectione	iii^v
	Tulerunt Dominum meum II	Domini	
4.	Ave stella matutina, mundi princeps et		iiii
	regina I		
	Tu es area compluta, cælesti rore imbuta II	5 tt; De beata	
		virgine Maria	
5.	Ego sum panis vivus qui de cælo descendi I	5 tt	v
	Caro enim mea vere est cibus II		
6.	Laudem dicite Deo nostro, omnes sancti eius I	5 ss	vi
	Laudate Dominum Deum, omnes gentes II		
7.	Peccantem me quotidie, et non pænitentem I	4	vii^v
	Commissa mea pavesco, et ante te erubesco II		
8.	Ave virgo gloriosa, stella sole clarior	4: De beata virgine	viii
		Maria	
9.	O intemerata et in æternum benedicta I	4; De virgine Maria	viii^v
	O virgo gloriosa, mater Dei, pietate		
	plenissima II		
10.	Paratum cor meum, Deus, cantabo et	4	ix^v
	psallam I		
	Exaltare in virtute tua, Domine II		
11.	Vias tuas, Domine, demonstra mihi I	4	x^v
	Eripe me de inimicis meis, Domine II		
12.	Domine, non secundum peccata nostra I	4	xi
	Quare memento nostri, Domine II		
13.	Ne reminiscaris Domine, delicta nostra	4	xii
14.	Proba me, Domine, et scito cor meum I	4	xii^v
	Respice in me, Deus, et miserere mei II		
15.	Ne derelinquas me, Domine, dominator		xiii
	vitæ meæ I	4	
	Propterea confitebor tibi, Domine II		
16.	Ecce odor filii mei sicut odor agri pleni I	4	xiii^v
	Esto Dominus fratrum tuorum II		
17.	Cantantibus organis, decantabat Cæcilia		xiiii^v
	virgo I	4	
	Cæcilia virgo gloriosa, semper evangelium		
	Christi II		
18.	Super montem excelsum ascende I	4	xv
	Judæa et Hierusalem nolite timere II		
19.	Usquequo, piger, dormies? I	4	xvi
	Vade ad formicam, o piger II		

Finis

i^v: Integerrimo ac doctissimo Viro Remigio Ruffo Cādido insignis / Ecclesie Turonen̄ canonico meritissimo P. Māchicourtius S. D. / . . .

Egidii de Sermisy ad P. Māchicourtium

For full text and translation of dedication see Appendix, Document 10.

For reprint see **119**.

Complete modern edition by A. Tillman Merritt in *Quatorzieme livre de Motets composés par Pierre de Manchicourt.* Paris and Monaco: Editions de L'Oiseau Lyre, 1964.

[1] Table: bbcc.

86

¶ Sixiesme liure contenant xxvij. Chansons nouuelles / a quatre parties en vng volume et en deux imprimees par / Pierre Attaingnant et Hubert Jullet libraires et Impri=/meurs de musique demourans a Paris en la Rue de la / Harpe pres leglise S. Cosme. M.D.xxxix. / [Table] / **Superius et Tenor.** /

2 vol. in-4° obl., 21 × 15.8 cm;. 16 f. numbered [i]–xvi
Sign.: x⁴–&⁴; X⁴–Æ⁴
RISM–I, 1539[16]

Castell: Fürstlich Castell'sche Schlossbibliothek (Ct-B)
Verona: Accademia Filarmonica, 207/I
Wolfenbüttel: Herzog-August-Bibliothek, 2.8.8 Mus. (Castell and Wolfenbüttel copies: Ct-B is foliated [i] iiii iii ii v)

			86, 87
1.	Amour perdit les traictz qu'il me tira	Maillart	i^{v}
2.	Fortune alors que n'avois congnoyssance	Certon	i^{v}
3.	Perrin, Perrinette et Perrot	Passereau	ii^{v}
4.	Encore ung coup, ung petit coup	Bon voisin	iii^{v}
5.	Sy contre amour je n'ay peü résister	Maillart	iii^{v}
*6.	Layssez-moy planter le may en riant	Bouteiller	iiii^{v}
7.	Humble et loyal vers ma dame seray		v^{v}
†8.	Plus je la voys moins y treuve a redire	Mittantier	v^{v}
9.	Hélas Amour, tu feiz mal ton debvoir	Peletier	vi^{v}
10.	Aymer ne veulx dames de grant beaulté	Certon	vi^{v}
‡11.	Je prens en gré la dure mort	Clemens	vii^{v}
12.	Asseurez-vous de mon cueur et de moy	Bourguignon	vii^{v}
§13.	Plus ne suys ce que j'ay esté	Certon	viii^{v}
14.	J'ay grand despit qu'elle m'a délaissé	Certon	viii^{v}
15.	D'amour me plains et non de vous m'amye	Rogier	ix^{v}
16.	Puisque de moy n'avez ferme fiance	Artins	ix^{v}
‖17.	Au temps heureux que ma jeune ignorance	Harchadelt	x^{v}
18.	O que je tiens celle la bien heureuse	Mittantier	x^{v}
19.	En m'en venant de la Fontarabie	Chevrier	xi^{v}
20.	Le rossignol plaisant et gracieulx	Mittantier	xii^{v}
21.	Las, qu'on congneust mon vouloir sans le dire	Sandrin	xii^{v}
22.	Quant ung travail surmonte le plaisir	Belin	xiii^{v}
23.	Le train d'aymer c'est ung parfaict déduyct		xiii^{v}
24.	Secouez-moy, je suys toute pleumeuse	Dambert	xiiii^{v}
25.	Layssons amour qui nous faict tant souffrir	Mittantier	xv^{v}
26.	Celluy qui veult en amour estre heureux	Courtois	xv^{v}
27.	On le m'a dict, dague a rouelle	Certon	xvi^{v}

Finis

* Modern edition in *Theatrical Chansons.*
† Modern edition as *Masterworks*, Vol. 9.
‡ Modern edition in *CMM 4*:X.
§ Modern edition in *Chorwerk, Vol. 82.*
‖ Modern edition in *Arcadelt.*

The Verona copy differs slightly in title, as follows:

¶ Sixiesme liure contenant xxvij. Chansons nouuelles / a quatre parties en vng volume et en deux imprimees par / Pierre Attaingnant et Hubert Jullet libraires et Impri-/meurs de musique du Roy demourãs a Paris en la Rue / de la Harpe pres leglise S. Cosme. M.D.xxxix. / [Table] / **Superius et Tenor.** /

The two volumes are bound with old leather-covered boards, stamped with the mark "Oloferne" on the front, and "Judic" on the back; the binding is illustrated in Giuseppe Turrini, *L'Accademia filarmonica dalla fondazione* (*Maggio, 1543*) *al 1600 e il suo patrimonio musicale antico*, Verona, 1941, Plate VIII. In the same work, p. 57, we learn that the set was purchased on Janurary 13, 1548: "per dui libri de cansone franzese coperte de corame L. 3, s. 12."

Contents same as **87**.

1539

87

Sixiesme liure contenant xxvij. Chãsons / NOVVELLES A QVATRE PARTIES, EN DEVX VOLVMES / *imprimees Par Pierre Attaingnant, libraire & Imprimeur de Musique du Roy* / *demourant a Paris en la Rue de la Harpe, pres leglise S. Cosme.* / *1539.* / [Table] / **Superius & Tenor** / *Auec priuilege du Roy pour six ans.*/

2 vol. in-4° obl., 21 × 15.8 cm.; 16 f. numbered [i]–xvi (S–T: [i] ii ii iiii)
Sign.: VI x⁴–VI &⁴; VI X⁴–VI *A*⁴
RISM–I, 1539[15]

Munich: Bayerische Staatsbibliothek, Mus. Pr. 4° 103

Contents same as **86**.

1539

88

¶ Septiesme liure contenant xxix. Chasons nouuelles a / quatre parties en vng volume et en deux imprimees par / Pierre Attaingnant et Hubert Jullet libraires et Impri-/meurs de musique demourans a Paris en la Rue de la / Harpe pres leglise S. Cosme. M.D.xxxix. / [Table] / **Superius et Tenor.** /

2 vol. in-4° obl., 21 × 15.8 cm.; 16 f. numbered [i]–xvi
Sign.: ☩ a⁴–☩ d⁴; ☩ A⁴–☩ D⁴
RISM–I, 1539[17]

Castell: Fürstlich Castell'sche Schlossbibliothek (Ct–B)
Wolfenbüttel: Herzog-August-Bibliothek, 2.8.8 Mus.

1.	O vous mes yeulx, qui fustes si long temps	Sandrin	i^v
2.	Voulenté fut en ton amour esmüe	Certon	i^v
3.	Le dur travail de ta longue demeure	Certon	ii^v
4.	Je suys tant bien, voire tant bien encore	Claudin	ii^v
5.	Ung doulx baiser je prins subtilement	Mittantier	iii^v
6.	Si j'eusse esté aussi prompte a donner	Mittantier	iii^v
7.	Si je vous ayme par amour ne le prenez	Maillard	iiii^v
8.	Languir me faiz en douleur et tristesse	Va. Sohier	iiii^v
9.	Qui peche plus, luy qui est éventeur	Claudin	v^v
10.	Celle qui fut de beaulté si louable	Sandrin	v^v
11.	Venons au poinct, c'est trop eu de langaige	Maillard	vi^v
12.	Mon seul espoir a tousjours prétendu	Maillard	vi^v
13.	Dictes pourquoy vostre amytié s'efface	Maille	vi^v
14.	Je ne pourroys ta fermeté blasmer	Morpain	vii^v
15.	Plus n'ay espoir je renonce a pitié	Certon	viii^v
16.	Las, me fault-il tant de mal supporter	Maille	viii^v
17.	Pleurez mes yeulx, pour la dure déffense qui rend l'amy	Sandrin	ix^v
*18.	O cueur ingrat qui tant m'est redevable	Certon	ix^v
19.	Tous bons pions commencez de trotter	Maillard	x^v
20.	Ung jour passé avec Collette	Le Hugier	x^v
21.	D'estre amoureux n'ay plus intention	Bouteillier	xi^v
22.	Le bon espoir guérist la myenne attente	Patinge	xi^v
23.	Reviens vers moy qui suys tant desolée	Lupi	xii^v
24.	Les fillettes de Tournay on dict qu'elles feront rage	Lupi	xii^v
25.	De tant aymer sans avoir joyssance	Maillard	xiiii^v
26.	Le souvenir de mon bien me rend triste	Maillard	xiiii^v
27.	Amour a faict ce qu'il ne peult déffaire	Cadéac	xv^v
28.	Toy seul sans plus peulx secourir l'amante	L'huyllier	xv^v
29.	Le doulx penser et regret langoureux [à 5]; S: Canon in subdyapenthe	Tetart	xvi^v
	Finis		

For reprint see **89**.

* Modern edition in *Chorwerk, Vol. 82.*

1540

89

Septiesme liure cōtenant xxx. Chansons/ NOVVELLES A QVATRE PARTIES, EN VNG VOLVME/ *& en deux, Imprimees par Pierre Attaingnant & Hubert Iullet / libraires & imprimeurs de musique du Roy, demourans a / Paris en la Rue de la Harpe pres leglise S. Cosme. / 1540.* / [Table] / **Superius & Tenor.** / *Auec priuilege du Roy, pour six ans.* /

2 vol. in-4° obl., 21 × 15.8 cm.; 16 f. numbered [i]–xvi
Sign.: ((a^4–((d^4; ((A^4–((D^4
RISM–I, 1540^{13}

London: British Museum, K.8.b.5 (5) (folios xii–xvi of Ct–B only)
Munich: Bayerische Staatsbibliothek, Mus. Pr. 4° 103
Verona: Accademia Filarmonica 207/II

1.	O vous mes yeulx, qui fustes si long temps	Sandrin	i^v
2.	Je suys tant bien, voire tant bien encore	Claudin	ii^v
3.	Si je vous ayme par amour	Maillard	ii^v
4.	Ung doulx baiser j'ay pris subtillement	Mittantier	iii^v
5.	Si j'eusse esté aussi prompte a donner	Mittantier	iii^v
6.	Le dur travail de ta longue demeure	Certon	iiii^v
7.	Le veoir, l'ouyr, le parler, l'attoucher	[1]Villiers	iiii^v
8.	Celle qui est dedans mon cueur emprainсté	Berchem	v^v
9.	Le bon espoir guérit la myenne attente	Patinge	v^v
10.	Venons au poinct, c'est trop eu de langage	Maillard	vi^v
11.	Mon seul espoir a tousjours prétendu	Maillard	vi^v
12.	Dictes pourquoy vostre amytié s'efface	Maille	vi^v
13.	Je ne sçay combien haine dure	Coste	vii^v
14.	Je ne pourroys ta fermeté blasmer	Morpain	viii^v
15.	Je ne pourroys promptement exprimer	Morpain	viii^v
16.	Plus n'ay espoir je renonce a pityé	Certon	ix^v
17.	Qui peche plus, luy qui est éventeur	Claudin	ix^v
18.	Celle qui fut de beaulté si louable	Sandrin	x^v
19.	Las, me fault-il tant de mal supporter	Maille	x^v
20.	Ung jour passé avec Collette	Le Hugier	xi^v
21.	Jehan de Lagny, mon bel amy	Berchem	xi^v
22.	Pleurez mes yeulx, pour la dure déffense qui rend l'amy	Sandrin	xii^v
23.	Est-il ung mal si rigoureux au monde	Villiers	xii^v
24.	Que feu craintif m'a causé grant martyre	Berchem	xiii^v
*25.	O cueur ingrat qui tant m'est redevable	Certon	xiii^v
26.	Reviens vers moy qui suys tant desolée	Lupi	xiiii^v
27.	Amour a faict ce qu'il ne peult déffaire	Cadéac	xiiii^v
28.	De tant aymer sans avoir jouyssance	Maillard	xv^v
29.	Le souvenir de mon bien me rend triste	Maillard	xv^v
30.	Languissant suis attendant que fortune	Villiers	xvi^v

Finis

Revised edition of **88** lacking nos. 2, 8, 19, 21, 24, 28, and 29. Nos. 7, 8, 13, 15, 21, 23, 24, and 30 are new.

* Modern edition in *Chorwerk, Vol. 82.*

[1] Certon in **161**.

1540

90

¶ Huitiesme liure contenant xix. Chansons nouuelles a / quatre parties de la facture et composition de maistre Cle=/met Jennequin en vng volume et en deux imprimees par / Pierre Attaingnant et Hubert Jullet libraires et Impri=/meurs de musique demourans a Paris en la Rue de la / Harpe pres leglise S. Cosme. M.D.xl. / [Table] / **Superius et Tenor.** /

2 vol. in-4° obl., 21 × 15.8 cm.; 16 f. numbered [i]–xvi
Sign.: ☩ e^4–☩ h^4; ☩ E^4–☩ H^4

Oxford: Christ Church, Mus. 515–516 (5)
Wolfenbüttel: Herzog-August-Bibliothek, 2.8.8 Mus.

		90, 91
1.	Ung gay bergier prioit une bergiere	i^v
2.	Jehanneton fut l'aultre jour au marché	ii^v
3.	L'espoir confus a plus hault désirer	ii^v
*4.	Il estoit une fillette qui vouloit sçavoir le jeu d'amours	iii^v
5.	Guillot ung jour estoit avec Babeau	iiii^v
6.	Secouez moy, je suys toute pleumeuse	v^v
7.	Une belle jeune espousée estoit une foys en devis	vi^v
8.	Ung jour Robin vint Margot empoingner	vii^v
9.	Plus ne suys ce que j'ay esté	viii^v
10.	Baisez-moy tost, ou je vous baiseray	ix^v
11.	M'amye a eu de Dieu le don	x^v
12.	Si celle-la qui oncques ne fut myenne	xi^v
13.	Las, qu'on congneust mon vouloir sans le dire	xii^v
*14.	L'amour, la mort et la vie me tourmentent a toute heure	xii^v
15.	O fortune, n'estois-tu pas contente	xiii^v
16.	J'atens le temps ayant ferme espérance	xiii^v
17.	Va rossignol, amoureux messagier	xiiii^v
*18.	Si come il chiaro sole fier' in un bel cristallo	xv^v
†19.	Ou mettra l'on ung baiser favorable	xv^v
	Finis	

Contents same as **91**.

In the Oxford copy, the device of an early owner appears on the back cover of 516: "Ung bon amy vault mieux que cent." Following 516 are three MS leaves bearing chansons printed elsewhere (**109**-3, **109**-4, **150**-25). The first two of these pieces are in "score" arrangement.

* Modern edition in *Anthologie.*
† Modern edition in *Trente Chansons* (*1928*).

1540

91

Huitiesme liure contenant xix Chansõs / NOVVELLES A QVATRE PARTIES DE LA FACTVRE ET / *composition de maistre Clement Iennequin en deux uolumes* / *imprimees par Pierre Attaingnant libraire &* / *imprimeur de Musique du Roy demourant* / *a Paris en la Rue de la Harpe pres* / *leglise S. Cosme. 40.* / [Table] / **Superius & Tenor.** / *Auec priuilege du Roy pour six ans.* /

2 vol. in-4° obl., 21 × 15.8 cm.; 16 f. numbered [i]–xvi
Sign.: VIII e^4–VIII h^4; VIII E^4–VIII H^4

London: British Museum, K.8.b.5 (1) (Ct–B)
Munich: Bayerische Staatsbibliothek, Mus. Pr. 4° 103
Contents same as **90**.

1540

92

¶ Neufuiesme liure cotenant xxvij. Chasons nouuelles / a quatre parties en vng volume et en deux imprimees par / Pierre Attaingnant et Hubert Jullet libraires et Impri=/meurs de musique demourans a Paris en la Rue de la / Harpe pres leglise S. Cosme. M.D.xl. / [Table] / **Superius et Tenor.** /

2 vol. in-4° obl., 21 × 15.8 cm.; 16 f. numbered [i]–xvi
Sign.: ☩ i[4]–☩ m[4]; ☩ I[4]–☩ M[4]
RISM-I, 1540[14]

Wolfenbüttel: Herzog-August-Bibliothek, 2.8.8 Mus.

*1.	O triste adieu qui tant me mescontente	Certon	i^v
*2.	O comme heureux t'estimeroys mon cueur	Certon	i^v
3.	Par ton seul bien ma jeunesse est heureuse	Maillard	ii^v
4.	Que gaignez vous a vouloir différer	Maille	ii^v
5.	Donne me fut des cieulx a ma naissance	De lattre	iii^v
6.	Avecques vous mon amour finira	L'huyllier	iii^v
7.	L'ardent désir du hault bien désiré	Certon	iiii^v
8.	Pauvre et loyal trompé par l'espérance	Mittantier	iiii^v
†9.	Que n'est elle aupres de moy celle que j'ayme	Certon	v^v
10.	Vous m'aviés vostre cueur donné	Mornable	vi^v
11.	O vin en vigne, gentil joly vin	Lupi	vi^v
12.	En revenant de Noyon la frelin frelorion	Lupi	vii^v
‡13.	Il n'est trésor que de lyesse	Lupi	viii^v
14.	D'ung amy fainct je ne me puys déffaire	Belin	viii^v
15.	La nuyct passée en mon lict je songeoye	Mornable	ix^v
16.	Si Dieu vouloit pour ung jour seullement	Mornable	ix^v
17.	Celluy qui fust du bien et du tourment	Mittantier	x^v
18.	Du corps absent le cueur je te présente	Certon	x^v
19.	Vouldriés vous bien estant de vous aymée	Maille	xi^v
20.	Ayant son cueur rompu la loyaulté	Maillard	xi^v
21.	Moins je la veulx plus m'en croist le désir	Mittantier	xii^v
22.	Contente ou non il fault que je l'endure	V. Sohier	xii^v
23.	Est-il point vray ou si je l'ay songé	Maille	xiii^v
24.	A qui me doibz-je retirer	Maille	xiii^v
25.	Ce moys de may au joly vert bouquet	Bouteiller	xiiii^v
26.	L'aultrier je viz par ung clair matinet	De porta	xv^v
27.	Trop plus que heureux sont les amans parfaitz	Le hugier	xvi^v
	Finis		

For reprint see **106**.

* Modern edition in *Chansons polyphoniques.*
† Modern edition in *Anthologie.*
‡ Modern edition in *Chorwerk, Vol. 15.*

1540

93

Missarū musicalium quatuor vocum cū suis / motetis Liber tertius. / [Table] / **Parhisiis in vico Cithare apud Petrum Attaingnant et / Hubertum Iullet musice typographos prope sanctorum / Cosme & Damiani templum. M.D.xl. / Superius.** /

4 vol. in-4° obl., 20 × 16 cm.; 12 f. numbered [i]–xii (B, T: xii^v blank)
Sign.: *i^4–*l^4; *ii^4–*ll^4; *II^4–*LL^4; *I^4–*L^4
RISM–I, 1540^2

Jena: Universitätsbibliothek
Noyon: Ancienne Bibliothèque du Chapitre

			93, 132
[1]1.	Missa Dulcis amica	P. Certon	i^v
	Dulcis amica Dei [à 3]		iiii
2.	Asperges me	[2]Claudin	iiii^v
3.	Amen. Et cum spiritu tuo	[2]Claudin	iiii^v
[3]4.	Quæ cæli pandis ostium	[2]Claudin	iiii^v
5.	[Missa Ave sanctissima]	Certon	v
	Ave sanctissima Maria [à 3]		viii
[4]6.	[Missa Domine quis habitabit]	Claudin	viii^v
	Domine, quis habitabit I		xi^v
	Ad nihilum deductus est II		
	B, T: Timentes autem Dominum glorificat		
	Finis		

Contents same as **132**.

[1] Based on the anonymous motet "Dulcis amica," first appearing in **27**-9. For modern edition of the motet and concordances see *Treize Motets.*
[2] Attribution in **132** only.
[3] "O salutaris hostia" in table of **132**; nos. 2, 3, and 4 are not listed in table of **93**.
[4] Based on Claudin's "Domine quis habitabit," first appearing in **12**-9. See G. Allaire, "The Masses of Claudin de Sermisy," unpublished dissertation, Boston University, 1960, p. 122.

1540

94

Second liure contenant xxvii. Chansons / NOVVELLES A QVATRE PARTIES, EN VNG VOLVME / *& en deux, Imprimees par Pierre Attaingnant & Hubert Iullet,* / *libraires & imprimeurs de musique du Roy, demourans a* / *Paris en la Rue de la Harpe pres leglise S. Cosme.* / *1540.* / [Table] / **Superius & Tenor.** / *Auec priuilege du Roy, pour six ans.* /

2 vol. in-4° obl., 21 × 15.8 cm.; 16 f. numbered [i]–xvi
Sign.: e^4–h^4; E^4–H^4
RISM–I, 1540[9]

Munich: Bayerische Staatsbibliothek, Mus. Pr. 4° 103

1.	Ung laboureur au premier chant du coq	Certon	i^v
2.	Vostre oeil a déceu ma pensée	Claudin	i^v
3.	N'espoir ne peur n'auray jour de ma vie	Claudin	ii^v
4.	Elle a mon cueur je croy qu'elle est contente	Mornable	ii^v
5.	Vaincre n'a peü le temps par sa rigueur	Sandrin	iii^v
*6.	Qui vouldra sçavoir qui je suys	Sandrin	iii^v
7.	Douce mémoire en plaisir consomée	Sandrin	iiii^v
†8.	Fini le bien, le mal soubdain commence	Certon	iiii^v
9.	Ce qui souloit en deux se despartir	Sandrin	v^v
10.	En lieu du bien que deux souloient prétendre	Quentin	v^v
11.	Je ne le croy et le sçay seurement	Sandrin	vi^v
12.	Je n'oserois le penser véritable	Villiers	vi^v
13.	Sy mon travail vous peult donner plaisir	Sandrin	vii^v
14.	Le doeul yssu de la joye incertaine	Villiers	vii^v
15.	Puis qu'il est tel qu'il garde bien s'amyc	Claudin	viii^v
16.	Qui se pourroit plus désoler et plaindre	Claudin	viii^v
17.	Ung seul désir ma volenté contente	Mornable	ix^v
*18.	L'heur d'amytié gist premier en la veue	Mornable	ix^v
[1],‡19.	C'est trop dormy, resveillez-vous	Jennequin	x^v
20.	Resveillez-moy mon bel amy	Garnier	xi^v
21.	Pilons l'orge, pilons la	Claudin	xii^v
§22.	Une fillette bien gorriere T & B: Tout au prez d'une riviere	Clemens	xiii^v
23.	Contentement, combien que soit grand chose	Jacotin	xiii^v
24.	Est-il possible que l'on puisse trouver	Morel	xiiii^v
§25.	Le départir est sans département	Clemens	xiiii^v
§26.	Ung jour passé bien escoutoye	Clemens	xv^v
27.	Ta bonne grace et maintien gracieux	Roquellay	xvi^v

Finis

Revised edition of **81**, lacking nos. 10 and 12. Nos. 10 and 12 are new.

* Modern edition in *Chorwerk, Vol. 61.*
† Modern edition in *Chorwerk, Vol. 82.*
‡ Modern edition in *Trente Chansons (1928).*
§ Modern edition in *CMM 4:*X.

[1] Table: Resveillez vous.

1540

95

Tiers liure contenant xxix. Chansons / NOVVELLES A QVATRE PARTIES, EN VNG VOLVME / *& en deux, Imprimees par Pierre Attaingnant & Hubert Iullet,* / *libraires & imprimeurs de musique du Roy, demourans a* / *Paris en la Rue de la Harpe pres leglise S. Cosme.* / *1540.* / [Table] / **Superius & Tenor.** / *Auec priuilege du Roy, pour six ans.* /

2 vol. in-4° obl., 21 × 15.8 cm.; 16 f. numbered [i]–xvi (S & T: xiii xxiiii xv xvi)
Sign.: i^4–m^4; I^4–M^4 (S & T: K instead of k)
RISM–I, 1540^{10}

Munich: Bayerische Staatsbibliothek, Mus. Pr. 4° 103

1.	Par ton parler n'auras sur moy puissance	Mittantier	i^v
2.	Le mal que j'ay rigueur me le procure	Le Moisne	i^v
3.	Au départyr m'amye a mauldit l'heure	Claudin	ii^v
4.	Mariez-moy mon pere, il est temps ou jamais	Godard	ii^v
5.	En grant douleur faict son triste demeure	Villiers	iii^v
6.	Mort ou mercy en languissant j'attens	Villiers	iii^v
7.	La, la, la, je ne l'ose dire	Certon	iiii^v
8.	Or n'ay-je plus crainte d'estre surpris	Bourguignon	iiii^v
9.	L'esté passé, Martine au dur téton	De porta	v^v
10.	Las, je ne sçay celle me laissera	Villiers	vi^v
11.	A bien compter ma joye abandonnée	Fresneau	vi^v
12.	En languissant je consomme mes jours	Cadéac	vii^v
13.	O doux reveoir que mon esprit contente	[1]Godard	vii^v
*14.	Vous perdez temps de me dire mal d'elle	Claudin	viii^v
15.	Tel en mesdit qui pour soy la désire	Mittantier	viii^v
16.	Ha, quel torment, quel peine et quel angoisse	Godard	ix^v
17.	Las, s'il convient si tost faire despart	Certon	ix^v
18.	Si l'amytié porte la suffisance	Mittantier	x^v
19.	Si j'ay du mal maulgré moy je le porte	Claudin	x^v
20.	Las, qu'on congneust mon vouloir sans le dire	Certon	xi^v
21.	Mon triste cueur puisqu'avec vous demeure	Jacotin	xi^v
†22.	Puis que de vous je n'ay d'aultre visage	Sandrin	xii^v
23.	Ung moins aymant aura peult estre myeulx	Certon	xii^v
24.	Faisons ung coup je vous en prie	Courtoys	xiii^v
25.	De ceulx qui tant de mon bien se tormentent	Maillard	xiiii^v
26.	Ce n'est a vous a qui je m'en prendray	Certon	xiiii^v
27.	Amour me feit longuement souffreteux	Certon	xv^v
28.	Le dur travail que je porte sans cesse	Certon	xv^v
29.	Cueur sans mercy, yeulx meurtriers de ma joye	Villiers	xvi^v

Finis

Revised edition of **82** lacking nos. 1, 3, 19, and 24. Nos. 6, 10, 21, 25, and 29 are new.

* Modern edition published by Akademische Druck- und Verlagsanstalt, Graz, 195–.
† Modern edition in *Quinze Chansons.*

[1] Certon in **161**.

1540

96

Quart liure contenant xxviij. Chansons / NOVVELLES A QVATRE PARTIES, EN VNG VOLVME / *& en deux, Imprimees par Pierre Attaingnant & Hubert Iullet,* / *libraires & imprimeurs de musique du Roy, demourans a* / *Paris en la Rue de la Harpe pres leglise S. Cosme.* / *1540.* / [Table] / **Superius & Tenor.** / *Auec priuilege du Roy, pour six ans.* /

2 vol. in-4° obl., 21 × 15.8 cm.; 16 f. numbered [i]–xvi
Sign.: n^4–q^4; N^4–Q^4
RISM–I, 1540^{11}

Munich: Bayersiche Staatsbibliothek, Mus. Pr. 4° 103

1.	Frere Thibault, séjourné, gros et gras	Certon	i^v
2.	Je n'en puis plus durer Marquet	Passereau	ii^v
3.	A cent diables la vérolle	[1]Heurteur	iii^v
4.	Ce moys de may sur la rosée	Godard	iii^v
5.	Amour, voyant l'ennuy qui tant m'oppresse	Claudin	iiii^v
6.	Plaisir n'ay plus mais vis en desconfort	Morel	iiii^v
7.	Mon cueur voulut dedans soy recepvoir	Claudin	v^v
8.	Preste-moy l'ung de tes yeux	Villiers	v^v
9.	Fine affinée, remplye de finesse	Vassal	vi^v
10.	Tristesse, ennuy, douleur, mélancholye	Villiers	vi^v
*11.	Je suys déshéritée puisque j'ay perdu mon amy	Cadéac [or Lupi]	vii^v
12.	Hélas, Amour qui sçays certainement	Heurteur	vii^v
13.	L'heur et malheur de vostre congnoissance	Villiers	viii^v
14.	Qui de tout bien vouldra choisir l'eslite	Villiers	viii^v
15.	Amour bruslé par son ardente flamme	Maillard	ix^v
16.	En espérant espoir me désespére	Mittantier	ix^v
17.	Layrras-tu cela, Michault	Bon voisin	x^v
18.	Tant est l'amour de vous en moy empraincté	Mittantier	xi^v
19.	Oncques amour ne fut sans grant langueur	Grenier	xi^v
20.	Puis que malheur me tient rigueur	Certon	xii^v
21.	Vaincu me sens et ton sert me reclame	Certon	xii^v
22.	Je veulx tousjours obéir et complaire	Claudin	xiii^v
23.	Est-il advis qu'on doibve estimer d'elle	Harchadelt	xiii^v
24.	Trop plus que la mort est aspre et dangeureux	Villiers	xiiii^v
25.	Satisfaict suys au long de mon mérite	Certon	xiiii^v
26.	Hélas Amour, je pensoye bien avoir	Godard	xv^v
27.	L'oeil trop hardy si hault lieu regarda	Cadéac	xv^v
28.	Ce me semblent choses perdues	Layolle	xvi^v

Finis

Revised edition of **83**, lacking nos. 2, 3, 4, 5, 10, 11, 15, 16, 18, 21, 25, and 27. Nos. 5, 6, 8, 9, 10, 11, 12, 13, 14, 15, 21, 24, and 28 are new.

* Modern edition in *Chorwerk, Vol. 15* and *GMB.*

[1] Bon voisin in **83**.

1540

97

Cinquiesme liure cōtenant xxv. Chāsons / NOVVELLES A QVATRE PARTIES, EN VNG VOLVME / *& en deux, Imprimees par Pierre Attaingnant & Hubert Iullet,* / *libraires & imprimeurs de musique du Roy, demourans a* / *Paris en la Rue de la Harpe pres leglise S. Cosme.* / *1540.* / [Table] / **Superius & Tenor.** / *Auec priuilege du Roy, pour six ans.* /

2 vol. in-4° obl., 21 × 15.8 cm.; 16 f. numbered [i]–xvi
Sign.: r^4–u^4; R^4–U^4
RISM–I, 1540^{12}

Munich: Bayerische Staatsbibliothek, Mus. Pr. 4° 103

1.	L'amour premiere en jeunesse innocente	Sandrin	i^v
2.	Quant je congneu en ma pensée	Sandrin	i^v
3.	Hélas amy, je congnoys bien que ne puis nyer mon offence	Sandrin	ii^v
4.	Amye, hélas, je suys dolent		ii^v
5.	Vivre ne puis content sans ma maistresse	Certon	iii^v
6.	Frere Thibault, séjourné, gros et gras	Jannequin	iiii^v
7.	Ung cueur vivant en langoureux désir	Mornable	v^v
8.	Deux cueurs voulans par fermeté louable	Sandrin	v^v
9.	Autant que moy heureuse pourrez estre	Villiers	vi^v
10.	Jamais amour ne peult si fermement	Mittantier	vii^v
11.	Veu le grief mal que longuement j'endure	Villiers	viii^v
12.	Continuer je veulx ma fermeté	Bourguignon	viii^v
13.	Si comme espoir je n'ay de guarison	Maillard	ix^v
14.	Puis que prier n'est de vous entendu	Certon	ix^v
15.	Nostre vicaire ung jour de feste	Heurteur	x^v
16.	Si j'ay aymé légierement	De porta	xi^v
17.	Par ton départ regret me vient saisir	Courtois	xi^v
18.	Si vostre amour ne gist qu'en apparence	Sandrin	xii^v
19.	Si mon vouloir ne change de désir	Maillard	xii^v
20.	Celle qui veit son mari tout armé	Jannequin	xiii^v
21.	Amour cruel de sa nature	Jannequin	xiiii^v
22.	O cruaulté logée en grant beaulté	Jannequin	xiiii^v
23.	Vostre oeil m'a dict cherchez ailleurs party	Certon	xv^v
24.	En vous voyant j'ay liberté perdue	Rogier	xv^v
25.	Une dame par ung matin	[1]Gentien	xvi^v

Finis

Revised edition of **84**, lacking nos. 9, 11, 19, 24, 25, and 27. Nos. 4, 9, and 23 are new.

[1] Belin in **84**.

1541

98

Missale ad vsū īsignis / ecclesie nouiomensis nouiter impressum / ac emendatum: per dé=/putatos a reuerendo in Christo patre / et domino / domino / Johanne ab hangesto Nouiom̄. Episcopo / et comite: / Francieqȝ pari: ac a venerabilib, decano et / capitulo eiusdem ecclesie canonicos. / Anno dn̄i Millesimo q'ngētesimo / quadragesimo primo. / [Cut] / **Venit Parisijs apud Petrū attaīgnā[t] et Hubertum Jullet musice typographos: commorantes in vico [Cy=]/thare: Nō procul a diuorum Cosme et Damiani templo: [in do]mo M[a]=/turinorum vico directe opposita. /**

1 vol. in-fol., 18.5 × 29 cm.; 218 fol. in four sections, as follows:

[Calendar]
8 fol. unnumbered
Sign.: [✠ i], ✠$^{2-8}$

[Proprium de Tempore]
Fol. i with cut, unnumbered; ii–l, ,lii liii, lii, liiii, lv–lix, lxi, lxi–lxiii, [lxiiii], lxv–lxviii, [lxix–lxxvi] (cuts on lxix^{v}, lxx), lxxvii–xcvi, xcvi, xcviii–cii, cvi, ciiii, cv–cviii, cx, cxv, cxvi.
Sign.: [Ai], A$^{2-8}$; B^{8}–E^{8}; F, F$^{2-8}$; G, G$^{[2]-8}$; H, H$^{2-8}$; I^{4}; kk^{1}, 7 unsigned folios on vellum; [L^{1}]$^{-8}$; M^{8}–P^{8}

[Proprium de Sanctis]
i–xi, xiii, xiii, xiiii–xviii, xviii, xx, xxi–xxxvii, xxxv, xxxix, xl–xlv, xlv, xlvii, xlviii–liiii
Sign.: a^{8}–g^{6}

[Commune Sanctorum]
i–xxi, xxiii, xxiii, xxiiii–xxxviii, [xxxix, xl]
Sign.: A^{8}–B^{6}; C^{8}–E^{10}

Description of cuts
Title page: Mater Dei
Fol. i: Celebration of Mass (See Plate V).
Fol. lxix^{v}: Crucifixion
Fol. lxx: God the Father in majesty with the symbols of the four Evangelists.

London: British Museum, 1484.g.7

This copy was obtained by the British Museum in November, 1956 (information supplied by John W. Jolliffe, of the Department of Printed Books). The title page bears at the top the shelf mark "(1) 308," identifying it as the former property of the Ancienne Bibliothèque du Chapitre, Noyon, from which it has been missing since before the Second World War. The manuscript catalogue of Alphonse Boulogne at Noyon describes the volume as follows: "(1) 308 Missale ad usum Ecclesie Noviomensis Anno Domini 1541, venit Parisiis. Petit in-folio."

1541

99

¶Dixiesme liure cōtenant xxviii. Chāsons nouuelles a / quatre parties en vng volume et en deux imprimees par / Pierre Attaingnant et Hubert Jullet libraires et Impri=/meurs de musique du Roy demourās a Paris en la Rue / de la Harpe pres leglise S. Cosme. M.D.xli. / [Table] / **Auec priuilege pour six ans / Superius et Tenor /**

2 vol. in-4° obl., 21 × 15.8 cm.; 16 f. numbered [i]–xvi
Sign.: ☨ m^{4}–☨ p^{4}; ☨ M^{4}–☨ P^{4}
RISM–I, 1541^{6}

Verona: Accademia Filarmonica, 207/IV

			99, 100
*1.	Ung jour que madame dormoit	Certon	i^v
2.	A ce matin ce seroit bonne estraine	Certon	ii^v
*3.	Mon pere my veult marier	Certon	ii^v
4.	O combien est malheureux le désir	Sandrin	iii^v
5.	L'oeil et le cueur contre leur ligue saincte	Certon	iii^v
6.	Je ne puis bonnement penser	Sandrin	iiii^v
7.	Amour lassif ne peult sa nourriture	Certon	iiii^v
8.	Las, que te sert ce doulx parler en bouche	Le Gendre	v^v
9.	O doulx raport si longtemps désiré	L'huyllier	v^v
10.	L'oeil dict assez s'il estoit entendu	Colin	vi^v
11.	Puisque de toy vient et non d'aultre place	Heurteur	vi^v
12.	L'oeil est a vous, le cueur et la pensée	Passereau	vii^v
13.	Amour et moy avons faict une dame	Cadéac	vii^v
14.	Si pour aymer et désirer	Sandrin	viii^v
*15.	Si j'ay eu tousjours mon vouloir	Certon	viii^v
16.	Comment mes yeulx ariez-vous bien promitz	Sandrin	ix^v
17.	Est-ce au moyen d'une grande amytié	Certon	ix^v
18.	Au feu d'amour je fais ma pénitence	La Rue	x^v
19.	Las, que plains tu, amy, de mon offence	La Rue	x^v
20.	Ung doulx regard, ung parler amoureux	Gervaise	xi^v
21.	Mort en malheur m'est seulle suffisance	Colin	xi^v
22.	Plus revenir ne puis vers toy ma dame	Lupi	xii^v
23.	Si l'estincelle en ung petit moment	Maille	xiii^v
24.	Je croy le feu plus grant que vous ne dictes	Maille	xiii^v
25.	Ung musequin d'ung assez beau maintien	Certon	xiiii^v
26.	Blanc et clairet sont les couleurs		xiiii^v
27.	Frisque et gaillard ung jour entre cent mille	Clemens	xv^v
28.	Si mon amour ne vous vient a playsir	Wauquel	xvi^v
	Finis		

Contents same as **100.**

* Modern edition in *Chorwerk, Vol. 82.*

1541

100

Dixiesme liure cōtenant xxviii. Chansōs / NOVVELLES A QVATRE PARTIES, EN DEUX / *uolumes imprimees Par pierre Attaingnant, libraire & Imprimeur / de Musique du Roy demourant a Paris en la Rue de la / Harpe, pres leglise S. Cosme. / 1541.* / [Table] / **Superius & Tenor** / *Auec priuilege du Roy pour six ans.* /

2 vol. in-4° obl., 21 × 15.8 cm.; 16 f. numbered [i]–xvi (S & T: ii unfoliated)
Sign.: X m^4–X p^4; X M^4–X P^4
RISM-I, 1541^5

Munich: Bayerische Staatsbibliothek, Mus. Pr. 4° 103

Contents same as **99.**

101

¶Onziesme liure cõtenant xxviii. Chãsons nouuelles a / quatre parties en vng volume et en deux imprimees par / Pierre Attaingnant et Hubert Jullet libraires et Impri=/meurs de musique du Roy demourãs a Paris en la Rue / de la Harpe pres leglise S. Cosme. M.D.xli. / [Table] / Superius et Tenor. / Auec priuilege du Roy pour six ans. /

2 vol. in-4° obl., 20 × 16 cm.; 16 f. numbered [i]–xvi
Sign.: ‡ q^4–‡ t^4; ‡ Q^4–‡ T^4

London: British Museum, K.4.g.1

			101, 107, 108
1.	Le jeu d'aymer ou jeunesse s'esbat	Certon	i^v
2.	Je le retiens tousjours pour moy	Mornable	ii^v
3.	J'ay veu que j'estoys franc et maistre	Certon	ii^v
4.	Si j'ay du bien, hélas, c'est par mensonge	Maille	iii^v
5.	Voulant Amour, soubz parler gracieux	Claudin	iii^v
6.	Est ce au moyen d'une grande amytié	Claudin	iiii^v
7.	Trop tost j'ay creu, y prenant tel plaisir	[1]Mornable	iiii^v
8.	O combien est malheureux le désir	Claudin	v^v
9.	Du mal que j'ay, las, qui m'en guérira	Maillard	v^v
10.	Si ta beaulté se garnist de prudence	Certon	vi^v
11.	Je n'ayme plus la mondaine plaisance		vi^v
12.	Jehanne disoit ung jour a Janinet	Garnier	vii^v
13.	De mon las cueur j'ay donné le pouvoir	Wauquel	vii^v
14.	En espérant je viz en grant langueur	Certon	viii^v
15.	Puis que fortune a sur moy entrepris	Mittantier	viii^v
16.	Las, je sçay bien que je feis grande offence	Harchadelt	ix^v
17.	Sy l'on doibt prendre ung bienfaict pour offence	Mornable	ix^v
18.	La loy d'honneur que nous dict et commande	Gentian	x^v
19.	C'est ung grand cas qu'amour qui a puyssance	Gentian	x^v
20.	Au feu, venez moy secourir	Maillard	xi^v
21.	Puis que d'amour reçoys élection	Maillard	xi^v
22.	Ung mesnagier, vieillard, recreu d'enhan	Sohier	xii^v
23.	C'est ung grant mal que d'ung refus	Certon	xiii^v
24.	En espoir viz et crainte me tourmente		xiii^v
25.	Elle a bien ce riz gracieux	Claudin	xiiii^v
26.	Apres avoir longuement attendu soubz le confort	Certon	xiiii^v
27.	Jamais je ne confesseroys qu'amour d'elle	Mornable	xv^v
*28.	Honneur sans plus en noble cueur prent place	Lupus	xvi^v
	Finis		

Contents same as **107**, **108**.

* Modern edition in *Chorwerk, Vol. 15.*

[1] Claudin in **163**.

102

[Cantica Canticorum Salomonis Guill. le Heurteur, etc. in quarto. Pierre Attaingnant, 1541.]

Jean de La Caille, *Histoire de l'imprimerie et de la librairie*, Paris, 1689, p. 116.

Fétis cites the same work giving as a date 1548, which is probably his error in copying La Caille rather than evidence of another edition. *Biographie universelle*, 2d ed., Vol. IV, p. 324.

103

CLAVDIN / **CLAVDII DE SERMISY, REGII SACELLI / Submagistri, Noua & Prima motettorum editio.** / INDEX VIGINTI OCTO MOTETTORVM. / [Table, by number of voices] / **Liber Primus.** ❧ **SVPERIVS.** ❧ / **Cum gratia & priuilegio Regis** / PARISIIS in vico Cythare. / EX OFFICINA PETRI ATTIGNANT ET HVBERTI IVLLET, / Typographorum Musices Cristianissimi Francorum Regis. / M.D.xlij. /

4 vol. in-4° obl., 25.5 × 19.4 cm.; 20 f. numbered [i 1]–xx 20
Sign.: a^4–e^4; aa^4–ee^4; AA^4–EE^4; A^4–E^4

Paris: Bibliothèque Nationale, Rés. Vm[1] 139 (S)
Rome: Biblioteca Apostolica Vaticana, Capella Sixtina 243, I
Vienna: Österreichische Nationalbibliothek, SA 78.C.1 / Lib. 1

1. O Maria stans sub cruce	[à 6]	i^v	1^v
2. Regina cæli lætare, alleluya I	[à 5]	ii	2
Resurrexit sicut dixit, alleluya II			
3. Quis est iste qui progreditur I	[à 5]	ii^v	2^v
Egredimini et videte, filiæ Syon II			
4. Quare fremuerunt gentes et populi meditati		iii^v	3^v
sunt inania I—Psalmus 2	[à 5]		
Ego autem constitutus sum rex ab eo II	[à 3]		
S tacet; Ct: EGO autem TACEO			
Et nunc reges intelligite erudimini qui			
judicatis terram III	[à 5]		
5. Verba mea auribus percipe Domine I—Psalmus 5	[à 4]	iiii^v	4^v
Adjuva me nequando miser audiam II			
6. Miserere mei, Domine, et exaudi orationem meam I	[à 4]	v^v	5^v
Miserere mei, Deus, secundum magnam misericordiam			
tuam II			
7. Cantate Domino canticum novum I—Psalmus 97	[à 4]	vi^v	6^v
Viderunt omnes termini terræ II	[à 3]		
Jubilate in conspectu regis Domini III	[à 4]		

8.	Domine Deus omnipotens qui ad principium	[à 4]	vii^v 7^v
9.	Misericordias Domini in æternum cantabo I	[à 4]	viii 8
	Universæ viæ tuæ misericordia II	[à 3]	
	Tribularer si nescirem misericordias tuas III	[à 4]	
10.	Regi seculorum immortali et invisibili soli Deo	[à 4]	ix 9
11.	Nos qui vivimus in exitu Israel de Egipto I—[1]Psalmus 113	[à 4]	ix^v 9^v
	Super misericordia tua et veritate tua II	[à 3]	
	Similes illis fiant qui faciunt ea III	[à 4]	
12.	Partus et integritas discordes tempore longo	[à 4]	xi 11
13.	Astiterunt reges terræ et principes I	[à 4]	xi^v 11^v
	Benedictus es, Domine Deus patrum nostrorum II		
14.	Audite reges et intelligite I	[à 4]	xii 12
	Inclinate aurem vestram ad illum II		
15.	Girum cæli circuivi sola I	[à 4]	xii^v 12^v
	Ego in altissimis habito II		
[2]16.	Aspice, Domine, de sede sancta tua	[à 4]	xiii^v 13^v
17.	Noe, quem vidistis pastores dicite annunciate I	[à 4]	xiii^v 13^v
	Dicite quidnam vidistis et annunciate II		
	De Nativitate Domini		
18.	Alleluya. Angelus Domini descendit de cælo I	[à 4]	xiiii^v 14^v
	Et introeuntes in monumentum II		
19.	Veni Sancte spiritus et emitte cælitus I	[à 4]	xv^v 15^v
	O lux beatissima reple cordis intima II	[à 3]	
	Lava quod est sordidum, riga quod est aridum III	[à 4]	
	De Sancto spiritu Prosa		
20.	Gaudent in cælis animæ sanctorum I	[à 4]	xvi^v 16^v
	O quam gloriosum est Regnum II		
21.	Michael archangele, veni in adjutorium	[à 4]	xvii 17
22.	Congratulamini mihi omnes	[à 4]	xvii^v 17^v
23.	Ave sanctissima Maria, mater Dei	[à 3]	xviii 18
24.	Regi seculorum immortali et invisibili I	[à 3]	xviii^v 18^v
	Et beata viscera Mariæ virginis II		
25.	Spes mea ab uberibus matris meæ	[à 3]	xix 19
26.	Euntes ibant et flebant mittentes semina sua I	[à 3]	xix^v 19^v
	Tunc repletum est gaudios nostrum II		
27.	Da pacem, Domine, in diebus nostris quia non est alius	[à 3]	xx 20
28.	Benedictum sit nomen Domini nostri	[à 3]	xx^v 20^v

Finis

Superius title page reproduced in *Larousse de la Musique*, Vol. II (1957), p. 348.

The same, with Superius, fol. xii, reproduced in Renouard, *Imprimerurs et Libraires parisiens du XVIe siècle*, Paris, 1964, plates A34–35.

The Paris copy is preserved in a 16th-century binding, stamped with the name *Philippes Hasart;* bound with it are **104**, **105**, and two other superius parts of the same format, *Liber Primus Collectorum Modulorum (qui Moteta vulgo dicuntur)*, Paris, Du Chemin, 1553, and *Liber Primus sex missas continens*, Paris, Le Roy and Ballard, 1552.

The Vatican copy is inscribed inside the back cover: "Melchioris sum maioris. Emptus scutis tribus dico Trit. zo" (abbreviation of a proper name?). And in another hand: "Isti libri erant Cardinalis Augustani posterius obitum emi scutis tribus." The reference is to Otto Truchsess von Waldburg, Bishop of Augsburg, created Cardinal in 1544 by Paul III, deceased in 1570.

[1] All books: Psalmus 311.
[2] De la fage in **63**.

104

CERTON / ❧ **Petri Certon Institutoris Symphoniacorum puero- / rum Sancti Sacelli Parisiensis recens modulorum editio.** / INDEX VIGINTI QVATVOR MOTETTORVM. / [Table, by number of voices] / **Liber Secundus ❧ SVPERIVS.** / ❧ / **Cum gratia & priuilegio Regis** / PARISIIS in vico Cythare. / EX OFFICINA PETRI ATTAINGNANT ET HVBERTI IVLLET, / Typographorum Musices Cristianissimi Francorum Regis. / M.D.xlij. /

4 vol. in-4° obl., 25.5 × 19.4 cm.; 20 f. numbered [i 21]–xx 40 (Ct numbered—xvii 37,—xix 39 instead of xvii, xviii, xix, xx; B: 18 folios, xviii 18 instead of xviii 38)

Sign.: f^4–k^4; ff^4–kk^4; FF^4–KK^4; F^4–K^4

Paris: Bibliothèque Nationale, Rés. Vm^1 140 (S)
Rome: Biblioteca Apostolica Vaticana, Capella Sixtina 243, II
Vienna: Österreichische Nationalbibliothek, SA 78 C 1 / Lib. 2

1.	Pater noster, qui es in cælis	[à 6]	i^v 21^v
	Quinta & Sexta Pars: Ave Maria, gratia plena [canon, 2 in 1]		
2.	Inviolata, integra et casta es, Maria I	[à 6]	i^v 21^v
	T 1: Canon in dyapenthe		
	Te nunc flagitant devota corda et ora II		
	T 1: Canon in subdyapenthe		
3.	Ave virgo gloriosa, stella sole clarior	[à 6]	ii^v 22^v
4.	Regina cæli lætare, alleluya I	[à 6]	iii^v 23^v
	Ct 2: Canon in subdyapenthe		
	Resurrexit sicut dixit, alleluya II		
5.	Angelus Domini descendit de cælo	[à 5]	iiii 24
6.	Non conturbetur cor vestrum, alleluya I	[à 5]	iiii^v 24^v
	Ego rogabo patrem meum II		
7.	Deus in nomine tuo salvum me fac I—Psalmus 53		vi^v 26^v
	Quinta Pars: Adjuva nos, Deus	[à 5]	
	Averte mala inimicis meis II		
8.	Quam dilecta tabernacula tua I	[à 5]	vii^v 27^v
	Memor fui dierum antiquorum II		
9.	Peccata mea, Domine, sicut sagitte I	[à 5]	viii^v 28^v
	Quoniam iniquitatem meam II		
10.	Domine, non secundum peccata nostra I	[à 5]	ix^v 29^v
	Domine, ne memineris iniquitatum II	[à 3]	
	Adjuva nos, Deus salutaris noster III	[à 5]	
11.	Cantantibus organis Cæcilia virgo I	[à 4]	x^v 30^v
	Benedico te, pater Domini mei Jesu Cristi II		
12.	Cæcilia virgo gloriosa semper evangelium Cristi I	[à 4]	xi^v 31^v
	Dum aurora finem daret Cæcilia dixit II		
13.	Jherusalem cito veniet salus tua I	[à 4]	xii^v 32^v
	Descendet sicut pluvia in vellus II		

14. Tulerunt Dominum meum I Dum ergo fleret inclinavit se II	[à 4]	xiii^{v} 33^{v}
15. Tanto tempore vobiscum sum I Domine, ostende nobis patrem II	[à 4]	xiiii^{v} 34^{v}
16. Cum sublevasset oculos Jesus I Accepit ergo Jesus panes II	[à 4]	xv^{v} 35^{v}
17. Laus et perennis gloria Deo patri	[à 4]	xvi 36
18. Ascendo ad patrem meum et patrem vestrum I Nisi ego abiero, paraclitus non veniet II	[à 4]	xvi^{v} 36^{v}
19. Verbum iniquum et dolosum I Ne forte satiatus euomam illud II	[à 4]	xvii^{v} 37^{v}
20. Laus Deo, pax vivis et requies defunctis	[à 3]	xviii^{v} 38^{v}
21. Ecce Maria genuit nobis salvatorem	[à 3]	xix 39
22. Ave Maria, gratia plena	[à 3]	xix^{v} 39^{v}
23. Sancta Maria, succurre miseris	[à 3]	xix^{v} 39^{v}
24. Ecce Dominus veniet et omnes sancti eius	[à 3]	xx 40

Bassus, i^{v} 21^{v}: **Petrus Certonius Phonascus** / SANCTI SACELLI PARISIENSIS CLAVDIO DE / Sermisy submagistro regij Sacelli foelicitatem perpetuam exoptat
For full text and translation, see Appendix, Document 14.

1542

105

LVPI / **IO. LVPI, CHORI SACRE VIRGINIS** / **Marię Cameracenis Magistri, Musicę Cātiones** / (QVE VVLGO MOTETTA NVNCVPANTVR) NOVITER OMNI / studio, ac diligentia in lucem editę / INDEX QVINDECIM CANTIONVM. / [Table, by number of voices] / **Liber Tertius, SVPERIVS.** / **Cum gratia & priuilegio Regis** / PARISIIS in vico Cythare. / EX OFFICINA PETRI ATTAINGNANT ET HVBERTI IVLLET, / Typographorum Musices Cristianisimi Francorum Regis. / M.D.xlij. /

4 vol. in-4° obl., 25.5 × 19.4 cm.; 20 f. numbered [i 41]–xx 60 (T: 22 folios; B: 18 folios)

Sign.: l^{4}–p^{4}; ll^{4}–pp^{4}; L^{4}–P^{6}; LL^{4}–PP^{2} (T = L; B = LL; T: P ii instead of L ii; final gathering marked P i, P ii, P iii)

Paris: Bibliothèque Nationale, Rés. Vm^{1} 141 (S)
Rome: Biblioteca Apostolica Vaticana, Capella Sixtina 243, III
Vienna: Österreichische Nationalbibliothek, SA 78.C. 1/ Lib. 3

1. Salve celeberrima virgo, Dei genitrix I Hæc est illa dulcissima quæ sanctarum sanctissima II	[à 8]	i^{v} 41^{v}
2. Ad nutum Domini nostrum I Ut vitium virtus operiret gratia culpam II	[à 6]	iii^{v} 43^{v}
3. Virgo clemens et benigna I Felix et beata Deo fecundata II	[à 6]	v^{v} 45^{v}
4. O florens rosa, mater Domini speciosa I Genitrix, virgo, mater salutis II	[à 6]	vi^{v} 46^{v}

5.	Felix nanque es, sacra virgo Maria I Ora pro populo, interveni pro clero II	[à 5]	vii^v 47^v
6.	Stirps Jesse virgam produxit I Virgo Dei genitrix virga est flos filius eius II	[à 5]	viii^v 48^v
7.	Vidi speciosam sicut columbam I Quæ est ista quæ processit II	[à 5]	ix^v 49^v
8.	Stella maris, luminosa virga florens et frondosa I O Maria singularis matertori expers maris II	[à 5]	x^v 50^v
9.	Tu Deus noster suavis et verus es I Nosse enim te consummata justicia est II	[à 5]	xii^v 52^v
10.	Angelus Domini apparuit Zachariæ I Vox clamantis in deserto, parate viam Domini II	[à 5]	xiii^v 53^v
11.	Isti sunt viri sancti quos elegit Dominus I Sancti per fidem vicerunt regna II	[à 5]	xiiii^v 54^v
12.	Gregem tuum, o pastor æterne I Ave præsul gloriose Deum venerari II	[à 5]	xv^v 55^v
13.	Quam pulchra es et quam decora I Veni, dilecte mi, egrediamur in ortum II	[à 4]	xvii^v 57^v
14.	Spes salutis pacis portus I Tu es enim decus honestatis II	[à 4]	xviii^v 58^v
15.	Benedictus Dominus Deus Israel I Honor, virtus et potestas sit Trinitati II	[à 4]	xix^v 59^v

Finis

Title page reproduced in *MGG* VIII, col. 1317–1318.

1542

106

Neufiesme liure cōtenāt xxviii. Chāsons / NOVVELLES A QVATRE PARTIES, EN VNG VOLVME / *& en deux, Imprimees par Pierre Attaingnant & Hubert Iullet, / libraires & imprimeurs de musique du Roy, demourans a / Paris en la Rue de la Harpe pres leglise S. Cosme.* / 1542. / [Table] / **Superius & Tenor.** / *Auec priuilege du Roy, pour six ans.* /

2 vol. in-4° obl. 21 × 15.8 cm.; 16 f. numbered [i]–xvi
Sign.: ((i⁴–((m⁴; ((I⁴–((M⁴ (S–T: ((I ii, ((K i, ((K ii, CT–B: () K ii)
RISM–I, 1542¹³

London: British Museum, K. 8. b. 5 (2) (Ct–B)
Munich: Bayerische Staatsbibliothek, Mus. Pr. 4° 103
Verona: Accademia Filarmonica, 207/III

1.	O comme heureux t'estimeroys mon cueur	Certon	i^v
2.	Par ton seul bien ma jeunesse est heureuse	Maillard	i^v
3.	Le train d'amour a l'incertain suivy	Maillard	ii^v
4.	Si fermeté qu'on dict estre en amours	Maillard	ii^v
*5.	Que n'est elle aupres de moy celle que j'ayme	Certon	iii^v

* Modern edition in *Anthologie.*

6.	Vous m'aviés vostre cueur donné	Mornable	iiii^v
7.	Avecques vous mon amour finira	L'huyllier	iiii^v
8.	L'ardent désir du hault bien désiré	Certon	v^v
9.	Pauvre et loyal trompé par l'espérance	Mittantier	v^v
10.	O triste adieu qui tant me mescontente	Certon	vi^v
11.	Que gaignez vous a vouloir différer	Maille	vi^v
12.	Force d'amour souvent me veult contraindre	Villiers	vii^v
13.	Espoir est grand mais contentement passe	Certon	vii^v
14.	Ce moys de may au joly vert bosquet	Bouteiller	viii^v
15.	L'aultrier je veiz par ung clair matinet	De Porta	ix^v
16.	Contente ou non il fault que je l'endure	Sohier	x^v
17.	Moins je la veulx plus m'en croist le désir	Mittantier	x^v
18.	O feu d'amour qui m'as tout consommé	Certon	xi^v
†19.	Il n'est trésor que de lyesse	Lupi	xi^v
20.	La nuyct passée en mon lict je songeoye	Mornable	xii^v
21.	Si Dieu vouloit pour ung jour seullement	Mornable	xii^v
22.	Celuy qui fust du bien et du torment de mes amours	Mittantier	xiii^v
23.	Du corps absent le cueur je te présente	Certon	xiii^v
24.	Ayant son cueur rompu la loyaulté	Maillard	xiiii^v
25.	Vouldriés vous bien estant de vous aymée	Maille	xiiii^v
26.	Est-il poinct vray ou si je l'ay songé	Maille	xv^v
27.	A qui me doibz-je retirer	Maille	xv^v
28.	Trop plus que heureux sont les amantz parfaitz	Le hugier	xvi^v

Finis

Revised edition of **92**, lacking nos. 5, 11, 12, and 14. Nos. 3, 4, 12, 13, and 18 are new.

† Modern edition in *Chorwerk, Vol. 15.*

1542

107

Vnziesme liure cōtenant xxviij. Chāsons / NOVVELLES A QVATRE PARTIES, EN VNG VOLVME / *& en deux, Imprimees par Pierre Attaingnant & Hubert Iullet,* / *libraires & imprimeurs de musique du Roy, demourans a* / *Paris en la Rue de la Harpe pres leglise S. Cosme.* / 1542. / [Table] / **Superius & Tenor.** / *Auec priuilege du Roy, pour six ans.* /

2 vol. in-4° obl., 21 × 15.8 cm.; 16 fol. numbered [i]–xvi
Sign.: † r^4–† u^4; † R^4–† V^4
RISM-I, 1542^{15}

Verona: Accademia Filarmonica, 207/V
Vienna: Österreichische Nationalbibliothek, SA 76 F49 (T ii instead of † T ii)

Contents same as **101**.

108

Vnziesme liure cõtenant xxviij. Châsons / NOVVELLES A QVATRE PARTIES, EN DEVX VOLVMES / *imprimees Par Pierre Attaingnant, libraire & Imprimeur de Musique du Roy / demourant a Paris en la Rue de la Harpe, pres leglise S Cosme.* / 1542. / [Table] / **Superius & Tenor** / *Auec priuilege du Roy pour six ans.* /

2 vol. in-4° obl., 21 × 15.8 cm.; 16 f. numbered [i]–xvi
Sign.: XI r[4]–XI u[4]; XI R[4]–XI U[4]
RISM–I, 1542[14]

London: British Museum, K. 8. b. 5 (3) (Ct–B)
Munich: Bayerische Staatsbibliothek, Mus. Pr. 4° 103

Contents same as **101**.

109

Douziesme liure cõtenant xxx. Châsons / NOVVELLES A QVATRE PARTIES, EN VNG VOLVME / *& en deux, Imprimees par Pierre Attaingnant & Hubert Iullet, libraires / & imprimeurs de musique du Roy, demourans a paris en la Rue / de la Harpe pres leglise Sainct Cosme.* 1543. / [Table] / **Superius & Tenor.** / *Auec priuilege du Roy, pour six ans.* /

2 vol. in-4° obl., 21 × 15.8 cm.; 16 fol. numbered [i]–xvi
Sign.: † x[4]–† &[4]; † X[4]–† Æ[4]
RISM–I, 1543[8]

Verona: Accademia Filarmonica, 207/VI (R instead of X, both books; y ii instead of † y ii; † & ii on f. xvi instead of f. xiiii)
Vienna: Österreichische Nationalbibliothek, SA 76 F49

			109, 110
1.	M'amye ung jour le Dieu Mars désarma	Certon	i^v
2.	Celle qui m'a le nom d'amy donné	Sandrin	i^v
3.	Ce qui est plus en ce monde amyable	Sandrin	ii^v
4.	J'ay veu que j'estoys franc et maistre	Sandrin	ii^v
5.	Cessez mon cueur de tant penser en elle	Colin	iii^v
6.	Longtemps y a que langueur et tristesse	Godard	iii^v
7.	Or sus Amour, puisque tu m'as attaint	Claudin	iiii^v
8.	Le cueur loyal en amour est déçeu	L'huyllier	iiii^v
9.	De ce brandon qui tant de cueurs enflame	Gentian	v^v
10.	L'oeil donne au cueur par son aspec	Certon	v^v

11.	Tant seullement ton amour je demande	Mittantier	vi^{v}
12.	Espoir est grand mais contentement passe	Claudin	vi^{v}
13.	Cessez mes yeux de tant vous tormenter	Morel	vii^{v}
14.	Celer ne puis ne monstrer par faintise	Ebran	viii^{v}
15.	Content seray quant elle sera mienne	Certon	viii^{v}
*16.	Si de bon cueur j'ayme bien une dame	Jennequin	ix^{v}
17.	Las, si amour, vertu, compaigne avoit	Maille	ix^{v}
18.	Peur de refuz de mon espérer bien	Certon	x^{v}
†19.	Celle qui a fascheux mari	Gentian	x^{v}
†20.	De long travail heureuse récompense	Certon	xi^{v}
21.	Quant ung bien par longtemps est attendu avoir	Sandrin	xi^{v}
22.	Mon cueur avez présent vous en ay faict	Ebran	xii^{v}
23.	Il est vray que vostre oeil qui pleure, le mien tente	Harchadelt	xii^{v}
24.	Voyez comment vous pourriez par rigueur	Le Moyne	xiii^{v}
25.	De tout le mal que d'ung vouloir constant	Certon	xiii^{v}
26.	Dieu des amantz qui mon feu congnoissez	Harchadel	xiiii^{v}
27.	Deux vrays amants n'ont q'ung vouloir ensemble	Certon	xiiii^{v}
28.	De faire bien et servir loyaulement	Gentian	xv^{v}
29.	Ta grand beaulté, ton amoureux maintien	Wauquel	xv^{v}
30.	Ou est le fruict que pres de vous pourchasse	Gosse	xvi^{v}

The Vienna copy differs slightly in title, as follows:

Douziesme liure cōtenant xxx. Chāsons / NOVVELLES A QVATRE PARTIES, EN VNG VOLVME / *& en deux, Imprimees par Pierre Attaingnant & Hubert Iullet,* / *libraires & imprimeurs de musique du Roy, demourans a* / *Paris en la Rue de la Harpe pres leglise S. Cosme.* / 1543. / [Table] / **Superius & Tenor.** / *Auec priuilege du Roy. pour six ans.* /

* Modern edition as *Masterworks, Vol. 8.*
† Modern edition in *Chansons polyphoniques.*

1543

110

Douziesme liure cōtenant xxx. Chansōs / NOVVELLES A QVATRE PARTIES, EN DEVX / *uolumes imprimees Par pierre Attaingnant, libraire & Imprimeur* / *de Musique du Roy demourant a Paris en la Rue de la* / *Harpe, pres leglise S. Cosme.* / 1543. / [Table] / **Superius & Tenor.** / *Auec priuilege du Roy pour six ans.* /

2 vol. in-4° obl., 21 × 15.8 cm.; 16 fol. numbered [i]–xvi
Sign.: XII x^{4}–XII &^{4}; XII X^{4}–XII Æ^{4} (S–T: x instead of z)
RISM-I, 1543[7]

Munich: Bayerische Staatsbibliothek, Mus. Pr. 4° 103

Contents same as **109**.

111

Tresiesme liure contenant xix Chansons / NOVVELLES A QVATRE PARTIES, EN DEVX VOLVMES / *Imprimees par Pierre Attaingnant & Hubert Iullet, libraires & / imprimeurs de musique du Roy, demourans a Paris en la / Rue de la Harpe pres leglise Sainct Cosme.* / 1543. / [Table] / **Superius & Tenor.** / *Auec priuilege du Roy, pour six ans.* /

Ct–B: 1545 / [Table] /

2 vol. in-4° obl., 21 × 15.8 cm.; 16 f. numbered [i]–xvi
Sign.: ∴ a^4–∴ d^4; ∴ A^4–∴ D^4
RISM–I, 1543[9]

Munich: Bayerische Staatsbibliothek, Mus. Pr. 4° 103
Vienna: Österreichische Nationalbibliothek, SA 76 F49

			111, 112
*1.	Ung jour ung galland engrossa	Certon	i^v
2.	Si j'estoys Dieu vous seriés tous mes anges	Guyon	ii^v
3.	Ung mari se voulant coucher	Jannequin	iii^v
4.	Ung compaignon joly et en bon poinct	Jannequin	iiii^v
5.	Ce tendron est si doulce chose	Jannequin	v^v
†6.	Martin s'en alla au lendit	Certon	v^v
7.	J'ay veu le cerf du boys sailly	Manchicourt	vi^v
8.	A ce joly moys de may	Jannequin	vii^v
9.	En m'en venant de veoir m'amye	Jannequin	vii^v
10.	Frere Lubin revenant de la queste	Jannequin	viii^v
‡11.	Hault le boys m'amye Margot	Godard	viii^v
12.	Jaquet ung jour voyant son poinct	Hebran	ix^v
§13.	Ouvrez-moy l'huys, hé Jehanneton m'amye	Jannequin	x^v
14.	Ung jour que madame dormoit	Jannequin	xi^v
15.	L'aultre jour ung gentil galland	Josselme	xii^v
16.	Maistre Roland fort de loysir	Peletier	xiii^v
17.	A ung Guillaume, apprenti, dist son maistre	Passereau	xiiii^v
‖18.	Il y a, non a, si a, il y a qui me chatoille	Clemens	xv^v
19.	S'il est ainsy que congnée sans manche	Vassal	xvi^v
	Finis		

* Modern edition in *Thirty Chansons (1960).*
§ Modern edition in *Trente Chansons (1928).*
‖ Modern edition in *CMM 4:X.*
† Modern edition in *Chorwerk, Vol. 82.*
‡ Modern edition in *Quinze Chansons.*

1543

112

Tresiesme liure cōtenant xix. Chansons / NOVVELLES A QVATRE PARTIES, EN VNG VOLVME / *& en deux, Imprimees par Pierre Attaingnant &*

Hubert Iullet, / libraires & imprimeurs de musique du Roy, demourans a / Paris en la Rue de la Harpe pres leglise S. Cosme. / 1543. / [Table] / **Superius & Tenor.** / *Auec priuilege du Roy, pour six ans.* /

2 vol. in-4° obl., 21 × 15.8 cm.; 16 fol. numbered [i]–xvi
Sign.: ∵ a⁴–∵ d⁴; ∵ A⁴–∵ D⁴
RISM–I, 1543[10]

Verona: Accademia Filarmonica, 207/VII
Contents same as **111**.

113

Quatorsiesme liure cōtenāt xxix. Chāsōs / NOVVELLES A QVATRE PARTIES, EN VNG VOLVME / *& en deux, Imprimees par Pierre Attaingnant & Hubert Iullet, / libraires & imprimeurs de musique du Roy, demourans a / Paris en la Rue de la Harpe pres leglise S. Cosme.* / 1543. / [Table] / **Superius & Tenor.** / *Auec priuilege du Roy, pour six ans.* /

2 vol. in-4° obl., 21 × 15.8 cm.; 16 fol. numbered [i]–xvi
Sign.: ∵ e⁴–∵ h⁴; ∵ E⁴–∵ H⁴
RISM–I, 1543[12]

Verona: Accademia Filarmonica, 207/VIII

			113, 114
1.	Le feu d'amour que grande confiance	Claudin	i^v
2.	Or veit mon cueur en grand tristesse	Jannequin	i^v
3.	Si de beaucoup je suys aymée	Sandrin	ii^v
4.	Mais pourquoy n'oze l'on prendre	Sandrin	ii^v
5.	Cesse mon oeil de plus la regarder	Ebran	iii^v
6.	Nostre amytié et nouvelle alliance	Poilhiot	iii^v
7.	Rien n'est plus cher que ce que l'on désire	Villiers	iiii^v
8.	Plus je le voy de beaucoup estimé	Belin	iiii^v
9.	La volunté si longtemps endormie	Sandrin	v^v
[1]10.	La doulce fin ou tend vostre pensée	Goudeaul	v^v
11.	A tous propos ou je pense venir	Mornable	vi^v
*12.	Bouche de corail précieux	Goudeaul	vi^v
13.	Le bien qu'on nous demande	Certon	vii^v
14.	Pleust or a Dieu celle qui tant a faict	Guyon	vii^v
15.	Hélas amy, je congnois bien veu l'amytié que tu me porte	Goudeaul	viii^v
16.	Dieu des amanz ton povoir est petit	Goudeaul	viii^v
17.	Dames d'honneur vouez mon adventure	Sandrin	ix^v
18.	Ce qui m'est deu et ordonné	Sandrin	ix^v

* Modern edition in *Chansons polyphoniques.*

[1] **113** only.

19.	L'aveugle Amour, ce petit envieux		x^v
20.	Vostre gent corps et précieuse face	Meigret	x^v
21.	Si elle fuit et se rend intraictable	Wauquel	xi^v
22.	Amour m'oyant souvent gémir et plaindre	Meigret	xi^v
23.	J'ai dict, j'ay faict pour sa beaulté	Jannequin	xii^v
24.	Le vin qui si cher m'est vendu	Romain	xii^v
25.	Cent mille fois et en cent mille sortes	Sohier	xiii^v
26.	La nuict passée ung songe m'assaillit	Meigret	xiiii^v
27.	Si l'amytié voire tant véhémente	L'huyllier	xiiii^v
28.	Le jour qu'Amour sur moy eut tant de force	Certon	xv^v
29.	Si franchement déclariés vostre cueur	Manchicourt	xvi^v

Finis

1543

113 bis

Quatorsiesme liure cōtenāt xxix. Chāsos / NOVVELLES A QVATRE PARTIES, EN DEVX VOLVMES / *Imprimees par Pierre Attaingnant & Hubert Iullet, libraires & / imprimeurs de musique du Roy, demourans a Paris en la / Rue de la Harpe pres leglise Sainct Cosme.* / 1543. / [Table] / **Superius & Tenor.** / *Auec priuilege du Roy, pour six ans.*

2 vol. in-4° obl., 21 × 15.8 cm.; 16 fol. numbered [i]–xvi
Sign.: ∵ e^4–∵ h^4; ∵ E^4–∵ H^4 (∵ g i, ∵ g ii, ∵ h i, ∵ h ii; ∵ F ii, ∵ Gi, ∵ H i ∵ H ii)

Vienna: Österreichische Nationalbibliothek, SA 76 F49

Contents same as **113**.

1543

114

Quatorsiesme liure cōtenāt xxix. Chāsōs / NOVVELLES A QVATRE PARTIES, EN DEVX VOLVMES / *imprimees Par Pierre Attaingnant, libraire & imprimeur de Musique du Roy demourant / a Paris en la Rue de la Harpe pres leglise S. Cosme.* / 1543. / [Table] / **Superius & Tenor** / *Auec prorogation du priuilege du Roy, De nouuel obtenu par ledit attaingnant / Pour les liures Ia par luy imprimez & quil Imprimera cy apres iusques a six ans.* /

2 vol. in-4° obl., 21 × 15.8 cm.; 16 fol. numbered [i]–xvi
Sign.: XIIII e^4–XIIII h^4; XIIII E^4–XIIII H^4
RISM–I, 1543^{11}

Munich: Bayerische Staatsbibliothek, Mus. Pr. 4° 103

Contents same as **113** except for substitution for no 10: "Vive sera pour jamais n'estre morte" (Du tartre) in place of "La doulce fin ou tend vostre pensée."

1543

115

[Jean Conseil. Livre de danceries à six parties. Paris, Pierre Attaingnant, 1543.]

1 vol. in-4° obl.

Fétis gives this information *s.v.* "Attaignant" and "Consilium." *Biographie universelle des musiciens,* 2d ed., Vols. I, II.

1544

116

Quinziesme liure cōtenant xxx. Chāsons / NOVVELLES A QVATRE PARTIES, EN DEVX VOLVMES, / *Imprimees par Pierre Attaingnant & Hubert Iullet, libraires & / imprimeurs de musique du Roy, demourans a Paris en la / Rue de la Harpe pres leglise Sainct Cosme.* / 1544. / [Table] / **Superius & Tenor.** / *Auec priuilege du Roy, pour six ans.*

2 vol. in-4° obl., 21 × 15.8 cm.; 16 fol. numbered [i]–xvi
Sign.: ∵ i^4–∵ m^4; ∵ I^4–∵ M^4 (S–T: ∵ K i, ∵ K ii)

Verona: Accademia Filarmonica, 207/IX
Vienna: Österreichische Nationalbibliothek, SA 76 F49

			116, 117	**118**
1.	Si le bon Dieu, protecteur d'innocence	Certon	i^v	i^v
2.	Si par désir bien désirer et le plaisir point n'empirer	Cętron	i^v	ii^v
3.	Sortez mes pleurs, hastez vous de descendre	Mornable	ii^v	vi^v
4.	En espérant souvent espoir m'asseure	Poilhiot	ii^v	iii^v
5.	En espérant qu'au nouveau temps d'ever	Maille	iii^v	iiii^v
6.	Corps s'esloignant faict son cueur approcher	Claudin	iii^v	v^v
7.	En n'aymant rien fors qu'elle seulement	Ebran	iiii^v	vii^v
8.	Le doulx regard du bien que je désire	Godard	iiii^v	viii^v
9.	O mal d'aymer qui tous maulx oultrepasse	Jannequin	v^v	xii^v
10.	Le cler soleil au plus hault degré luyt	Maille	v^v	ix^v

11.	Pleust or a Dieu pour fuyr mes malheurs	Poilhiot	vi^{v}	x^{v}
12.	Si j'ay aymé soubz espérance	Romain	vi^{v}	xi^{v}
13.	Dame d'honneur ou vertu se repose	Maille	vii^{v}	xiii^{v}
14.	O mes amys, n'ayez compassion	Mornable	vii^{v}	xv^{v}
*15.	Fy d'amours et de leur alliance	Claudin	viii^{v}	xvi^{v}
16.	L'enfant Amour n'a plus son arc estrange	De Marle	viii^{v}	xiiii^{v}
17.	La palme doulce avant que feulles rendre	Gardane	ix^{v}	xvii^{v}
18.	Si l'on me monstre affection	Belin	ix^{v}	xviii^{v}
†19.	Qui veult d'amour sçavoir tous les esbatz	Jannequin	x^{v}	xx^{v}
20.	En fut-il onc une plus excellente	Jannequin	x^{v}	xix^{v}
21.	Las, on peult juger clerement	Jannequin	xi^{v}	xxi^{v}
22.	Venez regretz, venez peine et soulcy	Meigret	xi^{v}	xxii^{v}
23.	Par le seul traict de voz yeulx	Meigret	xii^{v}	xxiii^{v}
24.	Hélas, tel feu dans le cueur m'avez mis	Gardane	xiii^{v}	xxx^{v}
25.	De peu assez a cil qui se contente	Gardane	xiii^{v}	xxxi^{v}
[1]26.	Au fort il ne m'en chault	Certon	xiiii^{v}	xxv^{v}
27.	Ung si grand bien c'est raison qu'il s'attende	L'huyllier	xiiii^{v}	xxviii^{v}
28.	Je sens l'affection qui a moy se vient rendre	Boyvin	xv^{v}	xxvi^{v}
29.	Oeil peu constant, messagier des pensées	D'Auxerre	xv^{v}	xxvii^{v}
30.	Si je n'avoys ung qui mon cueur contente	Belin	xvi^{v}	xxix^{v}
	Finis			

* Modern edition in *Anthologie*.
† Modern edition in *Trente Chansons (1928)*.

[1] Vienna copy and **118** read: O fort il ne m'en chault.

1544

117

Quinziesme liure cõtenant xxx. Chãsons / NOVVELLES A QVATRE PARTIES, EN DEVX VOLVMES / *imprimees Par Pierre Attaingnant, libraire & Imprimeur de Musique du Roy / demourant a Paris en la Rue de la Harpe, pres leglise S. Cosme.* / 1544. / [Table] / **Superius & Tenor** / *Auec priuilege du Roy pour six ans.* /

2 vol. in-4° obl., 21 × 15.8 cm.; 16 f. numbered [i]–xvi (Ct–B: v vi vii xv; xiii xiiii xv xi)
Sign.: XV i^{4}–XV m^{4}; XV I^{4}–XV M^{4}
RISM–I, 1544[7]

London: British Museum, K. 8. b. 5 (4) (Ct–B)
Munich: Bayerische Staatsbibliothek, Mus. Pr. 4° 103

Contents same as **116**.

118

Quinziesme liure cõtenant xxx. Chãsons / NOVVELLES A QVATRE PARTIES, EN VNG VOLVME, / *Imprimees par Pierre Attaingnant & Hubert Iullet, libraires & / imprimeurs de musique du Roy, demourans a Paris en la / Rue de la Harpe pres leglise Sainct Cosme.* / 1544. / [Table] / *Auec priuilege du Roy, pour six ans.* /

1 vol. in-4° obl., 21 × 15.8 cm.; 32 f. numbered [i]–xxxii
Sign.: ∵ R^4–∵ A^4
RISM–I, 1544^8

Erlangen: Universitätsbibliothek, 4° Kst. 24^c

Contents same as **116**.

The Erlangen set is bound with tooled leather and metal clasps, probably of the sixteenth century. It is inscribed at the bottom of the first title page: "Sum ex libris Johannis Theodorici Semleri fuit ingens diluvium Norimbergae."

119

Petri Manchicurtii Bethunii inclite / TORNACENSIS ECCLESIE PVERORVM SYMPHONIACORVM MODERA / *toris, modulorum musicalium* PRIMVS TOMVS. *Petri attingentis Regij musice calcographi / sumptu & labore nuper impressus. Parisiis in uico Cythare non procul a Sanctorum / Cosme ac Damiani templo.* / 1545. / [Table] / **Superius.** / *Cum priuilegio Regis ad sexennium.* /

4 vol. in-4° obl., 21.4 × 16 cm.; 16 f. numbered [i]–xvi (S, Ct, B: ix x xi xi; T: ix ix xi xi)
Sign.: I. Manchicourt a^4–I. Manchicourt d^4; I. Manchicourt aa^4–I. Manchicourt dd^4; I. Manchicourt AA^4–I. Manchicourt DD^4; I. Manchicourt A^4–I. Manchicourt D^4

Florence: Biblioteca del Conservatorio, Basevi 2496 (2)
Paris: Bibliothèque Sainte-Geneviève, Vm 93 Rés (S)
Vicenza: Biblioteca Bertoliana, FF. 2.7.23 (2) (S)

1.	Vidi speciosam sicut columbam I Quæ est ista quæ processit II	8 ss cc tt bb	ii
2.	Laudem dicite Deo nostro, omnes sancti eius I Laudate Dominum Deum, omnes gentes II	5 ss	iii^v

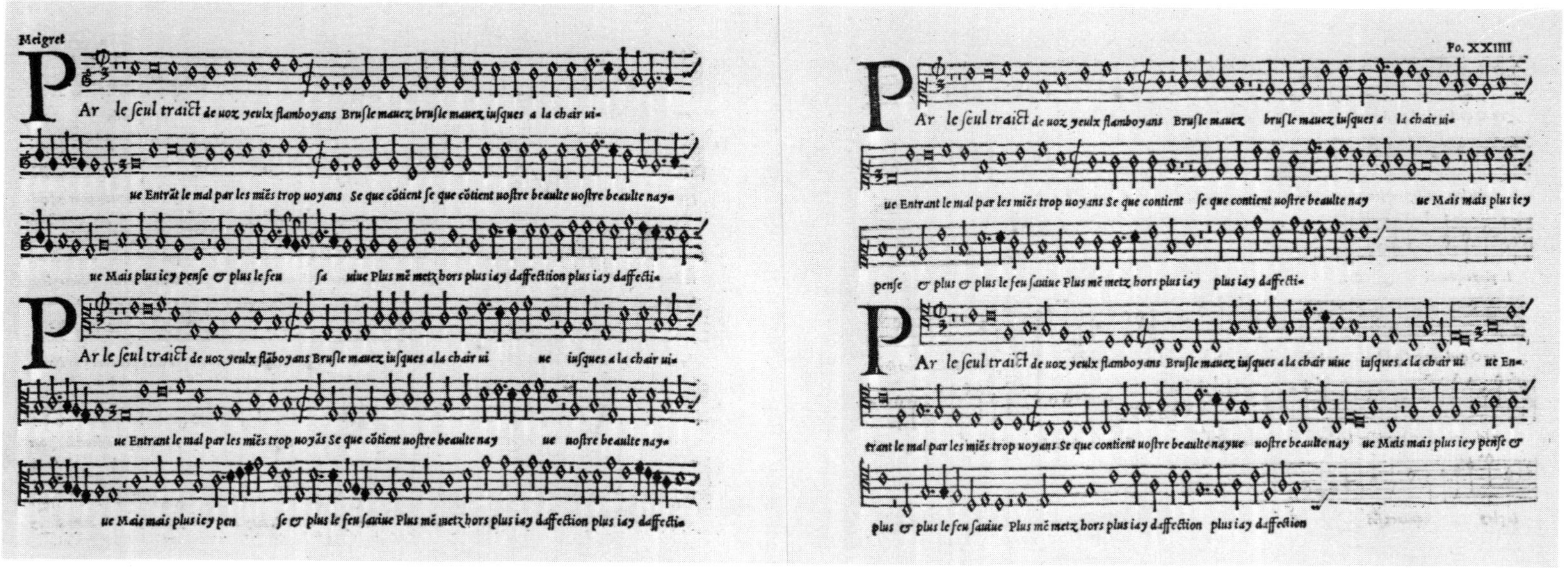

23 Double page from **118,** showing "En ung livre" format. (reduced) By courtesy of the Universitätsbibliothek, Erlangen.

3. Interrogabat magos Herodes quod signum vidistis I Et ecce stella antecedebat eos II	5 ss	v
4. Ave stella matutina, mundi princeps et regina I Tu es area compluta, cælesti rore imbuta II	5 tt	v[v]
5. Ego sum panis vivus qui de cælo descendi I Caro enim mea vere est cibus II	5 tt	vi[v]
6. Peccantem me quotidie, et non pænitentem I Commissa mea pavesco, et ante te erubesco II		vii
7. Ave virgo gloriosa, stella sole clarior		viii
8. O intemerata et in æternum benedicta I O virgo gloriosa, mater Dei, pietate plenissima II		viii[v]
9. Paratum cor meum, Deus, cantabo et psallam I Exaltare in virtute tua, Domine II		ix
10. Vias tuas, Domine, demonstra mihi I Eripe me de inimicis meis, Domine II		x
11. Domine, non secundum peccata nostra I Quare memento nostri, Domine II		xi
12. Ne reminiscaris, Domine, delicta nostra		xi[v]
13. Proba me, Domine, et scito cor meum I Respice in me, Deus, et miserere mei II		xii
14. Ne derelinquas me, Domine, dominator vitæ meæ I Propterea confitebor tibi, Domine II		xiii
15. Ecce odor filii mei sicut odor agri pleni I Esto Dominus fratrum tuorum II		xiii[v]
16. Cantantibus organis, decantabat Cæcilia virgo I Cæcilia virgo gloriosa, semper evangelium Christi II		xiiii[v]
17. Super montem excelsum ascende I Judæa et Hierusalem nolite timere II		xv
18. Usquequo piger, dormies? I Vade ad formicam, o piger II		xv[v]
19. Domine Jesu Christe, pastor bone		xvi[v]

Finis

i[v]: INTEGERRIMO AC DOCTISSIMO VIRO REMIGIO RVFFO / Cādido insignis Ecclesiae Turonēsis canonico meritissimo P. Māchicurtius. S. D. / . . . / Egidij de Sermisy ad P. Manchicurtium /

For full text and translation of dedication see Appendix, 10.

Concerning the Sainte-Geneviève copy see **141**.

Revised edition of **85**, lacking nos. 1, 2, and 3. Nos. 1, 3, and 19 are new. See **85** for modern edition.

1545

120

[—Secundus tomus. Ibid. 1545]

4 vol. in-4° obl.

121

[—Tertius tomus. Ibid. 1545]

4 vol. in-4° obl.

Sébastien de Brossard lists these volumes after describing **119**: "Manchicourt. Modulorum musicalium Primus tomus. Paris, P. Attaingnant, 1545. 4 parties 4° obl." Paris, Bibliothèque Nationale, MSS N.A. lat. 519–530. Brossard noted these volumes upon visits to the Ballards' publishing house in 1701–1702. See E. Lebeau, "La Bibliothèque des éditeurs Ballard" *XVIIe siècle* (1954), nos. 21–22, pp. 456–462.

122

Guillermi le heurteur, Ecclesiae diui / MARTINI TVRONENSIS CANONICI, ARTISQVE MODVLATORIE / *peritissimi professoris, Operum musicalium liber primus* / *XVII. modulorum index.* / [Table] / *Parisiis in uico Cythare nō procul a sanctorum Cosme & Damiani templo,* / *Apud Petrum attaingnant regium musicae calcographum.* 1545. / **Superius.** / *Cum Regis priuilegio ad sexennium.* /

4 vol. in-4° obl., 21.4 × 16.1 cm.; 16 f. numbered [i]–xvi (S: xiii xiv xv xv)
Sign.: I. Heurteur a4–I. Heurteur d4; I. Heurteur aa4–I. Heurteur dd4; I. Heurteur AA4–I. Heurteur DD4; I Heurteur A4–I. Heurteur D4
Florence: Biblioteca del Conservatorio, Basevi 2496 (1)

1. Surge, propera, amica mea I	6 ss tt	i^v
Veni de libano soror mea sponsa II		
2. Nesciens mater virgo virum I	6 cc bb	ii^v
Virgo verbo concepit, virgo permansit II		
3. Anima mea liquefacta est I-T: Canon	6 cc tt	v
Adjuro vos, filiæ Jhersualem II		
4. Noe, noe, noe, hodie natus est Christus I	6 bb cc	v^v
Hodie de cælo vera pax descendit II		
5. Antequam comedam suspiro I	5 tt	vi
Si bona suscepimus de manu Domini II		
6. Virgo Dei genitrix quem totus non capit orbis I	5 ss	vii
Te matrem pietatis opem te clamitat orbis II		
7. Congratulamini michi omnes I	5 ss	ix
Tulerunt Dominum meum II		
8. Jocundare, filia Hierusalem I		ix^v
Quem vidistis pastoris dicite II		
9. Ecce venit ad templum sanctum tuum I		x^v
Adorna thalamum tuum, Syon II		
10. Congratulamini michi omnes I		xi
Contremuerunt omnia membra mea II		
11. In te, Domine, speravi I		xi^v
Quoniam fortitudo mea II		
12. Christum ascendentem in cælum I		xii^v
Omnis pulchritudo Domini exaltata est II		
13. Tempus est ut revertar ad eum I		xiii^v
Non vos relinquam orphanos II		
14. Audite insulæ et attendite populi I		xiiii
Posuit os meum quasi gladium acutum II		

15.	Ego flos campi et lilia convallium I Ego mater pulchræ dilectionis II	xiiii^{v}
16.	Tota pulchra es, amica mea I Quam pulchræ sunt mammæ tuæ II	xv^{v}
17.	Vidi sub altare Dei I Divinum acceperunt responsum II	xvi

Finis

123

Seysiesme liure contenant xxix. Chansõs / NOVVELLES A QVATRE PARTIES, EN DEVX VOLVMES / *Imprimees par Pierre Attaingnant & Hubert Iullet, libraires & / imprimeurs de musique du Roy, demourans a Paris en la / Rue de la Harpe pres leglise Sainct Cosme.* / 1545. / [Table] / **Superius & Tenor.** / *Auec priuilege du Roy, pour six ans.* /

2 vol. in-4° obl., 21 × 16.8 cm.; f. numbered [i]–xvi (S–T: iv vi vi vii)
Sign.: ∴ n^4–∴ q^4; ∴ N^4–∴ Q^4
RISM–I, 1545[8]

Augsburg: Staats- und Stadtbibliothek (S–T), Tonk. Schl. 132
Vienna: Österreichische Nationalbibliothek, SA 76 F49

			123, 124	**125**
1.	Di moy Amour, si je fais mon debvoir	Le Gendre	i^{v}	ix^{v}
2.	Ma bouche n'oze dire mon amoureux désir	Certon	i^{v}	iiii^{v}
*3.	Je fille quant Dieu my donne de quoy	Gosse	ii^{v}	i^{v}
[1]4.	En fut-il oncque une plus excellente	Certon	iii^{v}	v^{v}
5.	Si vous la baisez, comptez quinze	Passereau	iii^{v}	iii^{v}
6.	La vraye amour cause persévéranse	Meigret	iiii^{v}	xv^{v}
7.	Loing de tes yeulx t'amour me vient poursuivre	Le Moyne	iiii^{v}	xii^{v}
8.	Pourquoy m'es-tu tant ennemye	[2][Manchicourt]	v^{v}	vi^{v}
9.	Ton doulx regard donne peine a mon cueur		vi^{v}	x^{v}
10.	Ce bon parler yssu de vostre bouche	Meigret	vi^{v}	xiii^{v}
11.	Tous les malheurs que j'ay pour l'amour d'elle	Sandrin	vii^{v}	xi^{v}
12.	J'ay court plaisir et longue patience		vii^{v}	viii^{v}
13.	Ung doulx regard, ung parler amoureulx	Meigret	viii^{v}	xvii^{v}
14.	Miséricorde au pauvre langoureulx		viii^{v}	xix^{v}
15.	Leur entreprinse est trop lourdement faicte	Certon	ix^{v}	xx^{v}
16.	Puisque ton dard m'a mis soubz ta puissance	[3]Léfé	ix^{v}	xxi^{v}
17.	Tu parle trop ma bouche, c'est trop faict	Wauquel	x^{v}	xviii^{v}
18.	Troys mois y a que j'attens ung bon jour	[3]Léfé	x^{v}	xxiii^{v}

* Modern edition in *Theatrical Chansons.*

[1] **124, 125:** En fut-il onc une plus excellente.
[2] Attribution after *Le Second Livre de Chansons* . . . , Antwerp, Susato, 1544, f. 2.
Attribution in **123** only.

[4]19. On le m'a dict, je ne l'ay pas songé	Mage	xi^{v}	
20. En contemplant ung jour ta grand beauté	Morpain	xi^{v}	xiiii^{v}
21. Dame Vénus rendz le cueur amoureulx		xii^{v}	xxv^{v}
†22. Ma peine n'est pas grande	Jennequin	xii^{v}	xxvi^{v}
‡23. Héllas mon Dieu, ton ire s'est tournée	Jannequin	xiii^{v}	xxii^{v}
24. Vous me laissez pour ung aultre	L'huillier	xiii^{v}	xxiii^{v}
25. Amour, héllas, on a pas d'avantaige	Hebran	xiiii^{v}	xxvii^{v}
26. Malheur me suit, fortune me pourchasse	Meigret	xiiii^{v}	xxviii^{v}
27. D'ung nouveau cas, belle, je m'esmerveille	Meigret	xv^{v}	xxix^{v}
28. Ung bien a moy si tres grand se présente	Mornable	xv^{v}	xxx^{v}
29. Si je n'avoys ung qui mon cueur contente	[Belin]	xvi^{v}	xxxi^{v}

Finis

† Modern edition in *Anthologie*.

‡ Modern edition in *Masterworks*, Vol. 13, and in O. Douen, *Clément Marot et le Psautier Huguenot*, Paris, 1879, Vol. II, pp. 78–82; also edited in keyboard score, transposed up a tone, and with attribution to Maillard in A. Souris and R. de Morcourt, *Adrian Le Roy. Premier Livre de Tabulature de Luth (1551)*, Paris, 1960, p. 75.

[4] This piece appears in **123** only.

1545

124

Sexiesme liure contenant xxix. Chansōs / NOVVELLES A QVATRE PARTIES, EN DEVX / *uolumes imprimees Par pierre Attaingnant, libraire & Imprimeur / de Musique du Roy demourant a Paris en la Rue de la / Harpe, pres leglise S. Cosme.* / 1545. / [Table] / **Superius & Tenor.** / *Auec priuilege du Roy pour six ans.* /

2 vol. in-4° obl., 21 × 15.8 cm.; 16 f. numbered [i]–xvi
Sign.: XVI n^{4}–XVI q^{4}; XVI N^{4}–XVI Q^{4}
(RISM–I, 1545[8])

Munich: Bayerische Staatsbibliothek, Mus. Pr. 4° 103

Contents same as **123**, with substitution for no. 19. The sequence of pieces at that point is as follows:

		124	**125**
18. Troys mois y a			
19. En contemplant			
20. La ne fauldra c'est chose toute seure	Manchicourt	xi^{v}	xvi^{v}
21. Dame Venus			

1545

125

Sexiesme liure contenant xxix. Chansōs / NOVVELLES A QVATRE PARTIES, EN VNG / *uolumes imprimees Par pierre Attaingnant, libraire & Imprimeur / de Musique du Roy demourant a Paris en la Rue de la / Harpe, pres leglise S. Cosme.* / 1545. / [Table] / *Auec priuilege du Roy pour six ans.* /

1 vol. in-4° obl., 21 × 15.8 cm.; 32 f. numbered [i]–xxxii (xxix xxx xxi xxxii)
Sign.: XVI R4–XVI &4
RISM-I, 1545[9]

Erlangen: Universitätsbibliothek, 4° Kst. 24c

Contents same as **124**.

1545

126

Dixseptiesme liure cotenāt xix. Chansōs / LEGERES TRES MVSICALES NOVVELLES A / *Quatre parties, en deux uolume. imprimees par Pierre Attaingnant, / libraire & Imprimeur de Musique du Roy demourant a / Paris en la Rue de la Harpe, pres leglise S. Cosme.* / 1545. / [Table] / **Superius & Tenor.** / *Auec priuilege du Roy pour six ans.* /

2 vol. in-4° obl., 21 × 15.8 cm.; 16 f. numbered [i]–xvi
Sign.: XVII r4–XVII u4; XVII R4–XVII U4
RISM–I, 1545[10]

Munich: Bayerische Staatsbibliothek, Mus. Pr. 4° 103
Vienna: Österreichische Nationalbibliothek, SA 76 F 49, (S–T: xiii, xxi, xv, xiiii)

			126	**127**
1.	L'aultre jour de bon matin je rencontray Guillemette	Jannequin	iv	iiiv
2.	Il estoit ung jeune homme qui avoit nom Jennet	Delafont	iv	iiiiv
3.	J'ay bonne grace et beau maintien	Meigret	iiv	[iv]
4.	Une nonnain fort belle et en bon point	Jannequin	iiiv	vv
5.	Ung laboureux sa journée commançoit assez matin	Senserre	iiiiv	[ixv]
6.	Pres d'ung buisson Robin et sa Robine	Vassal	vv	viiv
7.	Gaultier rancontra Janeton qui luy sembla coincte et jolye	Guion	viv	[xiv]
8.	Quelque frapart, homme de bonne mise	Jannequin	viiv	xiiiv
9.	L'aultre jour dedans ung jardin		viiiv	xviv
10.	Penser ne puis comment il se peult	Romain	viiiv	xviiiv
*11.	Au premier jour du joly moys de may	Jannequin	ixv	xviiv
12.	Ung jour Catin venant d'estre bactue	Jannequin	ixv	xvv
13.	Thenot estoit en son cloz resjouy	Senserre	xv	xixv
14.	Ung pelerin que les Teurs avoient pris	Jannequin	xiv	xxiv
15.	Ung jour d'iver Robin tout esperdu	Ebran	xiiv	xxiiiv
16.	En m'esbatant par ung joly matin	Gervaise	xiiiv	xxixv
17.	Une bergiere ung jour aulx champs	Demarle	xiiiiv	xxvv
18.	Hé, que faictes-vous, laissez-moy	Senserre	xvv	[xxviiv]
19.	Ung advocat dist a sa femme	Delafont	xviv	xxxiv

Finis

* Modern edition in *Trente Chansons* (*1928*).

The Vienna copy differs slightly in title, as follows:

Dixseptiesme liure cōtenāt xix Chansōs / LEIGERES TRES MVSIQVALLES NOVVELLES A / QVATRE PARTIES, EN DEVX VOLVMES / *Imprimees Par pierre Attaignant libraire & imprimeur / de musique du Roy, demourant a Paris en la / Rue de la Harpe pres leglise S. Cosme.* / 1545 / [Table] / **Superius & Tenor,** / *Auec priuilege du Roy, pour six ans.* /

Ct–B reads LEGERES and MVSICALLES.

1545

127

[**Dixseptiesme liure cōtenāt xix Chansōs** / LEGERES TRES MVSICALES NOVVELLES A / *Quatre parties, en ung uolume. imprimees par Pierre Attaingnant, / libraire & Imprimeur de Musique du Roy demourant a / Paris en la Rue de la Harpe, pres leglise S. Cosme.* / 1545. / [Table] / *Auec priuilege du Roy pour six ans.* /]

1 vol. in-4° obl., 21 × 15.8 cm.; 32 f. numbered [i]–xxxii (folios i, viii–xi, xxvi, and xxvii lacking)
Sign.: [XVII I]^4–XVII Q^4
RISM-I, 1545^{11}

Erlangen: Universitätsbibliothek, 4° Kst. 24^c

Contents same as **126**.

1545

128

Dixhuytiesme liure contenant xxviij. / CHANSONS NOVVELLES TRES MVSICALES A / *Quatre parties, en deus uolumes imprimees par Pierre Attaignant, / libraire & Imprimeur de Musique du Roy demourant a / Paris en la Rue de la Harpe, pres leglise S. Cosme.* / 1545. / [Table] / **Superius & Tenor.** / *Auec priuilege du Roy pour six ans.* /

2 vol. in-4° obl., 21 × 15.8 cm.; 16 f. numbered [i]–xvi (S–T: xiiii xiiii xv xvi)
Sign.: XVIII x^4–XVIII &^{4}; XVIII X^4–XVIII *A*^{4} (S–T: & i, XVIII & ii; Ct–B: *AA* i, *AA* ii)
RISM-I, 1545^{12}

Munich: Bayerische Staatsbibliothek, Mus. pr. 4° 103

			128	**129**
1.	Las, me fault-il tant de mal supporter	Certon	i^{v}	i^{v}
2.	Je cherche autant amour et le désire	Boyvin	i^{v}	iii^{v}
3.	Tant que le bleu aura nom loyaulté		ii^{v}	iiii^{v}
4.	Filz de Vénus, des amoureux support		ii^{v}	v^{v}
5.	Avant l'aymer je l'ay voulu congnoistre	Sandrin	iii^{v}	vi^{v}
6.	Comment puis-je ma départie	Claudin	iii^{v}	vii^{v}
*†7.	Je n'ay point plus d'affection	Claudin	iiii^{v}	viii^{v}
*8.	Voulant honneur que de vous je m'absente	Sandrin	iiii^{v}	viii^{v}
9.	Quel bien parler ou compter son affaire	Sandrin	v^{v}	x^{v}
10.	Peine et travail ne m'est que esjouyssance	Fresneau	v^{v}	xi^{v}
11.	Par bien servir j'ay dueil pour récompense		vi^{v}	xii^{v}
12.	Content seray quand elle sera mienne	Certon	vii^{v}	xv^{v}
13.	Vertu le veult, et Amour me commande		vii^{v}	xiiii^{v}
14.	O dur amour qui cueurs humains faict cuyre	Jannequin	viii^{v}	xvi^{v}
15.	J'ay double dueil qui vivement me point	Jannequin	viii^{v}	xvii^{v}
16.	Qui dict qu'au mal d'amour la jouyssance	Colin	ix^{v}	xviii^{v}
17.	On le voit bien le mal en quoy je suis		x^{v}	xix^{v}
18.	O cueur ingrat que nature et les Dieux	V. Sohier	x^{v}	xx^{v}
19.	De moy jouyr pour vous rendre joyeulx	V. Sohier	xi^{v}	xx^{v}
‡20.	De ta blancheur qui la neige surpasse	Sandrin	xi^{v}	xxi^{v}
21.	De vostre amour onc soulaige ne fuz	Certon	xii^{v}	xxii^{v}
[1]22.	En mon amour vous n'avez rien perdu	Certon	xii^{v}	xxiiii^{v}
23.	Depuis qu'Amour a son arc esgaré	Ebran	xiii^{v}	xxv^{v}
24.	Rigueur me tient, et doulx acueil m'attire	Claudin	xiiii^{v}	xxvii^{v}
25.	C'est trop pensé pour bien le sçavoir dire	Gentian	xiiii^{v}	xxviii^{v}
26.	Je sens mon heur, et si ne le désire	Gentian	xv^{v}	xxix^{v}
27.	Vénus avoit son filz Amour perdu	De la font	xv^{v}	xxx^{v}
28.	Si quelque fois devant vous me présente	Gentian	xvi^{v}	xxxi^{v}
	Finis			

* Modern edition in Adrian Le Roy, *Premier Livre de Tabulature de Luth*, ed. A. Souris and R. de Morcourt. Paris, 1960.

† Modern edition in *Anthologie*.

‡ Modern edition in *Quinze Chansons*.

[1] Table: En vostre amour.

1545

129

Dixhuytiesme liure contenant xxviij. / CHANSONS NOVVELLES TRES MVSICALES A / *Quatre parties, en ung uolume. imprimees par Pierre Attaignant,* / *libraire & Imprimeur de Musique du Roy demeurant a* / *Paris en la Rue de la Harpe, pres leglise S. Cosme.* / 1545. / [Table] / *Auec priuilege du Roy pour six ans.* /

1 vol. in-4° obl., 21 × 15.8 cm.; 32 f. numbered [i]–xxxii
Sign.: XVIII R^{4}–XVIII Æ^{4} (Z i, XVIII Z ii)
RISM–I, 1545^{13}

Erlangen: Universitätsbibliothek, 4° Kst. 24^{c}

Contents same as **128**, with addition of "Par toy Amour, hélas, je suis laissée de mon amy" (Fresneau) as no. 2, f. ii^{v}. (Not listed in index.)

130

[Jean Le Gendre. Brieve Introduction en la Musique tant au plain chant que choses faites; imprimée à Paris par Pierre Attaingnant, 1554 (sic., for 1545)]

From *La Bibliothèque d'Anthoine Du Verdier . . . contentant la Catalogue de tous ceux qui on escrit ou traduict en François*, Lyon, 1585, *s.v.* Jean Legendre. Du Verdier qualifies the author as "d'Orléans" and as "Mathematicien." La Croix du Maine in his *Bibliothèque* of 1584 has the following entry: "Jean Le Gendre, Parisien. Il a composé un briève introduction en la Musique, imprimée à Paris chez Nicolas du Chemin. Il y a un autre Jean le Gendre, natif d'Orléans, mais je ne sais s'il a rien composé."

Chansons by "Legendre" appear in **41**, **83**, **124**, and **145**.

Fétis in his *Biographie Universelle*, 2d ed. Vol. III, includes the following article:

> "Gendre (Jean Le) né à Paris, au commencement du seizième siècle, fut chantre de la chapelle des rois de France François Ier et Henri II. Il a publié: *Briefue introduction en la musique tant au plain-chant que choses faictes.* Paris, Pierre Attaingnant, 1545. in-8°. Du Verdier a confondu ce Le Gendre avec Jean Le Gendre d'Orléans, mathematicien . . . "

In *A Plaine and Easie Introduction to Practicall Music* London 1597, Thomas Morley among his "ancient writers" cites "Francois Lagendre."

In a revision of Claude Chappuys's *Discours de la court* (Paris, 1543), the following lines are added by François Gentillet (Paris, 1558). The passage follows the lines mentioning Claudin and Sandrin, quoted on p. 92, above:

Ou bien du fort sçavant Pierre Dauxerre
Chantre du Roy, digne de lierre
Ou le couronne, a fin de l'honorer
Pour les doux chants, qu'il sçait mesurer
Soit de motets composez par Le Gendre
Dont la douceur un appetit engendre
D'estudier au noble art de musique
Ou son esprit perfaictement s'applique.
(fol. xvi)

(Italics added)

1545?

131

[Clementis Iannequini Praelium ad Paviam, Alauda: Et alia iucunda. iv. Voc. Venet, ap. Hieron. Scotum. 54. Paris ap. Petr. Attaingnant]

Israel Spach, *Nomenclator scriptorum philosophicorum atque philologicorum*, Strasbourg, 1598, p. 574. Draud, *Biblioteca Classica*, 1611, p. 1203.

"54" should probably read "45"; "La Bataille" and "L'Allouette" appear in *Cl. Janequin . . . Libro Primo*, Venice, Gardano, 1545, and Scotto, 1550. Attaingnant may have brought out another printing of **4** at this time.

Janequin is not known to have composed a "Battle of Pavia" (1525—the worst defeat of Francis I). Subsequent generations interpreted his "La Bataille" or "La Guerre" variously, it appears, although it is beyond doubt that the piece was written in depiction of Marignano (1515—Francis's greatest victory).

1546

132

Missarum musicalium quatuor vocum / cū suis motetis Liber Primus. / [Table] / *Parisiis in uico Cithare apud Petrum Attaingnant / musice typographum prope sanctorum Cosme / & Damiani templum* M.D.xlvi. / **Tenor.** / *Cum priuilegio ad sexennium. /*

4 vol. in-4° obl., 21 × 15.8 cm.; 12 fol. numbered [i]–xii (Ct: vii–xii damaged.)
Sign.: ii^4–ll^4; II^4–LL^4; I^4–L^4 (B: II i, I ii)
RISM–I, 1546^1

Vienna: Gesellschaft der Musikfreunde, II 53300/3 (Ct, T & B)

Contents same as **93**.

1546

133

Missarum musicaliun quatuor vocum / Liber secundus. / [Table] / *Parisiis in uico Cithare apud Petrum Attaingnant / musice typographum prope sanctorum Cosme / & Damiani templum* M.D.xlvi. / **Tenor.** / *Cum priuilegio ad sexennium. /*

4 vol. in-4° obl., 21 × 15.8 cm.; 12 fol. numbered [i]–xii (B: v v vii vii; Ct: all folios damaged.)
Sign.: mm^4–oo^4; MM^4–OO^4; M^4–O^4
RISM–I, 1546^2

Missarum musicalium quatuor vocum cũ suis motetis Liber Primus.

Missa Dulcis amica	Certon	Fo. j
Missa Aue sanctissima	Certon	Fo. v
Missa Domine quis habitabit	Claudin	Fo. viij
Asperges me	Claudin	Fo. iiii
Amen. Et cũ spiritu tuo Et cetera	Claudin	Fo. iiii
O salutaris hostia	Claudin	Fo. iiii

Parisiis in uico Cithare apud Petrum Attaingnant musice typographum prope sanctorum Cosme & Damiani templum M. D. xlvi.

Contratenor

Cum priuilegio ad sexennium.

ii t

24 Title page (Contratenor) of the first volume of Masses "with their motets" **(132)**. By courtesy of the Gesellschaft der Musikfreunde, Vienna.

Vienna: Gesellschaft der Musikfreunde, II 53300/4 (Ct, T & B)

[1]1.	Missa Povre cueur	P. Manchicourt	iv
[2]2.	Missa C'est une dure départie	P. Manchicourt	v
[3]3.	Missa Ave regina	Math. Sohier	viiiv

T, after Agnus I: Trois testes en ung chapperon Deux apres / l'aultre suiveront Modulizans tout doulcement / Les semibreves seullement

Finis

[1] The titles of the first two Masses have been interchanged in the print. "Missa Povre cueur" is based on the anonymous chanson "Povre cueur," **8**-27.

[2] Based on Claudin's "C'est une dure departie," **14**-18.

[3] Based on Sohier's "Ave regina," **64**-1.

[1546?]

134

[Missarum musicalium quatuor vocum. Liber tertius]

A lost edition with at least one Mass by Pierre Colin; Fiches Brossard, Bibliothèque Nationale, MSS N.A. lat. 519–530 (see **121**). After giving the title of **133**, Brossard writes: "Le 3e livre de ce recueil de messes est sous le titre Petrus Colinus."

1546

135

Dixneufiesme liure cōtenāt xxii. Chāsons / NOVVELLES A QVATRE PARTIES, EN DEVX VOLVMES, / *Imprimées par Pierre Attaingnant libraire, & imprimeur / de musique du Roy, demourant a Paris, en la Rue / de la Harpe, pres leglise S. Cosme.* / 1546. / [Table] / **Superius & Tenor** / *Auec priuilege du Roy, pour six ans.* /

2 vol. in-4° obl., 21 × 15.8 cm.; 16 f. numbered [i]–xvi
Sign.: XIX a4–XIX d4; XIX A4–XIX D4
RISM–I, 1546[12]

Munich: Bayerische Staatsbibliothek, Mus. Pr. 4° 103

			135	**136**
[1]1.	Il me suffit de tous mes maulx S: Canon Superius in diapason; secondus Contratenor in diapenthe	Canis	iv	iv

[1] The three canonic pieces "Il me suffit" are based on the text and the Superius of the Claudin chanson first printed as **5**-34.

[2]2.	Secourés-moy ma dame par amour S: Canon A la quarte: Ce que l'ung faict l'autre defaict	Canis	ii^{v}	iii^{v}
3.	O mille foys la liberté heureuse	Mornable	iii^{v}	v^{v}
4.	Mes yeulx n'ont plus en beaulté jugement	Mornable	iiii^{v}	vii^{v}
5.	Mon cueur avez que ung aultre en ait le corps	Godard	iiii^{v}	xv^{v}
6.	Gentil esprit donnez-moy par raison	Mornable	v^{v}	xii^{v}
[1]7.	Il me suffit de tous mes maulx—Canon	Crequillon	vi^{v}	viii^{v}
8.	De varier c'est ung propre de femme	Godard	vii^{v}	xi^{v}
9.	Amour pence que je dorme et je me meurs	[3]Sandrin	vii^{v}	x^{v}
10.	S'il est vertu, loyaulté, courtoisie	Mornable	viii^{v}	xvi^{v}
11.	Trop malheureulx je dois estre estimé	Mornable	viii^{v}	xiiii^{v}
12.	Puis que mon cueur est vers toy mal venu	Gosse	ix^{v}	xviii^{v}
[1]13.	Il me suffit de tous mes maulx—Canon	Mornable	x^{v}	xxiii^{v}
14.	Par toy Amour, héllas, je suys laissée	[4]Guyon	xi^{v}	xxi^{v}
15.	Dictes ouy, madame et ma maistresse	Vulfran	xii^{v}	xvii^{v}
16.	Disant qu'aymer en gardant le debvoir	Vulfran	xii^{v}	xx^{v}
17.	Corps s'eslongnant faict son cueur approcher	Certon	xiii^{v}	xxv^{v}
18.	Travail j'endure en attendant	Vulfran	xiii^{v}	xxvi^{v}
*19.	Je ne sçay pas sy la longue demeure	Clemens	xiiii^{v}	xxvii^{v}
20.	Or me traictés ainsy qu'il vous plaira	Vulfran	xv^{v}	xxix^{v}
21.	A vous me suys de bien bon cueur donné	Mornable	xv^{v}	xxx^{v}
22.	A tout jamais vous faire humble service	Regnes	xvi^{v}	xxxi^{v}
	Finis			

* Modern edition in *CMM 4*:X.

[2] Based on the text and the superius of the Claudin chanson first printed as **2**-1.

[3] Godart in **136**.

[4] Fresneau in **129**.

1546

136

Dixneufiesme liure cōtẹnāt xxii. Chāsons / NOVVELLES A QVATRE PARTIES, EN VNG VOLVME, *Imprimées par Pierre Attaingnant libraire, & imprimeur / de musique du Roy, demourant a Paris, en la Rue / de la Harpe, pres leglise S. Cosme.* / 1546. / [Table] / *Auec priuilege du Roy, pour six ans.* /

1 vol. in-4° obl., 21 × 15.8 cm.; 32 f. numbered [i]–xxxii

Sign.: XIX A^{4}–XIX H^{4}

RISM–I, 1546[13]

Erlangen: Universitätsbibliothek, 4° Kst. 24^{c}

Contents same as **135**.

1546

137

Vingtiesme liure cōtenāt xxviii. Chansōs / NOVVELLES A QVATRE PARTIES, EN DEVX / *uolumes imprimees Par pierre Attaingnant, libraire & Imprimeur / de Musique du Roy demourant a Paris en la Rue de la / Harpe, pres leglise S. Cosme.* / 1546. / [Table] / **Superius & Tenor.** / *Auec priuilege du Roy pour six ans.* /

2 vol. in-4° obl., 21 × 15.8 cm.; 16 f. numbered [i]–xvi
Sign.: XX e⁴–XX h⁴; XX E⁴–XX H⁴ (Ct–B: XII F i; XII G i; XII H ii; S–T: XII g i; XII h ii)
RISM–I, 1546[14]

Munich: Bayerische Staatsbibliothek, Mus. Pr. 4° 103

1.	Du bien de vous toutes foys que j'y pense	Gardane	i^v
2.	Si au partir me convient congé prendre	Puy	i^v
3.	Vénus ung jour en veneur se déguise	Meigret	ii^v
4.	Amour, je sens tes doulx effors remectre	Gardane	ii^v
5.	Je ne le puis ny ne le veulx changer	Maille	iii^v
6.	Encore Amour ne m'avoit faict sentir	Guyon	iiii^v
7.	Au monde estoint douleur et volupté	L'huillier	v^v
8.	Le blanc et noyr ne doibt estre porté	Certon	v^v
9.	Avant l'aymer je l'ay voulu congnoistre	Certon	vi^v
10.	Dame qui as l'esprit et la beauté	Puy	vi^v
11.	Je suis content si la mort me veult prendre	Puy	vii^v
12.	Je ne veulx poinct pour mon plaisir	Certon	vii^v
13.	Ayant cogneu si haultes mes pensées	Certon	viii^v
14.	Bayser souvent n'esse pas grand plaisir	Symon	viii^v
15.	Que puis-je lors quand mon malheur consent	Manchicourt	ix^v
16.	Si la beaulté et doulce contenance	Meigret	ix^v
17.	Je suys trop satisfaict	Certon	x^v
18.	Je le sçay bien et si ne le puis croire	Vulfran	x^v
19.	Pleurés mes yeulx, pour la dure déffense qui de deux cueurs	Certon	xi^v
20.	J'ayme myeulx boire au pré bon eau	Certon	xi^v
21.	Comment mon cueur es-tu donc dispensé	Vulfran	xii^v
22.	Mon bon voloyr et mon loyal service	Manchicourt	xiii^v
23.	Le cueur, le corps, le sens, l'entendement	Symon	xiii^v
24.	Pareille au feu de non et cruaulté	L'huillier	xiiii^v
25.	Sy j'ay du mal pour bien aymer	Vulfran	xiiii^v
26.	Puis que mon cueur fermement continue	Morel	xv^v
27.	Puis qu'en amour Dieu n'est poinct offencé	Morel	xv^v
28.	Si la faveur a costumée	Meigret	xvi^v

Finis

1546, AUGUST

138

[Breviarum secundum insignis ecclesie Noviomensis usum, nuper recognitum multisque in locis auctum ac immutatum, tam in legendis octavarum Assumptionis beate Marie Virginis, commemorationibus ejusdem atque beati Eligii confessoris quam homelis evangeliorum quadregesime quarum tituli et lectiones (ut plurimum false et mendose erant) que quidem in melius ad exemplarium veritatem restitute fuerunt, ut legenti facillime patebit, M D X L V I, mense augusto. Venit Parisiis in vico Cythare, apud Petrum Attaingnant, musice calco-graphum, non procul a sanctorum Cosme et Damiani templo, pars hiemalis et pars estivalis.]

1 vol. in-16° [Pars hiemalis] 9 × 14 cm. c. 350 f. in four sections, as follows:

[Almanac]	7 f. unnumbered, of which the first two are lacking Sign.: ✠ iii–vii
Ordo servitii	148 f. numbered i–cxlviii (cxlii, cxliiii, cxlvi, cxlv) Sign.: *No* a^8–s^8, t^4
Ordo psalteri	108 f. numbered i–cviii (lacks lii, liii) Sign.: *No* A^8–N^8, O^4 Cut of King David (as in **1**) on f. ii^v
Officium sanctorum	84 f. (?), unnumbered Sign.: *No* A^8–J^8, K^3 (I^{6-8} and all after K^3 lacking)

Noyon: Ancienne Bibliothèque de Chapitre, V. 89 Rés.

The missing title page is quoted from René Pagel, *Bibliographie noyonnaise*, 1903, no. 1369. Pagel cites another copy at the Charterhouse of Montrenaud, in the vicinity of Noyon, which was destroyed in the First World War.

The manuscript catalogue of the Chapter Library of Noyon, compiled by Alphonse Boulogne in 1854, has this entry under V. 89: "Ancien Bréviaire de Noyon, gothique, dont le titre manque; 5 volumes, [sic] petit format. Les volumes paraissent être de plusieurs exemplaires différentes. Sur deux volumes se trouve cette indication manuscrite: *imprimé en 1546*."

1546

139

¶ Manuale insignis eccle= / sie Nouiomensis / auctum & recog= nitum: Cui / recenter Addita fuerunt que sequuntur. / Almanach cum Calendario. Precepta singulis dñicis diebus in prono / parrochialium ecclesiarum fieri consueta. Visitationes infirmorum. / Rescripta cura= torum / ¶ Venale habetur Parisiis / in vico cythare in domo Petri Attaingnant qua / prospectus est ad vicum Mathurinorũ: non pro=/cul a sanctorum Cosme & Damiani templo. / An. M.D.Xlvi /

1 vol. in-4°, 15.8 × 22.7 cm.; 120 f. in three sections, as follows:

[Almanac 1547–77]	[Part II]	[Part III]
8. f., unnumbered	96 f. numbered i–xcvi	16 f., unnumbered
Sign.: ✠ 8	Sign.: a^8–m^8	Sign.: aa^8

Cut of the Crucifixion on f. liii^v

Oxford: Bodleian Library, Douce BB. 183 (MS inscription on title page: "Istud manuale dedit communitati cappelanorum huius ecclesie Noviomensis dominus Simon Dablain presbiter cappellanus Noviomensis." Abbreviations and contractions realized.)

See fig. 6 above for facsimile of plainchant, f. 1 iii

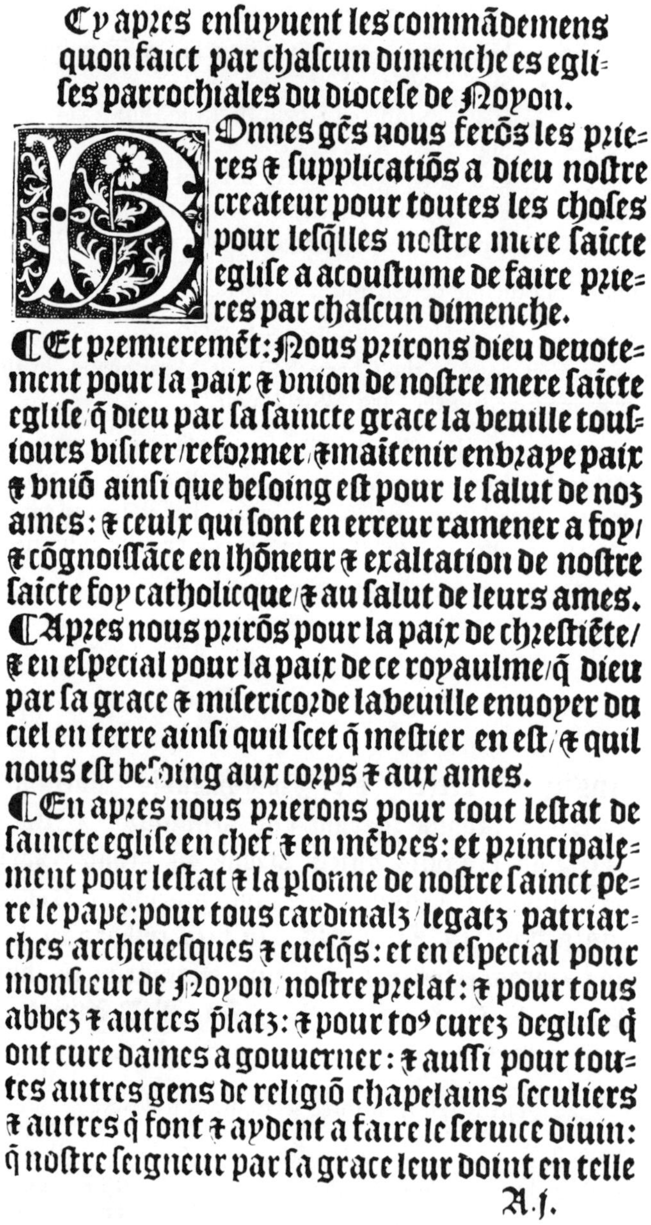

Cy apres ensuyuent les commãdemens
quon faict par chascun dimenche es egli=
ses parrochiales du diocese de Noyon.
Bonnes gẽs nous ferõs les prie=
res ⁊ supplicatiõs a dieu nostre
createur pour toutes les choses
pour lesq̃lles nostre mere saicte
eglise a acoustume de faire prie=
res par chascun dimenche.
¶Et premieremẽt: Nous prirons dieu deuote=
ment pour la paix ⁊ vnion de nostre mere saicte
eglise / q̃ dieu par sa saincte grace la veuille tous=
iours visiter / reformer / ⁊ maĩtenir en vraye paix
⁊ vniõ ainsi que besoing est pour le salut de noz
ames: ⁊ ceulx qui sont en erreur ramener a foy /
⁊ cõgnoissãce en lhõneur ⁊ exaltation de nostre
saicte foy catholicque / ⁊ au salut de leurs ames.
¶Apres nous prirõs pour la paix de chrestiẽte /
⁊ en especial pour la paix de ce royaulme / q̃ dieu
par sa grace ⁊ misericorde la veuille enuoyer du
ciel en terre ainsi quil scet q̃ mestier en est / ⁊ quil
nous est besoing aux corps ⁊ aux ames.
¶En apres nous prierons pour tout lestat de
saincte eglise en chef ⁊ en mẽbres: et principale=
ment pour lestat ⁊ la p̃sonne de nostre sainct pe=
re le pape: pour tous cardinalz / legatz patriar=
ches archeuesques ⁊ euesq̃s: et en especial pour
monsieur de Noyon nostre prelat: ⁊ pour tous
abbez ⁊ autres p̃latz: ⁊ pour to⁹ curez deglise q̃
ont cure dames a gouuerner: ⁊ aussi pour tou=
tes autres gens de religiõ chapelains seculiers
⁊ autres q̃ font ⁊ aydent a faire le seruice diuin:
q̃ nostre seigneur par sa grace leur doint en telle
A.j.

25 Dominical prayers at Noyon, from the *Manuale* **(139)**. (reduced) Courtesy of the Bodleian Library.

140

Premier liure contenant xxv. Chansons/ NOVVELLES A QVATRE PARTIES, EN DEVX VOLVME, / *Imprimées par Pierre Attaingnant libraire, & imprimeur / de musique du Roy, demourant a Paris, en la Rue / de la Harpe, pres leglise S. Cosme.* / 1546. / [Table] / **Superius & Tenor.** / *Auec priuilege du Roy, pour six ans.* /

2 vol. in-4° obl., 21 × 15.8 cm.; 16 f. numbered [i]–xvi
Sign.: Ia^4–Id^4; IA^4–ID^4
RISM–I, 1546^{11}

Munich: Bayerische Staatsbibliothek, Mus. Pr. 4° 103 (Rar. 900)

Contents same as **80**.

Concerning the make-up of the Munich set see p. 76 above.

141

Antonij de Mornable doctissimi musici / MOTETORVM MVSICALIVM, LIBER PRIMVS / XXV *Modulorum index.* / [Table] / *Parisiis in uico Cythare nō procul a templo sanctorum Cosmae & Damiani* / *Apud Petrum attaingnant regium musicae calcographum.* 46. / **Superius.** / *Cum Regio priuilegio ad sexennium.* /

4 vol. in-4° obl.; 20.5 × 16 cm.; 16 f. numbered [i]–xvi (Ct: [i] ii xiii iiii; all books: xiii xvi xv xiiii)
Sign.: Mornable m^4—Mornable p^4; Mornable mm^4—Mornable pp^4; Mornable MM^4—Mornable PP^4; Mornable M^4—Mornable P^4 (S, Ct: "Mornable" on first and last gatherings only)

Munich: Bayerische Staatsbibliothek, Mus. Pr. 175 / 4 (signature sometimes trimmed off in all books)
Paris: Bibliothèque Sainte-Geneviève, Vm 94 Rés (S, lacks fol. xiii–xvi)

1. Ecce Dominus veniet I	5 tt	i^v
Ecce apparebit Dominus II		
2. Ecce virgo concipiet		ii^v
3. Hodie Cristus natus est nobis	5 tt	ii^v
4. Congratulamini michi omnes I		iii^v
Et beatam me dicent omnes generationes II		
5. Nesciens mater virgo virum, peperit sine dolore	6 ss tt	iiii

6.	Joannes apostolus et evangelista I	5 bb	v
	Valde honorandus est beatus Joannes II		
7.	Postquam consummati sunt dies octo		v[v]
8.	Magnum hereditatis misterium		vi
9.	Videte miraculum matris Domini I	5 tt	vi[v]
	Virgo concepit peperitque virgo II		
	Quinta pars, I & II: Inviolata, integra et casta es, Maria		
10.	Peccantem me quotidie et non me penitentem	5 cc	vii
11.	De profundis clamavi ad te, Domine I		vii[v]
	Sustinuit anima mea in verbo eius II [à 3]		
	Quia apud Dominum misericordia III		
12.	Infirmitatem nostram, quæsumus, Domine		viii
13.	Judica me Deus et discerne causam meam I		viii[v]
	Et introibo ad altare Dei II		
14.	Jubilate Deo omnis terra I		ix[v]
	Laudate nomen eius quoniam suavis est II		
15.	Delicta juventutis meæ		x
16.	Angelus Domini descendit de cælo I	5 cc	x
	Venite et videte locum II		
17.	Laudate Dominum omnes gentes	5 cc	xi
18.	Ascendo ad patrem meum I	6 ss tt	xi[v]
	Et dum assumptus fuero II		
19.	Veni Sancte spiritus I	5 cc	xii[v]
	Emitte spiritum sanctum tuum II		
20.	Domine Jhesu Christe, seminator casti consilii I	5 cc	xiii[v]
	Dum aurora finem daret II		
21.	O mundi lampas et marguarita prefulgida I		xiiii
	Maria Magdalena semper pia II		
22.	Laudem dicite Deo, omnes sancti eius		xiiii[v]
23.	Timete Dominum omnes sancti eius		xv
24.	Ecce nunc benedicite Domino omnes servi Domini	8	xv[v]
25.	Virgo sancta Catherina, Græciæ gemma		xvi[v]
	Finis		

The copy at the Bibliothèque Sainte-Geneviève is bound with eleven other Superius part-books, **46, 47, 49, 50, 56, 57, 60, 61, 63, 64, 119.** There are several inscriptions in various hands, e.g., **46,** f. ii: "Ex libris Sta. Catharina Parisii"; **50,** f. xvi[v]: "Michel Prevost"; flyleaf following **141:** "Dessus. livre pour chanter sus l'orme. Appartenant a Jehan Bele[-]on, en l'eglise Saint Germain le vieul. Cité de Paris. A paris 1607."

1546

142

[Trente et un psaumes a quatre voix mis en musique par Pierre Certon. Paris, 1546]

4 vol. in-4° obl., 21 × 15.8 cm; 16 f. numbered [i]–xvi
Sign.: a^4–d^4

Lausanne: Succession A. Cortot (S, lacking folios i–iv)

1. [Ps. 6 Je te supplie, O Sire] [i^{v}]
2. [Ps. 32 O bienheureux celuy dont les commises] [ii]
3. [Ps. 33 Réveillez vous chascun fidele] [ii^{v}]
4. [Ps. 5 Aux parolles que je veux dire] [iii]
5. [Ps. 2 Pourquoy font bruit et s'assemblent les gens] [iii^{v}]
6. [Ps. 13 Jusques a quand as establi] [iv]
7. [Ps. 130 Du fons de ma pensée] [iv^{v}]
8. Ps. 114 Quand Israël d'Egypte sortit v
9. Ps. 143 [numbered 153] Seigneur Dieu oy l'oraison mienne v^{v}
10. Ps. 137 Estant assis aux rives aquatiques vi
11. Ps. 46 [numbered 45] Des qu'adversité nous offense vi^{v}
12. Cantique de Simeon [numbered Ps. 152] Or laisse, Créateur vii
13. Ps. 30 Seigneur, que de gens vii^{v}
14. Ps. 7 Mon Dieu j'ay en toy espérance viii
15. Ps. 51 [numbered 61] Miséricorde au povre vitieux viii^{v}
16. Ps. 91 Qui en la garde du hault Dieu ix
17. Ps. 22 Mon Dieu, mon Dieu pourquoi m'as-tu laissé ix^{v}
18. Ps. 1 Qui au conseil des malings n'a esté x
19. Ps. 36 Du maling les faictz vicieux x^{v}
20. Ps. 113 [numbered 112] Enfans qui le Seigneur servez xi
21. Ps. 43 Revenge-moy, prends la querelle xi^{v}
22. Ps. 104 Sus, sus, mon âme, il te faut dire bien xii
23. Ps. 118 Rendez a Dieu louange et gloire xii^{v}
24. Ps. 4 Quand je t'invoque, hélas, escoute xiii
25. Ps. 8 O nostre Dieu et seigneur aimable xiii^{v}
26. Ps. 19 Les cieulx en chascun lieu xiiii
27. Ps. 15 Qui est ce qui conversera xiiii^{v}
28. Ps. 103 Sus, louez Dieu mon cueur en toute chose xv
29. Ps. 12 Donne secours (Seigneur) il en est heure xv^{v}
30. Ps. 9 De tout mon cueur t'exalteray xvi
31. Ps. 10 Dont vient cela (Seigneur) je te supply xvi^{v}

Finis

The title of the collection is quoted from the card-catalogue of the Bayerische Staatsbibliothek, Munich, which no longer possesses a copy. Fétis cites a similar title under Certon in his *Bibliographie Universelle*. What remains of the now unique copy is described by Pierre Pidoux, "Les Psaumes d'Antoine de Mornable, Guillaume Morlaye et Pierre Certon," *Annales Musicologiques* V (1957), 179. Contents of the four initial leaves have been reconstructed after the *Premier livre de Psalmes mis en musique par Maistre Pierre Certon . . . reduitz en tabulature de leut par maistre Guillaume Morlaye*, Paris, Fezandat, 1554, edited as *Psaumes de Pierre Certon reduits pour chant et luth*, Paris, C.N.R.S., 1957. It seems that Morlaye merely started at the beginning and intabulated as many pieces as space allowed, corresponding to nos. 1–13 above. Pidoux chose to attribute the 31 Psalms to Mornable and made up a title calculated on the *Livre second* **(143)**. He disregarded the evidence of the Morlaye tablature and another concordance that confirms Certon's authorship: the 1546 superius parts fit the tenors in Certon's *Cinquante Pseaulmes de David*, Paris, Le Roy & Ballard, 1555, as pointed out by Howard Jay Slenk, "The Huguenot Psalter in the Low Countries: A Study of its monophonic and polyphonic manifestations in the sixteenth century" (Unpublished Ph.D. dissertation, Ohio State University, 1965, Vol. I, p. 135; I am indebted to Mr. Slenk for communicating his researches into the matter.) Pidoux's rejection of Certon in favor of Mornable was apparently influenced by the continuous signatures from one book to the other. He was perhaps unaware that Attaingnant commonly grouped different composers' works into a set having continuous signatures (cf. **103–105**).

143

Liure second contenāt XVII. pseaulmes / DE DAVID TRADVICTZ DE LATIN EN FRANCOIS PAR CLEMENT / *marot Et naguères mis en musique en quatre parties separees par maistre Anthoine de / Mornable Maistre de la chappelle & ualet de chambre de puissant seigneur / Monsieur le conte de Laual Imprimees par Pierre attaingnant libraire / & Imprimeur de musique du Roy, demourant a Paris en la / Rue de la Harpe pres leglise S. Cosme.* / 1546 / [Table] / **Superius** / *Auec priuilege du Roy, pour six ans.* /

4 vol. in-4° obl., 21 × 15.8 cm.; 16 f. numbered [i]–xvi
Sign.: e^4–h^4

Lausanne: Succession A. Cortot (S)

1.	Ps. 86 Mon Dieu preste-moy l'oreille	i^v
2.	Ps. 72 Tes jugements, Dieu véritable	ii^v
3.	Ps. 24 La terre au Seigneur appartient	ii^v
4.	Ps. 37 Désir aucun ne t'esmeuve et convie	iii
5.	Ps. 115 Non point a nous	iii^v
6.	Ps. 11 Veu que de tout en Dieu mon cueur s'appuye	iiii
7.	Ps. 14 Le fol maling en son cueur dict et croit	iiii^v
8.	Ps. 25 A toy mon Dieu mon cueur monte	v
9.	Ps. 45 [numbered 65] Propos exquis fault que de mon cueur sorte	v^v
10.	Ps. 101 Vouloir m'est pris de mettre en escripture	vi
11.	Ps. 128 Bienheureux est quiconques	vi^v
12.	Ps. 110 L'Omnipotent a mon seigneur et maistre	vii
13.	Ps. 79 Les gens entrés sont en ton héritage	vii^v
14.	Ps. 38 Las en ta fureur ague	viii
15.	Ps. 18 Je t'aymeray en toute obéyssance	viii^v
16.	Ps. 50 Le Dieu, le fort, l'Eternel parlera	ix
17.	Ps. 23 Mon Dieu me paist	ix^v
	Finis. des Pseavlmes.	
	[Folio x blank]	
18.	Les dix commandementz: Leve le cueur	x^v
	Les dix commandementz: Je suis dict-il [continued]	xi
19.	L'Oraison de N.S.J.C.: Pere de nous	xi^v
20.	La Salutation angelique: Resjouys toy Vierge Marie	xii
21.	Credo in unum Deum: Je croy en Dieu le Pere tout puissant	xii^v
	Credo in unum Deum: *Secunds Pars* Et qui de mort	xiii
	Credo in unum Deum: *Residuum* Au sainct Esprit	xiii^v
22.	Priere devant le repas: O souverain pasteur et maistre	xiiii
23.	Apres le repas: Pere eternel qui nous ordonne	xiiii^v
24.	Le cantique de la vierge Marie Magnificat: Mon âme loue et magnifie	xv
	Le cantique de la vierge Marie Magnificat: *Secunda Pars* Mais son bras est fort	xv^v
	Le cantique de la vierge Marie Magnificat [continued]	xvi
25.	Nunc dimittis: Quand Syméon fust Ihésucrist tenant entre ses bras	xvi^v
	Finis	

Title page and index after Pierre Pidoux, "Les Psaumes d'Antoine de Mornable, Guillaume Morlaye et Pierre Certon," *Annales Musicologiques* V (1957), 179.

1547

144

Vingt & ungiesme liure cōtenāt xxv Chā / SONS NOVVELLES A QVATRE PARTIES, EN DEVX / *uolumes imprimees Par Pierre Attaingnant, libraire & Imprimeur / de Musique du Roy demourant a Paris en la Rue de la / Harpe, pres leglise S. Cosme.* / 47. / [Table] / **Superius & Tenor** / *Auec priuilege du Roy pour six ans.* /

2 vol. in-4° obl., 21 × 15.8 cm.; 16 f. numbered [i]–xvi (Ct–B: ix x x xii; xi xiiii xv xvi)
Sign.: XXI i^4–XXI m^4; XXI I^4–XXI M^4 (S–T: XXI K i, XXI K ii)
RISM–I, 1547^8

Munich: Bayerische Staatsbibliothek, Mus. Pr. 4° 103

1.	O ma Vénus a ton Vulcain fidele	L'huillier	i^v
2.	Triste est mon cueur quant je voy enviellir	Meigret	ii^v
3.	En vous voyant j'ay liberté perdue	Meigret	ii^v
4.	J'ouys ung jour ung gros lourdault	Certon	iii^v
5.	J'ay supporté son honneur et son faict	Gentian	iii^v
6.	L'aller au ciel au moindre propose	Certon	iiii^v
[1]7.	Si sa vertu et grace		iiii^v
8.	Voyez le tourt que maulvaise fortune	Gardane	v^v
9.	Le grand désir que sentois approcher	Maille	vi^v
10.	Sy mon espoir vouloit désespérer	Certon	vi^v
11.	Je vous supplie, entendez-moy	Maille	vii^v
12.	O vous Amour, qui avez eu	Maille	vii^v
13.	A mon départ estoit de larmes plaine	Meigret	viii^v
[2]14.	J'ay veu que j'estoys cher tenu	Meigret	ix^v
15.	Oeil importum qui mon cueur a rendu	Fresneau	x^v
16.	L'oeil et le cueur n'eurent jamays povoir	P Symon	x^v
17.	Elle voyant approcher mon départ	Certon	xi^v
18.	Ung oeil riant ce matin m'a trouvé	Morpain	xi^v
19.	L'eureulx espoir qui contente ma vie	Romain	xii^v
20.	O seigneur Dieu, ta loy parfaicte et faicte	Gardane	xii^v
21.	Triste oeil menteur qui pour me decepvoir	Morpain	xiii^v
22.	Je sens mon heur, et si ne le désire	Gentian	xiiii^v
23.	Si l'endurer segret sans espérance	Meigret	xiiii^v
24.	O rossignol qui chante joliment	Morpain	xv^v
25.	Hélas amy, ta loiaulté poinct ne mérite cruaulté	L'huillier	xv^v
26.	Sois pour content que de moy joyras	Morpain	xvi^v

Finis

[1] Not listed in table.
[2] Table: Je veu que j'estoys.

145

Vingt deuxiesme liure cōtenāt xxvi. Chā / SONS NOVVELLES A QUATRE PARTIES, EN DEVX / *uolumes imprimees Par Pierre Attaingnant, libraire & imprimeur de / Musique du Roy demourant a Paris en la Rue de la Harpe, / pres leglise S. Cosme.* / 47. / [Table] / **Superius & Tenor.** / *Auec priuilege du Roy pour six ans.* /

2 vol. in-4° obl., 21 × 15.8 cm.; 16 f. numbered [i]–xvi (Ct–B: v vi vii vii; S–T: i ii iii ii; v vi vii vii)
Sign.: XXII n^4–XXII q^4–XXII N^4–XXII Q^4
RISM–I, 1547^9

Munich: Bayerische Staatsbibliothek, Mus. Pr. 4° 103

1.	Ung gros mignon espousa une fille		Sohyer	i^v
2.	Si pour vertu et ferme loyaulté		Gardane	ii^v
3.	C'est seurement que l'amour est certaine		Le Gendre	iii^v
4.	Rossignollet du bois qui chante au verd boscage		Gardane	iii^v
5.	Puis que mon cueur tu as choisi		Jannequin	iiii^v
6.	Réveillez-vous mes damoiselles		Sandrin	iiii^v
7.	Fleur de quinze ans (si Dieu vous saulve et gard)		Gardane	v^v
8.	En réveillant les damoiselles		Sandrin	v^v
9.	Quand j'ay la nuict plaisir en ma pensée		Ebran	vi^v
10.	Si j'ay du bien, hélas, c'est par mensonge		Sandrin	vii^v
11.	Amour m'avoit pourveue d'amy loyal et seur		Plisson	vii^v
12.	Comme le vent impetueux esvente la feulle		Delafont	viii^v
13.	Avecques vous mon amour finira		Puy	ix^v
14.	Au feu d'amour je fais ma pénitence		De Villa	ix^v
15.	Amour ayant de ma grand passion		Jannequin	x^v
16.	Vostre cueur je supply, ma dame, tant endurcy	L'amant	Gardane	x^v
17.	Amy cherchez vostre fortune	La dame	Gardane	x^v
18.	Justice, hélas, justice je demande		Certon	xi^v
*19.	Mort sans soleil tu as laissé le monde froid		Boyvin	xi^v
20.	Trop plus penser que bien escrire		Sandrin	xii^v
21.	Vuidez soulas, tout plaisir et liesse		Vassal	xii^v
22.	Marie monstroit a sa dame ung dizain		Passereau	xiii^v
23.	En te voyant ne fays que souspirer		Delafont	xiiii^v
24.	En l'eau plus froide que la glace		Du tertre	xv^v
25.	Puis qu'amour veult que vous soyez ma dame		Du tertre	xv^v
26.	Si vous voulez mon grief mal soulager		Delafont	xvi^v

Finis

* Modern edition in *Anthologie*.

1547

146

Vingtroisiesme liure contenant xvii. Chā / SONS NOVVELLES A QVATRE PARTIES, EN DEVX / *uolumes imprimees Par Pierre Attaingnant, libraire & imprimeur de / Musique du Roy demourant a Paris en la Rue de la Harpe, / pres leglise S. Cosme.* / 1547. / [Table] / **Superius & Tenor.** / *Auec priuilege du Roy pour six ans.* /

2 vol. in-4° obl., 21 × 15.8 cm.; 16 f. numbered [i]-xvi
Sign.: XXIII r⁴-XXIII u⁴; XXIII R⁴-XXIII U⁴
RISM-I, 1547[10]

Munich: Bayerische Staatsbibliothek, Mus. Pr. 4° 103

1.	L'espoux a la premiere nuict	Jennequin	i^v
2.	Le lendemain des nopces on vint veoir	Jennequin	ii^v
3.	A ce matin trouvay une fillette soubz ung buisson	Delafont	iii^v
4.	Michault avoyt aveu au curé convenu	Delafont	iiii^v
*5.	On vous est allé rapporter que j'avois faict amour nouvelle	Jennequin	v^v
6.	Je veulx que m'amye soit telle	Jennequin	vi^v
7.	Gros Jehan menoit hors de Paris en croupe ung jour	Jennequin	vii^v
8.	Le jeu m'ennuye, jouez m'amye	Jennequin	viii^v
9.	Ung amoureux de coucher eust envye	Maillart	ix^v
10.	Bouchez-le bien que la mouche n'y entre	P. Symon	x^v
*11.	Tu as tout seul, Jhan, Jhan, vignes et prez	Jennequin	xi^v
[1]12.	Qu'est la c'est le beau pere	Fresneau	xi^v
13.	Par ung matin d'esté sur la doulce roussé		xii^v
14.	Las, si j'ay failly, pardonnez-le-moy ma mere	Vassal	xiii^v
†15.	Ung verd galand garny d'arc et de trousse	Certon	xiiii^v
16.	La, la, la, que ne m'amye elle la don	Nicolas	xv^v
17.	Ceulx de Picardie ont trouvé la guyse de boire d'autant	Claudin	xvi^v

Finis

[1] Table: Trac trac trac.
* Modern edition in *Trente Chansons* (*1928*).
† Modern edition in *Chorwerk, Vol. 82.*

1547

147

Vingtquatriesme liure cōtenāt xxvi. Chā / SONS NOVVELLES A QVATRE PARTIES, EN DEVX / *uolumes imprimees Par Pierre Attaingnant, libraire & imprimeur de / Musique du Roy demourant a Paris en la Rue de la Harpe, / pres leglise S. Cosme.* / 1547 / [Table] / **Superius & Tenor.** / *Auec priuilege du Roy pour six ans.* /

2 vol. in-4° obl., 21 × 15.8 cm.; 16 f. numbered [i]-xvi (S-T: ix x xx xii)
Sign.: XXIIII x⁴-XXIIII &⁴; XXIIII X⁴-XXIIII A⁴
RISM-I, 1547[11]

Munich: Bayerische Staatsbibliothek, Mus. Pr. 4° 103

1.	Si je me plains si je souspire—Canon in Diapason	Mornable	i^v
2.	Si vous voyez ma joye convertye	Pagnier	i^v
3.	Auparavant que j'eusse congnoissance	Olivier	ii^v
4.	Toutes les fois que je pense au tourment	Gentian	iii^v

5.	Ha petit chien, tant tu as de bonheur	Meigret	iiii^{v}
6.	Amour voyant m'amye en fut si fort espris	Meigret	v^{v}
7.	N'est ce pas grand cruaulté	Maille	v^{v}
8.	Apres avoir longuement attendu si l'on povoit	De Villiers	vi^{v}
*9.	Voz huys, sont ilz tous fermez, fillettes	Godart	vi^{v}
10.	Craignant Amour de perdre le povoir	De Villiers	vii^{v}
11.	Fault-il pour ung verre cassé mettre dehors la chambriere	De Villiers	vii^{v}
12.	Si de long temps fortune a faict sur moy	Gardane	viii^{v}
13.	Ce raporteur et languart envieux		ix^{v}
14.	O vous souspirs, qui sortez de ce lieu		x^{v}
15.	On dict qu'Amour n'a plus fleche ne darde	Jennequin	x^{v}
16.	Amoureux suis dont pas ne me contente		xi^{v}
†17.	Toutes les nuictes tu m'es présente par songe doulx	Jennequin	xi^{v}
‡18.	Tirez soudain, tirez petit archer	Le Moyne	xii^{v}
19.	Pour loyaulment servir une maistresse	Jennequin	xii^{v}
20.	Est-il heureux, celuy qui de s'amye a bon recueil	De Villiers	xiii^{v}
21.	Sus approchez ces lebures vermeilet	Jennequin	xiii^{v}
22.	Nenny desplaist et donne grand soucy	De Villiers	xiiii^{v}
23.	Le souvenir de mes belles amours	Certon	xiiii^{v}
24.	Je ne vis pas mais je languis, belle, pour vous	Olivier	xv^{v}
25.	Pour avoir heu de ma dame refus	De Villiers	xv^{v}
26.	Si bon vouloir méritoit récompense	Mitantier	xvi^{v}

Finis

* Modern edition in *Theatrical Chansons.*
† Modern edition in *Trente Chansons (1928).*
‡ Modern edition in *Quinze Chansons.*

1547

148

Secōd liure contenāt trois Gaillardes, / TROIS PAVANES, VINGT TROIS BRANLES, / *Tant gays, Simples, Que doubles, Douze basses dances, & Neuf tourdions,* / *En somme Cinquante, Le tout ordonne selon les huict tons. Et* / *nouuellement imprime en Musique a quatre parties, en ung* / *liure seul, par Pierre Attaingnant, Imprimeur* / *de musique du Roy, demourant a Paris* / *en la Rue de la Harpe, pres* / *leglise sainct Cosme.* / 1547. / *Auec prorogation du priuilege du Roy, De nouuel obtenu par ledit attaingnant* / *Pour les liures Ia parluy imprimez & quil Imprimera cy apres iusques a six ans.* /

1 vol. in-4° obl., 20.9 × 15.4 cm.; 32 f. numbered [i]–xxxii
Sign.: II I^{4}-II Q^{4}

Paris: Bibliothèque Nationale, Rés Vm^{7} 376 (2) (MS inscription on the title page: "A maistre Claudin, Chapellain demourant a Langres. Et depuis a Franchoys Perin, sergent Royal en Leccan [?] de Langres.")

1.	Basse dance 1	i^{v}
2.	Basse dance 2	i^{v}
3.	Basse dance 3	ii^{v}
4.	Basse dance 4	iii^{v}
*5.	Basse dance Celle qui m'a le nom d'amy donné 5	iiii^{v}
*6.	Basse dance La volunté 6	v^{v}
7.	Tourdion 1	vi^{v}
8.	Tourdion 2	vi^{v}
*9.	Tourdion 3	vii^{v}
10.	Tourdion 4	vii^{v}
*11.	Branle [simple] 1	viii^{v}
12.	Branle [simple] 2	viii^{v}
13.	Tourdion 5	ix^{v}
14.	Branle [simple] 3	ix^{v}
15.	Branle [simple] 4	x^{v}
16.	Branle [simple] 5	x^{v}
*17.	Branle [simple] 6	xi^{v}
18.	Branle [simple] 7	xi^{v}
19.	Basse dance 7	xii^{v}
20.	Branle [simple] L'espoir que j'ay 8	xii^{v}
21.	Branle [simple] 9	xiii^{v}
*22.	Branle [gay] Mari, je songeois l'aultre jour 1	xiii^{v}
*23.	Branle [gay] 2	xiiii^{v}
*24.	Branle [double] 1	xiiii^{v}
*25.	Branle [double] 2	xv^{v}
*26.	Branle [double] 3	xv^{v}
27.	Branle [double] 4	xvi^{v}
28.	Branle [gay] 3	xvi^{v}
†29.	Basse dance Aupres de vous 8	xvii^{v}
*30.	Tourdion C'est grand plaisir 6	xviii^{v}
*31.	Tourdion Vous aurez tout ce qui est myen 7	xix^{v}
32.	Basse dance 9	xx^{v}
33.	Basse dance Content désir 10	xxi^{v}
*34.	Basse dance Par fin despit 11	xxii^{v}
*35.	Branle [simple] 10	xxiii^{v}
*36.	Branle [gay] Que je chatoulle ta fossette 4	xxiiii^{v}
*37.	Branle [simple] 11	xxv^{v}
*38.	Basse dance Trop de regretz 12	xxv^{v}
*39.	Tourdion 8	xxvi^{v}
[1]40.	Tourdion 9	xxvi^{v}
41.	Branle [simple] 12	xxvii^{v}
42.	Branle [gay] 5	xxvii^{v}
*43.	Branle [double] 5	xxviii^{v}
44.	Branle [double] 6	xxviii^{v}
45.	Pavane 1	xxix^{v}
46.	Pavane 2	xxix^{v}
47.	Pavane 3	xxx^{v}
48.	Gaillarde 1	xxxi^{v}
49.	Gaillarde 2	xxxi^{v}
50.	Gaillarde 3 [à 5]	xxxii^{v}

* Modern edition in *MMRF* XXII: nos. 5, 6, 34 and 38, pp. 2–9; nos. 9, 30, 31 and 39, pp. 10–17; no. 11, p. 54; no. 17, p. 58; no. 22, p. 73; no. 23, p. 75; no. 24, p. 63; no. 25, p. 64; no. 26, p. 68; no. 35, p. 56; no. 36, p. 69; no. 37, p. 55; no. 43, p. 66.
† Modern edition in D. Heartz, "The Basse Dance: Its Evolution circa 1450–1550," *Annales Musicologiques* VI (1958–1963), 323–325.

[1] The Contratenor bears the MS inscription: "Bon tordion pour faire danser et pour . . ."

Dances with vocal models are as follows:

No. 5	Celle qui m'a le nom d'amy donné	**109**–2 (Sandrin)
6	La volunté	**113**–9 (Sandrin)
20	L'espoir que j'ay	**14**–4
22	Mari je songeois l'aultre jour	**30**–18 (Jacotin)
29	Aupres de vous	**2**–24; **5**–3; **29**–3 (Jacotin or Claudin)
30	C'est grand plaisir	**10**–42
31	Vous aurez tout ce qui est myen	**30**–28
33	Content désir	**41**–23 (Claudin)
34	Par fin despit	**8**–21; another setting of the same tune, **54**–8 (Claudin)
38	Trop de regretz	**15**–2; **70**–28 (Hesdin)

Facsimile of title pages for this and the succeeding volumes of "Danceries" in *MMRF* XXII.

1547

149

Vingtcinquiesme liure cōtenāt xxviii. Chā / SONS NOVVELLES A QVATRE PARTIES, EN DEVX VOLVMES / *imprimees Par Pierre Attaingnant, libraire & imprimeur de Musique du Roy demourant / a Paris en la Rue de la Harpe pres leglise S. Cosme.* / 1547 / [Table] / **Superius & Tenor** / *Auec prorogation du priuilege du Roy, De nouuel obtenu par ledit attaingnant / Pour les liures Ia parluy imprimez & quil Imprimera cy apres iusques a six ans.* /

2 vol. in-4° obl., 21 × 15.8 cm.; 16 f. numbered [i]–xvi (S–T: xiii xiiii xv xv)
Sign.: XXV a^4–XXV d^4; XXV A^4–XXV D^4
RISM–I, 1547^{12}

Munich: Bayerische Staatsbibliothek, Mus. Pr. 4° 103

1.	D'avoir congneu la playe qui me blesse S: Resp. de Las, que te sert de doulx parler en bouche	Puy	i^v
2.	J'ay tant voulu ce que n'ay peu avoir	Gardane	i^v
3.	S'il advient que mon dueil me tue	P. Symon	ii^v
4.	Soyez seur que la repentence suyvoit de bien pres le peché	Bastard	ii^v
5.	Ce qui me fault pour mon contentement	P. Symon	iii^v
6.	Si vous avez de me veoir telle envie	Devilliers	iii^v
7.	Onques bon cueur ne fut sans grand amour	Ebran	iiii^v
8.	Si pour aymer l'on ne quiert que beaulté	Nicolas	iiii^v
9.	Si la beaulté de ma dame—Canon in dyapason	Arcadelt	v^v
10.	Le mal que sent une amye offensée	Du tartre	v^v
11.	Amour et moy avons faict qu'une dame	Jennequin	vi^v
12.	Ja commençoit a croistre l'espérance	Olivier	vii^v
13.	Sans y penser ne vouloir le vouloir	Jennequin	viii^v
14.	Si sa vertu et grace	Arcadelt	viii^v
15.	Ce n'est sans tort que me plains	Mitantier	ix^v
16.	En attendant qui tres mal me contente	Nicolas	x^v
17.	Il me prend fantasie de vous dire comment	Arcadelt	x^v

18.	Entendez vous point vostre amy	Arcadelt	xi^v
19.	Ton cueur s'est bien tost repenti	Claudin	xi^v
20.	Hélas mon Dieu, y a il en ce monde	Jennequin	xii^v
21.	Fault-il que pour nostre bonté	Gardane	xii^v
22.	Quand je vous ayme ardentement	Arcadelt	xiii^v
[1]23.	La mort plus tost que consentir le change	Jennequin	xiii^v
24.	L'heureux soucy de l'espéré désir	De Villiers	xiiii^v
25.	Je ne suis point amoureux de cent mille	Certon	xiiii^v
26.	O sotes gens qui s'en vont travailler	Jennequin	xv^v
27.	Lors tous ravy pour ce que je pensay	Arcadelt	xv^v
28.	Si en mes mains as liberté rendue	Nicolas	xvi^v

Finis

[1] Table: L'amour plus tost.

1548

150

Vingtsixiesme liure cōtenāt xxvii. Chan / SONS NOVVELLES A QVATRE PARTIES, EN DEVX VOLVMES / *imprimees Par Pierre Attaingnant, libraire & imprimeur de Musique du Roy demourāt / a Paris en la Rue de la Harpe pres leglise S. Cosme.* / 1548. / [Table] / **Superius & Tenor** / *Auec prorogation du priuilege du Roy, De nouuel obtenu par ledit attaingnant / Pour les liures Ia parluy imprimez & quil Imprimera cy apres iusques a six ans.* /

2 vol. in-4° obl., 21 × 15.8 cm.; 16 f. numbered [i]–xvi
Sign.: XXVI e^4–XXVI h^4; XXVI E^4–XXVI H^4 (S–T: XXVI h ii instead of XXVI g ii)
RISM–I, 1548^3

Munich: Bayerische Staatsbibliothek, Mus. Pr. 4° 103

1.	Aultant ou plus amour je quicte et chasse	Certon	i^v
2.	Je n'ay pas tort si j'ay mys mon amour	Certon	i^v
3.	La nuict passée en songeant me vint veoyr Juno	Du tertre	ii^v
4.	Estre peult-il que ne souspire	Vulfran	iii^v
5.	Si vous voulez estre aymée et servye	Certon	iii^v
6.	Honneur, beaulté, doulceur et bonne grace	Maille	iiii^v
7.	Pelerin suis d'un voyage ou j'ay trouvé maint passage	Maille	iiii^v
8.	Elle a le cueur entier et tres loyal	Du Muys	v^v
9.	Une amitié qui est bien commencée	Mornable	v^v
10.	Tout au rebours de mon affaire S: Canon Tout au rebours	Arcadelt	vi^v
11.	Elle voyant l'ennuy qui me tourmente	Belin	vi^v
12.	A ton départ ne me demeure rien		vii^v
13.	Si amytié n'est que conjunction	Du tertre	vii^v
14.	Il ne se treuve en amytié	Sandrin	viii^v
15.	De quoy me sert de tenter la fortune	Sandrin	ix^v
16.	Puis qu'ainsi est que d'un vouloir entier	Pagnier	ix^v
17.	Je cuyde bien qu'elle mourroit a l'heure S: Resp: de Qui la vouldra	Belin	x^v
18.	Qui de s'amye a le bien qui désire	Sandrin	x^v
19.	Si j'ay du bien l'ay-je pas mérité	Claudin	xi^v

20.	Puis que vivre en servitude	Sandrin	xi^v
21.	Montz et vaulx faictes moy place	Sandrin	xii^v
22.	Il est certain si fault tost que je meure	Pagnier	xii^v
23.	O doulx regard, ô parler gratieux	Jennequin	xiii^v
24.	Si ton plus grand désir n'est sinon d'estre tienne	Villiers	xiiii^v
25.	Toute la nuyct tu m'es présente par songe doulx	Belin	xv^v
26.	Je n'entendz pas de Cupido me plaindre	Villiers	xv^v
27.	Vostre doulx entretien, vostre belle jeunesse	Arcadelt	xvi^v

Finis

1548

151

Vingtseptiesme contenāt xxvij. Chansōs / NOVVELLES A QVATRE EN DEVX VOLVMES / *Par Pierre Attaingnant, libraire & imprimeur du Roy en musique En la / Rue de la Harpe pres leglise S. Cosme.* / 1548 / [Table] / **Superius & Tenor** / *Auec prorogation du priuilege du Roy, De nouuel obtenu par ledit attaingnant / Pour les liures Ia parluy imprimez & quil Imprimera cy apres iusques a six ans.* /

2 vol. in-4° obl., 21 × 15.8 cm.; 16 f. numbered [i]–xvi (S–T: x vi xii vii instead of v vi vii viii; Ct–B: v viii vii vi)

Sign.: XXVII i^4–XXVII m^4; XXVII I^4–XXVII M^4 (S–T: XXVII K i, XXVII K iii instead of XXVII k i, XXVII k ii)

RISM–I, 1548^4

Munich: Bayerische Staatsbibliothek, Mus. Pr. 4° 103

1.	Quel playsant songe ay-je eu la nuict passée	Du tertre	i^v
2.	Amy, héllas, je pensois bien	De la font	i^v
3.	Mon amy est en grace sy parfaict	Du tertre	ii^v
4.	Gentil petit rossignollet	Pelisson	iii^v
5.	Dieu la vouloit retire en son temple	Claudin	iiii^v
6.	Si ton amour viollant a souffert	De la font	iiii^v
7.	Celle que j'ay pour maistresse choisie	Meigret	v^v
8.	Héllas mon Dieu, et en quelle ignorance	Gentien	v^v
9.	Amour m'a mis en si grand desconfort	Vulfran	vi^v
10.	Grande en beaulté, en vertus tant heureuse	Belin	vi^v
11.	Tous les travaulx portés soubz espérance	Certon	vii^v
12.	Quand je regarde au peu de mon mérite	Belin	viii^v
13.	N'en parlez plus de l'amour en peincture	Meigret	viii^v
14.	Le fruict sans goust dont on me veult repaistre	Meigret	ix^v
15.	Quant ung vray cueur ne peult excécuter	P. Simon	ix^v
16.	Si a te veoir n'ay ausé entreprendre	Certon	x^v
17.	Vostre oeil tant doulx assez me faict entendre	Certon	x^v
18.	Si de mes os povoint estre les cendres	Vulfrant	xi^v
19.	Rien n'est certain en ce monde muable	Vulfran	xi^v
20.	Ce n'est malheur amy, sois asseuré	De la font	xii^v
21.	Cessés mes yeulx, de pleurer les ennuys	Plisson	xii^v
22.	L'oeil messager faict au cueur concepvoir	Meigret	xiii^v
23.	Le temps peult bien ung tainct effacer	Gentien	xiiii^v
24.	Si de mon mal n'avez compassion	Gentien	xiiii^v

25.	O gente brunette que Dieu gard	Mittou	xv^v
26.	Si le tourment ennvyeux mon corps lasse	Plisson	xv^v
27.	Elle voyant l'anuy qui me tourmente	Vulfran	xvi^v

Finis

1549

152

Vingthuitiesme contenāt xxviii. Chāsōs / NOVVELLES A QVATRE EN DEVX VOLVMES / *a Paris Par Pierre Attaingnāt, libraire & imprimeur du Roy en musique* / *En la Rue de la Harpe pres leglise S. Cosme.* / 1549 / [Table] / **Superius & Tenor** / *Auec priuilege du Roy pour six ans.* /

2 vol. in-4° obl., 21 × 15.8 cm.; 16 f. numbered [i]–xvi
Sign.: XXVIII n^4–XXVIII q^4; XXVIII N^4–XXVIII Q^4
RISM–I, 1549^{19}

Munich: Bayerische Staatsbibliothek, Mus. Pr. 4° 103

1.	Qui souhaitez avoyr tout le plaisir	Mornable	i^v
2.	Descens du ciel, o royne Calliope, vers ton poete	Meigret	i^v
3.	Si m'amie ha de fermeté	Certon	ii^v
4.	Vous qui voulés avoir contentement	Mornable	ii^v
5.	Des faictz d'amour je n'ay pas congnoissance	Colin	iii^v
6.	Si je te voy qui est-ce que désire	P. Symon	iii^v
7.	S'il est ainsy qu'on estaint la challeur	Meigret	iiii^v
8.	En discort sont l'oeil, la bouche et la grace	Mornable	iiii^v
9.	Gente mignonne de jadis qui tant fustes prudente	Certon	v^v
10.	Quand suis au lict pour prendre mon repoz	P. Symon	v^v
11.	Ung doulx nenny avec ung doulx soubrire	Crequillon	vi^v
12.	Sy a te veoyr n'ay ausay entreprendre	[Certon]	vii^v
13.	Vostre oeil tant doulx assez me faict entendre	[Certon]	vii^v
14.	Aussytost que je voy m'amye	Du tertre	viii^v
*15.	Je ly au cueur de m'amye une envye	Du tertre	viii^v
16.	De toy Amour je ne me veulx complaindre	Boyvin	ix^v
17.	Je ne cognois femme en ceste contrée	Du tertre	ix^v
18.	Certes l'amour grandement m'offensa	Boyvin	x^v
19.	Amour, Amour que ta force est estrange	Certon	x^v
20.	Je te supplie, ô celleste vainqueur	Boyvin	xi^v
21.	Ne craignés poinct qu'une beaulté nouvelle	Boyvin	xi^v
22.	Quelle prison au monde est plus cruelle	Mornable	xii^v
23.	Diane ceincte hault sa cotte attournée	Boyvin	xii^v
24.	Ung aultre et moy aymons en mesme endroit	Mornable	xiii
25.	Hélas, ne fringuerons nous jamais	Certon	xiii^v
26.	C'est trop presté sans jamais rendre	Guion	xiiii^v
27.	Entre vous gentilz hommes qui suivés la court	Certon	xiiii^v
28.	Et toy, beaulté tres élégant, ouvraige le plus exquis	Boyvin	xv^v
29.	Donnez m'en ung de ces yeulx bien aprins	Mornable	xv^v
30.	Ces jours la femme de Guillaume enceinte d'ung moyne	Delafont	xvi^v

Nos. 12 and 13 are lacking in the table.

* Modern edition in *Quinze Chansons.*

153

Vingtneufiesme contenāt xxix. Chansōs / NOVVELLES A QVATRE EN DEVX VOLVMES / *a Paris Par Pierre Attaingnāt, libraire & imprimeur du Roy en musique* / *En la Rue de la Harpe pres leglise S. Cosme.* / 1549 / [Table] / **Superius & Tenor.** / *Auec priuilege du Roy pour six ans.* /

2 vol. in-4° obl., 21 × 15.8 cm.; 16 f. numbered [i]–xvi (S–T: vi vi vii viii)
Sign.: XXIX r⁴–XXIX u⁴; XXIX R⁴–XXIX U⁴
RISM-I, 1549[20]

Munich: Bayerische Staatsbibliothek, Mus. Pr. 4° 103

1.	Qui souhaitez avoir tout le plaisir	Sandrin	i^v
2.	Partez regretz, puis qu'il plaist a ma dame	Mornable	i^v
3.	Tu pers amour et tes traiz et ta peine	Meigret	ii^v
4.	Je suis Robert le beau Robert	Gentiam	ii^v
5.	Héllas, frappez tout bellement	De la font	iii^v
6.	L'oeil pres et loing voyr vous désire	Certon	iii^v
7.	Or suis-je bien sur tous le misérable	Certon	iiii^v
8.	Ou cherchez-vous du Dieu d'amour l'empire	Certon	iiii^v
9.	T'en yras-tu, as-tu bien le couraige	Sohier	v^v
10.	O gent esprit qui gouverne ce corps	Morel	v^v
11.	D'amour me plains que je n'ay jouyssance	Morel	vi^v
12.	Je garderay jusqu'a mort endurer	Morel	vi^v
13.	Vous ressemblez au roc de l'aymant	Morel	vii^v
14.	La grant doulceur de vostre cler visaige	Meigret	vii^v
15.	Sa cruaulté me donne allégement	Vulfran	viii^v
16.	Je seuffre passion d'une amour forte	Gentiam	ix^v
*17.	La peine dure que tant j'endure	Gentiam	ix^v
*18.	Estes-vous de Clamessy, dame	Dambert	x^v
19.	Amour ung jour aparçoy congnoissant	Guion	xi^v
20.	S'il y eust onc en cueur contentement	Boyvin	xi^v
21.	J'ay tant de biens non plus que j'en désire	Boyvin	xii^v
22.	Asurez-vous, amye tant honneste	Boyvin	xii^v
23.	Héllas, mon Dieu, je te prie humblement	P. Symon	xiii^v
24.	O temps qui es vaincueur de mon martire	Gentiam	xiii^v
25.	Sy vous voulés user de l'entreprinse	Mittou	xiiii^v
26.	Puis que tu sens l'object de l'amoureuse flame	Harchadelt	xiiii^v
27.	Qu'est-ce qu'amour l'ung dict	Du tertre	xv^v
28.	En espérant plus l'espoir me tormente	Du tertre	xv^v
29.	De qui plustost maintenant me doibz plaindre	Sandrin	xvi^v

* Modern edition in *Chansons polyphoniques.*

1549, APRIL 20

154

Trentiesme liure contenāt xxviij. Chāsōs / NOVVELLES A QVATRE EN DEVX VOLVMES / *a Paris Par Pierre Attaingnāt, libraire & imprimeur du Roy en musique* / *En la Rue de la Harpe pres leglise S. Cosme.* / 20. *Aprilis.* 1549 / [Table] / **Superius & Tenor** / *Auec priuilege du Roy pour six ans.* /

2 vol. in-4° obl., 21 × 15.8 cm; 16 f. numbered [i]–xvi (Both books: ix x xi xii instead of v vi vii viii)
Sign.: XXX x^4–XXX $\&^4$; XXX X^4–XXX $\mathcal{A}^4$ (Ct–B: XXX & &i, XXX & &ii)
RISM–I, 1549^{21}

Munich: Bayerische Staatsbibliothek, Mus. Pr. 4° 103

1.	Rien au soleil la lune n'apartient	P. Symon	i^v
2.	Soleil qui tout voys par ma foy	Certon	i^v
3.	Si vous l'avez rendez le moy	Josselme	ii^v
4.	Quel Dieu du ciel ay-je tant irrité	Du tertre	iii^v
5.	Mon amy est en grace si parfaict	Certon	iii^v
6.	Ou se peult mieulx assoyr mon espérance	Harchadelt	iiii^v
7.	Si seul, je puis, une foys en ma vie	Ebran	iiii^v
8.	Je meurs allors que de vous ay perdu	Guyon	v^v
9.	M'amye est tant honneste et saige	Sandrin	v^v
10.	Si ce qu'avez vous le povyez avoyr	Morel	vi^v
11.	Mort et amour donnerent pris contraire	Gardane	vi^v
12.	Ce que l'oeil pert de vous voyr curieulx	Guyon	vii^v
13.	Si l'amour véhémente ne me tourmente	Morel	vii^v
14.	O doulx amour, ô contente pensée	Morel	viii^v
15.	Sy c'est amour de mourir en soy mesme	Morel	viii^v
16.	En contemplant de nature l'ouvraige	Gardane	ix^v
17.	Si vous eussiez seullement dict ouy	Ebran	ix^v
18.	Puys que je n'ay pour dire aultre nouvelle	Du tertre	x^v
19.	Vous souvient-il point, ma mygnonne	Du tertre	x^v
20.	Le dire ouy ne m'estoit raisonnable	Ebran	xi^v
21.	Ce moys de may soubz la belle verdure	Gardane	xi^v
22.	Si je me plains du mal que sens	Janequin	xii^v
23.	Si Dieu vouloit qu'eussions change	Du tertre	xii^v
24.	Mais en quel ciel fust si belle ame quise	Janequin	xiii^v
25.	Si le coqu en ce moys de may change	Janequin	xiiii^v
*26.	Las, viens moy secourir, ne tarde plus	Janequin	xiiii^v
27.	Je n'eu jamais de grandz biens le pouvoir	Janequin	xv^v
28.	Sçavez-vous quand je suis bien aise	Janequin	xvi^v
	Finis		

Under the Old Style, the date on the title page should read "20 Aprilis. 1548" (Easter fell on the following day, the 21st). It seems then that this volume, **152,** and **153** were dated according to the New Style.

* Modern edition in *Trente Chansons* (*1928*).

1549, MAY 22

155

Trente & vngyesme liure cōtenāt xxx. / CHANSONS NOVVELLES A QVATRE, EN DEVX / *Volumes De la Facture Et cōposition de Maistre Clemēt Iēnequin Imprimee / a Paris Par Pierre Attaingnāt, libraire & imprimeur du Roy en / musique En la Rue de la Harpe pres leglise S. Cosme.* / 22. *May* 1549 / [Table] / **Superius & Tenor** / *Auec priuilege du Roy pour six ans.* /

2 vol. in-4° obl., 21 × 15.8 cm.; 16 f. numbered [i]–xvi (S–T: ix xii xi xii)
Sign.: XXXI a^4–XXXI d^4; XXXI A^4–XXXI D^4

Munich: Bayerische Staatsbibliothek, Mus. Pr. 4° 103

1.	Las, si tu as plaisir en mon ennuy	i^v
2.	Petite damoyselle a amour donne lieu	i^v
3.	Je suys a vous mais sçavez-vous comment	ii^v
*4.	Quand contremont verras retourner Loyre	ii^v
5.	Ça, ces beaulx yeulx, ça ceste bouche	iii^v
†6.	Dur acier et diamant et l'aymant a la fin pouldre sera	iii^v
7.	Puys que vers vous aller je n'ause	iiii^v
*8.	Et vray Dieu qu'il m'ennuye	iiii^v
9.	Est-il possible, ô ma maistresse	v^v
10.	Las, si tu veulx en aultre part aymer	v^v
11.	Je me veulx tant a son vouloir offrir	vi^v
12.	Aussitost que je voy m'amye	vi^v
13.	Dieu doint le bon jour a m'amye	vii^v
14.	Je liz au cueur de m'amye une envye	vii^v
15.	Il s'en va tard, il pleut, il vente	viii^v
16.	Or as-tu bien raison de te douloir	viii^v
17.	Si a te veoir n'ay ausé entreprendre	ix^v
18.	Or ne différez donc pour ton amy	ix^v
19.	Malade si fut ma mignonne	x^v
20.	Faisons le dire mensonger	x^v
21.	Ne vous faschez si me voyez jaloux	xi^v
22.	Elle mérite pour ses graces	xi^v
23.	Puys que je n'ay pour dire aultre nouvelle	xii^v
24.	Ce disoit une jeune dame a ung viellart	xiii^v
25.	Elle voyant approcher mon départ	xiii^v
26.	Dont vient que ce beau temps, ces verdz prez, ces ruisseaulx	xiiii^v
27.	Par mes haultz cris je ne quiers advantaige	xiiii^v
28.	Je ne congnois femme en ceste contrée	xv^v
29.	Sy me voyez face triste et dolente	xv^v
30.	Quel Dieu du ciel ay-je tant irrité	xvi^v

Finis

* Modern edition in *Chorwerk*, Vol. 73.

† Modern edition as *Masterworks*, Vol. 3.

1549

156

Trente deuxiesme liure contenāt xxiiii / CHANSONS. NOVVELLES A QVATRE EN DEVX / *Volumes Imprimee a Paris Par Pierre Attaingnāt, libraire & imprimeur / du Roy en musique En la Rue de la Harpe pres leglise S. Cosme.* / 1549 / [Table] / **Superius & Tenor** / *Auec priuilege du Roy pour six ans.* /

2 vol. in-4° obl., 21 × 15.8 cm.; 16 f. numbered [i]–xvi (Ct–B: xi x ix xii)

Sign.: XXXII e^4–XXXII h^4; XXXII E^4–XXXII H^4 (S–T: XXXII I i instead of XXXII e i)

RISM–I, 1549[22]

Munich: Bayerische Staatsbibliothek, Mus. Pr. 4° 103

1.	Elle a voulu serviteur me nommer	Certon	i^v
2.	C'est a moy qu'en veult ce cocu	P. Symon	i^v
3.	Je vous diray que c'est de mon malheur	Gardane	ii^v
4.	Le jeu d'amours a court esbatement	Vulfran	ii^v
5.	Quand je me trouve aupres de ma maistresse	Harchadelt	iii^v
6.	Héllas Venus, trop tu me fuz contraire	Decapella	iiii^v
7.	L'on dict que la main tendre	Certon	iiii^v
8.	Combien est grand et en ditz et en faictz	Jacotin	v^v
9.	Tant de beaulté n'a elle pas	P. Symon	vi^v
10.	Sus, sus, ma seur, prendz bon couraige	Groussy	vii^v
11.	Si vous avez envye de congnoistre	Gardane	vii^v
12.	Ung amoureux de coucher eust promesse	Dubus	viii^v
13.	Bien est heureux le jour que je vous vis	Hebran	ix^v
14.	Las, est-il créature qui sente passion	Certon	ix^v
15.	Si me voyez face triste et dolente	Certon	x^v
16.	Ung doulx baiser m'est bien permis de prendre	Decapella	x^v
17.	Contentés-vous heureuses violettes	Harchadelt	xi^v
18.	Quand m'efforçay mettre la main	Certon	xii^v
19.	Si d'avanture ailleurs tu viens a veoir	Mornable	xii^v
20.	Las, si tu veulx en aultre part aymer	Du tertre	xiii^v
21.	Ung soir Guillot a sa Cathin a dict	Decapella	xiii^v
22.	O foible esprit, chargé de tant de peines	Gentiam	xiiii^v
23.	D'amour de vous, du temps et de moy mesme	Mornable	xv^v
24.	Elle s'en va dont tant triste demeure	P. Symon	xvi^v

Finis

1549, OCTOBER 12

157

Trente troysiesme liure contenãt xx. / CHANSONS. NOVVELLES A QVATRE EN DEVX / *Volumes Imprimee a Paris Par Pierre Attaingnãt, libraire & imprimeur / du Roy en musique En la Rue de la Harpe pres leglise S. Cosme.* / 12. *Octobris.* 1549 / [Table] / **Superius & Tenor.** / *Auec priuilege du Roy pour six ans.* /

2 vol. in-4° obl., 21 × 15.8 cm.; 18 f. numbered [i]–xviii (S–T: f. xviii numbered xix)
Sign.: XXXIII i^4–XXXIII m^4, XXXIII ꝫ^2; XXXIII I^4–XXXIII M^4, XXXIII ꝫ^2
RISM–I, 1549^{23}

Munich: Bayerische Staatsbibliothek, Mus. Pr. 4° 103

1.	Malade si fut ma mignonne		i^v
*2.	Cent mille foys estant dedans ma couche	Jennequin	ii^v
3.	Avant que partiez de ce lieu		iii^v
4.	Ce qu'il me faict si aysément jaloux	Symon	iii^v
5.	Il seroit bon planter le may	Jennequin	iiii^v
6.	En me baisant m'a dict m'amye	Jennequin	v^v
7.	Si je congnois que l'on ayme m'amye	Ebran	vi^v
8.	Il n'est que d'estre sur l'erbette	Du tertre	vi^v
9.	Si amytié n'est que conjunction	Gervaise	vii^v
10.	Qu'on m'appelle mal gratieulx		viii^v

* Modern edition in *Anthologie.*

11.	Or perdz-je celle en qui gist tout mon bien		ix^v
12.	Le moys de may sur tous est vigoureulx	Symon	x^v
13.	Sur l'aubépin qui est en fleur	Symon	xi^v
14.	Robin couché en mesme terre dessus l'herbette	Symon	xii^v
15.	Las vouldriez-vous si quelque sot en cause	Du tertre	xiii^v
16.	Qui veult sçavoyr qu'elle est m'amye	Jennequin	xiiii^v
17.	Or as-tu bien raison de te douloir	Gervaise	xv^v
18.	Ce qui pour moy en ce monde fut mis		xv^v
19.	Or sus pas je ne veulx refaire	Du tertre	xvi^v
20.	Petit jardin a Vénus consacré	Jennequin	xvii^v

1549, NOVEMBER 10

158

Trente quatriesme liure contenãt xx. / CHANSONS. NOVVELLES A QVATRE, EN DEVX / *Volumes, Imprimees a Paris, Par Pierre Attaingnãt libraire & imprimeur / du Roy en musique, En la Rue de la Harpe pres leglise S. Cosme.* / 10. *Nouenbris.* 1549 / [Table] / **Superius & Tenor.** / *Auec priuilege du Roy pour six ans.* /

2 vol. in-4° obl., 21 × 15.8 cm.; 16 f. numbered [i]–xvi
Sign.: XXXIIII n^4–XXXIIII q^4; XXXIIII N^4–XXXIIII Q^4 (S–T: signature of 1st two folios obscure; Ct–B: XXXIIII A i instead of XXXIIII N i)
RISM–I, 1549^{24}

Munich: Bayerische Staatsbibliothek, Mus. Pr. 4° 103

1.	Ce n'est poinct moy mon oeil qui te travaille	Symon	i^v
2.	Cent baysers au despartir, bouchette friande	Jennequin	i^v
3.	Quand vous yrez jouer au boys	Dubus	ii^v
4.	En Tour la feste Sainct Martin	Decapella	iii^v
5.	C'est grand cas que nostre voisin	Rene	iiii^v
6.	Que le sommeil a la mort soyt semblant	Besancourt	v^v
7.	Si vous eussiés le naturel préveu	Besancourt	v^v
8.	Mon bien et mal en toy gist seullement		vi^v
9.	Il n'est douleur qui tant soyt admirable	Alere	vii^v
10.	Poinct ne la debvez regreter	Gervayse	vii^v
11.	Raison le veult que fort je me contente	Gombert	viii^v
12.	O doulx regretz mon singulier plaisir	Gombert	ix^v
*13.	Mais languiray-je tousjours, vray Dieu	Clemens	x^v
14.	Belle commere, Dieu vous gard	Decapella	xi^v
15.	Si long travail méritte récompence	De la fons	xi^v
16.	Dieu qui conduictz l'amoureuse entreprinse	Gentian	xii^v
17.	Hault le boys myteine dondeine	De la font	xiii^v
18.	Alix a deux viellez disoit	Rene	xiiii^v
19.	Cathin en mal d'enfant cryoit	Rene	xv^v
†20.	O Atroppoz, viens bientost, je te prie	Lupus	xvi^v
	Finis		

* Modern edition in *CMM 4*:X.
† Modern edition in *Chorwerk, Vol. 15.*

159

Second liure cōtenāt xxix. chansons. / ESLEVES. POVR LES MEILLEV-RES ET PLVS FREQVENTES / *es cours des princes Conuenables a tous instrumentz musicaulz. Nouuellement / recoligees de plusieurs liures Et trescorectement imprimees a Paris, / Par Pierre Attaingnāt libraire & imprimeur du Roy / en musique, En la Rue de la Harpe pres leglise S. Cosme.* / 1549 3. *Decembris.* / [Table] / **Superius & Tenor.** / *Auec priuilege du Roy pour six ans.* /

2 vol. in-4° obl., 21.4 × 16.1 cm.; 16 f. numbered [i]–xvi
Sign.: Rec. r^4–Rec. u^4; Rec. R^4–Rec. U^4
RISM–I, 1549^{18}

Florence: Biblioteca del Conservatorio, Basevi 2496 (4)

1.	M'amye un jour le Dieu Mars désarma	Certon	i^v
2.	Je cherche autant amour et le désire	Boyvin	i^v
3.	Frere Thibault, séjourné, gros et gras	Certon	ii^v
4.	En fut-il oncques une plus excellente	Certon	iii^v
5.	Comment puis-je ma départie	Claudin	iii^v
6.	O triste adieu qui tant me mescontente	Certon	iiii^v
7.	O comme heureux t'estimeroys mon cueur	Certon	iiii^v
8.	Ce qui est plus en ce monde amyable	Sandrin	v^v
9.	Amour, voyant l'ennuy qui tant m'oppresse	Claudin	v^v
10.	Rien n'est plus cher que ce que l'on désire	De villiers	vi^v
11.	Plus je le voy de beaucoup estimé	Belin	vi^v
12.	Voulant honneur que de vous je m'absente	Sandrin	vii^v
[1]*13.	Je n'ay poinct plus d'affection	Claudin	vii^v
14.	Hélas amy, je congnois bien que ne puis nyer mon offence	Sandrin	viii^v
15.	La vouInté si longtemps endormie	Sandrin	viii^v
†16.	O passi sparsi, o pensier vaghi e pronti	Constantius Festa	ix^v
17.	Je ne le croy et le sçay seurement	Sandrin	x^v
18.	Si vostre amour ne gist qu'en apparance	Sandrin	x^v
19.	Au temps heureulx que ma jeune ignorance	Harchadelt	xi^v
20.	Si mon vouloir ne change de désir	Maillard	xi^v
21.	Au feu, venez moy secourir	Maillard	xii^v
‡22.	Hélas mon Dieu, ton yre c'est tournée	Maillard	xii^v
23.	Je sentz l'affection qui a moy se vient rendre	Boyvin	xiii^v
24.	Oeil peu constant, messagier des pensées	D'Auxerre	xiii^v
25.	Ce qui m'est deu et ordonné	Sandrin	xiiii^v
26.	Pleurez mes yeulx, pour la dure déffense qui rend l'amy	Sandrin	xiiii^v
27.	La palme doulce avant que feuilles rendre	Gardane	xv^v
28.	Si l'on me monstre affection	Belin	xv^v
29.	Ung advocat dict a se femme	De la font	xvi^v

Finis

* Modern edition in *Anthologie.*
† Modern edition in *Chanson and Madrigal*, with correct attribution to Sebastian Festa.
‡ Attributed to Janequin in **123–125**, q.v. for modern editions.

[1] Table: Je ne point plus.

160

Trente cincquiesme liure cōtenāt xxiiii / CHANSONS NOVVELLES A QVATRE PARTIES EN / DEVX *Volumes, Imprimees Nouuellement a Paris Par Pierre / Attaingnāt libraire & imprimeur du Roy en musique / En la Rue de la Harpe pres leglise S. / Cosme.* 22 *Ianuarij.* 1549 / [Table] / **Superius & Tenor** / *Auec Priuilege du Roy pour six ans.* /

2 vol. in-4° obl., 21 × 15.8 cm.; 16 f. numbered [i]–xvi
Sign.: XXXV f^4–XXXV i^4; XXXV F^4–XXXV I^4
RISM–I, 1550^5

Munich: Bayerische Staatsbibliothek, Mus. Pr. 4° 103

1.	Si m'amye ha de fermeté	Symon	i^{v}
2.	Si je n'avois de fermeté	Simon	i^{v}
3.	Je suis bien ayse qu'elle est belle	Symon	ii^{v}
4.	Amour m'a mis de tous reste des siens	De marle	ii^{v}
5.	J'ay d'un costé l'honneur tant estimé	Symon	iii^{v}
6.	Ung bon vyellard qui n'avoit que le bec	Certon	iii^{v}
7.	Frere Jehan fust un jour suprins	De marle	iiii^{v}
8.	Margot ung jour estant a ses ebatz dict a Robin	Maillard	v^{v}
9.	Ung gros lourdault de village espousa une fillete	De marle	vi^{v}
10.	Mon amytié tousjours augmente	Harchadelt	vii^{v}
11.	Laissez cela, laissez, je crainctz fort ceste troigne		vii^{v}
12.	Robin couché a mesme terre dessus l'herbette	Certon	viii^{v}
13.	Fault-il, hélas, sans l'avoir mérité	De marle	ix^{v}
14.	Adieu plaisir, adieu celle que j'ayme tant	Nicolas	ix^{v}
15.	Puis que tes mains et tes yeux bien apris	De marle	x^{v}
16.	Si refuz de joyssance a puissance	Belin	x^{v}
17.	Gros Jehan menoit hors de Paris en crouppe ung jour	Rene	xi^{v}
18.	Pour faire amour plus longuement durer	De marle	xii^{v}
19.	Elle a pour vray une si grand beaulté	Du tertre	xii^{v}
20.	Tu as tout seul, Jehan, Jehan, vignes et prez	Rene	xiii^{v}
21.	Mon pencement ne gist qu'en vostre faict	Gombert	xiiii^{v}
22.	S'advance qui veult s'advancer	Blancher	xv^{v}
23.	J'estimerois ma mort, ma vye	Blancher	xv^{v}
24.	Petite fille sans soucy passant	Du tertre	xvi^{v}

Finis

1550, FEBRUARY 14

161

Premier liure des chāsōs esleues en nobre / XXX. *Pour les meilleures & plus frequentes, es cours des princes, / Cōuenables a tous instrumentz musicaulz. Nouuellement recoligees / de plusieurs liures par cy deuant imprimez Dont aulcunes ont / este rechangees & mises au lieu des plus uielles & sont / beaucop plus correctes que les precedētes. Reimprimees / a Paris Par Pierre Attaingnāt libraire & im-/primeur du Roy en musique En la Rue / de la Harpe pres leglise S. Cosme.* 14 *Februarij*, 1549. / [Table] / *Auec priuilege du Roy pour six ans.* / **Superius & Tenor.** /

2 vol. in-4° obl., 21.4 × 16.1 cm.; 16 f. numbered [i]–xvi
Sign.: Rec. a⁴–Rec. d⁴; Rec. A⁴–Rec. D⁴
RISM–I, 1549[17]

Florence: Biblioteca del Conservatorio Basevi 2496 (3)

1.	Mon cueur voulut dedans soy recepvoir	Claudin	i^v
2.	Le voyr, l'ouyr, le parler, l'attoucher	[1]Certon	i^v
3.	Doulce mémoire en plaisir consomée	Sandrin	ii^v
*4.	Finy le bien, le mal soudain commence	Certon	ii^v
5.	Ce qui souloit en deux se départir	Sandrin	iii^v
*6.	Amour est bien de perverse nature	Claudin	iii^v
7.	N'espoir ne paour n'auray jour de ma vie	Claudin	iiii^v
8.	Le mal que j'ay rigueur le me procure	Le moyne	iiii^v
†9.	D'un desplaisir que fortune m'a faict	De la Rue	v^v
10.	Comme inconstante et de cueur faulse et lasche	Regnes	v^v
11.	Continuer je veuil ma fermeté	Bourguinon	vi^v
12.	Passions et douleurs qui suyvez tous malheurs	Pagnier	vi^v
13.	Sans liberté qu'un bon esprit regrete	Magdelain	vii^v
14.	Veu le grief mal que longuement j'endure	De villiers	vii^v
15.	O doulx revoir que mon esprit contente	[2]Certon	viii^v
16.	Amour me poingt et si je me veulx plaindre	Claudin	viii^v
17.	Force d'amour souvent me veult contraindre	De villiers	ix^v
18.	En espérant en ceste longue attente	Claudin	x^v
19.	Contentez-vous, amy, de la pensée	Claudin	x^v
20.	Plus je la vois moins y trouve a redire	Mittantier	xi^v
‡21.	Plaindre l'ennuy de la peine estimée Ct-B: Canon A quatre chantez A cincq si voulez	Hesdin	xi^v
§22.	Vous perdez temps de me dire mal d'elle	Claudin	xii^v
23.	Tel en mesdit qui pour soy la désire	Mittantier	xii^v
24.	Hélas, Amour qui sçais certainement	Le Heurteur	xiii^v
25.	Si mon travail vous peult donner plaisir	Sandrin	xiii^v
26.	Le dueil issu de la joye incertaine	De villiers	xiiii^v
†27.	Puis que de vous je n'ay aultre visaige	Sandrin	xiiii^v
28.	Ung moins aymant aura peult estre mieux	Certon	xv^v
29.	Hélas Amour, je pensoye bien avoir	Godard	xv^v
30.	Est-il possible que l'on puisse trouver	Morel	xvi^v

Finis

* Modern edition in *Chorwerk, Vol. 82.*
† Modern edition in *Quinze Chansons.*
‡ Modern edition in *Anthologie.*
§ Modern edition published by Akademische Druck- und Verlagsanstalt, Graz, 195-.
[1] Villiers in **89**.
[2] Godard in **82**.

1550, MARCH 14

162

Trente sixiesme liure cõtenãt xxx. chãsõs / *Tres Musicales, A Quatre Cinq & Six parties, En cinq liures, Dont le cinquiesme* / *liure contient les cinquiesmes & sixiesmes parties, Le tout de la cõpo-/sition de feu Iosquin des prez, Tres corectement Imprimees* / *Par Pierre attaingnant Libraire & imprimeur du Roy* / *en musicque En la Rue de la Harpe Pres* / *leglise S. Cosme* 14 *Martii.* 1549. / [Table] / **Superius.** / *Auec priuilege du Roy Pour six ans.* /

5 vol. in-4° obl., 21 × 15.8 cm.; 16 fol. numbered [i]–xvi

Sign.: Iosq. a^4–Iosq. d^4; Iosq. aa^4–Iosq. dd^4; Iosq. AA^4–Iosq. DD^4; Iosq. A^4–Iosq. D^4; Iosq. ()A^4–Iosq. ()D^4 (S: Iosq. B i; Ct: Iosq. A i; B: Iosq. A̱ i; Q & Sexta: Iosq. A i)

[1] Uppsala: Universitetsbiblioteket, Utl. vok. mus. tr. 511–515
Vienna: Gesellschaft der Musikfreunde II 53300/2 (Ct, T & B)

[2]1.	Cueur langoureux qui ne fais que penser	cc	i^v
2.	L'amye a tous et qui n'esconduit ame	tt	ii
	Quinta Pars: Je ne viz oncques la pareille		
3.	Vous ne l'aurés pas si je puis	tt bb	ii^v
4.	Parfons regretz et lamentable joye	tt	ii^v
5.	Plaine de deuil et de mélencolie	tt	iii
6.	Regretz sans fin il me fault endurer	tt cc	iii^v
7.	Incessamment livré suis a martire	tt	iiii
8.	Plusieurs regretz qui sur la terre sont	cc	iiii^v
9.	N'esse pas un grand desplaisir	tt	v
	T: Fuga. A la cincquiesme partie		
10.	Si vous n'avez autre désir	tt bb	v^v
11.	En non sachant se qui luy fault	cc	vi
	S: "Chantez une quarte plus bas"		
12.	Pour souhaiter je ne demande mieulx	tt cc	vi^v
13.	Je me complains de mon amy	cc	vii
14.	Se congié prens de mes belles amours	tt cc	vii^v
15.	Tenez moy en voz bras, mon amy, je suis malade	tt bb	viii^v
16.	Allégez moy doulce plaisant brunette	tt bb	ix
17.	Faulte d'argent c'est douleur non pareille	tt	ix^v
18.	Vous l'aurez s'il vous plaist madame	tt cc	x
19.	Petite camusete à la mort m'avez mis	ss bb	x^v
20.	Douleur me bat et tristesse m'afole	cc	xi
21.	Ma bouche rit et mon cueur pleure I	bb cc	xi^v
	Mon cueur pleure et ma bouche rit II		
22.	Baisés-moy ma doulce amy	tt bb	xii
23.	D'un mien amant le déppart m'est si grief I	cc	xii^v
	Or au facteur de toute créature II		
24.	Nimphes, nappés, neridriades venez plorer	tt cc	xiii
	Quinta & Sexta partes: Circumdederunt me gemitus mortis		
[3]25.	Cent mille regretz me poursuivent sans cesse	tt	xiii^v
[3]26.	Incassament mon povre cueur lamente	tt	xiii^v
[4]27.	Je ne me puis tenir d'aimer	tt	xiiii
28.	Cueurs désolez par toute nation	ss	xiiii^v
	Quinta pars: Plorans ploravit in nocte		
29.	Plus n'estes ma maistresse aultre servir me fault		xv^v
30.	Plus nulz regretz grandz moiens et menuz		xvi

All pieces included in the modern edition, *Josquin*, Wereldlijke Werken.

Fétis, *Biographie universelle des musiciens*, 2d ed., Vol. II, p. 481, gives this work under a Latin title (probably derived from one of the earlier general bibliographies, but one which we have not succeeded in identifying): "*Josquini Des Prez, musicorum omnium facile*

[1] At the end of each part-book at Uppsala: "Simoni Francisci Schillingij Ex dono Magistri Antonij Rod^t Vicarii Moguntiae. 1562 Telis Quod Potes."

[2] Quinta & Sexta partes: first five pieces printed in the sequence 1, 5, 2, 3, 4.

[3] The attribution to Josquin is doubtful. See H. Osthoff, *Josquin Desprez*, II, Munich, 1965, pp. 184–85.

[4] Ct, T. B: last four pieces printed in the sequence 28, 30, 29, 27.

principis tredecim modulorum selectorum opus, nunc primum cura solerti impensaque Petri Attingentis regii typographi excussum in-4° obl. goth. [sic] 1459." Fétis explains that the date should read 1549.

1550, JULY 1

163

Tiers liure contenant xxviij. chansons / ESLEVES POVR LES MEILLEVRES ET PLVS FREQVENTES / *Es cours des princes. Conuenables á tous instrumentz musicaulx Recol- / ligees de plusieurs liures par cy deuant imprimes. Et tresco- / rectement imprimees a paris Par Pierre Attaignant / libraire & imprimeur du Roy en musique, / En la Rue de la Harpe pres lesglise / S. cosme* 1 *Iulij* 1550 / [Table] / **Superius & Tenor.** / *Auec priuilege du Roy pour six ans,* /

2 vol. in-4° obl., 21.4 × 16.1 cm.; 16 f. numbered i–xvi
Sign.: III Rec. i^4–III Rec. m^4; III Rec. I^4–III Rec. M^4
RISM-I, 1550^6

Florence: Biblioteca del Conservatorio, Basevi 2496 (5)

1.	Trop tost j'ay creu y prenant tel plaisir	[1]Claudin	i^v
2.	O combien est malheureux le désir	Claudin	i^v
3.	Nostre amytié et nouvelle alliance	Poilhiot	ii^v
4.	Or sus Amour, puisque tu m'as attaint	Claudin	ii^v
5.	Je suys tant bien, voire tant bien encore	Claudin	iii^v
6.	Je ne puis bonnement penser	Sandrin	iii^v
7.	Quant j'ay congneu en ma pensée	Sandrin	iiii^v
8.	Longtemps y a que langueur et tristesse	Godard	iiii^v
9.	Vray Dieu tant j'ay le cueur gay	Vassal	v^v
10.	Las, me fault-il tant de mal supporter	Maille	vi^v
11.	Celle qui a fascheux mary	Jantian	vi^v
12.	Mort et fortune, pourquoy m'avez laissé	Gombert	vii^v
*13.	Je suis déshéritée puisque j'ay perdu mon amy	Cadéac [or Lupi]	vii^v
14.	Il est vray que vostre oeil qui pleure, le mien tente	Harcadel	viii^v
†15.	De long travail heureuse récompense	Certon	viii^v
†16.	Ouvrez-moy l'huys, hé Jehanneton m'amye	Janequin	ix^v
‡17.	Si j'ay eu tousjours mon vouloir	Certon	x^v
18.	Si pour t'aymer et désirer	Sandrin	x^v
19.	Puis qu'il est tel qu'il garde bien s'amye	Claudin	xi^v
‡20.	O cueur ingrat qui tant m'est redebvable	Certon	xi^v
21.	Hélas Amour, tu feiz mal ton debvoir	Peletier	xii^v
§22.	Si de bon cueur j'ayme bien une dame	Janequin	xii^v
23.	De tout le mal que d'un vouloir constant	Certon	xiii^v
24.	D'amour me plains et non de vous m'amye	Rogier	xiii^v
‖25.	Je prens en gré la dure mort	Clemens	xiiii^v
26.	Dieu des amantz ton pouvoir est petit	Goudeaul	xiiii^v
27.	Plus revenir ne puis vers toy ma dame	Lupy	xv^v
28.	Reviens vers moy qui suis tant desolée	Lupy	xvi^v

* Modern edition in *Chorwerk, Vol. 15* and *GMB.*
† Modern edition in *Chansons polyphoniques.*
‡ Modern edition in *Chorewerk, Vol. 82.*
§ Modern edition as *Masterworks,* Vol. 8.
‖ Modern edition in *CMM 4:*X.

[1] Mornable in **101**.

164

Quart liure de danceries, A quatre parties / Cotenant xix pauanes & xxxi gaillardes. / EN VNG LIVRE SEVL, VEV ET CORRIGE PAR / *Claude geruaise scauant Musicien. Et Imprimez par Pierre Attaīgnāt / Imprimeur du Roy en musique. Demeurant á Paris En / la Rue de la Harpe pres lesglise S. cosme.* / 19 *Augusti* 1550. / **Auec priuilege du Roy pour six ans** /

1 vol. in-4° obl., 20.9 × 15.4 cm.; 32 f. numbered [i]–xxxii (vii vi v viii)
Sign.: IIII A^{4}–IIII H^{4} (Second folio of each gathering except the first is numbered "III" instead of "IIII")

Paris: Bibliothèque Nationale, Rés. Vm^{7} 376 (3)

1.	Pavane La venissienne	i^{v}
2.	Pavane	ii^{v}
	Gaillarde	ii^{v}
3.	Pavane	iii^{v}
	Gaillarde	iii^{v}
4.	Pavane L'oeil pres et loing	iiii^{v}
	Gaillarde	iiii^{v}
5.	Pavane Vous qui voulez	v^{v}
	Gaillarde	v^{v}
6.	Pavane	vi^{v}
	Gaillarde	vi^{v}
7.	Pavane Qui souhaitez	vii^{v}
	Gaillarde	vii^{v}
8.	Pavane Plus revenir	viii^{v}
	Gaillarde	viii^{v}
9.	Pavane M'amyee est tant honneste et saige	ix^{v}
	Gaillarde	ix^{v}
*10.	Pavane O foyble esprit	x^{v}
11.	Pavane Le bon vouloir	xi^{v}
*12.	Pavane	xii^{v}
13.	Pavane Pour mon plaisir	xiii^{v}
14.	Pavane	xiiii^{v}
15.	Pavane	xv^{v}
*16.	Pavane	xvi^{v}
17.	Pavane	xvii^{v}
18.	Pavane DELLESTARPE	xviii^{v}
19.	Pavane	xix^{v}
20.	Gaillarde i	xx^{v}
21.	Gaillarde ii	xxi^{v}
22.	Gaillarde iii	xxii^{v}
23.	Gaillarde iiii	xxiii^{v}
24.	Gaillarde v	xxiiii^{v}
25.	Gaillarde vi	xxv^{v}
26.	Gaillarde vii	xxv^{v}
27.	Gaillarde viii	xxv^{v}
*28.	Gaillarde i	xxvi^{v}
29.	Gaillarde ii	xxvi^{v}
30.	Gaillarde iii	xxvii^{v}
31.	Gaillarde iiii	xxvii^{v}
32.	Gaillarde v	xxvii^{v}
33.	Gaillarde vi	xxviii^{v}
34.	Gaillarde vii	xxviii^{v}
35.	Gaillarde viii	xxviii^{v}
36.	Gaillarde ix	xxix^{v}
37.	Gaillarde x	xxix^{v}
38.	Gaillarde xi	xxix^{v}
39.	Gaillarde xii	xxx^{v}
40.	Gaillarde [xiii]	xxx^{v}
41.	Gaillarde xiiii	xxxi^{v}
42.	Gaillarde [xv]	xxxi^{v}

Dances which were written on chansons from Attaingnant's publications are as follows:

No. 4 Pavane L'oeil pres et loing, **153**-6 (Certon)

No. 9 Pavane M'amyee est tant honneste et saige, **154**-9 (Sandrin)

No. 10 Pavane O foyble espirit, **156**-22 (Gentiam)

No. 5 Pavane Vous qui voulez: Superius is related to the Superius of Gervaise, Vous qui voulez avoir contentement, **166**-2.

* These pieces edited in *MMRF* XXII: no. 10, p. 30; no. 12, p. 39; no. 16, p. 34; no. 28, p. 40. *Ibid.*, facsimile of S-T, f. xi^{v} of Ct-B, f. xii.

165

Cinquiesme liure de danceries, A quatre / PARTIES, CONTENANT DIX BRANSLES GAYS, / *Huict bransles de poictou, Trente cinq bransles de Champaigne, Le tout / en ung liure seul, Veu & corrige par Claude geruaise scauant / Musicien. Nouuellemēt imprimez par Pierre / Attaīgnāt Imprimeur du Roy en mu- / sique. Demeurāt á Paris En la / Rue de la Harpe pres / lesglise S. cosme. /* 28. *Augusti /* 1550. / [Table] /❧**Auec priuilege du Roy pour six ans** /

1 vol. in-4° obl., 20 × 16 cm.; 32 f. numbered [i]–xxxii
Sign.: V I^{4}–V Q^{4}

Paris: Bibliothèque Nationale, Rés. Vm^{7} 376 (4)

1. Bransle gay i — i^{v}
2. Bransle gay ii — i^{v}
3. Bransle gay iii — ii^{v}
4. Bransle gay iiii — ii^{v}
5. Bransle gay v — iii^{v}
6. Bransle gay vi — iii^{v}
7. Bransle gay vii — iiii^{v}
8. Bransle gay viii — iiii^{v}
9. Bransle gay ix — v^{v}
10. Bransle gay x — v^{v}
*11. Bransle de poictou i — vi^{v}
*12. Bransle de poictou ii — vi^{v}
*13. Bransle de poictou iii — vii^{v}
*14. Bransle de poictou iiii — vii^{v}
*15. Bransle de poictou v — viii^{v}
16. Bransle de poictou vi — ix^{v}
17. Bransle de poictou vii — x^{v}
18. Bransle de poictou viii — x^{v}
19. Bransle de champaigne i — xi^{v}
20. Bransle ii — xii^{v}
21. Bransle iii — xii^{v}
22. Bransle iiii — xiii^{v}
23. Bransle v — xiii^{v}
24. Bransle vi — xiiii^{v}
25. Bransle vii — xv^{v}
26. Bransle viii — xv^{v}
27. Bransle ix — xvi^{v}
28. Bransle x — xvii^{v}
29. Bransle xi — xvii^{v}
30. Bransle de champaigne [i] — xviii^{v}
31. Bransle ii — xix^{v}
32. Bransle iii — xix^{v}
33. Bransle iiii — xx^{v}
34. Bransle v — xxi^{v}
35. Bransle vi — xxi^{v}
36. Bransle vii — xxii^{v}
37. Bransle viii — xxiii^{v}
38. Bransle ix — xxiiii^{v}
39. Bransle x — xxiiii^{v}
40. Bransle xi — xxv^{v}
*41. Bransle xii — xxv^{v}
*42. Bransle xiii — xxvi^{v}
43. Bransle xiiii — xxvi^{v}
44. Bransle de champaigne [i] — xxvii^{v}
45. Bransle ii — xxviii^{v}
*46. Bransle iii — xxviii^{v}
47. Bransle iiii — xxix^{v}
48. Bransle v — xxix^{v}
49. Bransle vi — xxx^{v}
50. Bransle vii — xxx^{v}
51. Bransle viii — xxxi^{v}
52. Bransle ix — xxxi^{v}
53. Bransle x — xxxi^{v}

* These pieces edited in *MMRF* XXII: nos. 11-15, pp. 109–113; no. 41, p. 106; no. 42, p. 108; no. 46, p. 101.

1550, OCTOBER 23

166

Quart liure contenant xxvj .chansons / MVSICALLES A TROYS PARTIES A DEVX DESSVS / *& ung concordant, Le tout de la composition de Claude* *geruaise scauant / Musicien. Et imprimees Par Pierre Attaīgnant imprimeur du / Roy en musique, A Paris En la Rue de la Harpe / pres lesglise S. Cosme.* 23. *Octobris.* 1550 / [Table] / *Auec priuilege du Roy pour six ans,* /

1 vol. in-4° obl., 20 × 16 cm.; 32 f. numbered [i]–xxxii
Sign.: IIII Trio. A^{4}–IIII Trio. H^{4}

London: British Museum, K. 2. a 9

1.	Qui souhaitez d'avoir tout le plaisir	i^{v}
2.	Vous qui voulez avoir contentement	ii^{v}
3.	Sy j'ay du bien, héllas, c'est par mensonge	iii^{v}
4.	M'amye est tant honneste et saige	iiii^{v}
5.	Celle qui a le cueur haultain	v^{v}
6.	Au temps heureux que ma jeune ignorance	vi^{v}
7.	Puys qu'il est tel qui garde bien s'amye	viii^{v}
8.	Ou se peult mieulx assoir mon espérance	ix^{v}
9.	D'amour me plainctz et non de vous m'amye	xi^{v}
10.	Elle voyant approcher mon départ	xii^{v}
11.	Las, je sçay bien que je feis grande offence	xiii^{v}
12.	Sy l'on doibt prendre un bienfaict pour offence	xiiii^{v}
13.	Mon pencement ne gist qu'en vostre faict	xv^{v}
14.	Par bien servir j'ay dueil pour récompense	xvi^{v}
15.	Aultant que moy heureuse pourrez estre	xviii^{v}
16.	Vertu le veult et Amour le commande	xx^{v}
17.	Veu le grief mal que longuement j'endure	xxi^{v}
18.	Peine et travail ne m'est que jouyssance	xxii^{v}
19.	Contentement, combien que soit grand chose	xxiii^{v}
20.	O foyble esprit, chargé de tant de peines	xxiiii^{v}
21.	Honneur sans plus en noble cueur prent place	xxvi^{v}
22.	Puysque j'ay perdu mes amours	xxvii^{v}
23.	Sy franchement déclairez vostre cueur	xxviii^{v}
*24.	Tant qu'en amours tu seras ma maistresse	xxix^{v}
*25.	Trop de regretz pour vous seulle je porte	xxx^{v}
*26.	De trop penser en amour et richesse	xxxi^{v}

The volume is made up of re-arrangements of earlier chansons. See Lawrence Bernstein, "Claude Gervaise as Chanson Composer," *Journal of the American Musicological Society* XVIII (1965), Appendix A, 379–380. No model was found for no. 5.

* Modern edition in *Claude Gervaise: Three Chansons*, ed. Michael Grace. Colorado College Music Press, 1962.

1551

167

C Plinij Secūdi veronē -/ SIS IN XXXVII. LIBROS NATU- / *ralis historie sue ad Tit. Vespasianum Impera- / torem Prefatio. Commētarijs Leodegarij / à Quercu illustrata.* / PARISIIS, / *Ex officina Petri Attingētis, regij musices typographi, / in vico Citharae, non procul à templo D. Cosmae.* / M.D.LI. /

1 vol. in-4° obl., 14.8 × 20.5 cm.; 12 fol., unnumbered
Sign.: A^4–C^4

Paris: Bibliothèque Mazarine,*14743 (17); 14823; *A. 15361 (11)
Paris: Bibliothèque Nationale, *R. 7164

1553, JULY 24

168

PREMIER LIVRE CONTENANT xxvj. / Chāsōs nouuelles en musique à quatre parties en deux / VOLVMES IMPRIMEES PAR LA VEVFVE DE PIERRE / Attaingnant, demourant à Paris en la Rue de la Harpe, pres S. Cosme. / XXIII. de IVILLET, M.D.LIII. / [Table] / **Superius & Tenor / Auec priuilege du Roy pour neuf ans.** /

2 vol. in-4° obl., 23 × 16.5 cm.; 16 f. numbered [i]–xvi
Sign.: (∵)a^4–(∵)d^4; (∵)A^4–(∵)D^4
RISM–I, 1553[20]

Nantes: Bibliothèque du Musée Dobrée (S–T) ((∵) instead of (∵) a ii)
Paris: Bibliothèque Nationale, Fonds Rothschild VII (bas).1.17 (Ct–B)

1.	O doulx regard, o parler gratieulx	Gardane	i^v
2.	Souspirs errans, demonstrez luy ma peine	Gardane	ii^v
3.	D'ung cueur entier et d'un vouloir parfaict	Gardane	ii^v
4.	Amour muny de plusieurs divers traictz	Jacotin	iii^v
5.	En te contemplant je te prise	Lachenet	iii^v
6.	Et au surplus s'elle sçavoit combien	Jacotin	iiii^v
7.	Je ne me confesseray poinct d'avoir aymé	Mornable	iiii^v
8.	Plus ay désir oublyer sa présence	Du Buysson	v^v
9.	Je ne sçay que c'est qu'il me fault	Mornable	v^v
10.	S'il y en a qui peu louable	Du Buysson	vi^v
11.	Un gentilhomme, laid et fascheux	Le Rat	vii^v
12.	Adieu gentil corsaige ou nature a posé	La chenet	viii^v
13.	Las, oyez, piteuses dames, le tort	Mornable	viii^v
14.	Ce rossignol qui sa chere campaigne	Herissant	ix^v
15.	Sus donc, venez, embrassez-moy	Muret	x^v
16.	Fors de pitié tu es toutte remplye	Andrault	x^v
17.	Les mesdisantz par leur meschant langaige	Lachenet	xi^v
18.	Pour vous, amy, tousjours mon cueur souspire	Lachenet	xi^v
19.	L'amy certain au parler ne fault prendre	De Hauville	xii^v
20.	O mort, dont ma vie est captive	Goudimel	xii^v
21.	Qui pourra dire la douleur	Besancourt	xiii^v
22.	Je l'acolleray tantost celle que tant je désire	Goudimel	xiii^v
23.	Petite beste, je ne te nourriray jamais	Gervaise	xiiii^v
24.	J'en ay le mal d'aymer ces gentilhommes	Gervaise	xiiii^v
[1]25.	Mon pere me veult marier	Du Tertre	xv^v
26.	Passible corps, regarde a la constance	Du Tertre	xvi^v

The Rothschild volume is bound with *Premier* [—*Unziesme livre de*] *chansons nouvelles a quatre parties en deux volumes.* Paris, Du Chemin, 1549–1554.

[1] La gallande in table.

169

[Claude Gervaise. Premier Livre de Violle contenant dix chansons avec l'introduction d'accorder et apliquer les doigts selon la maniere qu'on a accoutumé de jouer, le tout de la composition de Claude Gervaise.—imprimé par la Veuve de Pierre Attaingnant demeurant a Paris près l'Eglise St Cosme le 14 fevrier 1554 avec privilege du Roi pour neuf ans.]

"Catalogue des livres de Musique Theorique et Pratique, vocalle et Instrumentale, tant imprimée que manuscripte, qui sont dans le Cabinet du Sr Sebastien de Brossard . . . 1724." MS in Paris, Bibliothèque Nationale, Rés. Vm^{8} 21.

Of the viol tutor, listed in IV Partie, p. 336, Brossard remarks: "Toutes ces chansons sont d'abord en tabulature par a, b, c, d, etc. pour la Violle, et en suite le Sujet est tres bien notté en Musique et Nottes ordinaires. 32 feuillets ou 64 pages."

Brossard lists the six volumes of *Danceries* after the "Premier Livre de Violle":

II° Item. Second livre contenant 3 gaillardes, 3 Pavanes etc.
III°—
IV°—
V°—
VI°—
VII°—

Thus the first edition of the viol tutor would appear to date back to 1547 or before; the signatures of the *Second livre*, **148**, I–Q, confirm that it was preceded in the same series by a volume of 32 folios (A–H).

1555, OCTOBER 2

170

SIXIEME LIVRE DE DANCERIES, / *MIS EN MVSIQVE A QVATRE PARTIES PAR* / *Claude Geruaise, nouuellemēt imprimé à Paris par la vefue de Pierre Attaingnāt,* / *demourant en la Rue de la Harpe, pres leglise sainct Cosme.* / [Table] / 1555. / **Auec priuilege du Roy, pour neuf ans.** /

1 vol. in-4° obl., 20.9 × 15.4 cm.; 32 f. numbered [i]–xxxii
Sign.: A^{4}–H^{4} (E instead of B, E iii instead of B iii)

Paris: Bibliothèque Nationale, Rés. Vm^{7} 376 (5)

*1.	Pavane Passemaize	i^{v}
	Gaillarde	i^{v}
2.	[1]Pavane des dieux	ii^{v}
	Gaillarde des dieux	ii^{v}
*3.	Pavane d'Angleterre	iii^{v}
	Gaillarde	iii^{v}
4.	ii Gaillarde	iiii^{v}
5.	iii Gaillarde	iiii^{v}
6.	iiii Gaillarde	iiii^{v}
7.	v Gaillarde	v^{v}
8.	vi Gaillarde	v^{v}
9.	Fin de Gaillarde	vi^{v}
*10.	Bransle simple i	vii^{v}
*11.	Bransle simple ii	viii^{v}
12.	Bransle de Champaigne i	ix^{v}
13.	Bransle de Champaigne ii	ix^{v}
14.	Bransle de Champaigne iii	x^{v}
15.	Bransle de Champaigne iiii	x^{v}
16.	Bransle de Champaigne v	xi^{v}
17.	Bransle de Champaigne vi	xi^{v}
18.	Bransle de Champaigne vii	xii^{v}
19.	Bransle de Champaigne viii	xii^{v}
20.	Bransle de Champaigne ix	xiii^{v}
21.	Bransle de Champaigne x	xiii^{v}
22.	Bransle de Champaigne xi	xiiii^{v}
23.	Bransle de Champaigne xii	xiiii^{v}
*24.	Bransle courant i	xv^{v}
*25.	Bransle courant ii	xvi^{v}
26.	Bransle gay i	xvii^{v}
27.	Bransle gay ii	xviii^{v}
28.	Bransle gay iii	xviii^{v}
29.	Bransle simple i	xix^{v}
30.	Bransle simple ii	xx^{v}
31.	Bransle simple iii	xxi^{v}
32.	Bransle simple iiii	xxi^{v}
*33.	Bransle gay i	xxii^{v}
*34.	Bransle gay ii	xxiii^{v}
*35.	Bransle de Champaigne i	xxiiii^{v}
*36.	Bransle de Champaigne ii	xxiiii^{v}
*37.	Bransle de Champaigne iii	xxv^{v}
*38.	Bransle de Champaigne iiii	xxv^{v}
39.	Bransle de Champaigne v	xxvi^{v}
40.	Bransle de Champaigne vi	xxvi^{v}
41.	Bransle de Champaigne vii	xxvii^{v}
42.	Bransle de Champaigne viii	xxvii^{v}
*43.	Bransle de Champaigne ix	xxviii^{v}
*44.	Bransle de Champaigne x	xxviii^{v}
*45.	Bransle de Champaigne xi	xxix^{v}
*46.	Bransle de Champaigne xii	xxix^{v}
47.	Bransle gay i	xxx^{v}
48.	Bransle gay ii	xxx^{v}
49.	Bransle gay iii	xxxi^{v}
50.	Bransle gay iiii	xxxi^{v}

Fol. 32^{v}: FIN DV SIXIEME LIVRE / de danceries, nouuellement imprimé à / Paris le ii iour d'Octobre, / 1555. / Auec priuilege du Roy, pour neuf ans.

* These pieces edited in *MMRF* XXII: no. 1, p. 28; no. 3, p. 18; no. 10, p. 59; no. 11, p. 62; no. 24, p. 78; no. 25, p. 80; no. 33, p. 72; no. 34, p. 76; no. 35, p. 94; no. 36, p. 95; no. 37, p. 98; no. 38, p. 93; no. 43, p. 99; no. 44, p. 102; no. 45, p. 104; no. 46, p. 97.

[1] The Contratenor bears the MS remark: "Qui est fait bonne pour les violons," in the same 16th-century hand as in **148**, fol. XXVII. Another inscription occurs on fol. V of the Contratenor, where the Roman numeral "V" has been surrounded by the letters "TABO" and "ROT," suggesting canon Jehan Tabourot (alias Thoinot Arbeau) of Langres.

1556

171

MISSARVM MVSICALIVM / *QVATVOR VOCVM LIBER III.* / [Table] / **Tenor.** / *De l'imprimerie de la vefue d'Attaingnant, demourant à Paris en la rue de la Harpe, pres S. Cosme* / **1556.** / **Auec priuilege du Roy, pour neuf ans.** /

MISSARVM MVSICALIVM

QVATVOR VOCVM LIBER III.

Dulcis amica.	*Gombert.*
Messe feriale.	*Paignier.*
Messe sur fantasie.	*Claudin.*
Messe de Requiem.	*Claudin.*

Tenor.

De l'imprimerie de la vefue d'Attaingnant, demourant à Paris en la rue de la Harpe, pres S. Cosme

1556.

Auec priuilege du Roy, pour neuf ans.

26 Title page from the last Mass volume **(171)**. By courtesy of the Newberry Library, Chicago.

[4] vol. in-4° obl., 20.6 × 15.7 cm.; 12 f. numbered [1]–12; 4 7 8 5 6 9
Sign.: Aa⁴–Cc⁴

Chicago: Newberry Library, Case-VM 2079 L63 L34 1571 P53 (T)

1. [Missa Dulcis amica]	Gombert	1ᵛ
2. [Missa sur fantasie]	Claudin	4
3. [Messe feriale]	[1]Claudin	6ᵛ
4. [Messe de Requiem]	Claudin	9ᵛ

The volume is bound with a copy of Lassus, *Primus Liber Modulorum*, Louvain, Phalesius, 1571.

[1] Attributed to Pagnier in table.

1557, JANUARY 17

172

TROISIEME LIVRE DE DANCERIES / *A QVATRE ET CINQ PARTIES, VEV PAR CLAVDE / Geruaise (le tout en vn volume) nouuellement imprimé à Paris par la vefue de Pierre / Attaingnant, demourant en Ia Rue de la Harpe, pres leglise S. Cosme.* / [Table] / **15. cal. Feb. 1556. / Auec priuilege du Roy, pour neuf ans.**

1 vol. in-4° obl., 20.9 × 15.4 cm.; 32 f. numbered [i]–xxxii
Sign.: III R⁴–III Æ⁴ ([III R], R ii, R iii; III S, S ii, etc.)

Paris: Bibliothèque Nationale, Rés. Vm⁷ 376 (2)

1.	Pavanne, Si je m'en vois. A cinq	iᵛ
	Gaillarde, Si je m'en vois	iᵛ
2.	Pavanne, Est-il conclud	iiᵛ
	Gaillarde, Est-il conclud	iiiᵛ
3.	Pavanne, l'Admiral	iiiiᵛ
	Gaillarde	iiiiᵛ
4.	Pavanne de la guerre	vᵛ
	Gaillarde	viiᵛ
	[1]Gaillarde	viiiᵛ
	[1]Gaillarde	viiiᵛ
5.	Gaillarde	viiiᵛ
6.	Gaillarde	viiiᵛ
7.	Bransle simple i	ixᵛ
8.	Bransle simple ii	xᵛ
9.	Bransle simple iii	xᵛ
10.	Bransle simple iiii	xiᵛ
11.	Bransle simple v	xiiᵛ
12.	Bransle simple vi	xiiᵛ
13.	Bransle gay i	xiiiᵛ
14.	Bransle gay ii	xiiiᵛ
15.	Bransle gay iii	xiiiiᵛ
16.	Bransle gay iiii	xiiiiᵛ
17.	Bransle gay v	xvᵛ
18.	Bransle gay vi	xvᵛ
*19.	Almande i	xviᵛ
*20.	Almande ii	xviiᵛ
*21.	Almande iii	xviiiᵛ
*22.	Almande iiii	xviiiᵛ
23.	Almande v	xixᵛ
24.	Almande vi	xixᵛ
25.	Almande vii	xxᵛ
26.	Et d'ou venez-vous madame Lucette, Almande viii	xxᵛ
*27.	Bransle de Bourgogne i	xxiᵛ
*28.	Bransle ii	xxiiᵛ
*29.	Bransle iii	xxiiiᵛ
*30.	Bransle iiii	xxiiiiᵛ
31.	Bransle v	xxiiiiᵛ

* These pieces edited in *MMRF* XXII: Almandes, pp. 46–51; Branles, pp. 82–92.

[1] Table: Deux gaillardes du ton de la guerre.

32. Bransle vi	xxv^{v}	[2]38. Bransle ii	xxix^{v}
*33. Bransle vii	xxvi^{v}	[2]39. Bransle iii	xxx^{v}
*34. Bransle viii	xxvii^{v}	[2]40. Branslc iiii	xxx^{v}
*35. Bransle ix	xxvii^{v}	[2]41. Bransle v	xxxi^{v}
36. Bransle x	xxviii^{v}	[2]42. Bransle vi	xxxi^{v}
[2]37. Bransle i	xxix^{v}		

Finis

The date "15. cal. Feb." under the Julian calendar must be read as fifteen days before February 1 (i.e., January 17).

[2] Table: Six autre bransles de Bourgongne.

1557

173

SEPTIEME LIVRE DE DANCERIES, / *MIS EN MVSIQVE A QVATRE PARTIES / par Estienne du Tertre, nouuellement imprimé à Paris par la vefue de / Pierre Attaingnant, demourant en la Rue de la / Harpe, pres l'eglise sainct Cosme.* / [Table] / **1557.** / **Auec priuilege du Roy, pour neuf ans.** /

1 vol. in-4° obl., 20.9 × 15.4 cm.; 32 f. numbered [1]–[32] (folios 20–32 lacking)
Sign.: I^{4}–[Q^{4}]

Paris: Bibliothèque Nationale, Rés. Vm^{7} 376 (6)

1. Pavane premiere	1^{v}	15. Bransle 4.	13^{v}
Gaillarde premiere	1^{v}	16. Bransle 5.	14^{v}
2. Pavane 2.	2^{v}	17. Bransle 6.	14^{v}
Gaillarde 2.	2^{v}	Troisieme suytte de Bransles	
*3. Pavane 3. [A cinq]	3^{v}	18. Bransle 1.	15^{v}
Gaillarde 3. A cinq	4^{v}	19. Bransle 2.	15^{v}
4. Pavane 4.	5^{v}	20. Bransle 3.	16^{v}
Gaillarde 4.	5^{v}	21. Bransle 4.	16^{v}
*5. Pavane 5.	6^{v}	22. Bransle 5.	17^{v}
Gaillarde 5.	6^{v}	23. Bransle 6.	17^{v}
6. Pavane 6. A cinq	7^{v}	Premiere suytte de Bransles d'Escosse	
Gaillarde 6. A cinq	8^{v}	*24. Premier Bransle d'Escosse	18^{v}
Premiere suytte de Bransles		*25. Bransle 2.	18^{v}
7. Bransle 1.	9^{v}	26. Bransle 3.	19^{v}
8. Bransle 2.	10^{v}	27. Bransle 4.	19^{v}
9. Bransle 3.	10^{v}	Table:	
10. Bransle 4.	11^{v}	Seconde suytte de bransles d'Escosse	xxi
11. Bransle 5.	11^{v}	Six bransles de Poictou	xxiij
Seconde suytte de Bransles		Huict bransles gays	xxvj
12. Bransle 1.	12^{v}	Cinq Gaillardes.	xxix
13. Bransle 2.	12^{v}		
14. Bransle 3.	13^{v}		

Facsimile of title page in *MGG*, Vol. XII, col. 1709–1710.

* These pieces edited in *MMRF* XXII: no. 3, p. 21; no. 5, p. 26; nos. 24 and 25, pp. 114 and 115.

174

LE / DIEVGARD DE / LA VILLE DE PARIS, A / Monseigneur de Guise, Pair, & grand Cham-/berlan de France, et Lieutenant Gene-/ral pour le Roy, à son retour de la / prise de Calais, par Sonnets he-/roiques. Autheur Fran-/cois Habert de / Berry. / *Avec une chanson en l'honeur de mondict Seigneur de Guise, / mise en musique par Francois Le Febure* / Francisci Haberti Distichon / Quidquid terra creat, tenues vanescet in auras, / Perpetua est, hominem quae ducit ad aethera, virtus. / A PARIS. / De l'imprimerie de la vefue de P. Attain-/gnant, demourant en la rue de la / Harpe, pres S. Cosme./MD.LVIII. /

1 vol. in-8° obl., 9.8 × 15.4 cm.; 15 f., unnumbered.
Sign.: A^4–C^4, D^3

London: British Museum, 238.m.3. (4.)
Paris: Bibliothèque Mazarine, 34 613 (1)

Chanson, fols. 12^v–15: Que dira l'on du noble advenement de ce vainqueur

Fol. 1^v: Pierre Habert Escrivain en l'université de Paris aux Lecteurs.
S'il est ainsi que la France reçoit . . .

Addendum Modern Editions

The edition of Janequin's chansons by François Lesure and A. Tillman Merritt (see **4**) totalled four volumes by 1968, extending through **155**–26.

A complete modern edition of **148** appeared in 1969: *Pierre Attaingnant Danceries à 4 parties (second livre, 1547)*, ed. Raymond Meylan. Paris, Heugel. (Le Pupitre, 9)

Editions of **41**–6, 16 and **42**–18, 19 appeared in *Chansons for Recorders*, ed. Howard Mayer Brown. New York, Galaxy, 1964. (American Recorder Society Editions, 52)

Two modern editions of chansons by Henry Expert have been omitted by oversight: *Florilège du Concert vocal de la Renaissance*, Paris, 1928; *Concerts du XVIe siècle*, Paris, 1938

SHORT-TITLE-LISTS

Chronological List

Catalogue Number	Date	Short Title	Reprint	Signature
1	1525	Breviarium secundum usum . . . ecclesiæ Noviomensis . . .		✠^{8}; a^8–d^8; ¶^{2}; A^8–L^8; M^6; A^8–R^8
2	1528, Apr. 4	Chansons nouvelles en musique a quatre parties . . .	**(9, 32)**	a^4–h^4
3	[1528]	[Chansons et motets en canon a quatre parties sur deux]		✠ 11^4
4	[1528]	Chansons de maistre Clement Janequin . . .	**(75)**	a^4–d^4
5	1529, Jan. 23	Trente et quatre chansons musicales . . .	**(29)**	e^4–h^4
6	[1529]	Trente et cinq chansons musicales . . .		i^4–m^4
7	[1529]	Trente et deux chansons musicales . . .		n^4–q^4
8	[1529]	Trente chansons musicales . . .		r^4–v^4
9	[1529]	Trente et sept chansons musicales . . .	**(2, 32)**	x^4– &^{4}
10	1529, Apr. 22	Quarante et deux chansons musicales a troys parties . . .		✠ a^4–✠ e^4
11	[1529]	Motetz nouvellement composez . . .		*a^4–*d^4
12	1529, Oct. 1	xii Motetz a quatre et cinq voix . . .		*ei; ✠ e$^{2-4}$–✠ h^4
13	1529, Oct. 6	Tres breve et familiere introduction . . .		A^4–P^4
14	1529, Nov. 1	Trente et une chanson musicales . . .		‡ a^4–‡ d^4
15	1530, Jan. 1	Trente et huyt chansons musicales . . .		‡ e^4–‡ h^4
16	1530, Feb. 1	. . . Dixhuit basses dances . . .		LA^4–LK^4
17	1530 (before Easter, Apr. 17)	Six Gaillardes et six Pavanes . . .		‡ i^4–‡ m^4
18	1530 (after Apr. 17)	Vingt et neuf chansons musicales . . .		‡ n^4–‡ q^4
19	1530 (July or after)	Trente et six chansons musicales . . .		‡ r^4–‡ v^4
20	1530	Neuf basses dances deux branles . . .		‡ x^4–‡ &^{4}
21	1530	Epithoma musice instrumentalis . . .		A^4–B^3
22	1531, Jan. 13	Dixneuf chansons musicales reduictes en la tabulature . . .		✠ a^4–✠ k^4
23	1531, Feb. 1	Vingt et cinq chansons musicales reduictes en la tabulature . . .		✠ l^4–✠ v^4
24	1531, Feb. 5	Vingt et six chansons musicales reduictes en la tabulature . . .		✠ aa^4–✠ kk^4
25	1531 (before Mar. 1)	Tabulature pour le jeu D'orgues . . .		‡ A^4–‡ K^4
26	1531, March 1	Magnificat sur les huit tons . . .		‡ L^4–‡ V^4
27	1531, April 1	Treze Motetz musicaulx . . .		‡ Aa^4–‡ Kk^4
28	1531 (before June 18)	Quatorze Gaillardes neuf Pavennes . . .		✠^{4}; ✠ AA^4–✠ BB^4; *CC^4–*HH^4; ‡ II^4
29	[1531?] (after Apr. 1530, and before June 18, 1531)	Trente et quatre chansons musicales . . .	**(5)**	34e^4–34h^4
30	1532, Feb. 1	Trente et troys chansons nouvelles . . .		ϕ a^4–ϕ d^4
31	1532, Feb.	Vingt et huit chansons nouvelles . . .		ϕ e^4–ϕ h^4
32	1532, Mar.	Trente et sept chansons musicales . . .	**(2, 9)**	x^4– &^{4}
33	1532, July 15	Primus liber viginti missarum . . .		A^7; B^6–E^6; F^8
34	1532	Secundus liber tres missas continet . . .		G^6–L^6; M^8
35	1532	Tertius liber tres missas continet . . .		N^6–S^6; T^4

Catalogue Number	*Date*	*Short Title*	*Reprint*	*Signature*
36	1532	Quartus liber tres missas continet . . .		AA^{6}–FF^{6}
37	1532	Quintus liber tres missas continet . . .		GG^{6}–LL^{6}; MM^{8}
38	1532	Sextus liber duas missas habet . . .		NN^{6}–RR^{6}; SS^{8}
39	1532	Septimus liber tres missas habet . . .		TT^{6}–𝒜𝒜^{6}
40	1533, Apr., (after the 13th)	Vingt et quatre chansons musicales . . .		ϕ h^{4}–ϕ l^{4}
41	1533, Apr., (after the 13th)	Chansons musicales a quatre parties . . .		ϕ n^{4}–ϕ q^{4}
42	1533, Apr., (after the 13th)	Vingt et sept chansons musicales . . .		ϕ r^{4}–ϕ v^{4}
43	1533	[Jannequin Cl. Sacrae Cantiones . . .]		
44	1534, Feb.	Trente chansons musicales . . .		ϕ x^{4}–ϕ &^{4}
45	1534, Mar.	Vingt et huyt chansons musicales . . .		Ͼa^{4}–Ͼd^{4}
46	1534, Apr., after the 4th	Liber primus quinqz et viginti . . . Motetos . . .		a^{4}–d^{4}
47	1534, May	Liber secundus; quatuor et viginti . . . Motetos . . .		e^{4}–h^{4}
48	1534, May	Missarum musicalium . . . Liber primus . . .		*a^{4}–*d^{4}
49	1534, June	Liber tertius: viginti . . . motetos . . .		i^{4}–m^{4}
50	1534, June	Liber quartus. xxix. musicales . . . modulos habet . . .		n^{4}–q^{4}
51	1534, July	Missarum musicalium . . . Liber secundus . . .		*e^{4}–*h^{4}
52	1534, Aug.	Liber quintus. xii. . . . magnificat . . .		r^{4}–v^{4}
53	1534, Sept.	Liber sextus. xiii. . . . magnificat . . .		x^{4}– &^{4}
54	1534, Sept.	Trente et une chansons musicales . . .		Ͼ e^{4}–Ͼ h^{4}
55	1534, Oct.	Vingt et huyt chansons musicalles . . .		Ͼ i^{4}–Ͼ m^{4}
56	1534, Nov.	Liber septimus. xxiiij. . . . modulos . . .		† a^{4}–† d^{4}
57	1534, Dec.	Liber octavus. xx . . . motetos . . .		† e^{4}–† h^{4}
58	1534	Hec figura omnes scientias et artes . . . in unam radicam . . . reducit . . .		
59	[1534?]	[Latin and French names of the rivers and towns of the three parts of Gaul]		
60	1535, Jan.	Lib. nonus. xviij. daviticos . . . psalmos . . .		† i^{4}–† m^{4}
61	1535, Feb.	Lib. decimus: Passiones dominice . . .		† n^{4}–† q^{4}
62	1535, Feb.	Vingt et six chansons musicales . . .		Ͼ n^{4}–Ͼ q^{4}
63	1535, Mar. (before the 28th)	Lib. undecimus. xxvj. musicales habet modulos . . .		† r^{4}–† v^{4}
64	1535, Mar. (29th–31st)	Lib. duodecimus. xvij. musicales . . . salutationes habet . . .		† x^{4}–† &^{4}
65	1535, Apr.	Trente et une chansons musicales a troys parties . . .	**(66)**	✠ f^{4}–✠ i^{4}
66	[1535?]	[Trente et une chansons musicales a trois parties en ung livre . . .]	**(65)**	
67	[1535?]	[Quarante et quatre chansons a deux . . .]		
68	1535, May	Lib. decimustertius. xviij. musicales habet modulos . . .		*a^{4}–*d^{4}
69	1536, Jan.	Livre premier contenant xxix. chansons a quatre parties . . .		A^{4}–H^{4}

Catalogue Number	*Date*	*Short Title*	*Reprint*	*Signature*
70	1536, Feb.	Premier livre contenant xxxi chansons . . .		a^4–h^4
71	1536, Feb.	Second livre contenant xxxi. chansons musicales . . .	**(76, 78)**	i^4–q^4
72	1536, Apr. (after the 16th)	Second livre contenant xxv. Chansons nouvelles . . .		I^4–Q^4
73	1536, May	Tiers livre contenant xxi. Chansons musicales . . .		r^4–$\&^4$
74	[1536]	[Chansons musicales, esleues de plusieurs livres . . .]		cc^4–dd^4
75	1537, May	Les chansons . . . Composees par maistre clement Iennequin . . .	**(4)**	$)(a^4$–$)(b^6$
76	1537	Second livre de chansons esleues . . .	**(71, 78)**	II e^4–II h^4
77	[1537]	[Jean-Louis Hérault. Antiphonæ sacræ B.M.V. . . .]		
78	1538, Feb.	Second livre contenant xxx. Chansons vieilles . . .	**(71, 76)**	aa^4–dd^4
79	1538, Mar.	Tiers livre contenant xxx. Chansons vieilles . . .		ee^4–hh^4
80	1538 (after Apr. 21)	Premier livre contenant xxv. Chansons nouvelles . . .	**(140)**	a^4–d^4
81	1538	Second livre contenant xxvij. Chansons nouvelles . . .	**(94)**	e^4–h^4
82	1538	Tiers livre contenant xxviij. Chansons nouvelles . . .	**(95)**	i^4–m^4
83	1538	Quart livre contenant xxvij. Chansons nouvelles . . .	**(96)**	n^4–q^4
84	1538	Cinquiesme livre contenant xxviij. Chansons nouvelles . . .	**(97)**	r^4–v^4
85	1539	Liber decimus quartus. xix. musicas cantiones continet / P. de Manchicourt . . . authore . . .	**(119)**	$*e^4$–$*h^4$
86	1539	Sixiesme livre contenant xxvij. Chansons nouvelles . . .	**(87)**	x^4–$\&^4$
87	1539	Sixiesme livre contenant xxvii Chansons nouvelles . . .	**(86)**	VIx ^{4}–VI $\&^4$
88	1539	Septiesme livre contenant xxix. Chansons nouvelles . . .	**(89)**	† a^4–† d^4
89	1540	Septiesme livre contenant xxx. Chansons nouvelles . . .	**(88)**	$((a^4$–$((d^4$
90	1540	Huitiesme livre contenant xix. Chansons . . .	**(91)**	† e^4– † h^4
91	1540	Huitiesme livre contenant xix Chansons . . .	**(90)**	VIII e^4–VIII h^4
92	1540	Neufviesme livre contenant xxvij. Chansons . . .	**(106)**	† i^4–† m^4
93	1540	Missarum musicalium . . . cum suis motetis Liber tertius . . .	**(132)**	$*i^4$–$*l^4$
94	1540	Second livre contenant xxvii Chansons . . .	**(81)**	e^4–h^4
95	1540	Tiers livre contenant xxix. Chansons . . .	**(82)**	i^4–m^4
96	1540	Quart livre contenant xxviij. Chansons . . .	**(83)**	n^4–q^4

Catalogue Number	*Date*	*Short Title*	*Reprint*	*Signature*
97	1540	Cinquiesme livre contenant xxv. Chansons . . .	**(84)**	r^{4}–u^{4}
98	1541	Missale ad usum . . . ecclesiæ noviomensis . . .		(See Catalogue)
99	1541	Dixiesme livre contenant xxviii. Chansons . . .	**(100)**	ǂ m^{4}–ǂ p^{4}
100	1541	Dixiesme livre contenant xxviii. Chansons . . .	**(99)**	X m^{4}–X p^{4}
101	1541	Onziesme livre contenant xxviii Chansons . . .	**(107, 108)**	ǂ q^{4}–ǂ t^{4}
102	1541	[Cantica Canticorum Salomonis Guill. le Heurteur . . .]		
103	1542	. . . Claudii de Sermisy . . . Nova & Prima motettorum editio . . .		a^{4}–e^{4}
104	1542	. . . Petri Certon . . . modulorum editio . . .		f^{4}–k^{4}
105	1542	. . . Jo. Lupi, . . . Musice Cantiones . . .		l^{4}–p^{4}
106	1542	Neufiesme livre contenant xxviii Chansons . . .	**(92)**	((i^{4}–((m^{4}
107	1542	Vnziesme livre contenant xxviii. Chansons . . .	**(101, 108)**	ǂ r^{4}–ǂ u^{4}
108	1542	Vnziesme livre contenant xxviii Chansons . . .	**(101, 107)**	XI r^{4}–XI u^{4}
109	1543	Douziesme livre contenant xxx. Chansons . . .	**(110)**	ǂ x^{4}–ǂ &^{4}
110	1543	Douziesme livre contenant xxx Chansons . . .	**(109)**	XII x^{4}–XII &^{4}
111	1543	Tresiesme livre contenant xix Chansons . . .	**(112)**	∵ a^{4}–∵ d^{4}
112	1543	Tresiesme livre contenant xix. Chansons . . .	**(111)**	∵ a^{4}–∵ d^{4}
113	1543	Quatorsiesme livre contenant xxix. Chansons . . .	**(113 bis 114)**	∵ e^{4}–∵ h^{4}
113 bis	1543	Quatorsiesme livre contenant xxix. Chansons . . .	**(113, 114)**	∵ e^{4}–∵ h^{4}
114	1543	Quatorsiesme livre contenant xxix Chansons . . .	**(113, 113 bis)**	XIIII e^{4}–XIIII h^{4}
115	1543	[Jean Conseil. Livre de danceries . . .]		
116	1544	Quinziesme livre contenant xxx. Chansons . . .	**(117, 118)**	∵ i^{4}–∵ m^{4}
117	1544	Quinziesme livre contenant xxx. Chansons . . .	**(116, 118)**	XV i^{4}–XV m^{4}
118	1544	Quinziesme livre contenant xxx. Chansons . . .	**(116, 117)**	∵ R^{4}–∵ *A*^{4}
119	1545	Petri Manchicurtii . . . modulorum musicalium Primus Tomus . . .	**(85)**	I. Manchicourt a^{4}– I. Manchicourt d^{4}
120	1545	[Manchicourt. Secundus tomus . . .]		
121	1545	[Manchicourt. Tertius tomus . . .]		
122	1545	Guillermi le heurteur . . . Operum musicalium liber primus . . .		I. Heurteur a^{4}– I. Heurteur d^{4}
123	1545	Seysiesme livre contenant xxix. Chansons . . .	**(124, 125)**	∴ n^{4}–∴ q^{4}
124	1545	Sexiesme livre contenant xxix. Chansons . . .	**(123, 125)**	XVI n^{4}–XVI q^{4}

Catalogue Number	*Date*	*Short Title*	*Reprint*	*Signature*
125	1545	Sexiesme livre contenant xxix. Chansons . . .	**(123, 124)**	XVI R^4–XVIA^4
126	1545	Dixseptiesme livre contenant xix Chansons . . .	**(127)**	XVII r^4–XVII u^4
127	1545	[Dixseptiesme livre contenant xix Chansons . . .]	**(126)**	XVII I^4–XVII Q^4
128	1545	Dixhuytiesme livre contenant xxviij. Chansons . . .	**(129)**	XVIII x^4–XVIII $\&^4$
129	1545	Dixhuytiesme livre contenant xxviij. Chansons . . .	**(128)**	XVIII R^4–XVIIIA^4
130	1545	[Le Gendre. Briefve introduction en la musique . . .]		
131	1545?	[Clementis Jannequini Praelium ad Paviam . . .]		
132	1546	Missarum musicalium . . . cum suis motetis Liber Primus . . .	**(93)**	ii^4–ll^4
133	1546	Missarum musicalium . . . Liber secundus . . .		mm^4–oo^4
134	[1546?]	[Missarum musicalium . . . Liber tertius . . .]		
135	1546	Dixneufiesme livre contenant xxii. Chansons . . .	**(136)**	XIX a^4–XIX d^4
136	1546	Dixneufiesme livre contenant xxii. Chansons . . .	**(135)**	XIX A^4–XIX H^4
137	1546	Vingtiesme livre contenant xxviii. Chansons . . .		XX e^4–XX h^4
138	1546, Aug.	[Breviarum secundum insignis ecclesiæ Noviomensis usum . . .]		(See Catalogue)
139	1546	Manuale insignis ecclesiæ Noviomensis . . .		(See Catalogue)
140	1546	Premier livre contenant xxv. Chansons . . .	**(80)**	Ia^4–Id^4
141	1546	Anthonij de Mornable . . . Motetorum Musicalium, Liber Primus . . .		Mornable m^4–Mornable p^4
142	1546	[Trente et un psaumes . . . Pierre Certon . . .]		a^4–d^4
143	1546	Livre second contenant xvii. pseaulmes . . . Mornable		e^4–h^4
144	1547	Vingt & ungiesme livre contenant xxv Chansons . . .		XXI i^4–XXI m^4
145	1547	Vingt deuxiesme livre contenant xxvi. Chansons . . .		XXII n^4–XXII q^4
146	1547	Vingtroisiesme livre contenant xvii. Chansons . . .		XXIII r^4–XXIII u^4
147	1547	Vingtquatriesme livre contenant xxvi. Chansons . . .		XXIIII x^4–XXIIII $\&^4$
148	1547	Second livre contenant trois Gaillardes . . .		II I^4–II Q^4
149	1547	Vingtcinquiesme livre contenant xxviii. Chansons . . .		XXV a^4–XXV d^4
150	1548	Vingtsixiesme livre contenant xxvii. Chansons . . .		XXVI e^4–XXVI h^4
151	1548	Vingtseptiesme contenant xxvij. Chansons . . .		XXVII i^4–XXVII m^4

Catalogue Number	*Date*	*Short Titles*	*Reprint*	*Signature*
152	1549	Vingthuitiesme contenant xxviii. Chansons . . .		XXVIII n^{4}–XXVIII q^{4}
153	1549	Vingtneufiesme contenant xxix. Chansons . . .		XXIX r^{4}–XXIX u^{4}
154	1549, Apr. 20	Trentiesme livre contenant xxviij. Chansons . . .		XXX x^{4}–XXX &^{4}
155	1549, May 22	Trente & ungyesme livre contenant xxx. Chansons . . .		XXXI a^{4}–XXXI d^{4}
156	1549	Trente deuxiesme livre contenant xxiiii Chansons . . .		XXXII e^{4}–XXXII h^{4}
157	1549, Oct. 12	Trente troysiesme livre contenant xx. Chansons . . .		XXXIII i^{4}–XXXIII m^{4}, XXXIII ꝫ^{2}
158	1549, Nov. 10	Trente quatriesme livre contenant xx. Chansons . . .		XXXIIII n^{4}–XXXIIII q^{4}
159	1549, Dec. 3	Second livre contenant xxix. chansons . . .		Rec. r^{4}–Rec. u^{4}
160	1550, Jan. 22	Trente cincquiesme livre contenant xxiiii Chansons . . .		XXXV f^{4}–XXXV i^{4}
161	1550, Feb. 14	Premier livre des Chansons esleues en nombre xxx . . .		Rec. a^{4}–Rec. d^{4}
162	1550, Mar. 14	Trente sixiesme livre contenant xxx. chansons . . .		Iosq. a^{4}–Iosq. d^{4}
163	1550, July 1	Tiers livre contenant xxviij. chansons . . .		III Rec. i^{4}–III Rec. m^{4}
164	1550, Aug. 19	Quart livre de danceries, A quatre parties . . .		IIII A^{4}–IIII H^{4}
165	1550, Aug. 28	Cinquiesme livre de danceries, A quatre Parties . . .		V I^{4}–V Q^{4}
166	1550, Oct. 23	Quart livre contenant xxvi. chansons . . .		IIII Trio. A^{4}–IIII Trio. H^{4}
167	1551	C Plinij Secundi veronensis in xxxvii. Libros naturalis historiæ . . .		A^{4}–C^{4}
168	1553, July 24	Premier Livre Contenant xxvi Chansons . . .		(∵) a^{4}–(∵) d^{4}
169	1555, Feb. 14	[Premier livre de violle . . . de la composition de Claude Gervaise. . . .]		
170	1555, Oct. 2	Sixieme Livre de Danceries . . .		A^{4}–H^{4}
171	1556	Missarum Musicalium Quatuor Vocum Liber III . . .		Aa^{4}–Cc^{4}
172	1557, Jan. 17	Troisieme Livre de Danceries . . .		III R^{4}–IIIÆ^{4}
173	1557	Septieme Livre de Danceries . . .		I^{4}–Q^{4}
174	1558	Le Dieugard de la Ville de Paris . . .		A^{4}–D^{4}

Alphabetical List

Title	*Catalogue Number*	*Date*
Anthonij de Mornable . . . Motetorum Musicalium, Liber Primus . . .	**141**	1546
Breviarium secundum usum . . . ecclesiæ Noviomensis . . .	**1**	1525
[Breviarum secundum insignis ecclesiæ Noviomensis usum . . .]	**138**	1546
C Plinij Secundi veronensis in xxxvii. Libros naturalis historiæ . . .	**167**	1551
[Cantica Canticorum Salomonis Guill. le Heurteur . . .]	**102**	1541
Chansons de maistre Clement Janequin . . .	**4**	[1528]

Title	*Catalogue Number*	*Date*
[Chansons et motets en canon a quatre parties sur deux]	**3**	[1528]
Chansons musicales a quatre parties . . .	**41**	1533
[Chansons musicales, esleues de plusieurs livres . . .]	**74**	[1536]
Chansons nouvelles en musique a quatre parties . . .	**2**	1528
Cinquiesme livre contenant xxv. Chansons . . .	**97**	1540
Cinquiesme livre contenant xxviij. Chansons nouvelles . . .	**84**	1538
Cinquiesme livre de danceries, A quatre Parties . . .	**165**	1550
. . . Claudii de Sermisy . . . Nova & Prima motettorum editio . . .	**103**	1542
[Clementis Jannequini Praelium ad Paviam . . .]	**131**	1545?
. . . Dixhuit basses dances . . .	**16**	1530
Dixhuytiesme livre contenant xxviij. Chansons . . .	**128**	1545
Dixhuytiesme livre contenant xxviij. Chansons . . .	**129**	1545
Dixiesme livre contenant xxviii. Chansons . . .	**99**	1541
Dixiesme livre contenant xxviii. Chansons . . .	**100**	1541
Dixneuf chansons musicales reduictes en la tabulature . . .	**22**	1531
Dixneufiesme livre contenant xxii. Chansons . . .	**135**	1546
Dixneufiesme livre contenant xxii. Chansons . . .	**136**	1546
Dixseptiesme livre contenant xix Chansons . . .	**126**	1545
[Dixseptiesme livre contenant xix Chansons . . .]	**127**	1545
xii Motetz a quatre et cinq voix . . .	**12**	1529
Douziesme livre contenant xxx. Chansons . . .	**109**	1543
Douziesme livre contenant xxx Chansons . . .	**110**	1543
Epithoma musice instrumentalis . . .	**21**	1530
Guillermi le heurteur . . . Operum musicalium liber primus . . .	**122**	1545
Hec figura omnes scientias et artes in unam radicam . . . reducit . . .	**58**	1534
Huitiesme livre contenant xix. Chansons . . .	**90**	1540
Huitiesme livre contenant xix Chansons . . .	**91**	1540
[Jannequin Cl. Sacræ Cantiones . . .]	**43**	1533
[Jean Conseil. Livre de danceries . . .]	**115**	1543
[Jean-Louis Hérault. Antiphonæ sacræ B.M.V. . . .]	**77**	[1537]
. . . Jo. Lupi, . . . Musice Cantiones . . .	**105**	1542
[Latin and French names of the rivers & towns of the three parts of Gaul]	**59**	[1534?]
Le Dieugard de la Ville de Paris . . .	**174**	1558
[Le Gendre. Briefve introduction en la musique . . .]	**130**	1545
Les chansons . . . Composees par maistre clement Iennequin . . .	**75**	1537
Liber primus quinqz et viginti . . . Motetos . . .	**46**	1534
Liber secundus: quatuor et viginti . . . Motetos . . .	**47**	1534
Liber tertius: viginti . . . motetos . . .	**49**	1534
Liber quartus. xxix. musicales . . . modulos habet . . .	**50**	1534
Liber quintus. xii . . . magnificat . . .	**52**	1534
Liber sextus. xiii . . . magnificat . . .	**53**	1534
Liber septimus. xxiiij . . . modulos . . .	**56**	1534
Liber octavus. xx . . . motetos . . .	**57**	1534
Lib. nonus. xviij. daviticos . . . psalmos . . .	**60**	1535
Lib. decimus: Passiones dominice . . .	**61**	1535
Lib. undecimus. xxvj. musicales habet modulos . . .	**63**	1535
Lib. duodecimus. xvij. musicales . . . salutationes habet . . .	**64**	1535
Lib. decimustertius. xviij. musicales habet modulos . . .	**68**	1535
Liber decimus quartus. xix. musicas cantiones continet/P. de Manchicourt . . . authore . . .	**85**	1539
Livre premier contenant xxix. chansons a quatre parties . . .	**69**	1536
Livre second contenant xvii pseaulmes . . .	**143**	1546
Magnificat sur les huit tons . . .	**26**	1531
[Manchicourt. Secundus tomus . . .]	**120**	1545
[Manchicourt. Tertius tomus . . .]	**121**	1545

Title	*Catalogue Number*	*Date*
Manuale insignis ecclesiæ Noviomensis . . .	**139**	1546
Missale ad usum . . . ecclesiæ noviomensis . . .	**98**	1541
Missarum musicalium . . . cum suis motetis Liber Primus . . .	**132**	1546
Missarum musicalium . . . cum suis motetis Liber tertius . . .	**93**	1540
Missarum musicalium . . . Liber primus . . .	**48**	1534
Missarum musicalium . . . Liber secundus . . .	**51**	1534
Missarum musicalium . . . Liber secundus . . .	**133**	1546
[Missarum musicalium . . . Liber tertius . . .]	**134**	1546
Missarum Musicalium Quatuor Vocum Liber III . . .	**171**	1556
Motetz nouvellement composez . . .	**11**	[1529]
Neuf basses dances deux branles . . .	**20**	1530
Neufviesme livre contenant xxvij. Chansons . . .	**92**	1540
Neufiesme livre contenant xxviii Chansons . . .	**106**	1542
Onziesme livre contenant xxviii Chansons . . .	**101**	1541
. . . Petri Certon . . . modulorum editio . . .	**104**	1542
Petri Manchicurtii . . . modulorum musicalium Primus Tomus . . .	**119**	1545
Premier livre contenant xxv. Chansons nouvelles . . .	**80**	1538
Premier livre contenant xxv. Chansons . . .	**140**	1546
Premier Livre Contenant xxvi Chansons . . .	**168**	1553
Premier livre contenant xxxi chansons . . .	**70**	1536
[Premier livre de violle . . . de la composition de Claude Gervaise . . .]	**169**	1555
Premier livre des Chansons esleues en nombre xxx . . .	**161**	1550
Primus liber viginti missarum . . .	**33**	1532
Quarante et deux chansons musicales a troys parties . . .	**10**	1529?
[Quarante et quatre chansons a deux . . .]	**67**	[1535?]
Quart livre contenant xxvi. chansons . . .	**166**	1550
Quart livre contenant xxvij. Chansons nouvelles . . .	**83**	1538
Quart livre contenant xxviij. Chansons . . .	**96**	1540
Quart livre de danceries, A quatre parties . . .	**164**	1550
Quartus liber tres missas continet . . .	**36**	1532
Quatorsiesme livre contenant xxix. Chansons . . .	**113**	1543
Quatorsiesme livre contenant xxix. Chansons . . .	**113 bis**	1543
Quatorsiesme livre contenant xxix Chansons . . .	**114**	1543
Quatorze Gaillardes neuf Pavennes . . .	**28**	1531
Quintus liber tres missas continet . . .	**37**	1532
Quinziesme livre contenant xxx. Chansons . . .	**116**	1544
Quinziesme livre contenant xxx. Chansons . . .	**117**	1544
Quinziesme livre contenant xxx. Chansons . . .	**118**	1544
Second livre contenant xxv. Chansons nouvelles . . .	**72**	1536
Second livre contenant xxvij. Chansons nouvelles . . .	**81**	1538
Second livre contenant xxvii Chansons . . .	**94**	1540
Second livre contenant xxix. Chansons.	**159**	1549
Second livre contenant xxx. Chansons vieilles . . .	**78**	1538
Second livre contenant xxxi. chansons musicales . . .	**71**	1536
Second livre contenant trois Gaillardes . . .	**148**	1547
Second livre de chansons esleues . . .	**76**	1537
Secundus liber tres missas continet . . .	**34**	1532
Septieme Livre de Danceries . . .	**173**	1557
Septiesme livre contenant xxix. Chansons nouvelles . . .	**88**	1539
Septiesme livre contenant xxx. Chansons nouvelles . . .	**89**	1540
Septimus liber tres missas habet . . .	**39**	1532
Sexiesme livre contenant xxix. Chansons . . .	**124**	1545
Sexiesme livre contenant xxix. Chansons . . .	**125**	1545
Sextus liber duas missas habet . . .	**38**	1532

Title	*Catalogue Number*	*Date*
Seysiesme livre contenant xxix. Chansons . . .	**123**	1545
Six Gaillardes et six Pavanes . . .	**17**	1530
Sixieme Livre de Danceries . . .	**170**	1555
Sixiesme livre contenant xxvij. Chansons nouvelles . . .	**86**	1539
Sixiesme livre contenant xxvii Chansons nouvelles . . .	**87**	1539
Tabulature pour le jeu D'orgues . . .	**25**	1531
Tertius liber tres missas continet . . .	**35**	1532
Tiers livre contenant xxi. Chansons musicales . . .	**73**	1536
Tiers livre contenant xxviij. Chansons nouvelles . . .	**82**	1538
Tiers livre contenant xxviij. chansons . . .	**163**	1550
Tiers livre contenant xxix. Chansons . . .	**95**	1540
Tiers livre contenant xxx. Chansons vieilles . . .	**79**	1538
Trente chansons musicales . . .	**8**	[1529]
Trente chansons musicales . . .	**44**	1534
Trente cinquiesme livre contenant xxiiii Chansons . . .	**160**	1550
Trente deuxiesme livre contenant xxiiii Chansons . . .	**156**	1549
Trente et cinq chansons musicales . . .	**6**	[1529]
Trente et deux chansons musicales . . .	**7**	[1529]
Trente et huyt chansons musicales . . .	**15**	1530
Trente et quatre chansons musicales . . .	**5**	1529
Trente et quatre chansons musicales . . .	**29**	[1531?]
Trente et sept chansons musicales . . .	**9**	[1529]
Trente et sept chansons musicales . . .	**32**	1532
Trente et six chansons musicales . . .	**19**	1530
Trente et troys chansons nouvelles . . .	**30**	1532
Trente et une chanson musicales . . .	**14**	1529
Trente et une chansons musicales . . .	**54**	1534
Trente et une chansons musicales a troys parties . . .	**65**	1535
[Trente et une chansons musicales a trois parties en ung livre . . .]	**66**	[1535?]
Trente et un psaumes à quatre voix . . . Pierre Certon	**142**	1546
Trente & ungyesme livre contenant xxx. Chansons . . .	**155**	1549
Trente quatriesme livre contenant xx. Chansons . . .	**158**	1549
Trente sixiesme livre contenant xxx. Chansons . . .	**162**	1550
Trente troysiesme livre contenant xx. Chansons . . .	**157**	1549
Trentiesme livre contenant xxviij. Chansons . . .	**154**	1549
Tres breve et familiere introduction . . .	**13**	1529
Tresiesme livre contenant xix Chansons . . .	**111**	1543
Tresiesme livre contenant xix. Chansons . . .	**112**	1543
Treze Motetz musicaulx . . .	**27**	1531
Troisieme Livre de Danceries . . .	**172**	1557
Unziesme livre contenant xxviii. Chansons . . .	**107**	1542
Unziesme livre contenant xxviii Chansons . . .	**108**	1542
Vingt deuxiesme livre contenant xxvi. Chansons . . .	**145**	1547
Vingt et cinq chansons musicales reduictes en la tabulature . . .	**23**	1531
Vingt et huit chansons nouvelles . . .	**31**	1532
Vingt et huyt chansons musicales . . .	**45**	1534
Vingt et huyt chansons musicalles . . .	**55**	1534
Vingt et neuf chansons musicales . . .	**18**	1530
Vingt et quatre chansons musicales . . .	**40**	1533
Vingt et sept chansons musicales . . .	**42**	1533
Vingt et six chansons musicales . . .	**62**	1535
Vingt et six chansons musicales reduictes en la tabulature . . .	**24**	1531
Vingt & ungiesme livre contenant xxv Chansons . . .	**144**	1547
Vingtcinquiesme livre contenant xxviii. Chansons . . .	**149**	1547

Title	*Catalogue Number*	*Date*
Vingthuitiesme contenant xxviii. Chansons . . .	**152**	1549
Vingtiesme livre contenant xxviii. Chansons . . .	**137**	1546
Vingtneufiesme contenant xxix. Chansons . . .	**153**	1549
Vingtquatriesme livre contenant xxvi. Chansons . . .	**147**	1547
Vingtroisiesme livre contenant xvii. Chansons . . .	**146**	1547
Vingtseptiesme contenant xxvij. Chansons . . .	**151**	1548
Vingtsixiesme livre contenant xxvii. Chansons . . .	**150**	1548

INDEXES

INDEX OF FIRST LINES

I. Latin Texts
II. Psalms and Related Pieces in French
III. Secular Pieces and Dances

The spelling of composer's names retains that of the original. Attributions in brackets come from outside the Attaingnant corpus and are noted in the Bibliographical Catalogue. Those that come from within the corpus are extended to cover all incidences of a given piece, except in the case of conflicting attributions. Reprints of the same piece come under the same entry, even if attributed to different composers. Intabulations for lute or keyboard also come under the main entry for the vocal model. Different settings of the same text receive separate entries. All vocal pieces are four-voiced unless otherwise indicated. Part III indexes only those dances that have an additional title beyond a class title such as "Branle" or "Basse dance." In Part III the author of the verse, if known, is given in italics at the right. For the major poets, collected modern editions were consulted. Conflicting attributions have been noted in some cases.

I. Latin Texts

Sicut malus	Moulu: **27**-4 (keyboard)
Sospitati dedit ægros olei perfusio I	Rousée: **56**-9
Vas in mari mersum patri II	
Spes mea ab uberibus matris meæ	Claudin: **103**-25 (à 3)
Spes salutis pacis portus I	Lupi: **105**-14
Tu es enim decus honestatis II	
Spiritus ubi vult spirat I	Gascongne; **47**-21
Charitas Dei diffusa est in cordibus nostris II	
T & B: Per Spiritum sanctum qui datus est nobis	
Splendor lucis æternæ et sol justiciæ *O Oriens*	G. Le Roy: **56**-14 (à 5)
Stella maris, luminosa virga florens et frondosa I	Lupi: **105**-8 (à 5)
O Maria singularis matertori expers maris II	
Stirps Jesse virgam produxit I	Lupi: **105**-6 (à 5)
Virgo Dei genitrix virga est flos filius eius II	
Sufficiebat nobis paupertas nostra	Richafort: **50**-22
Super flumina Babylonis illic sedimus I	De la fage: **49**-9 (à 5)
Si oblitus fuero tui, Hierusalem II	
Super montem excelsum ascende I	Manchicourt: **85**-18, **119**-17
Judæa et Hierusalem nolite timere II	
Surge Petre et indue te vestimentis tuis I	Jacquet: **68**-13 (à 6)
Si diligis me Simon Petre pasce oves meas II	
Surge, propera, amica mea I	Heurteur: **122**-1 (à 6)
Veni de libano soror mea sponsa II	
Surge, propera, amica mea, columba mea I	Mathias: **50**-26
Vox turturis audita est in terra nostra II	
Sustinuimus pacem et non venit	Claudin: **63**-13
Tanto tempore vobiscum sum	Verdelot: **50**-19
Tanto tempore vobiscum sum I	Certon: **104**-15
Domine, ostende nobis patrem II	
Te Deum laudamus	**26**-11 (keyboard)
Tempus est ut revertar ad eum I	Heurteur: **122**-13
Non vos relinquam orphanos II	
Tempus est ut revertar ad eum I	Consilium: **50**-20
Rex gloriæ, Dominus virtutum II	
Tempus meum ut revertar ad eum I	Cornesle Joris: **68**-2
Viri Galilei aspicientes in cælum II	
Thau. Reddes eis vicem (Sabbato in vigilia Paschæ)	Claudin: **61**-3
Gimel. Sed ex lamyæ	
Zay. Candidiores	
Timete Dominum omnes sancti eius	Mornable: **141**-23
Tota pulchra es amica mea	Claudin: **63**-20
Tota pulchra es amica mea I	Heurteur: **122**-16
Quam pulchræ sunt mammæ tuæ II	
Tu Deus noster suavis et verus es I	Lupi: **105**-9 (à 5)
Nosse enim te consummata justicia est II	
Tulerunt Dominum meum I	Certon: **104**-14
Dum ergo fleret inclinavit se II	
Unde veniet auxilium michi I	Passereau: **63**-14
Auxilium meum a Domino II	
Usquequo, Domine, oblivisceris me in finem? I	Lupus: **60**-11
Illumina oculos meos II	
Usquequo, piger, dormies? I	Manchicourt: **85**-19, **119**-18
Vade ad formicam, o piger II	
Veniat dilectus meus in hortum meum	**50**-3
T, Ct: Ut comedat fructum pomorum suorum	
Veni, electa mea, et ponam te I	Richafort: **57**-4 (à 6)
Quia concupivit rex speciem tuam II	

II. Psalms and Related Pieces in French

(*Translations by Clément Marot*)

III Secular Pieces and Dances

INDEX OF COMPOSERS

INDEX OF LIBRARIES